MYSTERIOUS PLACES
THE MASTER BUILDERS

MYSTERIOUS PLACES
THE MASTER BUILDERS

Philip Wilkinson & Michael Pollard

Illustrations by Robert Ingpen

DRAGON'S
WORLD

Dragon's World Ltd
Limpsfield
Surrey RH8 0DY
Great Britain

First published by Dragon's World 1992

© Text by Dragon's World 1992
© Illustrations by Robert Ingpen 1990 & 1992

Simplified text and captions by **Michael Pollard**
based on the *Encyclopedia of Mysterious Places*
by Robert Ingpen and Philip Wilkinson.

Editor	Diana Briscoe
Designer	Design 23
Art Director	Dave Allen
Editorial Director	Pippa Rubinstein

**British Library Cataloguing
in Publication Data**
The catalogue record for this book is
available from the British Library.

ISBN 1 80528 177 7

Printed in Italy

CONTENTS

Introduction

Everywhere we look, new buildings are being constructed and the builders seem to have a vast array of machines to aid them, from pile drivers to cranes.

Ancient builders had none of these machines, and yet they managed to create some extraordinary structures. One of the most famous is the stone circle at Stonehenge in southern England. It is made of enormous stone blocks, which the builders had to transport a long way to the site. And yet the people who built Stonehenge did not even have wheeled vehicles to help them carry the stones.

The same was true of the people who created the huge stone pyramids in many places in Central America, and the builders of the ancient temples on the island of Malta. How did they do it?

The builders' progress
This book shows how some of these mysterious buildings were created. It also explains why they were built – why people were prepared to put such great amounts of time and effort into making such strange structures. Some of the most basic buildings were made of simple materials that were easy to carry and use – the timber, straw and earth that were available near the site. And the reason they were made was the most basic of all – to give people shelter from the

rain and wind. The Iron-Age village of Biskupin in Poland shows how effective ancient buildings could be when created in this way.

But what if there was no local timber? In some places it was possible to use earth, making bricks out of mud and letting the warmth of the sun bake them hard. The buildings of the ancient Turkish town of Catal Hüyük were made in this way. Later on, bricks were baked in ovens.

An alternative was to use stone. At Skara Brae in the Orkney Isles, north of Scotland, stone was the only local material suitable for building. So the people made not only stone houses, but also stone furniture as well. Some of the stone cupboards and beds they made still survive.

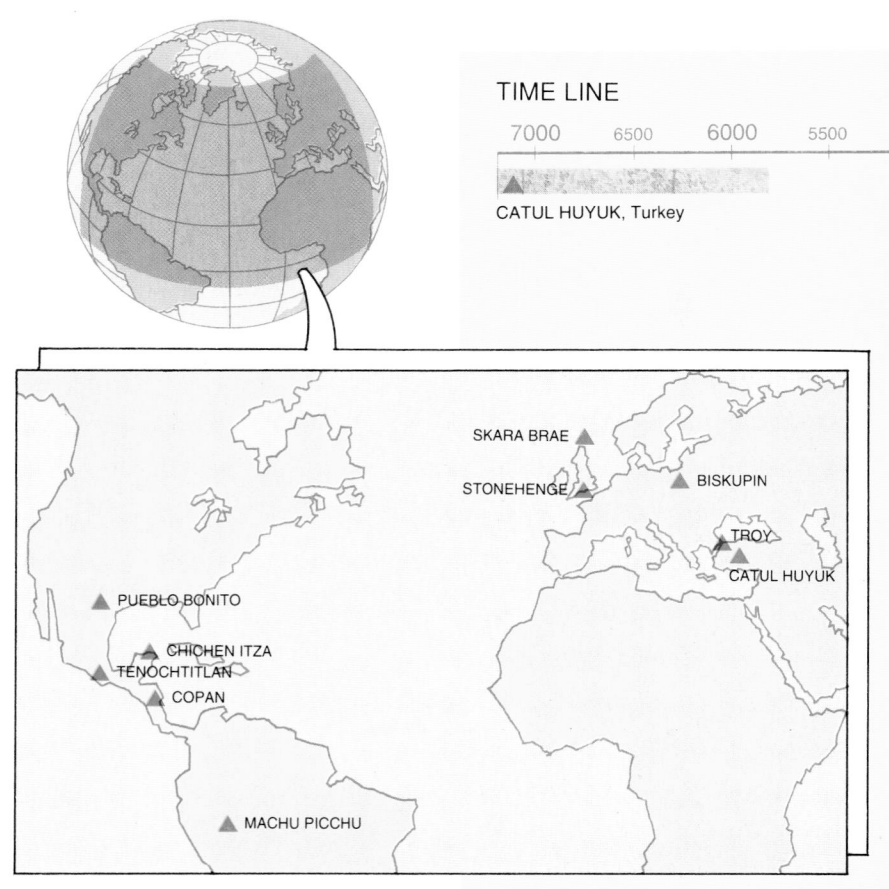

TIME LINE

7000	6500	6000	5500	5

CATUL HUYUK, Turkey

SKARA BRAE
STONEHENGE   BISKUPIN
TROY
CATUL HUYUK
PUEBLO BONITO
CHICHEN ITZA
TENOCHTITLAN
COPAN
MACHU PICCHU

Power building

Biskupin and Skara Brae are good examples of how builders adapted to their surroundings, but they are hardly amazing feats of construction. Soon builders were using buildings as a deliberate way of showing something about their society. A building was more than a way of protecting its owners from the wind, rain or sun. It was a statement of the beliefs or attitudes of the people who lived in it.

You can see this change if you look at some of the later places in this book, especially Copan, Chichen Itza and Tenochtitlan. These were places dominated by their great stone pyramids. The pyramids were temples, designed by the priests who had a great deal of power. Their towering height showed people how important the priests and their ceremonies were. The lavish carvings and the complex inscriptions also reminded people of the priests' importance.

Both types of building – those made simply for shelter, and those made to make a point – are fascinating. When we look at them today we can learn a lot about the people who lived in and around them.

Both needed their master builders. These were the people who could plan the work, supervise the artists who created the decoration, and organise the often vast labour forces needed to move the stone and build the walls.

Philip Wilkinson

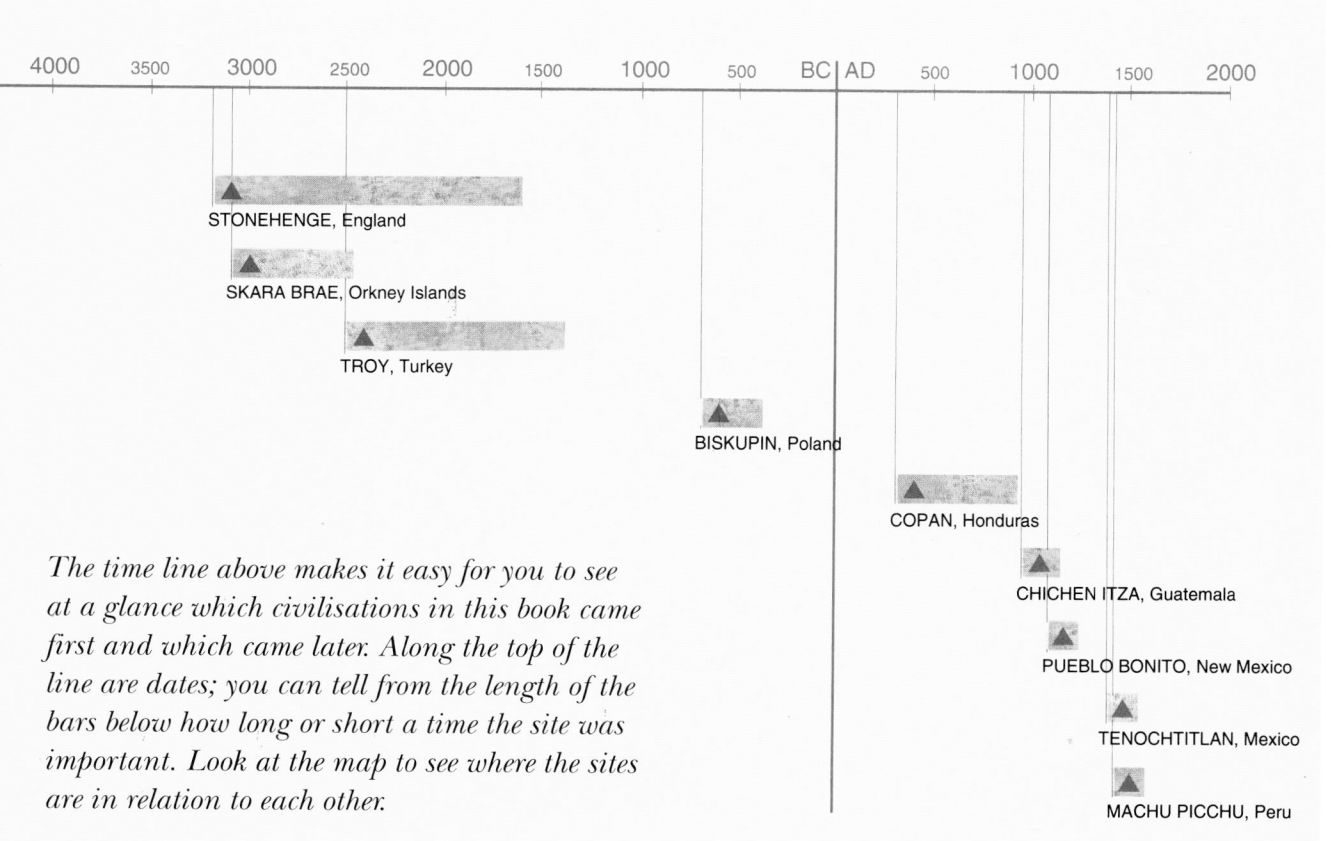

The time line above makes it easy for you to see at a glance which civilisations in this book came first and which came later. Along the top of the line are dates; you can tell from the length of the bars below how long or short a time the site was important. Look at the map to see where the sites are in relation to each other.

Catal Hüyük

Turkey, c. 7200-5800 BC

Archaeologists believe that Catal Hüyük, in southern Turkey, may have been the world's first city, built over 9000 years ago. So far its ruins have revealed only some of their secrets.

About forty years ago, archaeologists began to excavate a mound in a remote part of southern Turkey. Their fascinating discoveries changed what we know about the earliest civilisations.

As they worked, the team exposed the ruins of an ancient city older than any that had been found anywhere in the world. They called it Catal Hüyük.

Catal Hüyük dates back to about 7200 BC – over 9000 years ago. At least 6000 people lived there. Among them were skilled craftsmen – builders, weavers, potters and others.

City of mysteries

The people of Catal Hüyük had no written language, so they left behind no account of how they lived.

Archaeologists have had to piece together the story of their lives by sifting through what is left of the city. But there are still many unsolved mysteries about Catal Hüyük. Why was it built in such a remote spot? Why did the houses have their doors on the roofs? Why are so many of the buildings decorated with plaster models of bulls' heads? Who lived in Catal Hüyük, and what were their daily lives like?

Hunting country

Catal Hüyük was built on the site of a dried-up lake where the soil was good for growing crops. There were forests in the mountains about 80 kilometres (50 miles) away, so there was a plentiful supply of timber for building. Nearby there was good hunting country where gazelles and wild asses roamed – but there were also lions, leopards and bears, so hunting could be dangerous.

In many ways, the buildings of Catal Hüyük were like those in other ancient cities. They were made of mud bricks held together with a wooden framework.

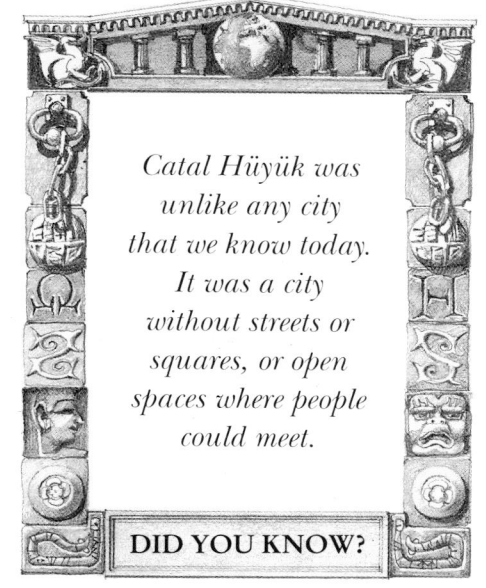

Catal Hüyük was unlike any city that we know today. It was a city without streets or squares, or open spaces where people could meet.

DID YOU KNOW?

This reconstruction of a shrine room at Catal Hüyük shows how richly decorated the shrines were, with real bulls' horns mounted in plaster heads and paintings of vultures on the walls. Offerings of precious objects are being made while a burial takes place.

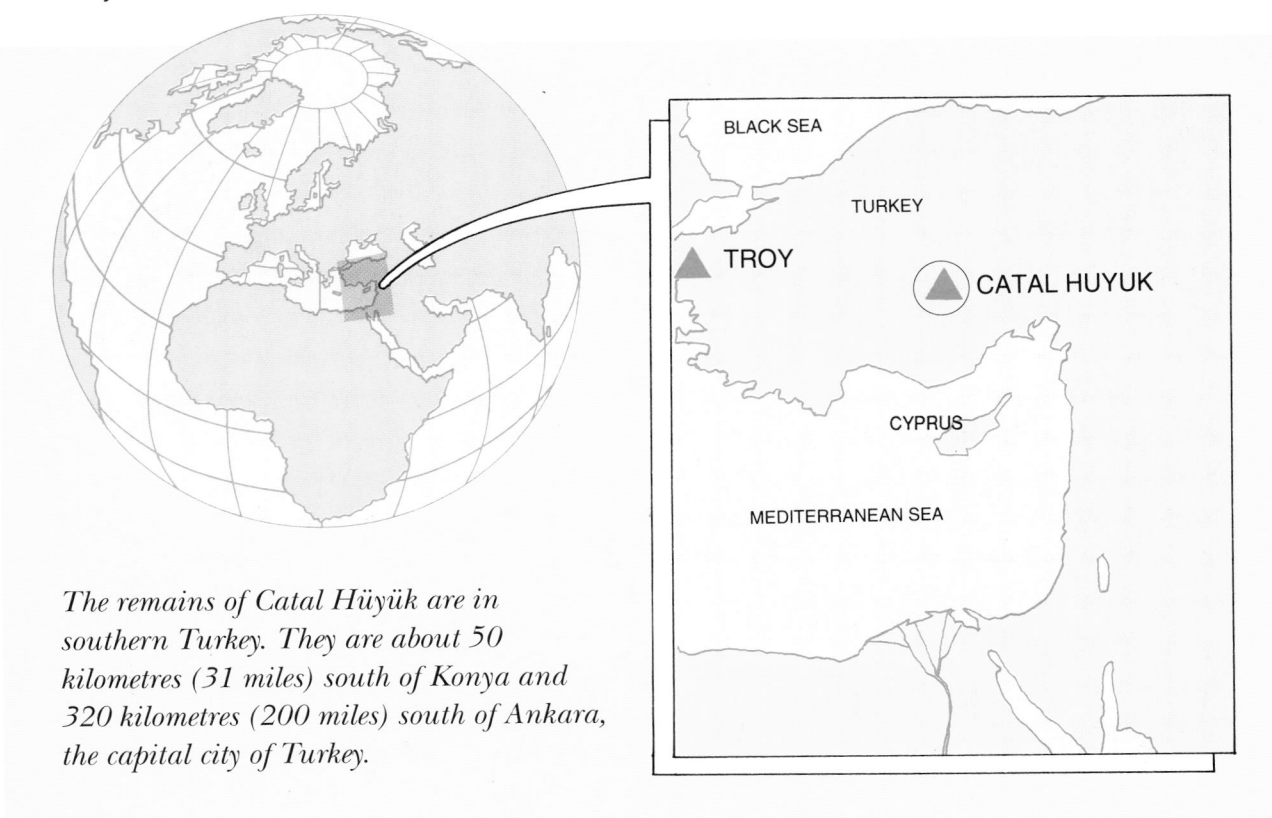

The remains of Catal Hüyük are in southern Turkey. They are about 50 kilometres (31 miles) south of Konya and 320 kilometres (200 miles) south of Ankara, the capital city of Turkey.

They had flat roofs, with plaster gutters to carry away rain water. But what made Catal Hüyük so different from other cities was that the houses had no doors at ground level. People went in and out through a trapdoor or through a door in a kind of hallway built on the roof.

The streetless city

Even stranger, people moved about the city by walking across the roofs. The houses were joined together, with no streets and few open spaces. Where buildings were different heights, they were connected by wooden ladders.

One advantage of having no doors at ground level was that the city needed no wall to protect its inhabitants from wild animals or human enemies. If they took away the ladders linking their homes, they were quite safe.

If this was the idea, it seems to have worked. Unlike most other ancient cities, Catal Hüyük does not appear to have been attacked or conquered.

Living on the roof

The houses of Catal Hüyük were small and must have been rather cramped, although in fine weather families could use their flat roofs as extra living space. Inside, much of the available space was taken up by large, raised platforms. The dead were buried in these platforms, which were probably also used as work benches and as seats and beds.

The people of Catal Hüyük seem to have taken great care of their homes. They kept them fresh and clean by renewing the plaster on the walls each year. They were also careful about disposing of their rubbish. Certain courtyards were set aside as rubbish dumps, and the refuse was covered with wood ash to stop smells and deter rats.

Measuring by hand

Although there was no written language in Catal Hüyük, the people seem to have worked out a system of mathematics which they used in building. They built most of their houses to standard sizes, usually about 6 metres (20 ft) long and 4.5 metres (15 ft) wide. Rooms, doorways, hearths and ovens were also made to standard sizes.

The basic elements of their system of measurement were probably the human hand and foot. The standard mud brick was four hands long, two hands wide and one deep.

Not all the buildings in Catal Hüyük were homes. There were also a large number of shrines built for religious ceremonies. These were decorated with paintings and sculptured clay panels which show that animals played an important part in the religion of Catal Hüyük. There were many hunting scenes, with deer being chased by leopards and human hunters. But the most prominent animals inside the shrines are plaster bulls, with real horns, mounted on the walls. It seems that to the people of Catal Hüyük, as to many other ancient civilisations, the bull was a symbol of life and action.

Sky burials

Other paintings in the shrines are more grisly. They show vultures picking the flesh off human bodies. The leader of the first excavation at Catal Hüyük, James Mellaart, believes that these pictures show how the people disposed of their dead. They gave them 'sky burials'.

The bodies of the dead were placed on tall platforms which kept them out of the way of animals such as dogs but allowed birds and insects to reach them. After the flesh had been stripped away, the skeleton would be brought down and buried beneath one of the platforms in the family's house or in a shrine. The women were buried under the larger platforms and the men under the smaller.

Female goddesses

Ancient civilizations like that of Catal Hüyük knew the importance of fertility of crops, animals and human beings. They depended on fertility for survival.

This would explain the number of female goddess statues found in the ruins of the city. Some of them are shown to be pregnant and others actually giving birth, sometimes to human babies and sometimes to animals.

Archaeologists can only guess at what these statues meant to the people of Catal Hüyük. But birth means new life – for plants as well as animals – and it is likely that these statues were made in the hope that they would bring continuing new life to the soil and to the families of the city.

Carving of a fertility goddess.

Life in the city

Archaeology is slow, careful work. Excavations at Catal Hüyük have been going on for about forty years, but so far only part of the city has been uncovered. Our picture of life in Catal Hüyük is still far from clear.

One mystery is what work the people of Catal Hüyük did. We know that many of them were priests and priestesses, but what did the others do? The burial platforms in homes and shrines contain many grave goods (the possessions with which people were buried). These include fine examples of weaving, pottery, copper jewellery, weapons, baskets and wooden vessels. But so far little evidence has been found of where these objects were made. Some may have been brought from outside the city, but it is likely that the working area has still to be excavated. Much more of this intriguing city remains to be explored.

Fourteen cities

Another of Catal Hüyük's secrets is how long its civilisation lasted. Although only a small part of the city has been excavated, fourteen different layers of buildings have been discovered, each layer built on the foundations of the previous one. But sadly, there is no way of knowing in detail the history of this mysterious city.

People of Catal Hüyük

Mainly by studying the skeletons and other contents of the burial platforms archaeologists have been able to find out a good deal about the people of Catal Hüyük, and especially about their skills.

They were taller than many other ancient peoples. The men were up to 1.7 metres (5 ft 7 ins) tall, and the women about 15 centimetres (6 ins) shorter. For those days, when there was no protection against disease, they had quite long lives. Men reached an average age of about thirty-four, and women about three years less.

What did they have to eat? Their diet included grain – probably made into a kind of porridge – and meat, and they drank milk, probably from sheep or goats.

A city of crafts

The big surprise about Catal Hüyük was the wide range of craft skills that its people developed.

One exciting discovery that the archaeologists made was a piece of cloth which had been used to fill a skull in one of the burial platforms. Although the cloth had been turned to ashes in a later fire, the pattern of the fibres could still be seen. This showed that the people of Catal Hüyük were expert spinners and weavers.

As well as cloth, they also wove mats out of rushes. The patterns made by these rugs can still be seen impressed in the clay floors of the

Above: a stone stamp used for making patterns on the walls of a house.

Left: wall painting from a shrine showing vultures and a headless human.

houses. The patterns are like those used in rugs still made today in that part of Turkey.

The Catal Hüyük people knew about making dyes, too. They used plants such as woad to give a blue dye, madder for red and weld for yellow. Some of the wall paintings in the shrines still show traces of these colours. Many of these paintings are of animals, particularly bulls, stags and leopards; but there are also pictures of people hunting and dancing, of flowers and abstract patterns.

Catal Hüyük's secret skill

Simple domestic crafts like weaving could not have provided the wealth that a city like Catal Hüyük needed to grow and survive. It must have made some valuable product that it could trade with the outside world.

A clue to what this might have been is provided by the nearness to Catal Hüyük of two volcanoes. These produced a hard, glass-like volcanic rock called obsidian, which could be given a sharp edge for tools and weapons and could also be polished to make mirrors. The people of Catal Hüyük seem to have mastered the skills of grinding and polishing obsidian, as well as drilling

Household objects including a decorated boar's tusk.

tiny holes into it. It may be that their work was so specialised that the city was able to export finished articles made of obsidian in return for other goods.

Another material the craftsmen learned to work with was copper. Before 7000 BC they had found out how to use hammers to make simple tools and pins. A thousand years later they were smelting copper ore to make small beads and other items. But it was probably their skill with obsidian – a difficult material to work with – that brought wealth to the people of Catal Hüyük.

The finding of Catul Hüyük

The ruins of Catal Hüyük were found buried beneath a mound about 320 kilometres (200 miles) south of Turkey's capital city, Ankara. The archaeologist who discovered the mound and decided to investigate it was James Mellaart. He began to dig in 1961.

Mellaart and his team worked slowly and carefully, taking one section of the mound at a time. As each layer of earth was stripped away, Catal

Hüyük's secrets were gradually revealed.

By 1967 Mellaart was able to publish his first book about what he had found at this important but previously unknown site. This news of a city even older than those along the Tigris and Euphrates rivers, such as Ur and Babylon, made archaeologists rethink their ideas about the ancient world and the beginnings of civilisation.

Stonehenge

England c. 3200–1650 BC

A great circle of stones has stood out against the sky on a hillside in southern England for 5000 years. But how did it get there and why was it built?

Archaeologists have been trying to unravel the mysteries of Stonehenge for over 300 years. But even the modern equipment available today has been unable to answer all their questions.

The first thing you see as you approach Stonehenge is a circle of huge, upright stones. But there is more to Stonehenge than that. There are many other stones placed inside and outside the circle. There is also a bank, which archaeologists call an earthwork, surrounding the stone circle, and inside the earthwork a circle of pits which have been dug and then filled in.

The work of centuries

Modern techniques which enable us to work out the age of archaeological findings, reveal that Stonehenge was not built all at once, but in stages.

The earthwork is all that is left of the first stage. This was built between 3200 and 2700 BC. Then, the bank was much higher and wider than it is today – probably about 2 metres (6 ft) high and 6 metres (20 ft) wide. Inside it, there was a large wooden building, probably with a thatched roof, up to 30 metres (100 ft) across.

What happened inside this building? No one can be sure, but it may have been used to store the bodies of the dead before they were cremated or buried. Between 2700 and 2200 BC, a circle of fifty-six pits was dug inside the earthwork. Some of these holes contained the ashes of people whose bodies had been cremated. But the pits are older than the ashes, so they must have been dug for some other purpose. What could it have been?

Stone Age computer?

One idea is that the circle of pits was a kind of calculator designed to predict eclipses of the moon. This theory was put forward in the 1960s by Gerald Hawkins, an astronomer. He showed that if stones are placed on six of the holes in a certain pattern and then moved on one hole each year, the dates of future eclipses can be calculated.

We do not know whether the people of 2000 BC had the mathematical knowledge to make such calculations, but it seems unlikely. A more probable explanation of the pits is that liquids, possibly rain water, were poured into them as an offering to the gods of the underworld. But this too is only a theory. The circle of pits remains another of the mysteries of Stonehenge.

The first circle

Round about 2200 BC the first stones were brought to Stonehenge. They were arranged in a double circle inside the ring of pits. The mystery about this part of Stonehenge's history is to do with where the stones came from. They were 'bluestones' from the Preseli mountains about 320 kilometres (200 miles) away in South Wales. There was plenty of other stone closer to Stonehenge that the builders could have used.

Why did they travel so far and go to the immense labour of transporting the stones all that way?

Finished at last

Between 2000 and 1600 BC the final stage of building was reached. This was the building of the circle of upright stones which now dominates the site. These huge stones rise to a height of

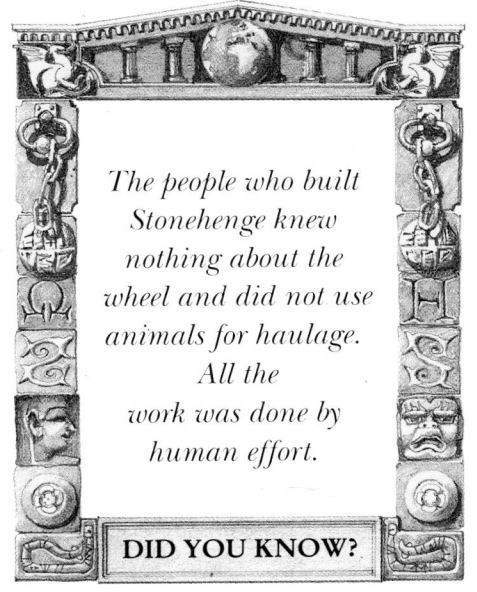

The people who built Stonehenge knew nothing about the wheel and did not use animals for haulage. All the work was done by human effort.

DID YOU KNOW?

4 metres (13 ft) and are buried up to 1.5 metres (5 ft) in the ground. Unlike the first stones, these came from the Marlborough Downs, only about 27 kilometres (17 miles) from Stonehenge, but transporting them must again have been a huge and difficult job.

When the great circle was finished, there were some more changes and additions. Groups of three even larger stones – two uprights and a lintel – were added in the centre, and the original bluestones were also moved to the centre. Work on Stonehenge then seems to have been complete.

Today, only about half of the stones are still in place. But Stonehenge still holds on to most of its secrets.

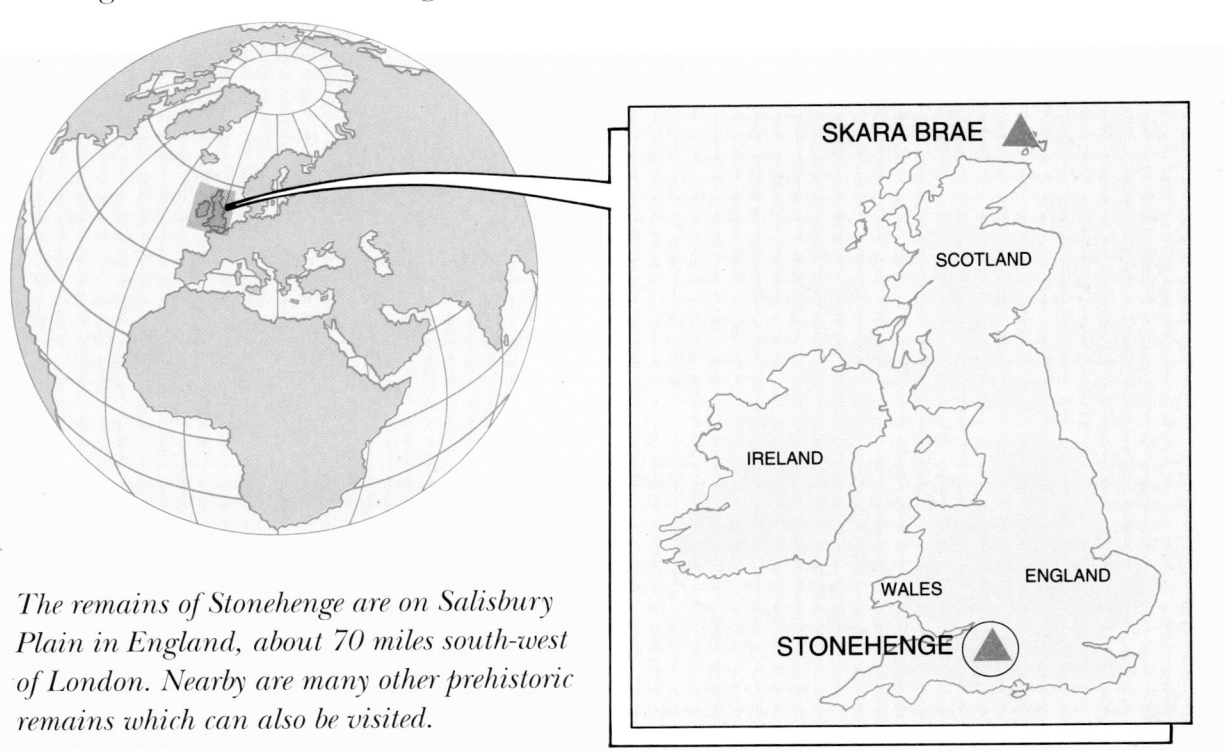

The remains of Stonehenge are on Salisbury Plain in England, about 70 miles south-west of London. Nearby are many other prehistoric remains which can also be visited.

Midsummer dawn

It seems certain that Stonehenge was a centre for religious ceremonies. It may also have been used to show off the power and skills of the people of the area. It was built with great care and accuracy, with the position of the pits and stones carefully worked out.

Stonehenge was built to last, as the centuries have shown. The stonemasons made sure that the lintels linking the upright stones were securely jointed. They were probably using skills they had learned as carpenters.

The rising sun

The most interesting thing about Stonehenge, and one which has fascinated people for centuries, is the way that the stones are arranged to make one particular day in the year important.

At the entrance to Stonehenge, just inside the embankment, is a stone called the Heel Stone. At dawn on Midsummer Day, June 24, the sun rises almost directly over the Heel Stone and points its shadow directly towards the great stone circle. We do not know what religious meaning this had for the people of Salisbury Plain thousands of years ago, but it is not hard to imagine them gathering before dawn and waiting in hushed silence for the sun to appear over the stone they had placed there for it.

Moving the stones

Even today, using cranes and trucks, bringing the stones to Stonehenge and placing them in position would be a major job. The people who built Stonehenge had nothing but their own strength and ingenuity to help them. Here is another of Stonehenge's mysteries – how did they manage?

We can only guess at the answer. It may be that the bluestones from South Wales were brought by sea and then by river, ending their journey on sleds which were dragged overland. But were Stone Age people able to build boats strong enough? How would they have loaded the stones on to the boats without sinking them?

Another idea is that, during the Ice Age, glaciers had carried the bluestones most of the way. But they would still have to be moved some distance across country, as were the stones from the Marlborough Downs. It has been shown that this could be done, using wooden levers and sleds, but it must have been a massive task involving thousands of people over a long period.

Then, once the stones had arrived, how were they erected, and how were

Merlin

Stonehenge is so strange and old that it is not surprising that many myths and legends have grown up around it.

Some of these stories are about Merlin, who was said to have been the chief magician at the court of King Arthur, the legendary ruler of southern Britain.

Merlin was such a clever wizard, the story goes, that he could do anything. He took charge of the building of Stonehenge, which he made out of giants he had turned to stone. At Merlin's command, the stones would turn back into giants, and dance.

It is a good story, but the dates are all wrong. Merlin, if he really existed, was alive around the year AD 500, nearly 2000 years after the building of Stonehenge was completed.

Stonehenge today.

the lintels placed in position? Again, we do not know, but there are several possibilities. Earth ramps might have been used – but if so, there would still be signs that the soil had been disturbed, and there are none. The builders could have used a wooden scaffold – but it must have been immensely strong to take the weight of the stones, and no traces of a scaffold have been found. A third idea is that each stone was hauled up in stages, with a temporary wedge to hold it in place between each pull.

Whatever the answer really is, we can only admire the planning and effort that went into the task.

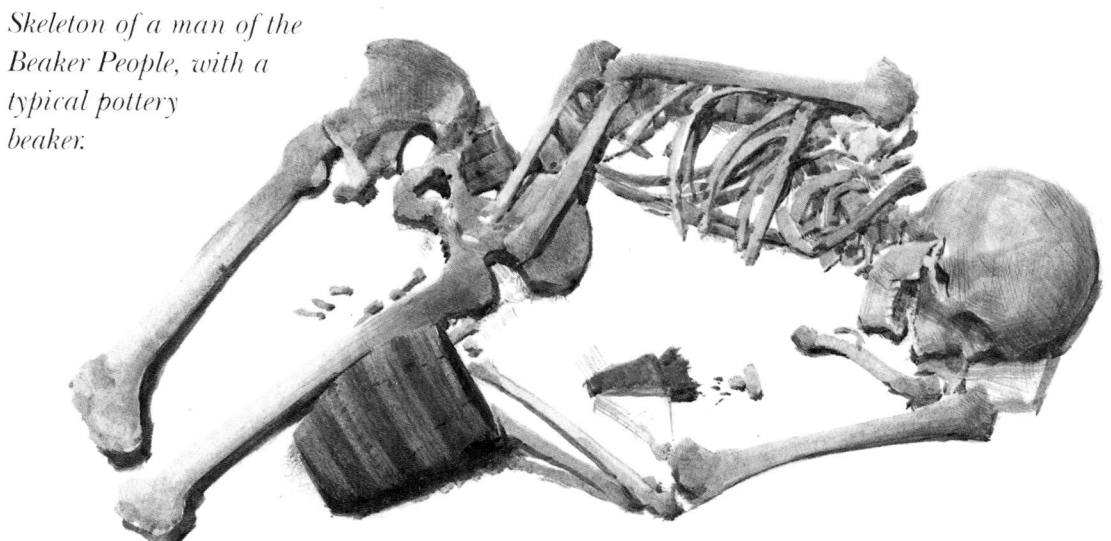

Skeleton of a man of the Beaker People, with a typical pottery beaker.

The Beaker People

The inhabitants of the country around Stonehenge at the time when the circle of pits was dug there are often known as 'the Beaker People'.

They get their name from a special kind of pottery jar. Many have been found in the graves of people who died around this time. Some archaeologists think that the beakers were used in religious ceremonies, perhaps to make offerings to the gods. This fits in with some ideas about the purpose of the circle of pits at Stonehenge.

At one time it was thought that the Beaker People were new settlers who arrived in the area. But it seems more likely that the beakers were merely a new style of pottery that began to be made about that time.

The Beaker People wandered far and wide in their search for pasture for their sheep and land which they could use for crops. In those days, the valleys were forested and could harbour wild animals or human enemies, so they travelled on higher ground along the ridges of the downs. Many of their tracks meet near Stonehenge.

John Aubrey

John Aubrey, born in 1626, was one of the first scholars to investigate Stonehenge. He discovered the circle of fifty-six holes inside the bank, which have since been called 'the Aubrey holes'.

But John Aubrey's guess at the age of Stonehenge was quite wrong. He thought that it had been built by the Celts, the people who lived in Britain when the Romans invaded in 55 BC. Many people continued to believe this until quite recently, but modern methods of dating have proved that Aubrey's guess was thousands of years out.

Skara Brae

Orkney Islands, c. 3100–2500 BC

On the shore of a windswept Scottish island,
a storm revealed the remains of a village built about 5000 years ago.
Who lived in this wild spot and why did they leave it?

The storm that hit the Orkney Islands, off the north coast of Scotland, one day in 1850 was one of the worst anyone could remember. When it was over, the people of one of the islands, Orkney Mainland, discovered an unknown and mysterious chapter in their history.

Village by the sea

Among the sand-dunes on the shore near the village of Sandwick the wind had blown the covering of sand away from the remains of an ancient village. There were about half a dozen houses, each between 4.6 and 6.4 metres (15 and 21 ft) across, with stone walls up to 1.8 metres (6 ft) thick. Around each house was a protective mound of earth. The houses had low doorways, but hardly any had window openings. The furniture inside was made of stone.

From each house door, a short passage led to a covered passageway which connected all but one of the houses. These passages were low, like the house doorways – only about 1.2 metres (4 ft) high.

Who were the people who had lived in this unfriendly place? Why did they leave their homes, and what happened to them?

All mod. cons.

One of the unusual things about the Skara Brae houses is how well they are equipped with furniture whose purpose we can easily understand today. There were shelf units similar to the dressers still found in many Scottish cottage kitchens – except that the Skara Brae units are made of stone. There are alcoves in the walls that were probably cupboards. There may have been a water supply in the form of storage tanks set into the floor, sealed with

Pieces of whalebone were found at Skara Brae, probably from dead whales washed up on the beach. What a find these huge creatures would have been for the villagers!

DID YOU KNOW?

It was a hard life for the villagers of Skara Brae.
The weather was stormy, and the winters were bitterly cold. They wrapped themselves in furs
and built earth banks to try to keep the draughts out of their homes.

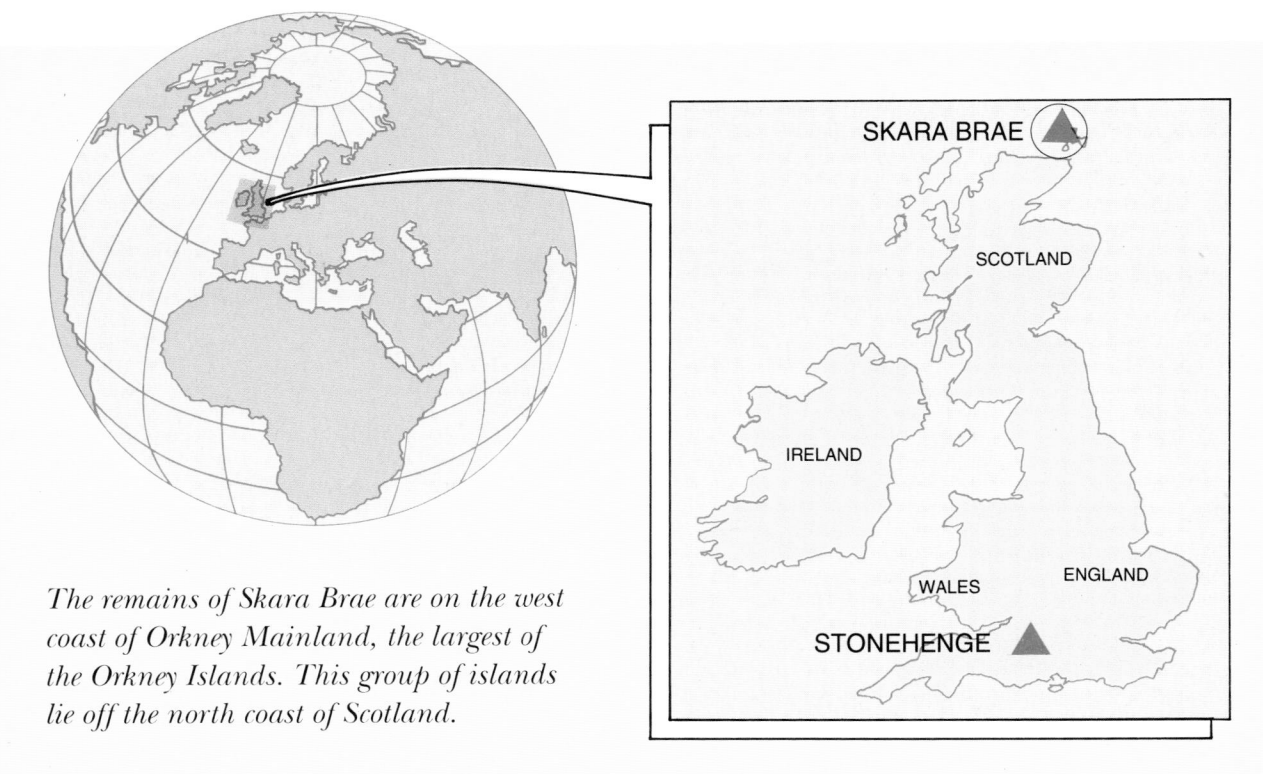

The remains of Skara Brae are on the west coast of Orkney Mainland, the largest of the Orkney Islands. This group of islands lie off the north coast of Scotland.

clay to make them watertight. The Skara Brae houses may even have had lavatories. There are small stone areas leading off the main rooms, with a drain to the village passageway.

A world of stone

The people of Skara Brae were experts in the use of stone, which the walls of their houses, and their stone furniture, were strongly and neatly made. The villagers made use of the material that was most easily found.

On the windswept Orkneys there are few trees, and wood was precious. It was kept for uses such as doors and roof supports where no other material would do. But there was plenty of stone.

What a load of rubbish!

It is not hard for a twentieth-century visitor to understand how the people of Skara Brae lived. But one fact about the village seems very strange to us today.

Skara Brae was built inside a mound which was actually an old rubbish dump (or midden), containing dung, bones, peat ash and other rubbish. What is more, the houses themselves were filled with rubbish. Among other things, there were shells, antlers and animal bones.

It seems strange that people, who in many ways seem to have lived such orderly lives, should have been content to live among their rubbish. But things become even more mysterious. First, the rubbish around the village is that of an earlier population. Why would people build their homes in their ancestors' rubbish dump?

Second, the rubbish inside the houses was not simply dumped there. It was arranged carefully in layers. The most likely reason why the village was built inside the midden of an earlier one is that it was easy to dig into. Within the mound there was shelter from the wind for the new houses. On this windy island, any extra protection from the weather was welcome. The explanation for the carefully layered rubbish in the newer houses is less easy.

Moving on

No one knows how the Skara Brae community came to an end, but at some time the houses were abandoned. As the village was very small, it may be that it was lived in by just one large, extended family.

Leaving a home is upsetting for anyone. In the harsh world of 2500 BC it must have been even worse. Some archaeologists have suggested that, to keep the family's link with its old home, the house may have been filled at some kind of ceremony with things connected with its owners. Sometimes these included the bodies or skeletons of dead members of the family.

We know nothing about the religion of Skara Brae, but perhaps the ash, shells, antlers and bones were put there in memory of the old life of the houses. Perhaps the people, as they left their homes, could not bear to think of other people moving in and living there. Filling up the house in this way would certainly make it difficult for a new family to take over.

The end of Skara Brae

Why did the villagers of Skara Brae decide to leave their homes? It cannot have been a sudden decision caused by a violent storm or some other disaster such as an outbreak of disease. There was time to take the roofs off the houses and fill them with careful arrangements of bones and shells. It looks as if the decision to leave the village was planned well in advance.

We do not know the answer. Some time later, other people lived in the houses for a while until they, too, left. But all the people of Skara Brae went away in the end, leaving us to rediscover their homes and furniture 5000 years later.

What did they eat?

We can tell, from the bones they left behind, that the people of Skara Brae were mainly meat-eaters. They raised sheep, cattle, and a few pigs. They were able to store enough feed to keep young sheep through the winter. The skins of their animals were used for clothes and bedding.

Hunting a wild boar.

Another important feature of the island's diet was fish. The battering of wind and waves has brought the sea nearer to Skara Brae than it was 5000 years ago, but it was only a short walk to the shore. There, cod and other fish could be caught. The stone containers in the houses may have been stores for bait – possibly limpets – which have to be softened in fresh water before being used. There is little evidence of plants in the diet. Some grains and hazelnut shells have been discovered, but not enough to suggest that they were important foods.

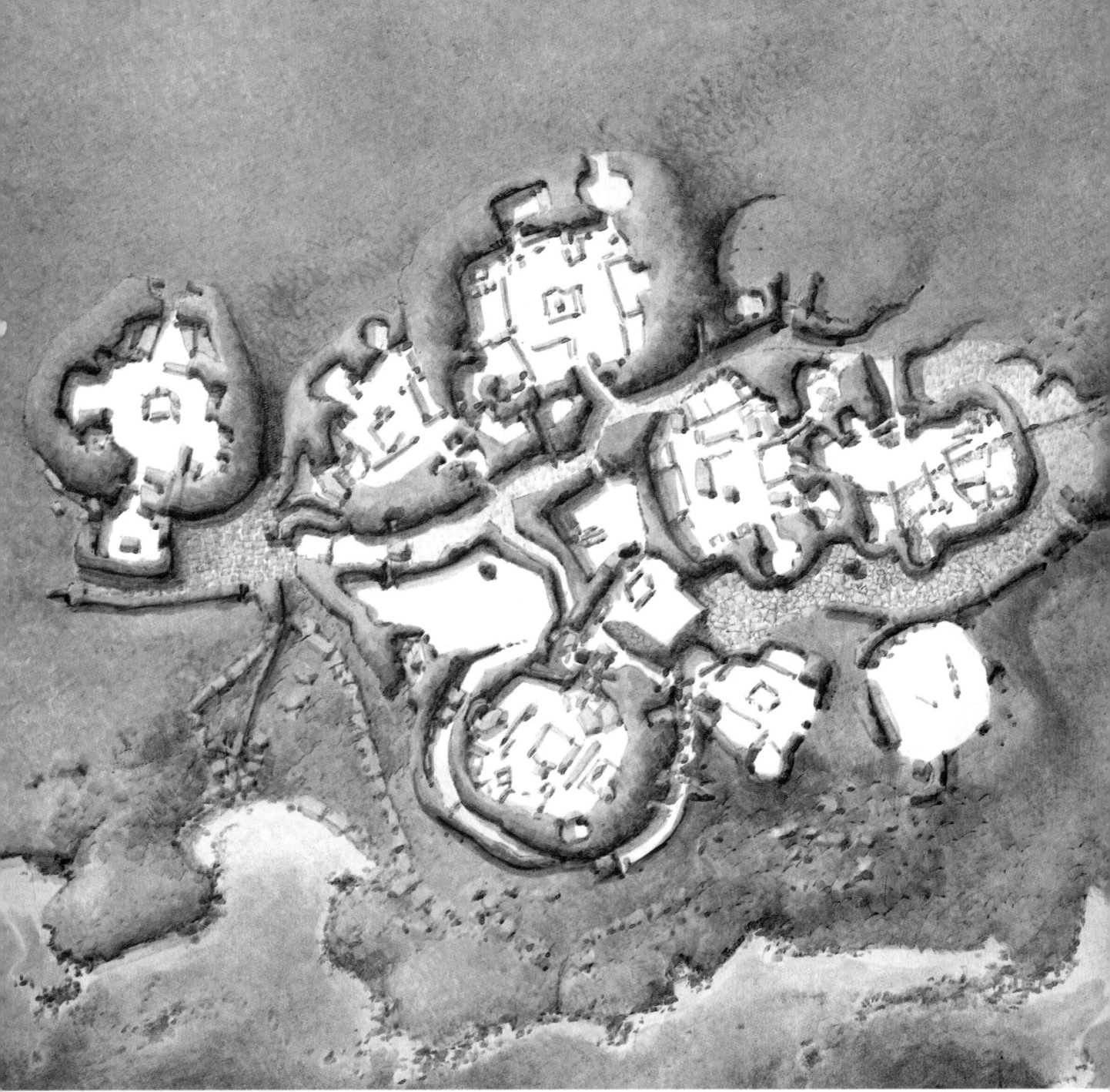

The village of Skara Brae

The ground plan of Scara Brae (above) shows the various houses and the connecting passage ways. House 7 is at the bottom in the middle; House 8 is at the bottom right. House 7 was especially well preserved. From it, we can put together a fairly clear picture of what home life in the village was like.

To enter your house, you opened the low, narrow door which was held in place with a stone bar. Inside you would find a square room about 5 metres (16 ft) across. The floor was of beaten earth, but there was a paving of stone slabs round the doorway. In the centre of the room was a square hearth, with four upright stone slabs to keep the fire in place. Peat was the fuel used in the fire. To one side was a raised area, which was probably used for preparing food and perhaps for eating.

Inside the house

Around the walls were stone box beds. These were frames made of stone slabs set on edge. They sound uncomfortable, but with a thick mattress of heather or straw to lie on, furs and skins as blankets, and the surrounding slabs to keep out the draughts they would have given the villagers a good night's sleep. Beds of a similar pattern, but with wooden frames instead of stone, were used on some remote Scottish islands until fairly recently.

The people of Skara Brae

Life at Skara Brae was hard. The villagers' main concern was with survival in a very hostile environment. Looking after their animals, making clothes, searching for food and keeping their homes in good repair would have taken up much of their time and effort. But some of them, at least, had time for various kinds of craft work.

Some of this work produced everyday items such as pots. Although Skara Brae pottery was not very good in quality, its makers showed some artistic sense by decorating it with simple patterns such as zigzags and wavy lines. The villagers' work with carved bone showed more skill, and they included items made purely for pleasure, as well as small tools such as scrapers used to clean animal skins. Among the finds at Skara Brae are bone beads, decorative pins and pendants, so some villagers must have had a liking for simple jewellery.

They also used their skill in working with stone to make hand tools and the mysterious carved objects that you can read about on the next page.

The village workshop

Stone working may have been carried on in a building specially set aside for it. House 8 at Skara Brae is the only building not connected to the main

Above: Bone beads, pendants and a dress pin.

Left: a leather cap.

passageway. It stands on its own at one end of the village. Like the homes, it has a hearth in the centre of the floor, but there are no beds and none of the other domestic furniture that the homes have. Perhaps this was a workshop for the making of stone tools and other things. On the floor a large number of pieces of chert, a flint-like stone, were found. When it was heated in the fire, and then plunged into cold water, chert could be broken into flakes or splinters which were ideal as small cutting and shaping tools.

House 8 may have been one of a number of workshops for different crafts. There are traces of other buildings separated from the main block of homes around the edge of the village, but there is now no way of finding out what they were used for.

Mysterious carvings

It is not very hard to make simple tools out of stone, but some of the examples of stone craft found at Skara Brae show that the villagers became very highly skilled at intricate stone carving.

These objects include stone balls with spiral designs carved on them, similar to those found in other places in the Orkney Islands and on the Scottish mainland.

But some objects are more cleverly made than those found elsewhere. One is an oval stone with double-pointed ends. Another is a ball covered with sharp spikes. It is hard to think of any use for these strange objects unless they had some religious meaning – though no one has been able to suggest what it was.

Some archaeologists think that the carvings on some of these stones may be an early form of writing. There are marks that look as if they have been arranged carefully in patterns of lines. Perhaps different patterns had different meanings.

There is no reason why the people of Skara Brae should have had a written language. They lived in a small village where they could communicate without writing to each other. The marks may be only decorations, like the patterns on Skara Brae pottery. But if they have any meaning, it could be some simple religious idea. For example, one pattern could represent one particular god.

Sadly, if the Skara Brae villagers were communicating with each other in writing, we will never know what they wrote.

Excavating Skara Brae

Excavations at Skara Brae began soon after the village was uncovered by the storm of 1850. But the major work on the site was done in 1928 and 1929 by a leading archaeologist of the time, Vere Gordon Childe.

Born in Australia, Professor Childe was an expert in prehistoric archaeology at Edinburgh University in Scotland. In 1928 he started work at Skara Brae, excavating another house and another section of the village passageway.

His discoveries added a great deal to our knowledge of Skara Brae, but he did not have today's equipment which makes it possible to date sites with great accuracy. Professor Childe believed that Skara Brae was a settlement of the Picts, a tribe who lived in the north of Scotland in Roman times. Modern radio-carbon dating of animal bones on the site have put the date of the village at between 3100 and 2480 BC, far earlier that Professor Childe could have guessed.

Troy

Turkey, c. 2500–1400 BC

*Everyone has heard of the ten-year war between the Greeks and the Trojans.
But what is the true story of the city that
held out for so long against an army determined to destroy it?*

The story of Troy is just one of the legends that have come down to us from Greek story-tellers. Many of these legends were retold by Homer, a Greek poet who was writing before 700 BC, many centuries after the events he described had happened. No one knows how many of the legends about Troy are true, but they have become part of world history and literature.

When the ruins of ancient Troy were discovered about 130 years ago, archaeologists were keen to try to link their discoveries with the stories. Which of the cities built on the same site, they wondered, was the Troy that Homer wrote about?

The strange answer may be: two.

Fortress Troy

Troy II, as archaeologists call it, was a living city somewhere between 2500 and 1400 BC. Only about 90 metres (300 ft) across, it was more like a fortress than a city. Great watch-towers were set in its walls. It was clearly built to withstand attack. Among its houses, one – probably the ruler's – was much larger than the others.

It was in Troy II that Heinrich Schliemann, the archaeologist who led the first excavations of Troy in 1870, discovered the hoard of treasure that you can read about on page 41.

Death and destruction

Homer's story about the Siege of Troy ends with the city being destroyed by the Greeks. There was no sign that Troy II had been attacked, but when archaeologists excavated the remains of the later Troy VI they discovered signs of destruction and fire. So perhaps Troy VI was the city that was overcome at the end of the Trojan War – in other words, Homer's Troy.

Homer described a city on a hill in the middle of

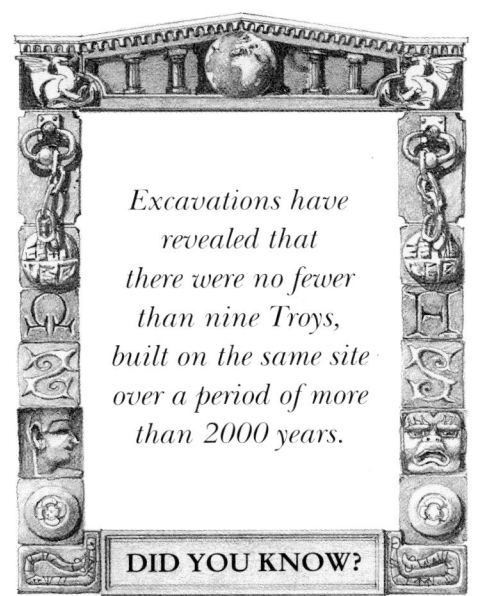

Excavations have revealed that there were no fewer than nine Troys, built on the same site over a period of more than 2000 years.

DID YOU KNOW?

*The story goes that the Greeks gave the Trojans a huge wooden horse.
Unknown to the Trojans, there were Greek soldiers hidden inside. When night fell, the soldiers
climbed out and opened the city gates to let their army in.*

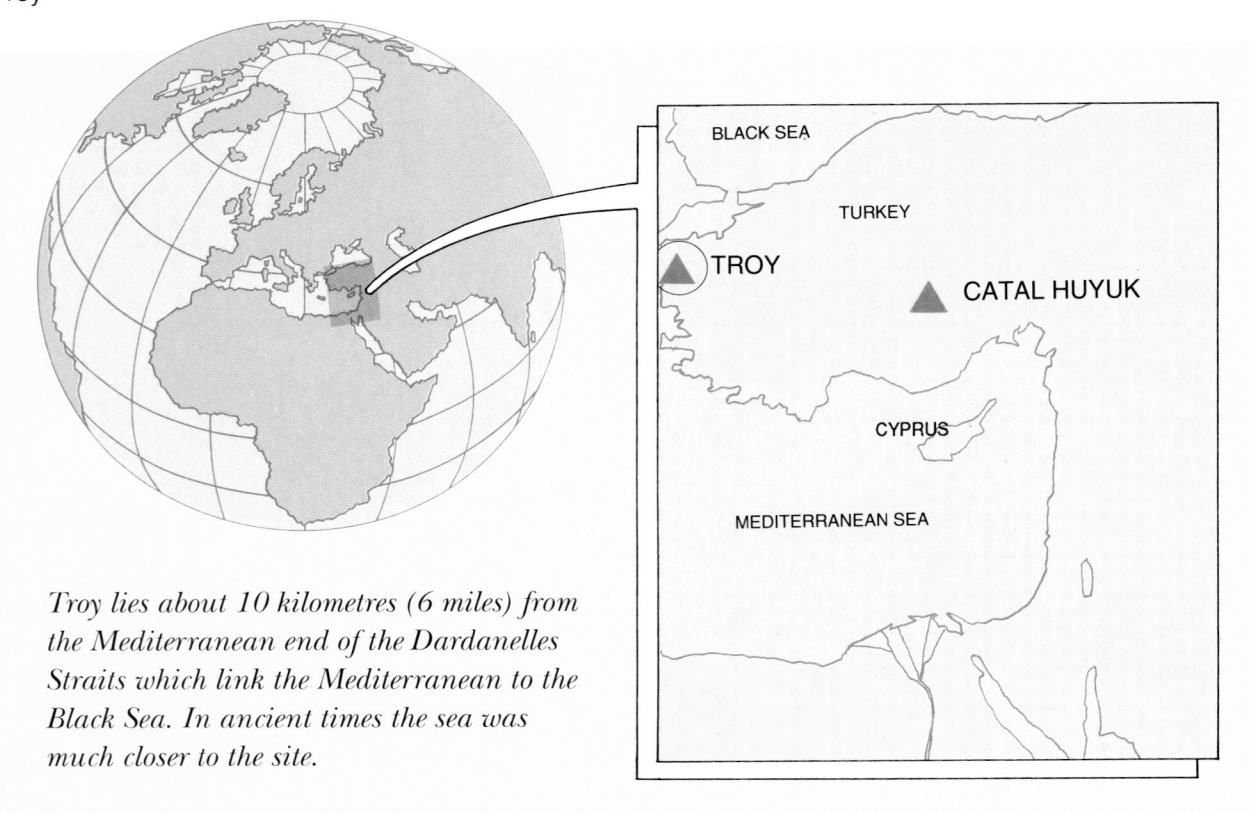

BLACK SEA

TURKEY

▲ TROY

▲ CATAL HUYUK

CYPRUS

MEDITERRANEAN SEA

Troy lies about 10 kilometres (6 miles) from the Mediterranean end of the Dardanelles Straits which link the Mediterranean to the Black Sea. In ancient times the sea was much closer to the site.

a windswept plain. Its wide streets were enclosed by a solid wall. At the top of the hill stood the magnificent castle of King Priam, its walls lined inside with marble. Was this Troy VI? It was certainly a city which had met with some kind of disaster.

Priam's city?

Although Troy VI was bigger than the earlier cities, it was still quite small. It contained enough houses within the walls for about 1000 people, though many more – perhaps up to 5000 – may have lived outside the walls in wooden houses which have since vanished.

The walls were immensely strong. In one place, the foundations went down 7 metres (23 ft). They could have supported a watch-tower over 20 metres (65 ft) high, which would have given the people of Troy good warning of any approaching enemies.

There were large houses, the homes of Troy's most important citizens, arranged in terraces on the slopes towards the centre. At the top of the slope stood the royal palace. Nothing remains of this, but a clue to where it was is provided by the fact that all the roads in the city seem to lead to this point.

The mysterious fall of Troy VI

What happened to bring the life of this prosperous city to an end? If it was Homer's Troy and his story is true, it was wrecked by the Greeks after they had conquered it. But there is evidence that other forces were at work.

The catastrophe happened between about 1300 and 1250 BC. Some archaeologists think that the cause was an earthquake as the ruins are in one of the world's major earthquake zones. There are cracks in the walls that could have been caused in this way, but that may not be the whole story.

The ruins also show signs of fire damage. This might have been the result of the earthquake, when roof timbers crashed down on to hearths, or it could have been caused by an enemy attack. There are two sets of clues that suggest that such an attack took place. First, some of the damage to the walls looks more like the work of battering rams than of an earthquake. Second, a large number of weapons, probably Greek, have been found inside the walls.

Hard times

The people of Troy VI, who had the wealth and skills to rebuild, do not seem the sort to let their city just fall apart. But the next Troy was a much poorer place in which the people seem to have struggled to survive. The large houses were divided into smaller units, and there are few signs of wealth. So whatever happened in Troy VI seems to have destroyed the spirit of the people as well as many of the buildings.

The destruction of Troy

According to Homer's story, the Greeks slaughtered the leading citizens of Troy before ransacking the city. Perhaps, at the end of a long and bitter war, they damaged it so badly that it looked like the wreckage of an earthquake. They may have finished off the job by setting fire to the ruins.

This would have left the survivors – perhaps people who lived outside the walls and had been able to flee into hiding – with the task of carrying on their lives in the ruins. The wealth and leadership of the rich were no longer there to help them. This would explain why the city was never again as magnificent as Troy VI had been.

Real Trojan horses

Where did the wealth of Troy VI come from? Objects found in the ruins show that goods flowed into the city from Greece and Cyprus, as well as from places closer to home. Some of these were luxury items such as a gaming board, silver pins, beads made from ivory and carnelian (a semi-precious stone), pottery and stoneware.

To obtain these goods, Troy VI must have traded other things in return, but there is less evidence of what these were. The city is said to have been famous for breeding horses, and these would have made a valuable export. The discovery of many horse bones on the site supports this idea.

Many pieces of spinning equipment have also been found, so the Trojans might have made and traded in cloth. A third possibility is fishing. In the time of Troy VI the sea was closer to the city than it is now. Perhaps, too, Troy exported its own pottery, which has been found in Cyprus and the Middle East.

A Trojan coin.

City of dreams

*The picture on the right is not
a reconstruction of Troy as it
really was. Instead, it shows
how the Greeks imagined it
from their legends and from
Homer's description. Homer
was writing centuries after
Troy had been destroyed, so his
picture of the city is also drawn
from stories he had heard.*

*The long flight of steps leads
to the royal palace among the
trees, protected by a massive
inner wall. The buildings
with pillars supporting
sloping roofs are temples to
the Trojan gods.*

*Apart from what looks like
a small market close to the
nearest city wall, and perhaps
a working area to the left of the
picture, there is little hint of
the trade that must have
provided Troy with its wealth.
This may have been carried on
outside the walls.*

The real Troy

*In reality, as the excavations
showed, none of the nine Troys
had streets as wide as those in
the picture. Nor, even at its
most magnificent, did the city
have so many impressive
buildings.*

*To us, the real Troy VI – the
largest of the nine – would
seem small. It covered an area
only about 200 x 120 metres
(650 x 390 ft). If it is true
that about 1000 people lived
inside the city walls, they must
have lived in very crowded
conditions.*

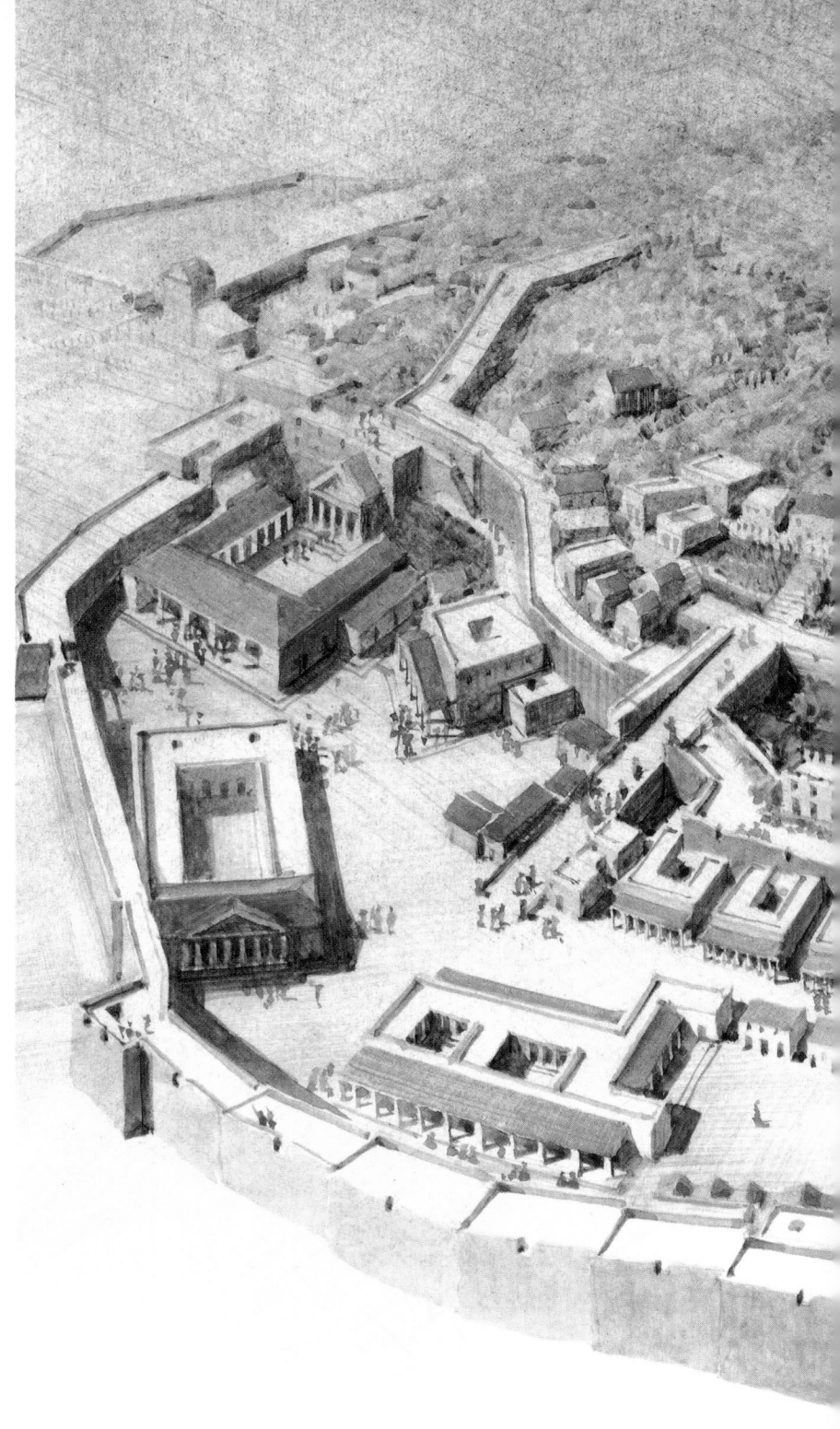

The Trojan Wars

According to Homer, the Trojan Wars began with a kidnap. The King of Sparta in Greece had a beautiful wife, Helen. Paris, the son of King Priam of Troy, fell in love with her and took her back to Troy.

This was the cue for an all-out Greek mission to rescue Helen and punish the Trojans. A great fleet of ships with warriors from all over Greece set out for Troy.

The Greeks expected a quick victory, but the fight proved harder than they had hoped. Landing on the coast, they reached the walls of Troy but were unable to break through. After a great battle, they surrounded the city and laid siege to it.

Stalemate

The siege continued for ten years. There were many battles but neither side gained the advantage. It began to look as if neither side could ever win. Then the Greeks had an idea. They built a huge wooden horse, large enough to conceal troops inside. The Greek fleet sailed away, leaving the horse behind on the shore.

The Trojans were delighted. They thought the horse was a peace-offering, and that the Greeks would trouble them no more. They hauled the horse through the city gates. At last, they thought, the long siege was over.

Darkness fell. As the Trojans celebrated the end of the war, the Greek ships sailed back under cover of night. Silently, Greek soldiers landed on the shore.

Their parties over, the Trojans went to bed. Then the doors of the wooden horse opened and the hidden Greek warriors jumped out. They crept to the city gates and opened them to let in their comrades. The siege of Troy was really over at last. Helen was reunited with her husband, and Troy was plundered and destroyed.

Greek and Trojan warriors locked in combat.

King Priam's treasure

One of the stories handed down from Greek legend is about the great storehouse of treasures belonging to King Priam of Troy. This story was very much in the mind of Heinrich Schliemann, the first archaeologist to excavate the mound that hid the ruins of Troy.

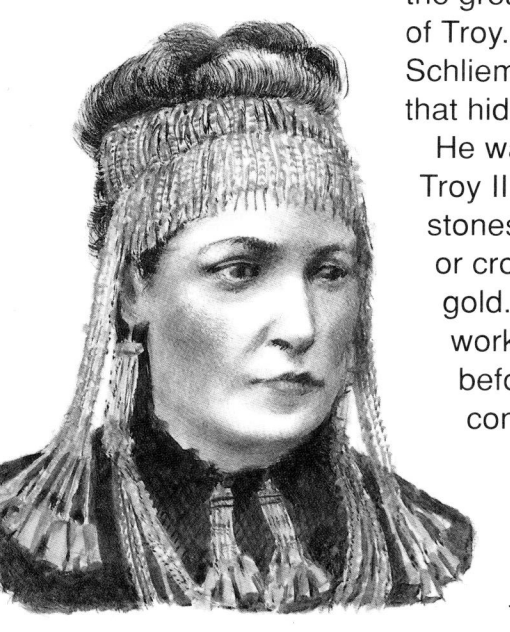

Mrs Schliemann wearing some of Priam's treasure.

He was not disappointed. As he worked on the site of Troy II, he found vast hoards of valuable objects – precious stones, gold jewellery, cups and salvers. One gold diadem, or crown, was made up of over 16,000 separate pieces of gold. Schliemann told how he and his wife Sophie worked secretly to dig out and remove these treasures before local people could steal them. The finds convinced him that he had found King Priam's Troy.

Later archaeologists doubted Schliemann's claims. He might, they said, have collected the treasures from more than one level of the Troy cities. He might even have gathered them in different parts of the site and saved them up until he had enough to make a good story. Archaeologists do not always trust each other.

An amateur archaeologist

Originally a German merchant, Heinrich Schliemann took up archaeology as a hobby. He had not been trained and his methods of working were clumsy by today's standards.

Instead of working slowly and recording his finds, he dug straight into the middle of the mound that hid the remains of Troy. In doing so, he destroyed evidence that could have told us more about the city, and the records he kept of his work were confused. He was determined to find the Troy that Homer had written about, and every discovery convinced him that he had succeeded.

To be fair, Schliemann was working in the 1870s before archaeology had become a science. He had been led to the mound that was Troy by a careful reading of Homer, and when he started work, excitement took over from caution. He was careless, but he was the first to find the site and lead others to follow him.

The saddest part of the story is what happened to 'King Priam's treasure'. This and Schliemann's other finds were collected together in a museum in Berlin, but during World War Two, they vanished. Unless they are found again some time in the future, the truth about their age will never be known.

Biskupin
Poland, c. 700–400 BC

By a Polish lake, the people of Biskupin built their wooden houses, with a sturdy wall to keep out intruders. But one of their most dangerous enemies was in their own homes.

Round about the year 720 BC, a group of people arrived by the shores of Lake Biskupin in central Poland. They were probably Slavs from the east. It would have been summer, as travelling through the bitter winter of central Europe was almost impossible.

They decided to make their homes beside the lake. There was a piece of marshy land jutting out into the water, and they chose this as the site. The fact that there was water on three sides, giving them protection from attack, might have helped them to make their choice.

Saved by mud

Lake Biskupin is a large stretch of water about 225 kilometres (140 miles) west of the Polish capital, Warsaw. In those days, the lake was smaller than it is now, and in the summer it may have shrunk to a watery bog.

If the people of Biskupin had not chosen this site for their village, we might never have known about it. Although the village was built entirely of wood, much of it was preserved when, years later, the lake grew in size and covered the houses with sand and mud. It was beneath these deposits that Biskupin was discovered in the 1930s.

Who were the enemy?

The people of Biskupin had chosen difficult land to work on, but perhaps the protection given by the water was more important to them. To make doubly sure of their safety, they surrounded the village with a wall 6 metres (20 ft) high and 3 metres (10 ft) across. It was a double wall made of wood, with earth filling the space between. The only opening was a single gate, probably with some kind of watchtower above it, on the landward side.

For people whose main activities were farming

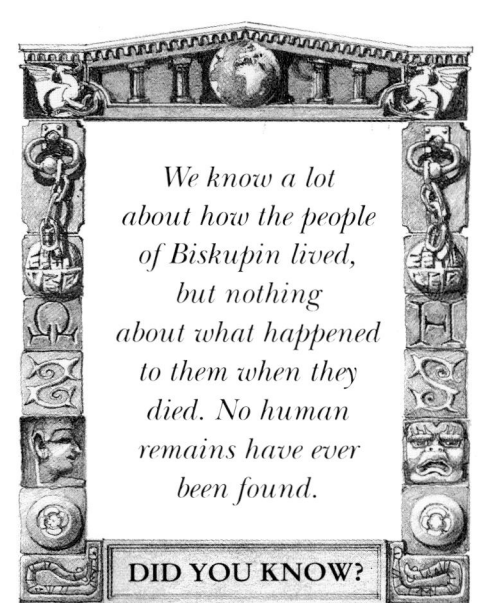

We know a lot about how the people of Biskupin lived, but nothing about what happened to them when they died. No human remains have ever been found.

DID YOU KNOW?

The Biskupin villagers had a strong sense of co-operation and teamwork. Here, they are working together to rebuild a house damaged by fire. The houses were so close together that a fire could spread very fast.

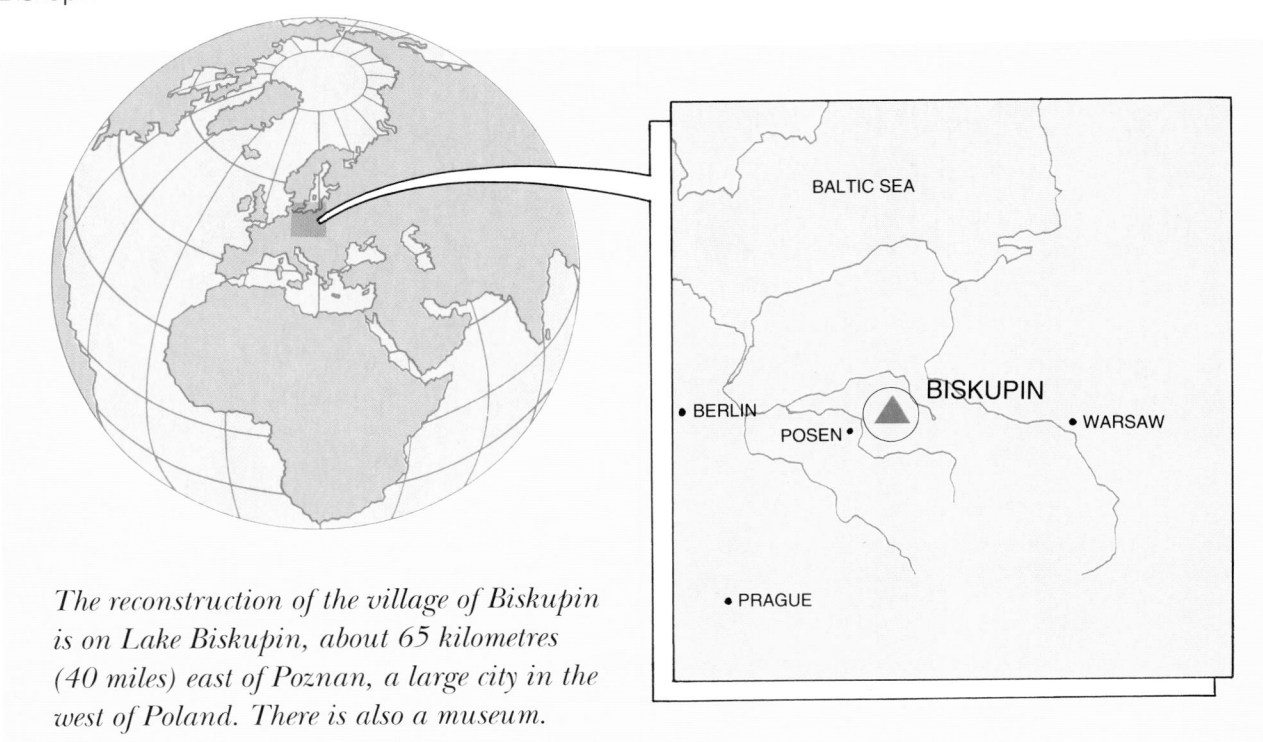

The reconstruction of the village of Biskupin is on Lake Biskupin, about 65 kilometres (40 miles) east of Poznan, a large city in the west of Poland. There is also a museum.

and craft work, this seems like a lot of effort to make to defend themselves. What were they afraid of? There are no signs that Biskupin was ever attacked. But other walled villages, not as well preserved, have been found in Poland. Probably any prosperous village like Biskupin was at risk from robbers.

Houses on stilts

As the ground was so soft, the builders had to sink supports deep into the marsh to keep the houses upright. They also paved the ground between the houses with logs so that people could move about more easily.

About one hundred houses were packed inside the wall in an area of about 2 hectares (5 acres). They were built in long rows side by side, rather like a terrace of houses today, with log pavements between them. There was a wooden road running round the village just inside the wall. Building houses in rows, which used less wood and space,

and took less time, than if the houses were separate, is interesting because it shows that the people of Biskupin must have been well organised and willing to work together on a community project.

Damp-proofing

Most of the houses had one large room, though some were split into two. They had wooden floors which rested on layers of birch sticks to stop dampness creeping up from the marshy land below. Each house had a stone hearth covered with a layer of clay to cut down the risk of fire.

The winters in this part of Poland were harsh, with heavy snow and biting winds from the east. The lake and marsh were frozen over for several months on end. There would be little activity out of doors at that time of year. In such a climate, building houses in rows, so that most of them had only two outside walls, would have helped to conserve heat.

Keeping themselves to themselves

The variety of objects found at Biskupin shows that the people there lived full, active lives. They kept cattle, sheep, pigs and goats. They ploughed the land nearby and grew wheat, barley and some kind of beans. They also made things. Spindles and loom weights for spinning and weaving have been found, together with leather-working tools and evidence of metal-working, at first in bronze and later in iron.

There are some signs that trade was carried on. Amber and glass beads found at Biskupin may have come from the Baltic, and other objects came from Hungary and Italy. But it is highly unlikely that the village was an important trading centre. It is possible that traders from other places passed by and exchanged goods.

The lives of the Biskupin people seem to have been very much rooted in their own community and they would perhaps have been put off exploring by the dangers of travel and trade.

Escaping the flood

Wooden buildings, especially in a harsh climate, need constant repair. We do not know how long the village of 720 BC lasted, but it seems that at some point, some houses had fallen down or been demolished.

By 560 BC, Biskupin was slightly smaller. One street had disappeared and the original houses had been replaced by smaller ones which were less well built. They were possibly sited at a higher level above the marsh, and it may be that the level of the lake was already rising.

If this happened in winter, it must have been a severe blow to the population, who would have had to build new shelter quickly. This could explain why the later houses were evidently put up in a hurry.

In the end there was no escaping the waters of the lake. They flooded the site and it had to be abandoned – but it was the rising water that preserved Biskupin for us to see today.

Victim of war

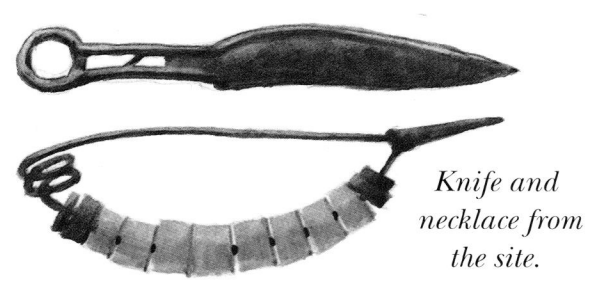

Knife and necklace from the site.

With a team from the University of Poznan, Jozef Kostrewski began work at Biskupin in 1933. Until the Nazi invasion of Poland in 1939, the excavation went well, with finds being carefully recorded. Sadly, the invaders destroyed the team's records and even some of the finds, so that our knowledge of Biskupin can now never be as good as it might have been.

When peace came, the Polish archaeologists returned and continued their work. They have since reconstructed of some of the buildings so that visitors can see what the original settlement was like.

A wooden plough.

The worst enemy

Although the people of Biskupin believed that there were enemies outside their village wall, their greatest enemy was inside. It was fire.

The entire village – even its roads and pavements – was built of wood. Every house had its hearth, and in some buildings the fires had to be stoked up to reach the high temperatures needed for metal-working. Fire was an ever-present risk, and evidence has been found that

Biskupin was several times partly destroyed. It is easy to imagine how panic would spread along the rows of houses if fire broke out in one of them. The buildings were so tightly packed together that any fire could easily have wiped out the entire village.

Perhaps it was the knowledge that they all depended on each other that bound the community tightly together. If they were to

survive as a village, they had to work together to stop fires spreading and to repair any damage. In the picture above they are rushing to put out a fire in one of the houses. It is not hard to imagine them forming a human chain to pass containers of water from the lake.

But this kind of teamwork usually needs a leader to organise it. In most ancient settlements there was a leader or chieftain, whose home stood out because it was larger than the others. There is no sign of a chieftain's house at Biskupin. Perhaps the village leader lived in the same kind of house as everyone else. It may be that the village was ruled by someone living outside. Although we can understand a lot about life at Biskupin from the objects found there, we know nothing about how its society worked or even what language they spoke.

Copan

Honduras, c. AD 300–900

*At the top of the pyramids, high above the city of Copan,
human and animal sacrifices were carried out in the hope of pleasing the gods
and bringing prosperity.*

Copan was built by the Maya people, a civilisation that flourished in Central America between AD 300 and 900. It was an advanced civilisation in many ways: it had a written language and used a calendar similar to ours. The Maya were also expert craftsmen in stone. However, there were strange gaps in their knowledge.

They knew about the wheel and used it on toys – but they had no wheeled transport and did not use wheels to make pottery. They were good arable farmers, but they did not raise animals. They hunted wild animals for their meat. Although in their later years they discovered how to work with metal, they used it only for decorative things and continued to make tools and weapons out of stone.

Worship and war

The two most important things in the life of the Maya were religion and war. Both were bloodthirsty.

The Maya cities fought savagely among themselves, and their battles ended with the beheading of the leaders of the losing side. Prisoners of war became slaves.

From early childhood, boys were trained for war. They were taken to live away from their families and taught to paint themselves black, the colour of Maya warriors. When they returned to their families, they married and exchanged their war paint for colourful body decorations and tattoos.

The Maya religion involved human and animal sacrifices, and ceremonies in which they tortured their own bodies. It seems that the Maya gloried in the sight of blood.

City in the forest

Copan was built about AD 725 in a clearing in the upland forest of what is now Honduras.

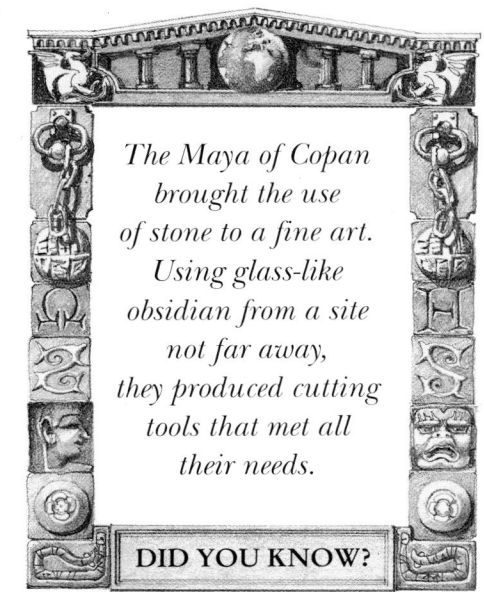

The Maya of Copan brought the use of stone to a fine art. Using glass-like obsidian from a site not far away, they produced cutting tools that met all their needs.

DID YOU KNOW?

A sacred ball game, played on a special court, was part of the religion of the people of Copan. This picture, based on carvings found at Copan, shows one of the players dressed for action.

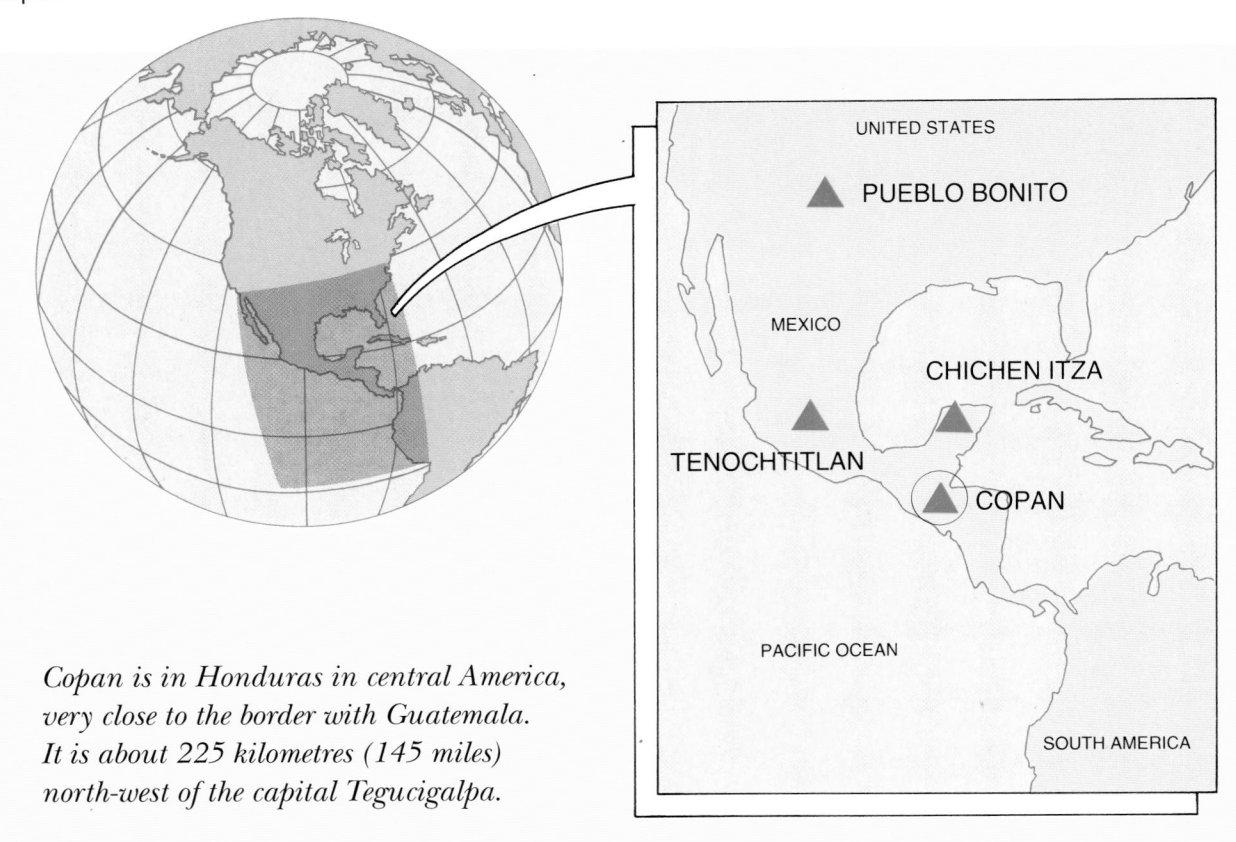

Copan is in Honduras in central America, very close to the border with Guatemala. It is about 225 kilometres (145 miles) north-west of the capital Tegucigalpa.

Its centrepiece was a collection of temples and pyramids set on a raised stone platform. Below this were the city's houses, which were built of wood and have long since disappeared. Copan was a large city, with many thousands of homes.

Good and bad days

Among the most important people among the Maya were the scribes. They were the scholars of Maya society. At least some of them were also priests. This double role gave them great power.

They were especially good mathematicians and astronomers. It was the scribes who worked out the Maya calendar, which you can read about on page 54. They were also responsible for keeping the records of Maya history.

To the Maya, the calendar was much more than a way of telling what day it was. It was closely linked with their religion. They believed that the days were gods, some bringing good times and others bringing disaster. There were also gods linked to the success of farming, such as the corn god and the rain god. It was to please these gods that sacrifices were made.

History in stone

The history of their people was important to the Maya. It brought together the ideas of time and religion.

The plaza or public square below the pyramids of Copan were dotted with stone stelae or pillars. On these was carved writing telling stories of Maya history and also the religious meaning of the calendar. The stelae were richly illustrated with pictures of the gods, who had life-like faces and bodies decorated in great detail.

Stone was not the only material the Maya used for their writing. They also wrote on animal skins and paper made of bark.

The fight to survive

Providing the essentials of life for a city of several thousand people, using very basic tools, was hard work, but the Maya were very active people.

They were enthusiastic arable farmers, cutting down the forest to make way for crops. Tree-felling must have been difficult without metal tools, and without wheeled waggons to haul the felled trees away. Once they had cleared the land, the farmers grew corn, beans, squashes – pumpkin-like vegetables – and chillies. In the remaining forests hunters caught deer and wild pigs, using darts, snares and traps.

The Maya had an unusual method of fishing. They put drugs, such as the leaves of the fish-fuddle tree, in the water to stun the fish so that they could be easily caught.

What happened to Copan?

The Maya civilisation was gradually overtaken, from around AD 900, by the more powerful Toltec people. But there is no sign that the Toltecs ever attacked Copan.

It seems that at some point the city began to lose its prosperity, and its people drifted away to new homes. The quick-growing tropical forests reclaimed the land that the Maya had used for farming, and it was deep in thick forest that the ruins of Copan were discovered about 800 years later. But it was not the end of the Maya people. Their descendants still live in parts of Guatemala and Honduras.

Plodding along

It is strange that, in spite of their grasp of practical skills such as building and their understanding of mathematics, the Maya people did not use wheeled transport or discover the use of the wheel for making pottery. Yet they knew about wheels and used them on toys. Somehow they failed to apply this knowledge to other things.

Trucks and wheel barrows would have been of great help to them in their huge building work. It may be that because they had a plentiful supply of slaves to do heavy carrying and lifting work, they saw no need to make these tasks easier.

As there was no contact between the Maya and civilisations in other continents, they knew nothing of the wheeled transport that had been used in Babylon 5000 years before.

There were no horses or cows in the Americas before the Spanish arrived in 1519. So the Maya had no pack animals either and relied on people power.

Wheeled toy from a Mayan tomb.

Death in the sky

Sacrifices and other religious ceremonies took place in the temples at the top of the pyramids which were dotted about Copan. Unlike Egyptian pyramids, those of the Maya civilisation were built in stepped layers, with a long flight of steps leading up to the top. The religious centre of Copan, seen here, is the only part to have survived.

Only scribes and a few other privileged people were allowed to climb the steps to the temples. Here, sweet-smelling incense was burned as the religious ceremonies were carried out.

Human sacrifices were attended by four men who were called chacs. Their job was to hold down the victim. But the sacrifice was not always human; dogs, squirrels, iguanas or birds were sometimes killed instead.

Looking into the future

Another ceremony performed in the pyramid temples involved a soothsayer or prophet, called a chilam, who would go into a trance and foretell the future.

These ceremonies would be watched by the people of Copan who gathered in the square below. The shape of the pyramids would have concentrated their attention and led their gaze upwards to what was happening at the top. Viewed from below, it must have seemed that the temples were up in the sky.

Experts on time

The Maya calendar, like ours, was based on the time that the earth takes to complete its journey round the sun. The scribes were able to calculate this very precisely. They made it 365.2420 days, which is only two-thousandths of a day (or just under three minutes) different from the most modern scientific calculations.

The Maya divided their year into twenty periods of eighteen days each. As this made 360 days, five days were left over at the end of the year. These days 'outside the calendar' were called the haab, and they had a special meaning for the Maya.

Days of danger

As the other 360 days all belonged to particular gods, the five days of the haab were particularly dangerous. The Maya took care not to fall asleep in daylight on these days, not to quarrel with anyone, and not to stumble or trip. If they could, they stayed at home and refused to do any work that they did not like. Only when the new year started was it safe to resume their normal lives.

The calendar had an important practical use in planning the sowing and harvesting of the farmers' crops. But Maya culture and religion were also closely tied to time. The Maya believed that time moved in a circle and that history repeated itself. Periods of war and political upheaval would occur regularly and could be predicted from what had happened in the past. Their calculations ranged from up to 400 million years into the past, and up to 4000 years ahead.

The scribes' study of the calendar produced some remarkably accurate forecasts of the future. One, for example, predicted the arrival of white men. In the sixteenth century, this is exactly what happened. Europeans arrived, and the old civilisations were destroyed.

Above: symbols from a Mayan calendar.

A Mayan scribe.

The Olmecs

The Maya borrowed many of their beliefs from the Olmec civilisation, which flourished in Central America from 1200 BC to about AD 400.

The first people to live in the area were probably from North America.

A huge Olmec stone head.

They had travelled from the north and moved from place to place as they hunted for their food. About 1500 BC these people began to settle in villages and farm the land around them. Their villages grew into towns, and this was the start of the Olmec culture.

The Olmecs lived in an area where there was little stone, so they used clay for their buildings, including the pyramid temples. Towards the end of the Olmec civilisation the people developed a calendar and a method of writing. The language was similar to that of the Maya, and many of the features of their religion, such as the importance attached to the jaguar, continued into Maya times.

The Olmec civilisation did not develop as far as building cities, though the village which grew into the city of Copan under the Maya was probably founded by the Olmecs. The earlier culture laid the foundations of a civilisation on which the Maya, with their greater skills and better resources, were able to build.

Lost in the jungle

Copan was first discovered in the 1830s by Colonel Juan Galindo. In 1839 two American explorers who specialised in the civilisations of Central America, John Stephens and Frederick Catherwood, made the first excavations there. But it was not until the 1880s that another American, Percival Maudslay, surveyed the site properly for the first time and made many new discoveries.

Between the visit of Stephens and Catherwood and that of Maudslay, photography had been invented. Maudslay was one of the first people to show how valuable the camera could be as an archaeological tool. His collection of pictures provides a record of what the ruins of Copan looked like as he uncovered them. Between 1935 and 1947 there were more excavations with American sponsorship, and some of the ruins were restored.

The legendary Quetzalcoatl

A huge and strange creature, half serpent and half bird, is the hero of many of the stories of the Central American civilisations. Its name is Quetzalcoatl (pronounced Kwet-sal-co-at-el) or Kukulcan. The stories of Quetzalcoatl began long before the time of the Maya, but they took them over as part of their own religion.

In the stories, Quetzalcoatl is the creator of law and knowledge and the inventor of the calendar. He taught people everything that they knew, including how to farm, weave and make pots. He showed the human race that corn was good food. Changing himself into a black ant, he stole some corn from the red ants and showed humans how to plant it.

Is the story of Quetzalcoatl based on a real person who at some time lived in Central America? We can only guess at the answer. It seems likely that there were a number of great rulers who each added something to Central American culture. Over the years, memories of these rulers were joined into one. Perhaps the idea was that Quetzalcoatl – who could change himself into anything he chose – inhabited each of these men in turn.

In one way, Quetzalcoatl was very different from the people who worshipped him. He was a kind leader who hated to hurt any living creature and who would not allow any but the smallest sacrifices to be made to him. By the time Copan was built, this side of Quetzalcoatl had been forgotten.

One of the myths about Quetzalcoatl was an explanation of night and day. In this story, Quetzalcoatl was the son of the Sun and Moon. As he grew up, he discovered that he had enemies – the stars of the Milky Way – who were determined to kill Quetzalcoatl's father. They succeeded, and buried the Sun's body in sand.

Vultures came to Quetzalcoatl, who was then nine years old, and told him what had happened. Helped by animal friends, he found the body and brought his father back to life.

Quetzalcoatl, the Feathered Serpent.

Tezcatlipoca

In most religions, different figures represent good and evil. In Central America, Quetzalcoatl, the son of the Sun and Moon, represented good. His main enemy was Tezcatlipoca (pronounced Tes-cat-li-po-ca), who was the god of the night and whose 400 star sons in the Milky Way had hunted down and killed the Sun, who was a god called Ah Kinchil. Tezcatlipoca then set out to destroy Quetzalcoatl himself and banish good from the world for ever.

Like Quetzalcoatl, Tezcatlipoca could change his appearance whenever he liked. He could also change the appearance of other gods. His own favourite disguise was that of a turkey, a bird which is native to Central and South America. In place of one of his feet he had a mirror, and it was this that helped him bring about Quetzalcoatl's downfall.

Tezcatlipoca, god of night.

Mischief with a mirror

First, he changed Quetzalcoatl into an ugly creature with wrinkled skin and sunken eyes, and made him look in the mirror. Quetzalcoatl was so ashamed of his appearance that he hid himself away from the world.

Then Tezcatlipoca came again and changed his enemy into a beautiful creature dressed in the finest clothes. Quetzalcoatl wore a robe made of green feathers and a splendid turquoise mask. Looking in the mirror, he felt that he was once again fit to go out into the world.

Death before dishonour

This was the wily Tezcatlipoca's chance to finish him off. He organised a party at which Quetzalcoatl drank so much wine and behaved so badly that when he awoke the next day he was filled with shame and decided to kill himself.

He ordered his servants to build him a funeral pyre on the beach. Meanwhile, he dressed himself in his feathered robe and turquoise mask. When the pyre was lit, he threw himself on it and the flames destroyed him. But as he burned, the ashes rose from his body as a flock of birds, carrying his heart with them. They flew high into the sky and Quetzalcoatl's heart turned into the planet Venus.

The story says that when Venus appears each evening, it shows that Quetzalcoatl is still on his throne, shining the light of goodness down upon the world. So the whole story – the death of the Sun and the coming to life of Venus – is replayed over and over again every night.

Chichen Itza

Mexico, c. AD 950–1150

*The Toltec city of Chichen Itza was strange and sometimes sinister.
Why were more than forty people, half of them children, thrown down the sacred well?
What was the purpose of the caracol, with its spiral staircase?*

After the Maya civilisation faded away, for reasons we do not know, a new culture took its place in Central America. The newcomers, known as the Toltecs, built splendid cities, of which Chichen Itza in Mexico was a fine example, although it was only their second city. Their capital was Tula, nearly 1200 kilometres (750 miles) away across the Gulf of Mexico.

City of death

In some ways, Chichen Itza is like Copan. There are similar paved squares or plazas, similar pyramid temples, a ball court and many stone carvings. But life at Copan, compared with Chichen Itza, seems quite calm and peaceful. To judge by the carvings, the Toltec filled their lives with war, death and human sacrifice.

Images of the serpent

Like the Maya, the Toltec people worshipped a god called Quetzalcoatl (see pages 56–57), and the image of the feathered serpent appears time and again in their sculptures and in the stone columns of the main buildings of Chichen Itza.

But the Toltec Quetzalcoatl had a different character from the god of the Maya. He was more warlike and demanded more human sacrifices. One story is that Chichen Itza was ruled by a king who called himself Quetzalcoatl, perhaps to make himself popular. But he was a fierce warrior and cruel tyrant, quite unlike the god whose name he had taken. This would explain why the Toltec Quetzalcoatl seems to have presided over a reign of terror.

The Fifth Sun

One clue to how Quetzalcoatl became linked with human sacrifice is provided by one of the Quetzalcoatl myths. This tells the story of the fifth sun.

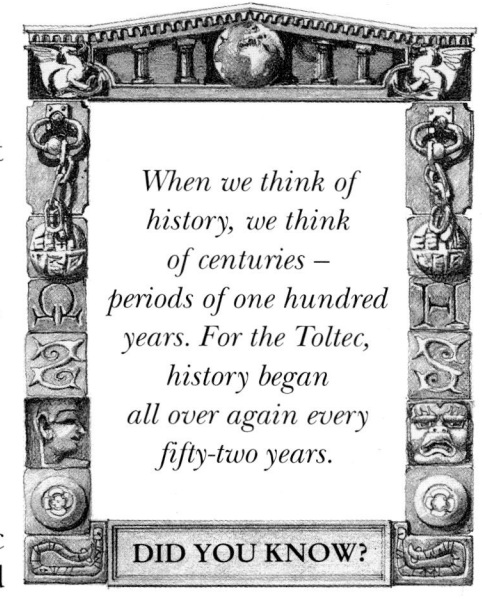

When we think of history, we think of centuries – periods of one hundred years. For the Toltec, history began all over again every fifty-two years.

DID YOU KNOW?

The procession at the top of the picture is passing a chacmool, or altar figure, which is waiting to receive the heart of a human sacrifice. Below a sculpture of Quetzalcoatl broods in the darkness of the old temple.

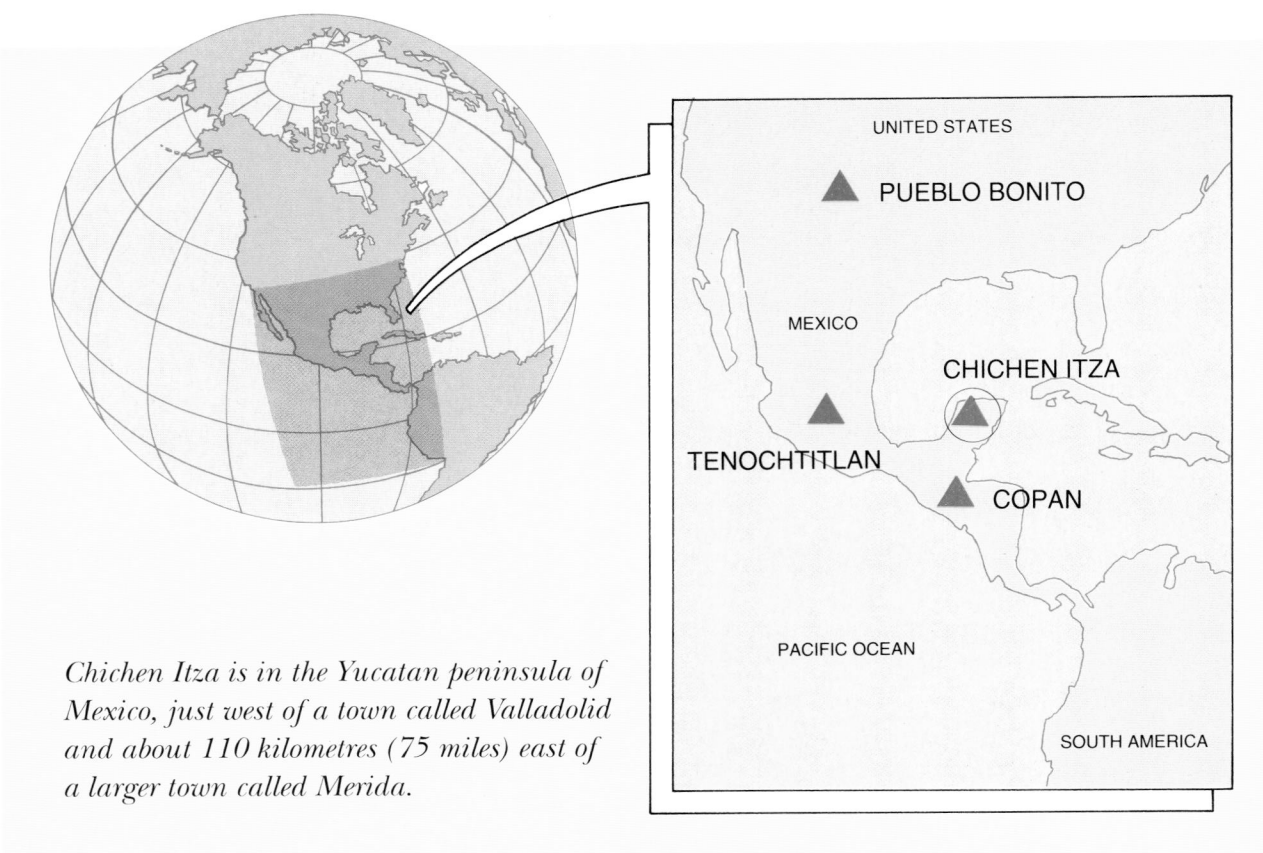

Chichen Itza is in the Yucatan peninsula of Mexico, just west of a town called Valladolid and about 110 kilometres (75 miles) east of a larger town called Merida.

The legend went that the sun that the Toltec knew was the fifth one. Four earlier suns had been destroyed in turn by jaguars, fire, wind and water. Each time, the earth returned to darkness.

Quetzalcoatl made the fifth sun, and gave light and life back to earth, by sacrificing himself and giving his heart and blood. The Toltec may have continued to offer human hearts and blood as sacrifices in the hope that these would enable the fifth sun to survive.

The temple of Quetzalcoatl

The main temple of Quetzalcoatl in Chichen Itza was a large pyramid in the centre of the city which is known today as the Castillo. It stood 24 metres (78 ft) high, and on each of its four sides there was a stairway leading to the temple at the top. Each stairway has 365 steps – one for each day of the year – and the

pyramid itself has nine steps or terraces, one for each of the nine regions of the underworld in Toltec myth. The outside is decorated with masks of gods and carvings showing Toltec warriors.

Inside the pyramid mound that the archaeologists excavated first, they found another. In the Toltec culture, the life of a temple was fifty-two years. At the end of that time, they either demolished it and put up another or, as at Chichen Itza, built a new one round the old. Among the treasures in the inner temple was a stone throne in the shape of a jaguar, with eyes of jade – a semi-precious stone – and teeth made of shell.

The sacred well

One of the grimmest finds that archaeologists made at Chichen Itza was the cenote or sacred well. It is thought that people were thrown into it in times of drought to please the rain-god Tlaloc (pronounced T-lal-ok). When the well was excavated, the skeletons of forty-two people were found, of which twenty were children. There were also pieces of jade and gold medallions with pictures of Toltec warriors.

Archaeologists say that we should read the evidence of the sacred well with care. Although human sacrifices were part of Toltec culture, the skeletons in the well date from a later time. But the gold medallions are clearly linked with the Toltecs.

The mysterious 'snail'

Of all the buildings at Chichen Itza, the most unusual is the caracol, or snail, so called because of its spiral staircase.

The caracol is the only circular building that has so far been found in the Maya or Toltec cities. Its spiral staircase is also unusual for these cultures. Archaeologists think it may have been an observation tower used by scribes to study the stars and check the calendar. Probably it was also a watchtower from which guards could warn of approaching enemies.

What happened at Chichen Itza?

What became of Chichen Itza is as much of a mystery as what happened to Copan. Both cities seem to have simply faded away for no real reason.

We know that the Toltecs' main city, Tula, was destroyed by fire around AD 1200. But there is no sign that such a disaster befell Chichen Itza, and no sign either that the city was attacked. Yet Chichen Itza began to decline in importance at about the same time.

It may be that once Tula had been destroyed, there was no future for the second Toltec city. We know that there was a good deal of trade between the two, and perhaps Chichen Itza could not survive without this. Whatever happened, neither their sacrifices to their gods nor the strength of their warriors could save the people of the city from the tide of history.

Cave of the rain god

The sacred well was not the only place in Chichen Itza dedicated to the rain god Tlaloc.

About 4 kilometres (2.5 miles) to the east of the city is a cave system with an underground stream. Water drips steadily from the ceiling, having filtered through the rock above. Perhaps the damp atmosphere made this a natural place for offerings to be made to Tlaloc. After all, it would be easy to imagine a rain god feeling at home there.

The people of Chichen Itza brought to the cave dozens of incense burners made of pottery or stone. Some of them were in the shape of Tlaloc's head. They were placed at various points through the cave system. Unusually for the Toltecs, this was a bloodless tribute; there is no sign of human sacrifices.

Pot showing the head of Tlaloc.

A hub of activity

This reconstruction shows the sacred buildings at the heart of Chichen Itza around AD 1180, before the city began to decline.

The tall, round building in the centre is the caracol, with its internal spiral staircase. It stands about 122 metres (400 ft) high. The tall pyramid to the left is the Castillo, the temple to Quetzalcoatl. Beyond, in the middle distance, the Temple of the Warriors, celebrating the Toltec people's warlike nature, stands on its smaller pyramid.

A corner of the court where the sacred ball game was played can just be seen on the left of the picture.

The city was mainly a place where ceremonies took place, and where the priests and military leaders lived. Farmers and craftsmen and their families lived some distance away in small villages near the land they worked on.

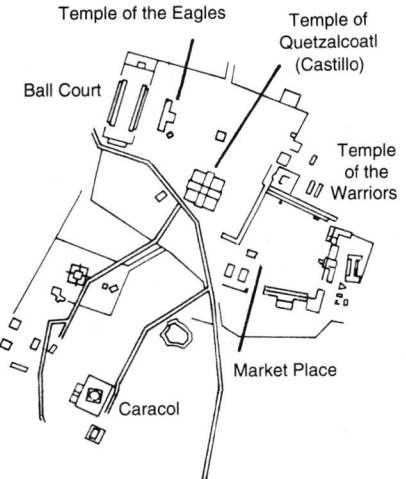

Temple of the Eagles

Temple of Quetzalcoatl (Castillo)

Ball Court

Temple of the Warriors

Market Place

Caracol

A deadly serious game

The importance the Toltecs attached to their ball game is shown by the carefully-planned arena they built for it. It is similar in some ways to a modern football ground except that there is no seating.

The playing area measured 128 x 60 metres (420 x 197 ft). This is not very different in size from a modern, full-size football pitch. The court was surrounded by a wall 8 metres (26 ft) high. Beyond the wall there was a viewing platform

for the important citizens of Chichen Itza, just as important visitors to football matches today have special places where they can get a good view of the play. Lesser folk had to watch the game from the terraces of nearby temples.

Playing for their lives

Two teams played the game with a solid, rubber ball. The aim was to score goals by passing the ball through stone rings placed

The ball court at Chichen Itza with a game in progress.

high on each side of the court. The rules of the game made scoring particularly difficult. Players were not allowed to let their hands or feet touch the ball. They had to move it with their shoulders, arms or knees.

It must have been a hard game to play, but each side probably had a great incentive to win. The locals told the Spanish invaders that the losers in Aztec games were sacrificed to the gods (see Tenochtitlan).

Skull relief from the ball court.

Chichen Itza rediscovered

The first archaeologists from the outside world to find Chichen Itza were the American travellers John Stephens and Frederick Catherwood. They did not excavate there as they did at Copan, but John Stephens published a description of the ruins in the 1840s.

The next archaeologist on the scene was E. H. Thompson, who discovered the grim secret of the sacred well and its skeletons. But this was not a careful, planned excavation, and Thompson's finds led to some false and exaggerated ideas about life in Chichen Itza.

In 1924 a team of United States archaeologists from the Carnegie Institute began the first planned excavation at Chichen Itza. Their work went on for seventeen years and examined the culture of the Toltecs from every point of view. Some of the buildings have been restored to their former glory.

Warlike city

Scenes of battle and processions of warriors were among the most common subjects of the carvings at Chichen Itza. A period of service in the army was compulsory for all men. Yet if these warriors ever went into action, it must have been well away from Chichen Itza. There is no sign among the ruins that battles were ever fought there.

The Temple of the Warriors, built to glorify war, is one of the great buildings of the city centre of Chichen Itza. There is a platform from which a stepped pyramid rises, with the temple at the top. Round the platform is a low building with its roof held up by columns, and it is these columns that give the temple its name. They are decorated with carvings of Toltec soldiers. The soldiers wear butterfly-shaped breastplates and bands of feathers on their heads, and have earrings and nose ornaments. Their weapons are javelins and spears.

Inside the temple on top of the platform are more warriors – but the columns at the entrance carry a feathered serpent design in tribute to Quetzalcoatl, showing that in the mind of the Toltecs war and religion went hand in hand.

Pueblo Bonito

New Mexico, United States, c. AD 1100–1200

In the pueblos of Chaco Canyon, the Anasazi people lived in huge, fortress-like buildings like modern apartment blocks. Why did they choose to live so close together, and what became of them?

In Chaco Canyon, in the mountains of New Mexico, are the remains of the oldest civilisation discovered so far in North America. Chaco Canyon is a strip of land no more than 1.6 kilometres (1 mile) wide and about 20 kilometres (12 miles) long. Nearly 1000 years ago, when a river flowed through the canyon, it was home to about 10,000 people. They were the Anasazi, the ancestors of the Pueblo people of today.

Living together

Most of the Anasazi lived in stone-built towns called pueblos. The pueblos were quite unlike the cities of any other ancient civilisation. They were large, fortress-like buildings on several levels, containing homes for hundreds of people.

A number of these pueblos were built along the Chaco Canyon, linked by a network of roads. The largest of these was Pueblo Bonito, alongside the River Chaco.

Around the outside wall of Pueblo Bonito, the building was four storeys high. Inside, there was a lower courtyard area. The people who lived there reached their homes by climbing up ladders on to the roof and then down again into their own rooms.

Built for defence?

Pueblo Bonito was massively built, with thick stone walls inside and out. These may have been for defence, but they would also have helped keep the rooms cool in the fierce desert heat.

Another possible reason for living together in the pueblo was that it used less land than if each family had had its own house. With so many people trying to survive on the narrow strip of fertile land in the canyon, every patch of land where crops

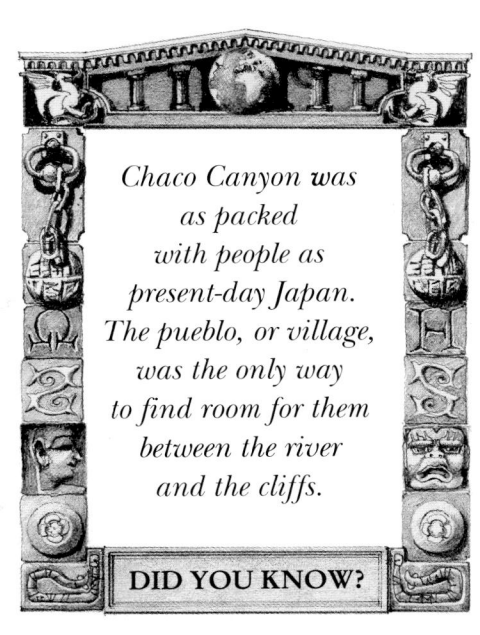

Chaco Canyon was as packed with people as present-day Japan. The pueblo, or village, was the only way to find room for them between the river and the cliffs.

DID YOU KNOW?

The thunder spirit looks down from the sky on Pueblo Bonito as an inhabitant makes an offering. To primitive peoples thunderstorms must have been terrifying, but they brought rain for the crops.

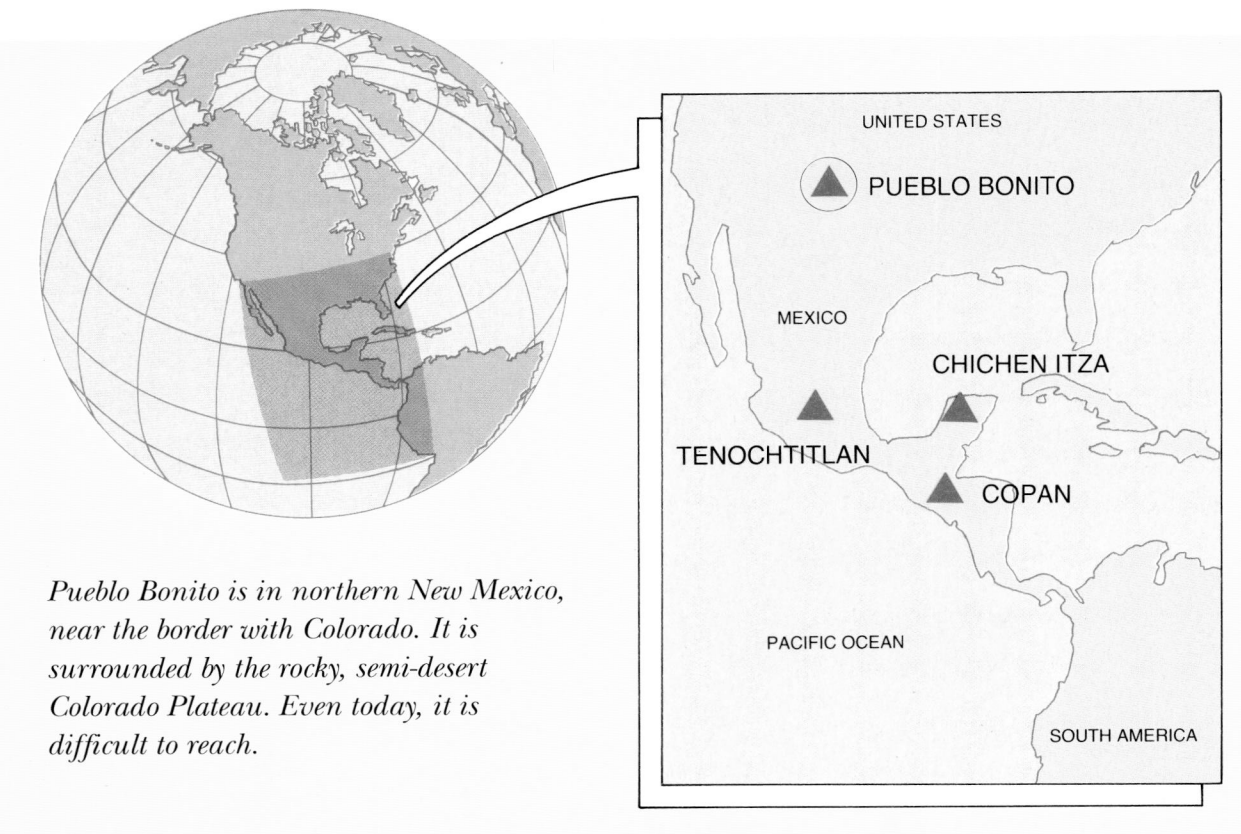

Pueblo Bonito is in northern New Mexico, near the border with Colorado. It is surrounded by the rocky, semi-desert Colorado Plateau. Even today, it is difficult to reach.

could be grown, would be valuable.

The Anasazi had no written language and they left behind no inscriptions and no stone carvings to give us clues to what their lives and culture were like. Our picture has to be pieced together from what the archaeologists found at Pueblo Bonito and the other twelve major sites in the canyon.

Learning by experience

One striking thing is the Anasazi's skill in building, all done with very basic stone tools. They must have had a system of measurement and an understanding of how weight is spread through a building in order to build a complex structure like Pueblo Bonito.

It is possible to see how their skill in building developed over the years. Deep inside Pueblo Bonito there is a core of older rooms built in the same style but more crudely. Here, the stone is more roughly cut and held together with mud. Handprints on the mud show how it was given a smooth finish by the simplest of methods. The newer houses around the original ones are better finished, and the tools found in them show that the Anasazi had made advances in their technology between the two phases of building.

Their skills extended outside their homes as well. They cut storage pits in the rock for water, which they channelled to the fields along irrigation ditches. Yet, although their ideas seem very modern in some ways, they continued to farm their land using only the most basic tools – digging sticks, stone knives and stone hoes.

Ladders to the outside world

When the people of Pueblo Bonito

were all inside, with their ladders stored away, they would have been completely safe from attack. We do not know who their enemies were, but possibly there were raiding parties of wandering people, who would have liked to plunder such a prosperous city. Some archaeologists think that this is what happened, but if so, there are no signs of a struggle.

Although Pueblo Bonito looks like a place lived in by people who were afraid of being attacked, the Anasazi did not cut themselves off from the outside world. As well as the road network linking the settlements in Chaco Canyon, they put ladders up the sheer rock faces and cut stone stairways so that they could climb out on to the plateau.

These routes were probably used by traders, but they would also allow the Anasazi to quarry precious stones like turquoise in the mountains. No doubt the meat, such as deer, elk, antelope and mountain sheep, which the people ate, also arrived in Pueblo Bonito this way.

A peaceful life

Despite the fortress-like appearance of the pueblos, there is nothing to suggest the religious violence or warrior-culture of the Central American civilisations. In fact, the picture that comes to us from the objects that the Anasazi left behind is of a peaceful life. The riverside land around Pueblo Bonito was carefully cultivated to produce maize and perhaps other crops.

Meanwhile, the women stayed at home, spinning, weaving, sewing and making baskets. Probably, except in the heat of midday, they used the roof of the pueblo as a workshop.

The Kivas

Not all the rooms in Pueblo Bonito were homes. There were also a number of larger underground rooms, known as kivas, which were used for religious ceremonies.

These were all built to a similar pattern, except that some were larger than others. Probably the smaller kivas were used by particular families. All had a stone bench built around the inside wall and a hearth in the centre. When they were found, they were open to the sky, but archaeologists think that they may have been roofed with logs, with a central hole for smoke from the fire.

Successful hunters.

What happened in the kivas?

We know very little about the religion of the Anasazi people, so we can only make guesses based on the objects found in the kivas. These include prayer sticks, which could have been used as offerings to the gods, plus torches and pipes. It may be that pipe-smoking had a ceremonial importance, as it did with Native Americans many centuries later.

Pueblo Bonito

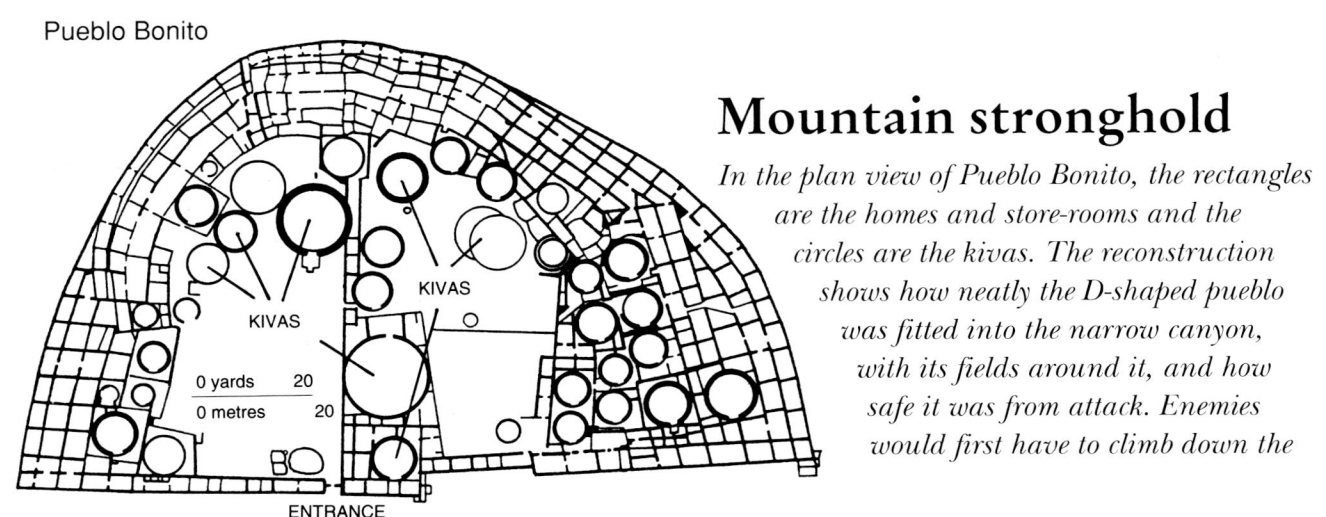

KIVAS

KIVAS

0 yards   20

0 metres   20

ENTRANCE

Mountain stronghold

In the plan view of Pueblo Bonito, the rectangles are the homes and store-rooms and the circles are the kivas. The reconstruction shows how neatly the D-shaped pueblo was fitted into the narrow canyon, with its fields around it, and how safe it was from attack. Enemies would first have to climb down the

sheer rock face, and then try to find a way into the building itself. Inside the pueblo, people were free to stroll about or visit each other using the roof as a thoroughfare.

Ideal home

The rocky plateau above Pueblo Bonito, reached by ladders, was a rich source of materials for the Anasazi. They built entirely in stone, except possibly for roofs, and seem to have had little wooden furniture. But they needed timber for ladders and fuel. Turquoise, jet and copper, which they used in their jewellery, also came from the plateau. So did their meat, as they did not breed animals. With the river beside them and the mountains above them, the Anasazi seem to have found a perfect environment for survival.

Life in Pueblo Bonito

If you think of hundreds of families living in single rooms in a large building with access to the outside only by ladder, it sounds like a cramped way of life. But it may have been less cramped than it seems to us.

Neat and cosy

The living-rooms in the pueblo were quite large – about 4 x 5 metres (13 x 16 ft). The higher rooms had windows, but the lower ones must have been dark and airless and may have been used only for storage.

Near the end of Pueblo Bonito's life some of the lower rooms were used as rubbish dumps – a valuable source of information for archaeologists.

Many of the rooms were linked to a system of ventilation which brought fresh air from outside and carried away smoke from the fires. There are hints that the people of the pueblo went to great efforts to make their lives as comfortable as they could. It seems that they frequently whitewashed the walls of their rooms, for example, to make them lighter and cover up the dirt from the fires.

They seem to have been tidy people. Many of their rooms had poles fixed to the walls to serve as clothes-racks. Some also had built-in shelves or cupboards hollowed out of the stone. They seem to have had little other furniture, but this would have left them more space for living in.

There were stone benches built into the walls of some rooms, but most people in Pueblo Bonito probably sat on the floor for their meals. They probably slept on the floor too, on mats made of rushes or willow shoots, or on blankets.

Because so many people lived in so small an area, it must have been very important to keep everything tidy and put clothes, bedding and cooking utensils out of danger.

Left: dressed for a religious ceremony.
Below: cutting maize.

Pueblo crafts

Spinning, weaving, pottery and jewellery-making were among the crafts carried on in Pueblo Bonito, probably by the women.

Around AD 1200, towards the end of the Anasazi civilisation, the pottery made at Pueblo Bonito was as good as was being made anywhere else in the world at that time. The potters had developed glazes and paints which enabled them to produce pots decorated with geometrical black-on-white designs.

They had also discovered how to make dyes and paints from different kinds of crushed rock and possibly also from plants. These were used not only on pottery, but also for cloth, and perhaps also as body paint.

Dressing up

The pueblo people were fond of adorning themselves with jewellery. They collected the brightly-coloured feathers of such birds as macaws, which they probably used in head-dresses. They particularly liked beads, and many thousands have been found in the ruins of Pueblo Bonito.

They liked to make beads out of turquoise (a semi-precious stone), but this was not found locally. Mining parties must have travelled to find it, unless it was obtained from traders. The jewellery-makers also used jet and copper, but these were also difficult to find, so they turned to materials such as shale, a soft rock found locally. The design of the jewellery was simple, but making it demanded great skill, for example in drilling the minute holes for stringing the beads.

Decorated jug.

Found on manoeuvres

Our present knowledge and understanding of Pueblo Bonito is due to the work of Neil M. Judd. He was an American archaeologist who carried out a thorough investigation of Pueblo Bonito in a series of expeditions between the 1930s and the 1950s.

His team experimented with local materials to try to find out how the Anasazi made their pottery and jewellery.

They were impressed with how skilled the Anasazi craftspeople were.

Pueblo Bonito had been discovered nearly one hundred years before. Around 1850, an American army officer, Lieutenant James Simpson, was taking part in an expedition against the Navaho people and came across the ruins. He published his account, with a detailed description of what he had seen, in 1852.

Tenochtitlan

Mexico, AD 1415–1520

*The Aztecs were such savage people that their neighbours drove them
into exile, where they built a new city. But neither its wealth nor the strength of
its army could save Tenochtitlan when the Spaniards came.*

'Go,' the god Huitzilopochtli told the Aztec people, 'and travel until you come to a place where an eagle sits on a cactus eating a serpent. When you have found it, build your city there.' (Huitzilopochtli is pronounced Whitzil-o-pock-tli.)

The Aztecs wandered for many years, looking for such a place. At last they found it, on an island surrounded by marshland. They called their city Tenochtitlan (pronounced Ten-ok-titlan), meaning 'the place of the cactus'.

Unpopular arrivals

The Aztecs were a wandering people who, some time around AD 1200, came from the north to settle in Mexico. They found themselves in the midst of a struggle for land between a number of warring tribes.

The Aztecs were so barbaric that these other tribes joined in expelling them from their new home, and by AD 1319

the Aztecs were again wanderers. It was then, Huitzilopochtli told them about the eagle.

At first sight, the place where he had led them was an unlikely spot to build a city. The site of Tenochtitlan was marshland surrounding Lake Texcoco. The water was salty and not fit to drink, and there was no wood or stone for building. But the site had good points, as well.

The land round about was good for farming, and the abundant wildfowl on the marsh promised a steady supply of meat. After their wanderings, the Aztecs were looking for a place of safety, and the marsh offered this also.

The Aztecs began building Tenochtitlan around 1350. They reclaimed land from the marsh by building platforms of mud and water plants, with basketwork barriers around the edges. Then

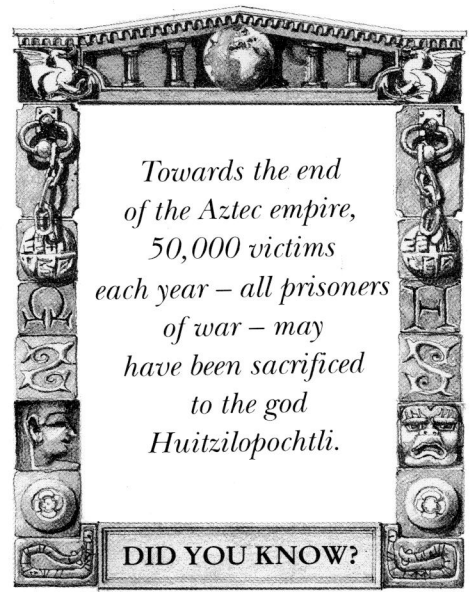

*Towards the end
of the Aztec empire,
50,000 victims
each year – all prisoners
of war – may
have been sacrificed
to the god
Huitzilopochtli.*

DID YOU KNOW?

*The eagle which showed the Aztecs where to built their new city dominates this
collection of figures from the legendary history of the Aztec people. In the centre background is
the great pyramid of Tenochtitlan, with its twin temples.*

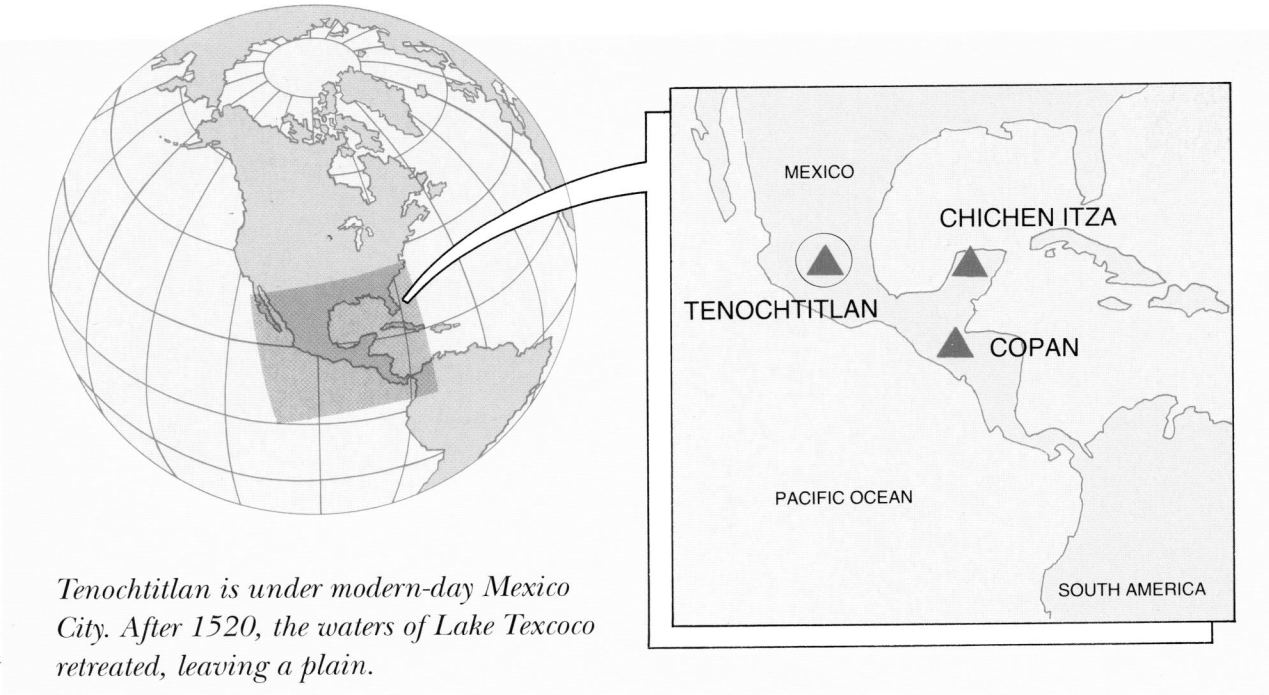

Tenochtitlan is under modern-day Mexico City. After 1520, the waters of Lake Texcoco retreated, leaving a plain.

they planted trees whose roots twined with the basketwork, and this stopped the reclaimed land from being washed away. They used the land for both farming and housing.

At first the Aztecs built wooden houses supported on poles sunk deep in the mud. But their skill at reclaiming land and building on it grew rapidly, and by about 1415 Tenochtitlan was a real city, with its main buildings made of stone from the mountains.

Over the next hundred years it continued to grow, until by 1520 it had a population of about 200,000. By then it had become a truly splendid city. But it was also a city of terror.

Trade and tribute

From the start, the Aztecs of Tenochtitlan had to trade with their neighbours for building materials and other supplies. It was not long before trade turned to war, and by 1400 the Aztecs had a huge empire.

They allowed the conquered peoples to keep their own leaders and worship their own gods, as long as 'tribute' – a kind of ransom – of such things as metal, jade, turquoise and cotton was paid. Tribes which failed to pay their tribute were attacked, and prisoners were taken. What happened to these prisoners is the most bloodthirsty part of the Aztec story.

Hearts for the sun god

In the Aztec religion, Huitzilopochtli was the god of creation and of war. He was represented by the sun. The Aztecs, correctly recognising that the sun was the source of life on earth, believed that only continuous sacrifices of human hearts and blood would keep them in the sun god's favour.

War provided victims for these sacrifices. Countless thousands of prisoners were brought back from the lands of the Aztec empire. They were taken up the steps to the temple of Huitzilopochtli at the top of the highest pyramid in Tenochtitlan. There, while they were still alive, their hearts were cut out by Aztec priests and their bodies thrown down the steps.

Some archaeologists have estimated that as many as 10,000 victims a year may have met their death in this way. Hundreds of skulls were found stored on shelves near Huitzilopochtli's temple.

A place for everyone

Tenochtitlan was a highly organised society in which everyone had his or her place. At the top was the king, who was so remote from the ordinary people that they were not even allowed to look at him. He had a council of advisers and military commanders who made up the government.

This group, together with the priests, made up the highest class of Aztec society and benefited most from the wealth of the empire. Below these people were judges, officials, merchants and army officers. Then came the skilled craftsmen, and finally, at the bottom of the ladder, the peasants who worked in the city or in the fields.

The merchants were a particularly powerful group. As they travelled far and wide, they made useful spies and often brought back information for the king about what was happening in the distant corners of his empire. Payment for this information added to the wealth they obtained from their normal trading activities.

The birth of Huitzilopochtli

Aztec legend tells how the sun god, Huitzilopochtli, drove the moon and stars from the sky.

His mother was Coatlicue (pronounced Co-at-li-queue) the earth goddess. She lived with her daughter

Carving of the Aztec earth goddess.

Coyolxauhqui (pronounced Coi-ol-how-kwee), the moon goddess, and the moon goddess's 400 star-god sons.

One day a ball of feathers fell from the sky on to Coatlicue, and she became pregnant. When Coyolxauhqui heard of this, she plotted with her 400 sons to kill her mother. But as the star gods crept up on Coatlicue, Huitzilopochtli sprang from her womb. He was already armed with a blue shield and a spear. On his left leg he wore humming-bird feathers, and on his head he wore a feathered headdress.

Huitzilopochitli first killed Coyolxauhqui with a single blow, and then chased her 400 sons until he had killed them too. And so the sun god, the Aztecs believed, defeated the gods of the night and established his rule over the earth. He became the god of creation and the god of war.

City of canals

Once the Aztecs had mastered the technique of reclaiming land, there was no limit to the number of islands they could build to cope with their growing population. This reconstruction shows what Tenochtitlan looked like round about AD 1475. By then, the city covered an area of almost 1000 hectares (4 sq. miles).

Like Venice today, Tenochtitlan was a city of islands connected by waterways. These canals were crossed by many bridges connecting the streets and alleyways, and three wide raised roads linked the islands with the centre. Water transport was used for everyday purposes: people and goods moved about the city by canoe, while rubbish was collected by big barges, which towed it away for dumping.

Many of the homes were built around courtyards where people grew vegetables and

reared turkeys. The windows of most of the houses opened on to the courtyards, giving the occupants protection from flood or attack.

Zoned city

In many ways, Tenochtitlan was organised like a modern city. It was divided into separate areas housing specialist craft workers or traders, or peasants who worked together. These areas were called calpulli. Each calpulli had its own temple and school, where boys were trained for the army. An elder from each calpulli was elected to the city government.

At the heart of the city, where the three wide roads met, was the Sacred Precinct, the area containing Tenochtitlan's main pyramid temples. It was surrounded by a high wall decorated with carved serpents' heads.

The Sacred Precinct

The walled collection of temples at the heart of Tenochtitlan was the centre of the Aztec religion. Its pyramids and courtyard temples were dedicated to the Aztec gods. There was also a court for the sacred ball game, a link with the earlier cultures of the Maya and the Toltec.

A carving of Tlaloc.

of Huitzilopochtli, skulls were picked out in white against a red background.

Tlaloc's temple was decorated with blue and white stripes.

Excavations have shown that there was a continuous programme of rebuilding and restoration to keep the great pyramid and its temples in good repair.

The great pyramid

The Sacred Precinct was dominated by a great pyramid covering an area of about 100 x 80 metres (330 x 260 ft) at its base and standing 30 metres (100 ft) high. Flights of steps led to the top, where there were two temples.

One was to Huitzilopochtli, the god of the sun and of war. It was there that the Aztecs sacrificed prisoners of war. The second temple was to Tlaloc (pronounced T-lal-ok), the same rain god that the Toltec worshipped at Chichen Itza.

The Aztecs used all their skill to decorate the pyramid and its temples. Painted heads of the feathered serpent – another reminder of Toltec culture – lined the central staircase. In the temple

Tributes to the gods

Other Aztec gods were also given temples in the Sacred Precinct. They included the Maya gods Quetzacoatl, the feathered serpent god of the wind and the morning star which we call Venus, and Tezcatlipoca, the god of the night sky (see pages 56–57). Another temple is to Huitzilopochtli's mother, Coatlicue the earth goddess.

Human sacrifice was not the only offering that the Aztecs made to their gods. Archaeologists have found more than 7000 other objects which were left at the temples in tribute. They include statues, masks, conch shells, pieces of coral, carved serpents and crocodiles.

A stone knife used for human sacrifices.

Doom foreseen

At the height of its wealth and power, the Aztec empire came to a sudden and terrible end.

The story goes that Moctezuma II, the Aztec king, had seen trouble coming. Some years before, soon after he became king, a comet had appeared in the sky. To Moctezuma, this looked like a rival to the sun, so he called for more sacrifices to give Huitzilopochtli strength to fight off the challenge.

The last years of the Aztec empire were the most bloodthirsty yet as Moctezuma's army swept through the lands they conquered taking fresh prisoners for sacrifice. The grisly ceremonies at the top of the great pyramid in Tenochtitlan were held every day. But it was all in vain.

In March 1519, an army of Spanish soldiers led by General Hernan Cortes landed in Mexico. Their arrival was welcomed by the people on the coast, who hoped that Cortes and his army would defeat the Aztecs and recover the land they had conquered. In fact, the coastal people joined forces with the Spanish to march on Tenochtitlan.

Aztec treachery

At first, Moctezuma seemed to welcome Cortes, but he sent a secret force to attack the Spanish camp on the coast. His soldiers returned with the head of a Spanish officer. Furious, Cortes ordered the entire secret army to be burned alive. Moctezuma's treachery had made enemies of the Spaniards.

Soon afterwards the Aztecs rebelled against the invaders, and Moctezuma was forced to appeal to his people to make peace. The angry crowd stoned him to death. With the Aztecs in revolt, Cortes attacked Tenochtitlan, helped by the Aztecs' local rivals. The end came in August 1521 when Cortes stormed the city, cut off its water supply, and set about levelling the hub of the Aztec empire to the ground.

Under the streets of a city

Forgotten by the Spanish invaders, Mexico City was built on the ruins of Tenochtitlan. The Spanish wrote detailed accounts of the Aztec civilisation they had discovered and conquered, but it was not until 1978 that the actual locations of temples and palaces were rediscovered.

Since then, there have been full-scale excavations involving the demolition of part of the modern city. Tenochtitlan has now been recognised as a World Heritage site by the United Nations.

An Aztec from the Codex Mendoza.

Machu Picchu

Peru, c. AD 1440–1570

*When Spanish soldiers conquered the lands of the Incas,
they overlooked Machu Picchu. Isolated on a mountain-top, frozen in time,
the site fills in our knowledge of Inca life.*

High on a mountain ridge in the Andes, the Inca stronghold of Machu Picchu (pronounced Match-oo Pee-shoo), was home, 500 years ago, to about 1000 people. It was not one of the Incas' most important cities – it was far too remote for that – but it is an important archaeological site today because it was almost undisturbed when it was rediscovered about ninety years ago. Almost all the other cities of the Incas were destroyed by Spanish invaders when they took over 400 years ago.

Machu Picchu is located in an earthquake area.

The mountain climate must have been very hard in winter. On top of all that, land for growing crops was in such short supply that terraces had to be laboriously cut out of the mountain.

However, the site had its good points. Surrounded on three sides by cliffs and mountains, it was a natural fortress. It could only be approached from the south, and here they built a massive wall to defend themselves against attack.

Why there?

We do not know what made the people of Machu Picchu choose such a hard place to settle in. It was separated from the Inca capital, Cuzco, by about 100 kilometres (60 miles) of difficult country. This in itself is surprising because the Incas paid great attention to ease of communication in their empire. In addition,

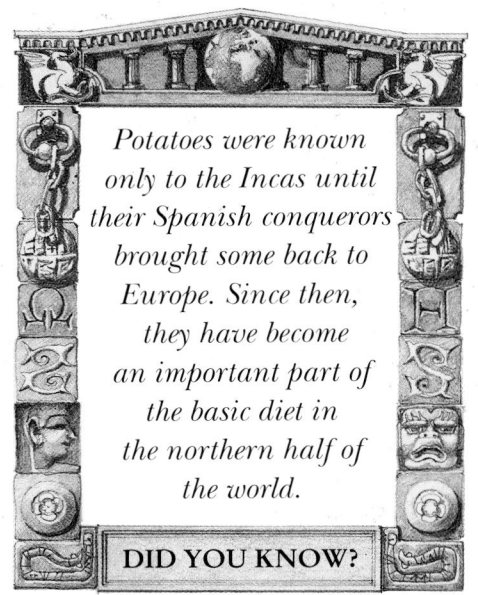

Potatoes were known only to the Incas until their Spanish conquerors brought some back to Europe. Since then, they have become an important part of the basic diet in the northern half of the world.

DID YOU KNOW?

A triumph of building

Another good thing about the site of Machu Picchu was that there was no shortage of stone for building. The people took full advantage of this, and their city was a triumph of the craft of stonemasonry. Not only the houses, but also temples and other ceremonial buildings were all beautifully made of

*What is the meaning of the intihuatana, the sundial cut out of rock in
its own temple in Machu Picchu? This picture suggests that it was a sacred stone
dedicated to the sun god Inti, and an object of worship.*

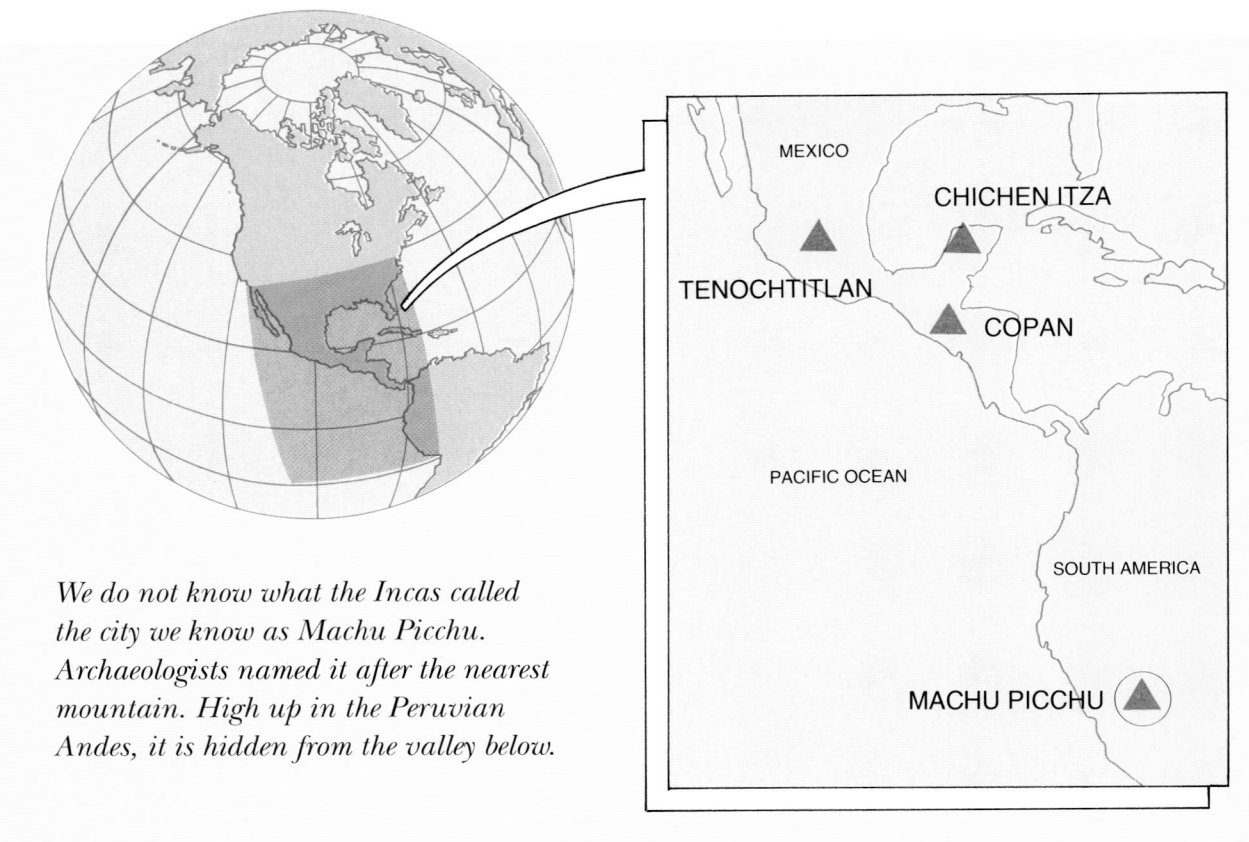

We do not know what the Incas called the city we know as Machu Picchu. Archaeologists named it after the nearest mountain. High up in the Peruvian Andes, it is hidden from the valley below.

blocks of granite cut exactly to fit without using mortar.

On the most important buildings the stones were polished with sand and water and the edges were rounded off, as if to show off the stonemasons' skill. All this was done using only the simplest stone tools.

On the topmost peak of Machu Picchu, the mountain that lent the city its name, the Incas built a tall watchtower which may also have served as a signalling station using smoke signals.

Stairways of rock

The stonemasons of Machu Picchu were equally skilled at cutting shapes out of solid rock. Different levels of the city were linked by flights of steps made in this way. Water channels and storage basins, ponds and fountains were also cut from the rock.

The Incas used their building skills to solve one of the major problems of the Machu Picchu site – the shortage of land for farming. To the south, outside the city wall, the mountain slopes steeply down. Here, the masons built a series of stone walls about 5 metres (15 ft) high. The gaps between these were filled first with gravel and then with topsoil, all transported with great effort from the river valley below. This made fertile terraces on which enough maize and vegetables could be grown to support the population.

Midsummer temple

In the centre of Machu Picchu was a large plaza or square which was probably used as a meeting place. Next to it was a separate, smaller plaza which was Machu Picchu's religious centre.

Here, there were open-fronted stone

shrines and a larger stone temple. One special structure, the intihuatana, looks as if it was positioned so that at dawn on Midsummer Day, the start of the religious year for the Incas, a stone set on an altar caught the first rays of the rising sun.

The son of the sun god

The Incas worshipped many gods, but the sun was the focus of their lives. One of their legends told how Manco Capac, the son of the sun god Inti, taught the Incas to build houses, irrigate the soil, plant crops and make shoes.

His sister, Mama Ocllo, taught the women how to spin, weave and sew.

The story went on to explain that Manco Capac founded the Inca capital, Cuzco, and ruled the world from there. The authority of the Incas' emperor came from this legend. Incas believed that their emperor was carrying out Manco Capac's orders, and so they must, in turn, obey him.

This belief that the Inca emperor was ruling in Manco Capac's place gave him enormous power. It also explains why he could easily gather together the large forces of labour necessary to build the empire's road system and the massive walls, stairways and terraces discovered at Machu Picchu and at many other Inca sites.

The Inca empire

The Incas' own story of how their empire began starts with Manco Capac. Armed with a golden rod, he searched South America for a place where the rod could be pushed deep into the ground and where the soil would therefore be good for crops. He chose the site of Cuzco, where the first Incas settled and which later became the centre of their empire.

Cuzco seems to have been founded around AD 1200. It was another 200 years before the Incas, under a new emperor, began to extend their power by conquering neighbouring tribes one by one. This process went on until, by 1525, Inca territory stretched along the Andes from Quito, in what is now Ecuador, to the River Maule in Chile, about 4300 kilometres (2700 miles) down the coast of South America.

This mountainous empire was not easy to control. The Incas built a network of roads so that troops could be sent to deal quickly with any trouble. The roads – and the bridges woven from climbing plants which were built to cross the rivers – were also used by government officials and by runners who carried messages to and from the capital to outlying parts.

An Inca sacrificial knife.

City in the clouds

Even the most simple houses in Machu Picchu were built to last, with sturdy stone walls. Most had only one storey and an open doorway covered with a cloth blind. The roofs were made of thatch, probably of grass found locally.

This reconstruction pictures Machu Picchu as it was around AD 1500. It shows how the builders made use of every available space on the mountainous site. Houses were often built in irregular shapes, narrower at one end than at the other, to fit their plots of land.

Like all aspects of the Incas' lives, their cities were highly organised. In the middle, surrounding the square or plaza, were the temples, other public buildings, and the homes of the most important citizens. In the foreground, near the city wall where the poorer people lived, the houses were smaller and packed more closely together.

Remote from other Inca settlements, the people of Machu Picchu had to be self-sufficient. The terraces on the hillside had to produce enough food to keep them through the winter. Any materials that were not available on the site – such as topsoil for the terraces – had to be painstakingly brought up the mountain from the valley below.

Living in Machu Picchu

Survival in an environment like Machu Picchu meant an endless struggle against all kinds of difficulties. Storms and torrential rains could undo months of careful work in the fields, and the mountain climate played havoc with thatched roofs. In winter it was bitterly cold.

The people used their homes only to eat and sleep in, and they had little furniture except for cupboard spaces cut out of the walls and sometimes a stone bench. Meals were prepared and eaten on the floor, which, covered with matting of reeds or grass, was also used for sleeping.

Early vegetarians

The Incas' diet was almost entirely vegetarian, though they would eat meat if they could get it. Maize – used to make flour and beer – was their basic food. They also grew pumpkins, chillies, beans, potatoes and coca, a shrub whose leaves were chewed as a drug, though the climate at Machu Picchu would not have suited all of these crops.

Building and farming were the main work for men, and these tasks were tackled with primitive tools. For building, they used stone chisels and scrapers, while the farmers used wooden digging sticks to till the soil and stone machetes for harvesting.

Skill with textiles

While the men were out building or farming, the women would gather together in the open spaces between their homes to spin, weave, dye and sew. The Incas loved colour, and they were good at making dyes out of plants. They also used the dried blood of the insect cochineal, which gave a bright red dye. The yarn they spun was made from the wool of llamas, alpaca and vicuna, which produced very fine, soft material.

The other great Inca craft was pottery, which they made both for everyday and for ceremonial use.

Jar for storing maize beer.

Cutting corn with stone tools.

Counting with string

Although the Incas had no system of writing, they developed a method of counting. This became necessary because of the need to keep a check on the number of men available throughout the empire for army service or for road-building projects.

This was done by teams of travelling officials called tucricucs (pronounced two-crik-ooks), who provided a link between the Inca capital, Cuzco, and the territories of the empire. When counting the Inca people, they recorded the results on knotted and coloured bundles of strings called quipus (pronounced kwee-poohs). Specially trained teams of accountants, or quipucamayocs (pronounced kwee-pooh-ka-may-oks), could translate the knots and colour codes back into numbers.

We do not know exactly how the Inca system worked, but it was probably similar to the abacus or counting-frame used by the Chinese. It was very efficient. The last Inca emperor was able to gather a room full of gold to ransom himself from the Spanish invaders within days of being told how much they wanted.

The last Inca city?

Machu Picchu was discovered in 1911 by a team of archaeologists led by Hiram Bingham, then professor of Latin American history at Yale University. It was one of the most exciting archaeological finds of all time. The next year, the Yale team carried out a full excavation of the site.

The setting of Machu Picchu on its mountain-top, and the superb condition of the buildings, led Hiram Bingham to believe that he had found the legendary 'lost city of the Incas', the centre of the Incas' sun worship and the first of their settlements.

The truth was discovered by later archaeologists. Machu Picchu was not the Incas' 'lost city'. That was Vilcabamba, far away in the Amazon rain forest. The reason Machu Picchu had been so well-preserved was its remote location; the Spanish army, marching through the Inca empire in the late 1520s, had simply failed to find it. But it was far too small and remote to have been a centre for religious life.

Although Hiram Bingham's conclusions were wrong, his reputation is still high. After all, it is thanks to his painstaking work at Machu Picchu that we know so much about the daily lives of the Incas. No where else in either South or Central America has a city survived intact.

Storage jar in the shape of a parrot.

Where to go

Although pictures will tell you a lot, it's much better to go to a museum and look at all the things that archaeologists have found from a vanished civilisation. You will get an even better idea of how a people lived and worked and what they thought was important by looking at the statues, jewellery, pottery and other remains.

Some museums have special visiting days when they let you actually touch these ancient things and examine them properly. Often school visits are allowed special access to items which are not usually on display if they are studying a particular period or culture. But **always** check the opening days and times before you try to visit a museum to avoid disappointment.

British museums
The following museums have good general collections on display from some of the civilisations featured in this book:
British Museum, Great Russell St, London WC1 (071–636 1555)
Museum of Mankind, 6 Burlington Gardens, London W1 (071–437 2224)
Birmingham Museum & Art Gallery, Chamberlaine Sq, Birmingham (021–253 2834)
University Museum of Archaeology and Anthropology, Downing St, Cambridge (0223–337733)
Ashmolean Museum, Beaumont St, Oxford (0865–278000)
Pitt-Rivers Museum, South Parks Rd, Oxford (0865–270927)
Royal Museum of Scotland, Queen St, Edinburgh (031–255 7534)
Hunterian Museum, Glasgow University, Glasgow (041–330 4221)

Specific sites
Catal Hüyük – most of the material from this site is in the Anatolian Civilisations Museum in Ankara, Turkey.
Stonehenge – there is an information centre at Stonehenge which explains how the site developed over the centuries. Nearby, the Alexander Keiller Museum at Avebury has displays about the Beaker People, while the Salisbury & South Wiltshire Museum at Salisbury has displays about Stonehenge and the people who built it.
Skara Brae – most of the things found by Professor Childe are in the Royal Museum of Scotland in Edinburgh. The Tankerness House Museum at Kirkwall on Orkney Mainland has a reconstruction of a house from Skara Brae.
Troy – there is a small museum at Troy showing some of the finds from recent excavations. Most of Heinrich Schliemann's finds went to Berlin and disappeared during the Second World War. For the ancient Greeks, the best collection is in the National Archaeological Museum in Athens.
Biskupin – most of the finds from the excavations before 1939 were destroyed during the Second World War. Since 1946 finds from excavations have been housed in a museum at Biskupin.
Copan – there is a small museum in the town near Copan but the best collection of Mayan material is in the National Archaeological Museum of Mexico in Mexico City.
Chichen Itza – the best collection of Toltec material is in the National Archaeological Museum of Mexico in Mexico City.
Pueblo Bonito – the best collection of material from the Pueblo culture is in the Smithsonian Institution in Washington DC, USA.
Tenochtitlan – all the finds from this site are in the Museum of Mexico City in Mexico City.
Machu Picchu – there is a small museum in Cuzco of finds from various Inca sites; but the best collection is in the National Museum of Peru in Lima. There is also a private 'Gold Museum' in the suburbs of Lima where gold and silver jewellery and feather garments are on display.

Find out some more:
Archaeology of North America – Snow, Dean R. (Chelsea House [available via Lutterworth Press, Cambridge CB1 2NT])
Atahuallpa and the Incas – Morrison, Marion (Wayland, 1986)
Aztec Warrior – Steel, Anne (Wayland, 1987)
Civilisations of the Americas – Williams, Brian (ed) (Cherrytree Press, 1990)
Everyday Life in Prehistoric Times – Quennell, Marjorie & C.H.B. (Batsford, 1959)
Growing up in Aztec Times – Wood, Marion (Eagle Books, 1991)
Growing up in Inca Times – Lewis, Brenda Ralph (Batsford, 1981)
Iliad, The – Homer (ed. Barbara Leonie Picard) (Oxford University Press, 1989)
Inca Farmer – Morrison, Marion (Wayland, 1986)
Luck of Troy, The – Green, Roger Lancelyn (Puffin, London)
Navahos, The – Iverson, P. (Chelsea House [available via Lutterworth Press, Cambridge CB1 2NT])
Poland through the Ages – Golawski, M. (Orbis, 1971)
Prehistoric & Ancient Europe – Williams, Brian (Cherrytree Press, 1990)
Prehistoric Britain – Marsden, Barry (Wayland, 1989)

Prehistoric People – Wood, Tim (Franklin Watts, 1980)

Sheldra: a child in Neolithic Orkney – Woodbridge, Teresa (Tempvs Reparatvm, 1988)

Warriors, Gods & Spirits from Central & South American Mythology – Gifford, Douglas (Peter Lowe, 1983)

Some adult books you might enjoy:

Ancient Turkey: a traveller's history of Anatolia – Lloyd, Seton (British Museum Publications, 1989)

People of Chaco: a canyon & its culture – Frazier, Kendrick (Norton, 1987)

The English Heritage Book of Stonehenge – Richards, Julian (Batsford, 1991)

The Great Temple of the Aztecs – treasures of Tenochtitlan – Moctezuma, Eduardo (trs Doris Heyden) (Thames & Hudson, 1988)

The Maya – Coe, Michael D. (Thames & Hudson, 1987)

Index

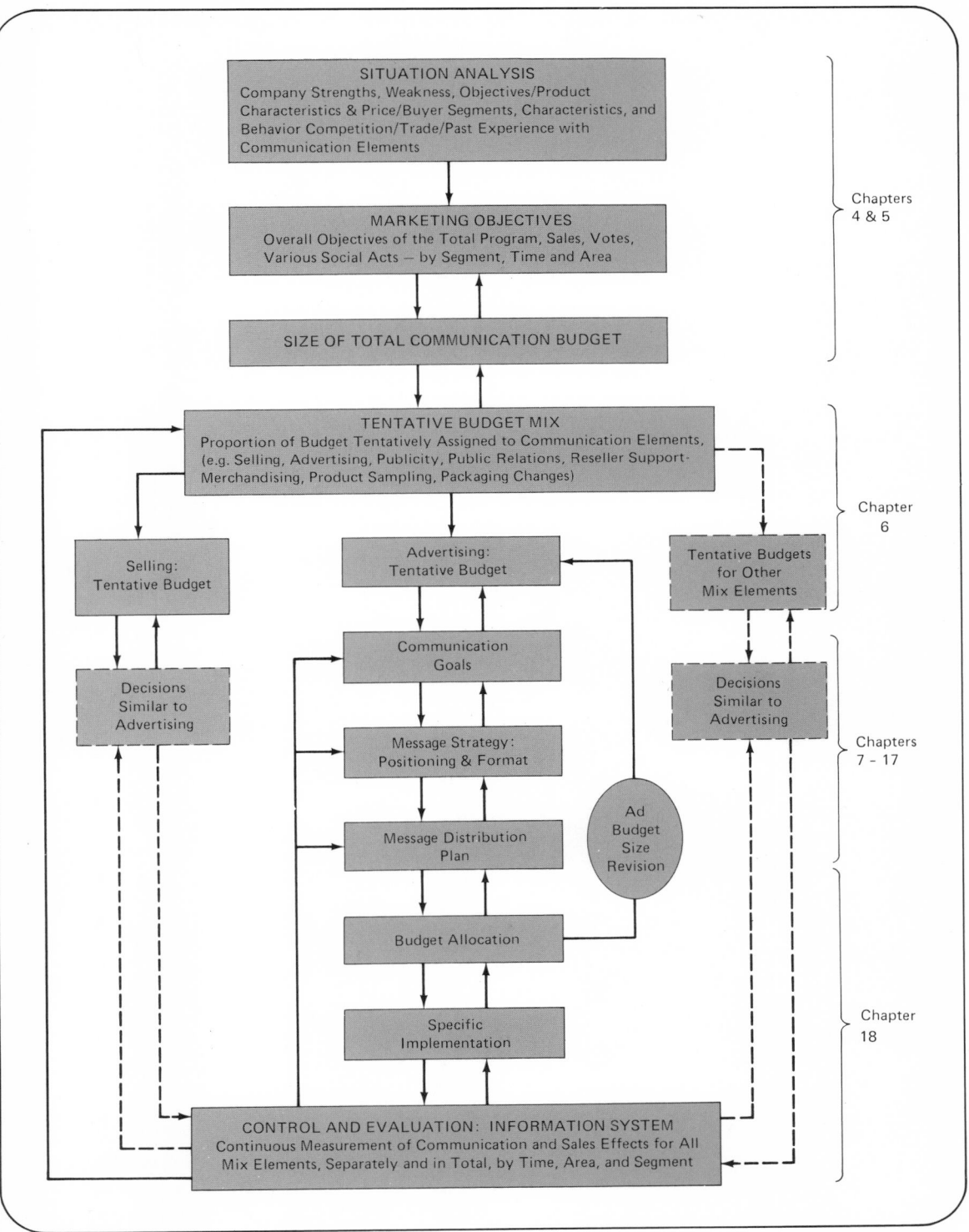

SITUATION ANALYSIS
Company Strengths, Weakness, Objectives/Product Characteristics & Price/Buyer Segments, Characteristics, and Behavior Competition/Trade/Past Experience with Communication Elements

MARKETING OBJECTIVES
Overall Objectives of the Total Program, Sales, Votes, Various Social Acts — by Segment, Time and Area

SIZE OF TOTAL COMMUNICATION BUDGET

Chapters 4 & 5

TENTATIVE BUDGET MIX
Proportion of Budget Tentatively Assigned to Communication Elements, (e.g. Selling, Advertising, Publicity, Public Relations, Reseller Support-Merchandising, Product Sampling, Packaging Changes)

Chapter 6

Selling: Tentative Budget

Advertising: Tentative Budget

Tentative Budgets for Other Mix Elements

Decisions Similar to Advertising

Communication Goals

Message Strategy: Positioning & Format

Decisions Similar to Advertising

Chapters 7 – 17

Message Distribution Plan

Ad Budget Size Revision

Budget Allocation

Specific Implementation

Chapter 18

CONTROL AND EVALUATION: INFORMATION SYSTEM
Continuous Measurement of Communication and Sales Effects for All Mix Elements, Separately and in Total, by Time, Area, and Segment

Michael L. Ray
Stanford University

Advertising
and
Communication
Management

PRENTICE-HALL, INC., Englewood Cliffs, New Jersey 07632

Library of Congress Cataloging in Publication Data

RAY, MICHAEL L.
  Advertising and communication management.

  Includes bibliographical references and index.
  1. Advertising. 2. Communication in
marketing. 3. Advertising media planning.
I. Title.
HF5823.R392   659.1′1   81-12075
ISBN 0-13-015230-7   AACR2

Editorial/production supervision
and interior design by **Esther S. Koehn**
Cover design by **Jayne Conte**
Manufacturing buyer: **Ed O'Dougherty**

Printed in the United States of America

10 9 8 7 6 5 4 3 2

ISBN 0-13-015230-7

Prentice-Hall International, Inc., *London*
Prentice-Hall of Australia Pty. Limited, *Sydney*
Prentice-Hall of Canada, Ltd., *Toronto*
Prentice-Hall of India Private Limited, *New Delhi*
Prentice-Hall of Japan, Inc., *Tokyo*
Prentice-Hall of Southeast Asia Pte. Ltd., *Singapore*
Whitehall Books Limited, *Wellington, New Zealand*

Contents

Preface

This book was born out of a realization of the growing need for better communication in marketing and a dissatisfaction with the materials available to students of advertising and communication planning.

The need is for direct, simple, effective, and honest mass communication because the world is changing and we are changing more rapidly than ever. A new decade has dawned. A new century is approaching. The very basis of communication and society is being altered with every year. On the one hand, there is the possibility of technological breakthroughs that will allow us to continue to live in the amazing affluence of the last three decades. On the other hand, even with such breakthroughs, there is a trend in the world toward a questioning of affluence for its own sake.

In this setting it is significant to be studying ways of improving mass communication, particularly advertising. There is a need now, more than ever, for efficiency in communication. We know that the basis of advertising, personal selling, sales promotion, and publicity–public relations is communication. But there is confusion as to how these components of the communication mix can be put together to get to the right people, at the right time, with the right message, for the right response.

In the context of this critical need it is painful to see advertising that is irritating, useless, and unethical. At the same time there is no doubt that advertising can be one of the most pleasurable, useful, and moral forms of communication confronting us.

Advertising is irritating, useless, and unethical when it too often reaches the wrong people with the wrong message at the wrong time.

Advertising is pleasurable, useful, and moral when it makes a meaningful communication with the people who need the message.

The purpose of this book is to minimize the incidence of the first type of advertising and marketing communication and maximize the second.

How is this done? It is done by concentrating on the basics as they are and should be practiced. Whether this book is used in an advertising management, campaign planning, marketing communication, or promotional strategy course, its value will be in providing students on both sides of the desk with a simple framework and the basic tools necessary to work within this framework.

Although this book uses advertising as the major component for outlining the steps that should be taken for effective communication, it is the coordination of these steps for all aspects of communication that makes this book unique. Advertising is the main example. The other aspects of the mix must and can be coordinated with advertising, because they each provide a special potential for communication which requires the same managerial decisions as does advertising.

This book takes a marketing communication approach to advertising management. Because of this approach, the book is relevant to potential managers in the public sector as well as those in consumer and industrial settings. Because the book covers the details of advertising planning and creative and media decisions, it allows a sophisticated understanding that will lead to sound management. Because it concentrates on the individual consumer and the latest knowledge of consumer information processing, the student will be able to deal with a variety of communication management situations.

Emphasis on Brand, Product, or Campaign Manager

Someone is ultimately responsible for the communication campaign. This person's title can be brand manager, or product manager, or campaign manager. Whatever the title, it is to that person or the person aspiring to that position that this book is directed. What this manager does is called marketing in business organizations, but the development of product, setting of prices, and overall distribution planning are tasks shared with other managers, certainly top management. The flexible part of the marketing mix—communication—is the part the brand manager works with most. It is emphasized here.

The problem is how the manager can coordinate all the aspects of the mix in order to make meaningful communication. The solution offered here is an ordered approach that makes certain that nothing is forgotten at the same time that no part of the mix is overemphasized. Within this ordered approach the student and manager can begin to be concerned with and understand the main target of communication: the individual members of the audience.

It is obvious that meaningful communication occurs when there is understanding of the audience on the part of the manager. Understanding can be achieved first by introspection and then by dealing with each individual communication situation with creativity. The goal is, as the communication theorists put it, to create "overlapping fields of experience."

The Decision Sequence

Chapter 2 presents the most distinctive aspect of this book—a decision sequence that allows an ordered approach to both studying and doing advertising and communication management. The sequence, which is also printed on the inside covers, moves the student from very general decisions to very specific ones as follows:

1. *Decisions about the whole marketing mix*—Part II, "Before Marketing Communication," presents the tools necessary to do a situation analysis and to make decisions about overall marketing objectives and total communication budget for individual campaigns. This is a managerial perspective that puts advertising and communication in the context of the entire marketing mix.
2. *Decisions across the communication mix*—Part III discusses decisions about the tentative weight (in dollars) and communication goals to be given to each of the elements of the communication mix, including advertising, personal selling, sales promotion, and publicity–PR. It is the tentative budget mix and the communication goals that allow managerial coordination of all mix elements.
3. *Decisions made for each mix element*—Parts IV–VII discuss the message, message distribution, and implementation decisions. Although advertising is most often used as an example, the unifying element of communication plan-

ning is that the same types of decisions are necessary for all elements of the communication mix.

Since the communication decision sequence is carried out in organizations, Chapter 3 deals with organizing for creative advertising and communication. The creative organization is something that fascinates us all but is difficult to treat adequately in most courses of this type. The focus of Chapter 3 is on organization from the brand or campaign manager's perspective, so that even the extensive treatment of the advertising agency is done from that viewpoint.

Integration of Behavioral and Quantitative Inputs to Management

The initial growth of marketing communication and promotional strategy courses was based on the availability of new behavioral and quantitative science tools. Unfortunately, these tools did not always apply easily to communication problems. People became concerned with learning about the tools and forgot about the critical decisions that need to be made. The decision sequence of this book allows an integration of these tools into the decision process. Thus virtually every chapter of this book has both behavioral and quantitative material that is applicable to the problems at hand. Examples include the following:

☐ Models of the communication process in Chapter 1 on the nature of communication.
☐ Results of research on the creative organization in Chapter 3 on organizations.
☐ Product life cycle, growth-share matrices, test market simulation, psychographic segmentation, conjoint analysis, consumer decision process models, and diffusion of innovation theory in Part II on "before marketing communication" decisions.
☐ Response function analysis, econometric budget, study results, decision calculus modeling in Chapter 6 on the tentative budget mix.

☐ Hierarchy-of-effects analysis, the compensation principle, and various social psychological theories, including learning, attribution, and dissonance approaches in Chapter 7 on setting communication goals.
☐ The essence of buyer behavior modeling, perceptual mapping, nonmetric scaling, and multiattribute decision process models is used to develop the concept of communication "positioning" in Chapter 9.
☐ The vast and disconnected literature of communication and attitude change research is applied to five critical questions of message format in Chapter 12.
☐ Computer simulation and media modeling are used as a framework to organize message distribution decisions in Chapter 16 on advertising media planning.
☐ Critical path scheduling in Chapter 18 on budgeting, implementation, and control.

No previous study of any of these behavioral and quantitative techniques is necessary to understand their use in the context of actual communication decision making. And it is easy to understand these tools here because there is a reason to understand them. By learning them in the context of the decisions to which they apply, the decisions will be improved; and improved communication will result.

Budgeting in Three Parts

Advertising and communication management students often find that budgeting is the most difficult concept to understand. Typically they are told that there are several suboptimal methods and that the optimal method is never truly possible even though the budgeting decision is the most important management task.

In this book, budgeting is divided into three parts, each of which can easily be handled with available methods:

1. The size of the total budget is first determined on the basis of the situation analysis outlined in Part II, "Before Marketing Communication."

2. Next a tentative budget mix is developed in order to indicate the importance or weight of each of the elements of the communication mix. Guidance for setting the tentative budget is given in Chapter 6.
3. Finally, the exact final budget is determined by an evaluation of the goals, message, and message distribution decisions made for each element of the mix. This part of budgeting is covered implicitly in Chapters 7 through 17 and explicitly in Chapter 18.

Thus the heart of management, *budgeting,* is fully integrated with other marketing communication decisions and divided into parts that students can understand and use.

Managerial Research Concern Throughout

Advertising research, like behavioral science and budgeting concerns, is a topic typically treated all at once in the study of marketing communication. In contrast, this book treats research to develop and test advertising throughout the book, wherever managerial concerns lead to questions answerable by research.

Developmental research tools, which provide the basic data for developing message ideas, are discussed primarily in Part II, "Before Marketing Communication," and in Part IV, "The Message Idea." For example, in Chapter 9, "Message Idea Positioning," tools are suggested for gathering data that would lead to the possibility of six positioning strategies.

Copytesting or pretesting research is discussed specifically in Chapter 13, "Advertising Format Implementation and Pretesting," where a framework is provided that will allow managers and students to put pretesting decisions in proper perspective.

Posttesting or evaluation studies, the third type of advertising-communication research, are one of the main topics of Chapter 18. Available posttesting methods are reviewed in the context of marketing communication information systems. Such systems, available for even the smallest of advertisers, could provide measurement of communication and sales effects of the campaign—thus providing information for later planning.

Creativity

Creativity is often thought to be part of just message development in advertising and communication management. Here, however, it is the underlying basis of almost every chapter. Organization issues are discussed from a creative perspective in Chapter 3. A creative problem-solving approach is made the basis for "before marketing communication" activities in Part II. Even the media-planning chapter, covering what is normally just an analytical topic, is distinctive for its appeal to creativity.

In addition, about a third of the total book is devoted to message idea and format considerations—the normal "creative" part of a text in this area. Although some of these message chapters will not be used in some courses, there are still more here than in most texts.

Why this emphasis on creativity? Primarily because it is the aspect of advertising and communication management that *is* both the most difficult and the most rewarding. It is creativity that offers the hope of efficient communication. Creativity can lead to campaigns that cut through clutter and deal with the problems and opportunities of the new media and new communication forms. Creativity equals leverage: As one company president said in my advertising management class, a great advertising idea is to dollar expenditures as a steam shovel is to a teaspoon.

The purpose of the creativity emphasis in this book, then, is to help managers and future managers to identify and contribute to the creation of great campaign ideas. And it is clear that this cannot be accomplished unless the managers understand the creative process intimately, particularly the area of message development.

In fact, it was a dissatisfaction with the repeated rediscovery of the "wheel" of creative procedures and fads in advertising that was largely responsible for this book's being written. It is hoped that students using this book will not be misled by advertising creatives and will at the same time be open to new directions in advertising and communication management.

A Situational Perspective

The great poet William Blake cautioned against generalities. Communication campaign planning is certainly one endeavor in which it is folly to overgeneralize.

The assumption in this book is that decisions can be made efficiently only by considering the specific communication situation. By taking a situational perspective, the student and the manager can deal more easily and realistically with communication planning situations.

The situational approach starts with vignettes at the beginning of most chapters, presents real examples within them, and lists various questions and projects at the end. Chapter 6, the main budgeting chapter, outlines the situational characteristics that lead to various types of tentative budget mixes. The issue of communication goal setting is resolved with a communication hierarchy situation analysis, which is carried through with many examples in the message chapters. Campaign scheduling is investigated in Chapter 16 in terms of nine situational characteristics that would lead to various strategies.

Ultimately the value of a campaign, both to the manager and to the target prospect, is related to how well the message and its delivery fits the situation.

Who Should Read This Book?

This book is for managers and those who aspire to management in advertising, marketing communication, promotional strategy, and overall campaign planning. More importantly, readers should want to do the job right, to be a service to others and themselves by creating efficient communication.

The question of the efficiency of communication was critical to the writing of this book. It was a struggle to complete, because I was not sure it would have value. Was there a need for another book ostensibly on advertising? Yes, there is a need for a book that takes human considerations into account in what promises to be a decade of great change. But would anyone want to read such a book? In the end I decided that the act of completing would in itself be of great value to me personally. Now only you can determine whether there is value for you too.

Acknowledgments

Too many people contributed to the making of this book to be mentioned here. One attempt at this acknowledgment section produced a document which was about a third as long as the whole preface and mentioned over seventy people. And it left out people of importance. So all I can say here is "Thank you" with great love to my family, teachers (many with whom I have never formally studied), students, colleagues, clients, enemies, lovers, and friends. You know who you are. And if you are not sure, send me a stamped, self-addressed envelope, and I will send you a copy of the long acknowledgment section. This is a hidden offer.

MICHAEL L. RAY

OVERVIEW
OF ADVERTISING AND
COMMUNICATION
MANAGEMENT

. . . The Nature

. . . The Decisions

. . . The Organization

The Nature
of Advertising and
Marketing
Communication

■ *If I were starting my life over again, I'm inclined to think I would go into the advertising business in preference to almost any other.*—Franklin Delano Roosevelt, thirty-second president of the United States

■ *I am the most superficial man on earth, and yet I am the dean of my profession.*[1]—Albert Lasker, legendary advertising man, often credited with giving birth to the modern advertising agency

■ *I know half the money I spend on advertising is wasted, but I can never find out which half.* —John Wanamaker, department store founder

■ *... advertising is much like electricity. We know a great deal about it and its uses, but we are not very successful in defining it or delimiting it.*[2]—Advertising Age

■ *... the aim of marketing is to make selling superfluous.*[3]—Peter Drucker

The field this book and all the quotations above are about is more than a little like the elephant in the Indian story of the blind men. In the story, one blind man touched the elephant's tail and said that an elephant was like a rope. Another touched the elephant's side and said that he was like a wall. A third touched the elephant's trunk and compared him to a big fire hose.

In the same way we are touched by and touch advertising and the other elements of marketing communication. If a particular television commercial irritates us, advertising is irritating. If we see that advertising expenditures increased over two and one-half times in the last decade to approach $50 billion per year, we think of advertising as being huge and powerful. This is especially true when we realize that nearly equivalent expenditures are made for other aspects of the communication mix. At the same time our exposure to marketing communication can seem quite small and intimate. Or we may look at it as an opportunity for employment, for creativity, or for influence.

The purpose of this chapter is not to explain away the discrepancies noted in the quotations or in our everyday experiences with advertising and marketing communication. Rather it is to show the nature of the whole beast. First it is necessary to understand the nature of communication itself. This is followed by sections on the tools of marketing communication and the marketing needs for communication in terms of consumer, industrial, and public-sector marketing of various types. Then the institutions of

marketing communications—the companies, the agencies, and the media—are examined. Finally, the meaning of all this for the individual reader and society is highlighted.

THE NATURE OF COMMUNICATION

Level One: The Individual

You know what communication is, because you have experienced it yourself. You have been startled, been bored, been made aware, learned, and simply perceived the many messages impinging on you almost constantly. Estimates are that the typical family is exposed to over one thousand advertising messages a day.[4] Certainly exposure does not equal effect. We ignore the overwhelming majority of communications messages of all types that confront us each day. But some get through. How?

Obviously your interest at this point should be in terms of how you as an advertising and communications campaign planner can get through with your own messages. In order to get a beginning idea of how this can be done, you must understand how all of us eliminate all but a small percentage of the messages confronting us.

First, we have biases against receiving most messages. Only a small proportion are attended to. These are the ones that stand out as being stronger (louder, brighter, sweeter, etc.) than others, different (but not so different that they might be rejected as strange), and of interest or value. Some theories indicate that we avoid messages that are opposed to our basic beliefs, but this depends on the strength, distinctiveness, and interest-value of the message also.

Second, once a message has received attention, we must process it to the extent of remembering it so that it can be related to what we already know, believe, and feel.

At this point there are limits to our processing ability. A wide variety of evidence indicates, for instance, that we can keep only about four to seven ideas in our minds at any given time. Just consider what happens when you look up a telephone number (seven ideas or numbers) and someone interrupts you just as you are about to dial. You forget the number, don't you? This is the limited ability we have to hold ideas in our minds.

When you consider that limitation and

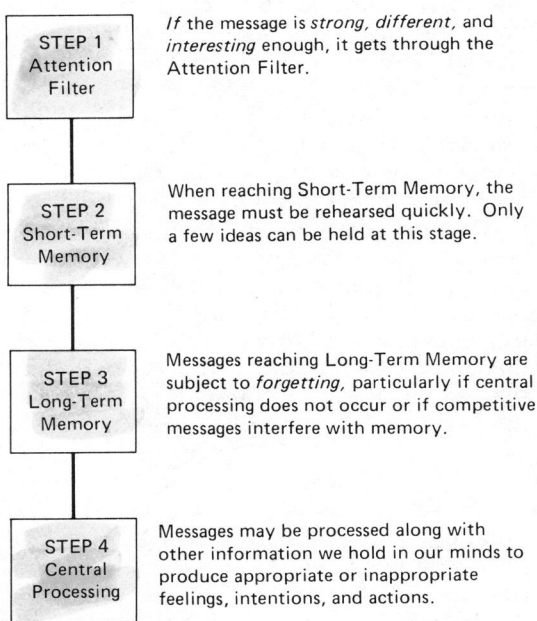

STEP 1 Attention Filter	If the message is *strong, different,* and *interesting* enough, it gets through the Attention Filter.
STEP 2 Short-Term Memory	When reaching Short-Term Memory, the message must be rehearsed quickly. Only a few ideas can be held at this stage.
STEP 3 Long-Term Memory	Messages reaching Long-Term Memory are subject to *forgetting,* particularly if central processing does not occur or if competitive messages interfere with memory.
STEP 4 Central Processing	Messages may be processed along with other information we hold in our minds to produce appropriate or inappropriate feelings, intentions, and actions.

Figure 1-1. Communication at the individual level

the fact that we must rehearse an idea in our minds so that it can be put into long-term memory within thirty seconds of receipt, it is easy to see why only outstanding television commercials can be recalled by as much as 25 percent of a television audience the day after exposure.

Of course memory alone is not the total process of communication. As marketing communicators we want specific kinds of memory—to affect feelings, intentions, and actions. In other words, the 25 percent remembering the supposedly "outstanding" commercial may remember it because they hate it, and because it gives them such a negative impression of the advertised product, service, or idea. At this level of communication processing, the newly processed message is affected by past knowledge, feelings, and actions. It is also affected by what happens next in terms of competitive messages, friends' opinions, experiences with products and brands, and the entire potentially confusing mass of impressions in the world.

In sum, communication at the individual level is a process that includes at least four stages. Although later chapters will show that the process is more complex, the four stages shown in Figure 1-1 are enough to prepare you for the task of advertising and communication management. Your messages must get through the initial Attention Filter, then survive the Short-Term Memory process to reach Long-Term Memory. After this, Central Processing occurs as the new impression interacts with other messages and possibly affects our beliefs, feelings, intentions, and actions. The most important aspect of Figure 1-1 to remember at this point is the fragility of communication at the individual level, the biases we bring to processing, the many limitations to our processing ability, and the interaction between the few messages that get through with what we already know, and so forth. These biases, limitations, and interactions lead to very few actual successful communication events out of all we attempt and receive.

Sometimes a communication campaign works just because so many messages are transmitted that even if a small proportion are successful, the campaign can have effect. The purpose of this book is to avoid this kind of campaign, however. By understanding the communication process at the individual level, we should be able to increase the proportion of successful communication events resulting from our campaign, thereby decreasing expenditures and the possibility that our campaign would be irritating, meaningless, or of low social value.

Level Two: Two-Person Communication

Communication is achieved when there is understanding. When there are *overlapping fields of experience* for the communicator (advertiser, salesperson) and the receiver (audience, prospect), there is communication.

What does "overlapping fields of experience" mean? You know what it means from your own experience. Communication does not occur when someone is speaking to you in a language you do not speak or understand. In such a situation the speaker and the listener do not have common experiences in terms of the labels or words that are attached to various objects. Communication does not occur.

In everyday life the instances of communication and noncommunication are both more subtle and more complex. A salesman trying to communicate the benefits of an automobile, for instance, succeeds only when you think and feel more or less the same way he does about it. This is overlapping fields of experience: Both of you feel the same way. Communication is easiest when the product is of interest to you and when its attributes are not different from what you expect and want. Communication does not occur in the strictest sense when the receiver experiences something different from what the sender intended—e.g., that the car is ugly, only for the rich, uneconomical, in poor taste, etc.

In communication planning, *the ultimate goal of the campaign is to cause some action on the part of a significant proportion or number of individuals in a target audience.* Each component of the marketing-communication mix can lead to some intermediate effect that will combine with others to effect the ultimate goal. Advertising can affect the awareness of a political candidate, for instance. A campaign worker can deal with specific questions and affect attitudes and intentions. The information from publicity releases and news reports can further increase comprehension. And all of these can combine to affect voting behavior in favor of the candidate by a majority or plurality of voters.

So communication at its base is an effect that is the result of overlapping fields of experience between sender and receiver. But it is also a process with several components critical to advertising and marketing communication. The early communication researcher Harold Lasswell pointed out that communication could be described by the sentence *"Who says What to Whom through Which Channels with What Effect?"* Another prominent communication observer, Wilbur Schramm, used the components of information theory to indicate that communication consisted of a *Source* (sender, advertiser, salesman), transmitting some *Message* (ad, sales pitch, label information) to a *Receiver* (consumer, industrial buyer, voter). Usually there is also some opportunity for *feedback,* that is, the Receiver communicates back to the original Sender with a message of response.

This two-way sort of communication is most easily seen in terms of a personal selling situation, as shown in Figure 1-2. Note that the overlapping fields of experience as well as the "noise" of other sounds and sights and thoughts are shown. In such a situation there is a constant flow of messages and feedback from salesperson to prospect and back.

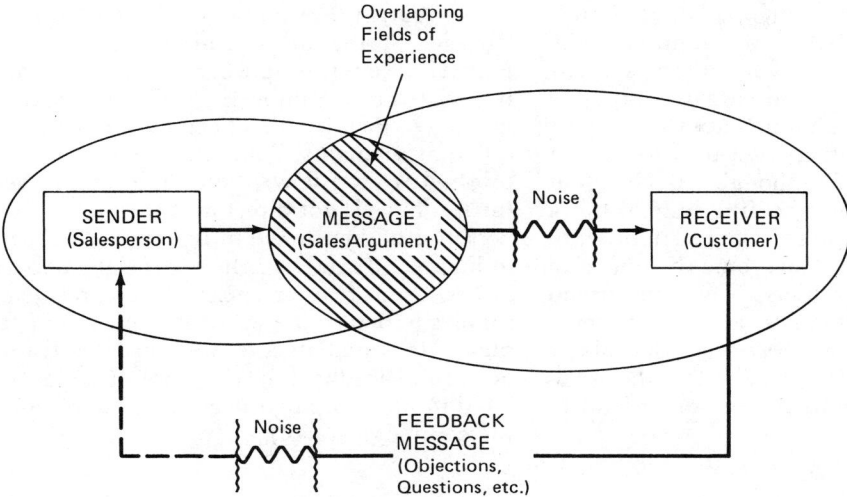

Figure 1-2. *Two-person communication*

Adapted from Wilbur Schramm and Donald Roberts, eds., *The Process and Effects of Mass Communications* (Urbana: University of Illinois Press, 1971) p. 23. Used with permission.

Level Three: Mass-Marketing Communication

In mass-communication situations the feedback is less clear and immediate. Eventually there is the ultimate action of buying or not, voting or not, and so on. But there are many intermediate kinds of feedback occurring in the personal-selling situation that occur only by a research effort on the part of the mass communicator in the advertising situation. Such kinds of feedback as awareness, comprehension, evaluation, intentions, objections, and perceptions are essential to know whether the messages are getting through in the mass situation.

In addition to a different kind of feedback, the mass-communication situation differs from the personal-selling one in several other ways. The marketing communicator is sending many different kinds of messages to

many different individuals. The "noise" in the marketing-communication situation is much more specific and damaging to appropriate communication. Competitive messages of all kinds can affect the success of any campaign. In fact, the noise has become so critical that in recent years it has been more logical to evaluate a communication campaign on the basis of how it "positions" a product, service, or idea in the prospect's mind in relation to competition as opposed to just what attributes, images, and so forth, are communicated. This "positioning" approach to communication will be presented throughout the book (see especially Chapter 9).

The mass communicator tends to think more of segments of people of various types rather than of an individual person. And people exist in relationships and groups, so that there is always the chance in some situations that the message will not affect people directly but instead be transmitted by word of mouth. This is what is often called the "two-step" or "multistep" flow of communication. It happens, for instance, when there is a new product and certain individuals may pay more attention to communications and pass the message on to others. Let us assume that you have never really thought much about installing a solar water-heating system. But a friend has thought about it, paid attention to news stories and ads, done some reading, and visited some retail outlets. Now your friend starts telling you about it, and you become interested and get a very clear idea about the products available. This is the two-step flow—from the media to your friend to you.

Figure 1-3 attempts to show all the intricacies of the mass-communication situation. There are multiple communicators, each transmitting a number of different types of messages. People are affected differently in different segments. Some people are affected by the two-step flow (the double lines). And the feedback is not direct as it was in the two-person situation shown in Figure 1-2. Instead, in Figure 1-3 there is either artificial feedback in the form of communication research (e.g., surveys to determine what proportion of people in key segments are aware of advertising) or natural feedback in the form of action related to the campaign (e.g., sales figures after the campaign starts.)

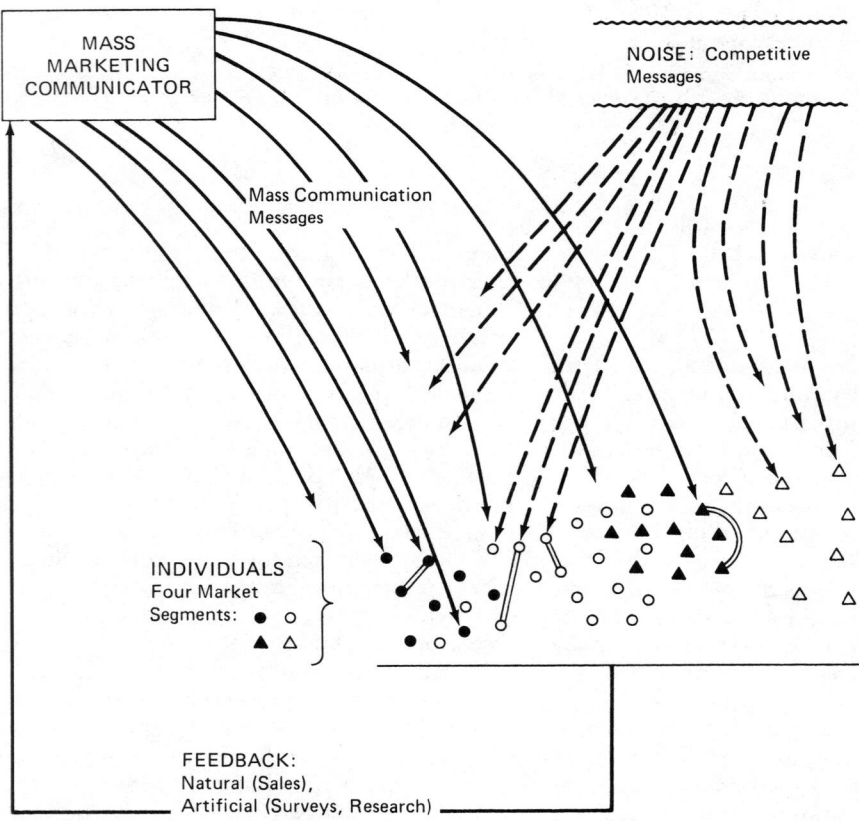

Figure 1-3. Mass-marketing communication

The Proper Attitude
for the Manager

In a sense, no diagram can adequately indicate the complexity of mass communication. Even if we take a very simple advertising situation with just one campaign ad and a number of magazines in which to place it to reach two segments, there are thousands of alternatives available. The purpose of this book is to narrow down these alternatives in specific situations so that you can make clear choices.

The proper attitude for the student and eventual manager of advertising and communication campaigns is to understand communication at the individual level in each situation first. Before attempting to develop and choose among all the alternates for reaching and affecting a large proportion of the total target segment or audience, it is critical to have understanding at level one, the individual. All the complexities of the campaign can be built on the foundation of this understanding.

Before anything can be done in communication, it is essential that we understand the biases, limitations, and present and future relevant experiences of the typical individual in each segment. The first step to achieving this is to understand how we ourselves would react in such a communication situation. Beyond this first step are all the other steps to understanding and creating communication in this book.

THE ELEMENTS OF MARKETING COMMUNICATION

This book is about advertising in the context of all the other potential tools in the marketing-communication mix. Looked at from the viewpoint of marketing as a whole, the communication components are the flexible part of the marketing mix, the ones typi-cally under the control of the brand, product, or campaign manager.

In virtually all marketing situations, whether they be product or service, consumer or industrial, private or public sector, there are four components to the marketing mix— *product, price, distribution,* and *communication.* The first three components are typically developed very carefully not only by the brand manager but also by many other top executives within the organization. Product, price, and distribution are not changed very often. One proof of this is that is is quite strange to think of annual product, price, or distribution plans. Of course each of these is affected by elements in the communication mix—product by sampling, and price and distribution by sales promotional activities. But the basic product, price, and distribution strategies for a particular brand, service, or organization are the fundamentals upon which the business operates. As the Drucker quotation on the first page of this chapter indicated, the purpose of marketing (primarily product, price, and distribution) is to make selling superfluous. The kind of communication mix required will be determined by these stable parts of the mix.

The communication mix, then, is what the brand or campaign manager controls, the relatively flexible part of the marketing mix, for which one-year or even shorter-term campaigns are developed.

Now, putting aside product, price, and distribution, what are the elements of the communication mix? There are essentially four parts to the communication mix—*advertising, personal selling, sales promotion,* and *public relations–publicity.* Each of these four parts comes in many forms and performs a distinctive type of communication.

Advertising

Perhaps the simplest definition of *advertising* is "paid, mass communication that is

11

identified clearly as to sponsor." It is important to pay attention to the "channels" of Lasswell's communication definition when defining advertising. It always goes through channels of advertising media, never in person from the sender to the receiver as in personal selling. In fact, one popular definition of advertising early in this century was "salesmanship in print." Advertising is, as the late advertising agency head Fairfax M. Cone used to say, what you do when you can't be there yourself.

We know advertising by its various media forms—newspaper advertising, magazine advertising, direct-mail advertising, outdoor advertising, specialty advertising, transit advertising, radio advertising, television advertising. Each of these represents an advertising medium, and each has particular benefits and limitations that will be revealed later in this book in the chapters on advertising media.

But all advertising in all media shares the same basic advantages and disadvantages. The advantages of advertising are its low cost per person reached, its ability to intrude where personal salespeople cannot reach, and its ability to create images that cannot be accomplished by a personal salesperson. Note in the print advertisement for Apple Computer in Figure 1-4 how a whole aura is created about this personal home computer. Consider also the magnificent visual and sound effects that are created by many television commercials, each a little program or play in itself, all in less than a minute.

But advertising has weaknesses. In virtually all marketing situations it must be supplemented by other elements of the communication mix because of these weaknesses. The main problem with it is that it can seldom be used to close the sale. It is usually used to develop awareness, possibly comprehension, attitude, or intention, but it alone cannot get the order.

The other weaknesses of advertising are closely related to the initial one. For instance, advertising is unable to hold a large part of

the potential audience. That is, advertising is identified as biased communication and is relatively easy to tune out at the initial Attention Filter stage of individual communication. We can turn away, turn the page, turn off the sound, turn off the set, turn off our attention when the advertising comes.

Not only is advertising deficient in ability to close the sale and hold attention but we often have, as the Wanamaker quotation indicated, difficulty in knowing whether it is having any effect at all. Feedback is not direct as with personal selling or somewhat automatic as with many sales promotions.

For all of these positive and negative reasons, it is folly to study or do advertising without parallel attention to the other aspects of the communication mix, each of which has characteristics complementary to advertising. The mix, including advertising, can be manipulated to produce the total effect necessary in each situation.

Personal Selling

While total U.S. advertising expenditures were estimated to be about 50 billion in 1980, total personal-selling expenditures were estimated to be about $80 billion. Of course many of the sales interactions are relatively inexpensive. Even considering retail clerk waiting time and extremely expensive industrial selling, average cost per sales interaction probably is not more than thirty dollars. Thus each year in the United States there are a minimum of 2 billion selling interactions of the type outlined in Figure 1-2 showing two-person communication.

Not all sales calls are alike, however. The brand or campaign manager has many alternatives for putting personal contact into his or her communication mix. The nature of personal selling depends first on what is being sold. For instance, one survey of 476 marketing executives indicated that personal selling and sales management were more important

What kind of man owns his own computer?

Rather revolutionary, the idea of owning your own computer? Not if your time means money. Because an Apple personal computer can help you make more of it.

Just like big computers, Apple manages data, crunches numbers, keeps records, processes information and prints reports. And it has three programming languages, including Pascal.

Not only that, Apple is less expensive than timesharing. More dependable than distributed processing. Far more flexible than centralized EDP. And, at less than $2500 (as shown), downright affordable.

Why not join the personal computer revolution by visiting us today?

apple computer

(Dealer name and address.)

(Courtesy of Apple Computer Incorporated)

Figure 1-4. *Advertising can create a world of its own*

than advertising in their companies' marketing efforts, but the degree of advantage differed by type of company. Selling was 5.2 times more important than advertising in industrial companies, 1.8 times more important in consumer durable companies, and 1.1 times more important in consumer nondurable companies' marketing efforts.[5]

In each of these companies the job description for each salesperson can range from intensive long-term selling with many calls and great involvement to simple order taking with the prospect coming to the salesperson. All varieties of sales effort, from intensive to order taking, could be used as part of a communication campaign in combination with advertising. Some of the types of sales roles discussed in later chapters include

☐ *Sales engineers,* who have technical knowledge, work with prospects in developing the utilization of products, coordinate research efforts, close the sale, and follow up to make sure that the product or service is operating properly and that the customer is satisfied.

☐ *Missionary salespeople,* who do not sell products or services but make sure that retailers have proper shelving, point-of-purchase materials, latest product information, and inventory.

Used particularly in pharmaceutical marketing where this type of salesperson is typically called a "detail man."

☐ *Door-to-door selling,* in which nearly the whole selling job is done by a person who simply knocks on doors. This is the method used mainly for high-priced specialty items such as encyclopedias and vacuum cleaners. It is also the method used by the nation's largest cosmetics company, Avon.

☐ *Telephone selling,* which is used for a variety of products and services but is typified by subscription and charitable sellers.

☐ *Clerks,* who are found in a variety of selling situations, from retail stores to industrial parts suppliers. Here the buyer has been moved substantially down the path toward purchase by other aspects of the communication mix. Although there is usually substantial opportunity for selling, it is often missed by clerks.

The advantages and disadvantages of personal selling and advertising are almost perfectly complementary, a fact that often leads to their being used together in communication campaigns. While selling can close the sale, hold the prospect's attention, and provide immediate feedback, it does all of this at an extremely high cost per prospect and is unable to reach certain people with the same impact as advertising. Thus advertising can be used to provide awareness and some favorable comprehension, in preparation for the sales visit or interaction.

This complementary use of selling and advertising is illustrated quite clearly by the McGraw-Hill ad in Figure 1-5. The message is simple: If advertising can make the prospect aware of all the facts on the left side of the ad, the sales call will be more efficient. This combined advertising-selling strategy is used successfully by a variety of marketers, including Avon, insurance companies, and the majority of industrial sellers.

Sales Promotion

Sales promotion consists of all forms of clearly sponsored communication other than advertising and selling. Thus it includes coupons, price-off packages, contests, samples, trade shows and exhibits, premiums, bonus packs, point-of-purchase materials, store demonstrations, consumer education services, trade allowances, and rebates.

Sometimes the line between sales promotion and other activities is blurred. Advertisements that contain coupons are primarily advertising, but some people would count them as promotion. Direct-mail advertising almost always includes promotional material. Trade shows, exhibits, and demonstrations almost always include some component of personal selling. Consumer education services are similar to many public relations activities except that the former are clearly sponsored.

Perhaps it is this blurring of distinctions that makes it hard to determine the actual expenditures for sales promotion. Several estimates indicate that some time in the 1970s sales promotion expenditures passed those for advertising and that 1980 expenditures were in the $55 billion range.

Neither the precise definition of sales promotion nor the exact expenditures on it are as important as knowing that this set of tools is available and how it can complement advertising as part of the marketing-communicaton mix.

The use of sales promotion tends to increase in difficult economic times simply because it combines the sales-closing advantages of personal selling with the mass reach of advertising at a low cost. In difficult economic times it is comforting to the brand or campaign manager to know that part of the mix offers lower prices (e.g., price-off coupons, rebates, trade allowances), provides quick feedback of effects (coupons used, number of demonstrations or visitors to an exhibit), and is often so efficient that only the messages that get through cause an incremental cost (as when a coupon is used).

But these advantages of sales promotion should be considered carefully against the main disadvantage—the possibility that sales promotion effects may be deceptively short

"I don't know who you are.

I don't know your company.

I don't know your company's product.

I don't know what your company stands for.

I don't know your company's customers.

I don't know your company's record.

I don't know your company's reputation.

Now—what was it you wanted to sell me?"

MORAL: Sales start **before** your salesman calls—with **business** publication advertising.

McGRAW-HILL MAGAZINES
BUSINESS • PROFESSIONAL • TECHNICAL

Figure 1-5. The complementarity of selling and advertising

(*Courtesy of McGraw-Hill Inc.*)

term or even meaningless in relation to the building of a market or franchise for a brand, product, service, or idea.

A price promotion (e.g., cents-off package, trade allowance, bonus packs) produces a quick increase in sales, for example, but it is usually followed by a decrease in sales below normal levels in the next period. And just as advertising effect cannot be measured by the dollar expenditure, sales promotion effect cannot be measured by the number of individuals visiting an exhibit, entering a contest, or sending for a premium.

Sales promotion devices differ in their

ability to communicate important product information at the same time that they offer important supplements to the other components of the communication mix. It is crucial that marketers realize that some sales promotion devices are better than others in potential for communicating distinctive brand, product, or service attributes. Those sales promotion activities that do communicate in this way are called *consumer franchise building* (CFB) activities. Some examples of CFB and non-CFB activities are shown in Table 1-1.

Marketers should also realize that all sales promotion devices can do nothing

Table 1-1. Sales Promotion Activities of Two Types

Consumer Franchise Building (CFB)	NON-CFB Effort

Consumer sampling expenditures
Cost of producing **samples and accompanying selling message, and distributing them to consumers** via:
    Direct mail
    House-to-house
    Inclusion with regular packages of another brand
    In-store handouts
    Print-media (space costs may be charged either to advertising or promotion)
	Reduced-revenue (price-off) packs
	Special packs for sale to consumers at less than regular price.
	
	Consumer premiums
	In-store
	In or on pack
	Mail ("Sendaway")
	Label-saving plans offering premiums or trading stamps
	
	Consumer contests/sweepstakes

Manufacturer's Couponing
Cost of producing, distributing, and redeeming coupons (cents-off) distributed to consumers by manufacturer—provided that an effective selling message about product and its advantages is included. Distribution may be via:
    Direct mail
    House-to-house
    Inclusion with package of same or different brand
    Print media (in-ad or pop-up); space costs may be charged either to advertising or promotion.
    Coupons may offer "00¢ off" or a low net price or free regular package.
	Consumer refund offers
	Consumer mails in proof of purchase for refund (cash or coupon good on next purchase).
	Label-saving plans offering cash refunds.
	
	Trade coupons
	Coupons placed by dealer in own ads or handbills (but paid for in whole or part by manufacturer). Trade coupons usually show only brand and price.
	
	Trade allowances
	Payments, credits, or extra merchandise given to dealers for buying, displaying, or featuring the product. Includes count-and-recount, "push money," etc.

Consumer demonstrations In-store Clubs Corporate sponsored classes or schools	*Other trade promotions* Premiums, prizes, and other incentives or activities that are *not* directed primarily to the consumer.
Consumer education material Cookbooks Teaching material Recipe or service material Materials distributed to consumers, home-economics classes, other authorities who can recommend brand.	*Other consumer promotions*

SOURCE: Adapted from Exhibit 1, *The Relationship between Advertising and Promotion in Brand Strategy*, Roger A. Strang (Cambridge, Mass.: Marketing Science Institute, 1975).

but supplement the other components of the mix. The marketers who depend too much on sales promotion devices such as price-off coupons soon find themselves losing their franchise.

Publicity-Public Relations

Publicity and public relations both involve mass communication that is not charged to any sponsor, nor is it identified with any particular sponsor. To the audience the news story, which may have been generated by a company's publicity department, has the full credibility of any editorial material.

Publicity and public relations differ primarily in their purpose and target audience. Publicity is of greater concern here because its purpose is to affect awareness, comprehension, attitudes, and so forth, about specific products, services, or ideas among target markets. Thus publicity's general purpose and market is not unlike that of advertising, selling, and sales promotion.

Public relations, on the other hand, typically has a broader purpose and target. The purpose is to communicate the nature of the organization to each of many publics, most of which would not be directly involved with the marketer's products, services, or ideas.

Publicity uses press releases and conferences, feature articles, newsletters, photographs, films, and tapes.

Public relations uses all of these but also includes annual report preparation, fundraising and membership drives, lobbying, special event management, public affairs activities, and even advertising.

Obviously publicity is more in line with the purposes of this book. But sometimes public relations activities are quite closely tied to product, service, or idea communication. One example is the Mobil advertising campaign that started in the early seventies on energy issues and auto safety issues. This is clearly public relations-corporate-institutional advertising within a product campaign. An example of one of these advertisements is shown in Figure 1-6.

Estimates for expenditures in publicity and public relations are difficult to determine because the actual communication messages are not paid for. Some idea of the minimum expenditure is provided by a series of rough estimates of about 150,000 "public relations and publicity writers" in the United States in 1980. If we assume that each writer requires $25,000 annual support, this gives a $3.75 billion minimum expenditure. This is a "minimum" estimate because it includes only writers' salaries—not all the other costs associated with publicity and public relations.

Publicity and public relations have the advantages of low cost and potentially great impact as a result of being part of the nonadvertising content of the media. Consumers are obviously going to have their guard down when a message appears as a news item or as a product used by a star in a popular movie, as opposed to when it appears as an advertisement. And a message that is part of the nonadvertising media content can seem more important than an ad.

Because of these advantages, publicity and public relations tend to be used more by small companies with limited budgets but with interesting new-product or other "stories" to tell. Publicity tends to be a relatively larger part of the budget for industrial and nonprofit public-sector organizations than for consumer organizations. The pages from a news release and the resulting *New York Times* article in Figure 1-7 are examples of a dramatic breakthrough for a technologically based company.

The disadvantages of publicity and public relations have to do with control and ethics. While the successfully placed news item probably has more effect in some ways than the average advertisement, there is much less control over whether the news item

On the death of cheap energy

Cheap labor is gone. So is cheap housing. Cheap land is vanishing fast, and cheap education is a nostalgic memory. Cheap medical and hospital care passed on some time ago. In each of these cases, there was widespread public consternation at their demise. And now time has caught up with cheap energy, and the bell tolls both the funeral and the attendant public outrage.

To some extent, we and many other oil companies must plead guilty to the accusation that we made energy too cheap for too long. We weren't alone, of course. On natural gas, for instance, the government maintained a policy on pricing that ignored the true worth and replacement cost, intentionally keeping it so cheap that conservation was foolish, capital investment was discouraged, and supplies of natural gas grew perilously short. And, in the meantime, we were searching everywhere for more energy. Whenever we found it, we marketed it at the lowest feasible cost.

Even when the prices of almost every other product were climbing steadily, energy prices stayed low—a little upward bump now and then, cushioned by long periods of stability. In economic terms, measured by the work a given unit of energy could accomplish, energy costs were a freak, an anomaly. Even today, government controls keep the cost of energy in the U.S. a bargain in comparison to its cost in most other countries.

Cheap energy was instrumental in creating a civilization—the one we now enjoy. Some say it made too much civilization, in too many places, on too many pristine shores and tranquil plains. These are the people who criticize Mobil, and companies like us, for having found and delivered all this cheap energy to America.

They do not care for the way America has used its cheap energy, and many agree with the view endorsed by Amory Lovins in *Nonnuclear Futures* that "even if we had an unlimited energy source, we would lack the discipline to use it wisely." Solar energy appeals to them, not so much as a technological solution, but because, as Lovins writes in the same book, "...it limits the amount of mischief we can get into."

It is as though Americans had proved themselves a gaggle of unruly children. We do not agree. Is the huge interconnected power grid that reaches out to every state in the continental U.S. some sort of blunder? Were we silly to build the great net of highways that made us a more unified people? Is the industrial might of this nation a gross mistake, one we should have passed by for the simpler, agricultural existence of the 19th century? Were our farmers deluded in using energy as the base for the most efficient and productive agricultural enterprise on earth? Of course not.

We think the results of the U.S. energy boom are a magnificent tribute to American enterprise and ingenuity, the envy of all the world. And, if we had our druthers, we think America, and every other country, would make good use of more cheap energy.

But at the moment there isn't any. And there is not likely to be any for quite some time to come. If there's any around, we hope to be the first to find it or develop and deliver it.

Until then, all we can do about cheap energy is join you in mourning the great times we had with it, and in wishing it had lasted forever.

Like fifteen-cent movies and $500 roadsters.

Mobil

(*Courtesy of Mobil Incorporated*)

Figure 1-6. Mobil institutional advertisement

---

is run and what it will say. Publicity just does not allow the sophisticated placement and scheduling of finely tuned messages that advertising does.

Finally there is the question of ethics. While advertising is clear to virtually all consumers as to its intent (there has always been controversy as to whether this applies to very young children), publicity placement of news items or brands in movies is not identified as having a commercial or special-interest backing. In one sense the media selection of items and the rewriting of them ensure that no particular marketer can have an unusual advantage. But there still is ample area for concern about the ethical aspects of publicity in some media.

In most advertising and marketing-communication situations, the role of publicity and public relations is limited because of the lack of control and interesting news to report. But publicity can play a key role in some situ-

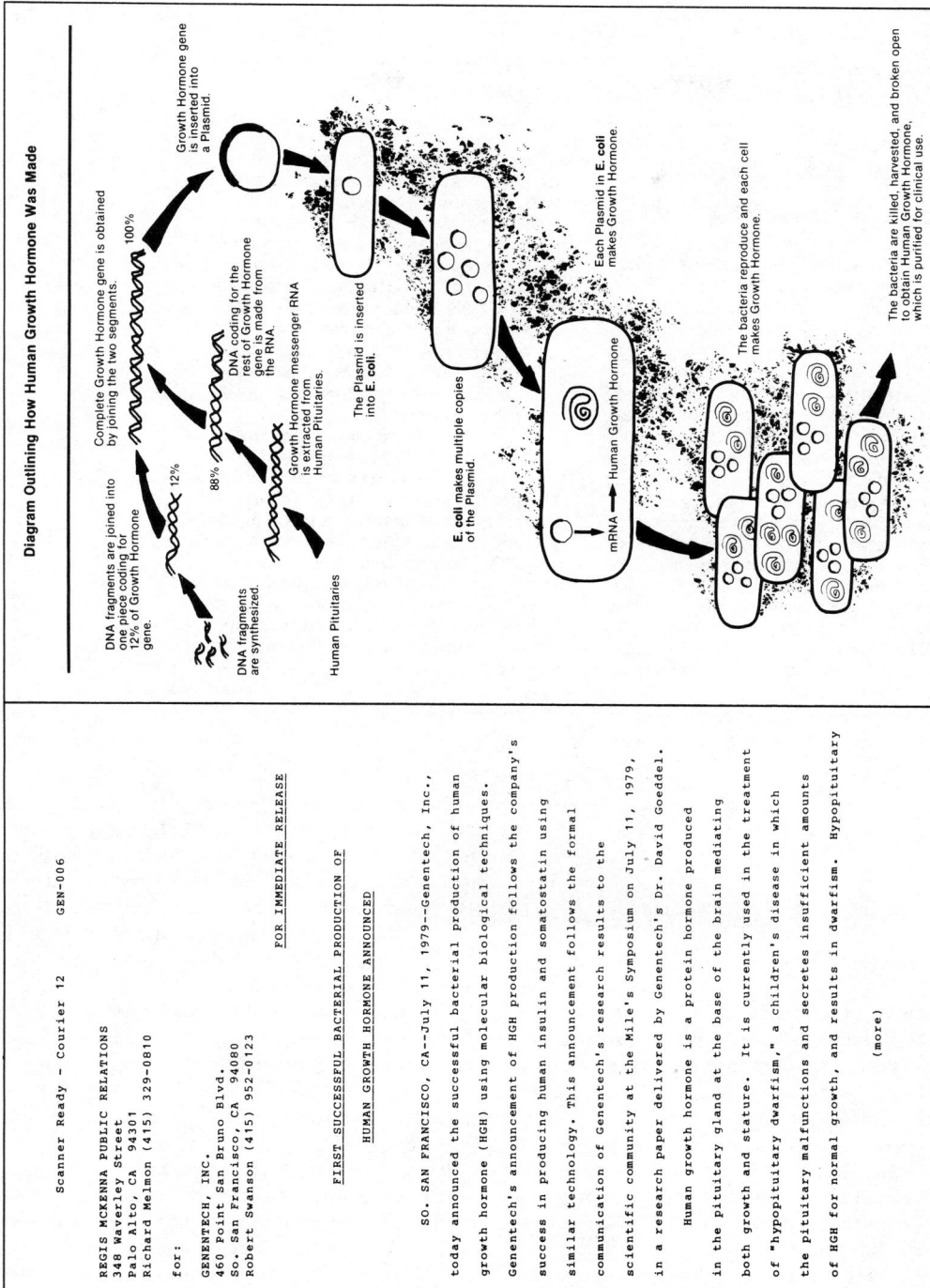

(Courtesy of Genentech Inc.)

Figure 1-7a Genentech news release

Bacteria Becoming A Growth Industry

Bacteria have been pressed into service once again to manufacture a human hormone vital to medical treatment but unavailable in sufficient supply. Dr. John D. Baxter and colleagues at University of California, San Francisco, reported that they obtained human growth hormone from specially manipulated one-celled organisms. Almost simultaneously, scientists at Genentech, Inc. announced bacterial production of the same hormone by slightly different techniques.

Human growth hormone, secreted by the pituitary gland, is essential for normal development. Children who lack it fail to grow unless they can receive hormone supplements, now available only from pituitary glands taken from cadavers — and 50 cadav-ers are needed to supply one child for one year. Some 20,000 Americans suffer from pituitary dwarfism.

The next step will be to make the hormone in quantity and then prove that it works as effectively as the natural substance. The researchers estimate that the hormone might be ready for general use within two years. Already, preliminary experiments indicate that human growth hormone could figure in the treatment of bleeding ulcers and bone fractures.

This is the third hormone to be produced with so-called gene-splicing techniques. The others were insulin, which controls the level of sugar in the blood, and somatostatin, a brain product that regulates other hormone functions. The human growth hormone experiments involved transplanting genetic material from pituitary gland tumors into bacteria, which then executed the instructions for making the hormone.

Figure 1-7b. *News item related to Genentech release*

ations, particularly where budgets are low and products are new.

How Elements Are Combined in Campaigns

The most important aspect of the preceding discussion was not the precise definition of advertising, personal selling, sales promotion, and publicity–public relations. Nor was it the examples or the expenditures. The most important aspect was the listing of the strengths and weaknesses of each element.

The real art of effective campaign planning is in making combinations of advertising, personal selling, sales promotion, and publicity–public relations. And the way this is done is by using the strength of each one to the hilt while playing those strengths against the weaknesses within the constraints of the situation—such as time, competition, size of market, nature of market offering, communication budget, position in market, consumer needs, present knowledge-attitudes, and decision-making procedures.

This is no easy task. You have to understand each of the elements thoroughly and understand the situation also. This book explains one of the elements, advertising, and provides a working knowledge of the others. This knowledge, plus a clear method and background for analyzing each advertising-communication situation, should provide a solid foundation for a career in this field— which is the only way to understand completely the elements of communication and their potential for combinations to solve marketing-communication problems.

THE NEEDS FOR ADVERTISING AND COMMUNICATION

This section is the first step in the attempt to understand the types of situations in which advertising and marketing-communication campaigns operate. There are essentially three global advertising-communication situations that are identified as being different enough to require different college marketing courses, different organizations or departments to carry out the work, and so forth. These three are *consumer, industrial,* and *public-sector* (sometimes called *nonprofit*) *marketing.*

Needs for Communication
to Consumers

The consumer market in the United States and the world is large, diverse, and changing. According to the 1980 census, the U.S. population is over 220 million people in over 88 million households.

Each one of these individuals represents an opportunity for consumer marketing. Each household is a potential consumer decision unit. For consumer marketing and advertising communication has to do with the ultimate user of a product, a service, or an idea for personal or family reasons. Thus each individual represents a prospect for consumer marketing communication.

It is the sheer size of the consumer market that leads to a need for efficient mass communication. Since our market structure provides adequate centralized shopping facilities, advertising can be used to stimulate awareness, comprehension, attitude, and intention, which should lead to a visit to the store to purchase.

But even within this typical advertising-dominated picture for consumer marketing, there is great opportunity for other aspects of the communication mix—personal selling at the retail store and in real estate or insurance; sales promotion devices such as samples to introduce a new product or contest and price-off coupons to revive an old one; and publicity–public relations to boost exposure for a new restaurant location.

While consumer marketing in general is different from industrial and public-sector marketing in terms of its greater emphasis on advertising, there are as many different consumer communication needs as there are brands of products and services. The key is the consumer decision process. When it is similar to that for industrial products—as it is for such consumer durables as real estate and automobiles—the communication mix begins to look more like the industrial one. There is less emphasis on advertising.

And even for many companies selling nondurable consumer items in grocery stores, the costs of sales promotion can equal or sometimes exceed those for advertising.

Industrial Communication Needs

Industrial marketing is the movement of goods and services for industrial or commercial (resale) purpose as contrasted to personal or family purposes.

Although there are not as many industrial consumers, the volume of industrial marketing is somewhat larger than that of consumer marketing.

This discrepancy—fewer individuals but larger dollar volume—immediately indicates a fact about industrial marketing that is significant for communication. There are fewer industrial prospects, but each is worth more in terms of potential business.

Thus it is possible to afford the higher cost per prospect of personal selling as opposed to advertising. All the aspects of sales promotion that are more personal can be used. And since there are many magazines edited for specific parts of the industrial market, publicity can be used quite effectively.

Just as in the consumer area, however, there is much diversity in the industrial area, which calls for a diversity of communication plans. Industrial products range from raw materials such as coal, oil, and iron ore to supplies such as nuts and bolts, fabricating materials, equipment such as motors or computers, and gigantic purchases such as factories or oceangoing tankers.

For all of these products and services, there is a tendency for industrial decision making to be more a group decision than is consumer decision making; for reasoning to be more technical, objective, logical, and long term (as opposed to impulse); and for more alternatives to be considered. All of this leads to the predominance of personal selling in the communication mix; but, as the McGraw-Hill ad in Figure 1-5 argues, there is a need for advertising to create awareness and comprehension and "open doors" for the industrial salesperson.

Indeed, just as advertising is not always totally predominant in consumer communication, personal selling is also supplemented in a variety of ways in industrial settings by other communication elements. No pat formula can be applied across-the-board.

Public-Sector Needs for Communication

Public-sector marketing is a blend of industrial and consumer marketing. It is primarily the selling of services and ideas (but also products) by nonprofit or government organizations not only to consuming individuals and families but to industrial organizations.

This is a rich and exciting area for marketing communication, which will undoubtedly become increasingly important during this decade. Some examples of public-sector situations would include

☐ Convincing voters to choose a particular senatorial candidate (and also convincing all kinds of individuals to contribute money to this candidate's campaign and volunteer to work for him or her).
☐ Increasing subscriptions for a ballet company season (and also increasing contributions and convincing promising newscomers to enter the ballet school and spreading awareness of the dance in the community).
☐ Switching a nation to the metric system with industrial sales promotion, publicity and public relations, and public service advertising.
☐ Packaging a special museum exhibit with advertising, promotions, personal selling to sponsors, and public relations that lead to magazine articles and special television shows.
☐ Positioning a university for prospective students and their families (and potential contributors, faculty, and staff) in the face of declining enrollments and support.

The list of fascinating examples could go on and on. What is common to all of these examples? Two aspects are essential to communication in the public sector.

First it is often hard to pin down precisely the *objective* of public-sector marketing. In the consumer and industrial sectors, the ultimate objectives are usually revenue and profit. In the public sector, the very label of the organizations is nonprofit. Sometimes the main goal is actually to reduce revenues. For instance, the objective of some public service advertising has been to increase the number of individuals who will refuse drugs, cigarettes, or alcohol when offered them.

Almost always in public-sector situations there are multiple objectives. For example, the dance company may have the multiple objective of improving the cultural climate, losing less money, increasing subscriptions, increasing the national rating of the particular company, and obtaining increased funding from the National Endowment for the Humanities.

And this brings us to the second distinctive aspect of public-sector marketing: *multiple publics* to go along with the multiple and often vague objectives. A museum, for instance, has to appeal not only to the prospective museum goer but also to the voting public, corporate sponsors, goverment agencies, collectors, educators, students, and so on.

This is more than the problem of multiple market segments in consumer or industrial marketing. In the public sector, the multiple publics differ in their potential relationship to the public-sector service. Some might use it. Some might contribute to it. Some might just verbally support it. Some might gain some cultural upliftment or feeling of security from it even if they did not directly use it. Others might be induced to work for it.

The implication for advertising and communication campaigns is that often each organization has several campaigns running simultaneously, with each campaign using different combinations of communication techniques. And public-sector campaigns tend to place a relatively greater emphasis on publicity and public relations than do consumer or industrial campaigns.

Again, however, just as with other types of marketing, there is a wide variation in communication needs in the public-sector area. Sometimes advertising is critical, as when it is necessary to introduce a new army program to a wide market of potential enlistees and their families. Personal selling can be important in getting large contributions; just as it is important in making large sales in the industrial area. Once again, the planner should concentrate on the prospect decision process and the communication job to be done, rather than some pat concept of public-sector communication campaigns in general.

Summary: Concentrate on the Individual

Table 1-2 shows the overall ranking of importance in a general sense for the various communication elements for each of the three types of communication need—consumer, industrial, and public sector.

There are, of course, many reasons why the ranking in Table 1-2 could be questioned. Few would disagree with the first ranking of advertising for consumer, personal selling for industrial, and publicity–public relations for public sector. But the rest of the ranking is quite subjective and cannot be determined by any objective information such as expenditures, employees, and ratings.

Thus this book, because it emphasizes advertising, will tend to emphasize consumer over industrial or public-sector problems. At the same time, however, all three communication needs require advertising in a mixture of communication elements, all of which are treated here.

Once again the reader should be reminded that it is important to consider the specific situation and particularly the individual prospect's decision-making process rather than relying just on a classification such as that presented in Table 1-2.

Table 1-2. Needs and use of various communication tools for three marketing types

Consumer Marketing	Industrial Marketing	Public-Sector Marketing
Most important: Advertising	Most important: Personal Selling	Most important: Publicity-PR
A close second: Sales Promotion	Tied for second: Advertising	Tied for second: Advertising
Third: Personal Selling	Tied for second: Publicity-PR	Tied for second: Sales Promotion
Fourth: Publicity-PR	Tied for second: Sales Promotion	Tied for second: Personal Selling

THE ADVERTISING AND COMMUNICATION INDUSTRY

Who puts together the advertising we see, the contest promotion we get in the mail, and the news releases that result in media items? What kind of organization comes up with National Pickle Week or the Uncola?

The answer to these questions is both simple and complex. The simple answer would paraphrase Martin Mayer, who said:

> Advertising is a tripartite business, composed of clients (the companies which make the branded products and pay to advertise them), agencies (which prepare and place the ads), and media (the newspapers, magazines, broadcasting stations)—each an individual *medium* for advertising—which carry the message to the public.[6]

The complex answer to the questions about the nature of advertising and communication management organizations would include all the elements of the communication mix—personal selling, sales promotion, and publicity–PR as well as advertising. There is a need to see how the three parts of the communication industry are each organized and how they are related to each other for the development of communication campaigns.

The complex answer is so important for the understanding of advertising and communication management that all of Chapter 3 is devoted to it. This section provides an introduction to the topic.

The Communication Function within Companies

The study of advertising and communication could be approached from any of at least three ways corresponding to the three parts of the industry outlined by Mayer—clients, agencies, and media. This book takes the perspective of the campaign planner, usually called the brand manager within companies. So the company or communicating organization's perspective is most important.

Advertising and marketing communication is handled in different ways in various companies depending on which communication element is most critical for that organization. While most companies have someone who is responsible for all four aspects of the communication mix, that person more often than not is given the title or sees the job responsibility in terms of one major function.

Therefore the main person in charge of advertising and communication might be called the brand manager, product manager, campaign manager, or communication director. But in a consumer-marketing company, this person will think of the job primarily in terms of advertising and might be called the advertising director. In the same way, in an industrial company, personal selling will be paramount, and the communication director might be called the sales manager. Further, in a public-sector organization publicity and public relations are paramount, and the key individual for communication might be called the public relations director.

The Advertising Agency

There are consulting organizations, or agencies that specialize in each of the four elements of communication. Here, however, we will concentrate on just the advertising agency, since advertising management is the main focus of this book and the most well-developed aspect of modern marketing communication.

There are nearly four thousand advertising agencies listed in the *Standard Directory of Advertising Agencies* in the United States. The same directory lists only about fifty sales promotion agencies. Advertising agencies range in size from the giant J. Walter Thompson Company (which annually spends the equivalent of about $1.5 billion worth of advertising) to the newest small agency (which has a staff consisting of one person who does writing and graphics work for advertising, sales promotion, or publicity).

Almost all kinds of agencies exist. Most concentrate on consumer business but will do other types. There are many large and small agencies that do primarily industrial advertising and communication work. A few concentrate on public-sector communication. And then there are all kinds of other specialties—fashion, pharmaceutical, agricultural, political. The types of advertising agencies indicate much about the various needs for communication.

There is more to the typical agency than account management and the creative and media departments. Agencies often have substantial research departments. And public relations and sales promotion are often covered by separate groups within agencies.

The job that agencies do is implemented in many different ways. Sometimes companies even have their own "in-house" agencies to do the advertising-communication job. The key fact, however, is that the agencies' job of account management, creative and media, has to be done by somebody or some organization. The client-agency relationship—with all its vagaries as described in Chapter 3—is still considered the best approach by the vast majority of companies doing advertising and marketing communication.

The Third Partner: Media

It is said that one of America's greatest exports is advertising. Certainly tied to this is the media structure that goes with advertising. In the United States there are approximately seven thousand radio stations, seven hundred television stations, eighteen hundred consumer magazines and farm publications, twenty-five hundred business publications, and eighteen hundred daily newspapers. These are the media, essentially a collection of opportunities for placing advertising.

You may have noticed that as we moved through the tripartite structure of the advertising and communication industry, we moved from general plans and the total marketing mix toward the implementation of communication. The media represent the last stop, where the ads are actually run.

The job of the media, then, from the viewpoint of the communication planner, is to provide an environment for advertising. This is not their job from the viewpoint of the consumer—who sees the media as a source of information or entertainment. Nor is the media's job seen in the same way by government officials. But advertising–marketing communication is the key here.

It is this split personality of almost all the media that produces the clearest aspect of media organization. Specifically it is divided at least in two: editorial and business. The editorial or program people are responsible for creating the content of the media that draws consumers. The business or advertising people are primarily responsible for selling advertisers and their agencies on each medium vehicle as an environment for advertising.

The most extensive research done on advertising effect is often done by the media. Of course much of this research is done for selling purposes and should be considered critically. On the other hand, the figures on media used throughout the industry are gathered by independent research contractors who are supported by all parts of the industry.

Almost every issue of such trade publications as *Advertising Age* is filled with advertising for various media vehicles. These ads might include advertising response as indicated by special studies, as in the *Good Housekeeping* advertisement in Figure 1-8. Or they might use generally available audience statistics, as in the *Sport* advertisement in Figure 1-9. If you examine any issue of *Advertising Age,* you will find that some of the most interesting advertising attempts are made for the media.

Good Housekeeping announces important new research on believability in advertising.

For every marketing or advertising executive, the key question these days is not just will she see the advertising, but even more important, will she believe it. And where the ad appears is more essential than ever to this belief.

Take magazines. A new national survey continues to show the strong confidence women have in magazines. The chart clearly indicates the large percentage of women who say they have "a good deal of or complete confidence" in the advertising in magazines – especially in the women's books. And most especially in Good

Magazine	% women with a good deal of or complete confidence
Good Housekeeping	78%
Reader's Digest	72
Parents	71
Better Homes & Gardens	70
Family Circle	64
Woman's Day	64
Ladies' Home Journal	63
McCall's	63
Redbook	53
TV Guide	42

Source: Herb Altman Communications Research, Inc. May 1979

Housekeeping. In fact, survey after survey after survey has shown that when it comes to stimulating confidence, an ad works best in Good Housekeeping.

This makes sense when you consider the unique editorial climate of Good Housekeeping.

These days when consumer skepticism may well be advertising's number one problem, it is clear Good Housekeeping remains advertising's number one opportunity.

It is the fundamental book on any print schedule that aims to inform and persuade women.

It's not just what you say-it's where you say it!

Good Housekeeping
Number one in consumer confidence.

© 1979 The Hearst Corporation.   Good Housekeeping is a publication of Hearst Magazines, a division of The Hearst Corporation.

Figure 1-8. Good Housekeeping *advertisement featuring a specially done study on audience responses*

(Courtesy of Hearst Corporation)

JOB OPPORTUNITIES IN ADVERTISING AND COMMUNICATION MANAGEMENT

There is an interesting contradiction with regard to advertising and communication management. No matter what objective gauge is used to measure the industry—expenditures, personnel, etc.—it comes out looking like a relatively modest industry. Yet it is accorded considerable attention worldwide because of its power.

This contradiction—between the objective economic measures and the obvious respect with which people treat the industry—is related to the quotations and the Indian story

FIGURE 1-9. Sport *advertisement using industry data to establish audience quality*

(*Prepared by Compton Advertising Inc., for* Sport *magazine. Used with permission.*)

of the blind men and the elephant at the beginning of this chapter. This contradiction also indicates why the advertising and communication industry is such an exciting one in which to work.

Each dollar expended by and each person working in the advertising and communication industry somehow has more power than in comparable industries. And there are two reasons for this: The dollars and people involved in advertising and marketing communication are (1) communicating and (2) creating.

As both the Preface and this chapter have indicated, communication can be extremely powerful and beneficial when it is done well. It is done well when it is done creatively. And the job opportunities in this industry are for people who know how to communicate creatively. The goal of this book is to guide people toward this type of communication.

SUMMARY

Advertising and marketing communication are one type of mass communication and one part of the marketing mix. More specifically, there are individual, two-person, and mass communication; and advertising and marketing-communication campaigns build upon a combination of individual communications for a total mass-communication campaign effect.

This particular type of mass communication constitutes the flexible part of the marketing mix for which yearly and even shorter-term campaigns are developed. These tend to be under control of the brand, product, or campaign manager, whereas the other parts of the marketing mix—*product, price,* and *distribution*—tend to be longer-term decisions that are made by higher-rank executives in concert with the brand manager. The brand or campaign manager perspective with emphasis on advertising is the one taken by this book.

There are three general types or needs for advertising and marketing communication: *consumer, industrial,* and *public sector.* Each tends toward a particular mix of four parts of marketing communication: *advertising, personal selling, sales promotion,* and *publicity–public relations.* Consumer marketing tends to emphasize advertising, industrial marketing tends to emphasize personal selling, and public-sector marketing tends to emphasize publicity and PR.

The reader should be warned, however, that although the three general types of need exist, each advertising and communication situation must be analyzed for specific needs. The basis of any campaign is communication at the individual level.

The advertising industry is a tripartite one consisting of clients-advertisers, advertising agencies, and media. This book takes the perspective of the advertiser or brand manager, but all three types of organizations are involved in management, creative, and media activities. Clients-advertisers conduct these activities at the long-term planning level. Agencies and media are more concerned with implementation.

The advertising and communication industry is said to have influence far beyond its numbers in either dollar or people terms. The reason for this contradiction is probably that creative communication can have synergistic effects—can multiply in effect if the total campaign is meaningful on an individual level. This type of powerful and responsible communication is the goal of this book.

ISSUES AND PROJECTS FOR DISCUSSION

1. Find an advertisement that you believe is great and another that you believe is terrible. Cut them out if they are print ads, or describe them briefly if you cannot obtain them physically. Indicate your reasons for believing that the terrible ad is terrible and the great ad is great.

2. You are an individual consumer. Describe in your own words how you reacted to the elements of a communication campaign for a product you bought recently. How did you first become aware of it? How did you get more detailed information? Did you get much information from television advertising? What and how were you eventually sold? What actions did you take?

3. What type of marketing communication, if any, are the following: (a) trade show exhibit, (b) direct-mail appeal, (c) the Fuller Brush man, (d) a press release, (e) a product sample, (f) an outdoor billboard, (g) a supermarket checker, (h) a matchbook cover?

4. Explain the apparent contradiction between the Roosevelt and the Lasker quotations on the first page of this chapter.

5. Describe the differences in the use of the four campaign elements for consumer, industrial, and public-sector marketing. Why do these differences exist? Under what conditions would these typical patterns not be observed?

6. What are the strengths and weaknesses of

each of the four elements of the communication mix?

7. What are the similarities and differences between individual, two-person, and mass communication? How would you know whether communication has occurred in each situation?

Notes

1. John Gunther, *Taken at the Flood* (New York: Harper & Row, Pub., 1960), p. 232.

2. *Advertising Age,* "World of Advertising" issue, November 15, 1963, p. 10.

3. Peter F. Drucker, *Management: Tasks, Responsibilities, Practices* (New York: Harper & Row Publishers, 1973), p. 64.

4. Steuart Henderson Britt, Stephen C. Adams, and Allan S. Miller, "How Many Advertising Exposures per Day?" *Journal of Advertising Research,* December 1972, pp. 3–9.

5. Jon G. Udell, *Successful Marketing Strategies in American Industry* (Madison, Wis.: Mimir Publishers, 1972).

6. Martin Mayer, *Madison Avenue, U.S.A.* (New York: Pocket Books, 1959), pp. 13–14.

Advertising
and
Communication
Decisions

• You are a brand manager about to prepare a budget for the introduction of a revolutionary new pharmaceutical. The product has already received wide coverage both in the popular media and in the medical journals. How will you determine the amounts to spend on journal advertising, detailing (drug salesperson distribution of samples and literature to doctors and pharmacists), and direct-mail promotion?

• It is June of the election year. As campaign manager for a gubernatorial challenger, you must make advance commitments for the purchase of radio-television time and outdoor advertising space. This must be balanced against your candidate's speaking schedule, print advertising, direct-mail programs, and fund-raising activities. How will you make these decisions?

• A strike interrupts the introduction of a new line of cars. How will you adjust the communication campaign in preparation for the settlement?

• You are concerned about drug abuse in your community, and as communications director of the local antidrug campaign, you are in a position to do something about it. What mix of messages and media, if any, will be used?

• As marketing manager for a new rapid transit system, you are responsible for maintaining and increasing usage despite recent system mishaps. Should you cut back on promotion, continue with present positive messages, or answer commuters' complaints directly?

• You are responsible for the marketing of a cake-mix line that has slipped from being the leading seller to being a poor third in sales. Now the number two brand is about to introduce a new premium line. How will you adjust your promotions, packaging, advertising, and trade selling to meet the new threat?

This book is aimed at individuals who are now or will be in positions like those described above. Whether they are in consumer, industrial, or public-sector fields, these brand managers, product managers, or campaign managers have become the controlling force in marketing communications. And the quantitative and behavioral tools that have evolved to support this control are the focus here.

This chapter is possibly the most important in the book because it presents a simple framework for solving problems like those presented on the first page of the chapter.

In a sense, everything you will learn from this book and this course is condensed in this one chapter. However, instead of trying to learn the details, just absorb the nature of the advertising and communication decisions presented here. To be able to make these decisions clearly and professionally should be your goal. The first step is to learn what the decisions are.

Also the framework this chapter presents is actually a method by which these decisions can be made for advertising in concert with the other elements of the marketing communication mix—*personal selling, sales promotion,* and *publicity–public relations.* Learning this framework in general should be the second step in reading this chapter. The framework is one way that all the various decisions of advertising can be integrated with other aspects of the marketing-communication mix. No other book in the field of advertising management, marketing communication, or promotion has presented such an opportunity for integration.

Throughout this chapter you will see references to various behavioral science and quantitative science tools. These are the bases for the framework, but it is not necessary for you to totally understand how these various tools work. This book represents what is useful now, based on these advanced tools. You can tell what is important to know now by reading the questions at the end of the chapter before you go on with the next section. You might also check back to these questions after each section—to see how the reading prepares you to make these decisions.

THE CONTEXT OF MARKETING-COMMUNICATION DECISIONS

The brand management organizational scheme was developed originally to give profit responsibility to one person on each brand in a multiproduct company. This is still true, but it is becoming increasingly clear that brand managers are really intermediaries between division and company top management and the organizations and tools of marketing communication. The brand or product manager is given a situation by the company and the market, and he or she must react to it by effective use of marketing-communication tools.

Our pharmaceutical product manager, for instance, can do little about the nature of the new product, its pricing, the overall weight of emphasis the company is giving to it, or the initial market response to research reports. What the manager can do, however, is react to the situation with appropriate use of journal advertising, detailing (selling), samples and literature, and direct-mail promotion—the marketing-communication tools at his or her command.

The same is true of the political campaign manager. This manager can do little about the candidate or the candidate's positions and activities. The stories of headstrong politicians going against media campaign efforts are legion. But the campaign manager can affect the media campaign, direct-mail efforts, collateral materials, and fund raising within the dictates of this candidate and the competition.

The automobile brand manager, drug-abuse campaign manager, transit system marketing manager, and cake-mix brand manager are all in the same intermediary position. They are given a situation, certain objectives for market share and/or profit, and certain resources. Their job is to allocate those resources to marketing-communication tools, and then supervise the planning, implementation, and control of those tools.

This book is designed to provide a structure for accomplishing these tasks.

In the next several hundred pages we will concentrate on the brand manager who uses marketing communication to sell products, usually consumer products in the convenience-goods category. We emphasize convenience-goods brand managers because most of the advanced tools have been developed for them and because these managers have clear-cut sales and profit objectives which are essential to the use of most of the developed tools.

This emphasis on consumer brand managers does not, however, exclude industrial, service, or public campaign managers. As in this chapter, we will continually use examples from these fields. The brand manager emphasis is taken in order to deal primarily with techniques that have actually been used, instead of just speculation. Also, as mentioned in the first chapter, the consumer area is the one in which there is the most sophisticated use of advertising, the central focus of this book.

COMMUNICATION WITHIN MARKETING DECISION MAKING

The outline for marketing communication in this book is based on the assumption that communication is the major and, in most situations, the only short-term action tool available to the middle manager in marketing. Let us review our definitions of communication in this context.

Communication is defined here as a process in which there is a sender-communicator, a message, a receiver-audience, and a response by the audience. In reality this is a two-way process. Usually the "receivers" become "senders" by reacting with a "message" of their own. Here, however, we will look at the process from the one-way perspective of the marketing communicator. Usually the communicator is working with mass communication in which he or she is responsible for many messages being sent to many receivers, virtually none of whom the communicator knows personally. What's more, each individual in the communicator's market segment is receiving many competing and supporting messages both from the mass media and from individuals. The audience is both influencing and being influenced by others.

In this kind of situation, "communication" is said to occur when a sufficient number of audience members react in the way the sender intends. This reaction or response can be in terms of awareness, comprehension, conviction, or action. In the aggregate, a communication campaign is composed of many messages and reactions, which together lead to increases in sales or votes, decreases in drug usage, increases in seat-belt usage, or other final measures of the success of a total marketing program.

Of course, all parts of the marketing program could be defined as "messages" and thus "communication." Certainly product, price, and channels of distribution are important messages in themselves. In reality, however, these aspects of the marketing mix are relatively stable. Once they are set, they are not changed as often as the communication parts of the marketing mix. Product, price, and distribution are typically "givens" to be considered in communication terms. But marketing communication itself is composed of those elements that middle managers can really affect in terms of a coordinated action campaign that might change many times for each time there is a significant change in product, price, and distribution. In marketing, the key communication campaign elements are personal selling, advertising, product sampling, coupons, promotions, retailer support-merchandising, publicity, and public relations.

Marketing communication, then, consists of a mix of communication elements or message types which are designed to evoke certain thoughts, feelings, or behavior—within the context of a given marketing mix and situation.

Considered in this way, the general steps of marketing decision making related to communication are as follows:

1. A *situation analysis* must be performed in order to determine the company's strengths, weaknesses, and general objectives; the product, price, consumer, and trade must be analyzed.
2. *Marketing sales objectives* are set.
3. A *total budget* for communication activities is set for this particular campaign.
4. *Resource allocation* must be considered for the kinds of communication activities necessary to accomplish the objectives. The manager must formulate a *coordinated plan,* with each component carrying its proper share of the burden.
5. A *series of specific decisions* must be made for each communication element. These will include the communication goals for each element, the communication positioning, the

message factors, and the message distribution plan.
6. *Budgets* are set for the communication elements and *control* procedures are instituted in order to evaluate the communication program.

Each of the following sections considers one or several of these six decision steps. A description is offered of the typical way the decisions are made. Then in each section there is an overview of the quantitative and behavioral supports that have been developed to aid the decision making. The final section of this chapter explains the full marketing-communication decision sequence and the plan of this book.

The intent of this second chapter is to give the reader a complete overview of the decisions, procedures, and techniques that are needed to answer the kinds of questions that were asked at the beginning of the chapter. With such an overview, the reader should be able to consider marketing-communication decisions in a realistic way as he or she learns about the decision-support tools that can be employed.

SITUATION ANALYSIS, MARKETING OBJECTIVES, AND TOTAL BUDGET

What has evolved along with the six-step decision process is an organizational environment in which the first three steps—situation analysis, marketing objectives, and total communication budget—are made with the brand or campaign manager as only a member of a team of people who are considering the manager's product or candidate or issue, along with others. Depending on the decisions of this team, the campaign manager will get a certain type of product and price and distribution. The manager's overall objectives will be clearly set in terms of final measures such as sales and votes. And the manager will have some idea as to how much weight the company is ready to put against his or her area of influence. The manager will also have an overall budget with which to do the job. Then he or she can begin to operate in a marketing communication sense.

The first three steps of decision making before actual marketing-communication work are shown in Figure 2-1. While these steps take place *before* marketing communication, they are critical to its success.

The cake-mix example above is typical. The product manager will not be able to act

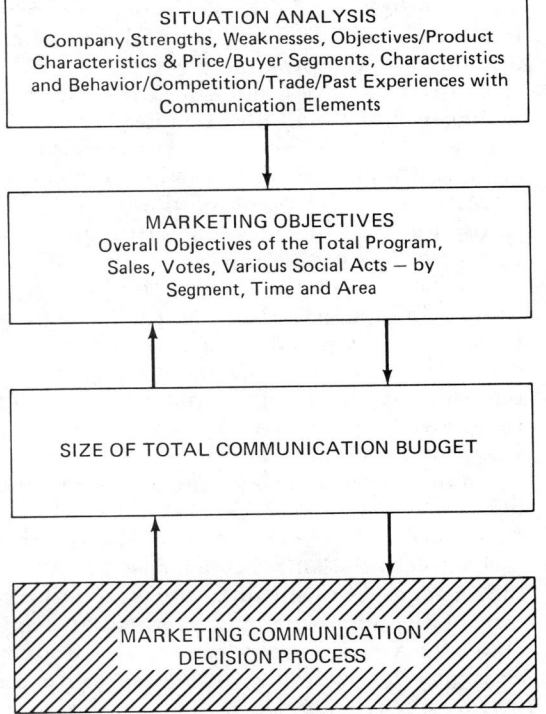

Figure 2-1. Before Marketing Communication. *Campaign Manager meets with other organization officials to use situation analysis to determine marketing objectives and size of total communication budget for his or her product. Main tools: Product Life Cycle Portfolio Analysis, Attitudinal Segmentation, and Consumer Decision Process Analysis.*

on communication until the company feels there is something to communicate. It may be that product development is necessary. Or a pricing change may be feasible. Or management may decide that very little can be accomplished with the brand. It may be best to "milk" it and put communication effort on other brands. The answer to the cake-mix question at the beginning of this chapter could not be made simply by action on the communication front.

In many situations communication is erroneously started before adequate attention to situation analysis and the setting of marketing objectives. The drug-abuse example is apt here. The main planner is called a "communication director." Therefore communication *will* occur. But what kind? This should depend on the nature of the drug problem. However, thorough analysis is seldom done and objectives are seldom set so it is possible to determine the appropriate role for communication.

Often preventive scare campaigns have been launched in the alcohol or drug area—without knowledge of such basic facts as the trial-to-repeat-user ratio. When this ratio is high, when very few trials or first uses of drugs result in repeat use—a preventive scare campaign is exactly the opposite of what is needed. In such a situation, some loosening of laws, followed by messages and treatment, may provide a better alternative. Of course there is no way to assess the viability of this strategy or any other without a situation analysis and marketing objectives. These are the main links between the more stable parts of the marketing mix and the communication components, which are more amenable to change and management.

In this book, situation analysis and marketing objectives will be treated in terms of three quantitatively and behaviorally based analytical procedures which can be used to determine the opportunity for effective communication. First, the product, price, and distribution will be considered in terms of the *product life cycle* and the *product portfolio con-*

cept. This will give a basis for considering the company and the market in an organized way.

Second, audience groups will be analyzed in terms of an *attitudinal framework for segmentation.* This behavioral-quantitative approach analyzes audiences in terms of their communication needs. Thus it is possible to establish information that can be used to position the product, service, candidate, or idea in the context of audience attitudes.

Third, each audience segment will be analyzed in terms of its typical decision process for buying the product or making relevant choices. *Logical flow charting,* computer simulation, and simple *models of consumer behavior* will be explained in practical terms. The purpose of these approaches is to determine the key steps in the decision process where communication can have a strong effect.

Situation analysis moves from a general examination with product life-cycle analysis to a more specific examination emphasizing segmentation to an even more precise study of audience decision processes. This allows an assessment of potentials, and marketing objectives can be set. Also, it is possible to determine the total communication budget, the weight of effort the company deems appropriate for the brand. Then the stage is set for marketing-communication activities to begin.

RESOURCE ALLOCATION: REALITIES AND SOLUTIONS

The first marketing-communication step is resource allocation. Its position and nature is shown schematically in Figure 2-2. For this step, the manager must decide how much of the total budget will be allocated to each of the various types of communication available to him or her. In most cases this allocation is done in a nonoptimal way, due to difficulties caused by most marketing organizations.

Essentially, the problem these managers have is one of budgeting. They are attempting to decide how much of their money they will commit to each element of the communication mix. In the ideal state, they would simply allocate on the basis of response. That is, they would keep allocating resources to aspects of the mix until the extra response they get is equal to the extra expenditure for that element of the mix.

This is the *marginal economic approach.* If the pharmaceutical product manager used it, he or she would take the total budget for promotion and allocate first to the most responsive part of the mix. This may be journal advertising. This allocation would be up to the dollar amount at which advertising is no longer responsive. Then allocations would be made to detailing, samples and literature, and direct mail in the same way.

In the case of the political campaign manager, direct mail may be most responsive because of its selectivity. Under the marginal economic approach, direct mail would receive allocations to the point of diminishing returns, and then other aspects of the political campaign mix could be covered.

These examples cover the ideal, of course. In practice, the scenario for setting budgets is quite different. In one survey of 267 corporations, some admitted to advertising budgeting on the basis of "that's about what we've always spent."[1] A more typical response was that advertising and other parts of the communication mix are budgeted on the basis of a *set percentage of last year's sales or expected sales* in the upcoming year. Almost none used a solely *competitive parity approach* in which they attempted to spend at the level and nature of their major competitors or, at least, above the average expenditure in the product class. The largest group attempted to use an *objective and task approach,* in which subobjectives were set for each component of the communication mix and the budget was set in terms of the tasks thought necessary to achieve those objectives.

Not one respondent to the survey claimed to be using anything close to the

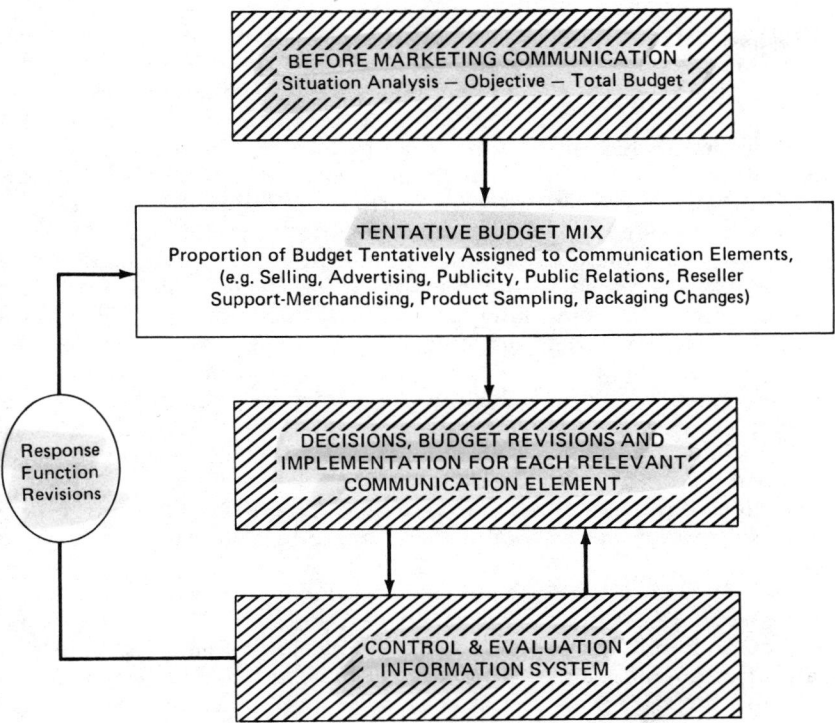

Figure 2-2. Resource Allocation. *Total communication budget is divided among communication elements in a tentative budget mix. This budget allocation is subject to revision on the basis of research and decisions for the individual elements, as well as on the basis of data from control and evaluation activities. Main tools: Response Function, Decision Calculus Situational Approach.*

ideal marginal economic method outlined above. Why? The usual answer is that there is inadequate information on response to expenditures for individual elements of the communication mix. Unless there is some information on response, it is clearly impossible to plan on its basis.

The realities of the resource allocation problem are not quite this simple, however. Budget allocation takes place within a difficult organizational setting.[2] This typical setting biases the definition of what is adequate information on response. Organizational pressures lead to certain communication mixes being used repeatedly despite data to the contrary.

Part of the difficulty comes from the campaign or brand managers themselves. They very often have had experience in managing one of the elements of the communication mix. They could have been advertising managers or sales managers. In many companies some experience in direct selling is considered to be an absolute requirement for managerial positions in marketing.[3]

Past experience can lead to a bias toward one particular communication element. In the pharmaceutical industry, for instance, there is a tendency to budget more for detailing and samples and literature than for, say, journal advertising. One company was shown to be spending in this way—in the reverse order of these tools' effectiveness as indicated by longitudinal research.[4] This tendency must be partially due to the fact that most pharmaceutical product managers started their careers as detail men on the sales side of the marketing effort.

Pressure for simpler, less optimal forms of research allocation come both from above and from below the campaign manager. From above, there is the usual pressure to get plans ready on time. Along with this, there is the cumulative past experience represented by top management. Since they have communicated successfully in a certain way in the past, there is reluctance to reassess communication in each new planning situation.

The political situation provides an example. Some candidates who had successfully used television advertising in past elections were slow to move to new possibilities offered by computerized direct-mail operations in the 1980 elections.

The political situation also offers some indication of the kinds of pressures at these managers get from groups and individuals below them in the chain of command. Both the advertising manager and the sales manager push for budgets to support their own activities. In the political organization, the state and local divisions ask for precinct work support. Various outside service organizations—such as advertising agencies, direct-mail agencies, broadcast stations, outdoor facilities, and public relations and campaign management organizations—all push for a share of the total communication budget.

As the capsule at the beginning of this chapter indicated, our campaign manager had to make commitments for outdoor space and television time in June of the election year, way ahead of the campaign season.

Similar commitments have to be made in other marketing areas. The automobile manufacturer marketing manager faced with a strike and subsequent settlement may opt for a television special just because of its availability. Or the manager may use print advertising because it can be bought on short notice when sufficient television time is not available. Or dealers may push for an after-strike promotion.

These pressures can lead to decisions in which managers attempt to balance requests rather than balance communication response in allocating resources. Managers get pushed toward "satisficing" rather than seeking optimal allocations in terms of response. They favor communication tools that can be measured in "units distributed" (number of pieces mailed, samples distributed, etc.) as opposed to response effectiveness. As surveys have indicated, there is a tendency to do what was done in the past rather than take advantage of changes, new opportunities, and the experience of response as it comes from the marketplace.

To a large extent this situation is inevitable. It is something that every brand, product, and campaign manager must face every time a new marketing-communication plan is developed. But, precisely because this situation is inevitable and because it occurs repeatedly, there have been management science tools developed to deal with it.

The tools developed fall under the heading of *decision calculus models*. These are simple models, usually computerized, which are designed to help managers utilize the data and judgments at their command, in order to plan in as close to the marginal economic way as possible.

Every manager has knowledge about the market that leads him or her to make assumptions about the response to be expected from advertising, promotion, selling, and so on. All the decision calculus approach asks the manager to do is to put these assumptions in a quantified form, to see if they make sense in terms of total market output. Only the data and judgments that the manager feels are valid are utilized in the model. Once this simple start is made, however, it is possible to evolve it into a powerful resource-allocation tool.

The distinctive aspect of this decision calculus approach is that it forces the manager to make conditional forecasts. Instead of first forecasting sales and then budgeting communication to fit these sales, the manager estimates response and then observes sales or profit outcomes given various communication budget mixes. With the decision calculus approach the "cart" is no longer put before the "horse." Response is estimated first, and then conditional forecasts are made.

To what extent is this approach a solution to the organizational realities of resource allocation outlined earlier? The brand manager is still under pressure. But if a decision calculus model has been developed, especially if it has been computerized, the manager has a quick way to respond to the pressure. If top management wants to put more emphasis into one aspect of the mix, its assumption of response can be utilized in the model to see if this increase is reasonable. If a new television or outdoor offering becomes available, then data or estimates of response can be put into the model to determine overall effect. If the advertising agency pressures for a new campaign, its pressure must be accompanied by estimates of response so that overall effect can be determined. If there is a strike or an equipment failure, then the brand manager or campaign manager can act intelligently by trying out various assumptions of response in the model. And the model helps to determine where response information is inadequate, that is, where research must be done.

Thus the decision calculus approach offers a good solution to many of the problems of resource allocation. In fact, it is central to coordination of the many activities of marketing communication. But it is not easy to implement. Chapter 6 of this book examines the decision calculus approach and the procedures for implementation, and it reviews the substantive findings on market response to various communication elements. A number of studies in the consumer, industrial, and public-sector area show how professionals actually use advertising and communication in various situations. This *situation analysis* can

provide clear guidelines for how much emphasizing to put against advertising and other mix elements. The result of the decision calculus situation and approach is a *tentative budget mix,* as shown in Figure 2-2. This mix gives direction to those individuals and organizations working on particular aspects of the mix such as advertising or selling. Those particular decisions, which are reviewed in the next section, eventually give a firmer idea as to how much should be spent for each element of the mix.

FOUR KEY DECISIONS OF MARKETING COMMUNICATION

The brand or campaign manager's pressure does not end once the tentative budget mix is determined. At that point the manager has a tentative statement of how much money will be allocated to each part of his or her communication mix. Next the manager must coordinate the activities of all the organizations involved in planning the specific ways this money will be spent.

This is easier said than done. Often the pressures of the individual organizations, such as the advertising agency, the sales representatives, and the public relations people, lead to gross changes in allocation—without intervening reassessment of response or full utilization of the organizations themselves. The "marketing-communication" plan can become an "advertising" plan or a "sales" plan, with only subsidiary attention being paid to most of the elements of the communication mix.

The activities of marketing communication seem, on the surface, to be multitudinous and variegated. How can a manager coordinate such activities as sales territory assignment, advertising copywriting, and liaison with publications for publicity purposes? One of the answers is in the decision

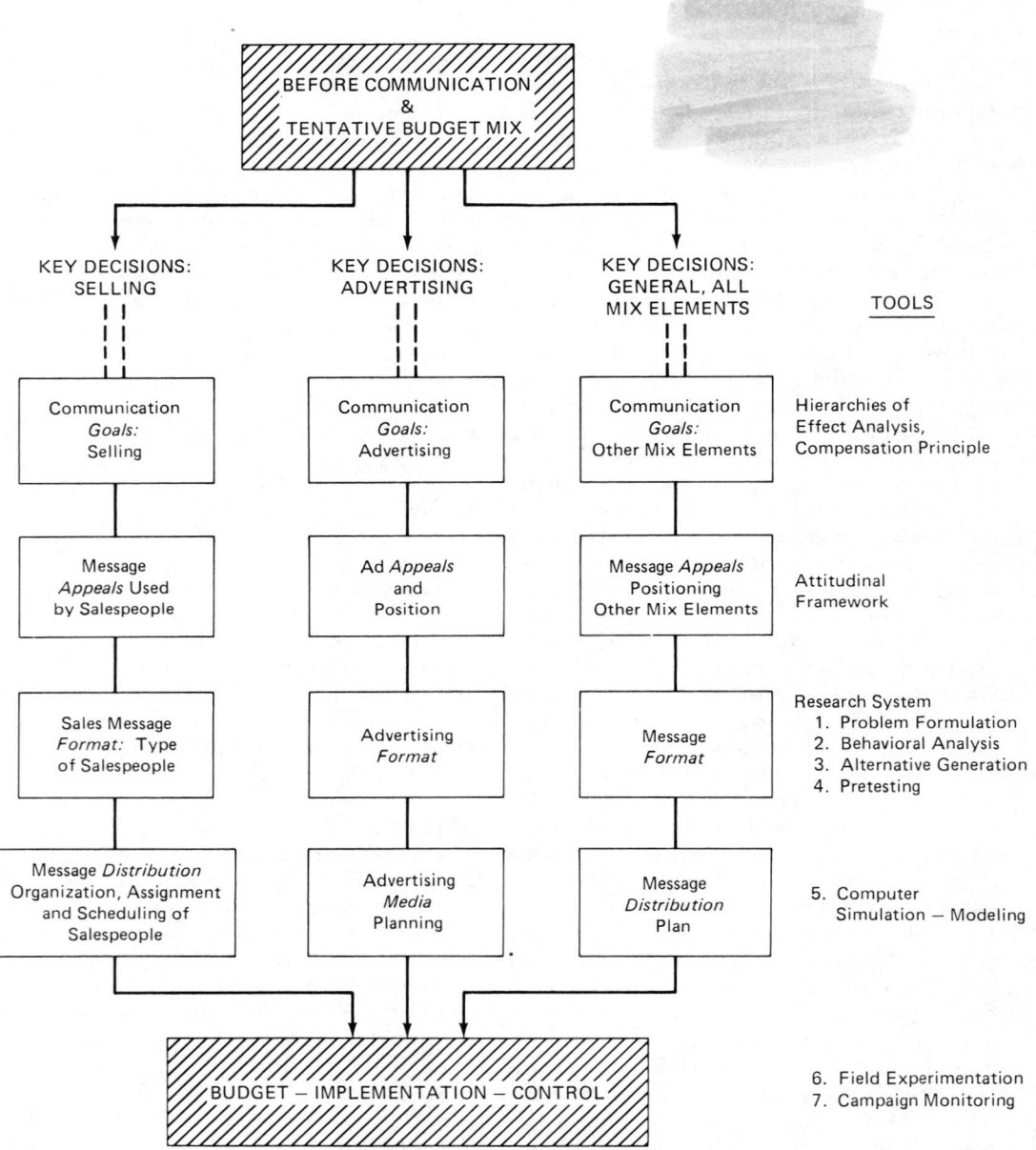

Figure 2-3. Four Key Decisions of Marketing Communication. *For every communication element there are decisions to be made on goals, appeals, format, distribution of communication. Examples for selling and advertising shown. Tools used for each decision level shown at right.*

calculus tentative budget mix itself. But the subsequent coordination is only possible because all the planning done on individual communication elements can be condensed into four key decisions: communication goals, message appeals-positioning, message format, and message distribution plan. These decision points, and their position in marketing communication and relevant quantitative-behavioral support techniques, are shown in Figure 2-3.

All communication elements have these decisions associated with them. This is true almost by definition. Recall that one of the founders of communication research, Harold Lasswell, once said that the field was concerned with *"Who said What to Whom through which Channels with what Effect."* This is identical with the definition of communication given earlier. The "Who" (source) and "Whom" (audience, consumer market segments) have already been discussed. Now the "Effect" (communication goals), and "What" (message appeals-positioning and format), and the "Channels" (message distribution plan) are seen as the key decisions to be made for each communication element and controlled by the brand manager.

The real advantage of a consolidated marketing communication as opposed to completely separate management of advertising, selling, and so forth, is that each communication element can be seen as part of the whole. For instance, the brand or campaign manager can balance the communication goals of one element of the mix against those of other parts of the mix to produce a greater overall effect in terms of marketing objectives.

This balancing of goals, positioning, format, and distribution depends greatly on the changing situation. Take our urban transit marketing manager mentioned at the beginning of this chapter. When this manager's new system first opened, he could depend on advance publicity to create awareness, with direct-mail and mass-media advertising adding comprehension and positive attitudes toward using the public mode of commuting.

As time went on, promotions would seem in order, to develop use in off-commuting hours. And personal sales representatives may work with administrators of large manufacturing plants, shopping centers, and outlying municipalities to develop public transportation packages.

When there are system mishaps, however, the transit manager must seek a different blend of goals, message, and message distribution across the group of communication elements. Most kinds of publicity will be negative to this manager's purposes. If the operating characteristics of the system have been markedly improved, the manager can begin to use advertising to get these ideas across. Then promotions, combined with advertising, might be used to induce trial. And point-of-service messages and passenger assistance crews may help induce a feeling of confidence on board the public vehicles themselves.

Success in mixing communication goals, message, and distribution is by no means automatic, however. It is easy to spin out examples of what might be done in any particular situation. But the very real art in marketing-communication decision making comes in combining elements in new ways. And in the past decade there has been a rapid development of tools that can help to make the four key decisions. Some of these decisions can be explained as follows.

Communication Goals

The subobjectives that have been emphasized in marketing communication have been those that fall into a *hierarchy of effects*. These are the states of mind and action people go through in response to ads. Many kinds of terms are used. Ad copywriters use the acronym **AIDA** (Attention-Interest-Desire-Action). The adoption process of awareness, comprehension, evaluation, trial, adoption is another one. So is the attitude structure of cognitive-affective-conative. Here we will talk primarily of the awareness-comprehension-conviction-action hierarchy, which has been used as a planning hierarchy within advertising.

There are two quarrels with the hierarchy approach to communication goal setting. One is that the hierarchy should be ignored and goals set only with regard to total marketing objectives such as sales and profit. The managerial advantages of using hierarchy goals are so obvious that not a great deal of time will be spent with this objection.

The second quarrel is with the assumed order of the awareness-comprehension-conviction-action levels. The question is whether awareness must precede comprehension which must precede conviction which must precede action. There is a great deal of evidence that people only sometimes go through this order of mental and physical states.

In this book a *three-orders model* is proposed, with directions for analyzing situations to determine which order of mental states is most likely to be operative. Also the *compensation principle,* which states that any particular message will probably have positive effects on one level of the hierarchy and negative or null effects on others, is used to indicate the possibilities of balancing the effects of the elements of the communication mix. Publicity may create product awareness; advertising can evoke brand recognition and comprehension; selling may change conviction; and promotion may evoke trial. The job of the brand manager is to make certain that the goals of communication for advertising, selling, publicity, and promotion blend together and balance each other to achieve overall marketing objectives.

Message Appeals-Positioning

Message strategy consists of two parts: what to say (appeals-positioning) and how to say it (format). The question of appeals has been answered in many ways in the past.

Here there will be some concentration on advertising agencies' *creative philosophies* which have indicated that the primary consideration is that communication be both distinctive and meaningful. More recent work with *perceptual mapping, nonmetric scaling* product positioning studies has not only quantified the typical creative philosophy but also made it relevant for a marketing-communication approach. If products are developed with perceptual mapping, then the attributes that should be communicated are already somewhat predetermined. Work on *summated attribute ratings* and *product positioning* has led to an *attitudinal framework* for message strategy.

That framework, which is the core of appeals-positioning development in this book, is based on the notion that each audience segment finds a limited number of appeals or product characteristics salient for purchasing each product and particular brands of that product. The brand manager's job is to determine these characteristics for each target segment. As mentioned earlier, if perceptual mapping, product development studies have been done, these key dimensions or characteristics are determined before marketing-communication planning begins.

In determining message appeals-positioning, however, more must be estimated than just the salient characteristics. Our cake-mix brand manager must face the threat of a new premium brand. This manager knows that there is a large segment of cake-mix buyers who use it for everyday family meals. They consider price, general quality, convenience-involvement, and taste-texture. Is this enough information on which to base a communication campaign? What further must be known?

The attitudinal framework for message positioning would suggest that three more bits of information are necessary. First, we must learn the ideal point and acceptable range of values for each characteristic. Take taste-texture for cake mix, for instance. The typical homemaker may want a chocolate cake for everyday family meals with about as much chocolate taste as a brownie but a bit drier. This is her ideal point for taste-texture. She might, however, be satisfied with cakes nearly as chocolate-flavored and moist as fudge on one end and chocolate cookies on the other end. This is her range of acceptable values.

The second bit of information we need for message positioning is how the consumer uses the characteristics. Does she use them all in an averaging or summative way, one at a time from most important to least important until a clear discrimination between brands is found or what? In the cake-mix situation, for instance, the homemaker may have found that taste-texture does not vary much across cake-mix brands. So she checks for availability of brands with particular convenience-involvement, then eliminates brands on quality and price to get to the one she buys. This is only one of many possible strategies we each take as consumers in making choices.

Notice that in order to make her decision, the cake-mix buyer must have some perceptions of brands on relevant dimensions. This is the third and final bit of information we need from consumers in order to make the message positioning decision. We need to know how consumers position our brand and others on the market.

Once the characteristics, ideal points and acceptable ranges, decision process, and brand perceptions are known, a framework for message positioning is complete. The cake-mix brand manager, political campaign manager, transit marketing manager, drug product manager, and all the individuals in the communication-planning role then have several clear strategies that might be used. Six are reviewed in this book. The communication planner may attempt to

☐ Emphasize a different goal for the product. If the "everyday family dinner" cake-mix segment is a large one, and your brand does not very well measure up to the segment's goals, it might be possible to communicate the possibility of using the mix for another purpose, say, "special occasions." By achieving com-

prehension of this new use, your product may be put into a better attitudinal framework position vis-à-vis the rest of the market.
☐ Add a characteristic for consideration, one that will be important, one that you have and your competition does not.
☐ Change the ideal point and acceptable range for a characteristic.
☐ Change the perception of some characteristic of your brand.
☐ Change the perception of some characteristic of your competitor.
☐ Change the way consumers combine perceptions to make decisions.

Much of the information for the framework and strategies is developed *before* marketing communication, at the situation analysis stage. Once weight is put against each of the communication elements and communication goals are set, it is possible to parcel out message position tasks to each of the mix elements. Some will only establish general brand awareness; others will attempt to affect perceptions directly; still others will attempt to convert these perceptions into feelings and actions. Each will carry out its positioning communication task in a somewhat different way. This brings us to format, the next of the four key marketing-communication decisions.

Message Format

This is perhaps the most creative and artistic aspect of marketing communication. "Show business" might be a better term for the decisions that need to be made in the message format area. The question here is, Given a goal and a position, what form should the message take? What kinds of salespeople are necessary and what kind of presentation should be used? What colors and visuals should be used on the new packages? Should the publicity release be long or short, and how many pictures should be included? Should the advertising be humorous, emphasize a personality, include a demonstration, evoke concerns or fears? What kind of premium can be used to generate trial and still get across the message position?

When managers are forced to deal with format questions, they often feel that they are out of their range of competence. It is often said that once budgets, goals, and positions are set, the manager should let the "creatives" to themselves.

While we would agree that there are times when "creatives" should be left alone, we would strongly disagree with the proposition that brand and campaign managers have little place in affecting message format decisions.

The managers should institute what is here called the *marketing-communication research system*. This procedure represents the appropriate managerial role in creative format development. It is designed to utilize all available information and quantitative-behavioral tools for format development and evaluation.

The research system consists of seven steps which correspond to the typical creative process, implemented with testing in order to reduce risk. Four of the steps are shown as format decision-support techniques in Figure 2-3. The first two steps—*problem formulation* and *behavioral analysis*—represent the manager's obligation to provide creatives with a clear structure of the problem and also a thorough behavioral analysis that indicates which format techniques have and have not worked in the past. This analysis would cover evidence from past campaign results, exploratory research, the situation analysis, and goals and positioning development, as well as broad and deep consideration of behavioral science findings on communication and persuasion.

Once those people responsible for creative development have this information, they can begin to develop many *alternative solutions*. This is the third step of the research system. Analyses indicate that much more effort and money should be put against format development than is now being spent. The emphasis in the third step should be on generating a large number of alternatives within the guidelines provided by the problem and analysis.

For instance, in the cake-mix and the public transit examples offered earlier, the problem may generally be phrased as, What format should be used in highly competitive situations? Those creative people working on advertising, publicity, packaging, sales presentations, and so forth, will know the general appeals and positioning. The behavioral analysis may indicate that a refutational format, in which competitive arguments are presented briefly and then refuted with strong arguments made for the seller's own brand, may be effective. This would be especially true of the transit situation, in which counterarguments to using transit would automatically occur to potential users and should be refuted if any form of marketing communication is to be effective.

At the alternative generating stage, then, several refutational-type aids may be prepared, along with some that are just supportive, others that are strong one-sided competitive messages, some that are attention-getting and humorous, and so forth.

Once alternatives are generated, one of the characteristic points of tension between managerial and creative personnel occurs. In advertising decision making, for example, the managers attempt to discern which of the alternatives is the best for the actual campaign. This kind of judging is so objectionable to creative workers that some advertising agencies give their clients only a single alternative. If the client doesn't like it, the agencies claim they tell the client to find another agency.

The research system idea obviously goes counter to this approach, since it argues, on the basis of good evidence, that not enough format alternatives are typically generated for any communication element. There is an important place for judgment, however. The brand or campaign manager should work closely with creative personnel to pare down the total number of alternatives for each communication element. This should be done on the basis of judgment and past experience. The chapters on message format deal with creative organization and then with what experience (advertising agencies' creative philosophies) and communication research suggest about the format. Once this experience is mixed with judgment to pare down alternatives, it is time for the fourth step of the research system.

The fourth step is *pretesting*. This consists of limited testing of format alternatives before large expenditures are committed to them. In advertising, this pretesting is known as "copytesting." What is needed in all areas of marketing communication is a quick and cheap method for determining which ad format, sales presentation, promotion idea, or direct-mail piece is best. Both managers and creatives need empirical estimates of response. Despite the large amount of behavioral evidence and past experience available, there is never any clear assurance as to how alternatives will work in a particular situation. Pretesting provides a way of testing in a specific situation.

For the mass-media forms of marketing communication, it is possible to do this pretesting with laboratory experimentation. Alternatives are each assigned to a respondent group representing the target market segment. Laboratory responses to the format alternatives provide an estimate of the segment's communication response in the natural campaign situation.

Later chapters review pretesting techniques that determine the effects of repetition, scheduling, distraction, media environment and mix, and competition on format effectiveness. All of this can be done within the managerial requirements of time, cost, and clear decisions between alternatives. More important are general guidelines for format development based on past pretesting results. They indicate the kinds of formats pretesting has shown to be optimal in particular situations.

Pretesting is not perfect, of course. Its results are only estimates, and these can be seriously biased if the testing is not done carefully. Even pretests that move out of the laboratory to, say, on-air, day-after recall tests in advertising can have major biases.

These imperfections should not lead to rejection of pretesting entirely, however. Since pretesting is being done within a system of managerial decisions on format, its imperfections are made less important. The pretesting results are not used alone to make decisions. Pretesting follows a great deal of information gathering and creative development. And after pretesting come the fifth, sixth, and seventh steps of the marketing-communication research system.

In the fifth step, the pretested alternatives are considered within the message distribution plan, sometimes in terms of some kind of *computer simulation* such as an advertising media *model*. The computer simulation allows management to use the pretesting results in a realistic way along with other inputs on the nature of market response.

The sixth step is *field experimentation,* sometimes consisting of test marketing. Those format alternatives that survive pretesting and simulation might need further testing in the natural but controlled setting of field experimentation. This could provide a final check on pretesting estimates before the selected format is actually used.

The last step of the research system is *campaign monitoring,* continuing communication research that is done to determine if the efforts are achieving objectives and goals.

The marketing-communication research system is a managerial tool that corresponds to key communication decision areas. The first four steps—problem definition, behavioral analysis, creative alternative generation, and pretesting—are part of the format decision. Computer simulation, the fifth step, is used in developing the message distribution plan. Field experimentation and campaign monitoring are done for implementation, information system, and adaptive control purposes.

The research system is merely a guideline for thinking about message format decisions in advertising. It is not necessary that the specific steps, such as pretesting and information systems, be fully implemented for every campaign or even the majority of them. The most important aspect of the creative format chapters is their situation analysis base. That is, the directions provided by the budgeting chapter and the communication goal chapter in terms of how to budget and set goals for advertising and communication in various situations are carried over to the format chapters. The situational guidance indicates in which situations such formats as the "honest-twist approach," testimonials, and humor should be used.

This book advocates that message format decisions become a part of the total flow of managerial decisions related to marketing communication. Creative people who develop format ideas should neither be left totally alone nor be totally controlled. Instead they should make their contributions within the flow of a research system that provides maximum possible information for undertaking their task and adequate checks in order to guard against costly failures. It is the brand or campaign manager's task to set up this research system and use its outputs to approve and balance the campaign.

Message Distribution Plan

Once messages are developed, it is time to determine how they will be distributed. Distribution is part of all communication elements, but in this book and in this section we will concentrate on advertising message distribution, called media planning.

In media planning, communication managers must deal with advertising agency staff and media people who will urge certain expenditure patterns. Managers must approve plans for a particular mix of media (e.g., magazines versus TV versus newspapers), class of media vehicle (e.g., types of television programs or magazines), and schedule during a time period. These three decisions—media, class of vehicles, and schedule—are the essence of media planning.

Developing media plans is a creative process. Plans are evaluated in terms of their ability to generate exposure to the campaign and response from that exposure. The planner must take into account not only the media costs and audiences but also multiple and cumulative exposure and the effects of media characteristics and audience mood on response.

The decision situation is complex. The number of alternatives is enormous. For instance, assume that our automobile campaign manager has an advertising budget of $1 million for poststrike activity. Further assume that he decides to consider one hundred prime-time television programs for the approximately twenty spot announcements he could buy with his money. This is actually a simplification of the media-planning decision the manager faces at the close of the auto strike. Even with this simplification, however, there are 770 *sextillion* ways he can spend his money![5]

How can this incredibly complex decision be handled? First, it should be realized that the previous steps of planning narrow down the number of alternatives considerably. On the basis of past experience, budgetary restraints, type of communication goal and audience, the nature of the appeals and format, and pretesting results—many media, vehicles, and schedules have been eliminated from consideration. Others loom as absolutely necessary to carry out the campaign. Also, in terms of broadcast media, there is a limit to the available options.

Despite these limitations, however, the total number of options is still very large. And the number of factors that affect the decision is even larger. In order to deal with this situation, managers have turned to the computer and the media model, which underlie the media-planning guidelines in this book.

While, for a variety of economic and organizational reasons, media models typically have not been used on a regular basis to make media plans or schedules, they are often used on a limited basis in media planning. They constitute an ordered approach to the problem of message distribution planning. When managers are forced to provide the information for a media model run, they are also forced to state their assumptions about how the media work. They are required to use a clear structure for media decision making. And they must bring to bear all available data on the media exposure and response patterns.

Media models, and corresponding message distribution models in other areas of marketing communication such as in the sales area, have forced a structure on message distribution planning. In addition, these models have become more and more practical as more data become available and costs decrease. Thus they are at the center of the application of behavioral and quantitative tools.

The requirements of these models are used to show the structure of planning. The models require estimates of exposure and impact of the media against market targets. This leads, in this book, to a discussion of the nature of the media for marketing purposes. Trends in terms of society and research are also covered. There is an attempt to review the behavioral data available for media planning.

Media models have forced advertising managers to consider the interaction between various message strategies and message distribution decisions. Some media models allow managers to make different estimates of the response to repetitive exposures, for each media vehicle and market segment. This kind of model puts new demands on behavioral research, necessitating the development of pretesting which provides estimation of the repetitive effects of various messages. These estimates can then be used in the models to present a sophisticated picture of what the message alternatives might mean in marketing terms. This is the "computer simulation" step of the marketing-communication research system. The results of repetition and forgetting research are directly relevant.

In the personal-selling area, models can be used to allocate sales effort among products, salespeople calls among prospects, and salespeople among geographic areas. As these models are developed, the type of message strategy-distribution combination that has been used in advertising will also apply to selling. In direct-mail promotion and sampling, computer use of data banks may also lead to the behavioral-model combination. The synergistic promise of marketing communication as originally conceived is finding potential realization in model and behavioral inputs at the message distribution decision point.

BUDGET-IMPLEMENTATION-CONTROL

The four key steps of marketing communication are, in large part, planning rather than implementation steps. Except for the relatively small amounts for research and development, there is no money spent and no regular use of communication elements as yet. Chapter 18 is concerned with tools that might be used by the manager to convert plans into actions and then control those actions into success.

At this point, perhaps more than at any other, the brand manager or campaign manager should be in control of activities. Both top management and those groups responsible for each communication element have made their contribution. Now it is up to the brand-campaign manager to mix these contributions into a campaign that can be funded, acted upon, and succeed.

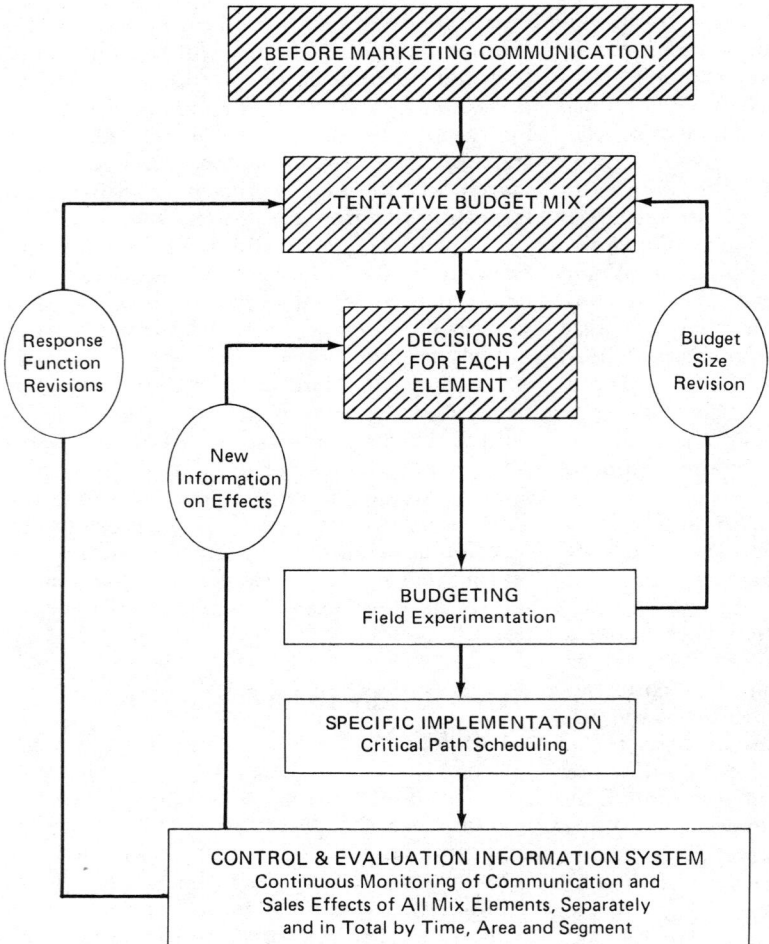

BEFORE MARKETING COMMUNICATION

TENTATIVE BUDGET MIX

Response Function Revisions

DECISIONS FOR EACH ELEMENT

Budget Size Revision

New Information on Effects

BUDGETING
Field Experimentation

SPECIFIC IMPLEMENTATION
Critical Path Scheduling

CONTROL & EVALUATION INFORMATION SYSTEM
Continuous Monitoring of Communication and
Sales Effects of All Mix Elements, Separately
and in Total by Time, Area and Segment

Figure 2-4. Budget-implementation-control. *Three feedback loops (identified by circles) provide an adaptive control system. Field experimentation is sometimes used at the budgeting stage. Critical path scheduling can be used to aid in specific implementation. Continuous campaign monitoring is the basis of a marketing-communication information system.*

As can be seen in Figure 2-4, the main suggestion made in this book is for extensive *feedback* in order to use all the information available. Feedback and reanalysis redevelopment is shown (1) for budgeting (revised budget and replanning for each communication element), (2) from the control-information system to the tentative budget, and (3) from the control-information system to the communication decisions.

Feedback is essential to *adaptive control systems.* This phrase is imposing, but it simply means that, during planning, managers naturally evolve estimates of how marketing-communication elements will work together in the particular situation. Then they adapt. By including feedback at several points, it is possible to adapt to new "data," such as pretesting and computer simulation results during message development, field experimentation at the point of revising the budget, or consumer panel and sales audit data during campaign monitoring. The new data or information need not be collected by means of sophisticated research techniques. The brand manager should set up procedures for adapting to estimates of other managers, creative developments, and new plans. Adaptive control systems exist for budgeting, implementation, and control.

Budgeting

For each communication element, the sequence of decisions about goals, message, and distribution ends in a budget allocation for media, time, geography, and segments. Repeating the sequence to incorporate revisions is the equivalent of what has been called the "objective and task" budgeting approach. Figure 2-4 gives this budgeting approach new significance by using it as a check on the planning that went into the tentative budget. The revised budget for each communication element is based on much more information and planning than was available at the time of the tentative budgeting. The manager must decide whether to accept any or all of these revised budgets, adjust total budget size, or fall back on original budget statements.

It is at this point that the manager may need to employ the sixth, or field experimentation, stage of the marketing-communication research system. Field experimentation is costly and can warn competitors, but it can be used from time to time to answer important general questions. For instance, it can be used to test or validate the less-expensive pretesting and computer simulation approaches. Weight tests can be done to determine if major increases or decreases in budget for any communication element will have a significant effect on results. Or the manager may have a specific question about the goals, message, and message distribution for particular elements. Then it is possible to do field experimentation—if the manager's question is important enough to merit the test. Typically, just major campaign developments merit field experimentation.

Whether field experimentation is done or not, it is likely that reconsideration of the budget will lead to a new set of decisions on communication goals, message strategy, message distribution, and allocation. All communication elements are considered together again in terms of the overall budget allocation. Then the cycle of decisions for each communication element becomes part of adaptive control. As in Figure 2-4, explicit and implicit models of the communication process are built, tested against decisions and the market, and then adapted to specific market situations.

Implementation

The problem of the implementation stage is one of coordination. The manager has so many organizations doing so many different things that it is possible for good plans to go awry. Several techniques offered in Chapter 18 can alleviate this problem.

In order to deal with scheduling, the manager and the manager's staff must clearly lay out each activity, as well as organizational responsibilities, timing, interrelationships, and importance. Since there are so many activities in a communication campaign, there is a tendency to oversimplify and ignore particular crucial aspects. When this happens, the entire campaign can falter.

The mishaps are similar to those that might occur at the tentative budget decision point. One communication element is ignored; it is done poorly or too late; and the whole campaign suffers. For instance, point-of-purchase materials may be ignored and arrive after the main impact of the mass-media campaign. Or they may be beautiful but too difficult to install. Or the television commercial may be excellent except for the information tag line which is thrown on at the last minute and is done with lettering that is too small to read. Or the salespeople and their presentations may be perfect, but they end up being directed against the wrong prospects—

because of the salespeople's convenience and lack of managerial pressures otherwise.

In the heat of the battle, managers might direct their efforts to the part of the communication mix they are most familiar with and miss certain other important aspects. Some parts of the mix are supported by consolidated organizations like advertising agencies, whereas others, such as the development of collateral material and trade shows, are done by a number of disparate organizations and individuals. The latter type of activity is less likely to be done effectively.

Beyond vigilance and care in implementation, the manager may want to apply some quantitative techniques that can reduce the implementation alternatives somewhat. Then the implementation problem will be more manageable.

One such technique is *critical path scheduling.* This entails a listing of all activities and their timing. Since there are so many activities involved in any campaign, the computer is used in order to find the critical path, that sequence of events that must be done in order for all other events to be done. Once the manager knows the critical path activities, he or she has a more manageable problem. There is a definite series of activities on which to concentrate.

Very often the act of implementation highlights previously unrecognizable opportunities. New materials, media availabilities, or markets open up that were not and could not be seriously considered during the planning stages. Usually when these opportunities occur at implementation, there is little time to take detailed consideration of them.

It is in such a situation that the planning tools mentioned earlier, such as the decision calculus approach and the research system, can help. If a computerized decision calculus model is available, the implications of the new opportunity can be assessed quickly. The pretesting and computer simulation aspects of the research system might also be used to make quick assessments. Field experimentation often reveals new opportunities and provides data for assessment. Once such tools become standard aspects of planning they can be used to solve problems, take advantage of opportunities, and, in general, support the organization of marketing communication.

Control

The last stage of marketing communication becomes a constant aspect of the campaign once initial implementation is undertaken. Control is necessary to determine (a) *how well* the campaign is doing and (b) *why* it is doing well or poorly. By knowing how well the campaign is doing, the manager knows when changes and other actions must be taken. By knowing the reasons for the results, the manager has a better understanding of what his or her next actions should be. This is the essence of communication control.

In order to exert this control, managers need information. Their information-gathering procedures can be as simple as a check of factory sales. Or they may have warehouse inventory records and sales audits at the point of purchase. More sophisticated approaches would involve collection of communication responses that relate to the communication goals of the campaign. Recall, comprehension, perception, beliefs, feelings, attitudes, intentions, and other related information may be collected on a regular basis. Such communication information is essential in determining the reasons for campaign success or failure. Even more sophisticated information gathering would involve the use of models that link data together with managerial assumptions on the workings of the market. These models can be quite simple, such as those about attitude-behavior relations. But they are powerful tools for determining actions in any specific situation.

The discussion of *information systems* in Chapter 18 considers not only their types but also the kinds of data that can be practically collected. As information moves from inside the organization (such as factory sales) to outside (consumer panel reports and models), the data collection requirements become more severe. The costs of collecting data must be balanced against their value in increased campaign control and efficiency.

THE FULL DECISION SEQUENCE AND THE PLAN OF THIS BOOK

Figure 2-5 shows the full marketing-communication decision sequence, which is a consolidation of the previous four figures and sections. The figure is both normative and descriptive. That is, marketing communication *should be* done in this sequence, and it *is* done in this way very often.

The sequence solves many problems that have hampered the development of marketing communication in the past. The field evolved primarily with a goal of consolidation. The idea was that if the communication functions of marketing were managed together, there would be many efficiencies. In addition, it was hoped that there would be a synergistic effect—i.e., that the "whole" of marketing communication would be more effective than the "sum" of the communication elements done separately. This synergistic effect seems reasonable, since the communication elements could be better coordinated and ideas from one element could be applied to others.

As the previous paragraphs have pointed out, however, there have been difficult organizational, informational, and conceptual problems. From an organizational standpoint, the brand or campaign manager is caught in the middle with a very complex decision task. He or she often does not have enough information or concepts to deal with the organizational problems or the decisions. Key organizational issues of advertising and communication are discussed in the next chapter.

This book presents quantitative and behavioral tools that can help solve the prob-

lems. These tools are represented in the sequence of decisions shown in Figure 2-5, and they are explained in detail in the chapters of this book.

In Chapters 4 and 5 there is an exposition of techniques that can be used to deal with the problems that arise "before" marketing communication. The situation analysis, marketing objectives, and setting of total communication budget must be done with the brand or campaign manager as part of a team. It is important that these activities be done with their communication implications clearly considered. This can be accomplished by use of product life cycle–product portfolio concepts, attitudinal segmentation, and buyer decision process analysis. All three of these techniques illustrate a main theme of the new techniques and of this book in general: Quantitative and behavioral approaches are increasingly being combined for greater efficiency and meaning to management. In the case of the activities before marketing communication, this combination provides strong solutions to the problems of coordination and lack of attention to communication that have existed in the past.

The heart of marketing-communication combination is found at the tentative budget-mix decision point, which is discussed in Chapter 6. Marketing communication cannot exist unless there is some common basis for combining its many different elements. The common basis that has evolved is the dollar. Information on sales response to dollar expenditures can be used to determine how the total budget will be allocated to advertising, sales promotions, and each of the other elements of the communication mix. A decision calculus situation analysis approach can be used to determine the efficiency of various mixes. The important aspect of this stage is that it is only tentative. As Figure 2-5 shows, the decision sequence is "adaptive" in the sense that as information analysis and decisions are made for each communication element, budgets can be revised and the entire budget mix reconsidered.

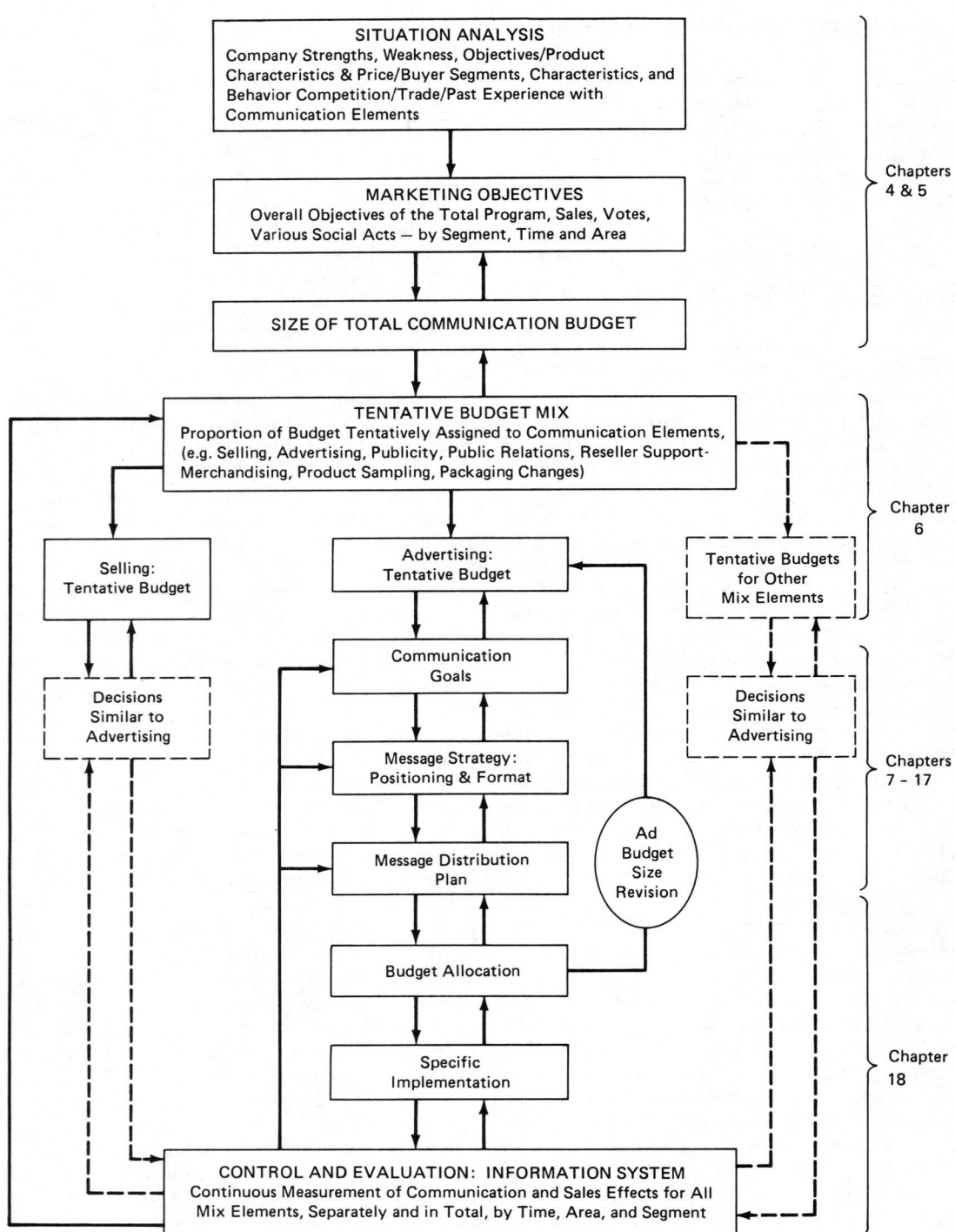

Figure 2-5. *The full decision sequence and the plan of this book*

Adapted from "The Full Decision Sequence" *Journal of Marketing*, January 1973, p. 31. Used with permission.

Chapter 7 deals with the goals of communication. The question is, What tasks can communication accomplish? A typical tool used to deal with this question has been the hierarchy of effects. In this book three possible orders of communication response are analyzed with regard to their communication implications. The manager's job is to balance the compensatory effects of the various communication elements in order to maximize overall communication effects.

Decisions on communication goals, message position, message format, message distribution, and budget are common to all elements of communication. That they are shown in Figure 2-5 for only the advertising element is representative of a bias of the middle chapters of the book. Advertising provides a clear setting in which to observe decision needs, and applications of quantitative and behavioral tools have often been made in advertising. So advertising decisions are the main focus of Chapters 7 to 13 as well as 15 and 16.

It is in Chapter 11 on message format that discussion of the marketing-communication research system begins. Once goals and message position are developed, the manager has many directions he or she might take in terms of format, distribution, budget, and implementation. Although creative personnel are responsible for many of the inputs to these decisions, this book suggests that the manager develop an ordered approach represented by the research system.

The system has seven stages. Four of these—problem formulation, analysis of past research implications, creative generation of alternatives, and pretesting—are done to aid the message format decision. The fifth stage is computer modeling and is used in message distribution planning. The sixth and seventh stages of the research system are field experimentation and campaign monitoring. They

are employed at the budgeting and control decision points.

The idea of the research system, and of the full sequence shown in Figure 2-5, is that managers should deal with the complexity of marketing communication by successive approximations. First the gross resource allocation is tentatively made, then goals, and so forth, all the way down to specific implementation and control. At each point in the sequence there is feedback so that the process is adaptive to new information. The same is true of the research system. First the problem is generally stated, and then it is continually refined and solved through a series of efficient stages and feedback. Application of quantitative-behavioral technology has been made possible primarily through what is an adaptive control system. It is an approach that can be applied by both the beginning student and the corporate brand manager.

The last chapter of this book represents extension of the marketing communication idea into social-effect concerns and the future. It traces the trends in communication technology, regulations, organizations, and research techniques—in order to indicate the way the procedures outlined in this book are likely to change in the future. Because of basic changes in telecommunications technology and attendant regulations, it is likely that control of the media will begin to shift from the sender to the receiver. Cable TV, satellite communications, videophones, computer-aided instruction, home computer installations, videotape, time sharing, holography—all of these and more promise to change not only the media but also the control of the media. Research techniques and organizations will develop in response to these changes, so that it will be possible to be much more responsive to consumer needs. This should be the goal of any marketing-communication effort.

ISSUES AND PROJECTS FOR DISCUSSION

1. Take any of the situations on the first page of this chapter and outline the steps of decision making specifically necessary for its solution. How do these steps compare with the more complex figures in this chapter? What is the most critical step? The next most critical?

2. What has to be done before marketing-communication decision making takes place? What tools can be used for the work before marketing-communication decision making? Indicate how the analysis and decisions before marketing communication can critically affect the nature and success of the total campaign.

3. According to a recent survey, what four methods are actually used for budgeting or resource allocations? What is the ideal marginal economic approach? What are some of the reasons this approach is not used? What tools can be used to lead to its application to resource allocation and budgeting?

4. What are the four key decisons of marketing communication? What are the advantages of considering them in a consolidated way, across elements of the mix?

5. What are some of the states of mind or hierarchies of effect we all go through in response to communication? Can you identify any of these happening to you when you first were exposed to information about a particular new product, service, candidate, or idea? How can knowledge of these hierarchies be used to set communication goals?

6. What six strategies for message positioning are reviewed in this book? Take any advertisement or commercial and indicate which of the strategies is being used.

7. To what extent should advertising decisions about the message format be made by campaign management at the client level as opposed to creatives at the agency? How can the proper balance be achieved with tools such as problem formulation, analysis of past communication efforts, alternative generation, and pretesting?

8. What are the three key message distribution decisions in advertising media planning? Take any of the situations on the first page of this chapter and suggest what choices you would make for the first two key media decisions. What are your reasons for your choices?

9. What is feedback? What are the three types of feedback in communication budgeting-implementation-control? How do these three types of feedback improve communication planning and implementation?

10. "The best laid plans of mice and men oft go awry." What is the difference between communication planning and implementation? How can communication plans go awry or wrong in implementation? What can be done to make sure that plans do not go wrong in implementation?

Notes

1. David Hurwood, "How Companies Set Ad Budgets," *Conference Board Record,* March 1968, pp. 34–41.

2. Seymour Banks, "Trends Affecting the Implementation of Advertising and Promotion," *Journal of Marketing,* 37 (January 1973), 19–25.

3. Ibid.

4. David B. Montgomery and Alvin J. Silk, "Estimating Dynamic Effects of Marketing Communications Expenditures," *Management Science,* June 1972.

5. Thomas Danbury, "How One Agency Uses Media Planning Models" (Paper presented to the Advertising Division, AEJ Meetings, Berkeley, Calif., 1969), pp. 2–3.

Organizing for Creative Advertising and Communication

■ *The Creative Organization*

Has idea men. Has open channels of communication. Has ad hoc devices, such as suggestion systems and idea units absolved of other responsibilities. Encourages contact with outside sources.

Has heterogenous personnel policy. Includes marginal, "unusual" types. Assigns non-specialists to problems. Allows eccentricity.

Has an objective, fact-founded approach. Ideas are evaluated on their merits, not status of originator. Ad hoc approaches: anonymous communications; blind votes. Selects and promotes on merit only.

Exhibits lack of financial, material commitment to products, policies. Invests in basic research. Has flexible, long-range planning. Experiments with new ideas rather than prejudging on "rational" grounds. (Everything gets a chance.)

*More decentralized; diversified administrative
slack; provides time and resources to absorb errors.
Tolerates and expects taking risks. Is not run as
"tight ship." Employees have fun, have freedom to
choose and pursue problems. Free to discuss ideas.*

*Organizationally autonomous. Has original
and different objectives. Is not trying to be
another "X."*

Security of routine allows *innovation.
"Philistines" provide stable, secure environment
that allows "creators" to roam.*

*Has separate units or occasions for generating vs.
evaluating ideas. Separates creative from
productive functions.*

Gary A. Steiner
The Creative Organization
(University of Chicago Press, 1965), pp. 16–18

Developing communication campaigns is essentially a creative activity. The decisions of the preceding chapter must be made creatively—with new combinations of ideas that break through to problem solution—in order to be successful. The question this chapter seeks to answer is, How can creativity take place when the organizations are so large, the decisions so complex, and the constraints so numerous?

The general answer to that question is that creativity takes place in marketing communication where the organizations have been developed to allow it to happen.

Few organization charts will be shown in this chapter. As Richard Stansfield has pointed out:

> Attempting to draw up a nice, neat organization chart for the typical industrial advertising department is something like trying to describe the average sunset. It can't be done because there isn't such a thing.[1]

Instead we are concerned here with the major issues in organizing the creative development of advertising and communication in marketing. Gary Steiner's list is instructive. Basically he says that the creative organization is open so that ideas can develop, allows eccentricity, is objective and separates the source from the content in evaluating information, suspends judgment and avoids early commitment, has slack that provides time and resources to tolerate risk and absorb errors, does not follow established patterns as to what it should be, and has disciplined routine within which "creators" can roam. Who

wouldn't want to work in such an organization?

When this type of organization is the goal for advertising and marketing-communication planning, there are essentially six questions that must be asked:

1. What part of the job should be done by the advertiser and what part by outside agencies?
2. How should the task be organized within the company?
3. What sort of outside partners, e.g., advertising agencies, should the company have?
4. How should the agency be chosen?
5. How should the agency be compensated?
6. How should the advertisers, agencies, and media work together to produce outstanding campaigns?

These are the six questions this chapter seeks to answer. Like Stanfield's average sunset, there is no one answer to any of these questions. But if we remember the goal of the creative organization—with its problem direction combined with freedom to roam—we will be able to learn what the choices are in various situations.

WHAT PART SHOULD THE COMPANY PLAY?

In Chapter 1 the point was made that, as we move through the three parts of the advertising industry from client to agency to media, we move from primarily planning at the client level to implementation at the agency and media organization levels. The basic idea of that sort of division of organizational responsibilities is that each type of organization has developed a specialization. The company should know its objectives, its market, and, most importantly, the product, price, and distribution strategies that underlie any great communication campaign. Thus the company does the basic planning, works with the agency to do the communication planning, approves creative output, and, through the agency, spends the budget in those media that fit campaign needs.

This is logical and the most common general division of labor between client, agency, and media. And it is easy to see how this general idea fits the concept of the creative organization. By using outside agencies, companies increase the flow of ideas from people who are not committed to any one product or service. The decentralization opens things up while the specialization of the agency provides a routine within which the men and women who can get ideas are free to roam mentally.

Not surprisingly, however, this common division of labor exists in a pure form nowhere. It is not uncommon for large consumer companies and many industrial companies to create their own sales promotion materials (such as brochures, point-of-purchase displays, and trade show exhibits) while working with outside graphics suppliers for implementation. It is quite common for companies to have their own sales forces instead of working with personal-selling intermediaries such as brokers and distributors. Many organizations, particularly the public-sector ones, have their own "public affairs" department which can do all the work, including implementation, in the publicity–public relations area.

Although less common than these other examples of the company taking up communication decisions and implementation, there are many examples of controlled company "in-house" advertising agencies. In the extreme example, all the creative advertising decisions on communication goals, message

theme and format, and media plan and scheduling are made by specialists within the company. Often outside suppliers—such as creative boutiques (doing only advertising copy and ad development), art studios, and media-buying organizations—are used to supplement the in-house agency. In-house agencies are particularly common for retailers.

Very often observers fail to note that, more common than the in-house agency, is the "in-agency marketing department"— with the advertising agency serving as the marketing department for a company. This certainly was typical in the early days of the modern advertising agency when some of the currently largest advertisers were guided by their advertising agencies in all aspects of marketing. Even today some agencies will help some clients with basic marketing research, the setting of objectives, and development of total marketing-mix strategy. This is particularly true of new companies founded and run by individuals who have no experience or ability in marketing planning. New industrial companies with an innovative product are a good example. The inventor often owns the company but does not know marketing. The agency becomes the marketing-planning and research department in such cases.

There are, then, three broad types of division of labor between the company and outside agencies. The most common has the company responsible for general marketing planning and research and outside agencies, particularly in advertising, responsible for planning and execution in their specialties. In contrast to this middle-of-the-road solution, there is the "in-house agency" on the one hand and the "in-agency marketing department" on the other. What factors would lead a company to select one of these three divisions of labor?

According to Steiner and many other writers on creativity, creative solutions are fostered in an environment with a balance between control and freedom (see Chapter 4).

In the company's choice of which activities to do in-house and which to assign to the agency, this balance of control and freedom is the key.

An organization should control those activities that it is best suited to do. In most companies this is the research, objective setting, and planning for each company's products and services. In contrast, some companies have a lack of marketing skill, and thus even some of the basic marketing research and planning is done by the advertising agency. Conversely, in some companies with technically oriented products, for instance, even the copywriting is not entrusted to an advertising agency.

Those companies that have in-house agencies obviously feel that control and skills are better if they do the work themselves. Also they may feel they can do the job more economically. This can be true of media work (see Chapter 15), but not of ad development.

In short, the in-house agency is outstanding in control, but it may stifle effective communication campaigns because of overcontrol, lack of freedom, closed lines of communication, limited viewpoints involved, overjudgment, overvaluing of traditional solutions, and a confusion of production with creation.

Most marketing companies, even those with extensive product lines that could support an in-house agency avoid this approach. Even extremely large consumer marketers like Procter and Gamble, who have large advertising staffs, use agencies extensively, probably because of the extra benefits mentioned above.

COMMUNICATION ORGANIZATION WITHIN THE FIRM

Given that the advertising and communication responsibilities at the client company usually tend toward research-objectives-planning rather than implementation, what are the alternatives for organization within the company?

There are truly as many alternatives as there are companies. This is because the structure of a company's product line and the nature of the markets it serves forces a certain structure. An example would be the E. I. Du Pont de Nemours and Company, a major chemical company which markets various fibers, paints, coatings (such as Teflon), and automotive products. At one point in the 1970s the company had thirteen staff departments including advertising. These departments served the company's twelve industrial departments (advertising served only ten).

Why all this complexity and people power in the Du Pont advertising department? Simply because there was so much to do in serving the Du Pont industrial departments (equivalent to product managers). These departments marketed about 1,250 product *lines!* And advertising was used for 90 percent of them. There were eighty-six separate advertising budgets at Du Pont. Working with agencies, Du Pont produced over twenty-three hundred new ads a year. These ads appeared in over two thousand different magazines for over 14,500 insertions.[2]

Despite all of this complexity at Du Pont, its department and communication organization is representative of one of two types of internal company organization for advertising and communication. These are the *functional* and the *brand* (or product, market, service, or campaign) *manager* systems.

Organization charts do not really fully convey the subtle differences between these two organizational structures. Charts tend to look alike, because both types are designed to coordinate marketing activities for any particular market offering that might be made.

In the *functional system,* the functional departments—such as finance, manufacturing, sales, advertising, and product research and development—are quite powerful. Profit responsibility for each market offering is diffused among functional division managers rather than centered on brand managers per se.

An example of the functional organization for Pepsi-Cola is shown in Figure 3-1. Note that the "brand marketing director" is at an equal level with a number of other functions, including primarily communication campaign-planning functions directly under the "brand marketing director" box on the left. Other functions to the right of that box are less communication-mix oriented. Note that field marketing (mainly personal-selling activities) is separated from brand manager responsibility somewhat.

The advantage of the functional organization is that experience from all the Pepsi-Cola brands can be brought to bear on all individual brands. The disadvantage is in terms of getting total commitment to individual brands in the total mix. Also, sometimes particular functions, such as personal selling, dominate the communication mix and decrease the effectiveness of the mix in total.

The other general type of organization, the brand manager one, was developed to get around the disadvantages of the functional organization. In the *brand management system* in its present form, each brand or product manager has profit responsibility and runs his or her brand or product like a separate company. In fact, at Procter and Gamble, the leading user of the brand manager system, there is great competition and secrecy maintained between the "companies" represented by the various brand groups. Sometimes the competition between various brand groups can be quite direct—as at General Foods where the leading decaffeinated coffee, Sanka, is attacked by Brim, another company brand in the same market. And in addition there are the other General Foods coffee brands, such as Maxwell House, Maxim, and Yuban, some of which appear in decaffeinated forms.

One example for the brand management system is shown in Figure 3-2. It is a simple view of a very complex organization, Procter and Gamble. In this type of organization the brand group is the key and, theoretically at least, controls and manages all resources for a particular brand.

The advantages of the brand management system are that each brand can demand its appropriate share of resources and that the balance in efforts will not be overweighed on any particular function, as might occur for the sales function in the case of Pepsi-Cola.

The disadvantages of the brand manager system are that experiences are less likely to be shared across brands, that brand managers may overemphasize some particular short-term communication tool such as trade deals (lower prices per case) at the expense of the long term, that market segmentation is sometimes avoided, and that consumerism and environmentalism concerns are ignored for brand objectives. Note also that overemphasis on one traditionally important part of the communication mix, advertising, is built in to the way the brand management system is organized at Procter and Gamble.

The balance between the functional and the brand (or product, market, etc.) management system of marketing and communication has been shifting back and forth throughout this century. At one time the advertising manager, if that title existed, would report to the sales manager. Then both sales and advertising would report to a vice-president of marketing, who would make sure the marketing concept was implemented for all the company's products. Even more recently there was a shift to the brand manager concept, with brand groups replacing departments. Instead of the advertising manager meeting with the advertising agency, for instance, the brand manager would. Still more recently, vice-presidents of marketing services have been added to oversee larger issues of communication that cannot be handled by individual brand managers. The most common form, however, is the brand management system imbedded within a functional system.

Thus the brand manager perspective offered by this book is important for those who

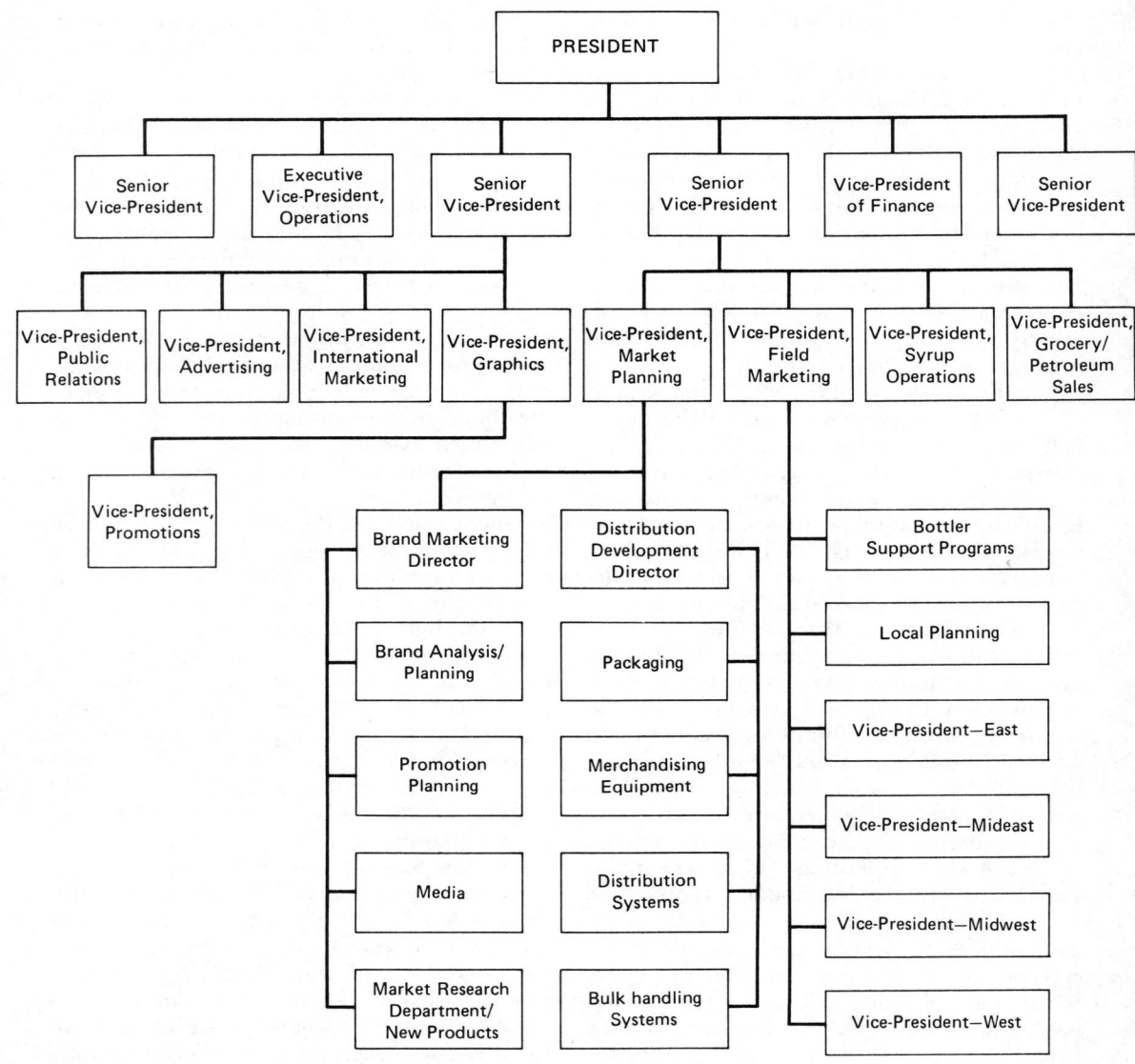

Figure 3-1. *Functional organization at Pepsi-Cola*

Reprinted from "The Brand Manager: No Longer King," *Business Week,* June 9, 1973, p. 59, by special permission. 1973 by McGraw-Hill, Inc. All rights reserved.

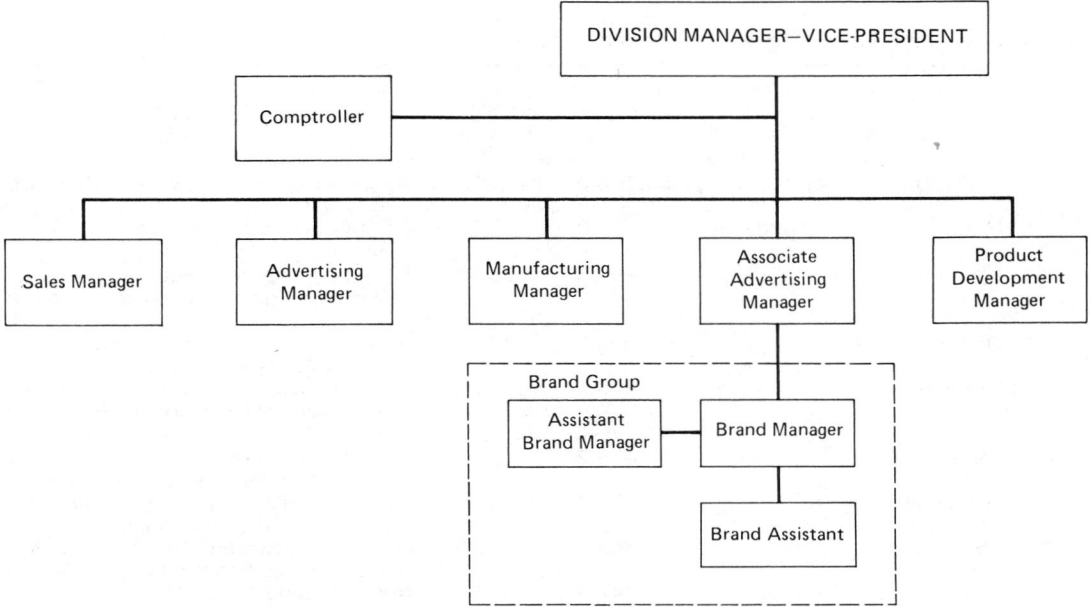

Figure 3-2. *The brand management system at Procter and Gamble*

Reprinted from "The Brand Manager: No Longer King," *Business Week,* June 9, 1973, p. 58, by special permission. © 1973 by McGraw-Hill, Inc. All rights reserved.

want to work in that campaign-oriented position in companies or in specific advertising and communication positions in both agencies and companies, no matter what their organization chart looks like.

THE OUTSIDE AGENCY

The third question about organizing for advertising and communication has to do with the advertising agency. What alternatives are available to the brand manager?

Size

The first answer would have to do with size. There are thousands of agencies in the United States and in the rest of the world, a changing group of small one-person shops

and medium-to-large agencies that are forming, dissolving, and merging almost constantly. The trend has been toward the average agency's becoming larger, primarily through merger. One executive commented in 1979:

> Of the ninety-two top agencies in 1966, forty-one are now owned by other agencies or have gone out of business. Moreover, the conditions are riper than ever for the trend to continue—for the big to get bigger as more pressures are put on agencies.[3]

As fascinating as the large agencies are, they do not necessarily fit the needs of all clients. You will notice in Table 3-1, for instance, that few of the top clients of the fifteen largest advertising agencies are industrial accounts. This is not to say that these "super-agencies" do not have industrial accounts. Rather, it is

Table 3-1. The Fifteen Largest U.S. Agencies in Mid-1979

Rank	Agency	Worldwide Ad Billings (millions)	U.S. Ad Billings (millions)	Top Five Accounts (alphabetically)
1	J. Walter Thompson	$1,476.0	$710.0	Burger King, Ford Motor, Kodak, Kraft, Unilever
2	McCann-Erickson Worldwide	1,405.0	397.0	Coca-Cola, Exxon, General Motors, Miller Brewing, Nestlé
3	Young & Rubicam	1,359.5	787.7	Ford Motor, General Foods, Johnson & Johnson, Procter & Gamble, Time Inc.
4	Ogilvy & Mather	1,003.7	472.3	American Express, General Foods, Sears Roebuck, Shell Oil, Unilever
5	Ted Bates	890.0	424.8	Brown & Williamson Tobacco, Colgate-Palmolive, ITT-Continental Baking, Mars, Warner Lambert
6	BBDO	876.2	529.5	Delta Airlines, General Electric, Pepsi-Cola, R. J. Reynolds, William Wrigley
7	Leo Burnett	871.4	604.0	Kellogg, Nestlé, Phillip Morris, Procter & Gamble, United Airlines
8	SSC&B/Lintas	840.5	175.9	Johnson & Johnson, Noxell, Rountree Mackintosh, Sterling Drug, Unilever
9	Foote, Cone, & Bending	747.9	504.7	Not available
10	Grey Advertising	703.0	434.7	Beecham Products, General Foods, Procter & Gamble, Revlon, Timex
11	D'Arcy-MacManus & Masius	698.7	333.7	Anheuser-Busch, Colgate-Palmolive, General Motors, Mars, Standard Oil (Indiana)
12	Doyle Dane Bernbach	593.0	411.4	American Airlines, G.T.E., Polaroid, Procter & Gamble, Volkswagen
13	Benton & Bowles	571.8	369.8	AMF, Fiat, General Foods, Procter & Gamble, Richardson-Merrell
14	Compton Advertising	557.4	246.2	AMC Jeep, I.B.M., Johnson & Johnson, Procter & Gamble, U.S. Steel
15	Campbell-Ewald Worldwide	466.7	233.1	General Motors, Goodyear, Henkel, Heublein, Phillips

SOURCE: Peter W. Bernstein, "Here Come the Super-Agencies," *Fortune*, August 27, 1979, pp. 46 and 47.

to point out that some advertisers' needs are better served by medium or even small agencies.

A recent issue of the *Standard Directory of Advertising Agencies* had *billings figures* (the value of the advertising placed and communication work done by an agency) for 2,785 agencies.[4] Of these, less than 4 percent (107) billed more than $25 million. Nearly 48 percent (1,302) billed between $1 million and $5 million; 35 percent billed under $1 million. So about 83 percent billed less than $5 million.

These are truly small agencies, since an agency gross income on even $5 million of billing would be only about $750,000; on $1 million dollars of billing it would be only about $150,000. Profits would be even smaller; as little as $7,000 for $1 million of billings. Yet these agencies can sometimes serve a number of clients. Some agencies with as little as $1 million or less billing handle twenty or more accounts.

Thus the small agencies are serving the needs of many marketers quite well. These marketers like the personal attention they get from a small agency. Their importance to their agency gives them control and the ability to spend money efficiently for exactly what they need in the communication mix.

Type

The largest agencies, as shown in Table 3-1, tend to be consumer oriented. Smaller agencies specialize more often. There are industrial, fashion, travel and resort, Black market, Spanish market, retailing, financial, and medical agencies.

Specialized agencies tend to stay smaller, because there are only a limited number of advertising accounts that do not conflict with each other. Account conflict occurs when one agency has more than one account (client, advertiser) in the same product market. It would not be acceptable, for instance, to Coke and Pepsi if their advertising were done by the same agency. How could they be open with the agency in terms of marketing data, objectives, and plans in such a situation?

Some advertisers become quite paranoid about account conflict and will refuse to do business with an agency that is doing business with a company that has a competing product—even if the agency is not doing business on that particular product. This would happen, for instance, if Armour Fresh Meat Company refused to place its business with an agency that had a soap account, because that account would be competitive with Dial soap, the product of another division of Greyhound Corporation.

Account conflicts are usually what make an agency grow away from specialization. This is true even though specialization can have definite advantages for the advertiser.

In the past, agencies grew from an initial specialization by adding accounts outside of that specialization. More recently, growth has often occurred by acquisition and merger. And in order to avoid account conflicts, the acquired agencies are kept as separate entities.

The best example of this merger strategy with separate advetising agency divisions is the Interpublic Group of Companies, the world's largest advertising organization (either J. Walter Thompson or Young and Rubicam is the largest single U.S. *agency,* depending on the latest figures). Interpublic is made up of

1. McCann-Erickson—the original Interpublic agency, second largest in the U.S., largest U.S. agency in income outside the U.S.
2. Campbell-Ewald—a separate agency network itself including four divisions—agencies such as Tinker-Campbell Ewald and Clinton E. Frank, Inc. C-E is the fifteenth largest U.S. agency in world billing. It has extensive international operations.
3. The Marshalk Co., Inc.—the thirtieth largest agency in the U.S.
4. SSC&B/Lintas—the eighth largest agency in the U.S.
5. Erwin Wasey Inc.—the eightieth largest agency in the U.S.

Interpublic also includes nine "Diversified Marketing Organizations," such as a research division called Marplan which does research for both clients and nonclients of the agencies, a division that assists advertisers in placing syndicated TV programs, a public relations organization, and a data-processing organization.

The size of Interpublic is staggering. Combined worldwide billings of the agencies alone approaches $3 billion. An account of one of the agencies, Chevrolet at Campbell-Ewald, has been the largest single advertised brand in the United States for nearly sixty years. It bills well over $100 million. The agency produces literally thousands of different ads for that one client alone each year.

Just how successful is the agency tendency to merge, grow, and keep separate operating units? In terms of individual agencies' growth, it has been quite successful. In terms of the possibility of carrying accounts for conflicting brands and/or companies, there have been some moderate successes, although potential clients still ask questions about conflicts. There is normally a loss of business when agencies merge even though their operations are kept separate, for instance. In terms of the advertiser, however, the new type of giant, multidivisional agency has its pluses and minuses.

The advantages of working with a large, multidivisioned, multiservice agency go mainly to marketing companies that are large and multidivisioned themselves. One need only glance at the list of top clients in Table 3-1 to see that these companies alone dwarf the entire advertising and marketing-communication industry. For instance, the sales of *either* Exxon or GM *alone* are about one third larger than total U.S. ad expenditures. Ford's sales alone are about equal to the ad industry; as are the combined sales of Sears, ITT, and General Electric.

But the real advantage of the large, full-service agency is in relation to creative balance. No matter how big the advertiser, there is a need to work with outside organizations that bring in new opinions and experiences unfettered by overdependence or overcommitment to the client. There is the need for a balance between control and the freedom to create. This means that the account must be important to the agency so that control is maintained. But the account should not be so important as to stifle new and unusual ideas and creativity in general.

The choice for the advertiser and the brand or campaign manager breaks down into one between agencies that service a broad range of accounts and those that specialize to some degree. The broad agencies tend to be larger, be more structured, and provide more services than the specialized ones.

Again, this choice can be made on the basis of creativity, on the basis of getting the best solutions to each campaign's communi-cations problems. A balance must be achieved between control and directly relevant experience, on the one hand, and freedom and outside experience, on the other. The specialized smaller agencies provide control through each account's importance. They have appropriate experience, because they work on one type of advertising and communication problem. The broad-range agencies have more freedom and bring more outside experiences to bear on each problem. The choice is up to the campaign manager, advertising director, and/or vice-president of marketing services in particular situations.

Services

With the exception of personal-selling management, there are advertising or communication agencies that will provide assistance to marketing organizations on all parts of the communication mix. In addition, most agencies will provide support services such as research and graphic production either directly or in a subcontracting or consulting role.

The basic job of the advertising agency is to do advertising. In short, agencies make ads and place those ads where people will see them so that communication and sales objectives will be met. An advertising agency is not really an advertising agency unless it provides these services.

But a brand or campaign manager in the typical situation should not want the advertising agency to be totally committed to advertising as the only solution. What's more, there is a need for an agency that can understand the total marketing context for a communication problem. Thus full-service agencies as well as limited-service agencies—for sales promotion, public relations, creative, media buying, research, etc.—have developed.

The advantages and disadvantages of various service configurations have already been discussed in terms of the division-of-labor question. For some advertisers, it will be advantageous to work with one outside agency that has broad expertise. Others will find that buying services from a variety of types of organizations (such as marketing consultants, sales promotion agencies, creative boutiques, media-buying organizations, and public relations agencies as well as advertising agencies) is best. The main criterion is the balance needed for creativity and better solutions.

Bias

Another aspect of the size, type, and services of advertising agencies is their bias or orientation. Agencies can be biased toward campaign planning in general, creative work, particular media such as television or magazines, merchandising, management, marketing, public relations, research and analytical promotion, or communication orientation.

All agencies are biased to some extent no matter what their size, type, or service configuration. There is no "best" bias unless it is a bias that is slight. The brand or campaign manager should just be certain that the agency is as balanced as possible, and that whatever bias it might have is particularly important to the need of the product, service, or idea being advertised.

From the late seventies to the present there has been a swing back toward the full-service agency and management-marketing–campaign-planning orientation. The Interpublic Group of Companies is now expanding in a way not really achieved in the earlier period. As an agency principal put it in 1979: "The people who run the business today are technocrats."[5]

Brand-campaign managers should make sure that their agencies do not bury their creative work with technocratic bureaucracy, mismanage the campaign effort with overemphasis on creative breakthroughs, bias the campaign effort toward short-term sales promotion or publicity efforts, or research the

life out of their advertising effort. Again, balance is critical.

Philosophy

All advertising agencies have a philosophy that is representative of their key personnel's understanding of how advertising and communication work. In a later creative strategy chapter, a number of these philosophies are reviewed in terms of what agency experience can tell us about how communication works. The actual application of the philosophies to particular marketing-communication situations varies. That is, ads for different clients do not look alike. But the agency philosophy can guide the brand or campaign manager in picking and using an agency. Examples include

- Benton and Bowles's "It's not creative unless it sells."
- Young and Rubicam's ". . . the sharpest advertising strategies provide the greatest creative freedom."
- McCann-Erickson's "Truth well told."
- D'Arcy-MacManus & Masius's "Belief dynamics."
- Kurtz & Tarlow's "Advertising is war."
- Ogilvy and Mather's series of print ads listing points as to "How to" do certain kinds of advertising.
- Ries Cappiello Colwell's "Positioning."

Organization

There are the functional and brand management alternatives within agencies just as in companies. In agencies the brand management approach is called the account group system. Most agencies have some form of this system.

The key aspect of the account group system is the account group itself. As depicted in Figure 3-3, each account group is the nucleus of an atom of each agency's activities. The account is defined by an advertising and

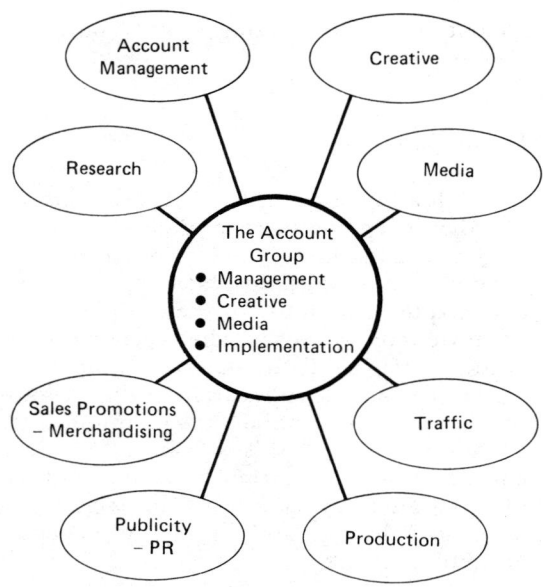

Account Management

Creative

Research

Media

The Account
Group
● Management
● Creative
● Media
● Implementation

Sales Promotions
– Merchandising

Traffic

Publicity
– PR

Production

Figure 3-3. *One account group and support departments in a full-service agency*

communication budget, usually for one brand.

In recent years agencies have become more efficient. It once took an average of ten people to service each million dollars of billing. Now the figure is down to about four and fewer people per million dollars of billing. This has led to and has been caused by a number of organizational aspects of agencies.

The most critical person in this system is the account manager, who organizes the effort at the agency and is the person who interacts most with the key decision maker from the client. The account manager must know business and marketing in general as well as the art of advertising and communication.

In the past there have been three and sometimes four levels of account management. Now there tend to be fewer levels. The person who leads a single brand account group is usually called an account executive. He or she may report to an account supervisor, who oversees the several accounts that a particular advertiser may have at an agency. For instance, General Foods may have several accounts of a particular type at Benton and

Bowles. An account supervisor would oversee these accounts, account executives, and account groups. Very often, in extremely large agencies, account supervisors are vice-presidents or even senior vice-presidents.

The issue of vice-presidents is often confusing to those outside the advertising agency business. Because the advertising business, like consulting and banking, is a personal service one, a title is used to give status to those people who must not only manage within the agency but make critical contact with clients. A brand manager or vice-president of marketing services likes to know that he or she is dealing with a vice-president or senior vice-president.

Virtually all agencies are organized in such a way as to give their clients the benefit of a creative organization in the broad sense that Steiner expresses on the first page of this chapter. Brand and campaign managers should be careful to determine that their agency, no matter what its size, has organizational features similar to the ones discussed here. The organization of the agency should lead to creative solutions.

Growth

All advertising agencies grow or they go out of business. Agencies differ in the way they grow, however. One of the two general strategies for agency growth is good for advertisers. The other usually is dysfunctional.

The two general strategies for growth could be called the *defensive* and the *offensive* strategies.

An agency using the defensive strategy puts its emphasis on serving present clients so well that their business will grow, that they will not be tempted to switch their accounts elsewhere, and that they will assign more of their business (additional or new products and services) to the agency. Certainly defensive agencies have to pick their clients well in the first place. They also have to seek new business. But when the defensive strategy is truly implemented, the best clients will seek out the agency, and new business seeking can be more efficient because the "product," the agency, is such a good one. The defensive agency is good for advertisers, because they come first in importance to this sort of agency.

This is in contrast to the offensive strategy in which work for present clients is compromised in the search for new business. There are probably no purely offensive agencies, but many have that tendency. And some normally totally defensive agencies will slip once in a while.

Clients are better off with agencies using the defensive strategy. Account switching may make some sense from the creative standpoint of getting more energy, new ideas, and a fresh approach. But brand and campaign managers should be aware of the other characteristics of a creative organization which should be in the agency chosen from the beginning. Studies show that large agencies have at least as much variation within as there is variation between agencies. Thus if a good partner, preferably a defensive agency, is chosen in the first place, a long and fruitful relationship should result.

CHOOSING AN AGENCY

The fourth question about organizing for advertising and communication management was, How should the agency be chosen? This question actually leads to three subquestions:

a. Under what conditions should a new or an additional agency be sought?
b. What are the criteria for choosing an agency?
c. What specific procedures should be used in soliciting, assessing, and taking the action of hiring an advertising agency?

Conditions

The conditions under which a new agency or additional agency should be selected can be considered in relation to the creative organization with its characteristics of openness, tolerance for eccentricity, objectivity and lack of judgment based on the source of an idea, avoidance of early commitment, slack to allow risk and absorb errors, avoidance of established patterns, and disciplined routine within which creatives can roam.

The issue of whether there should be an outside agency at all was discussed earlier in terms of the in-house agency. Although more and more advertisers are adding in-house agencies to do some of their work, total dependence on an in-house agency was not suggested. The creative organization is a balance between control and freedom. Even though in-house agencies can take accounts for other than the parent company, the in-house agency is overcontrolled, does not promote extensive idea production, and provides less freedom for creatives. There is also some evidence that the in-house agency is not as economical as its proponents would claim. If a wide variety of outstanding creative people are to be hired and kept, the costs can be extensive indeed.

In all but an extreme minority of instances, then, an outside agency should be employed to assist with communication campaigns.

Next we must ask whether more than one outside agency is needed. More than one is usually needed when a company has so many products and divisions that the work is too much for one agency. In other words, the account would become too important to a single agency to allow maximum creativity. Also there is the hope that, with multiple agencies, additional perspectives will be added. Finally, specialized agencies are used for particular markets when they are entered. A simple example is when a company markets to both consumers and industrial markets, possibly necessitating two agencies.

The final condition for seeking an agency—account switching—can seldom be supported by rational reasons. There are very good emotional ones, however. The client-agency relationship has been compared to a marriage. Although advertisers might have every rational reason to stay with their agency for new creative problem solving, the situation often becomes personal and leads to a split.

Criteria

It would seem that criteria for selection would be quite clear if a company is at a point where a need for a new or an additional agency becomes clear. In fact, there can be long lists of criteria that differ in importance for various groups within the company.

One such list, for instance, had thirty-five questions (criteria) grouped under six headings.[6]

Probably one of the best guides as to what characteristics to look for in any agency is the discussion in the preceding section about size, type, philosophy, bias, services, organization, and growth strategy. Each of these seven areas should be considered in light of developing a creative organization that is what the client-agency partnership should be.

Procedure

The procedure to be used for answering these questions is the key to whether they are answered well and whether, in fact, an advertiser's needs are met.

The procedure of selecting an agency goes through a series of stages—from a setting of criteria through initial screening to on-site visits by both sides through presentations by fewer and fewer agencies until one is selected. The variations on this process are fascinating.

Sometimes the agency is assigned the account without any of this procedure happening externally. This might happen if new top management decides to fire the company's agency and hire one immediately that it has worked with previously. The criteria-screening-visits-presentations part of the process has taken place before the new top management arrives at the company. The firing of the old agency and selection of the new one is made almost simultaneously and dramatically, with the procedure taking place in the new executive's head.

In other cases there is a long drawn-out procedure that is reported almost weekly in *Advertising Age* as the agencies are weeded out to a precious few. Then, shockingly, the original agency is retained. In such cases, which thankfully are infrequent, there are cries of "Unfair!" People in the industry accuse the company of using the selection procedure just to get new ideas (from the presentations of opposing agencies) while intending to retain the old agency all along.

Fortunately most advertisers are more professional than the first example and more ethical than the behavior of the second example indicates. The procedure starts with a listing of criteria within the areas suggested earlier. Lists should be gathered from all the relevant decision makers within the company. All the people who would be involved in working with the agency should be consulted.

Meetings with agencies change the criteria. Each agency will make presentations of what it thinks is important, and the advertiser

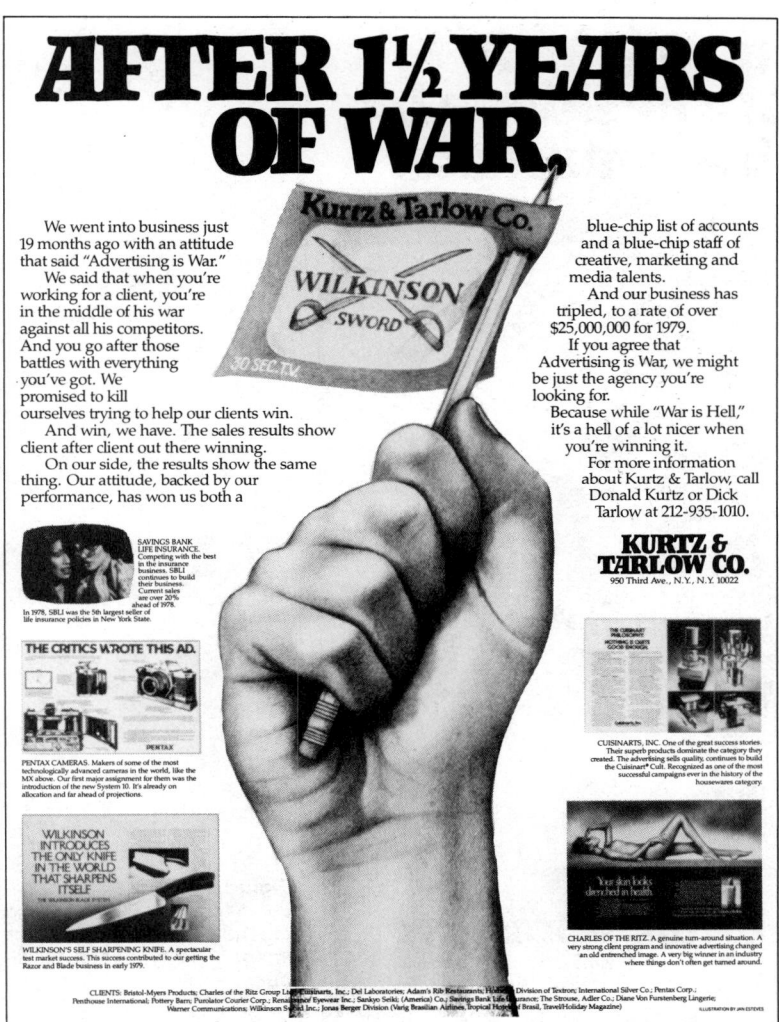

Figure 3-4. *Kurtz & Tarlow attempts to add a criterion to prospective clients' consideration*

(Courtesy of Kurtz & Tarlow Co.)

may become sold. Figure 3-4 shows an ad for Kurtz and Tarlow, a one and one-half year old agency that spent over $20 million for its clients and had over forty employees.[7] Notice that this ad presents what undoubtedly has to be a new criterion for any company considering the agency.

Images of agencies can change with direct experience also. It is not generally recognized that agency reputations sometimes do not fit their actual characteristics. An agency that has a reputation for being strong in creativity may actually provide very balanced services in other areas. An agency that is very large and thought to be primarily management oriented and conservative may actually produce outstandingly creative advertising.

Often agencies who see themselves as

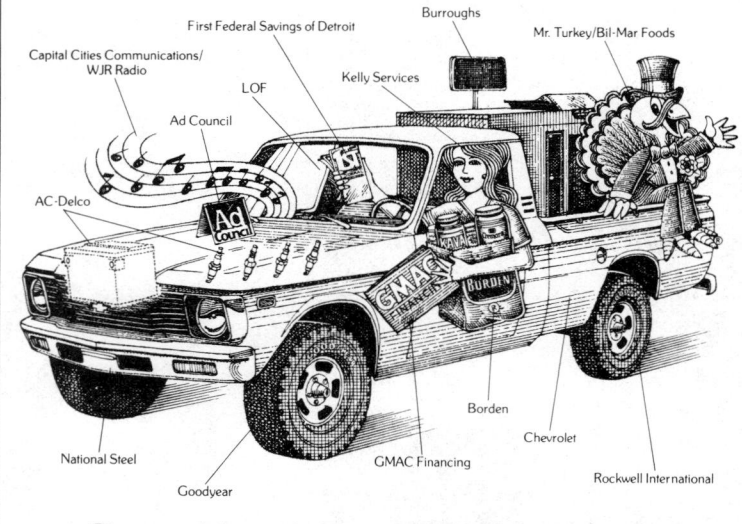

What do all these brands share besides a big share of their markets?

It's us, Campbell-Ewald. This "company car" features the fine clients we represent. And we think it makes a couple of important points about us.

Our clients' names are undoubtedly better known to you than our own. We think that's only fitting. It's evidence that we do our job pretty well.

Our clients are in a variety of fields: consumer products and services, consumer durables, industrial products and services, public service. We are a broad and balanced agency, qualified to perform in a variety of markets.

Our clients are major *brands*. And we are, quite frankly, brand-oriented. We emphasize long-term brand development and management.

Some of these brands, like Chevrolet, have been with us virtually since their inception. We helped create them. Others, like Goodyear, were household names before they hired us. They picked us to help them keep on growing.

If you'd like to know more about our brand of advertising, and the results it gets for our clients, please write or call our Vice Chairman, Dick O'Connor. Campbell-Ewald Company, 30400 Van Dyke, Warren, Michigan 48093. (313) 574-3400.

Perhaps we can help you to a bigger share of your market.

Burroughs

First Federal Savings of Detroit

Mr. Turkey/Bil-Mar Foods

Capital Cities Communications/ WJR Radio

Kelly Services

LOF

Ad Council

AC-Delco

National Steel

Goodyear

GMAC Financing

Borden

Chevrolet

Rockwell International

Campbell-Ewald Company

The Interpublic Group of Companies, Inc.

Figure 3-5. *Campbell-Ewald ad attempting to build on and change the agency's image for prospective clients*

(*Courtesy of Campbell-Ewald Company*)

creative are not seen by others in that way. For the fifteenth-ranked agency, Campbell-Ewald, its self-perceived strength in the automotive field is seen by others as a problem of being a "Captive of Detroit." In Figure 3-5 there is an example of how this agency attempts to build on the strength of having the world's largest single-brand advertising campaign, Chevrolet. The ad attempts to show that the Campbell-Ewald agency, despite its image, has a wide experience with many different types of accounts.

The question to the campaign manager is, How can the advertiser seeking an agency determine what an agency is really like? There are two broad ways. One that has often been attacked is to require *speculative presentations* from each agency competing for the business. When an agency does a speculative presentation, it actually presents a proposed advertising campaign. It shows the kind of advertising it would recommend for the client.

The other method is to visit each agency, meet with key people, and then see each agency's new business presentation. Such a presentation indicates agency personnel who might be working on the account, agency services and philosophy, the kind of advertising done for present clients, agency success stories, and so forth. No speculative presentation would be done, although it could be that there would be fairly detailed discussions as to how the business would be handled.

Both approaches include the visit and new-business presentation. The real question is whether the speculative presentation should be required. While it gives a sense of how the agency would actually work with the advertiser on the account, there is also the problem that the speculative presentation can be nothing more than a show. A complete communication campaign cannot be built on just brief client-agency meetings and a short time for development. The danger with a speculative presentation is that a long-term decision may be made on the basis of short-term responses.

In reality, of course, this is the problem with the whole agency selection process. Once criteria are checked, there are always at least several choices available. Fortunately the quality of all the remaining agencies is likely to be high if the original process was done carefully.

HOW SHOULD THE AGENCY BE COMPENSATED?

Compensation is a critical question in organizing for advertising and communication campaigns, because advertising agencies in particular have historically been compensated in a relatively strange way. How the advertiser compensates the agency will importantly affect the balance that can be maintained between control and freedom for creativity.

Since advertising agencies historically worked as sales agents for the media, they have maintained the media commission part of the payment. What this means is that for much of its compensation, the agency will receive a *15 percent commission* on the amount of advertising billed. That is, if an agency develops a four-color bleed (*bleed* occurs when there is no border around ads, it is printed all the way to the edge) full-page ad and places it in *Time* magazine for a cost of, say, $70,000, the agency will receive 15 percent, or $10,500 of that space cost as its compensation.

Note that with this 15 percent compensation system the advertiser does not directly control the advertising development, because the compensation is not directly for the work or time spent in development. This ad could run ten more times in *Time* or similar publications and without any additional conceptual, creative, or implementation effort (except actually placing the ad). The agency would then receive an additional sum of about $105,000.

Questioning of the 15 percent commission system started long ago on the part of smaller agencies doing many different ads for industrial or retail clients. Since almost every print insertion required a new advertisement and magazine space costs were low, the 15 percent commission did not provide adequate profit to the agency. Some sort of fee system, markups on purchased materials, or other contractual arrangement related to actual work was used to replace or augment the commission system. Thus a noncommission system is quite prevalent in the industrial advertising field.

More recently, large consumer advertisers have questioned the commission system also because the costs for television time in particular have become so high. If an agency develops one television commercial that runs many times on television networks, income without further creative work quickly reaches into the hundreds of thousands and millions of dollars. In fact, it may not be in the client's best interest to change the advertising, but the commission system may encourage change—just to get extra "value" for all the expenditures.

It is not surprising, then, that the vast majority (one estimate, 95 percent) of client-agency relations will have some form of compensation in addition to the 15 percent commission one. Some large consumer agencies on some accounts will agree to bargain the percentage down to, say 10 percent, even though the practice is severely frowned upon by the American Association of Advertising Agencies.

A more common compensation package would include fees, markup on materials and services purchased outside, and the standard commission. The compensation package is developed to fit the needs of the client-agency partnership in each particular situation. It is important to recognize, however, that compensation is certainly negotiable and flexible depending on the individual situation.

The ideal compensation would somehow be tied to the agency's contribution to sales or profits for the brand. Communication management, in concert with the agency, would determine what the overall marketing objectives were for the brand (in terms of sales, profits, etc.), what the contribution of advertising and the various campaign elements would be to those objectives, and what the tentative budget was for each of the campaign elements. Then the agency could develop advertising and communication programs and be compensated for its role in achieving objectives at some agreed-upon percentage of sales or profits.

There are several problems with this ideal approach, of course. It is difficult to set budgets based on solid determinations of the contribution of advertising, and so forth, to a brand's success. And such an approach may lead to lack of flexibility and an overemphasis on tools that can produce a short-term effect to the detriment of the long-term health of the brand.

But this ideal compensation plan and others highlight the effect of compensation on the degree to which creativity is manifested in solving the advertisers' problems. The 15 percent commission plan can provide great freedom to the agency. It leaves the matter of strict control up to the advertiser through other aspects of the relationship. Fees and markups lead to closer advertiser control. The ideal plan, with compensation tied to profits or sales, might constitute overcontrol. It might also lead to a close working relationship between advertiser and agency, with the advertiser being concerned about sales and profits and the agency being concerned about increasing the size of the pie from which it is compensated.

THE WORKING RELATIONSHIPS

In some sense all the discussion of this chapter points to the kinds of working relationships for advertising and communication that are necessary for outstanding campaigns over the long term. A review of the general answers to the first five of the main questions about organizing in this chapter provides a picture of the kind of working relationships necessary.

First, the discussion of this chapter was organized around the notion, primarily Steiner's, of the creative organization. All the individuals who work in a campaign—whether in an advertising department, in the management team, in sales management, or at the agency in all capacities—should strive to keep the organizational balance necessary for creative problem solving.

This means that channels of communication should be open. The various groups within the company and agencies should keep informed and inform. It is the responsibility of the campaign manager on each campaign to set a clear structure within which the campaign can be developed. If good products, services, and ideas are developed, a major part of communication is done. The job of people at the company is to communicate the qualities of these market offerings to people at the agency so that decisions can be made about objectives, goals, and themes.

Clarity of goals, markets, and themes provides the structure of the problem so that all the potential problem solvers can work together. Open information and structure are the key. Along with them there should be motivation driving everyone to work together creatively toward the solution. Compensation is the main motivator. But there should also be the feeling on the part of every individual that what he or she does makes a difference.

If everyone working on a campaign knows that the market offering is outstanding, what the campaign goals are, what his or her contribution may be, that all ideas will get a chance, that risks will be tolerated—there is a chance for strong solutions to occur.

Management should realize that the strength of having an outside agency is the potential for powerful new ideas to occur. The outside agency brings the outside point of view and allows unusual or marginal types to bring free thinking to bear on communication problems.

At the same time, however, the outside agency must be controlled in order for ideas to form. This means that people inside the company must know advertising and communication as well as do the people at the agency. Evaluation of the advertising effort must be based on knowledge. Those people approving agency work must have solid knowledge, experience, and reasoning to back their criticisms.

Overcontrol is seen in those situations in which agencies present, say, five or ten campaign alternatives and ask the client to pick one.

Undercontrol is seen in those situations in which agencies present one campaign alternative and expect the company to either take it or leave it.

Balanced control exists in those situations in which both sides work together in creating and evaluating alternatives. Too swift acceptance or rejection is dysfunctional.

Each side, company and agency, should be "great" at doing its own job and "good" at doing its partner's job. In the worst situation, people at the company think they know about advertising but actually do not. Campaigns are approved or rejected on whims, on personal prejudice, or on sticking to an outmoded formula.

Some say that the opposite situation, in which the company has a large group of outstanding advertising professionals, can also stifle creativity. One of the examples of this sort of staffing is Procter and Gamble, which has an extensive advertising department. It could duplicate the work of each of its ten agencies. The argument against this kind of staffing and organization is that it overcontrols and does not allow the agencies to create beyond the P&G mandated formula. In counter to this argument is P&G's amazing success and the creativity of its advertising in meeting particular problems. The company has created a balanced control and matches agency skills with skills of its own. Also, say those who criticize the creativity of P&G's advertising itself, the company markets outstanding products with tremendous advertising and sales promotion effort—more than any other company in the United States.

Some stories of agency-client interaction are sad. In one, for instance, the company had to be tricked into accepting the campaign idea by the account executive. He first told the company ad manager that the campaign idea was going to be used by the competition. Then once the ad manager was protesting and asking, "Why don't you people do advertising like this?" the account executive revealed that in reality the idea was not going to be used by the competition. It was actually one developed by the agency for the client. The idea was approved. But if clear lines of communication had been developed between the two sides, this kind of trickery would not have been necessary. The idea would have been evaluated on its true merits in relation to the marketing problem, rather than on the basis of jealousy of a competitive campaign.

Other stories of agency-client interaction show the kind of interaction that must go on. It is said that in seeking approval for the Clairol hair-coloring advertising line, "Does she or doesn't she," the copywriter, Shirley Polykoff, was faced by client objections. Would women read sexual meaning into the line? Polykoff bet that if women in

the client organization were asked directly, none would admit to having such thoughts. None did. The campaign was approved. Note that the copywriter was in the middle of negotiations with the client, who was posing an appropriate structural question. The result was an enormously successful campaign.

Campaigns are not developed all at once. Nor do all the parts fall together as clearly and simply as shown in the flow diagrams of the preceding chapter. If organization is developed as suggested in this chapter, the explosion of ideas that might occur all the time during campaign development not only happen but are heard, evaluated, and used to solve the complex puzzle that is communication campaign development.

ISSUES AND PROJECTS FOR DISCUSSION

1. What, in your own words, are the characteristics of the creative organization?

2. Some people say that organizations are being misled into seeking creativity, that they should simply use advertising ideas from other campaigns used in the past, that creative advertising and communication are often just too crazy to be effective. What do you think?

3. Take any one of the paragraphs on the first page of this chapter and indicate how this characteristic of the creative organization can be achieved or lost through advertising and communication organization.

4. What share of the advertising and communication campaign job should the company take?

5. What are the pros and cons of the in-house agency? Of the in-agency marketing department?

6. What are the advantages and disadvantages of the brand manager system of organization?

7. Under what conditions would a company want a very large advertising agency? Under what conditions would a company want a relatively small, specialized advertising agency?

8. Which is better for the company, an agency with a defensive growth strategy or one with an offensive growth strategy? Why?

9. Under what conditions should a new or additional agency be sought?

10. List the criteria you would use to select an advertising agency if you wanted one to advertise you for a job.

11. What are speculative presentations and under what conditions, if any, should they be used?

12. How does the form of compensation affect client-agency relations and ultimately the quality of the advertising and communication campaign?

Notes

1. Richard H. Stansfield, *Advertising Manager's Handbook,* 2nd ed. (Chicago: Dartnell Corporation, 1977), p. 17.

2. Ibid., pp. 21 and 22.

3. Peter W. Bernstein, "Here Come the Super-Agencies," *Fortune,* August 27, 1979, p. 46.

4. *Standard Directory of Advertising Agencies,* No. 186 (February 1979), p. A-5.

5. Bernstein, "Here Come the Super-Agencies," p. 47.

6. Stansfield, *Advertising Manager's Handbook,* pp. 69–71.

7. *Advertising Age,* March 14, 1979, p. 84.

BEFORE
MARKETING
COMMUNICATION

For Communication Planning
. . . Marketing Mix Diagnosis
. . . Consumer and Market Analysis

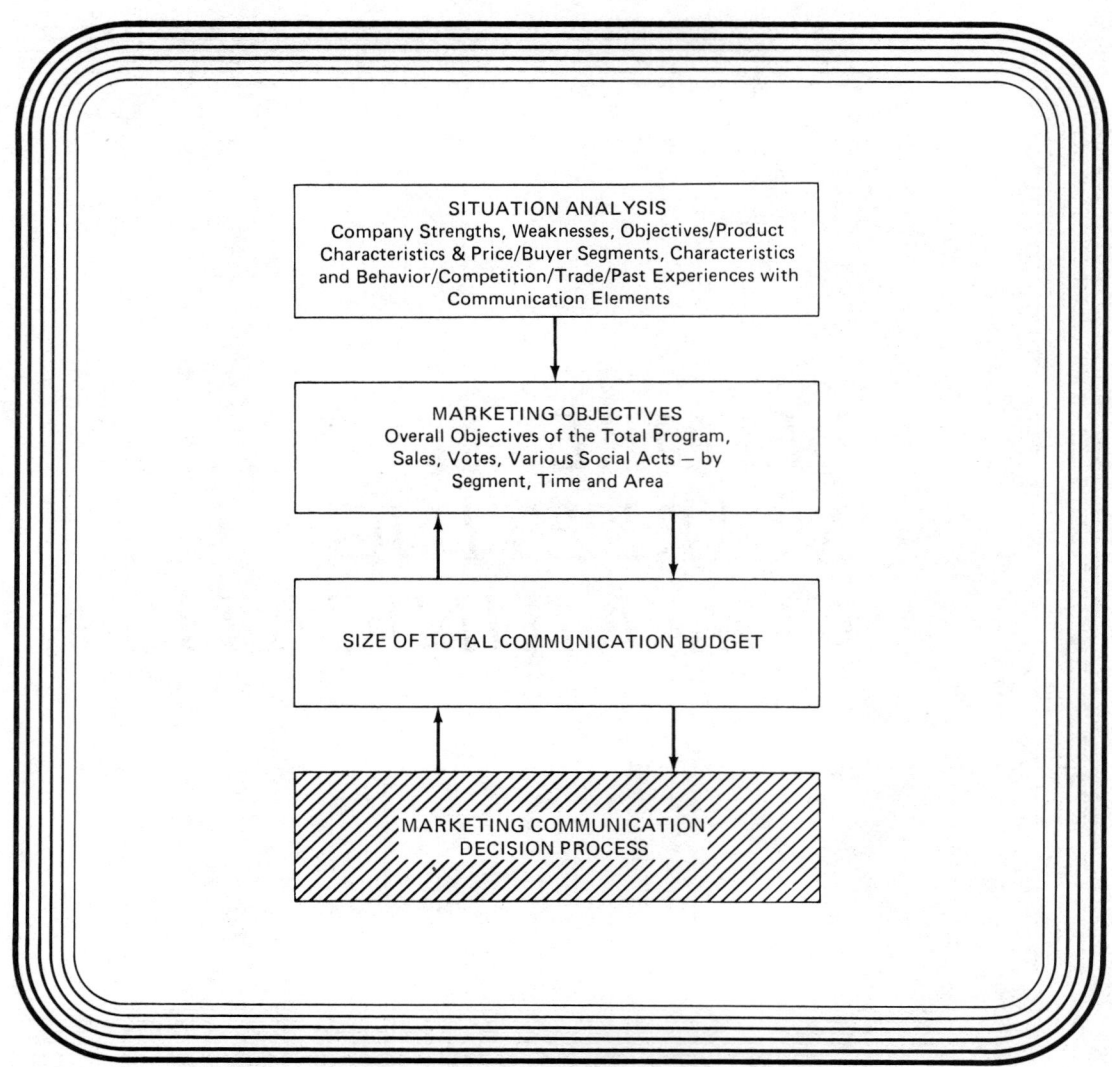

SITUATION ANALYSIS
Company Strengths, Weaknesses, Objectives/Product
Characteristics & Price/Buyer Segments, Characteristics
and Behavior/Competition/Trade/Past Experiences with
Communication Elements

MARKETING OBJECTIVES
Overall Objectives of the Total Program,
Sales, Votes, Various Social Acts — by
Segment, Time and Area

SIZE OF TOTAL COMMUNICATION BUDGET

MARKETING COMMUNICATION
DECISION PROCESS

Marketing-Mix Diagnosis for Communication Planning

- As brand manager of a toilet soap that has had fair success in the past, you are convinced that extra communication effort now will make it the leader in its field. What information can you present to members of management to dissuade them from spending the necessary funds on launching a new product in another category?

- Antidrug advertising can be directed either to preventing trial with fear appeals or to discouraging repeat usage with a variety of positive appeals. What information could help you make the decision between these two broad approaches?

- You are a product manager for a line of light industrial equipment and are not getting the sales support you deserve. The sales manager claims that the product is "hard to sell." The ad manager feels that increasing general advertising will help. What do you need to know to resolve these differences?

- Your line of dry-roasted products is far outselling your standard equivalent products. Now consumerists complain that your packaging deceives buyers into thinking that your dry-roasted line is lower in calories. How can you decide whether to change the packaging, the advertising, or both?

- Your agency has an opportunity to purchase for you a partial sponsorship of the telecasting of the Olympics. You are a low-budget industrial advertiser who has never used "consumer media." How can you evaluate this recommendation?

- A medical report indicates that your product is less dangerous than competing ones in terms of heart disease. How can you decide whether this potential appeal might be used instead of the fun-taste one you have been using?

- You are asked to consult with a wealthy, first-time political candidate. He wants to start heavy personal appearance and media campaigning six months before the primary election. What would you tell him to do?

If you are a brand, product, or campaign manager, you are constantly faced with questions similar to those above. Few of these questions fit neatly into the marketing-communication decision sequence presented earlier. In fact, one major point of this chapter is that a firm basis in the activities before marketing-communication planning—including situation analysis, setting overall campaign objectives, and setting total budget for the product—is the only way the constant stream of questions and opportunities and problems can be efficiently handled once communication planning begins.

All seven of the situations depicted above are situations that have actually occurred. It may be interesting to note what happened in some of them:

• The toilet-soap brand manager was not able to dissuade management from spending money on the new product. It was a moderate success, but the manager's soap brand went into a gradual sales decline from which it never recovered. Obviously, better life cycle and product portfolio analysis would have helped the company make better communication allocations.[1]

• Much antidrug advertising turned out to be of the fear-preventive variety. The effect of such efforts was uncertain, but some studies indicated a boomerang effect, with greater exposure to the campaign being related to greater drug abuse. In addition, a moratorium on producing more antidrug educational materials was called. Here the need seemed to be for better analysis of the decision process relating to drug use—particularly the trial-to-repeat-user ratio. If this information had been known, better communication planning could have been done.[2]

• The light-industrial-equipment product manager prevailed, developed new presentations and sales lists, and persuaded sales managers to run special campaigns on the product. Almost nothing happened to sales volume, and budget was taken from several promising products. Again, inadequate life-cycle analysis was done. It would have indicated the product was in a decline, and the communication budget would not have been misallocated.[3]

• The former low-budget industrial advertiser took the plunge into the Olympics sponsorship with great success. Tracking studies indicated that awareness levels were up sharply among prime prospects and the sales staff was converting this awareness into nearly more business than the company was able to handle in the short term. Attitudinal analysis and decision-process analysis were most helpful in making the media choice in the first place and then implementing it in such a successful fashion.

• The wealthy, first-time political candidate came from nowhere to nearly capturing the election. The success was due in part to segmentation and decision-process analysis, combined with abnormally high expenditures. In fact, if the analysis had been more complete, the expenditures would have been tempered in the later days of the campaign. With this, he might have won.

In every one of these situations, the success of the short-term communication decision was heavily biased by the quality of the situation analysis that was done before communication decision making began. Further, these short-term decisions often forced themselves upon the brand or campaign manager completely out of the order of decision making suggested in Chapter 2.

The possibility of a sponsorship, an attack by consumerists, a widely reported medical finding—these are all examples of communication opportunities and problems that can be acted upon successfully if there is a solid base of situation analysis–objectives setting–total budget. In exceptional cases it appears that a dramatic new idea has pushed beyond the realities and difficulties of the case to create a success beyond expectation. But usually when this occurs there is always a solid background of the before-communication fact gathering and analysis that allowed the creative breakthrough to happen.

In this chapter the logic of thorough situation analysis and planning in the context of the creative process is discussed first. Then the nuts and bolts of a situation-objectives-budget statement is examined in the context of a particular example. Specific discussion of market offering diagnosis plus competition and distribution components of situation analysis conclude this chapter.

Chapter 5 is concerned mainly with consumer and market analysis, the final components of situation analysis.

CREATIVITY, MANAGEMENT, AND EVOLUTIONARY PLANNING

The examples presented at the beginning of this chapter provide what may seem to be a dilemma of work in marketing communication; that is, that strict analysis and planning of a very mundane sort seem necessary on the one hand, while the "Great Crea-tive Idea" seems to be the essence of this area of business and management on the other.

Is this really a dilemma? Can these two seemingly disparate approaches of the creative insight and the planning framework fit together?

This book is not the place to review the vast behavioral and managerial literature on creativity and the creative organization. But some central ideas coming from this literature can illuminate the role of the before-communication activities in the creative communication decision process.

First, we should consider some definitions. What is an idea? What is a creative new idea? Have you ever had a new idea that solved a problem? If you begin to think about the situations in which you have had a good, problem-solving idea, you will begin to see what a new idea is.

Essentially, any new problem-solving idea is typically a new combination of old elements that fit together in a special way to solve a problem.

Considered in this light, creativity is the ability to see new, problem-solving relationships. Productivity is the ability to apply these relationships. Imagination is the ability to see new combinations, but not necessarily those that solve problems.

Under these definitions, the great creative genius of art and literature and the advertising agency copywriter have something in common. They are both trying to develop new combinations that uniquely solve a problem or fit a framework. The difference between the two types of creative individuals is that the fine artist has a great deal to do with choosing the problem and framework he or she will deal with. The copywriter has a problem and framework more or less handed to him or her by the market and the management. Still the copywriter creates.

Other people are merely productive. They keep applying, and applying well, good creative ideas that someone else has developed.

It is often said that children are highly

creative as a group. The definition of creativity here does not agree with this notion. Children are highly imaginative and can see strange new relationships that adults seldom comprehend. But very few children can see new relationships that solve particular problems. They are typically imaginative, but seldom creative.

If these definitions are accepted, the next question concerns the role of management in heightening creativity in planning communication. Obviously creativity can be increased if a solid problem framework is provided and if people are allowed the opportunity to see new relationships. The people who must come up with the ideas must be given a framework for guidance, but not so restricting a framework that it stops them from creating new combinations.

The literature of creativity gives many hints for how this proper balance can be achieved. One very simple suggestion was developed by an advertising man, James Webb Young, and consists of five steps: (1) gather raw material, (2) mental digestive process, (3) drop the problem, (4) the idea appears, (5) shaping and development.[4]

This procedure or "technique" for producing ideas has several major features that people managing and creating communication should be aware of. First, there is a great deal of emphasis on gathering raw material both on the particular situation and in terms of general information that *may* relate, however indirectly, to the problem. This is mirrored in this chapter's emphasis on doing a thorough situation analysis and clearly setting goals and budgets. It is also related to the suggestions made here to consider broader behavioral, communication research, and management science ideas, even though they may not be directly related to the problem at hand.

The second aspect of the Young "technique" and similar ones from the literature is that they consider idea production to be evolutionary, always tentative, adaptive, and growing. A highly creative individual typically withholds judgment longer than a less-creative individual. A management framework should allow the nonevaluative, highly creative approach in developing communication plans.

In his mental digestive process, Young urges that *all* ideas be considered but not scanned too closely. The process should go on even after you are tired of trying. Then, after dropping the problem, the idea appears. But after a good idea appears, there must be "shaping and development." A good idea grows under criticism. It generates other new ideas. It does not let you rest. It is worthless unless it is implemented, unless someone carries it the "final inch."

The decision sequence presented in the second chapter utilizes this concept of full analysis and evolutionary planning. Tentative statements are made at one stage and updated at others on the basis of new information. Implementation and control allow shaping and development of the entire campaign and its specific elements.

The same creative development process is repeated over and over in marketing communication. A United Airlines employee walks into a meeting that is dismal after extended fruitless effort to determine a communication plan that will get the airline back to normal business after a long strike. He is carrying a tube of toothpaste with a fifty-cents-off coupon for the next purchase. The idea was applied to United's problem with 50 percent-off coupons that brought the airline's volume back to prestrike levels in eleven days.[5]

An advertising copywriter nearly falls asleep as he listens to an engineer talk about washing machine characteristics. Suddenly he puts together the ideas of large machines and the low-suds characteristics of his client's detergent product.

In a perhaps apocryphal story, an account executive on the Schlitz beer account walked across the street for a drink. There he heard somebody at the bar exclaim angrily, "When you're out of *Bud*, you're out of beer." And thus, goes the story, the slogan, "When you're out of *Schlitz*, you're out of beer" was born. Later the ideas of attitudinal and life-style segmentation were used by Schlitz to target on the, "You only go around once in life" segment.

Again, creative communication can thrive within a managerial framework that allows evolutionary planning. It starts with facts and the direction provided by overall objectives and budget. This must be an open system if it is to be successful. It starts with very general fact-based analysis and moves progressively to fully shaped ideas. And the first step of the process is the situation analysis.

SITUATION ANALYSIS: AN EXAMPLE

What are the components of a complete situation analysis? What must be analyzed, and how can it be applied most efficiently? What is the form of a situation analysis statement?

In essence, it is necessary to analyze where the company has been and where it is going. This is done in a sequential fashion, starting with gross consideration of the market and company and followed by successively more and more specific cuts down to a consideration of past experience with communication elements. Thus even within situation analysis itself, the general to specific aspects of the creative process are followed.

The situation analysis that preceded the development of a campaign for Maytag washers and dryers provides an excellent example of how the situation analysis should be done.

When the Maytag campaign began, the advertising was different from any that had previously been seen in that industry. It was probably responsible for making Maytag a viable competitor in a situation in which it had formerly had trouble. The same major Maytag theme was still running in a variety of forms at the time this book was being written. The situation analysis that preceded that campaign development had the following elements:

1. *Company strengths, weaknesses, objectives.* Maytag's strengths were a high-quality product and a solid reputation for dependability. Its weaknesses were its high price and its distribution to independent dealers. Also the trend of sales was not good. The company's overall objective was to service the home laundry market with high-quality profitable products.

2. *Product and price characteristics.* High quality and price were major characteristics here. In addition, it might be said that the line was rather ordinary or fundamental. It offered all the advanced features but very few frills such as odd colors and sizes.

3. *Competition.* The main competition was Sears, Roebuck and Company with its vast distribution network, guarantee, readily available service, and low initial price. Considered in terms of the buyer's needs and segments, Sears and other mail-order or large merchandising chains appeared to offer the right combination of variety, confidence, and price needed in this market.

4. *Trade, distribution, channels.* The middleman is often a crucial factor in the nature and success of the marketing-communication campaign. In this case he was also a critical reason for the entire effort. The independent appliance dealer was Maytag's main distribution source. He was also in trouble in competition with large chains like Sears. Maytag had to support its dealers in a way that they had not been supported before. There was a need to help reduce large inventories and increase competitive position.

5. *Buyer segments, characteristics, and behavior.* In the Maytag situation the target segment with greatest potential was the young, growing family. This family had to be large enough to need a washing machine and affluent enough to be in the market for a high-quality one. Their main problem was keeping the machine going at a reasonable cost. The washing machine for the people in this target segment was like a valued member of the family. If it was in bad repair, it was necessary to fix it quickly. In purchasing, the housewife was a primary decision maker; and initial cost, features, and ease of service were important decision attributes. Also, word-of-mouth communication was quite important in influencing brand decisions.

6. *Past experience with communication elements.* It was clear from past results that promotions at the local dealer level would have only a short-term effect if any. There was a need for something dramatic and different at the national advertising level. The advertising agency, the Leo Burnett Company of Chicago, believed in advertising that spoke the language of the customer in a significant way. Much of Burnett's advertising was almost folksy in tone. The agency also had evidence that advertising that generated curious disbelief—believable-unbelievable advertising that caused a reaction—could be quite effective. Burnett favored honest testimonials to do much of the above advertising work. In terms of message distribution, the print magazine format had offered significant advantages for durable goods like washing machines.

The situation analysis, expressed in much greater detail than above, formed the basis for a series of communication decisions. The overall goal of the campaign was stated not only in terms of sales but also in terms of strengthening at the distributor level. The total communication budget was increased somewhat. Washers and dryers were virtually all that Maytag manufactured and sold at the time, so the survival of this mature product line was essential.

When it came time to decide on weight to be put on elements of the communication mix, all four communication-mix elements were considered: advertising, personal selling, sales promotion, and publicity. The bulk of the weight was tentatively put against advertising, with the other three elements considered to provide peripheral support should outstanding advertising be developed. For instance, if advertising could achieve the communication goal of comprehension of the unique advantages and benefits of Maytag, salespeople could convince dealers of the power of the new campaign, and the dealers could be supported with local promotions and sales that might induce buyers to come to the sales room. Publicity could add to the awareness level if the advertising were distinctive enough.

The analysis and decision making thus had successively moved down through tentative budget-mix and communication goals, always leaving the possibility that these decisions would be revised if outstanding advertising could not be prepared.

Next, appeals and positioning were decided upon. The situation analysis—focusing on Maytag's strengths, the competitive and trade situation, and the young-family segment—was entirely directed to the theme of outstanding dependability of a money- and time-saving sort. This theme was realistic in terms of actual product characteristics. It hit at the one vulnerability of the competitors. Their machines were not thought to be as dependable, and although initial cost was low and service was available, the service could be high priced and inconvenient. And the one weakness of the Maytag dealer in the eyes of the consumer—the lack of confidently available service facilities—could be overcome if the Maytag machines were shown to be unusually dependable.

Now the problem was well formulated for the creative people at the agency, and they began to generate alternative message formats or executions in the print magazine medium, this being most reasonable given cost considerations and objectives. They prepared over fifteen comprehensive layouts, each depicting a particular message format for the main theme and positioning.

Some of the layouts showed, for example, a shock test that was part of the quality-control program Maytag used, testimonials from well-known personalities, a picture indicating that the Maytag was the machine used by the Byrd expedition to the South Pole, the quality parts used in the Maytag versus the lower quality used by the competition, and unsolicited testimonials from actual Maytag owners. The last format approach was chosen because not only did Maytag have file draw-

It was uphill all the way for Mrs. Fericano's Maytag

No sooner did one little Fericano graduate from diapers than there was another to take his place.

Back in 1950, a new Maytag Automatic became part of the Frank Fericano family of San Francisco, California. Sal Fericano was 4 then, and Betty was 2, and together with Mr. and Mrs. Fericano they managed to keep the Maytag pretty busy. But things got a lot busier.

In the next 13 years, the Fericano's welcomed 8 more children (one year there were 3 children in diapers). This meant lots of work for Mrs. Fericano and lots of work for her Maytag. But they both came through in fine fashion. Through 13 years of at least a load of diapers a day — plus a load of other wash — the Maytag averaged less than $6.00 a year for repairs.

Last year Mrs. Fericano decided it was time to put her Maytag diaper specialist out to pasture. Not that it wasn't still running fine, but she wanted some of the new features Maytag offers.

Mrs. Fericano likes the Automatic Bleach Dispenser and Lint-Filter Agitator on her new Maytag. But what she really likes is Maytag's big-family load capacity.

It figures.

For a guide to all Maytag Washers and Dryers, send 10¢ in coin to: The Maytag Company, Dept. 365-L10, Newton, Iowa 50208.

MAYTAG
the dependable automatics

WALTZ THROUGH WASHDAY   with a dependable Maytag Washer and Dryer

Figure 4-1. Early ad in Maytag "dependability" campaign

(Courtesy of the Maytag Company)

ers full of these kinds of testimonial letters but the theme also fit what the agency believed to be effective communication. What's more, such an approach would be distinctive from that of the competition, who were using primarily price and features appeals.

One of the early Maytag advertisements is shown in Figure 4-1. A storyboard from a recent television commercial is shown in Figure 4-2. Notice that the approach has stood the test of time, changes in budget, competi-

tive appeals, and media. The "loneliest repairman" theme not only gets the dependability idea across but also shows that there *are* Maytag repairmen, should anything go wrong. And the disclaimer line at the end of the commercial is representative of government regulation, a given in communication in the 1980s.

Note also that minor creative breakthroughs were made all along the communication decision process for this company.

1. WOMAN: Meestaire Lonely Maytag Repairman,...

2. ...I see excitement ahead...

3. JESS: (Hopeful) Yeah?

4. WOMAN: I see Maytag Washer pumps going pffft!

5. WOMAN:...filtaires feezling... JESS: (Excitement builds) Yeah!

6. WOMAN:...and your telephone rrringing and rrringing!

7. JESS: (Ecstatically) Yeahhh!

8. (Gets Idea) Oh! I better get right back to the shop!

9. WOMAN: Five dollars, please.

10. JESS: (Embarrassed) Oh, excuse me.

11. WOMAN: (Philosophical aside to viewers) So I feebed a leetle.

12. A Maytag Repairman can use cheering up. (Laugh)

13. (Anncr VO) Not all Maytag Repairmen are this lonely. But we're trying.

14. Maytag,...

15. ...the dependability people!

Figure 4-2. More recent Maytag television commercial showing continued use and development of the "dependability" theme

They were made possible because there was a solid base of situation analysis which led to sequential refinements in the formulation of the problem.

In sum, the situation analysis consists of consideration of the six aspects reviewed in the Maytag example. Consistent with the Young "technique" for producing ideas, however, the analysis proceeded with much greater detail and concern for communication implications than was possible to illustrate here.

Detailed knowledge of the product and the way it is used and bought can lead to inspiration in communication that is available in few other ways. All competitive efforts must be reviewed to see where there is a distinctive opening for your product or service. The trade must be known not only as a set of statistics but also as people and organizations with certain strengths and weaknesses that figure in the total mix of communication effect. Communication planners must actually use the product, talk to consumers and dealers, and examine actual competitive efforts, as well as the statistics. The situation analysis is equivalent to the sort of total immersion process suggested by the "gather raw material" and "mental digestive" phases of Young's technique.

This process is more likely to be done well with the support of the behavioral and quantitative tools that are discussed in the following sections.

THE COMPANY AND THE MARKET OFFERING

The first two parts of the communication situation analysis given in the Maytag example were

1. Company strengths, weaknesses, objectives
2. Product and price characteristics

It may seem rather surprising that these are analyzed before the consumer. The consumer is analyzed first in developing general marketing strategy, of course. But communication is the fourth component of the marketing mix. Advertising and communication are planned in detail after the other components of the mix have been determined. The brand manager may have contributed to the research and planning effort to develop the product, price, and distribution plans. In the same way, communication is a critical consideration in the development of these plans. But they are givens that must be considered first in analyzing the situation to determine marketing objectives, the size of the total communication budget, and guidelines for advertising and communication planning itself.

How can the analysis of company and product and price aspects of the situation be done most efficiently? We start at a general level of analysis with the application of the product life-cycle concept. Then this concept is specified in company product portfolio analysis which gives an idea of where each product sits in the overall company picture. New-product development techniques are discussed next, since it is in this development process that many directions for communication are revealed. Hints from pricing development close out the section on the company and the market offering.

The Product Life Cycle

All products (brands, services, and ideas) in a specific form are conceived, are born, are matured into growth, lead active lives into maturity, and then decline and die.

This is the concept of the *product life cycle*—that any given product, service, or idea has a fairly predictable life with a well-defined pattern of introduction, growth, maturity, and decline. The life cycle was developed initially to take a minimal number of financial indicators and use them to forecast the growth and life of the product. The value of the cycle for the present purposes is that it organizes the first general look at the situation and can indicate what objectives, total communication budgets, and strategies should be for any particular market offering.

Typical textbook product life-cycle curves are illustrated in Figure 4-3. They show a flat preintroduction sales curve, an upward movement in introduction, rapid increases leading to the flattening late in the growth period, a flat maturity period, and, finally, decline. In this particular depiction the product begins to make money per unit in the growth period. The breakeven point is realized in maturity.

The value of the life-cycle concept is not so much in the particular curves but rather in the fact that there is a cycle and there are stages in it. In reality, the exact curves shown

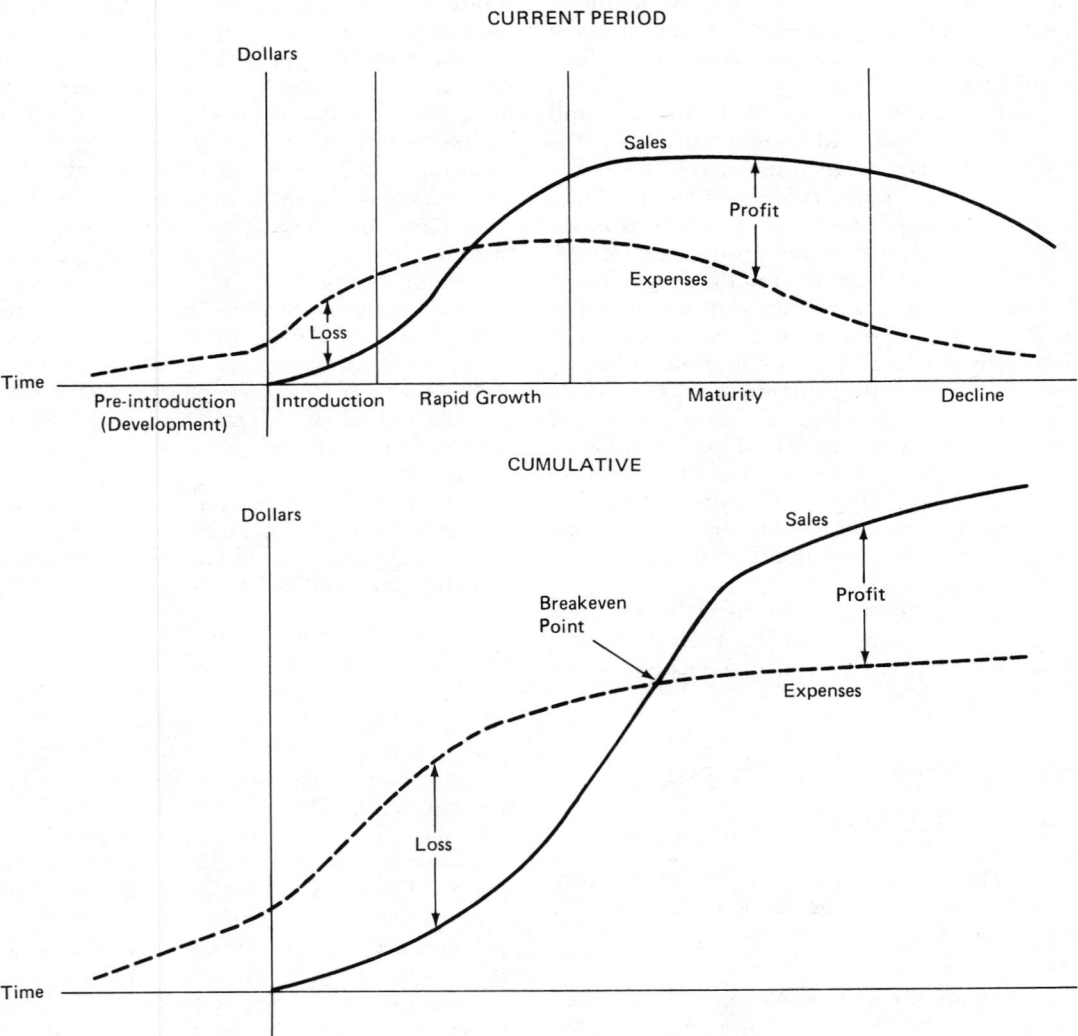

Figure 4-3. *Typical depictions of the product life cycle shown in terms of current period (above) and cumulative (below) sales, expenses, profit, and loss*

in Figure 4-3 occur in only a minority of situations. Some products and brands have been around so long that it seems as if they will never decline. The length and shape of the life cycle depend on the nature of the product situation and whether you are concentrating on an individual company offering or the entire class of offerings.

For instance, in most consumer convenience-goods categories, marketers are often concerned with introduction of new company brands of rather standard products. An example would be the introduction of Aqua-fresh toothpaste. In that sort of case the standard life-cycle pattern starts with almost no introduction period and an immediate growth in sales, since distribution is complete and heavy advertising starts the brand moving. The end of the growth period occurs some six to twelve months after introduction. Instead of flattening out into maturity, however, there is often a drop in sales to some steady maturity level that holds until the brand and/or the product reaches the declining phase. This up, down, and flattening is completed within some eighteen months. It occurs because many people try the convenience brand at least once or twice when it is introduced but do not actually become regular users. The triers boost the overall sales curves, but the brand then declines to a level that represents the steady state of a regular base of users plus some small rotating proportion of new triers.

One of the worst mistakes a convenience-goods marketer can make is to believe that the general sales trend for the first twelve months is representative of the strength of a brand. It could be that sales are shooting up because of many people trying only once and never again. Once a line of snack products experienced such a situation and began building plant capacity, only to see sales dip sharply after the supply of triers was exhausted. The solution was to repeatedly introduce and take off the market new versions of snack products. Thus the mature stage was never reached.

The job in analysis for new convenience brands is to quickly determine the proportion of households purchasing the new brand at various rates. Models are available for translating these proportions into predictions of what the steady state will be if everything, including communication, is held as is.[6] It is also possible with some types of these models to determine what effect various communication moves would have on the steady state of "maturity" eventually reached in eighteen months.[7] With or without such models, the concern of the communication planner in such situations should be to learn the rate of purchase of various market segments. Then communication can be planned to deal with the situation as it exists, in introduction, growth, or maturity.

In the industrial field there are many life-cycle patterns. Sometimes there are long preintroduction and introduction phases as new equipment, materials, and components are made known through publicity and journal articles. When a new version of a standard product is introduced in a rapidly changing field—e.g., small testing equipment—the product's sales move immediately into growth, hit a peak for a very short maturity period, and then decline as new products are introduced.

One study of life cycles in the pharmaceutical industry determined six different patterns, the most common of which was bimodal. That is, for these products there were two (thus the term "bimodal") mini life cycles. After the first cycle and some decline, the products would go through new introduction, growth, and maturity phases. The optimistic hint from that study is that rejuvenation can occur. Thus changes in basic strategies (product, price, distribution), as well as communication, can not only stop a decline but also boost the product substantially.

The product life cycle, then, is the first step in determining the nature of communication jobs required for a particular market offering. By knowing such factors as

☐ The length of time a product has been on the market,

☐ Sales and profit (loss) trends,

☐ Purchase behavior (e.g., trial vs. repeat buyers),

☐ Competitive activity (i.e., number and strategies),

☐ Technology development or product efficacy changes,

☐ Environmental factors (e.g., government support for certain energy sources),

☐ Alternative products and models,

☐ Cost structures, and

☐ The typical life cycles for the industry (e.g., the convenience goods, industrial and pharmaceutical ones discussed earlier),

we can begin to determine where a product, trend, service, or idea is in the life cycle. If we know these factors, it does not really matter whether we can name the stage of life cycle. We will have enough information to make a first cut at the objectives, total budget, and guidelines for communication strategy for the market offering.

The nice thing about the life-cycle concept is that it provides direction from limited knowledge combined with information as to what is required for a market offering at each stage of the life cycle. Table 4-1 shows the kind of direction that can be provided once campaign planners know what stage of the life cycle is involved.

When the life-cycle concept is used, there is an attempt to do the best possible job in terms of meeting objectives with appropriate budgets and strategy for each product at each stage of the cycle. It is not always necessary, however, to accept the eventual decline of the product. While Figure 4-3 and Table 4-1 show eventual decline stages, there are many ways product life can be extended. New uses can be developed, appropriate product modifications can be made, new market segments can be tapped, or new communication strategies can be devised.

There are many examples of products that were thought to be in the decline stage

Table 4-1. General Communication Directions at Each Life-Cycle Stage

Life-Cycle Stage	Marketing Objectives	Total Communication Budget	Typical Communication Strategies
Preintroduction	Generate awareness and interest Develop distribution, expertise, product quality	Small	Publicity–PR Sampling Selling to trade No advertising
Introduction	Expand distribution Generate trial Develop market	Large	Introductory promotions Heavy advertising Continued selling
Growth	Rapid share increase to dominant position Expand regular user segment Stave off competition	Large	Heavy advertising to establish image
Maturity	Hold total share • Largest segment • Develop smaller segments with new versions and approaches	Medium	Advertising: maintain image and help introduce changes, segments Promotions: introduce, hold distribution, used sparingly
Decline*	Gradually lose share while reaping profits	Smallest	Almost none

* Only if product is to be "harvested." See text suggestions for extending product life.

but eventually came back. The strategies suggested at the maturity stage in Table 4-1 are representative of those that can keep a brand going and avoid the high costs and loses of Preintroduction, Introduction, and Early Growth.

One chairman of Procter and Gamble claimed that it was product improvement to fit changing consumer needs that led to the continuing strength of the company's major brands. There were fifty-five significant product modifications in the first twenty-nine years of the life of Tide detergent, for instance.[8] Of course, appropriate advertising and communication strategies were used along the way.

Sometimes brands are assumed to be good for nothing but a natural and profitable death with what is called the "milking" or "harvesting" of profits. Even P&G does this. One former P&G market researcher gave Ivory Flakes as an example, saying:

> For years, P&G harvested Ivory Flakes, which received no noticeable marketing back-up but continued to hang on because the trade ordered it by mistake—so at least one investigation found—thinking they were asking for Ivory Snow.[9]

In another example, years of product, pricing, promotion, and advertising attempts failed to make Life cereal a viable brand for Quaker Oats.[10] A milking or harvesting strategy seemed appropriate. But then a creative breakthrough came in the form of a television commercial featuring a character called "Mikey." This one commercial was run repeatedly, the character was featured on the cereal's packages and the brand achieved a mature and solid position.

The point is that the life-cycle concept is a good first cut, but it is only a first cut. The disagreements between the emphasis of the chairman and the marketing researcher at P&G, the surprising turnaround of Life cereal, the vague direction of Table 4-1—all point to the need to search for better tools to

determine marketing objectives, total communication budget, and guidelines for communication planning for any particular market offering.

Company Product Portfolio Analysis

One tool that provides more specific situational information for communication planners is company product portfolio analysis. It builds on life-cycle analysis to show where each market offering fits in a company's total effort and picture of strengths and weaknesses. Each product is seen as being in a certain life-cycle phase, in a company that is attempting to allocate communication resources (budgets) across brands that have different life-cycle-objective requirements.

There are at least six different product portfolio approaches.[11] An early one most directly related to the life-cycle concept was proposed by Donald Clifford of McKinsey and Company. His was basically a sophisticated form of life-cycle analysis.[12]

The key addition Clifford made to this analysis was the suggestion that each individual product's situation be looked at in terms of the company's total product line, mix, or portfolio. By considering the profitability and campaign needs of all of the company's brands, it is possible to use resources more wisely. Again for the toilet-soap brand mentioned on the first page, the company may have had other profitable brands with positive cash flow which could have provided monetary resources for the manager's growth plans for the brand. The light-industrial-equipment brand, on the other hand, could have declined gracefully, providing funds for other company brands to grow into the more profitable maturity years.

One of the most popular of the product portfolio approaches is that suggested by the Boston Consulting Group. The BCG approach classifies products into four types depending on whether market share is high or low and whether growth rate is high or low. This classification, as well as the optimum cash flow (resources available), and success and disaster sequences of resource allocation are shown in Figure 4-4.

Based on BCG's application of the life-cycle product portfolio idea, it is possible to predict what the cash flow will be for each of the four product types. Any company should attempt to have a certain percentage of products in each of the categories represented so that cash developed by the maturity products ("cash cows" in Figure 4-4) can be utilized in the introduction of other products ("problem children"), which can then begin to move into the growth stage. Obviously maintenance is called for in the maturity phase when cash cows can be "milked." Growth objectives and larger budgets are called for in the introduction and growth stages where it is neces-

sary to not only grow along with the market but also establish a share position. Heavy communication expenses, even to the point of deficit spending, are called for in these two early phases because if high share is not established, there is a danger of dropping into the "dog" category shown in the figure.

One marketing consultant made suggestions for marketing moves, including communication, that should be made for each of the quadrants of the BCG matrix:

☐ Problem Child. Work on developing meaningful differentiation in product and positioning.
☐ Star. Keep advertising and promotion effort strong and competitive.
☐ Cash Cow. Develop leadership position, but also invest in line extensions, market segmentation.

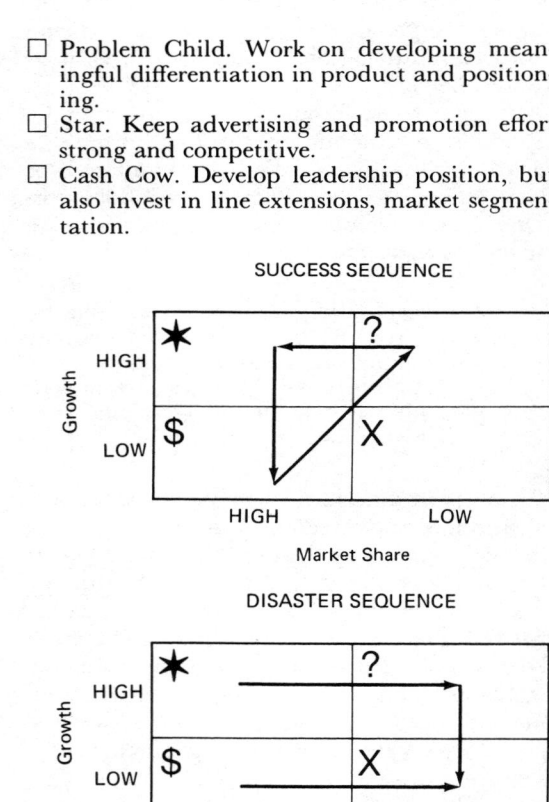

Figure 4-4. *The Boston Consulting Group growth-share matrix*
From Boston Consulting Group, "Perspectives No. 66, the Product Portfolio," 1970. Used with permission.

☐ Dog. Critique entire marketing mix, probably end up harvesting.[13]

The advantage of portfolio analysis over simple life-cycle analysis is seen best in the last three matrices of Figure 4-4. The "Optimum Cash Flow" matrix shows that the Cash Cow and the Problem Child have high positive and high negative cash flow, respectively. This means that once a brand gets to the Cash Cow or maturity stage, it produces money to use on other company offerings. The best use of the money is to put it into the development of Problem Children where money is needed. Then the Problem Children can grow into Stars, which can grow into Cash Cows, as shown in the "Success Sequence" matrix.

The "Disaster Sequence" occurs when the Cash Cow money is used in a too-late attempt to save the declining Dogs instead of being applied to developing the Problem Children into future Cash Cows. Another aspect of the Disaster Sequence is the use of money from Star or growth products, at a point in their development when they really need it, to bolster the introduction of Problem Children. In the Disaster Sequence money is taken too early from certain products and is insufficient to deal with the problems of either introductory or declining products.

The implications of portfolio analysis for communication management are numerous. It is easy to see why, for instance, the practice of determining the total communication budget for a brand on the percentage of past or future sales is so dysfunctional. If a brand is a Cash Cow it may not need as big a budget. And the money may be used for long-term profit on a Problem Child.

Portfolio analysis also illustrates why the brand manager's responsibilities have become limited. There is a need for overall company management in the form of a marketing VP or division manager to balance objectives and efforts across products of different types, as shown by the portfolio. There have been some horrendous examples of companies that became fat and happy with a stable of Cash Cows and let them age into decline while brand managers asked for ever more support to resuscitate inevitably dying beasts.

The very nature of the company and the kind of messages that should be used for each market offering are first revealed by the portfolio analysis. If company or corporate overriding objectives are clear, the products in the four quadrants are related. The introduction of a new product or the battle of a growth product can be made easier by linking them in communication to the mature Cash Cows. In essence, then, certain resources other than money can be transferred from the Cash Cows to the Problem Children and can affect all marketing objectives and total communication budgets accordingly.

There are several problems with the BCG approach as it applies to communication planning. First, of course, there is the question of what is "high" growth and share. One definition for *high growth* was 10 percent and above. *High share* was anything greater than or equal to the share of the number-one major competitor. But obviously these definitions would vary in their usefulness depending on the industry, market, company, and so forth.

Then there is the problem of whether the product portfolio can be defined adequately by just market growth and share. General Electric's business "screen" is another matrix approach to portfolio assessment. Instead of market growth, the GE screen uses "industry attractiveness." Instead of market share, the screen has "business strengths." Each of these factors has high, medium, and low levels, so the screen has nine cells of high-high, high-medium, high-low, and so forth.[14]

What is different about the General Electric screen is that a large number of factors are used to put each product into each of the cells. Assessment of these factors brings product portfolio analysis to life and provides more specific direction to communication planners.

In the GE approach, the factors considered for industry attractiveness are size, market growth, pricing, market diversity, competitive structure change, industry profitability, inflation vulnerability, technical role, social, environmental, legal, and human.

The "business strengths" factors that are considered by GE include size, growth, share, position, profitability, margins, technology position, strengths/weaknesses, image, pollution, and people.

Communication-planning situation analysis cannot stop with portfolio analysis. Planners must know more than just share and market growth. A market offering that is in a growth market and has a high share may actually have very different communication needs than are expressly called for in the BCG type of product portfolio analysis. Many higher-education institutions once constituted such a market offering. In the early 1970s such education was a growth market. Many colleges with high relative share would have begun increased development and communication effort if they had considered a more detailed analysis as suggested by the GE factors. The fact that they did not led to problems and much too tardy communication efforts.[15]

Life cycle and product portfolio are excellent initial steps. But they do not get to the "heart" of the matter because they do not have the "heart" of the consideration of how products and their communication affect people. Much of this sort of consideration, vital to communication planners, is implicit in product development itself.

Product Development and Communication

Where do new products, brands, services, and social ideas come from? The best answer is in the creative process itself. Someone gets an idea that can help to solve consumer, buyer, or constituency problems or fulfill their needs. Then this idea is subjected to a great deal of testing and development.

This process is like the life of a person. The market offering is conceived by the intercourse of ideas and problems. It is nurtured to birth. It takes its first steps in test markets, which are trials of the entire marketing mix in several markets before actual introduction on a wider basis. Then there is introduction with heavy support and later maturity, during which it can stand on its own and contribute to other "children." Finally there are the twilight years and eventually death.

A product is like a person, and it is kept alive by its meanings for and interaction with people. The goal of the before-marketing-communication analysis is to get to know the product intimately—the way one would know a good friend, with all of this friend's fascinating characteristics.

It is the job of the campaign manager to transmit to everyone working on the campaign as much information as possible about the market offering. And one of the best ways to do this is to allow advertising and communication people to be involved with the product's conception, birth, and upbringing either directly or in terms of knowing about them.

One view of the typical product's life that emphasizes the development, preintroduction, or conception-birth-upbringing aspects is shown in Figure 4-5. Note first that the growth, maturity, and death phases are shown on the right side of the figure in a very dramatic fashion. In fact, the author of this chart said that the headstone on the right might read "Chrysler Imperial: 1926–1975, died at age 49 of sales starvation."[16]

Communication planners should be more concerned with the left than the right side of Figure 4-5. It is in the research of the conception, development, evaluation, and test marketing stages that the actual character of the product is revealed. This is where there are many hints for communication.

Ideas come most often from consumers themselves. A typical research tool during this stage is the focus group interview. In order to determine consumers' problems and needs, small groups of target market individuals are

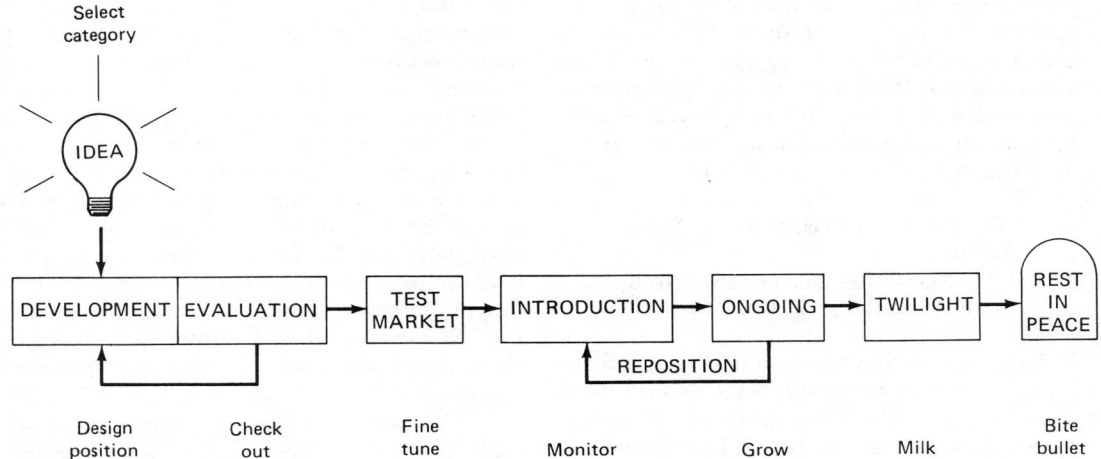

Figure 4-5. *Birth to death for a market offering*

From "Decision Support Systems for Marketing Managers," John D. C. Little, *Journal of Marketing,* Summer 1979. Used with permission.

brought together to discuss their experiences, problems, and needs.

Sometimes the groups are composed of people who are quite concerned about the buying area. For instance, a group talking about dental hygiene might be composed of those people who have their teeth professionally cleaned once a month. And sometimes just target market consumers are recruited, as in the case of the following comments from a group of women, mainly in their twenties and thirties, who had eaten pizza at a chain pizza restaurant within a month preceding the interview. These comments are on fast-food restaurants in general.

> "I've heard that Wendy's—I haven't been there yet, but everybody who goes there thinks it's terrific."
> "Really?" Nancy looks a little funny at Victoria. "Wendy's?"
> "I've been there." Anne says. "It's terrible."
> "Is it terrible?" Victoria asks sheepishly. . . .
> "Oh my daughter is the hamburger addict of the *world,* and she couldn't finish it," Nancy says. "It ran all down—it was so greasy—"

"I like Burger King," says Marlene, who has nine children in her 25-year marriage, "and I like Carl's Jr." She smiles nicely, relishing the impending heresy: "McDonald's I could *vomit* from." The women giggle. "I like Jack in the Box Super Tacos. And the onion rings. I know it sounds disgusting but the Super Tacos are really good." A couple of the women lean toward Marlene to assure her that they see nothing disgusting about liking Super Tacos. "What I'm hearing here is a lot of disagreement," says the moderator. "Most of you feel strongly about the ones you like and don't like."

Laura has seen a television news report on the quality control methods used by McDonald's. "They come in there frozen, the patties, and they put them right on the grill so there's no problem with spoilage," she says. "I think they have a special *process.* I love Big Macs. I love all that mayonnaisey stuff, the taste of the pickles. The onions. The sauce. I *love* that sauce."[17]

Such focus group interviews can give product and service planners ideas as to where consumers are having problems. For those involved in communication, focus groups can give an idea of how people actually talk about the product. This begins to give a sense of what the product is all about and what it is that must be communicated to prospective buyers. One can imagine such lines as the following coming from the above interactions:

"Go ahead, it's all right to love Super Tacos."

"Big Macs—the mayonnaisey stuff, the taste of the pickles. The sauce."

In fact, it is not hard to imagine such a focus group statement leading to McDonald's campaign for the Big Mac sandwich that featured the tongue-twister: "Twoallbeefpattiesspecialsaucelettucecheesepicklesonionsonasesameseedbun."

Such campaign ideas can come from a number of sources in addition to group interviews. One example mentioned earlier involved the Schlitz line "When you're out of Schlitz, you're out of beer," which supposedly came from a copywriter hearing a comment in a bar. But many ideas for campaigns and direction for objectives and budgeting come from the original research that led to the product idea.

Development, as indicated in Figure 4-5, is a stage in which the product idea is turned into a reality with design and positioning. This is the "shaping and development" stage of the creative process mentioned earlier in this chapter. Various forms of the product are designed. Alternatives in terms of pricing and packaging are considered. As the product is developed from an idea to an entity positioned within a market of products, there are even some attempts at possible message ideas for communication.

A variety of research techniques are used at this stage. Focus groups as well as more structured concept tests are employed. The approaches that lead to the attitudinal segmentation of the next chapter occur at this time. Consumers indicate how they perceive and prefer various new and old offerings in

the product class. Techniques such as perceptual mapping and conjoint analysis give estimates as to where the new product may fit in the market and what its important characteristics are to consumers. The point has been made that when a product is developed in this way, the actual words consumers use to indicate their perceptions of the new product should be employed in advertising. In this way there are likely to be the overlapping fields of experience, created by the ads, since they will be using the same words consumers use. As mentioned in Chapter 1, only when there are overlapping fields of experience does communication truly occur.

Products and packages are given to actual consumers during the Development phase for what are called in-home-use tests. Very often these tests show quite clearly the power of the package for certain types of products. The package can determine whether consumers say they are satisfied with the new brand in these in-use tests. This can show the importance of using the package in later advertising.

One in-use test during the development of Raid home and garden insecticide was designed to test the package but led to a discovery of a product characteristic that was used in advertising. A woman participating in an in-use test in a warm and muggy climate was irate about the dead insects on her kitchen floor. She said that before she used the new insecticide, she did not have any insect problems in her kitchen. A number of instances like this led to the conclusion that Raid would actually go behind cabinet walls and doors, behind refrigerators, and so forth, to get at pests that were not normally visible. This characteristic of the product was not really known before the in-use tests.

This in turn eventually led to the Raid advertising line "Hunts bugs down and kills them dead!" Now, of course, this line and the cartoon commercials of insects being exploded, and so on, came from many other sources than just the in-use tests. Consumers' desire to "kill with license" those pests about which they feel frustration and anger certainly led to the strength of the line and the implicit violence of the commercials. The "acceptable" violence in children's cartoons led to the use of cartoons as the medium through which violence against insects and the extra advantage of Raid could be depicted. The particular wording of the line has a feeling of finality about it that came as a result of many creative decisions along the way.

The discovery of the distinctive product characteristic during in-use testing was crucial for Raid, however. It led to possibly more ambitious marketing objectives and larger total communication budget for the product than would otherwise have occurred. The communication mix might have been changed. And the theme and positioning of the brand was ultimately affected.

These are the kind of insights about the product and direction for communication that can result from Development.

Evaluation is closely tied to Development. At this next stage in the process depicted in Figure 4-5, the various alternatives for *product* (and packaging), *price, distribution,* and *communication* are tested in some way short of actual test marketing or introduction.

Research approaches have been developed to expose consumers to parts of the proposed marketing mix in laboratory situations. Consumer responses indicate perceptions and preferences, and these are used to predict market share. If predictions are too low, alterations can be made on the basis of the research information.

One of these pretest market evaluation systems is called ASSESSOR.[18] With this system, consumers in shopping centers are asked to participate in a marketing research study in the center. If they agree, they are first screened by interview to see if they fit in the target market segment. Then they are asked about their awareness of brands in the relevant product class. This early questioning establishes the characteristics consumers use to choose brands, as well as their actual preferences.

Following this basic questioning, the consumer respondents are exposed to representations of the products in the form of commercials for the new and established brands and in the form of seeing the packaged products in a simulated shopping trip. Response to the new and old brands is determined by choice in the shopping trip, and after appropriate time has elapsed for home use, a new measure of repurchase, perceptions, and preference is taken through a telephone interview.

ASSESSOR provides two separate but related models for predicting market share in test marketing and introduction. This pretest evaluation system has proved to be quite accurate. Because of its accuracy, it provides the potential of much direction to the communication decisions, which must be made both before and during marketing-communication planning. Of course, such systems are applied best to low-cost package goods that are not revolutionarily innovative. Some other but similar form of evaluation is required for other types of products, services, and ideas.

Test marketing and *national introduction* show what can be expected for the market offering in the long term. Models that take early trial and repeat purchase rates and predict the steady state of purchase have already been mentioned. It is in the test market that it is possible to see how all the components of the mix work together. This sort of experience is essential for communication planning in the subsequent years of the brand.

Test marketing for package goods can be expensive. One estimate was that a ten to eleven month test in three cities would cost almost $1.0 million and could cost as much as $1.5 million. And from 40 to 60 percent of all products fail in test market.[19]

The primary contribution of test marketing is in terms of budget information and the interaction of components of the communication mix (see Chapter 6).

In sum, the process of product development is one that is rich in implications for the communication planner. Of course, this phase leads to overall marketing objectives and total communication budget. Just as important, however, are the hints that come as to the personality of the product, service, or idea. Ultimately the job of advertising and communication management is to transmit this personality to the audience so that overlapping fields of experience and communication can occur.

Pricing and Communication

Just as the product goes through a life cycle, so do its prices. In fact, one of the indicators of stage in the life cycle is trend of prices.

Pricing is critical to advertising and communication management for four reasons. First, pricing can indicate the character of the product. Second, it will affect the marketing objectives and total communication budget. Third, price can provide direction for the communication mix. Fourth, price can actually constitute an appeal in marketing communication.

Price meaning can be defined as assuming that price indicates quality; we are using price as the main indicator of the product's character. In virtually all consumer, industrial, and public-sector choice situations, price is a characteristic considered in some way. In the Maytag example earlier in this chapter, the high initial cost of Maytag relative to that of the competition was a major problem the campaign had to solve. Prices and costs in relation to value and in terms of initial and long-term consumer expenditures are critical issues relating to most advertising campaign situations.

The effect of price on the marketing objectives and total communication budget can be seen in terms of the life cycle. In the introductory stage, for instance, marketers have two broad pricing strategies available: skimming and penetration. *Skimming* means to price the product high for high profit per unit sold and "skim the cream" of the market willing to pay the high price. *Penetration* means to price low

for low-unit profit but high-volume "penetrating" into the mass market.

The pros and cons of these two introductory (and later) pricing strategies are discussed thoroughly in most marketing texts. Their differential effect on marketing objectives and communication budget is most important here. A skimming strategy implies a smaller share-of-market objective and, perhaps, a smaller total communication budget than does a penetration pricing strategy.

Price effect on communication mix occurs as the product or service matures, and there is a tendency for prices to decrease in a relative sense. Although the actual base or list price may not change much, some of the short-term pricing moves may be made in terms of sales promotion. Price discounts to wholesalers and retailers, coupon and multiple packs to consumers—are all examples of the types of sales promotion deals that might be used. And once there is a shift to this type of sales promotion, there is a chance that advertising and publicity will compose a smaller share of the total communication budget.

We have seen that overemphasis on price-off deals can lead to erosion of the consumer franchise and weakening of the brand. (This will be discussed in depth in Chapter 6). Before each new campaign is planned, it is essential to determine what the firm's pricing strategy is for the market offering. This may put a serious constraint on the advertising and communication mix.

Price appeal sometimes becomes the main or major appeal of the campaign. In some cases, direct comparisons are made with the competition. In others, the comparison is made with the value of the product. Even when price is not mentioned it can be the underlying dimension, as when qualities of widely known low-priced products are shown to be equivalent or even superior to those of the competitors' products. For example, Canada Dry ran an ad for its soda water that did not mention price but showed test results comparing its low-priced product with Perrier's product. Canada Dry's appeal was on the basis of the surprising result that its club soda tested as well as or better than high-priced imported waters.

Price, price strategy, and the meaning of price in relation to the product, consumer, and competition are critical to the development of communication strategy itself.

COMPETITIVE ANALYSIS

Competition, even more than price, is related to both life-cycle and portfolio analyses. In life-cycle analysis, it is clear that competition increases during the growth stage and must be combatted successfully so that the product may enter the profitable maturity years as a survivor. In product portfolio analysis, competition is the other side of high or low share for each product.

But the critical consideration of competition in the before-marketing-communication stage is in terms of competition as "noise." Noise was discussed in Chapter 1 as a component of mass communication that interferes with the audience's actually getting the message. And the main aspect of the noise is competition.

When competition is considered this way, it affects marketing objectives quite directly. Neither 7-Up nor Dr Pepper soft drinks can expect to make strong inroads against Coca-Cola or even Pepsi. But the two smaller-share brands are in a constant fight over the third position in share. In pursuing this third place, they must always relate their objectives to Coke, Pepsi, and each other. This part of the objective is known as *positioning*, a term and concept that are quite central in this book. Positioning here refers to how the marketing objectives in terms of share take competition into account.

The objectives must next be translated into a total communication budget, and here, again, competitive noise forms the context for the decision. The *competitive parity* form of budgeting actually takes this into account. The idea is that the total communication budget should be at least equal to (at parity) or greater than (by some amount) the average expenditures of major competition.

In the airline industry, for instance, there are five major domestic carriers. Their average annual advertising expenditure is something over $30 million. If you were budgeting for communication for one of those airlines, you would want to seriously consider that average figure. To spend much below, say, $20 million on a national advertising campaign might be wasting money just because of competitive noise. There might be a subsistence level for the total communication budget, below which expenditures would just be wasted.

Note that the last paragraph used the phrase "might be" in referring to the possible existence of a subsistence budget level. Budget, as will be discussed in Chapter 6, is only as powerful as the way the money is spent. Both creative and media strategy can affect the value of communication expenditures. And both creative and media strategy are effective in proportion to the way they deal with competition.

Creative strategy, basically the messages of the communication campaign, must be distinctive in order to be successful. In field after field, there is a sameness in the messages used. If one airline is featuring fares, the other ones seem to also. If all the ads for cigarettes, canned soup, insurance, automobiles, computers, political candidates, or copying machines were pinned together on a wall or run together as television commercials, a definite similarity would be observed. In such cases, consumers tend to see all ads as being for the major or dominant brand in the category.

The job of the communication planner and creative strategist is to break through this sameness with clear positioning. Competitive message analysis is the first step in developing such clear positioning and message strategy. You have to know what the nature of the noise is before you can be distinctive from it.

The same competitive sameness seems to exist for media planning. There is a standard way that various competitors in any industry divide their expenditures. Going back to the soft-drink example, it can be seen that Dr Pepper was able to make advances against the giants in the industry by concentrating its budgets in relatively few television specials.[20] This kind of break from the pattern can only be done if there is strong competitive communication analysis in the before-marketing-communication stage of campaign development.

TRADE ANALYSIS

Distribution strategy is such a given for most products and other market offerings that the trade—retailers, wholesalers, channels of distribution—are taken more or less as a given to be analyzed for their communication implications.

Distribution is normally a part of marketing objectives. The company is either trying to achieve distribution for the brand (in the earlier stages of the life cycle) or trying to maintain it (in the later stages). Distribution quality in terms of the type of retailer required is a given. Distribution quantity is an objective to be attained.

In this regard it is important to realize that there are many more products and brands than can fit on the typical grocery store's shelves, department store's counters, and so forth. Retail chain and store buying committees review whether products should be stocked. And some of these committees' key criteria are the size of the communication budget, the nature of the messages, and message distribution—the quality of the campaign. If the buying committee is impressed with the sales promotion and advertising to be done for a brand, this may lead to the product's being accepted by the retailer.

Thus a marketing objective for distribution can lead quite directly to effects on the total communication budget. Also, although it is true that store buying committee decisions should be made on the basis of product

quality and marketability, the quality of the communication campaign should be considered by campaign planners in terms of how the trade will judge it.

Trade analysis for communication should also be made in terms of consumer interaction with the trade. Is there some communication value in developing advertising, or publicity, or sales promotion that strengthens or uses the relationship consumers have with the trade?

Such use of the consumer-trade relationship can be of value. The famous Clairol haircoloring campaign said, "Does She or Doesn't She? *Only Her Hairdresser Knows For Sure*"—obviously playing on the credibility of the hairdresser and the status of having one, even though the Clairol product was most often used at home.

In Chapter 7 there is some discussion of another use of the trade, in advertising for P&Gs Charmin bathroom tissue. The "Please don't squeeze the Charmin" campaign reminded consumers of the one point in the buying process where they could easily identify brands of bathroom tissue—in the store. A side benefit was that the campaign led to trade-level sales promotions in which there were big end-of-aisle displays for Charmin, similar to the one shown in the commercials.

Before-marketing-communication analysis of trade, then, is similar to that for product, price, and competition. These factors directly affect marketing objectives and budget. In addition, they can give direction to the actual communication-planning effort.

SUMMARY

Activities *before* marketing-communication planning are critical to the success of the campaign. They fit the creative process and evolutionary planning. While situational analysis includes at least six categories, only the first four were covered in this chapter. Product life-cycle and portfolio analyses provide a first cut at analyzing the situation, particularly in showing company strengths and weaknesses. Product, price, competition, and trade analysis all provide direction for the two key decisions made by company management before actual communication planning—setting marketing objectives and determining

the size of the total communication budget for a particular market offering. In addition, this analysis and the research tools connected with it provide the basis on which the budget mix, communication goals, creative strategy, and media strategy decisions of communication planning are made.

ISSUES AND PROJECTS FOR DISCUSSION

1. Consider a time when you felt you had an especially good idea, one that solved a problem you were having. It does not necessarily have to be an advertising and communication management idea. How did you get the idea? How did this process relate to the definitions and steps of creativity discussed in this chapter? Did you go through any of the fact-gathering or situation analysis stages?

2. What are the six aspects of situation analysis? Which of these is the most important for each of the examples on the first page of this chapter?

3. Find a product, service, or idea that you believe is in each of the stages of the product life cycle. List as many reasons as you can that led you to feel that each market offering could be classified in each stage of the life cycle. Now, what are the most important marketing and communication elements for each of these market offerings? Are there clear differences in what you have said about the different stages? Why or why not?

4. What is product portfolio analysis and how

does it relate to communication decisions? Can you put each of your market offerings of Question 3 into one of the four cells of the BCG matrix? What are the advantages and disadvantages of product portfolio analysis?

5. In what sense do products, services, and ideas have personalities and lives like people? In what specific ways can before-marketing-communication product development indicate these personalities? What implications do they have for advertising strategy?

6. In what four ways can price affect communication? Explain how a skimming versus a penetration pricing policy can affect the nature of advertising and communication.

7. How can competitive analysis affect marketing objectives, budget, messages, and media? How is this effect different if you are the leading brand in the category as opposed to being a new and very small share brand?

8. In what sense is the trade an object of communication and in what sense is it a cause of the campaign character?

Notes

1. Donald K. Clifford, Jr., "Managing the Product Life Cycle," *European Business,* July 1969, p. 7.

2. Michael L. Ray, Scott Ward, and Gerald Lesser, *Experimentation to Improve Pretesting of Drug Abuse Education and Information Campaigns,* Part I, Marketing Science Institute, 1973.

3. Clifford, "Managing the Product Life Cycle."

4. James Webb Young, *A Technique For Producing Ideas* (Chicago: Crain Publications, 1960).

5. "The Toothpaste Tube That Saved United," *Advertising Age,* October 29, 1979, p. 14.

6. Philip Kotler, *Marketing Decision Making* (New York: Holt, Rinehart and Winston, 1971), Chap. 17.

7. Alvin J. Silk and Glen L. Urban, "Pre-Test-Market Evaluation of New Packaged Goods: A Model and Measurement Methodology," *Journal of Marketing Research,* 15 (May 1978), pp. 171–91.

8. "Good Products Don't Die P&G Chair-

man Declares," *Advertising Age,* November 1, 1976, p. 8.

9. Terry Haller, "Marketers: Strategically Plan Recovery of Corporate Power," *Advertising Age,* July 9, 1979, p. 56.

10. Milton Brown and others, "The Quaker Oats Company—Life Cereal," in *Problems in Marketing* (New York: McGraw-Hill, 1968), pp. 161–95.

11. Yoram Wind, "Marketing Oriented Strategic Planning Models," Marketing Department Working Paper No. 79-022 (Wharton School, University of Pennsylvania, 1979), pp. 16–20.

12. Clifford, "Managing the Product Life Cycle."

13. Haller, "Marketers," p. 59.

14. Main, Jackson & Garfield, Inc., "Market-Share-ROI Corporate Strategy Approach Can Be an Oversimplistic Share," *Marketing News,* December 15, 1978, pp. 1, 6, and 7.

15. Don Spech, "Colleges Take Swing Down Madison Ave.," *Los Angeles Times,* May 15, 1975.

16. John D. C. Little, "Decision Support Systems for Marketing Managers," *Journal of Marketing,* 43 (Summer 1979), pp. 9–26.

17. Charlie Haas, "Charlie Haas on Advertising," *New West,* November 5, 1979, p. 34.

18. Silk and Urban, "Pre-Test-Market Evaluation."

19. Ibid., p. 172.

20. Stephen A. Greyser, "Dr Pepper (A)," in *Cases in Advertising and Communication Management,* Second Edition (Englewood Cliffs, N.J.: Prentice-Hall, 1981), pp. 284–95.

Consumer
and
Experience
Analysis

Mistrust of ads spawning the "sensual consumer"

Researcher breaks society into "privilege levels"

IT'S WYETH, WARHOL AND MORE IN LIFESTYLES,
VALUES, EVEN DEMOGRAPHICS

"I want a weed-killer that will inflict a slow
painful death on crabgrass."

THE NEW FRONTIER OF THE AGING:
MARKETING IMPLICATIONS

Audience before image, beverage marketers urged

MEDIA & ADVERTISING/Discovering the over-50 set

ADVERTISING MUST ADAPT IN ORDER TO BE
EFFECTIVE IN CURRENT PREVAILING
CLIMATE OF CYNICAL DISTRUST

"Age of Me" poses new problems for marketers

MARKETS ARE CUSTOMER PROBLEMS
NOT GEOGRAPHY OR DEMOGRAPHICS

From "Me" Decade to "We" Decade

What every marketer should know about women

Trying to Reach Blacks? Beware of Marketing Myopia

Life style preview: San Diego family of the 80's

Headlines and captions[1]

When it comes to the consumer, "we" are "them." Even if we are not aged, beer drinkers, cynical, crabgrass haters, or members of San Diego families, we know what it means to be a consumer, to have wants, needs, and problems that might be satisfied and solved by products, services, and social ideas.

Why then is it so difficult to develop communication campaigns that simply let our fellow consumers know about solutions? Perhaps the reason is that when we advertise and otherwise communicate for marketing purposes, we forget that "we" are "them." We forget that we are consumers too.

The purpose of this chapter is to help you to remember what it is to be a consumer and to learn about those aspects of making problem-solving consumer decisions you may not know.

Once again, it is important to understand the concept in which consumer analysis takes place before communication planning. The product, price, and distribution strategies have already been largely developed on the basis of consumer, competition, and trade analyses. If these have been done well, all of the communication planners can learn much about the situation from the reports generated at the early stages. Basic strategy development, particularly in the product area, can tell a great deal not only about the marketing objectives and total communication budget but also about the market characteristics that lead to all the various communication decisions.

After perusing the strategy development materials on the consumer, the analyst and eventual planner should take four more steps in order to understand the consumer situation for consumer planning:

1. *Introspect*—immerse in the product and its buying process and the people most likely to buy it
2. *Segment*—determine the publics, markets, and segments most likely for communication attack
3. *Analyze* segments—determine their attitudinal structures and the perceptions and preferences that will be so critical in communication
4. *Understand* the buying process in the market—identify the key steps of decision making at which communication may have effects

This is essentially the procedure outlined for Maytag in the preceding chapter. Here there are more details. Planners must first immediately know what is being communicated—the product, price, and distribution. Then they should immerse themselves in the product and situation in a very personal way before considering any further research data. This immersion is followed by more specifically determining, for communication purposes, the Who (segments), Why (attitudinal structures, with perceptions and preferences), and How (consumer-buyer decision process) of the consumer. Once this is done, there is one more step before marketing communication:

5. *Reflect*—determine what has been successful and unsuccessful in similar communication situations in the past

This can provide broad direction for the advertising and communication management tasks ahead.

INTROSPECTION

The work of product, price, and distribution development leads to a reasonably good idea of the marketing program and particularly the product with which the communicators will be involved.

Once the relatively stable parts of the marketing mix are developed, it is time to eliminate the gap between those planning the campaign and those who will receive it, the consumers. Communication planners should realize, as the agency founder David Ogilvy is reported to have said, that "the consumer is no moron, she's your wife." (Obviously, custom developed since Ogilvy made that statement would require a second version, "The consumer is no moron, he's your husband," and so on through all forms of pronouns, relationships, and nonrelationships.) Finally, planners must realize that "the consumer is no moron, *you* are the consumer."

There is no deeper understanding of the consumer possible than *introspection,* the consideration of our own motives, needs, actions, and the like, in relation to a product. In order to introspect: (1) use the product yourself, (2) as a consumer, ask yourself a series of questions about your personal relationship to the product and its communication, and (3) question and observe others.

Of course, we are different from our potential customers in many ways. This is most true, for instance, when we are dealing with a product we are virtually incapable of using, such as one for the opposite sex. But just consider any product-communication situation as a consumer in terms of such personal questions as

☐ Do I really care very much about it or products like it?
☐ What do I know about it?

☐ What are my favorites and why?
☐ What really makes me mad about this type of product?
☐ What truly pleases me about this type of product?
☐ What happens when I myself am confronted by an ad, a commercial, a sample, a coupon for a brand of this type of product? Do I turn the page, turn away, or throw away the sample or the coupon?
☐ What do I wish "they," that somehow anonymous group of corporate decision makers, would do in this product area or in its communication?

Answering such questions for ourselves as consumers produces insights that are not possible in any other way. We cannot get into anyone else's head in the same way that we can get into our own. We do not know the feelings or lack of feelings other people have as well as we know or can feel our own.

Introspection can form a context of reality for the rest of consumer analysis. Looking into ourselves is only the first step. It clearly does not give all the information needed to make outstanding communication campaign decisions. It is, however, a check that can be used to understand the statistics and data of segmentation, attitude, and decision process analyses.

Introspection has been shown to be more accurate than executive guesses about how consumers may think and behave. In one study, consumers' actual ratings of product and brand characteristics for a number of product categories were compared with (1) marketing executives' guesses as to what the consumer ratings would be and (2) marketing executives' own ratings. The marketing executives' guesses as to consumer ratings were not very accurate. But the marketing executives' own ratings were very close to those made by the consumers. Thus, treating the consumers as "others" was not very accurate while considering ourselves as consumers was most accurate.[2] Of course we do not need to use our own ratings to predict those of consumers. Studies such as these just give us confidence in our own introspections as a start.

The less the planner himself or herself is a consumer for a product, the less likely it is that the introspection approach alone will be enough, even as a start. The less the planner is a consumer of the product, the more it is important to talk to friends and relatives, people who are likely to be in the market for the product and are also willing to reveal their personal thoughts about it. Observation of the way people buy in stores can help too. And talking to these people personally can add to the insights from more structured research-oriented approaches.

The creative process is quite personal. Without the insight provided by introspection, this personal element is missing.

Over and over again, creative workers in advertising and communication will talk about how their own experiences triggered an idea. In the preceding chapter the story was told of the United Airlines employee who bought a fifty-cents-off tube of toothpaste, considered how this offer had led to his buying an extra tube and becoming a regular user, and applied this to United's after-strike situation to develop a dramatically successful 50 percent-off coupon promotion. In a later chapter the story is told of the ad copywriter Jerry Della Femina and his art director realizing that their audience of retirement fund managers were terribly overworked and pressured, just as the two admen were. They turned this introspection realization into an extremely successful campaign![3] In all areas of marketing communication, the fruits of introspection are many.

SEGMENTATION FOR COMMUNICATION

Who is the target for communication? To paraphrase Lincoln, it is possible to communicate to some of the people all of the time and all of the people some of the time, but you can't communicate to all of the people all of the time. What this means is that there are virtually no communication campaigns designed to reach or capable of reaching all consumers well.

Even campaigns for soft drinks like Coca-Cola, which might be found in virtually all types of media and reach nearly all of us in some way weekly, reach certain people with greater effect, just because of the way they are designed. As introspection demonstrates, you cannot communicate with someone you do not know. And it is impossible to communicate with two or more very different people who have different needs, experiences, and ways of seeing the world. The person or advertisement that tries such communication ends up failing to communicate with anyone.

The reason for segmentation, then, is to find large groups of potential buyers, users, voters, and so forth, who are similar enough to appreciate the same communication. Segmentation is done at the time of developing a product. Further work on it is needed during the life cycle as communication is being developed. To understand the best segment for a product is to know the person with whom one is communicating.

Economic Basis For Segmentation

The clearest justification for segmentation is an economic one, similar to the marginal economic approach to budgeting mentioned in Chapter 2. This approach would dictate that resources or communication effort should be put first against a particular person or segment if that segment is likely to make the greatest response. And money should continue to be spent against that segment until the value of the response is less than the expenditure. Then the campaign should move to the next most responsive segment.

In almost every situation it is possible to find greater response for some individual segment than for the population as a whole.

Aside from the problem even the largest company has of spreading its money too thin, obvious weaknesses would be found in a campaign that attempted to reach and communicate with everyone equally. Much of the money would be wasted against, for instance, people who simply could not use the product. Thus segmentation is inevitable. It is just more economically sensible if it is planned.

Resource-Allocation and Self-selection Uses

Segmentation actually works in two ways. One is similar to the economic approach of *resource allocation.* Thus, certain segments are sent messages because those people are the most likely to respond. In advertising or sales promotion there is an obvious application when mailings are sent to a list of addresses of just people who own a certain type of automobile. Certain magazines, such as *Prevention,* deliver a particular type of audience very efficiently. That audience may correspond to the segment an advertiser is trying to reach.

The other segmentation strategy occurs because it is never possible to direct a message to exactly the right audience or segment. Television advertising is used because it reaches so many people at a relatively low cost per person reached. But it is not possible to direct advertising to a target segment with television in the same way as with direct mail or a special-interest magazine. Thus the advertising is designed for *self-selection* segmentation. That is, those people in the target segment who are in the total audience self-select themselves to be exposed to the advertising because it fits their needs. In a sense, segmentation occurs because the message itself constitutes an overlapping field of experience between the communicator and the people of the target segment. And this occurs for publicity, personal selling, and sales promotion in addition to advertising.

Of course, both uses of segmentation—resource allocation and self-selection—occur in every communication campaign.

Publics, Marketing Segments vs. Consumer Segments

All types of marketing communicators must be concerned about their various *publics.* These are the large groups of people who may or may not actually buy or use the market offering but may affect and be affected by the communicating organization. Publics are, as was pointed out in the first chapter, of greater concern to public-sector marketing organizations than to consumer or industrial ones. A urban mass-transit organization that is planning to introduce a new mass-transit plan, for instance, must be concerned not only with commuters but also with the commercial business public, the real estate and housing public, the government public, the mass-media public, the consumer organizations public, the investment public. Sometimes relatively simple, economical innovations like a carpool–bus lane on a freeway run into more trouble with these publics than complex, costly ones like new transit lines that might bring in business, increase housing values, and so forth.

Often consumer and industrial organizations find that their communication programs have had an unintended effect on some public they had not originally considered. Certain lines in advertising can offend particular racial, ethnic, or sex groups and must be changed because of the resulting uproar.

It is also true that communication can be directed at certain segments of particular publics. Publics are larger than segments. Some decision is made on publics for communication before segmentation is addressed. Since the market offering is always designed for the user, the issue of publics does not normally surface for consumer or industrial marketing until the communication stage. Then the issue is one of whether there should be a campaign for each of these publics or a general corporate campaign. In an award-winning corporate campaign for ITT, the target list included that

☐ General Public
☐ Business Community
☐ Financial and Investment Community
☐ Minority Groups
☐ Professional Community
☐ Academic Community
☐ Government Community[4]

Within each of these groups, certain segments are obvious targets. Even if resource allocation does not accomplish this, the design of messages will lead to self-selection by particular segments. Which publics and what segments within those publics are most likely to be reached by the television commercial and ads in Figure 5-1?

Marketing segments constitute another concept that should be kept separate from consumer segmentation, although the concepts are related. Marketing segmentation refers to the segmentation, primarily of trade, that occurs because of the way a firm chooses to do business or the way a product is marketed. For instance, L'egg's hosiery constituted a switch in marketing segment when the line was first introduced. Instead of the typical high-priced specialty and department store distribution for hosiery, L'egg's was relatively low priced and distributed through supermarkets. This was a move into a new marketing segment which involved different product, price, distribution, communication, competition, and, to some extent, consumer segments.

Segment Descriptors

People can be described and put into segments in many ways. This can be done on the basis of (1) where they live, (2) their socioeconomic class, (3) their personality, (4) their product-oriented problems and needs, (5) their product usage rates and characteristics,

and (6) their brand loyalty. All of these types of segmenting *descriptors* are useful in particular situations and for particular communication element decisions.

Geographic. Segments defined by where potential customers live are the easiest to determine and use in a resource-allocation sense. Certainly for personal-selling management, especially for industrial selling, geographic descriptors are enormously helpful. Quotas for salespeople can be set by geographic regions which then constitute broad segments. Certain parts of the country or of the world are more responsive to certain products than are other geographic areas. Concentration of certain industries and climate are two product-usage-relevant factors that are differentially distributed geographically, for instance. It is also true that certain appeals, types of promotions, and publicity approaches differ in efficacy by geographic area or segment.

Unfortunately, geographic segmentation, perhaps the easiest to implement, is also normally the least sensitive in terms of communication response. Since campaigns are generally done throughout the entire trading area of a company—be it regional, national, or worldwide—some other descriptor or combination of descriptors is usually used to get the benefit of segmentation. It should not be forgotten, however, that some of the following descriptors can be used on a geographic basis. People of certain socioeconomic segments, for instance, are likely to be concentrated in certain geographic areas.

Socioeconomic. Such descriptors as education, occupation, age, sex, religion, marital status, size of household, race, income, and ethnic origin can be used to segment the potential market for a product and its communication. These and others are socioeconomic or demographic descriptors.

Usually one of these descriptors alone is not enough. Despite the fact that several of the headlines on the first page of this chapter were for articles based on single sociodemo-

ITT
"Fiber Optics":60

Product: Fiber Optics

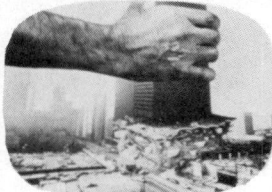

ANNCR (VO): In cities all over the world these days, there's congestion even underground.

The cables beneath the streets carry more and more phone calls, computer data, TV signals.

Do we have to keep tearing up streets for bigger and bigger cables?

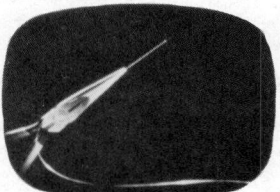

The people of ITT have an answer: optical fibers. Threads of glass, thin as human hair.

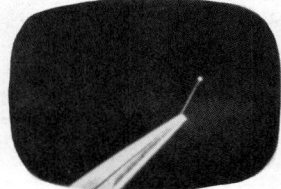

ITT has pioneered a practical way to communicate over these fibers by light—

laser light.

Eventually, today's underground cables...

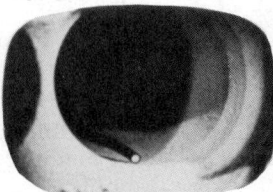

could be replaced by ITT optical fibers...

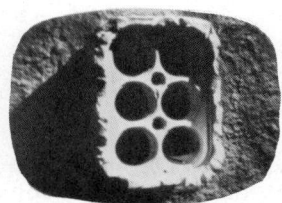

carrying thousands of times more information in the same space.

We could end that congestion below the streets...

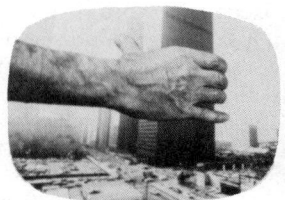

without tearing them up to do it.

(Courtesy of International Telephone and Telegraph)

Figure 5-1a. ITT television commercial—reaching publics with corporate advertising

(*Courtesy of International Telephone and Telegraph*)

Figure 5-1b. *ITT corporate print advertisements*

graphic descriptors such as age (over fifty), marital status and stage (families), and sex (women), these single descriptors alone are not the most sensitive indicators of potential communication response.

It is easy to see how these sociodemographic descriptors, especially when used in combination, can get communication planners closer to the people they wish to reach than would geographic segmentation alone. Data are available, moreover, on the reach of various media to segments with various socioeconomic descriptors. With such data, communication resources can be allocated efficiently. It is also easy to see how the nature of ads, sales promotions, publicity, and personal-selling technique could be varied so that members of key segments by sociodemographic descriptors would self-selectively respond.

One shortcoming of socioeconomic segmentation is that, although it is probably more predictive of product use than geographic segmentation, it is not as sensitive as planners would like. For instance, many communicators believed that the difference between housekeeping only and job-holding wives would be substantial in terms of purchase of labor-saving appliances and frozen foods, reading of magazines and newspapers, and so forth. Typically, however, the differences between these groups has not been

118

found to be great, with the exception, perhaps, of some decline in television viewing among job-holding wives.[5]

Social class is another combined variable that has not been shown to be terribly discriminating. Society is divided into, say, six social classes: upper-upper, lower-upper, upper-middle, lower-middle, upper-lower, and lower-lower. These divisions are usually *not* made with income as a consideration, although income is generally greater for higher social classes. Instead social classes are usually determined by asking people questions about their occupation, education, and age (since educational level means different things to different age groups).

This sort of social classing provides broad hints for communication, but it can be misleading. Many products and brands are purchased across all social classes. And types of communication have broad social-class appeal too.

One sociological researcher, Richard P. Coleman, has long advocated that social class be combined with income for more sensitive segmentation. He suggests that people of certain incomes could be overprivileged, average or underprivileged for certain social classes. An income of $100,000 might thus be overprivileged for some classes but would constitute underprivilege in the upper class. These people, says Coleman, would not be able to own a mansion, a second house, or provide private schooling. They would have to sacrifice, relative to their social-class position.[6]

Socioeconomic or demographic descriptors, then, provide something better than geographic ones but still leave something to be desired in terms of giving a personal understanding of the nature of the audience.

Personality. One hope for communication direction is in measures or descriptors that would allow segmentation by personality. Surely if sociodemographic segmentation is not enough, then certain variables—such as introversion-extroversion, passive-aggressive, achievement or power or affiliation orientation, inner-outer directed, high-low IQ, venturesomeness, innovativeness, and hypochondriasis—should provide a better division of segments for communication purposes. Shouldn't it be true, for instance, that more-aggressive people are more likely to drive certain kinds of cars, higher-IQ people to prefer certain kinds of entertainment, and extroverted–affiliation-oriented people to have particular fashion tastes?

The answer to this multiple-part question is "Somewhat" at best. For some reason it has not been possible to find measures that consistently divide people into personality segments that are truly different in terms of product use or communication sensitivity.[7] This lack of personality measure sensitivity has been shown primarily for low-cost convenience products but also for some durables such as automobiles.

Perhaps the main reason these personality measures are not as valuable as they may seem is that the measures for them are not actually developed for marketing application. Many are used to help people with behavior problems. When measures are developed to fit the consumer situation more precisely, the results are more satisfying.

In the area of new products, for instance, research on the diffusion of innovations proposes that consumers or buyers can be grouped according to their *innovativeness* or receptivity to new products or ideas. These groups, then, become important market segments. One major conclusion of diffusion research is that not only may customers be classified according to their receptivity to innovation but product adoption is a flow in which each customer group is cognizant of and influenced by the experience of those adopting the product before them ("demonstration effect").

The general implications of the theory are that speed of acceptance and market achievement depend on audience selection, the kind of information provided, and the media employed as the product progresses over its life span. The findings and some implications of marketing-communications strategy are summarized in Table 5-1.

One problem with these diffusion-of-innovation adopter categories is endemic to all personality segment descriptors. The problem is that these categories tend to exist *within* the segments that are most profitable for a particular market offering. Thus if a new form of home computer is offered on the market, the innovators are most likely to be found within those segments that are most likely to be in the market for a home computer. That is, there is not a separate segment of innovators (or any of the other adopter categories) that are innovators for a wide range of products. They tend to exist within specific product segments, which have to be determined on more than just personality grounds. When introducing a truly innovative product, therefore, the market must first be segmented for resource allocation. Then communication strategy along the lines of that suggested in Table 5-1 should be used successively over time to reach the particular adopter catego-

ries in the target segments. In this way the various adopter categories can self-select the communication that fits their needs.

Self-selection is typically all that can be hoped for with the use of personality segment descriptors, since adequate comparative data on the personality characteristics of the audiences of the various media are not available. It is only in the general sense that we are able to allocate, say, advertising expenditures to media on the basis of personality of the readers or viewers.

Personality descriptors, then, are probably closer to the consumer than geographic or sociodemographic ones. But adequate marketing-oriented personality measures have not been developed or used consistently with success.

Benefits. This type of segmentation is the first discussed here that is tied to the product or its use. Geographic, demographic, or personality descriptors are developed for other purposes and applied to marketing and communica-

Table 5-1. Adopter Categories, Characteristics, and Communication Implications

Adopter Category	Percentage of Population	Characteristics	Communications Strategy
Innovators	2½	• *Venturesome* • Cosmopolitan • Relate to other innovators	• Utilize published sources more than personal • Scientific • Encourage peer communication
Early adopters	13½	• *Opinion leader* • Secure • Extroverted • Empathy and imagination • Rational	• Utilize mass media, personal selling, and word of mouth • Stress product newness • Use clinical data
Early majority	34	• *Deliberate* • Less willing to take risks	• Show evidence of success and safety
Late majority	34	• *Skeptical* • Insecure • Respond to pressure	• Use personal information sources • Stress acceptance
Laggards	16	• *Traditional* • Introverted • "Eyes on rear-view mirror"	• Stress acceptance and low risk

tion. With benefit segmentation, the segments are developed on the basis of a similarity of needs among the people in a segment.

Benefits is not the only word used to describe these segment descriptors. *Needs, motives, problems, wants,* even *use occasions,* all fit in the same category. Basically the researchers, product management, and communication planners are concerned with the context within which someone would use the product.

The search is to define markets and segments not by products or geographic segment or by the frequent "upscale married working women aged 25–44" but by the reasons women have for using the product in the first place.

As one beer marketer put it, beverage segmentation "must be based on consumers' situation specific motivations or the [beer drinking] occasions."[8]

A cosmetics company president said that the best approach was to develop products based on problems or needs of the consumer. Showing how this approach applied to a successful new introduction, she said, "But then, you almost know it's going to be a success because it solved a problem."[9]

An agency president said, ". . . a market is really an aggregation of problems which certain people have in common . . . the function of advertising in any specific case is the communication of a solution to a problem."[10]

Once again, if a product is well developed, it will reach segments of people who are seeking the benefits it provides. Then the advertising and communication campaign must do just what the agency president said—communicate the product as a solution.

Usage. Consumers can be segmented into heavy, average, and light usage and also nonuser groups for any particular product. The difference between these groups is likely to be quite dramatic both in terms of product consumption and in terms of the types of people they are, the benefits and problems that concern them.

One study of heavy users indicated, for instance, that 17 percent of households accounted for 88 percent of beer purchasing, 39 percent for 90 percent of cola purchasing, and even just 49 percent for 74 percent of toilet tissue sales![11]

What can be done with heavy-user segments like these? Unfortunately options are limited. For one thing the heavy-user group is always changing, with different people moving in and out. Although there are data on product usage that can be related to media audiences, these data are of doubtful reliability and are used for resource allocation—expenditures by media to reach particular segments—primarily because they are the only thing available.

Furthermore there is the danger that in aiming campaigns at the heavy-user group we may be committing what is known as the "majority fallacy." In other words, we may be aiming at the same segment that all our competitors are trying to serve. Unless a distinctive approach can be found, it is likely that our communication will be lost among a number of similar appeals aimed at the same group.

The best way to incorporate usage segmentation into communication planning is to consider all usage segments, not just the heavy-user one. What causes shifts from one segment to another? What are the problems and benefits uppermost in the minds of people who happen to be in each segment? Answers to questions such as these can provide direction for communication that heavy and other usage segments will self-select.

Loyalty. Brand loyalty is the most sensitive and direct of the segmenting variables, because we are segmenting on the variable we wish to affect, purchasing behavior. Here we are concerned with whether consumers are loyal to our brand, loyal to our major competition, or loyal to neither (possibly a nonuser).

In most cases the target for communication is that segment composed of those people who are users but without strong loyalty to any particular brand. These people are movable in the sense that they are not totally committed to any particular brand. Of course we must maintain support from our present loyal customers while probably conceding those who are strongly in favor of the competition. Only a change in basic marketing strategy (usually a product change) is enough to affect those loyal to the competition. Communication efforts typically are not enough.

The size of the movable or switchable segment is enhanced by the fact that in most situations people are not loyal to one single brand or alternative. They have a "consideration class" or "evoked set" of acceptable brands or alternatives that they know and are willing to consider. This is seen most easily in convenience-goods purchasing where a consumer might be purchasing one brand in a fairly consistent way but might actually be willing to consider a variety of other brands. In categories like cake mix, beer, toothpaste, and soft drinks, there may be a substantial amount of switching within a set of brands in a consideration class.

This consideration class phenomenon occurs in other product or service classes also. Even when consumers make a decision such as buying a house, they may have an ideal in terms of location, number of rooms, type of construction, and so forth. But they and the real estate agent soon find that the ideal is actually a flexible and rather large set or consideration class of houses that might be acceptable.

The same is true of industrial purchasing, where the evaluation of bids for a contract is often affected by a variety of factors, making it clear that strict specifications are not really strict. There is actually a consideration class of acceptable alternatives.

In the public sector, one of the strongest examples of the consideration class and switchable segments is in voting behavior. Even in presidential elections there has been a segment of around one-third undecideds, which exists almost up to voting day. In other lesser races this undecided segment may even

be a larger proportion of voters. The job of the political campaign strategist is normally to hold on to those people in favor of his candidate (particularly if the candidate is a strong front-runner with a majority rather than a plurality) while putting the bulk of resources against the switchables segment which will turn the election.

It is clear that if product usage segments are not stable and are changing all the time, there may also be this type of vacillating in and out of loyalty classifications. The job for the communication strategist is to determine the nature of the situation in terms of loyalty. How fluid are the loyalty segments? What are the proportions loyal to specific brands and those who can be classified as switchers? How big is the consideration class for the target segment? Are there levels of consideration classes—top brands, medium brands that might be bought in a price-off situation, and brands seen as low quality and not worth purchasing under any circumstances?

The answers to such questions about brand purchasing and brand loyalty provide a variety of implications for marketing and communication strategy. In some situations, a brand is in a poor loyalty position because consumers correctly perceive the low quality of the product, price, distribution, and even communication. Communication moves in such situations may be dysfunctional. Overemphasis on sales promotion to keep the brand on the market may just further widen the segment eliminating the brand from its consideration class. In such situations, basic surgery or even conception and birth of a new product are necessary.

In most situations, however, communication can help. Share increases are called for in objectives, with a general strategy of holding the presently loyal segment and switching undecideds and product nonusers into the loyal segment. These objectives lead to a substantial total communication budget, a communication mix centering on consumer franchise-building activities like advertising mixed with promotion to generate trial. The general message is one that positions the advertised brand as part of the consideration class first and then as the top brand. There are some reasonable data that indicate brand usage by media, so some segmentation by resource allocation can be done. But the main use of brand loyalty segmentation is to construct the campaign and its elements so that segment members self-select the messages. This is especially important, since brand usage segments, particularly the switchers, are so shifting and changing.

Segment Descriptors: Dilemma and Opportunity. The dilemma is that while brand purchasing loyalty segmenting is the *most* useful and sensitive, it is also the *least* accessible and applicable, particularly in terms of response allocation. Geographic segments are easy to know and apply because one almost needs to do nothing other than look at a map. Sociodemographic descriptors are a bit more difficult, but many are almost a matter of public record. Personality descriptors are even more difficult to get, but perhaps a bit easier than benefit ones, and so on down the list. The difficulty or dilemma, then, is that communication planners have easy access to those descriptor measures that are of least ultimate value to them.

Wherever there is a dilemma there is an opportunity. As Edison said, "Necessity is the mother of invention." In segmenting for communication planning, there have been two "inventions" or solutions to the segmenting descriptor problem.

One solution is *psychographics,* which is essentially the combined use of all the types of descriptors. Through psychographics it is possible to get a detailed insight as to the type of person in the target segment. This insight can lead to efficient communication resource allocation.

The other solution is *attitude structure analysis,* basically a combination and extension of the benefits, usage and loyalty descriptor types. Attitude structure analysis involves determination of benefits, perceptions, and preferences for various usage and loyalty segments. Then communication strategy can be developed to affect the benefits sought and brand perceptions and preferences of each of the target segments.

Psychographics: Meeting the Message Receiver

Ever since Albert Lasker discovered that advertising was "salesmanship in print,"[12] it has been clear that in mass communication we should strive to understand and know our audience in the same way as we might in a personal-selling situation. The whole purpose of segmentation is to group the total potential audience in such a way that we might understand each segment as individuals with all their complexity and reality. Psychographic segmentation is a giant step toward such understanding.

"Psychographic" is really a misnomer. This form of segmentation does not restrict itself just to personality and benefit segment descriptors, the two most clearly psychological types of the descriptors discussed earlier. While psychographic segmentation may have begun with long questionnaires asking about psychological concepts such as attitudes, interests, and opinions, the psychographic approach now includes all types of variables to give accurate and lifelike pictures of people for communication planning.

An indication of the types of variables collected and related to each other to give pictures of consumers is shown in Table 5-2. As indicated in the table, the characterization of heavy users of eye makeup and shortening is given in terms of four descriptors: demographic characteristics; product use; media preferences; and activities, interests, opinions. This is typical of the life-style form of psychographic segmentation. It is easy to see how the two descriptions in Table 5-2 could lead to different appeals, different messages, and different media for an advertising campaign to

Table 5-2. Psychographic Differences between Heavy Users of Eye Makeup and Shortening

Heavy User of Eye Makeup	Heavy User of Shortening
Demographic Characteristics	
Young, well-educated, lives in metropolitan areas	Middle-aged, medium to large family, lives outside metropolitan areas
Product Use	
Also a heavy user of liquid face makeup, lipstick, hair spray, perfume, cigarettes, gasoline	Also a heavy user of flour, sugar, canned lunch meat, cooked pudding, catsup
Media Preferences	
Fashion magazines, *Life, Look,* Tonight Show, adventure program	*Readers Digest,* daytime TV serials, family situation TV comedies
Activities, Interests, and Opinions Agrees more than average with	
I often try the latest hairdo styles when they change	I love to bake and frequently do
I usually have one or more outfits that are of the very latest style	I save recipes from newspapers and magazines
An important part of my life and activities is dressing smartly	The kitchen is my favorite room
I enjoy looking through fashion magazines	I love to eat
I like to feel attractive to all men	I enjoy most forms of housework
I want to look a little different from others	Usually I have regular days for washing, cleaning, etc., around the house
Looking attractive is important in keeping your husband	I am uncomfortable when my house is not completely clean
I like what I see when I look in the mirror	I often make my own or my children's clothes
I comb my hair and put on my lipstick first thing in the morning	I like to sew and frequently do
I take good care of my skin	I try to arrange my home for my children's convenience
Sloppy people feel terrible	Our family is a close-knit group
I would like to take a trip round the world	There is a lot of love in our family
I would like to spend a year in London or Paris	I spend a lot of time with my children talking about their activities, friends, and problems
I like ballet	Everyone should take walks, bicycle, garden, or otherwise exercise several times a week
I like parties where there is lots of music and talk	Clothes should be dried in the fresh air and out-of-doors
I like things that are bright, gay, and exciting	It is very important for people to wash their hands before eating every meal
I do more things socially than do most of my friends	You should have a medical checkup at least once a year
I would like to have a maid to do the housework	I would rather spend a quiet evening at home than go out to a party
I like to serve unusual dinners	I would rather go to a sporting event than a dance
I am interested in spices and seasonings	
If I had to choose, I would rather have a color television set than a new refrigerator	
I like bright, splashy colors	
I really do believe that blondes have more fun	

SOURCE: William D. Wells and Arthur D. Beard, "Personality and Consumer Behavior," in *Consumer Behavior: Theoretical Sources,* ed. Scott Ward and Thomas Robertson (Englewood Cliffs, N.J.: Prentice-Hall, 1973), p. 195. Reprinted by permission of Prentice-Hall, Inc., Englewood Cliffs, New Jersey.

reach these two types of people. It is likely that the mix of the communication campaign would be different too—with publicity and personal selling (in a department or specialty store) being added to advertising for the heavy users of eye makeup; and sales promotions such as coupons and contests being added for the heavy users of shortening.

Since psychographic segmentation is difficult to measure in a reliable way, it should only be used for the general directions it provides for communication planning—rather than for precise resource allocation. It provides limits and directions rather than precise population percentages that can be depended upon.

In a sense, psychographic segmentation adds information to that which comes from a review of product and market strategy development research and from introspection. Psychographic information can provide confirmation and expansion of this earlier work to the point where communication targets are known in a very intimate way. One example of such a portrait or "personal profile" of a target segment individual (the people are actually fictitious) is shown in Figure 5-2, which is concerned with the all-purpose cleaner market. It is so representative of the mixture of introspection and data that the advertising agency people who wrote this profile cited four data sources and then invoked their introspection citing "the personal experience of a third generation Czech and a third generation Italian."

The degree of understanding shown in Figure 5-2 is the goal of segmentation. The team at the company and at the agency should always attempt to put down on paper, as a guide for everyone working on the campaign, a characterization of target segment individuals. Then the members of the team will begin to know the people they are trying to reach with a solution to consumer problems. Going back to the definition of communication in Chapter 1, we are trying to understand the "field of experience" of the target segment or segments. In this way campaign messages of all types can constitute overlapping fields of experience.

Communication planners should not be overinfluenced by reported trends in segments. The headlines on the first page of this chapter having to do with women, older consumers, the me-generation, cynical consumers, sensual consumers, and the life styles of the 1980s are all examples of such trend information. Psychographic segmentation can provide a balancing of such emphases on particular trends. For instance, although there seemed to be a boom in jogging and running in the late 1970s, a psychographic study at the time indicated that a very small proportion of the population actually ran regularly as recreation. Running was eclipsed by more standard forms of exercise in terms of people ever doing it and in terms of ratings of importance. At the same time the small proportions of, and slight increases in, running may have been critical for certain communication situations. Segmentation for communication planning must be done very carefully and thoroughly.

Psychographic segmentation can be critical in industrial as well as consumer marketing. But if communication planners think there is only one target segment in an industrial-marketing situation, they are sadly mistaken. Careful psychographic segmentation in the industrial field may indicate that there are more than one or several segments requiring quite different approaches.

In Figure 5-3 there are two ads for Spectra-Physics, a laser products company. The "Laserman" cartoon ad was meant for the construction industry. The campaign stood out in the magazines and led to personal-selling and sales promotion innovations with Spectra-Physics salesmen wearing jackets that were of the same yellow color as Laserman's costume.

The Spectra-Physics ad for the scientific community also used art, but of a very modern, almost science fiction kind—again perfectly meeting an industrial psychographic segment.

Rosemary and Frank LaSala were childhood sweethearts. They grew up on the same block in Bayonne, New Jersey; attended the same schools; dated steady since they were 16 and, to no one's surprise, were married right after high school. Frank got a job at Bayway refinery at age 19 and by "working his tail off and being a spunky little guinea" (as he puts it) was next in line for shop foreman at age 25. Rosemary bore and raised three children (they wanted at least one more, but the doctor advised against it). And she cared for her home—a simple but attractive two-family house in Bayonne that Frank's father had built and given them as a wedding present.

Now their oldest was 6 and all were out of diapers so Rosemary had a little more time to herself. One of her neighbors suggested she get a parttime job next year when her youngest entered kindergarten but Rosemary couldn't see that. "Frank's making a decent salary, $12,000 plus overtime. We've got the rent from the family upstairs, and the house and family keep me going all day."

In fact, Rosemary took great pride in her home. She did some cleaning just about every day, but once a week she gave it a thorough cleaning—all the floors, kitchen cabinets, vacuumed the upholstery and so on. That day was usually Thursday—Frank's bowling night and her night to have the girls over ("just to relax and gab a little"). Rosemary's parents were first generation Italian, as were Frank's, and Rosemary's attitude toward her housekeeping was shaped by her mother. Her whole world revolves around caring for her house and her family. It bothers her if Frank has to go to work with his coveralls stained from his work at Bayway (even if it doesn't bother him). It bothers her if everyone doesn't eat a meal. It bothers her because it's a reflection on her role as a mother and a wife. But Rosemary feels she's less of a "slave to her house," more modern in her outlook than her mother.

"My mother used to say 'you can eat off this kitchen floor.' And it was true. She scrubbed that floor on her hands and knees with a brush, a bar of Fels Naptha soap and ammonia water. And then she'd put down newspapers in a little path through the kitchen to keep it clean. That's the way she cared for the whole house. She always worried about company arriving unexpectedly. It had to be clean. I'm not that bad. I use a mop, except for the really tough spots. I try a lot of different products, unlike my mother who stuck to a few tried and true ones. But I think some of the old ones are still the best. Nothing beats a powder like Spic & Span for floors and walls. If there's really tough dirt, I'll add Lestoil or Mr. Clean to the Spic & Span or even some ammonia. On door knobs and light switches I use a spray. I don't care what the TV says, there's no such thing as one cleaner for everything. You've got to use different ones for different jobs. They make it look easy on TV, but if you want a clean house, you've got to do the work. Like they say 'no rinsing,' but I always rinse. Otherwise you're just wiping the dirt around. I like the way my house smells when it's really clean. And Frank notices it too. He'll say, 'Hey, honey, you've been working today haven't you?' I make believe I didn't hear that, but it makes me feel kind of proud. I know I'm doing my job."

Figure 5-2. *Personal lifelike description of an all-purpose detergent segment member*

ATTITUDE STRUCTURE ANALYSIS

Once segments are discovered and understood in an intimate, lifelike, and significant way, it is important to understand how these segment people think about the problems and market offerings very specifically.

This is done through attitude structure analysis. In this type of analysis, target segment attitudes are determined in terms of importance of product attributes along with perceptions of presence or lack of these attributes in competing brands and the resulting preferences. Such analysis is possible because there is typically one or just a few target segments with

Figure 5-3a. Spectra-Physics ad for construction market

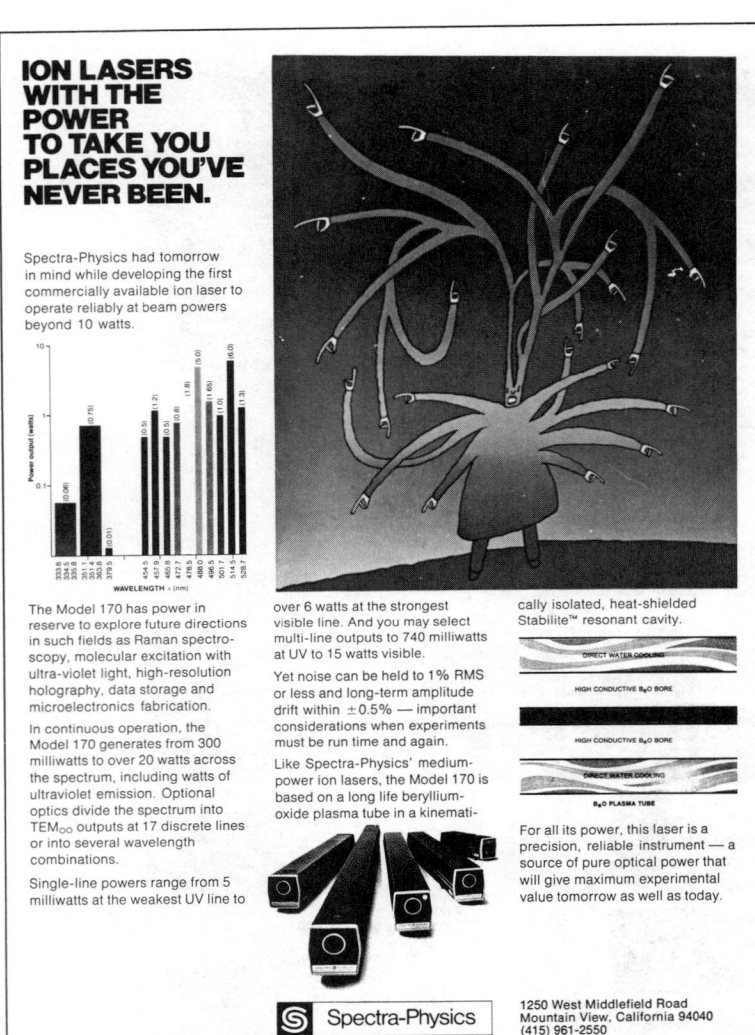
(Courtesy of Laser Instruments Division, Spectra-Physics)

Figure 5-3b. *Spectra-Physics ad for scientific segment*

quite homogenous attitudes in terms of attribute importance, perceptions, and preferences.

Product Development Technique Contributions

Good products are developed on the basis of consumer needs and problem solving. In order to develop good products, marketers have developed a number of techniques that can indicate the attitude structure for the target segment(s). The preceding chapter, for instance, reviewed ASSESSOR, a new product developed early market evaluation approach that is representative of a number available to marketers. One part of ASSESSOR is a perceptions and preferences interview and model which can provide direction to attitude structure analysis for communication planning.

Product development is sometimes

based on *perceptual mapping, product structure studies,* which also provide attitude structure information. In this research, consumer preferences and patterns of competition are observed, usually in large-scale samples. Then a smaller group of consumers representing each relevant segment indicate how they perceive the brands and products presented in the market and, possibly, how they also react to some new product concepts. These perceptions are indicated simply by the consumers indicating how similarly or differently they see various brands, products, and concepts. Then these similarity evaluations can be put into a perceptual map to give a physical "picture" of how consumers perceive a market.

Another product development tool that provides attitude structure information is called *conjoint analysis.* In this procedure focus groups and various forms of interviewing are used in order to determine what product attributes are considered by consumers. Then in one conjoint analysis approach, product descriptions with all levels of all the attributes are rated by target segment consumers. The ratings of the descriptions are then mathematically manipulated to indicate the most popular dimensions and/or levels of dimensions and can aid, among other things, product or service development and communication.

In one conjoint analysis study of airline service to Paris, for example, twenty-seven different flight descriptions or profiles were evaluated on a seven-point scale of desirability by members of the segment of people who had flown at least once across the Atlantic in the twelve months before the study. Two of the profiles follow. If you were going to Paris on business, which flight would you choose?

☐ A B-707 flown by British Airways that will depart within two hours of the time you would like to leave and that is often late in arriving in Paris. The plane will make two intermediate stops, and it is anticipated that it will be 50 percent full. Flight attendants are "warm and friendly" and you would have a choice of two movies for entertainment.
☐ A B-747 flown by TWA that will depart within four hours of the time you would like to leave and that is almost never late in arriving

in Paris. The flight is nonstop, and it is anticipated that the plane will be 90 percent full. Flight attendants are "cold and curt," and only magazines are provided for entertainment.

The respondent ratings of the twenty-seven descriptions indicated that only four of the attributes implied by the descriptions were important. These were departure time relative to ideal, punctuality of arrival, number of stops en route, and crew attitudes. The other four—airline, aircraft, passenger load, and entertainment—did not produce big differences in evaluation of the alternative flights.

By the way, if you chose the second flight, the TWA one, for your trip to Paris, you were close to the average of the respondents in the study, who preferred that particular TWA flight over the British Airways one by a small margin.[13]

Perceptual mapping and conjoint analysis are only two of a number of interview and analysis techniques that can be used to produce statistical evidence of target segment attitude structure. All such techniques assume that consumers can accurately verbalize in some way their perceptions of and preferences for products. If consumers cannot do this verbalizing, then it may be that they do not have detailed attitude structures in relation to the product to be advertised. Such situations are rare for the target segment, however. And the techniques are such that the verbalization task is not too difficult.

Perceptual mapping and conjoint analysis are each appropriate for different marketing situations. Perceptual mapping requires just simple judgments about product-brand similarity. It best fits those situations such as grocery store purchasing where choices are not reasoned thoroughly and there are a fairly large number of brands that could be considered. The perceptual-mapping technique takes the similarity judgments in such situations and decomposes them into the dimensions or attributes on which consumers are making judgments—even if consumers actually could not accurately verbalize what these attributes are.

Conjoint analysis, on the other hand, best fits those situations in which there is a reasoned choice, like the international airlines flight. In such situations, consumers can indicate which attributes are considered, descriptions made up of salient attributes can be formulated, and consumers can make realistic judgments of the descriptions.

No matter what the situation, however, description of attitude structure for the market offering and competitors can provide direction for campaign creative strategy.

Attitude Structure Strategy Implications

Attitude structure analysis provides information on the attributes that are important to the target segment, just how important each attribute is, and how the consumer perceives the advertised product and its key competition. If campaign planners have this kind of information, they can then decide what the campaign should attempt to do.

If the campaign is for TWA, for instance, and the results of the conjoint analysis about Paris flights did not turn up "speed of check-in" as an important attribute, the campaign strategy might be to *add that attribute* to the target segment's decision process.

On the other hand, respondents did not see "type of aircraft" as very important while TWA had the slightly favored 747 type. Thus the campaign strategy might be to *increase the importance of that attribute* for the target segment. Campaign messages showing the advantages of 747s, particularly TWA's, would be appropriate.

TWA is already doing very well in the previous description on one of the most important attributes, "punctuality." Thus the communication should let target segments know about TWA's punctuality. This strategy is called *increasing favorable perceptions*.

Note that the same strategy could be used for another important attribute, "crew attitude," if TWA had a plus in that area. Unfortunately, the description earlier indicated that the TWA crew was "cold and

curt." So crew attitude would have to be improved first *and then* advertised. The worst thing that could be done, of course, would be to advertise an attribute that the product, service, or idea does not have. This would be a mistake both morally and in terms of marketing success.

One other strategy TWA might use would involve making a clear comparison with competition. If punctuality is important to the target segment and TWA is normally on time while British Airways is often late, advertising strategy can be used to *decrease the rating of competition on that attribute.*

There are other strategies which will be discussed in relation to "positioning" in Chapter 9. What is important right now is that knowledge of target segment attitude structure is necessary before creative strategy planning can be done. In fact, even marketing objectives and budgets can be planned on the basis of attitude structure. A market offering already perceived in a favorable way by a vast majority of consumers, like TWA on punctuality, needs only a maintenance marketing objective and relatively low-cost reminder advertising. But if the task is to add an attribute to consumers' consideration, the total communication budget will be much larger.

Attitude structure analysis should be done even if there are no precise quantitative figures on attributes considered, attribute importance, and perceptions of market alternatives. No matter whether communication planners have data or not, they have to make assumptions of target segment attitude structure in developing creative strategy. Note, for instance, that four creative strategies for TWA were discussed above without referring to exact numbers.

Summary: Attitude Structure Analysis

Attitude structure analysis is a method for determining why certain target segments purchase or do not purchase the market offering at various rates. Once attitude structure, the "why" of purchasing, is known, it is possible to plan communication more precisely.

Simply stated, attitude structure analysis is an attempt to link perceptions and preferences. It is assumed that attitudes are essentially predispositions (preferences) to respond given certain situations and that the situations are defined by the way people perceive them (perceptions). Thus the communication planner analyzing segments takes essentially four steps:

1. Define groups that differ in past or future propensity to consume the product, use the service, or act on the idea you are supporting. This can be done by questionnaire, by past sales (especially possible in industrial marketing), and by general analysis of both of the above factors. The groupings discussed earlier—in terms of heavy to light and ours versus switchers versus theirs—are adequate for this purpose and can be stated quite tentatively.
2. Determine the perceptions of the different preference-consumption groups formed in the first step. This again can be done tentatively and can be based on the judgment and experience of the analyst. Or this judgment can be tempered by marketing research data. The kind of perception information necessary has two general parts:
   a. Perceptions relevant to the product class, the attributes sought, and the relative importance of the attributes in the product or service category; and
   b. The perceptions of the individual brands or company offerings that relate to the product class offerings. Thus the assumption here is that the product class perceptions define the buyer's need, and the perceptions of the brands indicate how well each brand fulfills the need.
3. Adjust the preference groups established in the first step by the perceptions information developed in the second step. The goal is to establish homogenous groups. The theory here is that buyers will prefer those products and brands they see as fitting their needs. So the different purchasing groups formed in the first step should be homogenous in terms of the perception analysis of the second step. But it

may be that groups with slightly lower or higher propensity to consume may be brought into the main ones on the basis of their perceptions. Or it may be that the main preference groups have imbedded in them more than one perception group. So the groups might have to be split.
4. Analyze the resulting segments in terms of their typical purchase and use behavior and resultant communication needs.

THE CONSUMER DECISION PROCESS

After segmentation and attitude structure analysis, one more type of consumer analysis should be done before marketing communication. This next step is analysis of the decision process taken by the typical consumer in each segment. If the campaign coordinator knows the steps the consumer takes to make a decision, then it will be possible to plan the campaign to provide information for each relevant step. Fortunately there has been evidence that introspection and relatively simple research techniques such as focus group interviewing can provide a picture of the buyer decision process which is accurate enough for communication planning.

The Typical Process

It is feasible to determine the buying process in individual situations without extensive research, because virtually all consumers go through the same steps in a typical decision process. Not all of these steps are relevant for each particular purchase. But they all occur at some time in a consumer's experience with each product, service, or idea market offering.

There are four common steps:

1. Developing need
2. Searching for and comparing alternatives
3. Purchasing
4. Postpurchase

Developing Need. At some point consumers must realize they have a need, a problem, or an occasion for which they require a solution in the form of a product, a service, or an idea. Once this happens, it is necessary to learn more about exactly what the need requires or could require. High-school seniors may know they have a need for further education. But then they have to consider what kind of education, whether it is important that schooling be close to home, if it has to be inexpensive, if it should be similar to what their parents had, and so forth. In short, developing need consists primarily of determining which attributes are important and how important they are in making the eventual purchase decision.

The need development stage tends to be important in communicating with particular segments—most easily classified as the nonuser or the new consumer segment. Nonusers could be nonusers because they have not paid attention to the problem or have not developed their need sufficiently to require the attributes the product offers. People who do not drink wine may not be aware of all the attributes it might possess. As they try some and like it, they begin to realize that it has many attributes they first ignored.

Advertising, in particular, is a useful communication tool because it can help the consumer to understand the detailed nature of the problem, the attributes that should be considered. Such advertising is sometimes called *primary demand* advertising, since it attempts to stimulate demand for the product class rather than an individual brand. But some of this advertising can emphasize individual brand or *selective demand,* as would TWA advertising that attempted to add an attribute to consumers' consideration like speedy check-in, which was a real plus only for TWA.

Other parts of the communication mix can be important at this first step. Promotion and sampling can force a trial that might develop need. Publicity or public relations can provide information about attributes and the broad range of alternatives for nonusers or new consumers. Personal selling sometimes is the only way to jog consumers into considering a particular need. Although in most cases advertising is more efficient at the developing need stage, personal selling seems to be almost required for certain segments in developing need for such products and services as encyclopedias, vacuum cleaners, and insurance.

Searching for and Comparing Alternatives. One part of need development is the determination of the general classes of alternatives available for satisfying a need. There is a constant mental interplay between need, attributes, and possible alternatives. Once a high-school senior learns that there are colleges near ski slopes or trade schools that concentrate on preparing people for stage careers, whole new sets of attributes come to mind. Then these attributes lead to a search for more types of alternatives, which leads to the discovery of more attributes.

At the search and comparison stage, the consumer has some idea as to the general class of product desired. The attributes and attribute importance weights usually eliminate most product classes. High-school seniors may find themselves comparing just Ivy League schools. Intermediate-level wine consumers may be looking among high-quality Zinfandels. Office managers could be investigating small business computers and, as another broad alternative, computer service bureaus that sell computer time. Home buyers may have restricted their search to houses in a particular geographic area, price range, and architectural style. Similar narrowing will occur for other choices.

While the need development stage consisted mainly of determining attributes and their importance in general, the search and comparison stage is done to form perceptions of alternatives on those attributes. For the airline flight example this would mean, for instance, that the potential passenger would know that punctuality was important. Using the telephone to communicate with Paris and sailing to Europe have been eliminated. Now, at search and comparison, he or she would try to find out how punctual each of the individual airlines were on their Paris flights.

The best strategy for marketers at this stage is to have a product, price, and distribution that perfectly fits the needs of the target segment. Then if communication is adequate, that target segment will make a favorable comparison of the market offering. Sometimes this can lead to direct comparisons within individual ads as is shown in Figure 5-4.

Purchasing. The act of purchasing itself can be quite complex. Consumers in most situations need help in making the decision to actually purchase. This calls for personal selling so the sale can be closed. In other situations where there are almost no salespeople, such as in the supermarket, sales promotion incentives and point-of-purchase materials can help to move the consumer to purchase state. This is a stage in which advertising and publicity are of minimal help. Other than urging the consumer to contact or welcome a salesperson or go to a store, advertising can do relatively little at this stage where many very personal decisions and accommodations are made.

Postpurchase. For many consumers this stage is the critical one of evaluation. The product must stand on its own, of course, but many communication moves can be made to ensure that the postpurchase experience is a good one.

For one thing, it is true that those people who own or are using a particular product or service are more likely to be exposed and pay attention to its advertising. All types of communication should assure customers that they have made a good choice and guide them toward satisfactory use. With good ex-

perience, a powerful form of two-person communication called *word-of-mouth advertising* (although it is not advertising) takes place. Good products, good service, and good communication can encourage customers to spread the word with personal testimonials to their friends.

Varieties of Decision Making

Introspect for a moment. When making a purchase, how often do you actually go meticulously through all four stages of decision making? Do you develop your need, then search and compare, then purchase, and then evaluate in postpurchase every time you buy? When are you thorough and when are you more impulsive?

It is questions like these that lead advertisers, marketers, and researchers to consider how the flow of decision making varies in different situations. As you would discover if you answered the questions above carefully, in some situations—such as in buying a home, buying a stereo, or making an industrial purchase—all the stages are done quite thoroughly. In other situations, when you are making an infrequent but economically unimportant decision, you go through the stages but with none of the intensity discussed earlier. In still other situations, the need development, search, and postpurchase activities are almost nonexistent and repeated purchases are made.

The consumer behavior theorists Howard and Sheth call these types of decision making *extensive problem solving, limited problem solving,* and *routinized buyer behavior.*[14] The names are quite descriptive of the situations. What is amazing is that we consumers use the "limited" and "routinized" approaches for the vast majority of our decisions. It is not that we are being sloppy or irrational. Partly it is because we simply could not do extensive problem solving for every purchase. Also, it is because few purchases are important enough

The NP-L7 with Automatic Document Feeder:

Canon's proof that actions speak louder than words.

	One copy from one original	One copy from ten originals	One copy from thirty originals	Ten sets of ten page report*
Canon NP-L7 with ADF	14.0 sec.	32.0 sec.	72.0 sec.	284.0 sec.
Savin 780	7.5 sec.	34.0 sec.	94.0 sec.	465.0 sec.
Xerox 3100	12.0 sec.	102.0 sec.	302.0 sec.	528.0 sec.
Xerox 3600-I with 10 Bin Sorter	11.5 sec.	115.0 sec.	345.0 sec.	288.0 sec.

(Courtesy of Canon U.S.A. Inc., Copier Div.)

This offer's been in effect since last November, and we haven't had to give away a single copymaker.

AM beats Xerox or you get our copymaker free for a year.*

(Courtesy of Addressograph Multigraph)

Figure 5-4. *Direct comparison ads appropriate for consumers in the search and comparison stage*

---

to merit it. Finally, we seldom do extensive problem solving, because at some time in the past or over a period of time we have gathered the information and made all the comparisons that allow present purchases to be made with a minimum of effort, routinely.

The varieties of decision making have implications for objectives, budgets, and the nature of communication. If the target segment is engaged in extensive problem solving, many of the suggestions of the preceding section should be followed. Communication budgets should be large per prospect, although possibly moderate in total. Messages

would be full of detail and be carried by salespeople and print media. Effort would be made at almost all stages of the buyer behavior process.

With limited and routinized behavior, however, there is an effort to find the stage of the process at which communication can have an effect—usually advertising at the search-comparison stage and/or sales promotion at the purchase stage. Budgets are small per prospect per exposure, but larger overall than with extensive problem solving. Messages are brief in the hope that the product name and some attribute get through to add to the consumer's store of information. Rather than personal selling and print, it is advertising and sales promotion and the broadcast media that are most important.

Flow Charting and Simulation

The communication planner should not stop with identification of any particular situation as being extensive, limited, or routine. These labels can provide direction for specific analysis. But, in the end, communication is planned best when labels are avoided and those working on the campaign have an intimate feeling for exactly what target segment consumers are going through as they make decisions.

This can be developed verbally in the form of *written descriptions* of the steps target segment consumers take. Sometimes it is also possible to use a more formal *flow chart,* a step-by-step drawing of consumers' steps. Finally, it is possible for the flow chart to be turned into a *computer simulation,* which mathematically estimates how the market of consumers will behave if the implications and assumptions of the descriptions and flow charts are accepted.

These three techniques—written descriptions, flow charts, and computer simulation—are closely related. It is not necessary to get into flow charting and computer simulation, but each successive technique provides greater power with which to make marketing and communication decisions.

An example is provided by a case called Hinesbury Mills.[15] The name Hinesbury Mills is a fictitious one made of three competitors' names: Duncan *Hines,* Pills*bury* and General *Mills.* The case depicts an actual situation. Hinesbury Mills had to make a series of decisions relating to its cake-mix line which was foundering in the market. Essentially it needed to predict how consumers would react to various new-product formulations it and its competitors had developed.

Description of the cake-mix buying process was accomplished by introspection, past knowledge of the market, and use of the results of several focus group interviews. The management team sketched out the following steps:

☐ First, the consumer determines the use opportunity for the cake mix. That is, will it be used for snack purposes, for an everyday family meal, or for a special occasion.
☐ Second, acceptable or desired attributes of the cake mix are determined for each use. The key attributes were thought to be price, quality, convenience-involvement, and taste-texture. These differed in terms of acceptable levels, depending on the use opportunity.
☐ Third, consumers either had or developed perceptions of each product and brand alternative worth considering before going to the store. These perceptions were not general good-bad but rather on the basis of the four attributes.
☐ Fourth, the process of purchasing in the store was one of buying a brand that matched needs in terms of acceptable attributes for a particular cake-serving occasion. But, importantly, the executives had observed the power of price-off deals and believed that the matching process was heavily affected by them.
☐ Fifth, in some cases it was not possible to find a cake mix that matched need. Then either the perceived need was changed or the cake mix was not purchased.

Aside from the fact that this description could be classified as a *limited problem-solving* version of the typical decision-making process, it in itself could have a number of product and communication strategy implications. This is particularly true if the description is made more detailed—which it was—with such information as the proportion of purchases for each of the various serving occasions and the numerical importance of the attributes for each type of situation.

A logical flow chart is the description in the form of a chart that shows the precise relationships between and within steps. Such a chart can illustrate inconsistencies, show

when more information is needed, and highlight the points at which marketing and communication effort is needed.

One chart developed from the Hinesbury Mills case is shown in Figure 5-5. Note
that the first three steps are quite straightforward and depend on the proportion of individuals in each use occasion, related to the
attribute importances, related to the probability of various brand perceptions. Predictions of what biases consumers will have when
they enter the store depend, then, on the
quality of information, on the occasion percentages, attribute weights, and brand perceptions. If these are accurate and this depiction of the need development and search-
comparison in the cake-mix process is correct,
there are some clear alternatives for communication—such as affecting occasion percentages, attribute importance, or brand perceptions.

Some of the most interesting new implications come from the flow chart in the in-
store purchasing situation. Here the more detailed implications of the description's emphasis on the importance of deals is seen. Big
deals and small deals seem to have the power
to override pre-shopping-trip perception-preference matches. And there is some possibility
that perceived need may be changed or that
no cake mix will be bought. Just this in-store
part of the flow chart underscores the importance of sales promotion in the communication mix.

A computer simulation involves attach-
ing numbers and probabilities to each stage of
the flow chart. Then these probabilities are
mathematically combined to produce a number of simulated consumers and shopping
trips in the computer. The simulations developed for Hinesbury Mills could provide an
estimate of the shares of market that would be
expected for each competing brand-product
given certain estimated inputs.

The Hinesbury Mills simulation accurately predicted the market shares for two
types of new cake-mix entry. Once this sort of

positive result is achieved and repeatedly
confirmed, it is possible to use the simulation
for other purposes, including communication
planning. For instance, the model used an estimate of 20 percent for the proportion of
times a special occasion was the use for a cake
mix. Communication planners could run the
model with, say, 25 or 30 percent to see if a
campaign urging the use of cake mix for special occasions would be worth the effort in
terms of share for the campaign's brands.

The same kind of test run could be done
for possible changes that could be caused by
campaigns emphasizing various attributes or
perceptions of the brands themselves. Sales
promotions could be planned by seeing the
effect of increasing or decreasing the probability that in-store deals would be Hinesbury
ones or be seen.

Such model runs would give planners
some idea as to what share objectives might
be achieved by various campaign effects on
steps in the consumer decision process. It is
then up to the planners to determine if it is
economically possible to achieve these effects
with communication.

Everyday Decision Process Analysis

It certainly is not always possible to do a
computer simulation. It is always possible,
however, to take the decision process into account with descriptions of the steps that target segment consumers go through. Even a
successful simulation should be tempered by
careful consideration of real consumers and
all the little problems they have that cannot
be covered by a simulation. Many of the
breakthroughs in advertising and communication involve getting consumers to change
the way they think and act with regard to a
particular need or problem area.

Such breakthroughs, of course, come
from a basic understanding of the situation,
which is represented well by such a simulation. The only way to start the creative pro-

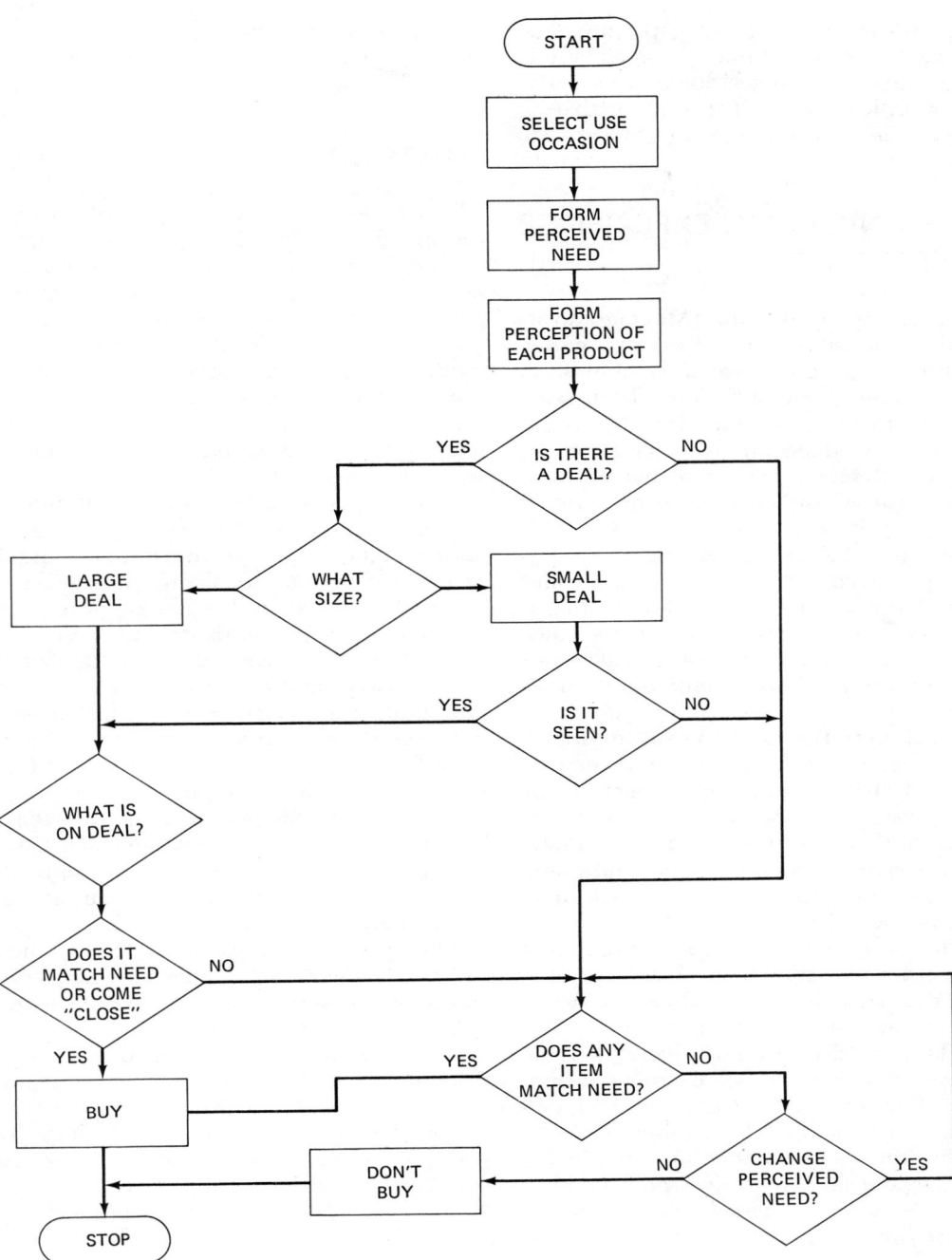

Figure 5-5. *Hinesbury Mills flow chart of the cake-mix decision process*
From Eskin and Montgomery, "Hinesbury Mills," p. 11. Reprinted by permission of Scientific Press.

cess is with outstanding fact gathering. The consumer analysis—segmentation, attitude structure analysis, and decision process analysis—is a critical aspect of this fact gathering before marketing communication.

COMMUNICATION EXPERIENCE AND RESEARCH

It will be recalled that Maytag and its advertising agency followed certain guidelines from their past experience and from communication research findings. Their experience told them, for instance, that *Life* magazine was a good beginning vehicle for the campaign. Research indicated that ads that created a curious disbelief would be quite effective.

At the before-marketing-communication stage the company people should transmit, and the agency people should review, whatever experience and research have shown to be effective communication practice—for this brand and for similar communication situations.

This suggestion is not meant to support rigid restrictions on advertising and communication. In most cases a requirement for the use of a specific phrase in every ad is a hindrance. And rigidly staying with essentially the same budget, communication mix, and media schedule year after year can lead to missed opportunities.

But, once again, the results from past experience and research form a base from which new creative directions can be developed. In each of the following parts of this book there is a discussion of what experience and research tell about such decisions as budget mix, message positioning and format, and efficiency of various media combinations.

At the before-marketing-communication stage, the share objective and total budget estimate should be based somewhat on experience and research. As the campaign goes

through various stages of development, more and more detailed use of experience and research findings is possible.

SUMMARY

Development and diagnosis of the marketing mix are based largely on consumer concerns, but more detailed consumer analysis is necessary for communication campaign planning. Six broad steps are suggested: review of consumer analysis materials from product and marketing strategy development, introspection, segmentation, attitude structure analysis, decision process analysis, and review of communication experience and research findings.

Introspection involves each communication planner's totally immersing himself or herself in the product, its use, and communication in a very personal way. Introspection can lead to lifelike understanding of the people who are in the campaign audience.

More structured understanding of communication prospects comes through segmentation, attitude structure analysis, and decision process analysis. Segmentation is used to identify communication targets. Attitude structure analysis identifies the way target people think about products, services, ideas, brands, and so forth, in terms of their needs and problems. Consumer decision process analysis identifies the steps people go through in buying a product or service, voting for a candidate, or accepting an idea. Communication can be developed to affect attitude structure at key steps in the decision process of valuable target segment members.

Although the activities described in Chapters 4 and 5 are done before marketing communication, they form a setting for communication that structures everything that goes on in the communication-planning process. In the tradition of the approach to creativity mentioned earlier, the situation analysis, overall objectives, and total budget statement form a rough and flexible framework within which communication planning can be done. In other words, the activities before marketing communication actually state the problem that is to be solved by the new ideas of the communication plan. A good problem statement can go a long way toward a good solution.

ISSUES AND PROJECTS FOR DISCUSSION

1. What is introspection and how is it relevant to communication planning? Introspect about *any two* of the following: McDonald's, home videotape recorders, your local commuter service, contributing to the American Cancer Society, Vantage cigarettes, Green Giant canned peas, Cadillac Seville. From your introspection, what did you learn that may assist you in communication planning?

2. Which publics and which segments within those publics are most likely to be reached by the television commercial and ads in Figure 5-1?

3. Finds ads (or describe broadcast commercials) that seem to be attempting to appeal to each of the six segmenting descriptors (other than psychographics) discussed in this chapter. How effective do you feel each of these ads is? Why or why not?

4. What is psychographic segmentation and what are its advantages and disadvantages in comparison with each of the other six segment descriptors? Can you find an ad of any sort that seems to be appealing to a psychographic segment? How would you characterize this target segment?

5. What are perceptual mapping and conjoint analysis? How might they provide information relevant to communication planners?

6. How can attitude structure analysis affect objectives, budget, and campaign messages?

7. Compare primary and selective demand advertising. How would primary and selective advertising differ for an airline, a television-set marketer, a restaurant?

8. Consider a recent purchase. Did you go through the four stages of decision making at any time in a way that would have affected that purchase? Which of the three types of decision making was this purchase decision? Can you identify times when you used the other two types? What kind of advertising and communication campaign should be directed to "your segment" of purchasers, making decisions in the way you did?

9. Find an advertisement for a cake mix or describe one you have seen on television. How could this be justified by the Hinesbury Mills description, flow chart, and simulation? What alternatives to this ad approach could you suggest? How could the Hinesbury Mills simulation be used to test the validity of your suggestion?

Notes

1. Headlines and captions came from, in order: *Advertising Age,* February 17, 1975, p. 32; *Advertising Age,* June 11, 1979; *E&L Marketing Today,* 16, No. 3 (December 1978), 1; *Palo Alto Times,* June 4, 1979; *Wall Street Journal* cartoon; *Grey Matter,* 49, No. 1 (1978), 3; *Advertising Age,* August 27, 1979, p. 63; *Business Week,* November 19, 1979, p. 194; *Media Science Newsletter,* 1, No. 5 (June 15–30, 1979), 1; *Marketing News,* June 30, 1978, p. 3; *Advertising Age,* September 2, 1974, p. 29; *Advertising Age,* December 3, 1979, p. 59; *Harvard Business Review,* May-June 1978, p. 73; *Advertising Age,* May 21, 1979, p. 59; *Advertising Age,* November 5, 1979, p. 78.

2. Yoram Wind, personal communication, August 1978; and Russ Haley, personal communication, April 1979.

3. Jerry Della Femina, *From Those Wonderful Folks Who Brought You Pearl Harbor; Front-Line Dispatches from the Advertising War* (New York: Simon & Schuster, 1970).

4. *Advertising Campaign Report Newsletter* (New York: American Association of Advertising Agencies, September 1979), p. 2.

5. Myra H. Strober and Charles B. Weinberg, "Use of Strategies to Reduce Time Pressures: Some Non-Differences between Working Wives and Non-Working Wives" Research Paper No. 465 (Graduate School of Business, Stanford University, 1978); and Peter Clarke as quoted in "Researcher Breaks Society into 'Privilege Levels,' " *Advertising Age,* June 11, 1979, p. 20.

6. Richard P. Coleman, "The Significance of Social Stratification in Selling," in *Advertising Management: Selected Readings,* ed. Harper W. Boyd, Jr., and Joseph W. Newman (Homewood, Ill.: Richard D. Irwin, 1965), pp. 205–16; and as quoted in "Researcher Breaks Society into 'Privilege Levels,' " *Advertising Age,* June 11, 1979, p. 20.

7. Harold Kassarjian, "Personality: The Longest Fad," in *Advances in Consumer Research,* ed. William L. Wilkie (Ann Arbor: Association for Consumer Research, 1979), VI, 122–24.

8. Allin W. Proudfoot, quoted in "Audience before Image, Beverage Marketers Urged," *Advertising Age,* August 27, 1979, p. 63.

9. Linda Wachner, quoted in "Max Factor's President Brings Company Back to Basics in Cosmetics Market," *San Francisco Business Journal,* 1, No. 13 (Week of December 3, 1979), 18.

10. Tom Dillon, "Markets Are Customer Problems, Not Geography or Demographics," *Advertising Age,* September 2, 1974, p. 29.

11. Dik Warren Twedt, "How Important to Marketing Strategy Is the 'Heavy User'?" *Journal of Marketing,* January 1964, pp. 71–72.

12. John Gunther, *Taken at the Flood: The Story of Albert Lasker* (New York: Harper & Row, Pub., 1960).

13. Paul E. Green and Yoram Wind, "New Way to Measure Consumers' Judgments," *Harvard Business Review,* July-August 1975, pp. 107–17.

14. John Howard and Jagdish Sheth, *The Theory of Buyer Behavior* (New York: John Wiley, 1968).

5. Gerald Eskin and David Montgomery, "Hinesbury Mills," *Cases in Computer and Model Assisted Marketing: Data Analysis* (Palo Alto, Calif.: Scientific Press, 1977), pp. 1–28.

ACROSS
COMMUNICATION
MIX PLANNING

... *The Tentative Budget Mix—resource allocation based on sales response*

... *Communication Goal Setting—based on three hierarchies of psychological response*

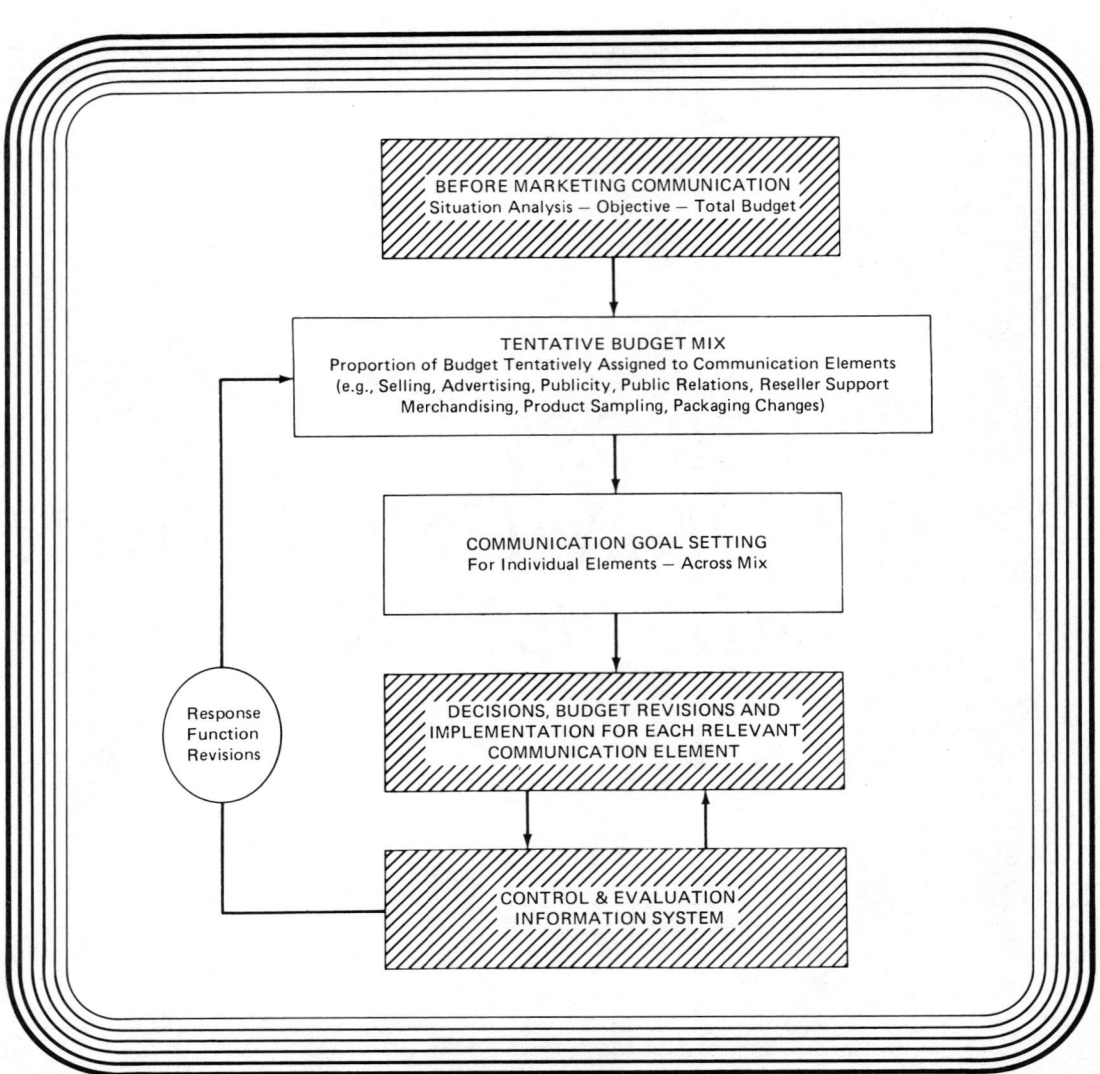

The Tentative
Budget Mix

• Your food products company is ready to introduce a revolutionary new toilet soap. There are indications that food stores will resist the introduction but the drugstores may welcome it. How can you take this information into account in planning the allocation of communication budget across sales, advertising, trade deals, and consumer promotions?

• For years your pharmaceutical house has been depending primarily on detailmen and direct distribution of samples and literature. Now a longitudinal study indicates that journal advertising produces greater response. How can this be taken into account in resource allocation?

• You are asked to consult with a campaign team for a congressional candidate. Since he has run before and has a past record of success, a campaign team has a fairly clear idea as to what to do in the effort.

But several large potential contributors have varying views as to how their money should be allocated to mass-media efforts, direct mailing, and precinct work. How can you reconcile this resource-allocation problem?

• Your budget is $50,000 for a new and, to some, controversial dairy product. A regional dairy has developed a good-tasting low-fat milk that through the addition of a special food culture has certain medicinal advantages. How can this small budget be utilized through media advertising, publicity, and sales promotion to introduce the brand?[1]

• You must develop a communication program for a company marketing small computers to businesses that think computers are too complicated. How will you spread the limited budget among media advertising, publicity-PR, personal selling, and educational programs?[2]

All the examples on the two preceding pages are real ones which you should be able to solve by the time you have finished reading this chapter. They all involve a particular kind of budgeting—resource allocation—which is one of three budgeting decisions in communication management. The preceding two chapters, particularly Chapter 4, concentrated on the decision to put a particular share of a company's resources against an individual market offering. Later chapters will investigate how this specific final budget is built up for each element of the communication mix.

The budgeting decision considered in this chapter, however, has to do with the very structure of the communication mix. Here the brand or campaign manager must decide upon the general weight that will be put against the various elements of the communication mix. As indicated in Chapter 2, the resource-allocation decision must be made tentatively so that later information and opportunities can be utilized to improve the allocation. Also in Chapter 2, it was noted that the decision as to allocation of the total budget is often made in a far from optimal way because of organizational pressures and lack of information. In this chapter, we review procedures that might be used to improve the practice at this initial stage of communication decision making.

Tentative budget setting has always been a part of marketing-communication decision making. But, until recently, it has not been given the main role in organizing the marketing-communication effort. While both practitioners and academicians have talked about somehow combining the activities of marketing communication, there has not been a common basis for doing so. Now both data on the sales response to communication tools and procedures for using these data in judgments have provided that common basis.

There is no doubt that if the campaign manager can give everyone working on the campaign proper direction with creative resource allocation, the results can be exciting. The new toilet soap mentioned at the start of this chapter became the leading selling toilet soap. The miserly $50,000 budget for the new low-fat milk was turned into a combination radio, publicity, and promotion campaign which the campaign manager said was the most successful introduction of a new product he had ever seen in his more than twenty-five years in the dairy business. Within days of the product's going into local dairy cases, it soon matched or bettered sales of the existing 2 percent low-fat milk.

With a combination campaign that overlapped all of the components of the communication mix, the computer company sold over fourteen hundred computers to businesses with as little as $500,000 in annual sales.

Unfortunately, however, many marketing organizations still tend to budget each component of the communication mix separately. There is a tendency to overemphasize the communication element which has traditionally been used in the industry—e.g., advertising in consumer marketing, personal selling in industrial marketing, and public relations in nonprofit marketing.

Top-management people, after doing the job of strategic planning that leads to a communication allocation for the brand, tend to urge that the brand manager keep doing the same thing that has always been done. Brand managers have a tendency to want to maintain share for their brands. So they allocate a disproportionate share of their resources to the trade deals that produce short-term share at the expense of long-term consumer franchise. Another effect of this short-term maneuvering on the part of brand managers is highly volatile profits in certain consumer goods markets while shares are stable.

Adding to the picture of dysfunctional resource allocation are the organizations and executives who represent individual communication elements. Each of these is clamoring for its share of the budget pie. Sales managers, advertising agencies, sales promotion people, and public relations organizations all urge the brand manager for their specialty. If procedures such as those suggested in this chapter are not utilized, the real needs of the situation are not reflected in the tentative budget mix.

This chapter has four parts. First, the standard allocation methods and the general form to be used in this chapter are discussed. Second, since it is critical to know what response can be expected from the use of various communication elements, there is an outline of the types of responses expected from individual communication elements—i.e., advertising, personal selling, sales promotion, and publicity-PR. Third, there is a review of the types of situations within which various tentative budget mixes have been used. This third section is the heart of this chapter and this book's suggestion for resource allocation in communication. Until workable resource-allocation models such as those discussed in the fourth and last section of this chapter are

developed and used more frequently, it will be critical for communication decision makers to know what kinds of mixes to use in certain kinds of communication situations. This chapter is a guide toward doing the right thing in each situation in terms of communication resource allocation.

STANDARD BUDGETING ALTERNATIVES

Virtually all budgeting approaches in the communication area have been developed for dealing with one communication element at a time. None of them were truly appropriate for the decision already discussed about the total size of the budget. Instead product life-cycle and product portfolio approaches—when corrected by information on competition, trade, consumer, and past communication experience—should be used to allocate funds for communication to particular market offerings.

Some of the standard budgeting approaches can be applied to the work that has to be done to make budgets more specific and vital. At the time of developing the tentative budget mix, however, they are of limited value as they are normally constituted, because the tentative budget mix is "tentative" and involves an estimate of the interaction between all elements of the communication mix.

Thus the consideration of standard budgeting alternatives in this section is done with full attention on the key goal of the tentative budget mix. This goal is to provide a general direction to the people who will be working on advertising, personal selling, sales promotion, and publicity–PR. By allocating a certain budget to each of these communication element groups, the campaign planner helps them to start their more detailed planning.

The six standard approaches used for budgeting in communication can be divided into two groups depending on whether they are more judgment or data oriented.

The three judgment-oriented approaches are the arbitrary, percentage of past sales, and percentage of future sales methods. They all have serious problems for across-mix resource allocations, but they may actually provide some starting point for tentative budget-mix building.

The three data-based approaches are the competitive parity, objective and task, and marginal economic methods. They each provide a particularly valuable perspective in setting budgets, even though complete data are not always available.

Judgmental Approaches

Arbitrary budgeting consists of budgeting on the basis of what has always been spent for the market offering or what is normally spent for such a product if the product happens to be new. Surprisingly, a large proportion of budgeting is still done on this basis. One study indicated that 60 percent of a sample of nonconsumer advertisers used either the arbitrary approach or the closely related "affordable" approach. Forty-two percent of the consumer advertisers responding to the same survey used something close to the arbitrary or affordable approaches.[3]

Close in popularity to the arbitrary method are the two percentage-of-sales methods, *percentage of last year's sales* and *percentage of expected future sales*. All three of these methods have some arbitrary or judgmental component to them. The arbitrary method has no relationship to the needs of the present year's situation. Although the arbitrary expenditure may be related to the needs of a combination of past situations, it may be quite misleading in terms of the present one.

The two percentage methods are judgmental in terms of what the percentage is and in terms of whether past or future sales should be used. Using last year's sales seems rather dysfunctional, since the purpose of every element of the communication mix is to produce sales in the upcoming year. Using expected future sales has a related problem, since the manager is putting the "cart before the horse." The manager estimates sales and then assumes a standard percentage for, say, advertising, which is supposed to be a variable controlling or producing sales, not controlled by sales.

Like the arbitrary budget amount, however, the percentage itself can be the result of historical information and experience as to what importance each component of the communication mix should have. In industrial marketing, for instance, personal selling is typically given the largest percentage, and one study indicated that if a company wanted to take full advantage of the potential of advertising, it should spend more than 20 percent and probably not more than 33 percent of its marketing budget on industrial advertising.[4] Another rule of thumb, this time from the consumer field, is that putting less than 50 to 55 percent of the combined advertising/promotion budget in media advertising and certain types of consumer franchise-building promotion will lead to long-term drops in sales and profits.[5]

In sum, then, the judgmental methods are not adequate for planning budgets for either single elements or resource allocation across the entire communication mix. They do not use data that might be available to deal with the present communication problem situation. They may, however, provide the guidelines within which a current budget-mix decision might be made. In particular, arbitrary amounts for the various elements of the mix may reflect the weight of past communication experience. While past or future sales are not good bases upon which to apply the percentages, there are certain industry guidelines for how the total communication budget pie should be divided among the various elements of the mix. Data can be used to alter industry guidelines to fit specific situations. This is the contribution of the following data-based approaches.

Competitive Parity

The competitive parity approach, which was reviewed briefly in both Chapters 2 and 4, consists of budgeting for each element of the mix in relation to what the competition is spending. The idea of a "subsistence level" of spending is critical here. That is, as was discussed in Chapter 4, unless a company's share of expenditures for a particular communication element like advertising reaches a certain level, it is likely that the money will be wasted. This is because of the substantial "noise" that would be developed by the sum total of competitive advertising, sales promotion, publicity, and selling.

The competitive parity approach is also related to what has been called the "fundamental determinant of market share."[6] This idea is that market share is likely to be due to some proportion of share of marketing effort. One study looked at thirty-four new convenience good brands over their first two years of life. These were all successful brands that were thought to have received a respectable market position. The average share of advertising for these successful brands was approximately 1.5 times their successful market shares. That meant that in order to achieve a 10 percent market share, you had to spend at a level representing a 15 percent share of all advertising in the category.[7]

Presumably the kind of data gathered by the study above for advertising could be gathered within a particular industry for all the components of the mix. Then an average budget mix in terms of percentages devoted to each of the elements could be constructed. The next decision would be whether each particular campaign should have percentages just like the average or emphasize certain components of the mix more than the average company does.

It should be clear to the reader that this sort of competitive parity approach is not adequate to the task of communication resource allocation. In the first place, the average competitive budget mix may apply to no

one competitor in the market! In the study cited above, for instance, only three of the thirty-four brands had the average 1.5 ratio of share of advertising to share of sales. That ratio varied among eleven brands of household products from 1.1 to 3.0. That latter household product brand achieved only a 6 percent market share with an 18 percent share of advertising.[8]

Budgeting by the competitive parity method alone, therefore, is a mistake. It does not take into account the particular capabilities and position of the brand being communicated. The competitive parity approach can be a useful guideline only when used in combination with the other approaches to be discussed.

Objective and Task

The objective and task approach is sometimes called the communication buildup method. This is an apt term also, because the approach concentrates on setting marketing objectives, then communication goals, and then determining what tasks will be necessary to achieve those goals. Once the tasks are determined, it is possible to determine costs and the budget expense for that particular element of the communication mix.

This objective and task approach, moving from communication goals to creative strategy to message distribution or media allocation to final budget, is the one recommended in this book—but only *after* resource allocations have been determined to develop the tentative budget mix.

The reason the objective and task approach is not recommended for setting the tentative budget mix is that the objective and task method requires too much detailed analysis and creative development for a *tentative* budget. Also since this detailed approach builds primarily from communication goals and information for each individual element of the mix, it necessarily misses the opportunity to use sales-response information to determine the general character of the communication mix with a cross-element resource allocation.

As has already been indicated, the objective and task approach is therefore the one implicitly being used in all that follows this chapter. It consists of all the communication decisions that are made separately for each element of the mix after all the elements have been considered at the resource-allocation stage.

Marginal Economic Budgeting

From an ideal economic point of view, we would spend money for any communication tool until the last dollar spent makes exactly a dollar. This budgeting approach is similar to the "marginal revenue equals marginal cost" criterion often mentioned in economics courses.

Of course the resource-allocation problem at the tentative budget-mix stage in communication involves the next dollar spent in any number of communication elements. The ideal marginal economic approach in this case would be to add a prespecified amount to the budget for the communication element with the greatest marginal effect. This would be done over and over again until no further profit improvement could be obtained.

These of course are the "ideal" marginal economic budgeting approaches to the single communication element and multiple communication element budgeting problems. The word "ideal" is used because in virtually no cases are data available on the marginal response that one would get from each additional dollar expenditure in advertising, personal selling, sales promotion, or publicity–PR. Perhaps the most heavily studied communication element is advertising. Even for advertising, there is only a limited number of published research results showing how profit increases and then decreases for various levels of advertising.[9]

Such precise data are almost never available. And this is the key problem with the marginal economic approach. Recently, however, enough data have been amassed and, more importantly, procedures have been developed for getting estimates of the kinds of sales response expected for particular kinds of communication situations.

Not only have experimentation and test marketing been used extensively, but there have been extensive analyses of campaign data which provide clues as to how individual communication elements affect marketing response and how elements work together.

Thus the "ideal" economic approach is not the one that could honestly be recommended in this book. Instead the basic idea of allocating resources at the tentative budget-mix stage on the basis of response to communication is recommended. If it is possible to determine the way each element and combinations of elements produce sales response in various situations, then it will be possible to make more intelligent tentative budget-mix decisions. When such decisions are based on data about market response combined with managerial judgment, they lead to a process in which more and more is learned about communication response.

CHARACTERISTIC RESPONSE TO INDIVIDUAL COMMUNICATION ELEMENTS

> Advertising and price promotion work a lot like farming. The farmer must invest in seed in order to grow a crop. To make a profit he must reap. He can't reap more than the value he put into the ground. It takes both sowing and reaping to be a successful farmer. A poor balance of sowing and reaping wastes money and ruins the farm.[10]

The first step in response-oriented situational resource allocation is to learn what the general response is to each communication element. As the quotation above indicates, some elements of the communication mix perform a "sowing" function. They characteristically have a slow-growing long-term effect which can be the basis on which other "reaping" or short-term aspects of the mix can be used. Obviously there must be a balance between these two types of communication efforts. In general, advertising and publicity are seen as sowing-type activities, while personal selling and certain types of price promotions are seen as "reaping" activities.

The purpose of this section is to go a bit beyond these generalities and indicate something of the sort of response that might be expected from each communication element.

Advertising

The relationship between advertising and sales is not a direct one. That is, there are very few ads, only some mail-order ones really, that can actually close a sale. The jobs that advertising can do in relationship to a sale determine the shape of sales response to advertising.

First, all other aspects of the marketing and communication mix must be adequate. If the product, package, price, distribution, and other elements of the communication mix are right, then advertising can work to perform certain functions, as follows:[11]

☐ For new products, advertising can help consumers to *consider a trial*. This may then lead to sales changes shown in general advertising response curves.

☐ For products that are established in the market, it is possible that advertising can help consumers to *consider intensifying their usage*. Advertising for Johnson and Johnson's baby products in terms of new uses sent many of these products to the top of various markets.

☐ When a brand has been around for a long time, such as the Procter and Gamble brands mentioned in Chapter 4, advertising can help to *remind people of their reason for preferring the brand*. In other words, advertising can help to sustain preference, and this will lead to response function of a very different shape.

Brands that are at the top of their category tend to need lower incremental advertising expenditures in each given year.

☐ Some products are bought because they have a high-quality reputation which is confirmed by their price, past experience, and the people who tend to use them. In such cases advertising can help to *confirm this reputation*. Just as in the preference sustaining function of advertising, there is a tendency for reputation-confirming advertising to be at a lower budget level than that meant to induce trial or intensify usage.

☐ In other cases advertising is necessary because the product will be used only if people change their thinking about it. In the terms used in Chapter 5, this function of advertising would be to *add attributes or change the importance of attributes for a particular need*. Examples would include Greyhound bus or commuter line advertising, which asks travelers to consider attributes like relaxation and the ability to see scenery; wine advertising, which often suggests that a particular red wine can be chilled or a particular white wine can be used with any dish; Clairol's campaign, which made dyeing one's hair acceptable; and Bic's campaigns for pens and lighters, which made throwing them away when they are empty acceptable. Such campaigns, which tend to change traditional thinking, require moderate to heavy levels of advertising spending.

☐ For marketers who use a family branding approach, when all of their brands use the same name, advertising can help to *build acceptance for the brand family*. Normally each individual product in a brand family requires less advertising expenditure because of the acceptability built up by the advertising of other products in the family. Examples of such families include Kraft, Sears, and Levi. And expenditures for each brand can be lower for this ad function.

☐ For most industrial and some consumer products where personal selling is critical, advertising can help *pave the way for a personal salesperson*. This was the point of the McGraw-Hill advertisement shown in Chapter 1. In the consumer ad area, television advertising for Avon is representative of such pathbreaking for the sales force. Such advertising does not require heavy advertising expenditures.

☐ If advertising is being done for service establishments, such as restaurants, clothing stores, or banks, it can *portray an aura of what it is like to be in such a store.* The feeling of friendly personnel, pleasant surroundings, and appropriate status can be transmitted through the ads. Once again, the retail establishment has to actually have these characteristics, and, even then, budgets usually have to be substantial for advertising alone to carry the burden.

These are only some of the functions that might be served by advertising on the way to sales effect. The point is that the sales response that might be observed or expected from advertising is dependent on the function advertising is performing within the context of the total marketing mix.

Given this necessary setting, it might be said that the general relationship between advertising and sales is an S-shaped one. There is really no need to even have a figure showing this shape. What the S-shape indicates, however, is that at low levels of expenditure in advertising there is a very gradual increase in sales. At successively higher levels of advertising expenditure there is a very dramatic increase in sales, and at extremely high levels of

expenditure there is little further increase and possibly a decline in effect as a limit in the number of possible customers and individual consumer use is reached.

In reality, the entire S-shaped curve as depicted in Figure 6-1 is seldom seen in a single situation. Usually the advertising situation dictates that only a part of the response curve will be shown. Figure 6-1 lists some examples of the situations that would apply to each part of the curve. Most research findings exhibit just the middle, concave part of the overall curve.

The first part of the curve, which is relatively flat and shows a slow buildup, would occur early in the life cycle for brands with lower share, strong competition, lower budgets, difficult selling jobs, and a relatively weak marketing mix.

The second part of the curve, which shows a sharp increase and final leveling off, is characteristic of a number of situations and would occur for established brands, in the growth period of the life cycle, with medium shares, medium budgets, a new appeal that is exciting, and/or a strong overall marketing

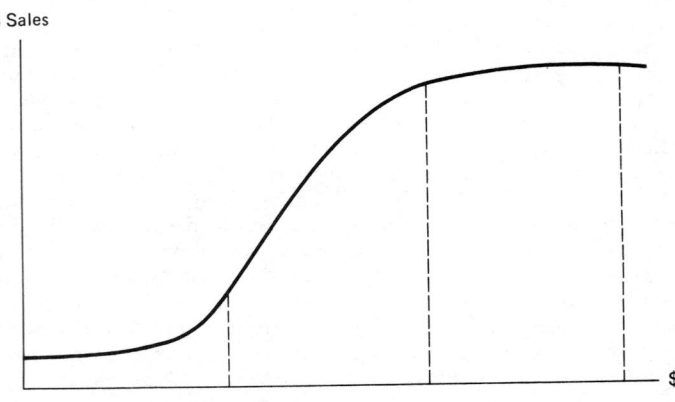

$ Sales

$ Advertising

Early Life Cycle	Growth Life Cycle	Maturity
Lower Share	Established Brands	Market Leaders
Strong Competition	Medium Share	Strong Image
Lower Budget	Medium Budget	High Budget
Difficult Selling Job	New/Exciting Appeal	Familiar Appeal
Weak Marketing Mix	Strong Mix	Appropriate Mix

Figure 6-1. *General S-shaped sales response to advertising with situational factors leading to observation of particular parts of the curve*

mix. The majority of situations seem to produce this part of the curve.

The third part of the curve, which is fairly flat and at a high level, is representative of brands in the maturity period which are market leaders, have established a strong image, are in the high-budget range, and are using appeals that are relatively familiar to most consumers.

In addition, advertising, unlike other aspects of the mix, tends to have a longer-term effect. That is, it has the capability of developing an image or general awareness of the product that might not be accomplished with, say, price-off coupons. It is this long-term component of advertising that leads to its sometimes being considered as an investment. This long-term aspect of advertising is also the reason that campaigns are usually thought to be weak without it. This is not to say that products and services are not marketed without advertising. If advertising is not used, however, there is a need for some communication or other marketing element to take its role.

Personal Selling

Most personal selling consists of reaping the benefits of the selling of advertising and other parts of the mix: Personal selling is the part of the mix that most often closes the sales.

As indicated in Chapter 1, there are basically three types of salespeople. One is the stereotype of the salesperson, the one who actually sells in the sense of convincing a buyer to pay for or make some other effort to own a market offering. A second type is best characterized by the word "clerk." These people take orders and do a minimum of selling. A third type performs the same sort of function that advertising does, but in a personal way. These people, typically called missionary salespeople, will visit stores and prospects and distribute sales promotion literature, check on displays, answer questions, and so forth.

The sales response to increasing personal-selling efforts of the first two types, field salesperson and clerk, is usually found to be quite dramatic up to a point. That is, as the sales force begins, each salesperson has a large number of potential prospects and can produce a large number of sales. As salespeople are added, however, each additional salesperson has fewer prospects, and so the sales response to each additional salesperson decreases up to a point where the value of the last salesperson is less than his or her cost.

Such a response is shown in Figure 6-2. Note that the curve is not an S-shaped one. That is, there is no slow-buildup period. The assumption of the curves in Figure 6-2 is that once a salesperson is in the field, he or she can sell. This is a big assumption. Salespeople can differ in efficacy, and there are possibilities of each new salesperson's getting into territories that are ripe for selling. But the curve in Figure 6-2 assumes away all of these complexities, many of which will be discussed in following chapters. The key thing to notice is that there is a constantly diminishing sales return as salespeople are added.

The third or missionary type salesperson performs the same sort of function as advertising. Instead of closing sales, the missionary salesperson performs a variety of duties which involve exposing prospects to the product in better ways. Thus in marketing fields where there are relatively few prospects and personal contact is important, missionary selling can do the advertising job. And the response of the market to this type of selling is similar to that described above for advertising.

Personal selling composes an important part of the communication mix in those situations in which personal contact is necessary to close the sale. Most areas of industrial marketing provide a perfect example. In the consumer field, large durables are another example where personal contact is important. Once again, however, it is important to point out the proper balance between the sowing and reaping aspects of the mix.

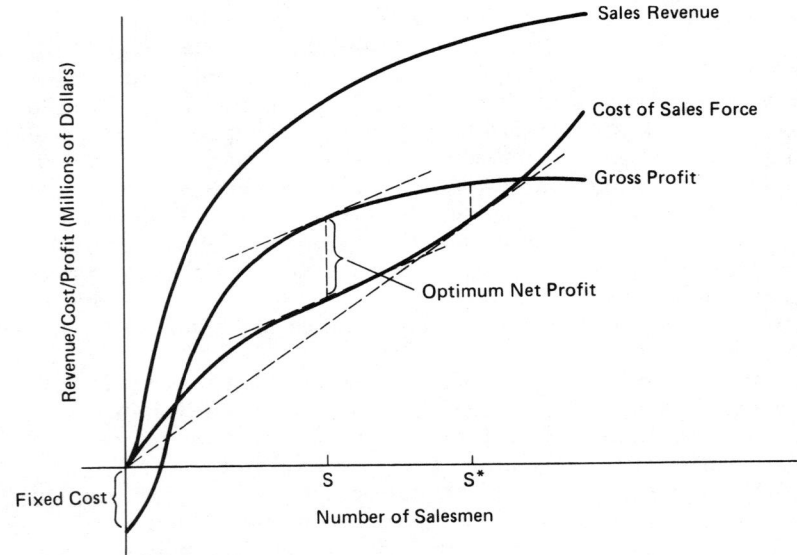

Figure 6-2. Typical shape of response to personal-selling increase. Sales force size–sales revenue curve is at top.

Adapted from *Marketing Management* by Harper W. Boyd, Jr. and William F. Massy © by Harcourt Brace Jovanovich, Inc. Reproduced by permission of the publisher.

Sales Promotion

As mentioned in Chapter 1, sales promotion consists of a number of very different marketing-communication activities. *Sales promotion* is defined as all forms of clearly sponsored communication other than advertising and selling.

Sales promotion activities can be divided into two parts, based on whether they have a long-term (consumer franchise-building) effect or not. Included in the consumer franchise building would be such activities as consumer sampling and couponing to consumers that is accompanied by a clear selling message, consumer demonstrations, and consumer educational material—e.g., cookbooks, teaching material, recipe or service material, and materials distributed to educators. Included in the short-term, nonconsumer franchise-building effort would be price-off or giveaways to the consumer that do not include a selling message or promotions that go to the trade or retailers. These would include price-off packs, consumer premiums, consumer contests, sweepstakes, consumer refund offers, trade coupons, trade allowances, and other incentives to the trade.

The sales response to the first type of sales promotion tends to be similar to that of advertising, with the exception that cents-off coupons can usually have a very quick response.

The response to nonconsumer franchise-building sales promotion activities is very quick. Typically the finding is that there is a very sharp increase in sales, dropping down to a decrease below the level of sales normally expected, later rising back up to the normal level or perhaps a little lower. Figure 6-3 shows the daily market shares of two national brands in a supermarket chain. The sharp peaks for both brands are the effect of store specials, a type of sales promotion. Notice that for brand A, sales drop below the normal level after the store-special peak, and the normal level seems to be going down over time.

This decrease in the normal level of sales over time is the danger of nonconsumer franchise-building sales promotion activities. These types of activities are clearly "reaping" activities. If there is too much emphasis on such sales promotion activities, people will begin to respond to the brand on the basis of price alone. Once this happens, the brand's franchise is melted away.

Sales promotion should be included in the tentative budget mix carefully with re-

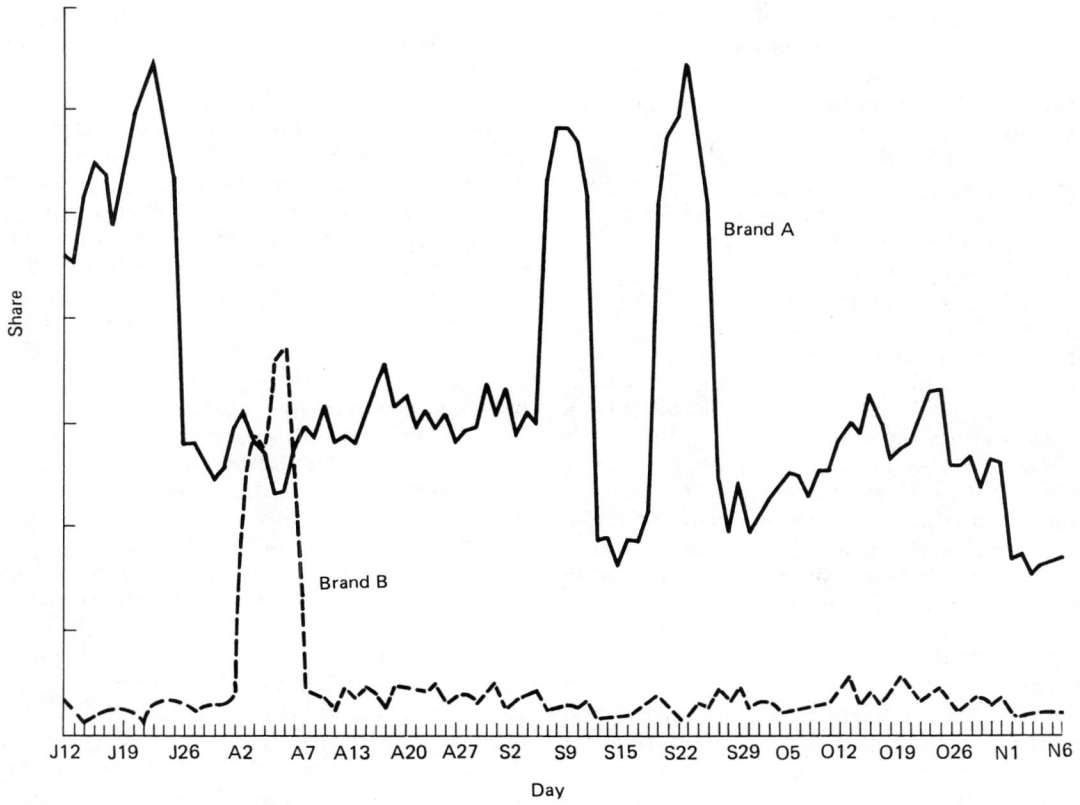

Figure 6-3. *Daily market shares of two national brands in one supermarket. Chain store specials effects shown by peaks. Data collected by electronic checkout equipment.*

From John D. C. Little, "Decision Support Systems for Marketing Managers," *Journal of Marketing,* 43 (Summer 1979), 16. Used with permission.

gard to the two types of functions that the various activities of sales promotion can perform. The franchise-building types of activities, such as sampling, can be very important at certain times in the product's life. In many ways, sampling can be the best possible introduction to a new product. There are definitely times when the nonconsumer franchise-building types of activities should be used. After all, there must be some way to fully reap the potential of a brand developed through advertising and other means. But the communication planner should be careful not to overemphasize such activities just on the basis of achieving a short-term market-share objective. The long-term viability of a brand is seriously affected by an overemphasis on such sales promotion activities.

Publicity and Public Relations

The publicity and public relations type of communication element is the most difficult to deal with in a tentative budget mix. Since most publicity and public relations activities are only viable when there is something newsworthy about the market offering, it is difficult to build up the sort of repetition over time that is characteristic of advertising.

And since publicity and public relations activities are dependent upon the judgments of editorial and program people in the media, there is little control over what will exactly be said about the product.

Therefore while publicity and public relations can have enormous effects, it is difficult to draw a sales-response curve for them. Publicity efforts tend to lack continuity or the potential for a sustained drive.

Chapter 1 mentioned that publicity and public relations were second in importance for industrial marketing and first in importance for public-sector marketing. This indicates that while it is not possible to draw a sales-response curve for publicity–PR, these communication elements can have a major effect in certain situations. For instance, in the new low-fat milk product example at the beginning of this chapter, the budget was so small that television advertising could not be utilized. But the product was so new and revolutionary that publicity was used to get television air time for the product. This is the kind of use that makes public relations and publicity so important in both industrial and public-sector marketing. When budgets are small but the story is interesting, it is possible to use these tools to increase the awareness and comprehension of the market offering. In such situations a substantial amount of the budget should be allocated to publicity and public relations, at least for the early part of the campaign. Perhaps the only curve that would be relevant would be to show that the use of publicity would increase the level of sales response from all the other components of the mix.

Summary: Two Kinds of Communication Elements

This section began with a quotation indicating that some communication elements are "sowing" ones and others are "reaping" ones. Another way of looking at this dichotomy is in terms of consumer franchise-building versus nonconsumer franchise-building activities.

All of advertising, missionary selling, some types of sales promotion, and probably all of publicity could be considered to be in the consumer franchise-building or "sowing" category. These types of communication have a long-term effect in building up awareness, comprehension, attitudes, intentions to behave, and general preference for a brand or market offering. This is the sort of sowing that can be reaped in the form of pricing, distribution, and communication activities of the nonconsumer franchise-building type.

The general implication is that most of the tentative budget mix should be composed of consumer franchise-building activities. Of course this can be affected by the particular situation at hand. In industrial marketing, for example, personal selling sometimes takes up a larger than 50 percent share of the communication budget.

One pair of terms that has been used to describe the two general alternatives and tentative budget mix is "push and pull." A *push strategy* consists of pushing the product through the distribution to the consumer by using personal selling and price-off sales promotion, typical nonconsumer franchise-building activities. A *pull strategy* involves improving the image of the product in a variety of ways so that consumer demand pulls the product through the distribution with less need for personal selling and sales promotion pushing.

Each situation has to be examined carefully to determine the potential role of each communication element in the tentative budget mix. The next section is based on the assumption that specific response functions are seldom available to communication decision makers. Instead analysis of the situation can be used to determine how resources will be allocated among the various components of the mix. Some of the general situational characteristics that might be used in such an analysis are reviewed in the next section.

SITUATIONAL TENTATIVE-MIX GUIDELINES

One of the best ways to see the effect of the situation on budgeting is to look at expenditures as a percentage of sales. For instance, if two companies each had a million dollars in sales and one spent $100,000 in advertising while the other spent $50,000 in advertising, their advertising-to-sales ratios would be 10 percent and 5 percent, respectively. The difference between these percentages would be due to the differing situations these two companies faced as perceived by their communication decision makers. Advertising-to-sales ratios vary widely, as do situations. The following are some of these ratios for fairly well known companies.[12]

Noxell Corporation (toiletries, cosmetics)	22.3%
Alberto-Culver (toiletries, cosmetics)	18.8
Miles Laboratories (drugs)	11.6
William Wrigley (gum)	8.5
Unilever (soaps, cleansers)	8.8
General Foods Corporation	6.2
Joseph Schlitz Brewing Company	5.4
Time, Inc. (communications)	4.5
Coca-Cola	3.2
K-Mart	2.1
Chrysler Corporation	1.4
American Airlines	1.1
Du Pont (chemicals)	0.6
General Electric Company	0.6
American Telephone & Telegraph	0.4
General Motors Corporation	0.4
Mobile Corporation (oil)	0.4

What is it that causes the Noxell Corporation to value advertising nearly fifty-six times as much in relation to sales as does AT&T, GM, or Mobil? More importantly, what situational characteristics affect the balance in the communication mix that is given tentatively to those people planning each communication element?

Obviously a great deal of analysis would have to be done before enough would be known about situations to pinpoint each specific situation. This section reflects the result of a series of situation analyses that provide guidelines for the construction of the tentative budget mix.

Consumer Advertising Situations

Determining the percentage of sales spent on advertising produces information on more than just advertising budgeting. The amount spent on advertising is an indicator of the extent to which a pull strategy is being used as opposed to a push one. It is an indicator of the extent to which all types of consumer franchise-building activities, not just advertising, are being used in the mix. As such, if we could determine what situational variables lead to high advertising-to-sales ratios, we could determine what kind of tentative budget mixes are required in such situations.

The most thorough work in attempting this sort of situation analysis has been done by Paul W. Farris with the sponsorship of the Marketing Science Institute.[13]

Farris's review of the marketing literature indicates that the budget for advertising is affected by the nature of the product, market, customer, marketing strategy, and profit margins. In all, he found twenty-four different variables that seem to have a significant effect on the proportion of sales that companies spent on advertising. In a later correlational study of 103 consumer businesses during the 1970–73 period, he was able to substantiate the nature of the situation variable/advertising–sales ratio relationship for twelve variables.

Once these relationships are seen, they are not too surprising. And it should be noted that all of this analysis is correlational. This means that advertising could cause the situational variable as well as the other way around. For instance, Farris finds that when there is active competition—with unstable market shares for the major competitors from year to year—there is more advertising. It is clearly possible the high advertising expenditures could have caused the unstable shares as well as the other way around.

So the following listing and justification of situational factors should be taken with a grain of salt.[14] They are not a replacement for using knowledge of communication element response to set the tentative budget mix. On the other hand, knowledge of response can be tempered by these factors to guide the communication decision maker toward a budget mix.

Product Factors. Both past literature and recent empirical findings indicate that advertising's share of the communication budget is larger when the product provides some basis for differentiation, has hidden qualities, relates to emotional buying motives, is purchased with a moderate degree of frequency, is purchased in relatively small dollar amounts, and is a nondurable item.

Product Factors	*Relationship with A/S*
Basis for differentiation	+
Hidden qualities	+
Emotional buying motives	+
Purchase frequency	curvilinear
Amount of purchase	−
Durability	−

These relationships are not hard to understand. Advertising is more important when there is differentiation, hidden qualities, and emotional buying motives, because these product qualities give something substantial to talk about in advertising—thus larger budgets for this communication tool. Advertising is probably allocated more heavily to those products with medium-purchase frequencies for negative reasons. That is, advertising is not necessary for those purchasing at a low frequency, since more personal forms of communication are utilized, while high-frequency purchase products communicate their attributes through use and therefore do not require as large budgets. Finally, the rela-

tively lesser importance of advertising in the communication mix for products that constitute a large dollar purchase and are durable probably relates to consumer needs for greater, more personalized information for these important products.

Market Factors. Early life-cycle stages seem to require more advertising emphasis than do later life-cycle stages. When price is not important as a demand factor, advertising seems to gain in importance. Advertising emphasis also increases when there is a concentration of large competitors and competition is active. On the other hand, advertising receives less emphasis when market share is already large and the company was a pioneer in the market.

Market Factors	*Relationship with A/S*
Introductory stage of product life cycle	+
Growth stage of product life cycle	+
Maturity stage of product life cycle	−
Decline stage of product life cycle	−
Inelastic demand with respect to price	+
Concentration of competitors	+
Market share	−
"Active" competition	+
"Pioneer" in market	−

The relatively greater emphasis on advertising in the early stages of the life cycle was examined in Chapter 4. Obviously also, if price is not an important variable in the market, then advertising increases in importance. And if large competitors are active, then counteracting with advertising expenditures would seem natural. Finally, the value of having a large market share and being a pioneer in a market is that each dollar expended on advertising has greater leverage than those of lesser share or later entrant competitors.

Therefore, less is spent on average for advertising in the communication budgets of large share, pioneer entries.

Customer Factors. If the product is sold to industrial users, advertising's importance tends to diminish; and when a brand's business is concentrated among small proportions of heavy users, advertising's emphasis tends to be increased.

Customer Factors	Relationship with A/S
Products sold to industrial users	−
Concentration of users	+

Industrial selling, as has been pointed out, emphasizes personal selling, probably because users require personalized attention. Thus advertising is less important.

It may be more surprising that an important heavy-user segment increases advertising. The explanation may be the "majority fallacy" where heavy advertising expenditures are necessary to reach a small segment with distinctive appeals in the face of heavy competitive activity.

Strategy Factors. When a brand's price and quality are high relative to competition, long distribution channels are used, and it is in the early stages of its own life cycle, the advertising expenditures tend to be relatively high. If trade margins are high and the product is sold regionally, however, advertising expenditures tend to be relatively low.

Strategy Factors	Relationship with A/S
High relative prices	+
High relative quality	+
Long distribution channels	+
High channel margins	−
Early stages of *brand* life cycle	+
Regional markets	−

The effect of high prices, high quality, and early stage of the life cycle in increasing advertising expenditures seems to be due to both the need and the ability to "talk about" something in advertising. Long distribution channels, on the other hand, seem to make a push strategy much less viable than the pull strategy which would be implemented by advertising. The negative relation between high channel margins and advertising expenditures probably relates to the fact that those channels that have high margins are expected to push the product to the consumer as opposed to depending on a pull strategy of advertising. One need only look at any two companies in the same product category that are using different distribution strategies to see the impact on advertising expenditures. Revlon and Avon both sell cosmetics, but Revlon has relatively long distribution channels and Avon sells door to door. Revlon has extremely high advertising budgets, while Avon spends relatively little on this communication activity.

Cost Factors. If manufacturing and other costs are relatively low so that the marketer has high profit margins on sales, advertising expenditures as a percentage of sales tend to increase. The reason for this is quite simple—high profit margins afford more money to spend on advertising and all parts of the communication mix.

Resource-Allocation Implications. To some extent the findings reported in this section can be used as guidelines for establishing the importance of advertising in the communication mix. At this point, of course, these are only general guidelines. As mentioned earlier, advertising expenditures in the case of some of these variables may be the cause rather than the effect of the factor. Also it is possible that these factors could increase the importance of other communication elements as well as advertising. It is likely that any of these variables that increases the importance of advertising would also increase the importance of any consumer franchise-building type of communication activities, for instance. Thus personal selling and nonconsumer franchise sales promotion activities are likely to have a relationship exactly the opposite of that of advertising to these factors, but there are several gray areas.

Therefore if you are planning a campaign for a product or market offering that has all or virtually all of the factors relating positively to advertising expenditure, then you can be quite certain that advertising should constitute a large proportion of the tentative budget mix for communication. Also if all or virtually all of these factors look negative for advertising expenditure, then it is probably clear that advertising will constitute a small proportion of the tentative budget mix.

It is in those situations in which factors are half and half, or only weakly pointing in the direction of advertising expense, that it is hard to use the above analysis for tentative budget-mix allocations. Only two published studies have given specific weights or coefficients to the various situational factors so that a communication planner might apply them to his or her situation to determine the specific advertising-to-sales ratio.[15] And these authors point out quite carefully that using such coefficients in a model to determine advertising expenditure as a share of sales would be a chancy undertaking at best.

Therefore the situation analysis provides general guidelines. More specific information in each situation, particularly with regard to other aspects of the mix, is needed for tentative budget-mix determination.

Industrial Advertising Situational Factors

The position of advertising in industrial marketing is so different from that in consumer marketing that it demands a separate section of situational analysis for tentative budget-mix determination. Guidelines for consumer communication simply do not apply to the industrial one.

The prime reason for the difference in implications for communication resource allocation is that industrial marketing advertising is such a small share of the budget. As was mentioned earlier, the range of 20 to 33 percent of the marketing budget being composed of advertising was indicated as an optimal range.[16] In one study of industrial advertising expenditures, the median advertising expenditure for sixty-six products was $92,000 and only six-tenths of one percent of sales—a far cry from the multimillion-dollar consumer advertising budgets.[17]

Because advertising expenditures are so relatively small in industrial marketing, the question is not so much advertising's relationship to sales but rather what proportion of the marketing budget is taken by advertising. In one study three relationships are reported, the ratios of (1) marketing to sales, (2) advertising to marketing, and (3) advertising to sales. In this way it is possible to see how important marketing or campaign effort is to a particular product situation, how important advertising is within that marketing effort, and, finally, how important advertising is in a general sense.

The results of this study are shown in the following table.[18] Six variables—product quality/uniqueness/identification with the company, frequency of purchase, stage in the life cycle, market share, concentration of sales, and growth in customer base—are related to M/S (the ratio of marketing expense to sales revenue), A/M (the ratio of advertising expenditures to marketing expenditures), and A/S (the ratio of advertising expenditures to sales revenue). Note that these six factors cover most of the areas of the factors that affected consumer advertising expenditures. By looking at three ratios instead of one, it is possible to determine more about the factors that affect resource allocation. The A/M column in the table is the one that indicates the proportion of communication mix effort devoted to advertising. For three of the six factors, the A/M ratio has a different relationship to the factor than does the A/S ratio. When there is a plus sign in the table, it means that as the variable increases, the ratio increases. When there is a minus sign, it means that the ratio decreases as the variable increases. A zero indicates that there is no significant relationship.

Situational Factor	Relationship with		
	M/S	A/M	A/S
Product quality/unique-ness/ID with company	0	+	+
Frequency of purchase	0	+	+
Stage in life cycle	−	0	−
Market share	−	0	−
Concentration of sales	−	+	0
Growth in customer base, 1972–73	+	+	+

From "Advisor 2: Modeling the Marketing Mix Decision for Industrial Products," by Gary Lilien in *Management Science,* February 1979, pp. 191–204. Used with permission.

The table should be interpreted as follows:

☐ *Product quality/uniqueness/identification with the company.* While the size of the marketing budget in relation to sales does not seem to vary depending on industrial product quality or uniqueness, higher quality and uniqueness seem to be related to a greater proportion of the marketing budget being devoted to advertising. Advertising as a proportion of sales revenue also increases with product quality, etc. Just as in the consumer area, advertising's emphasis in the communication budget increases as there is an increase in what can be said about the product.

☐ *Frequency of purchase.* This second product factor has the same relationship to the ratios that product quality does. That is, total marketing budgets on average do not change as frequency of purchase increases. The emphasis on advertising in the communication mix did increase with frequency of purchase, however.

In the industrial area, this relationship may be explained by the lower importance of each purchase as frequency increases. In such situations, where there is high frequency, personal selling no longer is as viable a communication tool.

☐ *Stage in the life cycle.* As a product ages and goes through the life cycle, the marketing budget for it decreases. This phenomenon has been discussed both in this chapter and extensively in Chapter 4. In the industrial area, the additional finding is that advertising as a proportion of that budget stays pretty much the same through the life cycle. Therefore advertising use decreases over the life cycle—a finding that was reported for the consumer field also. The driving force for this finding seems to be the fact that less marketing effort is needed to promote a product once it is established on the market in the mature and certainly in the declining stages of the life cycle.

☐ *Market share.* Once again, as a large part of the discussion in Chapter 4 indicated, as a market share goes up, marketing costs in general go down. This is shown in the table in terms of a negative relationship between market share and the marketing-to-sales ratio. For industrial products, advertising's part of the marketing or communication budget seems to stay about the same no matter what the market share. These two relationships result in the advertising sales ratio's decreasing as market share increases.

☐ *Concentration of sales.* This variable was defined as the percentage of a product's sales purchased by the three largest customers. For products or brands having a large proportion of their business sold to the three largest industrial customers, total marketing or communication budgets are small, thus producing the negative relationship for the marketing/sales ratio shown in the table. Surprisingly, however, the advertising proportion of the communication budget increases as concentration increases. Perhaps this is due to these marketers using advertising as an instrument to reach their potential customers beyond the three largest. Recall that for consumer marketing, greater concentration led to greater advertising weight also, but the explanation for that surprising finding was somewhat different.

☐ *Growth in customer base.* This was measured by

the percentage increase in number of customers in 1973, as compared with 1972. In one sense, this is the same variable as stage in life cycle. It indicates whether this is a growth market or not. When a market or brand is growing in terms of number of customers, the marketing, communication, and advertising costs also go up. The growth period is the time that advertising is used more than other parts of the mix.

This study was one of the few in either industrial or consumer marketing to look at more than just the advertising-to-sales ratio and give some indication of situational effects on the emphasis of advertising in the communication mix. One other study that concentrated on the ratio between advertising *plus promotion* to sales in industrial marketing did find three additional situational factors to be related to this ratio.[19] These factors were

☐ *Amount of purchase.* As the amount spent on each purchase increased, the degree to which personal selling as opposed to advertising and promotion was emphasized in the mix increased. This is not too surprising. Personal selling can be used when the value of the sale is high.
☐ *Percent of sales direct to end users.* Not surprisingly, as this percentage went up, emphasis on advertising went down.
☐ *Price relative to competition.* As this went up, advertising and promotion emphasis went up also. Apparently the advertising and promotion is necessary to support the quality claims underlying the higher price.

Once again, the implications of the above findings for industrial-communication campaign planners are not absolutely clear. Although both of the studies cited in this section offer models that can take their findings on industrial-communication expenditures and apply them to specific new situations, the communication planner would be well advised to be cautious in using them. Rather, as was suggested for consumer situations, the findings indicated above should be used as guidelines. If in a specific instance all nine of

the factors mentioned above are such that advertising should be considered an important part of the mix, then the guideline is fairly clear. Situations in which there is a mixture of positive and negative signals, however, call for great care and further analysis.

Advertising versus Promotion in the Communication Mix

During the last decade there was a substantial increase in the amount of communication budgets devoted to various types of sales promotion. The main increase seemed to be in trade promotions, which are generally considered to be nonconsumer franchise-building activities.

A number of general and economic reasons have been given for the increase in sales promotion spending.[20] Basically it was felt that there were more new brands and that this situation led not only to promotions to introduce the brands but also to an increasing number of brands, each of which was fighting for space on supermarket shelves. This in turn led to competitive pressures with competitors heavily using sales promotion tactics. The economy, with the combination of inflation and recession, and economy-minded consumers led to the popularity of price-reduction-type promotions. New promotion techniques were developed which contributed to the increase in use. And trade pressure for more promotions fueled the sales promotion fire in the 1970s.

Of course it is possible that such factors could always increase the emphasis on sales promotion in the communication mix. What is critical here, however, is identification of those factors that might tip the balance toward a greater emphasis on sales promotion, no matter what the general economic and marketing conditions may be.

Few empirical studies such as those reviewed above for advertising emphasis in industrial budgets have been done for sales promotion. A survey conducted by Strang among fifty-four executives from seventeen companies did uncover a few factors that seem to affect the promotion-to-advertising ratio. These executives indicated that the promotion-to-advertising ratio was higher in situations when profit margins were slim, brand loyalty was low, and the product was considered to be something of a commodity. This is not hard to understand, since the price promotions, particularly to the trade, could be used by those manufacturers who feel that they have to cut price to maintain distribution.

Supporting this interpretation of Strang's findings is the fact that the executives indicated that promotion expenditures were higher when a brand's market share was low, competitive promotions were extensive, and there was strong private-label competition. Again, all of these factors would force a marketer to use promotion to stay in the market, at least in the short term.

Strang's survey also indicated that the promotion/advertising ratio was affected by stage in the life cycle. In the introductory stage, the balance between promotion and advertising seemed to be about equal. In the growth stage, advertising dominated. In the maturity stage—when the total market was growing at 5 percent or less—the ratio depended on whether there was brand loyalty. If there was high brand loyalty, advertising dominated. If there was low brand loyalty, sales promotion became more important in the maturity stage. In decline, sales promotion once again became more important as a device to keep brands in distribution while they were being milked for profits.[21]

These indications on the factors affecting the balance between promotion and advertising in the mix should be taken as only the most general suggestion. It is always possible that heavy advertising may have led to brand loyalty rather than the other way around.

In determining how to balance advertising and promotion in communication strategy, it is better to consider how the two communication elements interact in relation to sales. Strang's review of the literature and individual spending studies indicates that there can be important interactions between advertising and promotion. For instance, in one experiment, half of the homes in a city exposed to advertising purchased significantly more during the sales promotion period than the other half. The increased sales more than outweighed the extra cost of advertising.[22]

Another study, while concentrating on personal selling-advertising interactions, indicated that sampling plus coupon sales promotions that preceded advertising for a new brand could dramatically affect the effectiveness of the introductory advertising.[23]

Most research indicates that communication planners should be careful in their use of promotion, however. It seems that increases in promotion beyond a certain level (often indicated to be 45 percent) can lead to a long-term decline of the brand, despite the deceptive short-term gains that might be obtained by promotion.[24]

It is important, however, not to group together all sales promotion in terms of lack of franchise-building effectiveness. Some, as in the case of samples with coupons at the time of a brand's introduction, can be critical in building a franchise among consumers for the brand.

The idea that different types of promotion vary in the relative franchise-building effectiveness is supported by Peckham in his study of Nielsen audit data.[25] He ranks different types of promotion in order of their franchise-building effectiveness and says that promotions can be most effective in building a consumer franchise under the following conditions:

☐ New brands or established brands with a major product improvement;
☐ Established brands already enjoying an improving competitive trend;
☐ In conjunction with a sales drive to increase store distributions;

☐ When used on infrequent basis, limited to a campaign with rigidly controlled quantities, at intervals not closer than eight to ten months;

☐ In addition to, rather than as a replacement of, brand advertising support.

Peckham warns against the overuse of promotions, particularly as a replacement for advertising and as a major competitive tool.

Others take these general rules and make very specific suggestions:

☐ *High loyalty, high share.* Both advertising and promotion can be low, since buyers are loyal and probably to your brand.

☐ *High loyalty, low share.* Advertising probably won't help, but promotion might draw some people to your brand for trial and later loyalty.

☐ *Low loyalty, high share.* Advertising should be used to hold share, and price promotions should be diminished.

☐ *Low loyalty, low share.* Both advertising and promotion are valuable tools.[26]

When planning the tentative budget mix, communication decision makers should be aware that there are different types of sales promotions and that they can interact in creative ways with advertising and personal selling. Consider, for example, the promotion for Texize's Spray 'n Wash, which was called the "incredible guarantee." The offer was: "If Spray 'n Wash doesn't remove any stain from any shirt, we will refund the price you paid for the shirt."

This offer, combined with a television commercial and extensive trade selling, established the credibility of the product and what it could do. As a result there was a separate stain remover section developed within the laundry products aisle, inventories were doubled, and this became the largest-selling brand for Texize.[27]

Communication planners should never forget that components of the mix can work together in creative ways based on the devel- opment that goes on after the tentative budget mix.

Situations for Personal Selling

While advertising and sales promotion are dominant forces in consumer communication, particularly for low-price convenience goods, personal selling is the mainstay of industrial products and many consumer durables. Although not a completely accurate rule of thumb, a situation analysis that indicated that personal selling was more important in those situations in which advertising was of lesser importance would not be far wrong.

Some factors are clearly indicative of greater personal-selling emphasis and lesser advertising emphasis. For instance, when the amount of purchase is large and the product is a durable one, advertising weight has been shown to be less and certainly personal selling would be more important. One study showed that as the growth in the customer base increased, the importance of advertising increased. One would guess that the importance of personal selling would decrease in terms of share of the mix. And, of course, with shorter distribution channels or direct selling as the distribution method, advertising becomes less important and personal selling more important. The example comparing Revlon and Avon is apt again at this point.

There is ample evidence to indicate that, whatever the mix, personal selling interacts in important ways with advertising. One study showed a very clear type of advertising-selling interaction in the public-sector field of recruiting charitable volunteers.[28] In the industrial field, personal selling is so dominant that advertising is often thought to be a necessary evil. To combat this folklore, the business magazine publisher McGraw-Hill sponsored a series of correlational studies that showed the positive personal selling-advertising interaction.

THE PROCESS OF TENTATIVE BUDGET-MIX SETTING

The previous sections of this chapter have actually represented successive steps in the resource-allocation task of setting the tentative budget mix. Each section has considered a successively more precise way to determine the emphasis that will tentatively be put on each element of the communication mix— advertising, sales promotion, personal selling, and publicity.

The process of setting the tentative budget mix should almost always move through these stages:

1. *Arbitrary, about what was always spent.* Past allocations of budgets to the communication mix are indicators of what experience has told managers about the correct allocation for each particular situation. Of course the situation has probably changed from that in which many of these past allocation decisions were made. And staying with the same budget year after year is ridiculous. But the arbitrary approach represents a first step.

2. *Set percentage of last year's or expected future sales.* Once again, the percentages themselves can indicate, even more precisely than the arbitrary budget amount, what the needs for particular types of communication are in each situation. Of course, it is almost as dysfunctional to stay with a particular percentage as it is to stay with arbitrary amounts. Again, however, these percentages can be a good start. The only danger is that communication planners often stop with the percentages and do no further analysis.

3. *Competitive parity.* The competitive parity method offers an advance over the percentage one. Not only do competitive budget allocations give some idea of what your budget should be, but they also indicate the needs of the situation and how intensive each component of the communication mix must be to get above the "noise" of competition. Again, however, this level of resource-allocation analysis is not sufficient, since there are wide variations in the budget mix even within very small well-defined industries.

4. *Response analysis.* Next it is important to fully understand how each of the potential elements of the communication mix produce responses in sales. Advertising tends to produce a general S-shape; personal selling, a diminishing returns function; and sales promotion, a spiked response with a very quick up in sales, then a decline, and a later return to normal levels. This sort of analysis, which should extend to the reasons for particular kinds of responses, is a definite advance beyond the first three steps of tentative budget-mix setting. Response analysis alone, however, is not enough because it often is not related to a specific situation.

5. *Situation analysis.* Much is known about the way the various elements of the mix have been used alone and in combination in various situations. This information could be used in a very quantitative way to point to a specific budget level or at least a range of budget levels that are appropriate for the individual situation at hand. In a general sense we know that there is a particular kind of budget mix for consumer convenience goods which differs from that for durables which differs from that for many kinds of industrial products. As the preceding section showed, many factors seem to determine the importance of advertising, sales promotion, and personal selling within a communication budget. The balance between franchise-building and nonfranchise-building activities can certainly be established in a general way with the guidelines provided from situation analysis.

In virtually all cases these five steps form an adequate process for developing the tentative budget mix. Remember that this mix is *tentative*. It is meant to provide direction for those people working on the specific components of the communication campaign. Therefore a scientifically precise budget split is not necessary. Remember also that an excellent form of the objective and task budgeting approach will be applied for each component of the mix. Any errors in setting the tentative budget mix can potentially be corrected by the remainder of the communication-planning process.

Of course the better the tentative budget mix is in terms of reflecting the role each communication element can play in the campaign, the more efficient the planning process is and the more likely the campaign will have a positive outcome. Campaign managers who are not fully confident of the tentative budget-mix allocation can be pushed toward disproportionate expenditures later by overzealous advocates of particular communication elements. The advertising agency, for instance, may not be aware of what can be done with personal selling, sales promotion, and publicity. In such instances the agency people may plan in such a way that advertising is asked to do too many tasks, and the end result is that that communication element is given a dysfunctionally large share of the budget.

One guard against such occurrences is to extend the resource-allocation process and the five steps listed above. Two more sophisticated steps might be undertaken. These are market experimentation and decision calculus modeling.

Experimentation can be done to determine what levels of spending are necessary on each communication element to achieve particular sales objectives. In experimentation, various advertising weights, for instance, can be assigned to various separate metropolitan markets. Or certain cities have "split-cable" facilities in which it is possible to give different advertising weights to different parts of the market. In either case the sales resulting from certain advertising expenditures are recorded. This gives information as to what the response to advertising will be in a particular

situation. Sometimes tests are done with combinations of advertising and sales promotion.[29]

Campaign planners who have the results of such experiments can obviously do a better job of developing the tentative budget mix. Experiments are extremely costly in terms of time and money, however. And they cannot be done unless there is a reasonable sense of what the nature of the communication elements will be. In other words, it is essential to know what the advertising messages will be, the media, the specific types of sales promotions, and so forth, so that expenditure experiments can be done.

In some cases experiments seem to lead to dramatic changes in the emphasis companies put on various communication elements. Du Pont, a leader in marketing experimentation, conducted an experiment to determine whether Teflon-coated cookware could be reintroduced to the market after a disastrous first introduction. The experiment gave confidence that the reintroduction could be done and also gave specific directions as to budget.[30]

One of the most dramatic marketing and communication experiments involved Budweiser and advertising expenditures. An extensive multicity and long-term experiment showed that variations in the Budweiser advertising expenditure from 0 to 300 percent of normal expenditures made little significant difference in Budweiser sales.[31] This indicated that Budweiser was spending above optimal levels for advertising and also that other parts of the communication mix, such as distributor selling efforts, which differed from market to market, were having a major effect. Of course the net result was a decrease in advertising expenditures on Budweiser and a direct increase in the company's profits.

Weight or expenditure tests, then, can provide valuable information, but they normally cannot be done at the resource-allocation stage. They are just too costly in terms of time and money. Their results, however, can be used along with judgments and another sophisticated approach to resource allocation: the decision calculus model.

Decision calculus models are simply mathematical and computer approaches to putting together the data and judgments available to campaign planners at the resource-allocation stage. These models can project what sales results will occur with different combinations of communication elements.

Decision calculus models are not mysterious. Instead they are tied quite directly to managerial judgment in rather plain language. Instead of asking a communication planner to draw a response curve for each communication element, the management scientist working with a decision calculus model asks managers to guess at the averages and the extremes in terms of sales response. If you were using such a model for advertising, for instance, you would ask yourself what the level of sales would be at the maximum or sat-

uration level of advertising, what it would be if advertising was dropped completely, and what it would be if advertising was increased by 50 percent. These three points plus the present advertising-sales point would allow a decision calculus model to infer a tentative advertising response curve.

Figure 6-4a shows the kinds of estimates a manager might give for one particular decision calculus model having to do with advertising and communication budgeting.[32] In the Figure 6-4b, a smooth response curve is shown which is the one that would be used in the model for estimates as given by the manager.

Similar curves or effect indices could be developed for other parts of the communication mix. The decision calculus model then consists of a combination of such response curves, data on the market, present advertising and communication levels, and the present market share situation. Once such a

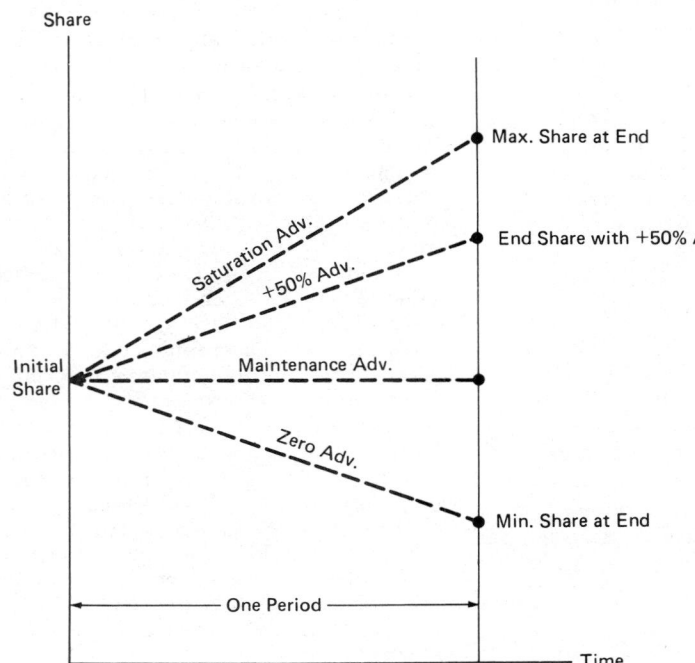

Figure 6-4a. *Input data for fitting a sales-response-to-advertising function in a decision calculus model*

From "Models and Managers: The Concept of a Decision Calculus" by John D.C. Little in *Management Science,* April 1970. Reprinted by permission from Scientific Press.

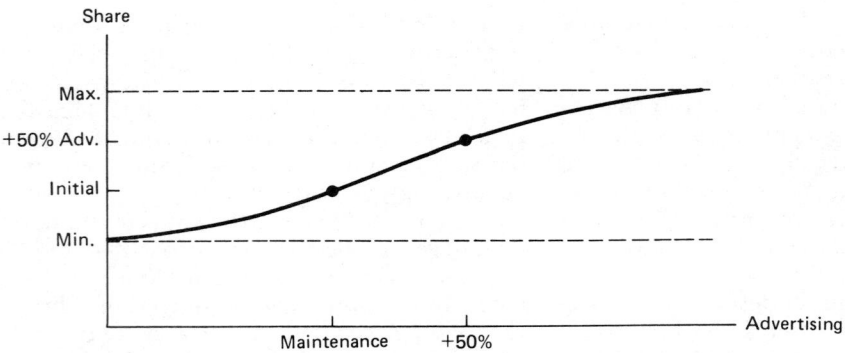

Figure 6-4b. *A smooth curve of share versus advertising put through the data of form shown in Figure 6-4a*

model is developed, it is possible to try various tentative budget mixes to get predictions of what sales levels will be. By tinkering with components of the mix, it is possible to see whether the model predicts past market shares accurately. If it does, then it is possible to see how changes in the tentative budget mix will affect future shares. In tests of such models, used almost exclusively in the consumer supermarket products area, predictions have been accurate and the models have been quite useful for planning the tentative budget mix. Such models can also be used to evaluate proposals that occur later in the communication-planning process for various copy, media, personal selling, sales promotion, and publicity approaches.[33]

The decision calculus approach is not really different from the approach used by communication planners long before computers were used extensively in marketing. It is not necessary to use computers to arrive at the tentative budget mix. All that is necessary is to apply adequate knowledge of the sales response to be expected from each communication element. For example, the following quotation is nearly twenty-five years old and expresses basically the same managerial approach recommended in this chapter.

In such a situation, you should approach the problem of a final expenditure decision by slow stages. As a first step, you might begin by establishing in your mind a mental "range" between the highest total expenditure you can practically consider and the lowest, which as a practical matter should be zero dollars. In the case of a new advertiser, the top or ceiling of that range would be strongly influenced by financial considerations. Thus it would tend to resemble in a way the "all we can afford" approach mentioned earlier.

It is suggested that you set the low end of the range at zero because the possibility that careful consideration of advertising approaches open to you may lead you to conclude that your soundest course is to do no advertising at this time is always strongly present. Today a small sum for advertising—say an expenditure much below $25,000—is unlikely to be productive except in a rare case, other than in a very restricted geographic area. A small-space advertiser selling direct by mail might be such an exception. In today's blue-chip advertising world, such a sum is likely to disappear without causing even a small ripple on your sales curve or on your competitive situation. The likelihood that a small expenditure may be completely unproductive should be weighed carefully against the objectives which those who recommend a very small appropriation feel that appropriation can achieve for your company.

With a top and bottom limit on your possible advertising appropriation set in your mind, you should select some central value within that range—say a figure halfway between the top and the bottom. Use that figure as your tentative advertising appropriation for planning purposes. You need some such definite figure to use in discussing with advertising agencies, for example, the possibility that they might handle your account. The figure you use in your discussions should be a realistic one. You should know (but generally you should not communicate that knowledge to an agency early in your negotiations or work with them) that if their recommendations seem to you sound and carefully planned you are prepared to go considerably higher than that figure.[34]

SUMMARY

The tentative budget-mix decision is the most important of three budgeting decisions made in communication planning. It is the link between the total communication budget established for the brand and the more specific and final budgets made for each communication element. At the tentative budget-mix stage the planner makes tentative allocations of the total communication budget to elements of the mix.

Of six standard budgeting approaches only the "marginal economic" one is perfect, and it can seldom be used since adequate data are usually not available. The "objective and task" approach is essentially what is being suggested by this book in using the decision sequence for individual communication elements. If the objective and task method were used at the tentative budget-mix stage, the stage would lose all its value of

giving general tentative direction to the planner of each mix element.

Thus instead of any of the standard approaches, this chapter recommends situation analysis to determine the potential sales response to each of the major elements of the communication mix.

An examination of the general response expected from the various elements indicated that they are basically of two types: (1) "sowing," or "consumer franchise building," types, which build the general, long-term health of a brand, and (2) "reaping" types, which have basically short-term sales effects. The "sowing" category consists mainly of all of advertising and publicity–PR, some types of sales promotion, and missionary personal selling. The implication is that most of the tentative budget mix should be allocated to these types of activities.

More specific indications for the tentative budget mix are gained from an analysis of situations. The advertising, sales promotion, and personal-selling proportions of the tentative mix depend on a variety of product, market, customer, strategy, and profit margin situation factors. These factors operate quite differently in consumer and industrial settings. The situational analysis can provide direct guidelines for the tentative budget mix.

A five-step process is derived for setting the tentative budget mix. Each step is a successively more precise way to determine the emphasis that will tentatively be put on each element of the communication mix. In some instances two more-sophisticated steps—market experimentation and decision calculus modeling—may be taken. Decision calculus modeling is simply a convenient way to organize the data and judgments used for setting the tentative budget mix.

ISSUES AND PROJECTS FOR DISCUSSION

1. How does the tentative budget-mix decision differ from the other two budgeting decisions in marketing communication?

2. What is the value of the judgmental and competitive parity budgeting methods in a process of tentative budget-mix setting? What are their serious disadvantages when used alone?

3. Why are the objective and task method and experimentation not appropriate at the tentative budget-mix stage?

4. Describe the marginal economic approach to budgeting, why it normally cannot be directly done for tentative budget-mix setting, and how it is approached by the procedures suggested in this chapter.

5. Which communication elements do you see as fitting in the "sowing" and "pull strategy" categories and which in the "reaping" and "push strategy" categories?

6. Characterize the general sort of response one would expect to get from advertising, personal selling, sales promotion, and publicity–PR. Are there variations in response for different types of each of these communication elements? Give some examples.

7. Use the situational factors discussion of this chapter to generally explain the differences in advertising-to-sales ratios shown on page 157.

8. Now take one of the company ratios that is extremely high and one that is extremely low on page 157. What are the most important situational factors in that difference? Why is it dangerous to use these situational factors alone to establish the tentative mix?

9. Describe the general approach to tentative budget-mix setting suggested in this chapter. How could decision calculus models be used over the long run to improve it?

10. How is it possible to do tentative budget-mix setting without having precise data on sales response to elements of the communication mix?

Notes

1. Richard J. Westman, "A Quart of Advertising for a Pint of Money," *Broadcasting,* August 23, 1978, p. 11.

2. "Basic/Four Corp. Uses Ad, Sales, PR, and Education Methods to Show Small Businesses How to Increase Their Productivity with Its Competitors," *Marketing News,* April 11, 1975, p. 7.

3. Andre J. San Augustine and William F. Foley, "How Large Advertisers Set Budgets," *Journal of Advertising Research,* 15, No. 5 (October 1975), 11–16.

4. John W. DeWolf, "A New Tool for Setting and Selling Advertising Budgets" (Paper presented at the Eastern Regional Meeting of the American Association of Advertising Agencies, November 7, 1963), p. 21.

5. Robert M. Prentice, "How to Split Your Marketing Funds between Advertising and Promotion," *Advertising Age,* January 10, 1977, p. 41.

6. Philip Kotler, *Marketing Management: Analysis, Planning and Control* (Englewood Cliffs, N.J.: Prentice-Hall, 1980), p. 218.

7. James O. Peckham, Sr., *The Wheel of Marketing* (Chicago: A. C. Nielsen Company, 1973).

8. Ibid.

9. John D. C. Little, "Aggregate Advertising Response Models: The State of the Art," Working Paper No. 1048-79 (February 1979).

10. William T. Moran, personal communication, May 4, 1979.

11. These advertising functions and some of the examples are from Paul C. Harper, "What Advertising Can and Cannot Do" (Marketing Conference of the Conference Board, New York Hilton, New York City, October 20, 1976).

12. "100 Leaders' Advertising as Per Cent of Sales," *Advertising Age,* September 6, 1979, p. 8.

13. Paul W. Farris, "Determinants of Advertising Intensity: A Review of the Marketing Literature," Report No. 77–109 (Cambridge, Mass.: Marketing Science Institute, 1977); Paul W. Farris, "Advertising Intensity in Consumer Goods Businesses: An Empirical Analysis," Report No. 78–118 (Cambridge, Mass.: Marketing Science Institute, 1978); Paul Farris and Robert

D. Buzzell, "Why Advertising and Promotional Costs Vary: Some Cross-Sectional Analyses," *Journal of Marketing,* 43 (Fall 1979), 112–22.

14. The relationships discussed in the following paragraphs are adopted from Farris, "Determinants of Advertising Intensity." Only some of these relationships have been subjected to actual empirical tests by Farris, "Advertising Intensity on Consumer Businesses"; and Farris and Buzzell, "Why Advertising and Promotional Costs Vary." All of those that were adequately tested were substantiated.

15. Farris, "Advertising Intensity in Consumer Goods Businesses"; and Farris and Buzzell, "Why Advertising and Promotional Costs Vary."

16. DeWolf, "New Tool for Setting and Selling Advertising Budgets."

17. Gary L. Lilien, "MIT Plan Helps to Budget, Allocate Promotion Dollars," *Marketing News,* February 25, 1977, p. 7.

18. Ibid.; and Gary L. Lilien, "Advisor 2: Modeling the Marketing Mix Decision for Industrial Products," *Management Science,* 25, 2 (February 1979), 191–204.

19. Farris and Buzzell, "Why Advertising and Promotional Costs Vary."

20. Roger A. Strang (with contributions by Robert M. Prentice and Alden G. Clayton), "The Relationship between Advertising and Promotion in Brand Strategy," Report No. 75–119 (Marketing Science Institute, October 1975).

21. Ibid.

22. Ibid., p. 133.

23. William R. Swinyard and Michael L. Ray, "Advertising-Selling Interactions," *Journal of Marketing Research,* 14 (November 1977) 509–16.

24. David B. Montgomery and Alvin J. Silk, "Estimating Dynamic Effects of Marketing Communications Expenditures," *Management Science,* June 1972; Prentice, "How to Split Your Marketing Funds"; and Richard J. Weber, "How Trade Allowances Are Making Mincement out of Project Objectives" (New York: Association of National Advertisers Financial Management Workshop, 1973).

25. Peckham, *Wheel of Marketing,* p. 34.

26. Moran, personal communication.

27. "Creative Sales Promotion Vital in Marketing Mix," *Marketing News,* November 30, 1979.

28. Swinyard and Ray, "Advertising-Selling Interactions."

29. Strang, "Relationship between Advertising and Promotion"; John Adler, "How to Test and Measure the Sales Effectiveness of Television Advertising," *Advertising Age,* July 14, 1975, pp. 27–29; and Gerald Eskin, "Some Results from BehaviorScan," Stanford University, June 15, 1981.

30. James C. Becknell, Jr., and Robert W. McIsaacs, "Test Marketing Cookware Coated with Teflon," *Journal of Advertising Research,* 3 (September 1963), 2–8.

31. Russell L. Ackoff and James R. Emshoff, "Advertising Research at Anheuser-Busch, Inc. (1963–68)," *Sloan Management Review,* 16 (Winter 1975), 1–16.

32. John D. C. Little, "Models and Managers: The Concept of a Decision Calculus," *Management Science,* 16 (April 1970), B466–85.

33. Ibid.; and John D. C. Little, "BRAND-AID: A Marketing-Mix Model, Parts 1 and 2," *Operations Research,* 23 (July-August 1975), 628–73; and Little, "Aggregate Advertising Response Models."

34. Richard D. Crisp, *How to Increase Advertising Effectiveness* (New York: McGraw-Hill, 1958), pp. 77–80.

Communication Goals
and Three Hierarchies

• Two life insurance companies faced decidedly different situations. New England Life ranked relatively low among the fifty largest U.S. insurance companies in terms of life insurance in force. Northwestern Mutual Life ranked seventh in assets and was the largest company specializing in individual life insurance. On the other hand, they both were in the bottom half of the top fifty insurance companies in terms of consumer awareness. Both companies used approximately the same mix of advertising, agents, direct mail, and promotions. This was standard in the industry. But now their top executives began to wonder about the value and purpose of advertising in their communication mix.

• Texize's Spray 'n Wash stain remover pioneered a whole product category. What combination of communication elements should have been used to lead to awareness, comprehension: and believability of what the product would do?

• Marketing managers at L'egg's Products, Inc., were concerned about the role of advertising and price-off promotions (both in-store and via coupons) in the context of their dual marketing objectives of staving off increasing competition and developing share in their relatively weak markets while still expanding distribution nationwide.

• Executives of Hewlett-Packard, Inc., the large Palo Alto, California, based electronics firm, were concerned about their regular marketing communication package which included publicity, journal articles and advertising, direct mail, trade show activity, and sales engineer support. They were forced to reassess the purpose of all of these communication elements, particularly advertising, for those products in the mature state of the life cycle and new products like hand calculators, for which the situation resembled consumer marketing.

• Communication planners at Crown Zellerbach were readying campaigns to combat the coming onslaught of Procter and Gamble's Charmin against their Zee brand toilet tissue. What was there about the communication situation for this product that led to the enormous success of the Charmin television commercials?

• It was a presidential election year and the Democratic chairman for a medium-sized county in Massachusetts was concerned about the purpose that precinct workers, advertising, and candidate speeches could fulfill for, alternatively, his state legislature candidates and his party's presidential candidate.

No one element of the marketing communication mix is alone responsible for the end result of the campaign in terms of sales, votes, donations, or whatever. As was seen in the preceding chapter, it is a combination of selling, publicity, promotions, advertising, packaging changes, public relations, and other aspects of the communication mix that produces success or failure or, more likely, something in between. And in order to develop the best combination or communication elements, the campaign manager must determine exactly what role each element will play, in terms of *communication objectives,* such as awareness, comprehension, positive image, conviction, attitude, intention, or initial behavior response.

Communication objectives are the primary issue in each of the situations described at the beginning of this chapter. The insurance companies must decide whether advertising can accomplish just a goal of awareness or also generate comprehension and stimulate action of some sort. The political campaign manager has the same kind of problem, with the added difficulty that the objectives of various elements of the mix are likely to be radically different for the state legislature candidates as opposed to the presidential one. The L'egg's executives should realize that as they move from the introductory to the growth stages of their product's life, they will also have to be considering new roles for the various parts of their communication mix. The same kind of reassessment was faced by Hewlett-Packard when it realized that it could no longer put almost sole reliance on the highly innovative nature of its products and the great publicity this would generate in the trade press. Mature products and products facing competition comparable to that found in consumer marketing forced the company to consider new communication objectives.

This is the first of twelve chapters that deal quite specifically with marketing-communication decisions. While the situation analysis and tentative budget mix are obviously of basic importance, it is at the communication goals stage that we must first assess the actual nature of communication response in the problem situation at hand.

The campaign managers for the situations described at the start of this chapter knew the situation and the budget mix. Then they had to determine what each part of the mix was to do, in communication terms instead of sales.

Communication goal setting in the past has been considered in terms of one communication element at a time. Only for mass-media elements such as advertising has there been considerable controversy as to what goals should be. In this chapter we will deal first with advertising goals and then move to a consideration of a situation analysis that would allow an assignment of goals across elements in the communication mix. The basis of this process is a three-order hierarchy model of communication effects which states that target segments can respond in any of three ways to marketing-communication campaigns. The particular order of response depends on the nature of the campaign situation.

The managerial procedure for communication goals setting suggested here has three steps. First, the situation must be further analyzed in order to determine which of three orders of communication response is likely to be operating. This is done by consideration of buyer involvement, product differentiation, the importance of mass media, and the product life-cycle stage. Second, communication goals are set in general for each element of the mix. This means that achievement of a particular communication response is assigned to each communication element. And third, specific goal statements are developed for each component of the communication mix. This is done in terms of a written statement that indicates the target segment, a specific percentage change in the assigned communication response, and a definite time period during which the change is to be attained.

THE VALUE
OF COMMUNICATION GOALS

Once the tentative budget mix is set, a consideration of objectives other than sales is important for three related reasons: measurement, planning, and coordination.

The measurement value of communication objectives can be seen in a negative way—by considering the difficulty of determining the effectiveness of communication expenditures without communication objectives. One example of this difficulty is represented by the frustration of the legendary retailer John Wanamaker, who was purported to have said, "I know that half the money I spend on advertising is wasted, but I can never find out which half."[1] Somewhat more recently the researcher Charles Ramond observed, "The sales effect of advertising is like the unicorn or mermaid—something we all have heard of but few of us ever expect to see."[2]

The same kind of frustration and bewilderment is present for all the other aspects of the communication mix, in varying degrees and ways. While they all have their final goals as some contribution to sales, they make that contribution by communicating. The trouble that most managers have in measuring and determining the objectives of the communication mix in terms of sales is that the communication elements work together to produce sales, but they do this individually by affecting some communication goal such as awareness, comprehension, conviction, intention, or initial search activity. Thus measurement cannot be accomplished unless we know what we are measuring, and that is usually some communication objective.

These more specific objectives not only aid measurement but are also invaluable in planning. Stated simply, sales goals do not indicate what should be done by each component of the mix; communication goals do. There are a series of message, message distribution, budget, and implementation moves that can be made in, say, publicity to affect awareness, advertising to affect comprehension, and personal selling to affect intentions. These moves are not directly related to sales. But once the staffs and outside organizations connected with each of these activities are aware of what they are supposed to do in terms of communication, they begin to plan communications.

The final reason for relying on communication objectives is that they allow coordination and balancing among the elements of the communication mix. Of course, one purpose of the tentative budget mix is to provide this type of coordination, at least in terms of how much of the company's resources are to be laid against each element of the mix. But the decision of communication goals gets more specific as to what each element of the mix is to accomplish and how these goals relate to each other in accomplishing the final task of the total campaign in terms of sales. The tentative budget mix just indicates, on the basis of past sales response, that each part of the mix is to make some contribution to sales. The communication objectives statements indicate what the precise nature of each mix element's contributions will be in the upcoming campaign. The brand or campaign manager can then use these statements to coordinate and balance the contributions in achieving the final campaign goal.

AN EXAMPLE OF ADVERTISING HIERARCHY GOAL SETTING: DAGMAR

One advertising goal-setting publication was so widely circulated and used in the field that its title, *Defining Advertising Goals for Measured Advertising Results,* was almost immediately collapsed into the acronym DAGMAR. This book, by Russell H. Colley is representative of the suggestions made by a whole series of communication goals publications.[3] Its approach can be summarized in terms of the following seven points.

1. *Advertising goals are virtually always communication goals.* Here Colley pointed out that advertising is only one part of the marketing mix for virtually all companies. It seldom is a dominant enough force in the mix so that it can be directly related to sales. Therefore, Colley assumed, the specific goal for advertising in virtually all situations would have to be represented in terms of some communication objective short of sales.

2. *Goals should be written down.* Unless everyone in the planning process for advertising and communication is clear about what the goals for a particular effort are, it is unlikely that they will all be working on the same problem or developing mutually supportive campaign components. An important aspect of DAGMAR, then, is that goals should be made very clear and solid in the form of writing, so that everyone understands what is being done.

3. *Advertising should be measured in terms of effects, not exposures.* The second chapter reported the results of research on pharmaceutical marketing communication in which the

company was spending in exactly the reverse order that was indicated by a longitudinal study on the effectiveness of journal advertising, samples and literature, and direct mail. One way that such a misallocation of resources could have occurred is by the brand manager's being more concerned about physical "units distributed" than about effectiveness. In pharmaceutical marketing it is possible to see a certain number of samples and pieces of literature and direct mailings as an indication of the effectiveness of a brand manager's work. Similarly, in national consumer advertising it is common to justify a campaign on the basis of the size of the audience that will be reached. Colley's point here, however, is that reaching a certain number of potential consumers, no matter how astronomical that number seems to be, is meaningless unless there is some effect in terms of communication goals.

4. *Advertising operates through a hierarchy of communication effects.* Colley was very specific as to the levels of this hierarchy and their relationship over time in response to advertising effort. Figure 7-1, taken from one of Colley's articles, indicates both the levels he posited and the linear relationship between the levels as they are affected by both marketing and countervailing forces. One example he offered in the same article is the following. It illustrates a very strong reliance on a stairstep relationship among levels of a hierarchy.

Suppose an automobile manufacturer is about ready to bring out a new compact car which he has named, let us say, "Venus." At the moment nobody has ever heard of Venus. His first communication job is therefore to make the consuming public aware of Venus. Next, he has certain information and mental impressions he wants to convey; Venus is a light, spirited, beauty; a roomy, economical compact. He wants *comprehension* of these features. Then he wants to create a favorable disposition (emotional or rational) towards the purchase of his product; he wants to develop public *conviction* about it. Finally, he wants to spur the consumer to *action*, which, in

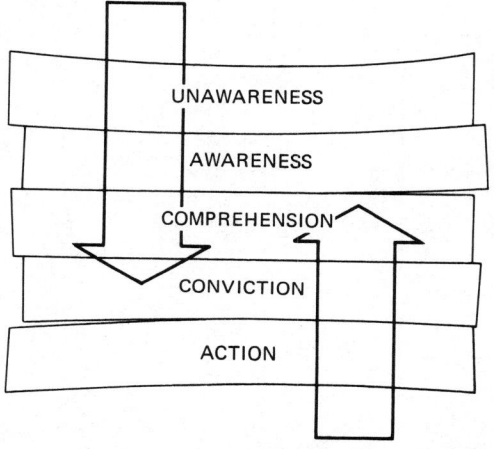

MARKETING FORCES
(Moving People Toward Buying Action)

Advertising—Promotion
Personal Selling—Publicity
User Recommendation
Product Design
Availability—Display—Price
Packaging—Exhibits

UNAWARENESS

AWARENESS

COMPREHENSION

CONVICTION

ACTION

COUNTERVAILING FORCES
Competition—Memory Lapse
Sales Resistance
Market Attrition
(Transfer, Death, etc.)

Figure 7-1. *The Colley–DAGMAR hierarchy of communication effects*

From Russell H. Colley, "Squeezing the Waste out of Advertising, *Harvard Business Review*, September-October 1962. Copyright © 1962 by the President and Fellows of Harvard College; all rights reserved. Reprinted by permission.

this case, might mean persuading the consumer to visit a dealer's showroom and ask for a demonstration.[4]

Obviously, this was a very strong statement for the stairstep hierarchy as a research and planning tool.

5. *Creative planning considerations should come before media decisions in the advertising planning process.* When media considerations come first, there is a tendency to be concerned about the amount of reach an advertising campaign can develop rather than the effects that are to be generated. The creative or message strategy

decision is always intimately related to the communication effects that are intended. Therefore the creative planning decision should occur first, exactly in the same order as in the decision sequence emphasized in this book.

6. *Benchmark measurements should be developed before the campaign is implemented.* Colley suggested a particular research procedure for measuring advertising effectiveness. This involved developing a measurement of the level of an objective before the campaign and then measuring deviations from the measurement as an indicator of campaign effect.

7. *Specific criteria must be developed.* This suggestion follows quite closely from the preceding one. That is, it is impossible to develop benchmarks unless the objectives are stated specifically in terms of some operational measurement. This means that the advertising objective should state the specific target market segment, the marketing goal in some percentage terms over some time period, and the advertising goal(s), again in terms of a percentage attainment in a particular time period. Figure 7-2 shows three case examples that are taken from the Colley book. Most of these come close to the kind of specificity he is suggesting. The actual companies claimed success in measuring advertising effect, although there are some shortcomings in the particular examples we have shown. As others have noted, it is difficult to develop the kind of specificity that would be required for the Colley system. On the other hand, it is difficult to see how advertising can be measured, planned, or coordinated with the other aspects of the communication mix unless such specificity is developed.

DAGMAR: ATTACKS AND COUNTERS

Colley's position as represented by the above seven points was accepted enthusiastically by a wide variety of scholars of the advertising process and by advertising agency people, as well as several large advertisers such as General Motors.[5]

Use Sales Instead?

On the other hand, the approach suggested by Colley and the other books in the early 1960s was attacked from several positions. One was the very familiar position that

any of the marketing-communication elements should be measured in terms of its sales effectiveness rather than some intermediate goal. Those management scientists and managers who suggested this approach felt that it was possible to measure sales effects by a variety of experimental and analytical techniques. Some of these techniques have already been discussed in Chapter 6 of this book. Therefore we are not arguing that sales goals be ignored, but rather that sales goals should be integrated with the more textured indications that are provided by communication effects.

Does Communication Relate to Sales?

Another line of attack emphasized that substitution of communication goals for sales goals did not really eliminate the need to determine the relationship between achieving any particular communication goal and ultimate sales effect. In this same area was the attack that it is one thing to say that sales are inadequate measures because they are affected by many other parts of the mix, but it is making an enormous leap to assume that communication responses are somehow immune from these other effects. Both of these arguments seem to miss the point of adding communication goals to sales objectives for the marketing-communication campaign. Of course, if we posit communication goals, we have to begin to understand the linkage between these goals and sales on one side and the effects of the other aspects of the marketing mix on the other side. But an understanding of these fundamental linkages is critical to developing more effective campaigns in any particular communication situation. To say that communication response should be ignored because it is difficult to understand is taking a position not unlike that of the proverbial drunk who loses his keys by his darkened front doorway but looks for them under the lamppost because that is where there is light. Communication goal setting helps us cut through the murky area of the nature of communication response.

Only for Large Companies?

Still another objection to the approach suggested by DAGMAR is the one that has to do with practicality and managerial consider-

ations. Colley's insistence on setting specific goals, writing them down, and researching with benchmarks and specific measurable criteria all suggest a very expensive and rigid managerial and research program. Many people looking at DAGMAR and other communication goal approaches in the early 1960s felt that this was indeed a system that could be considered only by academics and very large companies such as General Motors. The research that Colley is suggesting could be quite expensive, and there is some question as to whether his approach is really a valid research technique. It is weak, for instance, in accounting for lag and interaction effects. Fortunately, however, there have been an enormous number of developments in the field of measuring advertising effectiveness since the early 1960s. Thus the type of measurement necessary to follow the communication objectives strategy is now realistic for a wide variety of firms. And it is possible to imagine a systematic approach to goal setting and measurement being done by the smallest of companies.

Inhibits Creativity?

Another part of the managerial objection to the DAGMAR approach was that rigid goal setting would inhibit creativity. This is an easily handled objection within the communication decision sequence presented in this book. The goal-setting procedure is not the overriding one in the total sequence. It is only one of a number of steps and provides a broad framework within which to create all types of message and media strategies. Also there is the opportunity for feedback from later steps in the decision sequence process. Therefore, if an outstandingly creative message strategy is developed that can achieve more than the communication goals that were originally established for it, a revision in the communication goals can be made. Similar variations can be developed on the basis of striking ideas in the message distribution plan and budget allocation.

A NEW PERSPECTIVE ON THE HIERARCHY

Underlying all of the above objections and their variants was one quarrel with the DAGMAR approach that went to the very heart of its assumption about the nature of communication response. As shown earlier in Figure 7-1, Colley's assumption is that there are a series of possible reactions and that these reactions occur in some predetermined order as people are exposed to advertising about a product. Several other similar hierarchy conceptions for advertising effect are shown in Table 7-1. All of these hierarchies have two aspects in common. First, they all contain three types of levels: *cognitive* (attention, awareness, comprehension, learning, belief), *affective* (interest, feeling, evaluation, conviction, yielding), and *conative* (intention, trial, action, adoption, behavior) components. And second, they all assume that cognitive reactions must precede affective which must precede conative in a stairstep fashion. In other words, these models assume that learning comes before attitude change which leads to behavior.

The first of these two assumptions—i.e., that the three types of variables always

exist—is a quite reasonable one. The second or stairstep assumption, however, is not always reasonable.

Findings Against the Stairstep Hierarchy

Both empirical evidence and theory indicate that the stairstep "learning" hierarchy is, at the very least, too simple. Many studies both in psychology and in marketing communication indicate that learning or cognitive response is often not a measurable precedent to either affect or conation.[6] Similarly, the affective-conative link is questioned by studies of the attitude-behavior relationship that have been done over the last fifty years.[7]

These deviations from the stairstep hierarchy can be due to either theoretical or methodological shortcomings. Clearly, there are some conditions and measurements under which the stairstep hierarchy will occur and others in which it will not.

Other Possible Orders

What is critical from a marketing-communication management perspective, however, is that there are some marketing-com-

Table 7-1. Several Variations of the Standard Hierarchy of Effects: McGuire's Information-Processing Model, the Lavidge-Steiner Hierarchy, and the Diffusion of Innovation Adoption Process Model

Information-Processing Model	Hierarchy of Communication Effects	Adoption Process Model
Presentation of message		
Attention to message	Awareness	Awareness
Comprehension of conclusion	Knowledge	Interest
Yielding to conclusion	Liking	
	Preference	Evaluation
Retention of the belief		
	Conviction	Trial
Behaving on the basis of the new belief	Purchase	Adoption

SOURCE: George S. Day, "Theories of Attitude Structure and Change," in *Consumer Behavior: Theoretical Sources*, ed. Scott Ward and Thomas Robertson (Englewood Cliffs, N.J.: Prentice-Hall, 1973), p. 330. Reprinted by permission of Prentice-Hall, Inc., Englewood Cliffs, New Jersey.

munication situations in which the stairstep order of the hierarchy will occur and there are others in which some other order of the communication responses is dominant. Consider, for instance, the three major levels of response: cognitive-learning, affective-attitude, and conative-behavior. If we knew nothing about them, it would be reasonable to assume that they could be ordered in all six possible permutations of three things. The fortunate fact for communication goal setting, however, is that we know a great deal about the levels of response and the way they are ordered in particular situations. We know, for instance, that there are some products in certain market situations for which the bulk of the market's purchasing is done on impulse with little or no advance awareness or attitude related to the brand. This, then, might be the reverse of the stairstep hierarchy and is the sort of process that might have made up a large part of L'egg's sales during the early part of its introduction.

In other situations, it is reasonable to assume that people develop a gross awareness about a brand or a candidate without even thinking about it. Then, when they are faced with a buying decision, they make a trial without really developing an attitude or feeling about their choice until after use experience. This is the common process that is likely to be occurring for convenience packaged goods which are purchased often and require a low cash outlay in order to achieve trial. It also appears to be the kind of situation that holds true for lower-level political races like the state legislature ones mentioned in the example on the first page of this chapter. People tend to get a gross and imperfect impression of candidates in these kinds of races and then make a ballot choice on election day without really developing an attitude about the candidate they have chosen.

The Crown Zellerbach Zee versus P&G Charmin situation mentioned at the beginning of the chapter turned out to be something quite different from the stairstep learning hierarchy. Analysts decided that if the standard hierarchy could be characterized by "Learn-Feel-Do," the hierarchy in the toilet tissue market could be called "Do-Do" (pun intended!). This meant that when we purchase and use toilet paper, we really do not get any brand identification as we use it. The only time is at the purchase situation in the store. This is why the Charmin advertising and communication worked so well. The television commercials featured a character named Mr. Whipple who implored buyers to "Please don't squeeze the Charmin!" The commercials showed the critical in-store situation and shoppers actually handling and squeezing the product. P&G personal-selling and promotion efforts could build on the commercials by establishing end-of-aisle displays of Charmin similar to those in the commercials, along with introductory deals. This, plus the spending power of P&G, is what Crown Zellerbach faced.

In still other situations it is possible to imagine people developing a feeling about a product without really being able to know much about it. This might be the case in marketing to young children. Advertising may get them emotionally excited about a product without their even having the ability to cognitively process the specific information about it. They might take some action on their feeling by urging their mothers to buy the product when they are in the store. But it is only after purchase that the children really develop any detailed knowledge or awareness.

Of course, there are situations in which the original stairstep hierarchy occurs. Of the examples on the first page of this chapter, it is most likely to be applicable for the insurance companies and for many of Hewlett-Packard's industrial products. But the planning perspective that is being suggested by this chapter is that managers should first analyze the situation to determine which hierarchy order, the stairstep or some other, is predominant. Then it will be possible to assign communication goals to all aspects of the mix in such a way that the marketing objective of the total campaign can be maximized.

ANALYZING SITUATIONS: A THREE-ORDER HIERARCHY MODEL

The first step in setting communication goals, then, is a further analysis of the situation to determine what type of hierarchy situation exists and how it might be affected by a combined communication goal strategy.

At first glance, it might seem that such an analysis would be an imponderable task. Not only are there six possible orders of the three general hierarchy levels but there are usually more than three hierarchy levels that might be considered. And when you add to this complexity the fact that different hierarchies might exist for different target segments in a campaign situation, the communication goal situation analysis seems difficult indeed.

Fortunately for the planner, however, a great deal is known about the characteristics of situations that lead to particular hierarchy orders. In particular, there are three hierarchy orders that are each supported by a great deal of research. There is the standard stairstep Learning hierarchy; the Dissonance-Attribution hierarchy, which consists of action occurring first followed by attitude change and learning; and, finally, the Low-Involvement hierarchy, which consists of a gross awareness occurring first and then action and attitude development in that order.

The existence of solid knowledge on these three hierarchies makes the situation analysis and communication goal-setting task a viable one. In order to set communication goals, the planner need only examine those characteristics of the situation that have proven in the past to lead to the operation of one or the other of the three major hierarchies. Once one of the hierarchies or a variant has been identified as operating in the situation, the planner can efficiently assign goals to elements of the communication mix.

This section explains the nature of the three hierarchies and the kinds of conditions under which they are most likely to occur.

The Learning Hierarchy: "Learn-Feel-Do"

The Learning hierarchy is the equivalent of the original stairstep one discussed above. It is called the Learning hierarchy because with it there is the assumption that learning must occur before attitude and behavior change happen. That is, "learning" is posited to be essential to subsequent responses. For instance, William McGuire's "information-processing" approach is based essentially on a hierarchy, and he characterizes his approach as a learning one.[8]

While it has been posited as a basic progression of reactions to communication, even those individuals who examine the Learning hierarchy most thoroughly will caution that it exists only under special conditions. McGuire, for one, mentions several other approaches to attitude research, and he then points out that he would lose all credibility as an attitude researcher if he claimed that the Learning hierarchy (he does not use this particular term) existed for a majority of communication situations.

Under what conditions does it exist? Research by McGuire and others seems to indicate that it typically occurs when the audience is *involved* in the topic of the campaign and when there are *clear differences between alternatives*. Research on the diffusion of new products and innovations provides the best illustration of such conditions. Those market segments that are most interested in new ideas are involved, and new products or ideas offer clear alternatives. It is under such conditions that audience members first become aware, then develop interest, make evaluations, try, and adopt—the adoption process hierarchy.[9] This hierarchy as well as McGuire's is shown in Table 7-1.

Of the examples shown on the first page of this chapter, then, the Learning hierarchy is most likely to occur for those in which there is audience involvement, product differentiation, and an emphasis on the *mass media* in communication and in which the product is in the *early stages of the product life cycle,* such as those situations for which the adoption process hierarchy is most applicable. These situations would include the presidential political campaign. L'egg's in the early stages of its introduction, and the Hewlett-Packard hand-held calculator when it was introduced.

The nature of the Learning hierarchy and the situational characteristics that predict it are summarized in Figure 7-3. It is not too surprising that most of the examples offered for this hierarchy happen to be new-product introductions in which there is a tremendous amount of mass-media advertising. Recall that Colley used the hypothetical new car Venus as an example. And one of the most successful applications of the hierarchy planning approach was by General Motors in regard to a new-car introduction. A noted new-

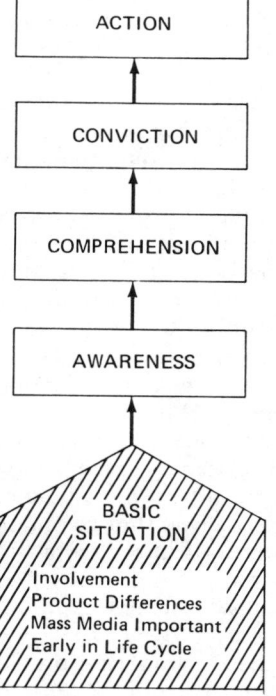

Figure 7-3. *Learning hierarchy*

product planning model was developed by N. W. Ayer based primarily on the Learning hierarchy.[10] And the first example in Figure 7-2 was for a new brand of hosiery.

Of course, there are exceptions to the Learning hierarchy even in the adoption situation, and these usually occur where there is varying availability of mass-media sources of information.[11] Marketing communication is more concerned with mass-media messages. In the adoption process it is sometimes true that personal sources of information and persuasion cause a behavior change before attitude change and learning from the mass media can take place. It is such situations that are covered by the second type of hierarchy.

The Dissonance-Attribution Hierarchy: "Do-Feel-Learn"

The "Dissonance-Attribution" hierarchy is the exact reverse of the standard Learning one. That is, both dissonance and attribution theorists have posited and examined situations in which behavior occurs first, then attitude change, and, finally, learning—a conative-affective-cognitive relationship.[12]

The basic idea of *dissonance theory* is that people are very often put in a situation where they are forced to make a choice between two alternatives that appear to be very close in quality but are complex and have many hidden or unknown attributes. When the choice is important enough, the very act of making that choice leads the person to try to bolster or rationalize the decision he or she has made by developing an improved attitude on the chosen alternative. On the basis of this "dissonance reduction," people will tend to seek out information favorable to their choice and avoid information that is counter to it. This then leads to a behavior-attitude-learning hierarchy. In marketing, the dissonance theory idea has been applied primarily to postpurchase behavior. One of the most often-quoted studies is one relating to the automobile area, for which we have already indicated that the Learning hierarchy works best for new-car purchasing. The quoted and often-criticized study by Ehrlich and others indicated that automobile advertising was more likely to be read by recent purchasers of the respective automobiles than by those who were at some point prior to purchase. Such studies indicate that marketing-communication planners should be concerned about the communication goals for segments that have bought the product and need reinforcement in their purchase as well as support for future purchases. Ehrenberg has indicated that one of the major functions of advertising is to reinforce a pattern of purchase.[13]

Attribution theory is really a more up-to-date explanation for dissonance phenomena as well as a wider variety of other psychological situations. The basic idea of the theory is that people tend to balance a whole series of internal and external stimuli to determine or "attribute" the causes of events that they observe. The basic balancing is between internal, personality, or "dispositional" causes and external or situational causes. One of the most important subtheories in the attribution area is Daryl Bem's "self perception theory." The basic idea of his theory is that people determine that they have attitudes by perceiving their own behavior. Therefore, if someone has made a choice as in dissonance theory, this person will say to himself or herself, "I must have a positive attitude toward that alternative because in fact I have chosen it." If subsequent to that choice and attitude development, individuals are exposed to marketing-communication messages, they will tend to develop information that will support the attitudes. Thus we would have a Dissonance-Attribution hierarchy: choice, then attitude formation and, finally, cognitive development. One study that was done in the dissonance area but can be explained quite readily by attribution theory is one by Doob and others on the effect of low introduction prices. Their conclusion, which may have applications to the marketing-communication

element of price promotions, was that low initial prices induce people to buy the product for inadequate product characteristics reasons. Therefore there is no opportunity for the individual to "attribute" the purchase to dispositional or motivational reasons. In the Doob study, the low initial prices led to less aggregate purchasing behavior in the long run than did higher prices. Thus, as with dissonance theory, the attribution theory notion can be applied most readily to those situations and segments who have already made a purchase.[14]

Now, in what situations could the manager expect the Dissonance-Attribution hierarchy to occur? These have typically been situations in which the audience has been *involved* but the *alternatives have been almost indistinguishable*. In research, consumers or pseudoconsumers are forced to make a choice of behavior caused by some *non-mass-media marketing-communication source*. In addition, the products involved tend to be those in the *mature stage of the product life cycle*. Many dissonance and attribution studies have been done with durable goods, such as automobiles, household appliances, and home entertainment equipment. In the research itself, the consumer is asked to make some choice, then he or she changes attitude in order to bolster that choice—often on the basis of experience with the chosen alternative. Finally, learning itself occurs on the selective basis, in order to bolster the original choice by response to messages that are supportive of it. The Dissonance-Attribution hierarchy and situation characteristics are shown in Figure 7-4.

Obviously, the mass media can have an effect in promoting the original choice behavior and attitude change, but both dissonance and attribution theorists argue that the main mass-media effect is in terms of reducing dissonance or providing information for attribution or self-perception—*after* behavior and attitude change have occurred.

For the third type of hierarchy, on the other hand, mass-media learning is the key initial step.

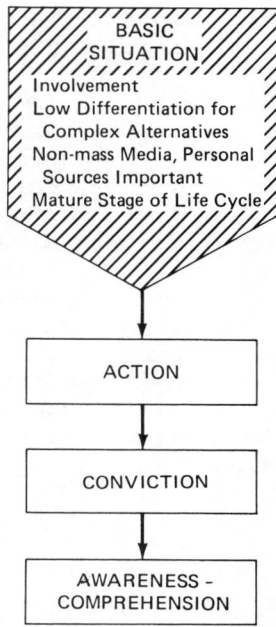

Figure 7-4. Dissonance-Attribution hierarchy

The Low-Involvement Hierarchy: "Learn-Do-Feel"

Herbert Krugman is most responsible for recognizing what is here called the Low-Involvement hierarchy.[15] Krugman was interested in determining why television advertising seemed to have such a strong aggregate effect, although laboratory research often indicates little effect of TV ads on individuals' attitude change.

He concluded that most television viewers are *not involved* with either the advertising or the topics. This means that there is very little perceptual defense against the messages. Although television ads may not directly change attitude, they may, after overwhelming repetition, make possible a shift in cognitive structure. Consumers may be better able to recall the name or idea of a product. Then the next time they are in a purchasing situation, that name comes to

mind, they buy, and attitude is subsequently changed as a result of experience with the product. Thus the Low-Involvement hierarchy is a cognitive-conative-affective one, as shown in Figure 7-5.

In addition to the obvious situation characteristic of low consumer involvement, there are several others that characterize the situations in which the Low-Involvement hierarchy tends to occur. Perhaps the best general guide to the planner is that products that are likely to be advertised on broadcast media tend also to be those that follow the Low-Involvement hierarchy. For these products there tend to be *minimal differences* between alternatives, *mass-media advertising is important,* and they are usually in the *mature stage of the product life cycle.* Both the N. W. Ayer model and research by Ehrenberg on such products find substantial evidence for the Low-Involvement hierarchy.[16] This does not mean, however, that this hierarchy is restricted to broadcast communication about low-priced consumer goods. Nor are all low-priced consumer goods

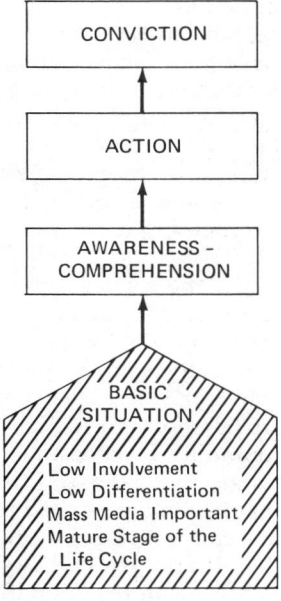

Figure 7-5. Low-involvement hierarchy

subject to the Low-Involvement hierarchy. In fact, the low-involvement situation does hold for a variety of purchasing situations and social acts, including part of the insurance purchasing process, voting for candidates like those for the state legislature, and many industrial purchasing decisions made by purchasing agents.

In addition, the Low-Involvement hierarchy has been found quite often by recent research studies, which are the subject of the next section.

Recent Research Findings on the Three-Order Model

Although there is a great deal of evidence of each of the hierarchy orders within the research traditions that have developed them, only recently has there been research that has compared the relative incidence of each of the hierarchies in particular marketing-communication situations.

Some of this research has been correlational. That is, the search for sequences of communication responses have been done with cross-lag correlation, recursive regression models, distributed lag models, and various other econometric techniques.[17] Most of these correlational studies have searched for the Learning hierarchy and found that it exists in some situations.

Despite the fact that the correlation-regression approach has provided valuable information, there has been a need for experimental research that directly compares the existence of the hierarchy in a variety of situations that are posited to be importantly different in terms of their communication response. Such research is necessary to "validate" the three-order model. That is, managers need to know if the situational characteristics represented in Figures 7-3, 7-4, and 7-5 and suggested by the previous discussion really do in-

dicate differential communication response and the need for particular communication goal-setting strategies.

Fortunately, some research has been generally supportive of the model and planning approach suggested here. This research program has centered on determining the repetition response function for advertising. This "repetition project" has involved a series of laboratory and field experiments in which consumers in different situations have been exposed to advertising at various repetition levels. In the course of these studies, all of the four situational characteristics—involvement, product differentiation, mass-media importance, and stage of the product life cycle—have been varied with results that are supportive of the model presented earlier.[18]

Advances in Communication Goals Situation Analysis

One result of the increase in solid information on the communication process has been that managers can now analyze situations more precisely. The four factors that have been mentioned in this chapter are the result of the great deal of research on communication response. And the long-run potential is for a more ordered analysis of situations. Thus it would be possible to develop a matrix representing all levels of the four situational factors mentioned here. Then a manager could examine any particular situation and determine in which cell of the matrix it was located. Past experience with such situations could then be brought to bear in order to make a first cut in determining the type of communication campaign that is necessary. Far from replacing the manager or making the campaign development too mechanistic, such a procedure would allow the manager to spend more time on the creative pursuits that are discussed in the following section.

BALANCING ELEMENTS OF THE COMMUNICATION MIX AND THE COMPENSATION PRINCIPLE

Once the situation has been analyzed to the point that there is some basic understanding of the type of communication response that is likely to occur, it is necessary to determine how the communication mix will operate in order to move this response toward the final marketing objectives of sales, and so forth. Essentially, what needs to be done is an assignment of one particular level of the hierarchy to each of the components of the communication mix over time. This is done at a general level at this point, without the sort of specificity that is called for in the end set of communication goals statements. The attempt here is to balance the effects of the elements of the communication mix in such a way that they work together and produce a sort of synergy for maximum output in marketing objective terms.

The three-order model provides a first cut at this balancing job. We know, for instance, that if the situation is a low-involvement one, advertising will be the main tool used to create awareness and possibly some positive comprehension. There will be little concern with attitude development except to make sure that the product is an excellent one so that it helps to develop product satisfaction after purchase. Point-of-purchase materials, product sampling, and price promotions will be used to induce trial.

Similar types of analyses might be done for the Learning hierarchy and the Dissonance-Attribution one. The Learning hierarchy offers the potential of using mass-media efforts to move people through several of the stages of the hierarchy. It also brings into play the possibility for the use of publicity, which is not a viable alternative in low-involvement situations. Publicity can create comprehen-

sion as well as attitude about the brand in the Learning hierarchy situation. Personal selling can also become an important factor, as it is in those Learning hierarchy situations that exist in the industrial-marketing area. With industrial advertising and other components of the mix creating awareness and general comprehension and interest, the personal-selling component can develop conviction, intention, and additional action.

In the Dissonance-Attribution hierarchy situation, some of the emphasis should be on providing information and attitudinally oriented material that supports the choice that present users have made. Again, personal selling, sampling, and promotions can be effective vehicles for developing additional action response.

Beyond these general indications from the three-order model for communication-mix balancing, there is interesting potential for dramatic creative moves in breaking the standard patterns of using the elements of the communication mix. This potential is based on an idea developed by William McGuire, which he calls the *compensation principle*.[19] In examining his Learning hierarchy–information-processing approach to communication, McGuire had the insight that any communication variable that had a strong effect on one level of the hierarchy would tend to have an opposite effect on some other. He called this idea the "compensation principle" and used it to explain such phenomena as the non-monotonic (first increasing and then decreasing) effects of increasing levels of fear appeals.

Stated in compensation principle terms, the effect of great fear in a message may be to *increase* attention and awareness but correspondingly to *decrease* attitudinal effects—because the audience may reject such high fear as being unreasonable. The interaction of these two effects leads to a nonmonotonic effect, with moderate levels of fear being most effective.

The repetition project has produced a number of results that might be characterized as compensation ones. For instance, ads that tended to use "borrowed interest" produced strong effects in awareness but null or even negative ones on attitude and purchase intention. This compensation principle result that has been noticed for advertising probably can hold for other aspects of the mix also. Salespeople who learn how their product relates to all aspects of their client's business may effectively apply this knowledge in generating conviction and search action, but the emphasis on their client's business may draw attention away from their own product. Another example of this compensatory relationship between hierarchy levels occurs in publicity that generates comprehension of product features but fails to generate name registration.

The compensation principle is a problem if the manager is considering just one part of the communication mix at a time. It becomes an exciting opportunity, however, when a campaign manager considers a balancing of all the aspects of the mix. If compensation between hierarchy levels is inevitable or even frequent, then the elements of the communication mix can be used selectively to deal with it. Extremely high awareness and negative attitude generated by advertising may be complemented by personal selling, product sampling, and point-of-purchase efforts with contrasting effects. In fact, "negative" byproducts of advertising such as mild disbelief may be converted to positive effects if other aspects of the mix are of high quality.

One illustration of this compensation principle at work is the solutions that were developed for the two insurance companies, New England Life and Northwestern Mutual Life, that were mentioned on the first page of this chapter. Both companies attempted to achieve extremely high levels of awareness and comprehension with advertising, realizing that the negative byproducts of such a move could be compensated for by their agents and collateral material.

New England Life developed an advertising campaign that featured wild cartoon illustrations of a New England policyholder who is about to face disaster. This advertising was so different from all other insurance advertising in magazines that it generated a great deal of awareness for the company, although much of this awareness may have been negative because of the frivolous and somewhat strange nature of the advertisements themselves. Presumably the rationale for the approach was that there was a necessity to break through the extreme "noise" level in the media so that New England Life's agents would have a strong awareness level to work with when they called on prospective customers. The extremity of the New England Life approach was so great that it might also have been necessary to use other communication elements, such as direct mail, to soften the possible negative impact before agents came to call on prospective customers (Figure 7-6).

Northwestern Mutual, on the other hand, did its creative work in media as opposed to copy. It increased its annual advertising budget by 50 percent and proceeded to put all of this money into forty-six messages which were exposed during the seventeen days of the 1972 Olympics. Its advertising was far from being the strange and unusual type that was featured by New England Life. Instead the commercials promoted NML as being the "quiet company." Thus this overwhelming and concentrated media plan, which might have caused negative reactions from viewers, was turned into an invitation to meet with agents who could then make this a more positive overall effort. The extremely difficult and strong job of creating and developing awareness beyond all previous imagination for Northwestern was assigned to the advertising component. The other parts of the communication mix were used to convert this strong impression into something more positive in terms of overall campaign effect. NML has continued this balancing into the 1980's with ad placement on Super Bowl broadcasts.

The kind of creativity that might be exercised in setting communication goals could

"My insurance company? New England Life, of course. Why?"

Figure 7-6. New England Life advertisement showing intense implementation of a strong awareness goal for advertising to be balanced by different goal achievement by other communication elements

(Courtesy of New England Mutual Life Insurance Co.)

actually change the very terms that are used to describe those goals. For instance, one communication goal is typically to get some segment to comprehend something about the brand or product being promoted. But it might be possible to change the goal from one of developing comprehension to one of developing intrigue. If advertising can create the response "I wonder if that's true?," then it might be possible to lead consumers to try the product and find out more about it. This trial and information seeking can be facilitated by other aspects of the mix. Therefore a response something less than complete comprehension and belief might actually be converted by compensatory moves of other elements of the communication mix.

A strong "credibility" comprehension

goal was assigned to sales promotion for the early Spray 'n Wash campaign ad balanced and extended by other communication elements. As mentioned in Chapter 6, the promotion was called "The Incredible Guarantee"—a refund of the price *of the shirt* if Spray 'n Wash did not remove any stain from that shirt. This strong guarantee was presented convincingly in a television commercial along with sales force selling and publicity, which contributed to literally creating a new subsection in the supermarket.[20]

Application of the compensation principle is especially necessary in today's marketing-communication environment in which there are so many messages for so many different types of products. In such an environment, it is often necessary to "go out on a limb" on some particular aspect of the mix in order to have any effect at all. But the creative campaign manager can balance such an unusual communication goal with creative strategy and goal setting for other aspects of the mix. This is essentially the task of the second step of communication goal setting.

CONCLUSION: MAKING GOALS SPECIFIC

It is not enough to simply analyze the communication situation and balance the goals across the elements of the communication mix. As was mentioned in Chapter 4, any creative act requires a "shaping and development." Too many strategists stop at the level of a general statement of communication goals. In order to fully implement the goal statement throughout the campaign development stages of message, message distribution, budget, implementation, and especially measurement and control, it is necessary that the campaign goals for each element of the mix be stated in terms of specific percentage increases for specific market segments in specific time periods.

What is really necessary at this stage is to make the communication goals operational in the sense that there will be something to measure with control procedures that are used to assess the effects of the campaign. Evidence indicates that most marketing-communication campaigns operate on too general and subjective a set of communication objectives. The kinds of objective statements that were offered for advertising campaigns in the three examples of Figure 7-2 are a fine first step in this effort. In addition, each of those advertisers developed specific measurements that were to be used to determine if the campaign had indeed had any effect. Part of the goal statement should also be a statement of the measurement that would be used to determine each effect.

In one study that was made of 135 campaigns done by forty advertising agencies, it was shown that almost none of the agencies stated their objectives in such a way that they could really know whether or not their campaigns were successful. The author of this study pointed to four major deficiencies of the stated campaign objectives:

1. Failure to state the objective or objectives in quantifiable terms.
2. Apparent failure to realize that the results of the advertising could not be measured in sales.
3. Failure to identify the advertising audience.
4. Use of superlatives (which are unmeasurable.)[21]

Managers should go through the exercise of very precisely stating the objectives in communication terms for every element of the communication mix. They will find that this exercise provides a great deal of extra information and insight into communication response in the particular campaign under study.

The development of communication goals is a continuing process both at the communication goal stage and throughout the communication decision sequence. The three-order model allows a gross analysis of each situation and a development of outlines of communication response. But as has been noted before, there are six possible permutations under the three levels of the communication hierarchy. In addition, there are often more than three levels, and the compensation principle can further complicate each situation. Thus the major conclusion and suggestion of this chapter is that the steps of communication goal setting suggested in this chapter—situation analysis, balancing elements of the mix, and specifying goals—should be the first ones in a continual sharpening process that goes on throughout the development of efficient campaign strategy.

SUMMARY

A three-step procedure for setting communication goals has been advocated.

First, the situation should be analyzed in terms of which hierarchy of communication effects is likely to be operating. Three

types were discussed in this chapter. Others probably exist. They can be identified by analyzing involvement, product differentiation, consumer information sources, and consumer degree of experience with the product (life cycle).

Second, once the hierarchy situation is identified, planners should set general communication goals for each element of the mix. Recognizing that when advertising, personal selling, sales promotion, and publicity work together they can produce great final sales results—the campaign manager must creatively use the compensation principle to set extreme goals for some parts of the mix which can be balanced by other parts.

Third, very specific communication goal statements should be written for each mix element in terms of segment, percentage change in communication response expected in what time period, by clearly specified measures (even if market research measurement is not possible).

ISSUES AND PROJECTS FOR DISCUSSION

The Discussion questions for this chapter are in the form of a hierarchy situation analysis assignment. You are to answer the following questions for a particular communication campaign situation, either one you have picked or one assigned by your instructor.

1. What is the brand-product?
2. Describe the target market for which this campaign is being developed.
3. How involved is the typical person in this segment? Is this person actively looking for information, is this purchase of great importance to him or her, how routine is the purchase? Is this purchase:

☐ Most involving purchase?
☐ One of the most involving?
☐ Above average?
☐ Average?

☐ Below average?
☐ One of the least involving?
☐ Least involving?

Reason for your response?

4. Does the typical person in this segment perceive that there are big differences between alternative brands in the product category? To this person:

☐ Is every brand distinctive?
☐ One or two brands stand out?
☐ Good, medium, and bad brand groups perceived?
☐ Good and bad brands perceived?
☐ All brands pretty much the same?

5. Where do consumers in this segment get their main information for purchasing? TV ads, friends, POP, articles, past experience, salespeo-

ple? In other words, what is the main "medium" through which their beliefs are affected?

6. How experienced are the segment consumers in purchasing this product? Are they relatively inexperienced so that it is a new experience to them? Or, on the other hand, are they so experienced that it is routine? Or are they somewhere in between?

7. On the basis of the above, which hierarchy response to advertising would you say exists for this brand-product and segment? Is it Learning (Know-Feel-Do), Low-Involvement (Know-Do-Feel), Dissonance-Attribution (Do-Feel-Know), or some other?

8. Now, on the basis of your answers to the above questions, what general communication goals should be assigned to each element of the mix?

9. Write a specific communication goal statement, similar to those in Figure 7-2, for advertising for the market offering.

10. What implications does your situation analysis and goal statement have for message content (positioning), message format, message development and testing, media weight/scheduling, media selection, use of promotion, advertising research (recall testing), etc.?

Notes

1. Martin Mayer, *Madison Avenue, U.S.A.* (New York: Harper, 1958), p. 259.

2. Charles K. Ramond, *American Marketing Association Bulletin,* 17 (April 1964), 2.

3. Robert J. Lavidge and Gary A. Steiner, "A Model for Predictive Measurements of Advertising Effectiveness," *Journal of Marketing,* 25 (October 1961), 59–62; Russell H. Colley, *Defining Advertising Goals for Measured Advertising Results* (New York: Association of National Advertisers, 1961); Rosser Reeves, *Reality in Advertising* (New York: Knopf, 1961); Harry D. Wolfe, James K. Brown and G. Clark Thompson, *Measuring Advertising Results* (New York: National Industrial Conference Board, 1962); and Darrell B. Lucas and Steuart H. Britt, *Measuring Advertising Effectiveness* (New York: McGraw-Hill, 1963).

4. Russell H. Colley, "Squeezing the Waste out of Advertising" *Harvard Business Review,* September-October 1962, pp. 76–88.

5. Gail Smith, "How GM Measures Ad Effectiveness" in *Readings in Marketing Research,* ed. Keith Cox (New York: Appleton-Century-Crofts, 1967).

6. Anthony G. Greenwald, "Cognitive Learning, Cognitive Response to Persuasion, and Attitude Change," in *Psychological Foundations of Attitudes,* ed. Anthony G. Greenwald, Timothy C. Brock, and Thomas M. Ostrom (New York: Academic Press, 1968); Jack B. Haskins, "Factual Recall as a Measure of Advertising Effectiveness," *Journal of Advertising Research,* 4 (March 1964), 2–28; and Peter L. Wright, "On the Direct Monitoring of Cognitive Response to Advertising," in *Buyer/Consumer Information Processing,* ed. G. David Hughes and Michael L. Ray (Chapel Hill: University of North Carolina Press, 1974).

7. Donald T. Campbell, "Social Attitudes and Other Acquired Behavior Dispositions," in *Psychology: A Study of a Science,* ed. S. Koch (New York: McGraw-Hill, 1963), Vol. 6; George S. Day, *Buyer Attitudes and Brand Choice Behavior* (New York: Free Press, 1970); Leon Festinger, "Behavioral Support for Opinion Change," *Public Opinion Quarterly,* 28 (Fall 1964), 404–17; Martin Fishbein and Icek Ajzen, "Attitudes and Opinions," *Annual Review of Psychology,* 23 (1972), 487–554; and Robert T. LaPiere, "Attitudes versus Actions," *Social Forces,* 13 (1934), 230–37.

8. William J. McGuire, "An Information-Processing Approach to Advertising Effectiveness," in *The Behavioral and Management Sciences in Marketing,* ed. H. Davis and A. J. Silk (New York: Ronald Press, 1978).

9. Ibid; Thomas S. Robertson, *Innovative Behavior and Communication* (New York: Holt, Rinehart & Winston, 1971); and Everett M. Rogers with F. F. Shoemaker, *Communication of Innovations; A Cross-Cultural Approach* (New York: Free Press, 1971).

10. Henry J. Claycamp and Lucien Liddy, "Prediction of New Product Performance: An Analytical Approach," *Journal of Marketing Research* (November 1969), 414–20.

11. Robertson, *Innovative Behavior;* and Rogers and Shoemaker, *Communication of Innovations.*

12. Elliott Aronson, "The Theory of Cognitive Dissonance," in *Advances in Experimental Social Psychology,* ed. L. Berkowitz (New York: Academic Press, 1969) Vol. 4; Daryl J. Bem, "Self Perception Theory," in *Advances in Experimental Social Psychology,* ed. L. Berkowitz (New York: Academic Press, 1972), Vol. 6; and Harold H. Kelley, "The Processes of Causal Attribution," *American Psychologist,* Vol. 28, pp. 107–28.

13. Aronson, "Theory of Cognitive Dissonance"; Danuta Ehrlich, I. Guttman, P. Shoenbach, and J. Mills, "Post Decision Exposure to Relative Information," *Journal of Abnormal and Social Psychology,* 54 (1957), 98–102; James F. Engel and M. Lawrence Light, "The Role of Psychological Commitment in Consumer Behavior: An Evaluation of the Theory of Cognitive Dissonance," in *Applications of the Sciences in Marketing Management,* ed. F. M. Bass, C. W. King, and E. A. Pessemier (New York: John Wiley, 1968), pp. 179–206; and Andrew S. C. Ehrenberg, "Repetitive Advertising and the Consumer," *Journal of Advertising Research,* 14 (April 1974), 25–34.

14. Bem, "Self Perception Theory"; Kelley, "Processes of Causal Attribution"; and Anthony M. Doob, J. Merrill Carlsmith, Jonathan L. Freedman, Thomas K. Landauer, and Tom Soleng, Jr., "Effect of Initial Selling Price on Subsequent Sales," *Journal of Personality and Social Psychology,* 11 (April 1969), 345–50.

15. Herbert E. Krugman, "The Impact of Television Advertising: Learning without In-volvement," *Public Opinion Quarterly,* 29 (1965), 349–56.

16. Claycamp and Liddy, "Prediction of New Product Performance"; and Ehrenberg, "Repetitive Advertising."

17. David A. Aaker, *Multivariate Analysis in Marketing: Theory and Application* (Belmont, Calif.: Wadsworth, 1971); Claycamp and Liddy, "Prediction of New Product Performance"; Terrence O'Brien, "Stages of Consumer Decision Making," *Journal of Marketing Research,* 8 (1971), 283–89; and Kristian S. Palda, "The Hypothesis of a Hierarchy of Effects: A Partial Evaluation," *Journal of Marketing Research,* 8 (1966), 283–89.

18. Michael L. Ray, Alan G. Sawyer, Michael L. Rothschild, Roger M. Heeler, Edward C. Strong, and Jerome B. Reed, "Marketing Communication and the Hierarchy of Effects," in *New Models for Mass Communication Research,* ed. Peter Clark (Beverly Hills, Calif.: Sage Publications, Inc., 1973), pp. 147–76; and Rajeer Batra and Michael Ray, "Advertising Situations," in *Information Processing Research in Advertising,* ed. Richard J. Harris (Hillsdale, N.J.: Erlbaum, 1982).

19. McGuire, "Information-Processing Approach."

20. "Creative Sales Promotion Vital in Marketing Mix," *Marketing News,* November 30, 1979, p. 8.

21. Steuart H. Britt, "Are So-Called Successful Advertising Campaigns Really Successful?" *Journal of Advertising Research,* 9 (1969), 3–9.

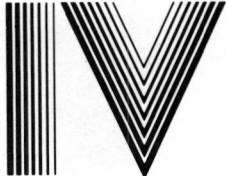

THE MESSAGE IDEA

. . . Its Nature and the Copy Platform

. . . Positioning

. . . Tone

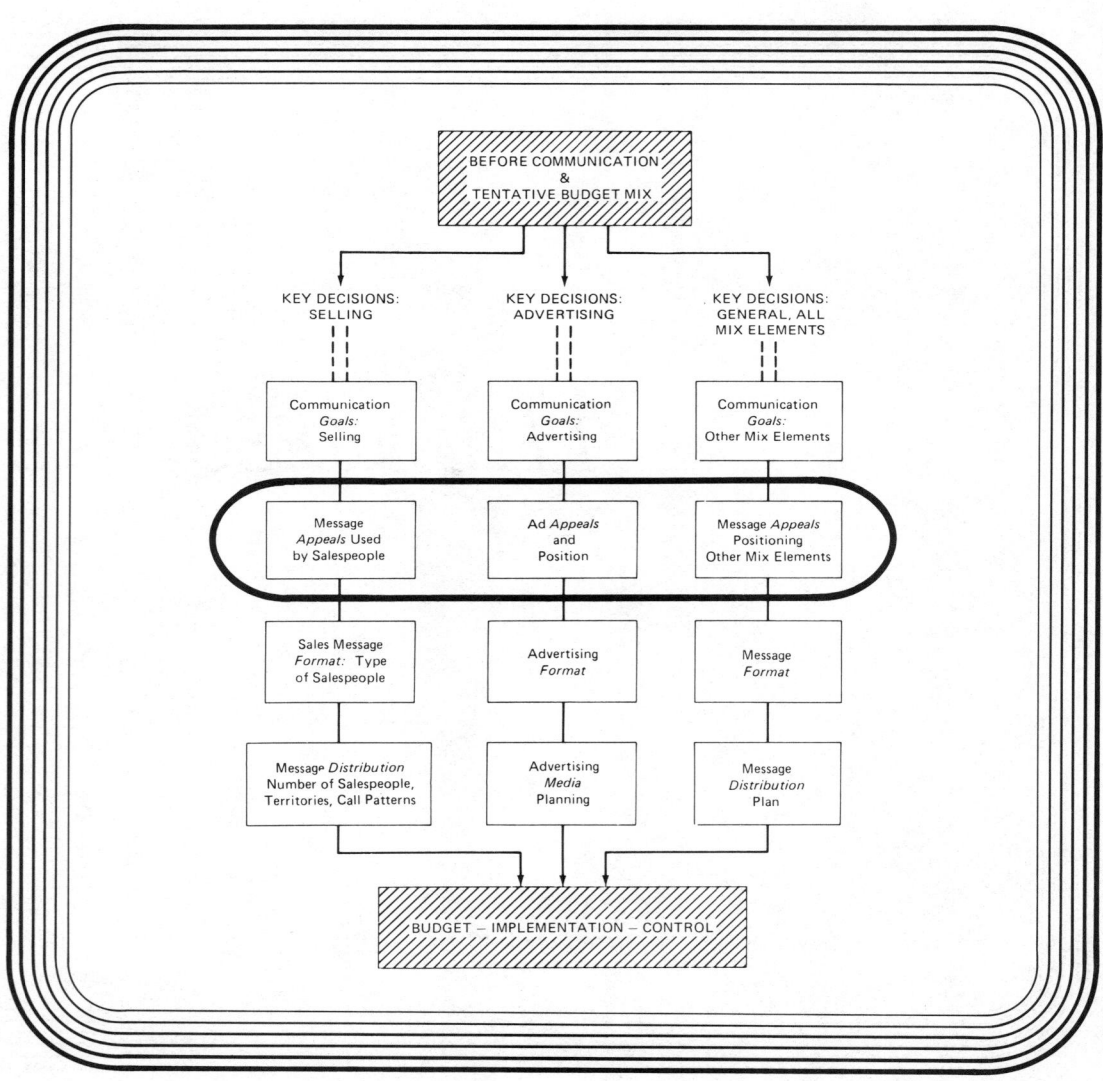

The Message Idea and the Copy Platform

Ford aims at young car buyers
with muscle, fuel economy mix

Schaefer uses
"people" theme
in new effort
to boost sales

A&P apology
kicks off drive;
phase II will
stress service

Listerine now says it's
"more than a mouthwash"

J&J will stress expanded
baby lotion uses

Mazola adds tie-in with
lower cholesterol diets

Eastern's next ad campaign
to stress schedules, not extras

Campbell tries
new ad theme
for soup line

Goodyear ads
combine tires,
service; ''more''
good years

—*Advertising Age* headlines

It has been said that "nothing is as powerful as an idea whose time has come." In marketing, and particularly in marketing communication, this is especially true. The entire campaign and its success revolve around the position of the brand, product, service, or candidate. If the message idea is outstanding, then other parts of the marketing-communication mix will be multiplied in their effect. Great message ideas have a tremendous amount of "leverage"; that is, relatively small expenditures on message ideas development can multiply back many times in terms of returns to the company possessing the idea.

In this chapter we will learn how to develop great campaign ideas that have this sort of leverage. Although we have been discussing creativity and the creative development of campaigns throughout this book, it is important to realize that the message idea or creative strategy is the keystone of the campaign because it is what is communicated. Let us look at the nature of the message idea in terms of the nine examples that are represented by the headlines on the first page of this chapter. In all cases there is a building on the nature of the product, consumer, competition, trade, and past experience. But the campaign idea is more than these things, more than the physical reality of the market offering itself. For example:

1. *Ford.* In an automobile market in which the product offerings are quite similar, the campaign ideas of the major American manufacturers differ quite markedly. Ford, as the above headline indicated, decided to aim at young car buyers with a "muscle, fuel economy mix." Obviously attacking the foreign car inroads into the American small-car market, Ford was building on its cars' names (Pinto, Stallion, Maverick, Mustang), styling, and engineering to reach the young car buyer. In the automobile market the communication message idea is closely tied to the product offering itself, whether it be the Ford type of offering or the AMC Buyer Protection Plan.

2. *Schaefer.* In contrast to the automobile market, the beer market offers an example in which the message idea of the communication campaign is the key factor in consumer perception of and reaction to the brand. The Schaefer "people" theme was this regional beer's reaction to the success of its competitor, Genesee beer. Schaefer had aimed its advertising in the past at the heavy beer drinkers segment with the theme-slogan "The one beer to have when you're having more than one." Genesee countered with a campaign that featured nearly 130 commericals in its first five years, all using a personal testimonial from someone who had lived in the Genesee marketing area but moved elsewhere and missed the beer. This "fantastic fan" campaign coincided with five straight years of sales increases while Schaefer lost sales in the last year, fired its advertising agency, and started with a theme similar to Genesee's ("I'm Schaefer people").

3. *A&P.* The giant food chain's campaign theme or message idea had been based almost entirely on the consistent price reductions which had been the chain's policy. The headline on the first page of this chapter points out that A&P developed a new theme which was in reaction to the lack of consistent effect from the price-cutting program. The new theme featured an "apology" for diminishing the service and pride of A&P while cutting prices. The new theme stressed the service that people could expect from a store like A&P. This theme was related to a complete image-building campaign for A&P.

4. *Listerine*. The leading mouthwash brand tried the theme, "More than a mouthwash" in response to heavy competitive activity and the Federal Trade Commission ruling that the brand could no longer use the cold preventive theme that it had used for more than half a century.

5. *Johnson & Johnson*. This company provides a perfect example of a message idea that opened up tremendous new markets. The Johnson & Johnson baby powder, baby shampoo, and baby oils had been positioned for all family and adult usage. This led, for instance, to the baby shampoo's becoming the leading selling shampoo. Subsequently, as the headline on the first page of this chapter suggested, Johnson & Johnson attempted to do the same thing with its baby lotion by using copy lines in women's magazine ads suggesting "Outrageous ways to help save your softness with Johnson's baby lotion."

6. *Speed Queen*. This company's washing machines were sold with a durability or long-lasting theme. This was obviously in response to the reliability theme that had been developed so successfully by Maytag in the past (see description in Chapter 4). These two washing machine campaigns illustrate that the theme or message idea is only one part of the creative strategy. Campaigns like these two can have very similar themes, yet their message formats may be quite different. The Maytag campaign used strong testimonials to emphasize the reliability theme. Speed Queen's durability theme was "Built better to

last longer." The advertising featured a rugged presenter, actor Chuck Connors, selling the well-built components of the Speed Queen washer.

7. *Mazola*. Although there are other cooking oils high in polyunsaturates, Mazola was the only leading one made of pure corn oil and capitalized on this with a theme that featured the use of Mazola in a university-developed low-cholesterol diet.

8. *Eastern Airlines*. This airline had vacillated between selling the total idea of air travel and selling Eastern's extra services. Then it moved away from image campaigns to a schedule one, as did TWA. At the same time Braniff had a famous artist painting its planes in special colors, and National Airlines was continuing to sell its no-frills fare. In airline advertising the campaign theme can be very closely tied to service or pricing characteristics, or it can attempt to build on these characteristics with an image approach.

9. *Campbell Soup*. This company holds 80 percent of the condensed soup market but feels that it needs continual rejuvenation in its campaign themes in order to get the entire market moving. The company first tested a number of themes on television and then selected one entitled "Campbell life." The message idea attempted to relate to changing eating habits and positioned condensed soups as the "Popular choice for today's quick and easy life style."

The competitive give and take in response to market needs represented by these case examples is the essence of creative strategy development. Earlier, in Chapters 4 and 5, we discussed the way a product or service can be positioned in a market due to its characteristics or to the way it is distributed and priced. In this chapter and the next we discuss creative strategy and the way any given market offering may be positioned in the mind of the consumer through the use of a communication campaign.

The reason that a great creative idea for

communication messages can have such great leverage is that consumers have preferences for products that are based on their perceptions. A product does not really exist for any given consumer unless he or she knows about it. And what consumers know about a product is what that product consists of for them. Beginning marketers often make the mistake of believing that if a product is superior, is inferior, satisfies a particular need, or looks better than any other market offering, these characteristics alone will ensure the same perceptions on the part of consumers. However, the achievement of any particular level of the hierarchies we talked about in the preceding chapter is based on the communication of some particular product position, appeal, or theme. If it were possible to have identical market offerings (which it is not), the one with the more appropriate theme, communicated effectively, would capture a larger share of market.

THE COMMUNICATION ENVIRONMENT

Not only must a marketer communicate about his or her market offering in order to affect perceptions and thus preferences but communication is more difficult today than in the past because there are an increasing number of competitive messages.

The Explosion of Messages

The estimates for the total number of commercial messages of all types seen by any given consumer on any day range from three hundred to sixteen hundred. It is estimated, for instance, that the volume of advertising in the United States has increased about 500 percent in the past twenty years, while the population has increased only 50 percent. Cost per message has increased, but the fig-

ures presented earlier in Chapter 1 are strong testimony to the increasingly cluttered media environment. Estimated ad volume has pushed above $50 billion, personal selling over $70 billion, and promotion (depending on how it is defined) expenditures also exceed $50 billion. Advertising expenditures have been growing at an average rate of 5.5 percent per year since 1969, while sales promotion expenditures have increased an average of 9.2 percent per year. Promotions are obviously something that is increasingly being done to cut through the cluttered communication environment. The A. C. Nielson Company estimates that over 25 billion coupons are distributed each year, for example.

At the end of the 1960s, a local Chicago television station, monitored continuously by a media research agency, interrupted its nightly movie five times to present thirty-six different messages to viewers. Four years later, the same station's movie contained eleven breaks with an average of fifty-three separate messages. From the bginning of the 1960s to the beginning of the 1970s, television commercial expenditures increased more than 300 percent, not to mention the increase in public service and program promotional messages. The available time has been cut up into smaller segments, with the common commercial length going from sixty seconds down to thirty seconds, and the latest predictions indicate that ten seconds will be the common commerical length in the future. The American Association of Advertising Agencies conducted a spot check and found 50 percent more commercials and 33 percent more commercial minutes than in a similar check conducted eight years earlier.

Such "clutter" is also found in the media other than television. For many magazines, there is actually more advertising than editorial material. At one time in the past it was possible to gain extra attention in newspapers by using full-color preprints. Now preprinters are concerned that this usage is too common and that attention value is lost.

Decreases in Consumer Recall

It appears that all of this clutter is having an effect on the consumers' ability to notice and remember advertising. A study sponsored by the Americn Association of Advertising Agencies indicated that of the sixteen hundred commercial messages consumers are exposed to each day only eighty make some conscious impression. And only 15 percent of these have some perceptively positive or negative effect on the consumer.[1] A study done by Quaker Oats indicated that 97 percent of the audience for six high-rated television shows could not remember what was being advertised. Daniel Starch and staff, in a study conducted in Atlanta in the early 1970s, found that 25 percent of those noting a television commercial attributed it to the competition. Another study found no difference in the number of ads recalled when there were great increases in the number available to be recalled in cluttered conditions.[2]

There are good psychological reasons for the consumer's inability to process the increasing information load represented by commercial communication. Numerous studies have indicated in general that the maximum number of ideas that a person can keep aware of or consider at any given time ranges from three to seven. This means that there is a definite limit to the number of messages and ideas about products and services that people can keep in their minds. Thus although the number of products has been increasing along with the number of messages that are generated for each product, the consumer's ability to absorb messages has stayed about the same.

How Consumers Cope

People have developed a number of methods for coping with the information explosion, however. It has been shown that by classifying, or "chunking" as the psychologists call it, people can keep a large number of objects in mind. In a simple research study, for example, people were confronted by literally hundreds of words, some of which were names of animals and others were names of colors, and were able to play back a large percentage of the list because they were able to classify the words in those categories. In a similar way, according to the consumer behavior theorists Howard and Sheth, consumers have an "evoked set" of brands that come to mind when they are considering any particular product category. Much consumer behavior research has indicated that the number of brands or categories of brands that a consumer is willing to consider is usually in the range of three to five. And consumers have a tendency to rank or position the product offerings they are willing to consider. Consumers seem to be combining and simplifying the world as they view it in order to be able to make purchases without great cost in time, effort, money, and product satisfaction.

An Example: Soft Drink Purchasing and Communication

Perhaps an example of how one consumer may organize a product category for purchasing may help to explain the importance of creative strategy in this process. Let us take the soft-drink category. In one eight-year period the number of soft drinks advertised on network television increased from seven to twenty-two! How would a typical soft-drink purchaser deal with this explosion of products and messages? First it would be important to determine the use occasions for soft drinks, in a way similar to that in the purchasing process for cake mixes discussed in Chapter 5. But next the consumer would have to consider the types and brands of soft drinks he or she is aware of. Fortunately this process would be aided by the fact that soft drinks fall into fairly well defined categories. A typical consumer can either choose one of the soft-drink categories or consider all the brands recalled across all categories.

The basic thrust of much soft-drink advertising is to get the consumer to consider a particular category and a particular brand as being representative of that category. Coke's "The Real Thing" campaign, with variations in copy and style, consistently pointed out that Coca-Cola is the leading soft drink in the leading category, cola. Seen in this light, 7-Up's "Uncola" campaign was really an attempt to position 7-Up in relation to the cola category with a new category including only 7-Up. The same may be said about the attempt to position Dr Pepper in a category of its own. Starting with a short campaign with the theme, "The most misunderstood soft drink in the world," the advertising went on to feature such positioning lines as

Dr Pepper!
It's not a cola.
It's something much, much more.
It's not a root beer.
There are root beers by the score . . .
It's the most original soft drink ever
in the whole wide world.

This theme was carried through radio, television, print presentations at bottler's meetings, posters, outdoor advertising, and record albums.

Such is the development of a creative idea that positions a product to fit consumer information-processing needs in an increasingly complex environment.

THE NATURE OF CREATIVE STRATEGY

Creative strategy has two parts:

☐ *What is said:* the theme, the appeal, the copy platform, the position, or the message idea
☐ *How it is said:* the copy, the message, the message implementation, the execution, or format

This and the next two chapters discuss the first, or message idea, part of creative strategy. Subsequent chapters cover message format.

It is important to remember that the message idea decision is based on a particular set of research data and prior decisions. Although the message idea decision is the second of four communication decisions that are made more or less separately for each communication element, it is really the first that is given over by the brand or campaign manager to some outside group, usually the advertising department or an advertising agency, to develop for the manager's approval.

The theme or positioning or message idea is most successful when it is carried out through all elements of the marketing-communication mix. As Gerald Zornow, former chairman of the Eastman Kodak Company and of the Marketing Science Institute, has pointed out:

You see, products have no selling message apart from their total sales personality. And once the product's basic sales personality is defined, the specific choice of marketing alternatives falls readily into place. The basic question in evaluating an alternative is how efficient a job it does of reinforcing the product's basic sales personality.[3]

Usually the "basic sales personality" or message idea is developed by that team of people working on the advertising part of the campaign. Then the theme is carried out through all the elements used in the marketing-communication mix.

Examples in Figure 8-1 show how Boschert carries a theme throughout its entire communication and promotional program. As mentioned above, Dr Pepper's theme was also carried throughout all activities of the communication mix. The same can be said of the Ford campaign mentioned earlier, which flowed from the style and names of the cars through the advertising to the promotions.

(a)

(b)

(c)

(d) *(Courtesy of Boschert Inc.)*

Figure 8-1. *Boschert's basic sales personality carried through various campaign elements: (a) advertising, (b) coffee cup premium, (c) buckle premium, stick-on labels, (d) catalog page, tag.*

Because of the centrality of the message idea in developing a successful campaign, the campaign manager must be involved to some extent in (1) developing an adequate advertising department and selecting an appropriate advertising agency, (2) ensuring that these groups use all available resources (including the inputs of other communication element groups) in developing message ideas, and (3) evaluating the message ideas that are submitted to him or her for approval.

The goal in this first stage of creative strategy is to develop a clear statement of the message idea that can be used by all of those people who have to develop coordinated message formats for all the elements of the communication or promotional mix.

The Message Idea Statement and Copy Platform

No matter what it is called—message idea, main appeal, theme, copy platform, or positioning—the statement must be a blueprint or, at the very least, a structure upon which the copywriters in advertising, the promotional managers, the salespeople, the public relations people, and all others in the campaign organization can build their specific messages. We already know from the discussion of creativity in Chapter 3 that the message idea or copy platform statement cannot be too specific or it will stifle creativity. At the same time, the message idea statement cannot be so general that it provides no direction and leads to what Gerald Zornow calls "communication islands" of advertising doing one thing, promotion another, salespeople another, and so forth.

It is best if the message idea can be stated at some point in terms of a single sentence or phrase. This is not to say that the message idea statement should consist only of this single sentence or phrase. This statement should indeed be a "copy platform"; that is, it should provide a thorough elaboration of the

key phrase. But, time and again it is found that the campaign message idea that can be expressed concisely in a sentence is the one that will be successful.

One can imagine the message idea statements behind the nine campaigns discussed at the beginning of this chapter:

☐ Ford: "Build on the styling, engineering, and nomenclature of our new line in order to sell the young and young-at-heart market with a combination of the muscle styling of our cars and their fuel economy."

☐ Schaefer: "Keep aiming at the heavy-beer-drinking market with a campaign showing this particular type of person in contrast to the Genesee type, while continuing the 'One beer to have' ideas."

☐ A&P: "Attempt to win back customers who were disenchanted by the WEO price-cutting program by showing that A&P's distinctiveness is a unique combination of both price and service with pride."

☐ Listerine: "Differentiate Listerine from other mouthwashes, implying that it offers more without making specific claims similar to those being challenged by the FTC."

☐ Johnson & Johnson: "Utilize the same combination of innocent safety and excitement to show how our baby lotion product can be used for adult cosmetic care."

☐ Speed Queen: "Show that proportion of the market considering the Sears low-cost offering and the Maytag quality reputation that Speed Queen washing machines have superior durability to make them the best buy in the long run."

☐ Mazola: "Demonstrate with convincing evidence that Mazola's 100 percent corn oil characteristics make it the best choice for those who are concerned about a low-cholesterol diet."

☐ Eastern: "Get out of the frills competition and show that Eastern is an airline that has schedules meeting the needs of the prime target business and pleasure travelers."

☐ Campbell: "Counteract the leveling off of per capita consumption of condensed soup by showing that Campbell's soup should be an integral part of the new American life style."

The Five Parts
of the Copy Platform

Such theme statements can become the linchpin for all of those working on the campaign. Each theme statement should have five components which are elaborated in the copy platform: target market, appeal(s), competitive consideration, tone, and rationale.

First, there should be some statement of *target market.* Everyone working on the messages for all parts of the marketing-communication mix should have some idea of the key market segments toward which the campaign is being aimed. But part of the creative work done at the message idea stage is the further delineating of these targets as an "audience." Communication occurs when there is shared experience. If those people developing the messages for the campaign are to create this shared experience, they must understand, quite intimately, those people to whom they are communicating. When the Ford theme statement above mentioned the "young and young-at-heart," it implied a specific type of car buyer. The copy platform could discuss not only the numerical incidence of these people but also their possible frustration at wanting a car with style and power that also gave them good economy. One small creative breakthrough in the development of such a campaign would be to realize that there are people with such frustration and combine this with the fact that the Ford line may provide an answer.

Second, both the theme and the copy platform should have a statement of the key *appeal or appeals* of the campaign. The Eastern, Schaefer, and A&P themes all represented a change in appeal for these advertisers. Eastern moved from an emphasis on the extras of its airline service to one on its schedules. Schaefer, while retaining its previously successful "The one beer to have when you're having more than one" appeal, decided to shift gears somewhat with an "image" approach showing the kind of people who are Schaefer drinkers. A&P also made a slight shift from featuring just price to including service-pride along with price. In the copy platform, of course, there would be much more detail about the nature of the appeal. Eastern's appeal of schedules, for example, would probably be expanded into an explanation that Eastern is not just an East Coast airline but one that serves many key destinations. This appeal could be expanded further to point out that Eastern is the second-largest airline in the free world. Thus a message idea including the appeal of schedules could be expanded into one that inspires confidence, makes one aware of the airline for a wide variety of purposes, and implies "extras" without specifically stating them.

Third, both the theme statement and the copy platform should be a reference to *competition.* Of all the theme statements above, the one for Listerine is most specific in dealing with the competitive situation. By saying that the message should "differentiate Listerine from all other mouthwashes," the theme statement is asking for a creative "positioning." The word *positioning* is a popular one in marketing communication. Basically, when used in terms of the message idea, it is concerned with establishing a frame of reference of the product in the consumer's mind. If there is a great deal of clutter and noise in the communication environment, then a message idea that can establish a brand in a particular position in the consumer's mind will cut through the noise and confusion. Listerine was under considerable competitive pressure when the above campaign was developed. If the advertising can succeed in positioning this brand of mouthwash in a category of its own, there is little that competitive mouthwashes can do to counter this in a communication sense. There remains, of course, for the copy platform and message format development to turn this positioning idea into a reality that works.

For both Mazola and Speed Queen it

can be seen that there may be some problems with their message idea vis-à-vis competition. In fact, Mazola's low-cholesterol diet approach was somewhat countered by Fleischmann's magarine, which also used the same diet approach. Earlier the Maytag reliability approach was clearly delineated. Obviously the Speed Queen emphasis on durability will do little to differentiate Speed Queen from Maytag and its long-term campaign. The copy platform must contain a clear statement of the way the message idea will differentiate each market offering from that of the competition.

Tone is the fourth component of the message theme and copy platform. This is what was meant in the Maytag example in Chapter 4 in which the statement was made that the advertising should be "believable-unbelievable." Again, this could be done in a variety of ways—with testimonials, unusual demonstrations, information about the quality parts, etc.—but all of these message formats would have to fit within the "believable-unbelievable" tone dictated by the original message theme and copy platform for Maytag. The same sort of direction is provided by the Johnson & Johnson message theme stated above. By mentioning "innocent safety and exitement" and referring to past Johnson & Johnson campaigns for baby products in the adult market, the theme gives clear direction to subsequent creative workers. It is precisely this combination that has worked for other Johnson & Johnson products in the past, and the copy platform should provide some detail as to the particular type of tone needed for the creative work for baby lotion. The copy platform should provide extensive support for any particular tone suggested for the message idea. It is especially important that subsequent creative people understand how and why a particular tone will work.

The last component of the message theme and copy platform should be the *rationale*. In other words, there should be some indication of how all the components of the message idea will work together to achieve both communication and total campaign objectives. To some extent, the copy platform descriptions of each of the other four components of the message idea give some explanation of how the message idea will work. But the creative people need to be reminded of the campaign goals and objectives. And there should be a pep talk of sorts included in the message idea statements in order to keep all subsequent creative work on target. The rationale combines all of the aspects of the message idea and shows how they would work together. If the message idea is a good one, the rationale should convey a certain amount of excitement to the creative people. It should fall together quite easily.

The great creative idea has to be manifested in the message idea as represented by the theme statement and the copy platform. It is always possible that the message format can develop a breakthrough that carries a mundane message idea through to a successful campaign. But when this is true, it is usually the result of a reworking of the message idea on the basis of a message format change. A distinctive message format without an idea behind it consists purely of borrowed interest. It might be successful with enough dollars behind it in a parity product area. But this is, in essence, giving up the powerful leverage that a great creative strategy can have. As three executives from the McCann-Erickson advertising agency put it in a white paper entitled "A Point of View on Advertising Strategy":

> So much advertising sinks without a trace in today's competitive and cluttered environment. The key lesson: advertising that stands out from the crowd, that commands attention and involvement, begins with a distinctive *idea* and does not depend on a distinctive execution alone.[4]

The remainder of this chapter delineates the way a campaign manager can evaluate message ideas and the way message ideas themselves can be developed from fact gathering.

HOW TO EVALUATE MESSAGE IDEAS

The campaign manager, as mentioned above, has the responsibility for making sure that the creative process and the creative organization for his or her campaign are set up in such a way that the development of good creative ideas is likely. Approval, however, is actually the most important role the manager has in the development of creative strategy. It is not an easy task. Few individuals are born with the instinctive ability to look at a message idea and know whether it is a good one.

Fortunately there do seem to be characteristics common to all "great" message ideas. By learning and applying these characteristics, a campaign manager can develop the ability to judge message ideas accurately.

The Role of Research and Intuition

The characteristics that a manager should look for in a good message idea cannot be applied in any mechanical sense with long-term success. To a great extent it is impossible to verbalize the nature of a great creative idea. It may be that, as a result of continuous application of the nine characteristics listed here, the manager may develop a sense or intuition as to what a great creative idea is.

It may also be true, however, that great creative ideas come too seldom to allow the campaign manager to develop any ability to recognize them. Most "great" message ideas were somewhat unusual when they were first proposed. Consider, for instance, the idea of advertising Volkswagen as an ugly small car, the idea of stating that Avis was number two in rent-a-cars, or the idea of using Sunkist oranges as a drink. Although these famous campaigns seem part of American culture now, they probably at one time seemed very strange to a campaign manager who had to approve them.

For the very nature of the creative process is based on the ability to take rather mundane facts and put them together in new ways. It has been said that the good creative individual has the ability to see "unexpected likenesses." If this is true, how can the creative judge, the campaign manager, determine whether the message idea is just strange or a strange idea that will work? And how can this manager differentiate between the many moderate-to-good ideas that may be presented? When should he or she reject all ideas and push those people developing the message idea to work harder toward something better?

It is in response to questions like these that some managers attempt to fall back on theme-testing research. The idea of such research is that consumers in the target market segment can be presented with representations of alternative themes and indicate whether or not those themes would affect them.

The track record for theme-testing research has not been good. For instance, it has been said that the "We're number two, we try harder" campaign would have been rejected on the basis of copy research. The reason for this frequent failure of copy research, especially at the theme or message idea stage, is that consumers are not very good judges of how particular messages may affect them in the future. Unless advertising or other aspects of the communication mix are presented to people in a natural way, so that they can react to messages as they normally do, it is unlikely that test results will be significant.

Research has great value at the beginning and the end of the creative process. At the beginning, situation analysis research can provide the basic material to define the problem and delineate possible alternatives. It is from this material that the creative intuition takes over and makes new combinations that have the potential of being a great problem-solving idea. At the end of the creative process when there is finished or near-finished advertising, promotion, and so forth, it is possible to test campaign ideas in a relatively natural surrounding. But at the stage of message idea development, research is unrealistic and unfair to those creative individuals who may have come up with an unusual and effective new combination.

Creative individuals often resist judgment by managers who have not been a part of the intuitive development of an idea. Some advertising agencies claim that they use all the situation information available, come up with the best message idea, present it to the client-manager in such a way that he or she can see how it would be implemented (e.g., using comprehensive ad layouts or rough-cut commercials or storyboards), and offer the manager the option of either taking the campaign or firing the agency. The assumption being made is that the advertising agency is the expert in creating advertising and that if it is given the proper information it will create the best campaign for the situation.

It is unlikely that many agencies have resigned advertising accounts in exactly this way. This does illustrate, however, the importance of clear and forceful presentation of the message idea to the manager. At the same time it shows that creative people are very sensitive about their ideas being judged. The best communication campaign manager will create an aura of openness while keeping the creative people within the restrictions dictated by the situation.

There are no formulas for judging proposed message ideas. The ideas cannot really be researched at the theme stage. Instead the manager and the creatives must agree on the factual basis of the situation and should use the following criteria to eliminate those ideas that are inappropriate. Identification of the great idea from those that remain is an art that comes both naturally and with experience.

Criterion One: Fits Strategy

The message idea decision comes after a number of other strategic decisions have already been made. A good message idea must fit those other decisions or alter them in a positive way. If very little money is to be spent on communication for a product, the message idea must overcome this handicap or so fit the situation that each dollar spent will be effective. If the communication objective for the advertising part of the campaign is simply awareness while that for promotion is attitude change, the message idea should fit these objectives.

In essence, this criterion relates to the "rationale" portion of the theme–copy platform statement. The manager should consider whether the message idea fits the needs of the situation. Will it work within the budget restraints that have already been set, within the particular mix of communication elements that has tentatively been chosen, and to achieve the particular communication and total campaign objectives that have been set?

This is perhaps the most important criterion because it is concerned with whether the message idea is "appropriate" to the situation. Instead of merely asking whether the idea is good or not, the manager is asking whether this is the message idea that can achieve the particular objectives that have been set. Further, the manager should be asking whether the message idea is at variance with the present image and position of the brand in the market. If a product has been developed for a particular position in the market, the message idea should fit within that position. For instance, in one research study it was found that the Chase Manhattan Bank was the leader in consumers' minds in terms of fast service. If indeed this is an important attribute to consumers, it may be foolish for the message idea to ignore it or go counter to it.

Criterion Two: Fits Target Segment

The theme statement and copy platform must show that the message idea is aimed directly at a particular segment. If it has been determined that mothers are the key decision makers for toothpaste purchasing, for example, the message idea that is aimed at children or adult singles may not be effective in the long run. A message idea that fits a segment well is one that fits that segment's problems and the very language that the segment uses to talk about those problems. Take, for example, the initial advertising for Aim fluoride toothpaste, which was directed toward mothers. It included such lines as

☐ "Great news for mothers of cavity-prone children!"
☐ "Most children don't brush properly or often enough."
☐ "If you have children, read on:"
☐ "How new Aim encourages children to brush longer."
☐ "Ask your dentist about Aim."

These lines had to come from a theme and message idea statement that was directed quite clearly to women who were mothers and had problems getting their children to brush often and thoroughly enough with fluoride toothpaste.

In every situation the campaign manager should check carefully to see that the message idea is directed at the target market or markets.

Criterion Three: Appropriate for the Total Marketing Communication Mix

As has been mentioned earlier, the message idea is usually developed for the advertising part of the communication mix and then applied to other communication elements. Unfortunately, however, there sometimes are separate message ideas developed for each component of the mix. Or it sometimes happens that the advertising message idea is not applied to other communication elements. This is unfortunate because the hallmark of a successful communication campaign is a clear image or position that is consistently communicated throughout all aspects of the mix. If different ideas are operating in different parts of the mix, the potential consumer will become confused or get no impression at all.

A strong message idea translates easily to all aspects of the communication mix. For instance, 7-Up's Uncola positioning led quite easily to "uncontests," a variety of premiums and publicity stunts. Not only did the theme fit the teen-age audience well but it was also possible to keep emphasizing it in a variety of ways.

In some cases it is difficult to see how a message idea will work in the various elements of the communication mix. For instance, the whimsical theme of Benson & Hedges 100-millimeter cigarettes was the "disadvantages" of the longer cigarette. This theme worked very well in advertising because it was possible to demonstrate the extra length of the cigarette in a variety of ways. Surprisingly, this theme worked very well in a sweepstakes promotion also. The headline for the sweepstakes ad said:

> "Oh, the disadvantages of having to make a choice of Benson & Hedges 100s sweepstakes."

The prizes in the contest were all one hundred of a variety of items. One could imagine the difficulty a manager might have had in foreseeing the wide applicability of this message idea. Managers should be careful in exploring the potential of such ideas before rejecting them too early.

Criterion Four: Leverage

The fact that a great creative idea can multiply its effect many times cannot be overemphasized. Most great ideas accomplish leverage by utilizing consumers' present beliefs in a powerful way.

Consider the well-known Volkswagen Beetle. The agency creating this campaign could have suggested a message idea that involved telling people about the advantages of a smaller car, few design changes, the particular shape of the Beetle, the low initial price, and so forth. This strategy would have been correct and would have fit the three criteria discussed above. It would not have had leverage, however. The strategy used, in which people's present attitudes about the Volkswagen were taken to make fun of the car and then turn the laughter into positive advantages, again fit the situation but had a great deal of leverage. The same can be said of the Uncola idea and the Benson & Hedges disadvantages idea, as well as many others recognized as being an enormous success. The manager should look for that extra twist that gives the message idea the power and involvement to make it stand out from the noise of the communication environment.

Criterion Five: Simplicity

Beginning copywriters and campaign managers have a tendency to want to say as many positive things about a product as they can. Such a complex message, however, may only confuse the consumer.

Simplicity is therefore an important criterion to consider in the development of both great advertising and the message idea that underlies the communication campaign.

The best message idea is one that is not only simple but stands for a large number of positive aspects about the product or market offering. A list of appeals for a rent-a-car company might be very long indeed. But the Avis theme, "We're number two, we try harder," implies almost every one of the positive attributes a rent-a-car company might have. If a company is trying harder to get ahead, it probably has better service, cleaner cars, wider variety of cars, increasingly better locations, and so forth.

In a similar way, all great message ideas

have the ability to sum up the advantages of a product for a particular segment in a single statement. As Marker, Powers, and Lessler point out:

> If you have a lot of trouble describing or explaining your strategy, chances are that you don't have a strategy, or at least not the right strategy.

Great and simple strategic positionings are usually easily and effectively translated into great and simple copy lines:

- ☐ "It 's the real thing. Coke."
- ☐ "Come to Marlboro country."
- ☐ "Wouldn't you really rather have a Buick?"
- ☐ "If you think all the good wines in the world are imported . . ."
- ☐ "We try harder."[5]

A message idea that can be stated simply, yet pulls together all the attributes of a situation, is likely to lead to campaigns and copy lines such as those mentioned above.

Criterion Six: Specificity

Inadequate message idea statements often confuse words with ideas. When you see such words as "quality," "new," "convenient," "good tasting," and "best" without any supporting statement related to the situation, you should be concerned that the message idea is not specific enough.

Continental Airlines could have had a message idea statement that said, essentially, that Continental would be portrayed as the best all-around airline over its routes. Instead the message idea statement must have said something equivalent to: "Show that Continental's record has demonstrated that Continental people feel compelled to go beyond the normal service expected from an airline." This kind of message idea would have led to Continental's, "We really move our tail for you!" campaign. Thus the airline was able to move away from generalities to a series of specific reasons and records relating to the kind of service air travelers wanted from an airline.

Criterion Seven: Mass-Communication Potential

Often in industrial advertising a message idea can be communicated through the give and take of a personal-selling encounter but has little potential for the essentially one-way message situation of mass media. For instance, the creative director on the Detroit Diesel account was given this product description:

> Detroit Diesel has announced a major improvement to the cyclinder block design of all its V-type, Series 71 engines. Made feasible by more modern foundry techniques, the improvement results in additional engine cooling through a new water jacket surrounding each cylinder liner below the air intake ports.[6]

Obviously, this is not a mass-media message idea. Instead, this product description was translated into the message idea and copy line "The cool engine is coming." This idea could be used for a series of advertisements in various media.

The message idea must be one that can easily be translated into effective messages by those people concerned with the message format.

Criterion Eight: Resistance to Counterattack

Marketing communication is a competitive situation, much like war. The word *strategy* itself is a military term. Thus, when considering a message idea, you should be concerned about whether it is vulnerable to counterattack. Exclusivity of a position or an appeal is not the only consideration in determining whether a message idea will be resis-

tant to counterattack. Timing and the position of the brand in the market are also important. If a brand is first with a particular appeal and communicates it with a great deal of strength, it is likely that counterattack will be difficult. This is especially true if a brand is a leader in the marketplace. Although Chase Manhattan was seen as the bank with faster service in New York, First National was the leader and could have, with a strong advertising campaign, preempted the fast-service idea.

Some ideas are, by their very nature, resistant to counterattack. Avis's "We're number two, we try harder" campaign is an example. If either Hertz or National attempted to attack the campaign, it would just be giving free advertising to Avis. This kind of message idea, which automatically carves a position for the brand, should be the goal of campaign developers.

Criterion Nine: Durability

Communicators tend to change their campaigns too often. One reason for this may be that the message ideas are not durable enough to be used over a long period of time. Coca-Cola's campaigns have run over five- and ten-year periods. The theme "A certain kind of woman" for the Peck & Peck clothing stores was used in over twelve hundred ad versions.

The campaign manager must seek a durable message idea because, as Rosser Reeves points out:

1. Changing a story has the same effect as stopping the money, as far as penetration is concerned;
2. Thus, if you run a brilliant campaign every year, but change it every year, your competitor can pass you with a campaign that is less than brilliant—providing he does not change his copy; and
3. Unless a product becomes outmoded, a great campaign will not wear itself out.[7]

Evaluation versus Creation

One of the personal interaction difficulties in the creative process is that between the people who evaluate the message ideas and those who create them. Perhaps the reason is that the two procedures are essentially different. It is true, however, that those developing the message idea should keep the nine criteria listed here in mind. In the following sections of this chapter we deal more directly with the steps that should be taken to develop the great creative idea.

THE FACTUAL BASIS FOR THE MESSAGE IDEA

There are essentially six types of information that should be utilized in order to develop the message idea, both theme statement and copy platform. These factual components were discussed under "Situation Analysis" in Chapter 4. But here they have a somewhat different meaning because they are not related to such global decisions on marketing objectives or total communication budget. Instead, these decisions are taken as given and the components of the situation are now examined for hints they might provide for the message idea. The specific way this can be done is discussed in the following paragraphs.

Nature of the Product

While all successful marketing is based on a detailed analysis of consumer needs and perceptions, it is the product and not the consumer that deserves first consideration at the stage of developing the message idea. Presumably the product and its packaging and branding have been developed prior to the message idea stage on the basis of consumer consideration. Now those people who have the job of developing the message idea must carefully consider the product's attributes as they relate to the consumer. One should be reminded here of the steps of creative development and creativity discussed in Chapter 4. The first step is to "gather raw material." Remember that the suggestion was to gather *all* material that is both directly relevant to the problem and tangentially relevant.

The second step of the creative process is the "mental digestive process." At this time the creative individual or the group members are supposed to turn all the facts over and over in their minds. The earliest stages of the creative process are the most difficult and require the most work. Usually the people attempting to create the message idea are different from those people who develop the product in the first place. Therefore it is important for them to work especially hard in understanding the product and all its attributes in relation to the consumer and possible communication appeals.

The history of marketing communication contains many examples of successful message ideas blossoming from an exhaustive examination of the characteristics of the product. Take, for example, the development of the advertising campaign for Raid insect spray discussed in Chapter 4, in which product-testing findings surprisingly led to the line "Hunts bugs down and kills them dead." This came, of course, after a series of other creative decisions were made.

Another example involves Hughes Airwest and its agency Foote, Cone & Belding/Honig, whose personnel introspected, interacted with consumers, and continually heard them say, about Airwest's yellow airplanes, "It looks like a banana to me." This was usually said with a pleased, friendly smile. So the agency turned this common observation into the "Top Banana in the West" campaign (see Figure 8-2). Awareness of the airline doubled a month after the campaign started; travelers' preference for Airwest increased almost 70 percent.

In order to learn about the product and its characteristics for communication, creative people must not only pour over every

Figure 8-2. Hughes Airwest billboard, which grew from consumer comments such as "It looks like a banana to me"

(Courtesy of Hughes Airwest, now Republic Airways)

written fact about it but also, when possible, use the product itself, take it apart, and visit at the factory with those people who know about its production and development at the most basic level. In one of the earliest examples of this, the legendary copywriter Claude Hopkins visited the brewery of a beer for which he was writing copy. He learned that part of the brewing process involved a steaming of the liquid. This evolved into the message idea and copy line "Washed with live steam," an idea that purportedly was quite effective in the sales success of the brand.

One of the most successful marketing-communication companies, Procter and Gamble, is legendary for its requirement that agency creative people visit the factory and learn about the product in detail from technical people. This process led to a reawakening for the low-suds detergent Dash, which had been experiencing sluggish market performance. Two representatives from the company's advertising agency listened almost sleepily as a technician talked about the advantages of the product in larger-load and larger washing machines. Suddenly the agency copywriter snapped to attention. He realized that this was a new potential message idea for Dash. Instead of being sold just as a low-suds detergent, Dash could be sold as a product ideal for large-load washing machines. This message idea led to further growth for the Dash brand.

The Consumer and the Product

Although the first consideration at the stage of message idea development is the product, the interaction of the product and the consumer is always important. Product characteristics are meaningless unless they relate to consumer needs.

Earlier in this book we conceptualized marketing communication in terms of the radio electronics, information theory model of sender-signal-receiver. This model works quite well when describing personal selling in

a two-person interaction situation. In considering the consumer for all other parts of the communication mix, however, it is necessary to imagine artificial types of feedback and interaction. This is why two of the most successful copywriters of the early part of the century decided that advertising was actually "salesmanship in print." This concept represents the state of mind the message idea developer should be in when he or she is digging into consumer information. Considering that you have to come up with an idea for a sales pitch, whatever the media or type of communication, can you find consumer concerns that directly relate to your product in a distinctive way?

Since all competitors in a particular product area are usually looking at the same target market segment with only slightly different products, it is difficult to find an unusual but profitable segment or a distinctive relationship between any particular market offering and the segment of interest to most competitors in the market. A distinctive segment, a distinctive appeal, or both can catapult communication beyond the noise in the environment. Digging for distinctiveness at this point is worth a great deal. Everything about the message idea and format will be distinctive if a new relationship can be discovered at the very basic stage of consumer and product.

Of course, as was discussed in Chapter 4, the relationship between the consumer and the product is already well determined in the development of the product and in initial marketing efforts. When the whole subject of communication—total budget, allocation to elements of the communication mix, communication goal setting, etc.—is discussed, there is already a clear understanding of the nature of the target segment. Those people developing the message idea, however, must look in detail at this target segment in terms of the idea of salesmanship-in-print and in terms of interacting with the segment in distinctive ways.

Take for example the message idea situations headlined at the beginning of this chapter. Surely all automobile manufacturers face the same sort of target segment for the advertising of at least part of their line. But Ford looked at this young-driver segment and the particular frustrations it might be experiencing because of wanting to drive a "muscle" type of car while still needing fuel economy. This is the kind of frustration that would surface in a one-to-one personal-selling interaction. In order for Ford's advertising to be salesmanship-in-the-media, the message idea developers have to seek out this frustration on the part of the consumer to see how it relates to their own product offering.

In the case of Schaefer beer, one executive for its agency described the target segment as the "20 percent of the public who drink 80 percent of the beer. Men by and large. Blue collar guys. And their average per cap is 45 cases a year." But the outstanding aspect of the Schaefer campaign development was not that this target segment had been identified. All beer manufacturers would like to be first in this segment. The outstanding characteristic of the original Schaefer campaign was that it recognized that men who were drinking beer that heavily often had the problem that it lost taste after they had had several. Thus the perfect fit of the Schaefer theme "One beer to have when you're having more than one."

There are almost no great campaigns that are not based on an understanding of the thinking and language of the target segment. Good creative people learn that it is essential to have this understanding and to empathize with the target segment.

It was important to know, for instance, that the prime prospects for Wisk laundry detergent included "the 25 percent of all housewives who are so finicky about getting clothes clean that they actually scrub the inside of shirt collars by hand with a toothbrush." This kind of knowledge led quite directly to such themes as Wisk's "Ring around the collar."

In the cold remedy area almost all competitors know that their product has to be portrayed as one that will cure a cold quickly. But the advertiser and agency for Dristan recognized that most of us have a streak of hypochondriasis. That is, many of us have a tendency to imagine that we are sick when we actually are not. The Dristan agency noted this characteristic and actually invented a disease or, more accurately, pointed out an aspect of the common cold that might otherwise have been ignored. By showing "eight sinus cavities" in television advertising and pointing out Dristan's ability to drain them, the company made cold sufferers aware of an aspect of the common cold that Dristan could cure. For a good deal of time during the course of this campaign, Dristan was the best-selling cold remedy in the United States.

Perhaps the advertising agency creative philosophy that best fits the discussion here belongs to Batten, Barton, Durstine and Osborn. Executives of this advertising agency have made the point that it is difficult to develop a distinctive message idea on the basis of just positive attributes of the product. Instead they suggest that we should seek the *prime prospect's problem*. The assumption of the BBD&O philosophy is that if you ask people what they want from a product category, they will give you their reasons for using a product but really no information that would cause them to switch to a particular brand in the product category.

If you ask heavy users of dandruff-removing shampoo to tell you what they want from the product, they will say that they want effective protection against dandruff. Unless your brand is the leader in the product category, this information is of little use. The prime, heavy-using prospect is in that category because he or she has already found a product that somewhat satisfies his or her needs. However, if you ask prime prospects to tell you what their main *problem* is with the product category, you will often find information that provides an opening into the market. In the dandruff-removing shampoo market, for instance, heavy users often came up with the complaint that this particular type of shampoo left their hair in poor condition and unmanageable. This complaint was an important one within the product category and provided an opening for that shampoo that actually had the dual characteristics of protection against dandruff and conditioning. Of course, if the leading company in the product category is carefully monitoring this situation, it also has the opportunity of product and/or communication message change.

Trade

While the message idea must be aimed directly at the consumer and fit that individual's concerns and needs, it would be a mistake for it to ignore the reaction of the trade—wholesalers, retailers, and other types of intermediaries. And it is sometimes possible for particular kinds of distribution and distributors to be part of the message idea itself.

It is axiomatic that the nature of the communication campaign—its size, excitement, and likelihood of success—will have a major effect on how the trade reacts to a particular product or market offering. If the campaign looks good or great, retailers are more likely to stock the product, salespeople are likely to work harder in selling it, and the whole process of marketing at the trade level will be improved. In a real sense this consideration is equivalent to the criterion of extendability mentioned earlier in this chapter. That is, the message idea must be appropriate for all aspects of the communication mix, including those that most directly interface with the trade.

In this section, however, we are more concerned with the message idea developer analyzing the trade as a factor that must be considered in developing the message idea.

The Maytag campaign discussed in Chapter 4 provides a clear example of how the trade can be considered in developing the message idea and, in a later phase of a campaign, actually be used as part of the message idea. Initially the concern with the trade was

that retailers had large inventories of Maytag washing machines. Part of the problem was actually Maytag's distribution itself. The largest competitor, Sears, offered consumers a sense of security because a Sears store would always be available to service their washing machines. Maytag had to come up with a distinctive campaign that would help the trade move inventory but would also allay consumers' fears about lack of service. The outstanding message idea that solved this problem was the theme of outstanding dependability of a money and time-saving sort which was expressed in a believable-unbelievable way.

By concentrating on the lack of service necessary for the Maytag, the creative strategists were able to get around the problem that consumers perceived, possibly incorrectly, that the trade did not offer the kind of consistent and ready service that Sears did. Later, after the campaign had run for some eight or nine years, the focus was shifted somewhat to deal with the service problem more directly and tied in with the reliability theme. The new humorous approach featured the "Loneliest man in town." Advertising showed a Maytag service man whiling away the long hours with nothing to do because the Maytag is such a dependable washing machine. Thus did Maytag deal quite directly with the trade problem by making it clear that there was a readily available Maytag service network and at the same time reminding consumers that this network was largely unnecessary because the Maytag is such an extremely dependable machine.

Once again, as in the case of the product and the consumer, it is critically important that creative strategists not only look at research results but also have direct contact with the trade. Trade people who interact with the consumer can not only tell you about their problems, but they also have a definite idea about how the consumer goes about buying the product. Very often this point of view can be expressed in the message idea.

Discussions with people in the trade, "store checks" to determine how the product is being sold and displayed and priced, observation of consumers interacting with people in the trade—all of these kinds of fact gathering at the trade level can provide important input into message idea development.

Competition

The very idea of positioning is that the purpose of communication messages should be to firmly position the product in the consumer's mind vis-à-vis competition. It is impossible for creative strategists to position products adequately without knowledge of the positions competitors hold in the consumers' minds.

The competitive environment contains not only the advertising and communication messages for direct competitors in the product category but also messages for related product categories, as well as a plethora of totally unrelated communications. Unfortunately, in many product categories there is low product differentiation. Thus all competitors are looking at almost the same set of information about the product, the consumer, and the trade. This produces a sameness in message ideas and a lack of differentiation among products in consumers' minds. There is a sort of "major fallacy" for message ideas in which all competitors attempt to get across the same idea (which, incidentally, is the most central appeal related to the product, is most important to consumers, and fits the trade situation).

The inevitable result of common message ideas is that the leader in the market will inevitably benefit somewhat from everyone else's advertising. Consumers have a tendency, in their way of simplifying the plethora of messages about any particular product category, of attributing all communication to the brand most clearly connected to the category. If consumers are shown unidentified print advertising for prepared soup products, over 80 percent will attribute it to Campbell soup, even though the unlabeled advertising

may be for some other brand. If the advertising was for Lipton's Cup-of-Soup when this brand was the first on the market with single serving packages, however, Campbell would not have the commanding lead. In fact, single-serving soup advertising is likely to be attributed to Lipton.

Two things have to be done in considering competition in developing the message idea. First, you must learn how the consumer positions not only your product but also competitive products in his or her mind. This takes careful consumer research, but it is not the sort of research that is reserved only for large-budget marketing operations. We will discuss the positioning process in the next chapter.

The second step that must be taken in considering the competition is to analyze competitive communication campaigns. One very sobering approach to this analysis would be to tack up on a large wall all the advertisements and promotional materials used by competitors. The reason this approach is so bering is that it shows, quite clearly, the miserable monotony of the creative strategies used in any particular area.

The solution to the problem of competitive sameness is best developed out of a careful examination of competitive messages and their effects on consumers. In some cases it is impossible to be different in the message idea itself, and creative strategists have to leave the job of creating a distinction of other parts of communication. The beginning of creating that distinction at any level, however, is analysis at the competitive stage.

Past Experience

Creative strategists can be helped enormously by knowing what has and has not worked in past communication campaigns. This experience can be specific to the particular market offering being considered, or it can be experience of a more general sort.

Past experience is of greater value to

those individuals developing the message format than it is to those concerned with the message idea. In the chapters on message format we will discuss a series of creative philosophies that relate to the particular types of devices that advertising agencies have found useful in various communication situations.

There is, however, some general agreement that the development of a strong and distinctive message idea is critical to a successful campaign.

Beyond this, however, is it possible to transfer a successful idea from one campaign situation to another? The answer is, "Perhaps, but only in the most general way." The trouble with most unsuccessful campaigns is that they are using tired, old ideas.

Message ideas do not transfer well from one campaign to another because they are designed to fit a particular situation. One of the mistakes commonly made by beginning students in communications is to attempt to apply their favorite advertising idea to an inappropriate situation. This kind of transfer never works. Not only is the fit to the situation bad but the "new" campaign idea ends up reminding consumers of the original.

Some general rules about message ideas can be learned on the basis of experience, but they are really no different from the suggestions that have been made above about learning from the product, the consumer, the trade, and the competition.

Communication Research

Although communication research studies often have shortcomings in terms of realism, they offer hints and suggestions for the nature of the message idea. We have already mentioned the communication research support for the "believable-unbelievable" message idea that was used for the Maytag campaign.

It is generally believed that the creative person knows more about the problem situation and facts in general than does the noncreative person. It follows from this general belief that a knowledge of the findings of research about communication can help to develop effective message ideas. A solid basis in fact—product, consumer, trade, competition, past experience, communication research—always underlies the great creative idea. Hard work at the fact-gathering stage of message idea development will provide enormous returns.

THE PROCESS OF MESSAGE IDEA DEVELOPMENT

In the difficult, noisy environment of marketing communication, the message offers some hope of getting more value for the marketing dollar in turning around a situation that otherwise may not be good. The first step in creating a message with leverage is the message idea statement, including the theme and copy platform.

The message idea statement is a blueprint for the people who implement it in terms of the message format. Message ideas are often developed within advertising and translated to other parts of the marketing-communication mix. The people who develop the message idea are usually closer to management than those who implement it in terms of the message format. Usually the campaign manager is more intimately involved with the message idea than with the message format. As such, the message idea is a vital link between the overall goals and concerns of the campaign and the implementation in terms of format and message distribution.

The informational components that go into the message idea reflect the overall development of the campaign. In order to develop outstanding message ideas, it is important to consider the product, the consumer's relationship to the product, the trade, the competition, past experience, and relevant communications research findings. Of course it is true that these same components were considered very early in the development of the general strategy and budget for the campaign. But at this point these components are examined for their relevance to creative strategy and the development of the message idea. For instance, in the "before marketing communication" situation analysis, the product was considered primarily in terms of its stage in the life cycle, market share, and growth potential. In message idea development, on the other hand, the product is considered in terms of its potential for particular appeals, tone, and competitive positioning that might lead to a distinctive message within the communication environment. Similarly, in the initial situation analysis, the consumer was considered in terms of economic potential and general marketing-communication strategy. In fact-gathering message development, the consumer's specific problems and ways of looking at the world are considered in a manner that allows the language of the message to relate quite directly to target market segments. Thus, in a sense, an entirely new situation analysis is done, building upon the initial work. In this particular process of creativity, the message idea developer is looking for unexpected likenesses and new combinations that will provide a great idea and a breakthrough message with high leverage in the difficult competitive environment.

The campaign manager and the creative strategists have the job of developing a theme statement and copy platform for those who implement the message format. Both the brief theme statement and the more fully articulated copy platform should have five components. These consist of a statement of target market, the key appeal or appeals of the campaign, reference to competition, tone, and rationale.

Although the development of the message idea is a creative process and therefore cannot really be fully codified, some general guides might be used to eliminate those ideas that are inappropriate. Identification of the great idea and those that remain is an art that comes both naturally and with experience. Among the criteria that might be used to develop and judge potential message ideas would be the following. A good message idea should:

1. Fit strategy
2. Fit the target segment
3. Be appropriate for the total communication mix
4. Have leverage
5. Be simple
6. Be specific
7. Have mass-communication potential
8. Be resistant to counterattack
9. Have durability

ISSUES AND PROJECTS FOR DISCUSSION

1. What is the difference between the message idea and the communication goals? In what sense does the message idea affect all elements of the communication mix?

2. Describe the nature of the communication environment in terms of the demands it puts on the message idea.

3. What is the organizational and managerial function of the message idea and the copy platform? How does that function affect them?

4. For a campaign you select or are assigned, write a concise message idea statement and a copy platform.

5. Evaluate that campaign (and your statement and platform) on the basis of the nine criteria for evaluating creative strategy.

6. What is the nature of the interaction between campaign management, research, and creativity in the development and evaluation-selection of the campaign message idea?

7. What is the difference between fact-gathering message development in this chapter and in Chapters 4 and 5 of Part II?

8. Compare the ads for one product category. Is there a miserable monotony? Analyze the competitive environment in this category.

9. What do you know about a product or service you use that you believe could be made into a great campaign for that market offering?

Notes

1. Raymond A. Bauer and Stephen A. Greyser, *Advertising in America: The Consumer View* (Boston: Division of Research, Graduate School of Business Administration, Harvard University, 1968).

2. Peter H. Webb and Michael L. Ray, "Effects of TV Clutter," *Journal of Advertising Research,* 19, No. 3 (June 1979), 7–12.

3. Gerald B. Zornow, "Planning the Total Sales Personality" (New York: Association of National Advertisers, 1967), p. 3.

4. Robert S. Marker, John A. Powers, and Richard S. Lessler, "White Paper I: A Point of View on Advertising Strategy" (New York: McCann-Erickson, October 1972), p. 15.

5. Marker, Powers, and Lessler, "White Paper I," p. 6.

6. Ray C. Blackwell, Jr., "The Cool Engine Is Coming" (New York: American Association of Advertising Agencies, 1971).

7. Rosser Reeves, *Reality in Advertising* (New York: Knopf, 1961), p. 32. (Second edition, 1981).

Message Idea Positioning

- You consider with some trepidation the situation facing the Honeywell computer division. Giants of the industry such as GE and RCA have failed in their assaults on the entrenched leader, IBM. Can anything be done in message idea positioning and tone to establish Honeywell in a market where others have failed?

- Although you know that your company, B. F. Goodrich, has made most of the discoveries and innovations in the tire industry, the leader in the market, Goodyear, seems to get all the credit. Can anything be done in message idea positioning and tone to deal with this confusion in names and overwhelming market lead of Goodyear?

- All signs look negative for American Motors Corporation as you consider the message idea decision. Just the dismal share and low-experience curve situation of AMC puts the company in an impossible competitive fix. Is there a positioning and tone that can solve this seemingly insurmountable problem?

- As a campaign manager for an incumbent mayoral candidate, you are faced with a difficult task. He is either loved or hated. The feelings are so strong that he has already lost his own party's nomination! Now he has to run as an independent. The message idea positioning and tone have to be particularly appropriate and effective, because the small amount of money he has to spend must be used on messages that will convince potential workers, contributors, and voters of the viability of his candidacy. What should be done?

  - You are working with the creative staff at the Leo Burnett advertising agency to develop a message idea (theme and copy platform) for the Royal Crown Cola account. You know that the major competitors—Coke, Pepsi, 7-Up, Dr Pepper—have distinctive positions and large shares of market. How can you develop a distinctive position for RC; and should the message idea be emotional, competitive, and strong in tone?

The quest in the initial stages of creative strategy work is for the great idea that will have outstanding leverage. In many cases it is necessary to find something that will catapult a weak brand or market offering into a viable market position on the basis of limited funds. Although the message idea is of critical importance to all communication campaigns, it is especially so for weak brands because of all the components of the communication mix, the message can have the greatest multiplier effect on money expended.

The positioning and tone of the message are its most important aspects in creating leverage. *Positioning* is the combination of the appeal and competitive considerations that can give a brand a distinctive perception or position in the consumer's mind. *Tone* is the way a position is stated.

For RC Cola the Leo Burnett agency decided upon an intimate, personal, and "loyalist" position with the "Me and my RC" campaign. The tone was belligerent and confident, tempered with a folksy flavor. The ads showed successful ordinary but likable people, and country music was used to reinforce the theme idea.

Honeywell positioned directly against the overwhelming leader, IBM, with a campaign featuring the line "The other computer company vs. Mr. Big." This position put the company in the same category with the leader. At one point it was reported to be the only other large company making money on computers. (See Figure 9-1.)

Goodrich used the name confusion with Goodyear to its advantage by positioning itself as the company whose name is confused with the market leader but should get credit for being the actual leader in tire innovations and quality. The tone was humorous. This resulted in messages capitalizing on the fame of the Goodyear blimp. Characters in television commercials continually confused the two and talked about the "Goodrich" blimp.

Mayor Lindsay of New York faced a situation almost identical to that faced by the mayoral candidate discussed above. Lindsay's campaign positioned him as a candidate who had made some mistakes because the job of running New York was so difficult. But the message idea was that the mistakes should not be allowed to overshadow the many good things Lindsay had done for the city. This message, competitive and cocky in tone, seemed to capture people on both sides of the love-hate dichotomy, generated workers and contributions, and, most important, was one of the major factors in Lindsay's reelection.

AMC cars were positioned as "different" or "unusual" while the whole line was given the aura of respectability and economic viability with the AMC Buyer Protection Plan. The tone was humorous and, at the same time, competitive in a reasonable, nonbelligerent, way.

In this chapter and the next, the methods that might be used for developing high leverage positioning and tone for a message idea are discussed. Once the fact-gathering situation analysis is done, it is necessary to put the message idea together. And this is done with positioning analysis and the added touch of direction in message tone.

When you haven't got all the customers, you fight for all the customers you've got.

The way we see it, the only way to get ahead in this business is to do right by the business you've got.

So we make sure our customers are happy customers. We make sure our computer systems are doing what our customers expect them to do: solving the right problems—faster, better, more economically.

We've got a world-wide force of support specialists who make sure your investment in a Honeywell computer system pays off for you. Now. And in the future.

And best of all, Honeywell offers basic software, systems support, application packages, and education at no extra cost.

Sure, we'll fight for new customers. More aggressively than any other company in the business.

But after we get the business, we knock ourselves out.

The Other Computer Company:
Honeywell

Honeywell Information Systems (MS 061), 200 Smith Street, Waltham, Massachusetts 02154.

A banker can take better care of the money if a Honeywell computer is taking care of the paperwork.

Our computer systems can make you a better banker because they have better ways to handle your paperwork.

Our large-scale Series 6000 computers, for example, offer multi-dimensional processing, which lets you handle up to six high speed MICR reader-sorters at one time on one control unit, accept transactions from terminals, and run several other jobs all at once.

Since MICR hardware is important to your paperwork transactions, Honeywell offers an extensive MICR product line. For example, our low-cost MICR reader-sorter features six-pocket sorting. It's ideal for either a branch or a correspondent bank, because it works off-line or on-line to a local or a remote computer. And our high speed MICR reader-sorters offer the optimum number of pockets to meet your sorting needs.

Honeywell has many more hardware and application systems for banks of all sizes. And we're working on a lot more systems just to help bankers do what bankers do best: make money make more money.

We're not about to curl up and go to sleep on a job well done when we can do it even better.

The Other Computer Company:
Honeywell

For our brochure, "Honeywell in Banking," write: Honeywell Information Systems (MS061), 200 Smith Street, Waltham, Massachusetts 02154.

(Courtesy of Honeywell Information Systems)

Figure 9-1. *The Honeywell positioning putting the company in a class with IBM without actually meeting it head on*

POSITIONING ANALYSIS

In past years the message idea was called the appeal, theme, brand, personality, image, or, simply, idea. But most recently the standard term has been *position*.

That the word *position* has become part of standard terminology in market communication is evidenced by the slight change that David Ogilvy has made in statements about creating advertising campaigns. As was reported in the preceding chapter, Ogilvy's first commandment for creating advertising campaigns in his 1963 book was:

What you say is more important than how you say it.[1]

In the early 1970s the wording of this same point was changed to:

. . . The results of your campaign depend less on how we write your advertising than on how your product is positioned.[2]

Increasing use of the term *positioned* or *positioning* is due to a change in the marketing-communication environment as well as increased information about how consumers process messages for use in making decisions.

As was noted in the preceding chapter, there is increasing noise in the communication environment. There are more advertisements, more salespeople, more promotions, and more packages and products on the supermarket shelves. Because of increases in costs, marketers are forced to use shorter and shorter messages. All of this means that consumers are being faced with many more messages, each with less impact for a wider variety of products. And consumers seem to have developed ways of classifying, simplifying, ordering, and remembering just a few prominent brands in any particular category.

This is where positioning comes in, because communication, particularly advertising, must establish the brand in some position in that mental set consumers have developed to deal with the noise and confusion in each product category. It is no longer enough to communicate a brand image or a set of appeals. The image and appeals must be related to the way consumers have of possibly thinking about a brand and positioning it in their minds.

In a real sense, then, positioning analysis takes all the materials that have been developed about the situation and puts them together into the message idea.

Psychological and marketing research has led to a series of developments that provide a clear-cut series of steps that can be taken, following the situation analysis, to delineate clearly the alternative strategies available in the situation. These research developments were outlined in Chapter 5 under the heading "Attitude Structure Analysis."

The basic assumption of attitude structure research is that people's actions are governed by the way they view the world. Stated in another way, perceptions lead to preferences. Or, in a more general sense, there is some relationship between learning about a product area and brand attitudes and purchasing behavior. As we saw in Chapter 7, it is sometimes true that critical behavior comes before clear preferences and distinguishing peceptions. Several different orders of these mental states are possible, depending on the situation. The critical aspect is that communications can have some effect on the way people view the market offering, and this can

be instrumental in achieving total campaign goals.

The positioning concept is related most directly to the perceptions part of attitudinal segmentation. Without positioning, it is argued, consumers will have no clear perception of the market offering, and all will be lost. In order to develop a clear position, the communicator must somehow put together all aspects of the product, consumer, trade, competition, and communication situation in a distinctive way for that brand.

Three developments in attitudinal segmentation research have led to a relatively simple and clear procedure for positioning analysis and development.

1. *Buyer behavior modeling.* Researchers attempting to develop comprehensive theories of buyer behavior have independently developed flow chart models which essentially trace the growth of perception-preference relationships over the course of the consumer decision process. These models have evolved more recently into more small-scale decision process conceptualizations in which researchers are concerned with how people combine their perceptions to come up with certain preferences that lead to behavior. In this research, consumers are asked to indicate what their alternative choices would be to solve a particular problem, what characteristics they want in the best alternative for problem solution, and how they see the current alternatives in terms of these characteristics. As will be pointed out later, these three pieces of information—the choice alternative (competitors), desired characteristics, and perception of alternatives in terms of these characteristics—when combined with knowledge of how the consumer makes his or her decision, are all that a message idea developer needs to know in order to put together a creative strategy position.

2. *Perceptual Mapping, Nonmetric Scaling.* Another thrust of research leads to the creation of "pictures" of the consumer's perception of any particular problem area or product category. These pictures or perceptual maps are developed by asking consumers how different or similar they see various brands or possible products within a particular product area. These similarity judgments can then be made into a perceptual map that shows how far apart various brands are and how they relate to the ideal brand. Communication positioning is really an attempt to locate the campaign brand somewhere on that consumer's perceptual maps that makes it distinctive and close to an ideal. The assumption is that the brand that is seen as a distinctive representative of some ideal cluster will be the brand that is purchased.

3. *Multi-attribute Decision Process Models.* The multiple-attribute approach is most directly related to the positioning analysis suggested here. The assumption is simply that the likelihood of purchasing in a product category is indicated by the extent to which that product category contains the attributes the segment thinks are important for solving a particular problem, achieving a particular goal, or fitting in with a particular event. Correspondingly, the extent to which a brand is perceived as having those attributes indicates the likelihood that it will be purchased. Just as in the buyer behavior modeling area, multiple-attribute researchers have become more sophisticated recently in determining how it is that consumers combine attributes and evaluate them in order to make a buying decision. The example in the following section will clarify how this is done.

These three developments in communication research have provided a relatively simple way for message idea developers to put together the facts of a situation to lead toward a successful positioning. The creative strategists must know how people see a particular problem and the alternative solutions (products, brands, or market offerings). Once this is known, several alternative strategies might be taken in order to position the brand.

The Perceptual Matrix

As outlined in Chapter 5, attitude structure analysis assumes that each target segment has a common way of looking at the product category that can be represented by a perceptual matrix. That is, there is a set of salient product characteristics that are desired to various degrees, and these desired characteristics are related in some way to how each competing brand in the marketplace is perceived. In Chapter 5 it was suggested that for any problem-solving decision, it might be true that consumers go through a series of stages. Decisions must be made as to which goals and events are critical, which product categories will be considered, and, finally, which brand should be purchased within the relevant product category. For each of these steps—goals, product category, brand—a perceptual matrix might be developed. And on the basis of these attitudinal structures along with purchasing behavior, it is possible to determine clear market segments that might be acted upon in communication terms.

At present we are concerned with developing the message idea, once these segments have been determined and much of the communication campaign has been developed. Consider, for example, the perceptual situation that might have existed for two segments of the dentrifice market at about the time that Lever introduced Aim toothpaste. Figure 9-2 shows graphically how the "mother with younger children" segment and the young singles market may have perceived the three leading brands.

First, note the form of this perceptual information. Instead of a two-dimensional perceptual map or a table showing the perceptual matrix, the figure is a bar graph showing the ideal rating and brand perceptions for each of four product characteristics. As noted in Chapter 5, it is important that the creative individual see the situation in his or her own terms and in terms of concepts that best represent the problem. It may be true

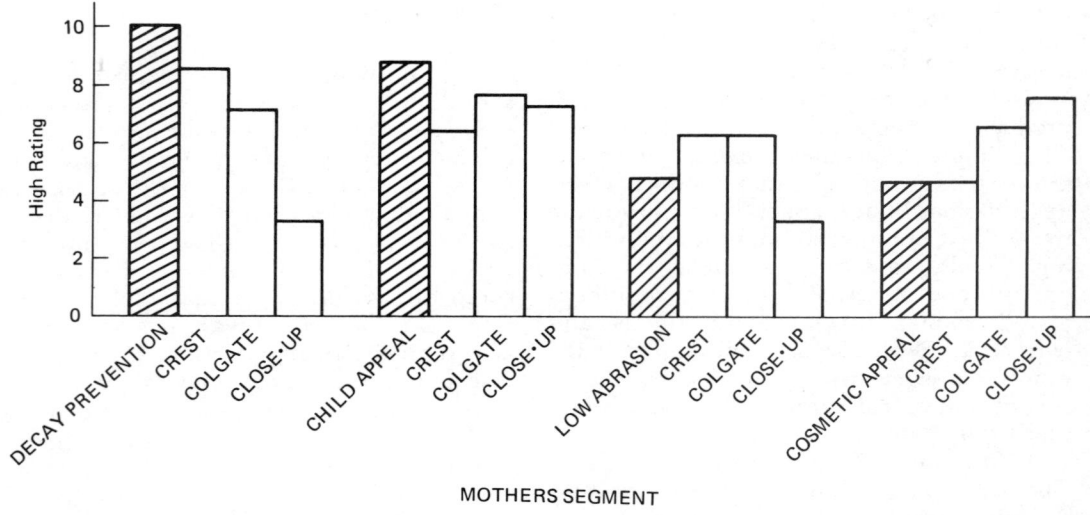

MOTHERS SEGMENT

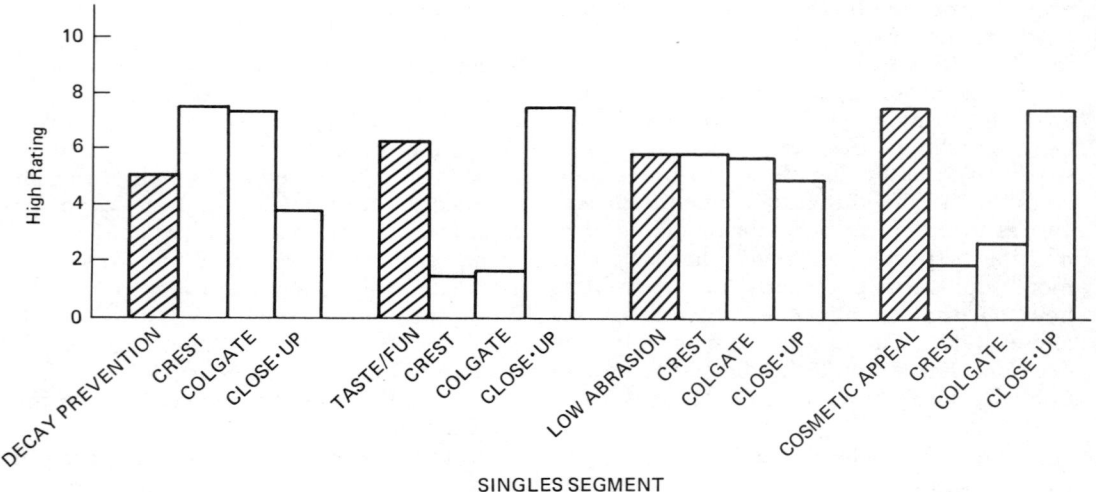

SINGLES SEGMENT

Figure 9-2. Depiction of perceptions of the toothpaste market for two consumer segments and three leading brands

that the kind of bar graph shown in Figure 9-2 is a clearer representation, for problem-solving purposes, of the consumer's view of the toothpaste market than those representations mentioned in Chapter 5. It would be possible with this representation to lay charts of the various segments over each other to compare perceptions quickly. It also allows quick analysis of the relative importance of various characteristics as well as the relative standings of various brands. As James Adams says in *Conceptual Blockbusting,* new ways of looking at a problem can produce better solutions.[3] It is also true, however, that Figure 9-2 may not represent the full richness of relationships that a two- or greater-dimensional figure might.

Looking more carefully at the figure now, it is possible to see clear differences between the two segments depicted. The "mothers" segment is most concerned with decay prevention for their family and the method of its delivery, which is expressed in the child appeal characteristic. This segment does not seem to be concerned about the low-abrasion characteristic, probably because this has not been pointed out as a problem with decay-preventive toothpaste. The cosmetic characteristic, including breath freshening and whitening, is also of no great concern to this segment. Note that there are very few characteristics considered. Usually two or three are more than enough to characterize the key perceptions influencing decisions in a product category. In this case, decay prevention and child appeal would probably be enough to describe the perceptions relevant to purchasing behavior for the mothers segment.

Turning to the singles segment, one sees an almost exact opposite pattern to that exhibited for the mothers segment. In the singles segment, decay prevention is relatively unimportant, while the cosmetic characteristics of toothpaste are most important. The characteristic analogous to child appeal, taste and fun, has a fair amount of importance for this segment, as does low abrasion. The pattern of brand perceptions was developed for this figure to relate to the market-share picture that was present in 1971 when Lever was first considering the introduction of a new brand. At that time the therapeutic brands had nearly 65 percent of the toothpaste market. Cosmetic and other types of brands held the rest.

The therapeutic brands, represented by Crest (with a 37.1 percent share in 1971) and Colgate (with a 20.0 percent share in 1971), best fit the mothers segment. Crest was the leading selling brand probably because, as depicted in the figure, it was the overwhelming leader in decay prevention. This leadership was based on the brand's being the first fluoride toothpaste in the market to have the American Dental Association's approval. Crest's ratings for all other characteristics are not outstanding, although it is possible to observe the carryover affect of the leadership position on the ratings for other characteristics. It might also be true that other parts of the marketing mix, such as in-school toothbrushing-testing promotions, might affect other characteristics such as child appeal.

Colgate, the second-selling brand in the product category, had vigorously entered the therapeutic part of the market after years of effort on the cosmetic side ("Cleans your breath while it cleans your teeth"). These two efforts are clearly seen in the ratings for the mothers segment. Colgate has a relatively high decay prevention rating and is stronger than Crest on child appeal as well as the cosmetic characteristic. Colgate had used its past advertising effect to support a secondary child appeal in its advertising, and the residual of the breath-freshening claim still seemed to affect the mothers segment, with a relatively high cosmetic score for the brand in that segment.

Close-Up was the third brand in the market and the leading brand using a cosmetic appeal. The reason for this, as depicted in Figure 9-2, is the brand's high scores on taste-fun and cosmetic characteristics. This is especially true in the singles segment, which is most concerned with these two characteristics.

Lever had no brand actually competing in the therapeutic segment of the market when it developed Aim. The company capitalized on the product characteristics of Close-Up and added the characteristics necessary to compete in the therapeutic part of the market, particularly for the mothers segments. Like Close-Up, Aim was a clear gel product rather than a paste, and it had the taste appeal of the other Lever product. To this was added fluoride, which gave Aim the ability to claim decay prevention in addition to child appeal. Fortunately, too, the combination of the gel formulation and fluoride provided the first really new and distinctive fluoride toothpaste at that time. The reason is that in the gel formulation, the fluoride ion activity was significantly higher than in Crest. This meant that the product dispersed faster in the mouth and had less abrasion than Crest.[4]

SIX STRATEGY POSSIBILITIES

As often happens with a new product, the creative strategy for Aim could have been taken directly from those product characteristics that were developed to fit a particular attitudinal segment, in this case the one of mothers concerned about dental care for their children. This is usually a mistake, however, because a wide variety of message ideas might be considered even within the constraints offered by a new product and its characteristics. By fully considering the consumer's view of the world along with trade and competitive factors, the message idea developer can create an especially distinctive message idea. In the perceptual matrix represented in Figure 9-2, there are essentially six strategies a message idea developer can consider. He or she can seek to

1. Affect those forces that strongly influence the choice criteria used for evaluating brands belonging to the product class;

2. Add characteristic(s) to those considered salient for the product class;
3. Increase/decrease the rating for a salient product class characteristic;
4. Change perception of the company's brand with regard to some salient product characteristics;
5. Change perception of competitive brands with regard to some particular salient product characteristics; or
6. Change the "composition rule" or the way people go about using characteristics and brand perceptions to make a purchasing decision.

The following sections discuss these strategies.

Strategy 1: Affect Product Class Linkages to Goals and Events

The first strategy relates to the formulation of advertising that attempts to stimulate primary demand. As was noted above, there are perceptual matrices that determine the goals a consumer will seek to reach, the product class considered in order to reach the selected goal, and, as demonstrated in Figure 9-2, the brand he or she will buy within the selected product category. This first strategy relates to the first two kinds of matrices, that is, the decisions relating to goals and product category.

If the message idea developer knows (1) the goals of a given market segment with regard to (2) the choice criteria (salient product characteristics) used to evaluate the alternative product classes considered as ways of achieving the goals and (3) the perceptions regarding each product class, he or she can better decide what action to take to stimulate demand for the product class. Inevitably, message idea developers must link the product class to relevant goals. But they might also seek to change the consumer's rating of their product class versus others with respect to the choice criteria involved.

The message idea developer could seek to change the saliency of the consumer's goals and thus increase the demand for the product class. However, most of the change associated with goals comes about through environmental factors operating over long periods of time, although communication campaigns can undoubtedly accelerate the trends.

Thus far no distinction has been made between *goals* and *needs*. Products are ultimately judged on the basis of their function or role in helping the individual attain some goal or in meeting a need. In the case of dentifrices, the goal of many consumers is to improve or maintain their appearance with shining white teeth and clean fresh breath. Other consumers may have the goal of good personal health through dental care. Still others, like the mothers segment, may have the goal of caring for loved ones by making sure that they regularly brush their teeth with an effective dentifrice. Many other goals could be outlined, but their importance lies, first, in that the goal(s) will partly determine what product class characteristics are salient (as well as how salient), and second, that the goal(s) will ultimately be reflected in the individual's attitudes toward alternative brands of the product. Thus if goals are known—however imprecisely—they help to explain attitudinal ratings, or if salient product characteristics and ratings are known, goals may be deduced.

After the message idea developer has differentiated individuals on the basis of goals and translated this differentiation into a preference for one product class over another via saliency or ideal point ratings, the developer could try to alter these saliency ratings or product-class choice criteria in the hope of attracting more consumers to a product class and ultimately to a brand. In the dentifrice example, Crest attempted to invoke the caring goal with the appeal "Look, Ma, no cavities." Ultra-Brite, on the other hand, invoked a goal of good interpersonal relations with the appeal "Ultra-Brite gives you sex appeal." Crest tied goals to product-class criteria, while Ultra-Brite simply stressed the goal to be attained.

Other examples of attempting to change, influence, or create additional goals as they relate to the use of product classes or brands are safety in automobiles, health protection by eliminating oral bacteria and germs through the frequent use of mouthwash, reducing the financial burden of decentralized inventories through the regularized use of air freight, and the reduction in air pollution through the use of low-lead gasoline.

Once goals are set, consumers will proceed to select products that will help them obtain their objectives. But there is an intervening consideration, since most products are consumed as part of an "event"—that is, as part of a situation that occurs at certain places at certain times and often involves the presence of more than one individual. The situation may be social or work oriented and often involves more than one product. The event is, of course, tied to the goal and is prescribed and constrained accordingly.

The possibility presented for strategy formulation at this level is the use of communication to change the individual's attitude toward the use of a product class *within* a particular period. In other words, the salient product characteristics of alternative product classes will be judged according to how well they "fit" with the event to be pursued. The event itself is perceived by the individual as being associated with certain salient product characteristics, and the decision process is similar to the notion of perception and brand choice. The advertiser seeks to change or modify the attitudes toward salient product-class characteristics that the individual associates with the event, in order to increase the probability that the product class of interest will be chosen.

It is at the event level of demand that social or group influence on the individual's choice of brand becomes more apparent. This is only natural, because social encounter is viewed as an "event" by individuals, whether people gather for some jointly agreed purpose (specific goal-related activities) or merely meet "by chance." Frequently, a modification or influence of attitude sets at the event level entails changing attitudes of the group or at least changing the individual's perceptions of attitudes held by the group. A prominent example of such attempted influence involves the social acceptability of women's smoking small cigars in public. Others include the serving of margarine to guests, the serving of wine at family meals to bring greater enjoyment to a commonplace affair, and the drinking of milk after strenuous exercise to reduce body temperature.

The first broad strategy alternative is a complex one, and the message idea developer needs procedures to allow him or her to be certain that the full range of goals and events has been considered. Two such procedures that can help are Maslow's *need hierarchy* and Maloney's *message generation framework.*[5]

The advantage of Maslow's hierarchy of needs is that it provides a classification for the message idea developer to use in assessing the alternative needs within any particular situation. In addition, Maslow pointed out that the needs are ordered in a hierarchy of "prepotency," so that lower-order needs must be satisfied to some extent before higher-order needs can be considered.

The five needs in the Maslow system label the rows of Table 9-1. The most basic, or physiological and safety, needs are listed first. These needs must be satisfied to some extent before someone can be concerned about satisfying the other needs, such as self-actualization.

Maslow's system is only one of a number of classifications of needs. Some of these classifications offer many more types of needs, running into the dozens. Others are very simple and are based on essentially one need. Carl Rogers, for instance, based his personality system essentially on the idea that people are searching for self-knowledge, something similar to Maslow's fifth category, self-actualization. Others believe that all human activity is based on a drive or need for variety tempered by the opposing need for order. Maslow's classification scheme is perhaps most useful for marketing communication, however, because it represents a balance between the too simple and the too complex.

Table 9-1. Framework for Considering Various Goal-Event Combinations for Strategy 1.

Goals*	Events		
	Effect of Buying and Owning	*Process of Consumption*	*Effect of Consumption*
Physiological	Peace of mind from a well-stocked medicine cabinet	Toothpaste tastes and looks good	Nutritionally rich foods; natural foods
Safety	Fire and smoke detectors	Toothpaste has low abrasion	Toothpaste prevents tooth decay
Belongingness-love	Diamond rings and jewelry	Sharing a certain wine	Toothpaste gives fresh breath and white teeth
Esteem-status	Buying right toothpaste for children	Driving a certain automobile	Certain college education
Self-actualization		A meditation or yoga course	A particular career path

* Goals are in terms of Maslow's need hierarchy; events are in terms of Maloney's classification. Cell entries are just examples.

Most needs that could be used for Strategy One can be classified within Maslow's scheme.

The first two needs are physical ones. The most basic, the physiological, would include hunger and thirst as well as those sensory experiences that relate to the physiological. It is almost impossible to think of a marketing-communication campaign that is directly related to promoting the life-giving physiological appeals of products. In most cases in our society, these needs are so well met that it is necessary to sell food products, for instance, on the basis of higher-level needs. Perhaps the only good example would have to do with natural foods and nutrition appeals, in which the ability of a particular product to satisfy the body's physiological need is promoted. Message idea developers should consider whether it is logical to fall back to a more basic need in a product category that for a long time has been sold on the basis of higher-order needs. This is often a real possibility when new ingredients are added to food products, for instance.

Although Maslow did not specifically discuss the sensory aspects of physiological needs, the message idea developer should consider them. People do seem to have a physiological need for variety and pleasant sensory aspects in their environment. The basic fact that food looks good, smells good, tastes good, and so forth, is extremely important in consumer choice. Although this brings in a broad classification of need, the message idea developer should consider general sensory needs as a possibility for taking a new Strategy 1 type of direction.

The second physical need, safety, relates to an individual's concern about physical survival. This would include protection from the elements as well as medically related products. If it is possible to imagine a toothpaste market segment that is buying the product just for personal use in preventing tooth decay, then a safety-related Strategy 1 for Aim might be imagined. Instead, the two segments mentioned earlier for the toothpaste market each are concerned with higher-order needs. The "mothers" segment is really motivated by an esteem need, since good care of children will lead to self-respect. The "singles" segment would be motivated by a belongingness or love need, which the cosmetic benefits of toothpaste might provide. When Crest was first given ADA approval as being an effective decay-preventing fluoride, the individual safety need was perhaps the most realistic. As the market developed, however, all toothpaste had some potential for filling this need, and higher-level needs have been invoked.

For many products it may be true that early in the life cycle the more basic needs are of concern in marketing communication, while later in the cycle social needs may be invoked.

The third and fourth of Maslow's needs, belongingness-love and esteem-status, are in the social category that encompasses most consumer product advertising appeals. We have already identified the two toothpaste segments discussed earlier as fitting in these social categories.

The last of Maslow's needs, self-actualization, is the desire to become a full person in terms of the outer limits of one's capabilities.

Maslow's scheme provides a helpful framework for considering the possibility of using Strategy 1 in terms of goals or needs. What about events, however? In Table 9-1 each column represents a particular event classification that might be considered by the message idea developer. These three types of events—the effect of buying and owning, the process of consumption, and the effect of consumption—are categories originally developed by John Maloney. Table 9-1 shows the kinds of events that fit in with particular goals. For instance, a consumption effect that relates to the safety need is the ability of a toothpaste to prevent decay. A process of consumption effect in terms of a physiological need is the fact that a toothpaste may taste and look good. By considering this table for any particular marketing offering, a message idea developer can first classify the positionings that are now present on the market and look for new potential positionings relating to Strategy 1. Although Strategy 1 is difficult to implement, this framework should provide some assistance.

Strategy 2: Adding a Salient Characteristic

The strategist who observes that his or her brand does not "fit" the ideal product-class characteristics is faced with the alternatives of adding a salient characteristic or altering the perception of existing ideal product characteristics. Strategy 2 is concerned with the first of these alternatives.

Through marketing communication, primarily advertising, a firm can make consumers aware of an attribute of a product class that has previously not been considered salient or may not even have existed. Examples of this strategy's application include the use of additives to gasoline, the adding of fluorides to toothpaste, the adding of vitamins and minerals to cereal, and the incorporation of light meters into cameras.

This type of positioning strategy is most often attempted when a product is at the mature stages of its life cycle, since by this time consumer attitudes pertaining to choice criteria have been well established. The communication positioning change is frequently combined with the product modification, although this may not be necessary. As mentioned above, such a new product ingredient is usually related to physiological or safety needs and the effect of product use. These changes also often start a new life cycle for the brand introducing the new characteristic. Later in that cycle other needs are invoked in order to create the position.

Clearly, research must show that the new characteristic has the potential of becoming salient; further, the communicator must believe that his or her brand can obtain a high relative rating on the new characteristic. Ideally, the communicator would like to appropriate it so that competitors who followed would reinforce the claims made for the brand while simultaneously building the saliency of the product characteristic. The continuing success of Crest in the toothpaste market, for instance, seems to be due to this brand's ability to appropriate the fluoride characteristic. Brands like Colgate, in attempting to gain share in the market following Crest's success, have had to do so by positioning against another segment with a slightly different mix of appeals. Aim was eventually able to capture a good share of the market by being positioned as the product that had fluoride but also had the fun-child appeal characteristics that Crest did not have. This apparently was a very effective positioning against the "mothers" segment. More recently Aqua-Fresh carried the Aim strategy even further. (See Figure 9-3.)

Strategy 3: Altering the Perception of Existing Product Characteristics

Increasing Salience. The communicator who observes that his or her brand rates well on a product-class characteristic that consumers do not consider too salient may wish to try to effect an increase in its salience. This strategy is an extension of the previous one and requires careful research to determine how the marketer's brand and competitive brands are positioned by the market segment. This kind of comparative examination is necessary, since research has indicated that changing the importance of a product-class characteristic will not affect preference for it unless one brand rates high and competitive brands are low with respect to that characteristic. For example, an airline company that noted that "on schedule" was not given a high saliency rating might seek to increase the rating of this product-class characteristic provided that it felt that its "on schedule" performance was

Since 1955 Crest has helped over 40 million kids prevent cavities.

Over 19 years ago Crest toothpaste with fluoride was introduced. And since then, Crest has helped over 40 million kids prevent millions and millions of cavities.

We know Crest's fluoride works

because there have been over 20 clinical studies proving it. The kids who have been helped by Crest know it works because they have the good checkups to prove it.

So make sure your kids cut down

on treats. Take them to the dentist every six months for a regular checkup and have them brush regularly with a fluoride toothpaste you know you can trust. Have them brush with Crest.

Why trust your family's teeth to anything else?

Crest

You can't beat Crest for fighting cavities.

(Courtesy of Procter & Gamble Co.)

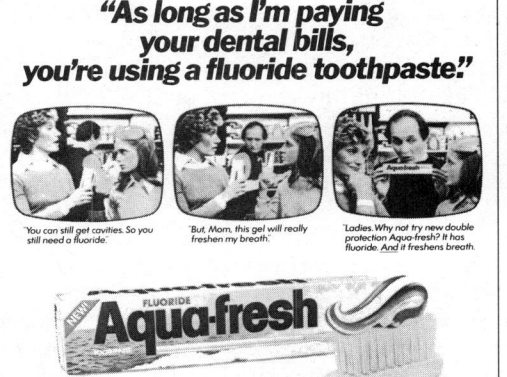

"As long as I'm paying your dental bills, you're using a fluoride toothpaste."

"You can still get cavities. So you still need a fluoride."

"But, Mom, this gel will really freshen my breath."

"Ladies. Why not try new double protection Aqua-fresh? It has fluoride. And it freshens breath."

FLUORIDE
Aqua-fresh

HERE'S HOW IT WORKS: Aqua-fresh gives you all the cavity-fighting fluoride of the leading paste.

And all the breath freshener of the leading gel.

Concentrated in one toothpaste. That's double protection.

New double-protection Aqua-fresh fights cavities and freshens breath.

© 1979. Beecham Inc.

(Courtesy of Beecham Products)

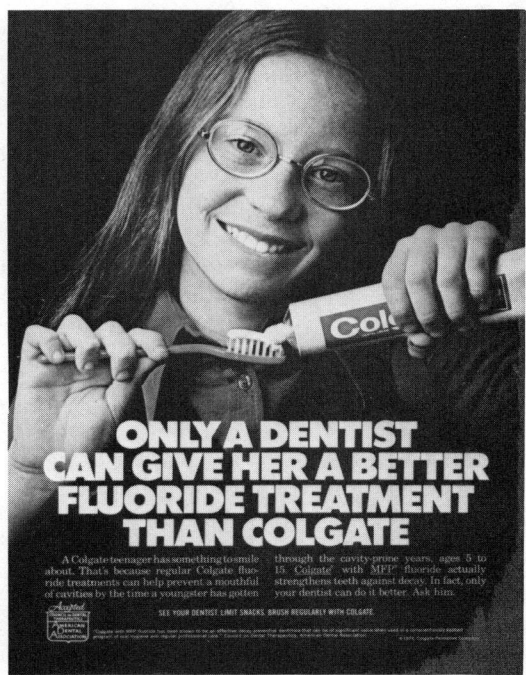

ONLY A DENTIST CAN GIVE HER A BETTER FLUORIDE TREATMENT THAN COLGATE

A Colgate teenager has something to smile about. That's because regular Colgate fluoride treatments can help prevent a mouthful of cavities by the time a youngster has gotten through the cavity-prone years, ages 5 to 15. Colgate with MFP fluoride actually strengthens teeth against decay. In fact, only your dentist can do it better. Ask him.

SEE YOUR DENTIST. LIMIT SNACKS. BRUSH REGULARLY WITH COLGATE.

(Courtesy of Colgate-Palmolive Co.)

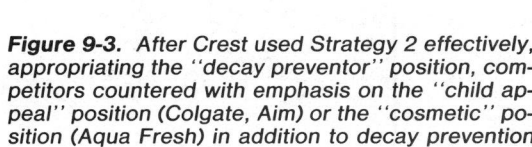

Figure 9-3. *After Crest used Strategy 2 effectively, appropriating the "decay preventor" position, competitors countered with emphasis on the "child appeal" position (Colgate, Aim) or the "cosmetic" position (Aqua Fresh) in addition to decay prevention*

better than that of its competitors. In another example, the Ries, Cappiello and Colwell research on New York banks showed that Chase Manhattan was seen by the market as being the leader in "fast service," an attribute that the bank had ignored in the past. A Strategy 3 approach that would attempt to increase the importance of fast service in the bank customer's mind seemed indicated in that situation.

Changing the Optimal Range. Underlying much of the above is an assumption of how communication relates to brand and product perceptions and of how these relate to brand preference. Specifically, the purchase probability of any particular brand is assumed to be the sum of the salient characteristics ratings multiplied by the brand ratings across all characteristics considered by the segment. In other words, the assumption is that the higher a brand is rated across all ideal characteristics, the more likely it is to be preferred and purchased.

This assumption probably holds true in only a few markets because, in order for it to be correct, consumers would have to desire an unlimited amount of any characteristic. And since the communication environment is so noisy, consumers tend to simplify the way they look at products and the way they use those perceptions. Therefore the detailed consideration of numerous characteristics compared with a series of brand perceptions is not likely to be too frequent an occurrence. Strategy 6, discussed later, deals with the actual mechanisms that consumers use to put together their ideals and brand perceptions in order to make purchasing decisions. This section considers a form of Strategy 3 in which it is assumed that consumers have an optimal range in which they are willing to consider market offerings.

Since there are probably optimal ratings below or beyond which preferences would fall off, a reasonable strategy may be to attempt to change that range rather than a particular

rating point. For instance, in the toothpaste example given earlier, it is likely that for the characteristics "decay prevention" and "cosmetic effect," the more a brand is perceived as having the characteristic, the more a consumer is likely to buy the brand. But, for the characteristic "low abrasion," a point probably exists beyond which the consumer is not willing to go; that is, a toothpaste could have too little abrasion. Possibly the relationships are also somewhat different on either side of the optimal point. In the toothpaste example, the "singles" segment may be willing to accept almost any deviation above the ideal point on the characteristic "decay prevention," but deviations too far below the ideal may cause rejection of the brand.

These relationships can vary across the ideal characteristics within any given market. For instance, when price is considered as a variable, the ideal product rating usually represents a maximum level above which the consumer may not move and below which the consumer would happily go. For "quality," on the other hand, the ideal rating is usually a minimum level, with higher-rated brands acceptable and lower-rated brands nonacceptable. Moreover, interactions between the characteristics often occur—e.g., consumers will accept infinite drops in price so long as no clearly perceptible quality decrease occurs. A price drop in some instances will affect the consumers' perception of the product's quality.

The same sort of reciprocal interaction probably exists between "decay prevention" and "child appeal" for the mothers segment, and between "low abrasion" and "cosmetic effect" for the singles segment. That is, mothers may feel that it is inevitable that as decay prevention increases, child appeal must decrease. In the same way, singles may feel that as abrasion goes up, so does cosmetic effect. Truly successful positionings often consist of a breaking of such a natural mental link between two characteristics in the consumer's mind.

A manager must consider the optimal product rating not only with regard to its relation to brand perception and preference but also with regard to (a) a distribution of that relationship around the ideal point and (b) the relationships between distributions for all the characteristics that consumers consider important. While this may appear to be extremely complex, the process is simplified by the fact that few product characteristics seem to be utilized in any single product purchase decision. Also, the characteristics by which products are identified and conceptualized are fairly stable over time. Further, managers have demonstrated their ability to understand and predict very well with the use of a few very simple variables.

Once the meaning of the saliency of product-class characteristics is established, it is possible to consider the process that entails an attempt to change the nature of the ac-

ceptable distribution around the ideal point for a characteristic. If a marketer is selling a higher-price product than competitors, for instance, he or she may not be able to change the ideal rating a segment would want for price. But the marketer may be able to get consumers to consider a range of prices *above* the ideal rating by affecting the price-quality relationship that is perceived by many. Advertising could point out the quality that is possible only with the higher-priced product. An example, for Chivas Regal, is shown in Figure 9-4. Similar positioning examples could be cited for all the negative relationships discussed above. Thus one could attempt to deal with the potential negative relationship between the perception of decay prevention and child appeal for toothpaste, initial cost and upkeep for machinery, horsepower and safety for cars, taste and effectiveness for mouthwash, and so forth. The goal of

If you think people buy Chivas Regal just for the bottle,
try selling this one.

Figure 9-4. Chivas Regal ad showing a variation of Strategy 3 in which the optimal range for price may be changed by relating it to quality received

this type of positioning is to change the nature of the range around the ideal point. Typically this is done with communication using two or more of the product characteristics.

A substantial amount of research has been conducted by psychologists on latitudes of acceptance and rejection in attitude. Since this research is examined in the next chapter, it will suffice here to emphasize that the research indicates the significant value of considering positioning strategies not only in terms of rating points but also in terms of distribution around those points.

Strategy 4: Changing Perceptions of the Brand

Whereas Strategies 2 and 3 were concerned with changing consumer perceptions of the ideal brand, the present positioning strategy focuses on changing consumer perceptions of the market offering itself. In both cases, the strategy objective is to develop a better "fit" between the "ideal" brand and the advertiser's brand.

Little can be said about this strategy that has not been said already. Several significant suggestions, however, come from recent attitudinal research. An obvious one is that advertisers should not attempt to change perceptions for their brand when the brand itself does not possess an adequate quantity of the characteristics in question. The basic assumption of some of the product development systems mentioned in Chapter 4, for instance, is that the purpose of a campaign is to communicate the characteristics that a brand actually has. The positioning work of Trout and Ries also makes the assumption that a brand should lead from strength, not only in terms of characteristics the brand actually possesses but also in terms of those characteristics that are already perceived as being possessed by the brand.[6]

The framework suggested here provides

a clear and measurable set of criteria for selecting the particular brand perceptions to be emphasized. Analysis of the optimal points and ranges for the salient product characteristics can indicate those characteristics that are most crucial in their effect on preference— and can do so by segments. Indeed such a process would appear to be at the very core of any segmentation scheme. Within this set of characteristics, the message idea developer should seek to emphasize those for which he or she has the most relative advantage. Ideally, these would be characteristics for which both the campaign brand and the competitors have low brand perceptions. These characteristics provide an opportunity for profitable change in brand perception. This is especially true of those characteristics that the brand possesses and which will be difficult for the competition to copy.

These conditions—high salience of a characteristic and exclusive possession of it by one brand—occur so seldom in marketing that their absence constitutes good reason to believe that there is substantial opportunity for product development. Certainly there is no room for trivial claims in positioning strategy. There is, however, an opportunity to preempt a position that other brands have not taken, even though they *could* have. At the time that Avis started its "Number Two" campaign, National could have actually used this appeal, but the force and effectiveness of the Avis campaign were such that, once it started, National no longer had this positioning alternative.

Strategy 5: Changing Perceptions of Competing Brands

Under some conditions, success may be achieved by altering perceptions for a brand with regard to salient characteristics that are perceived as being possessed to a greater extent by a competitive brand. There are techniques that boost the brand while pointing out the fallibility of competitive claims. Specifically, two-sided and refutational messages provide a vehicle for fairly presenting both sides of an issue while at the same time improving the perceptions of the brand being communicated.

Examples are Avis's and Hertz's advertising dealing with the advantages of first or second position in the rental-car industry; Volkswagen's refutation of the small and ugly car counterclaims; Bayer Aspirin's counterattacks against other forms of headache remedy, and, in the political arena, any incumbent's messages that refute claims of his or her alleged mishandling of affairs. The strategy of dealing with competitive claims also occurs in industrial selling through the presentation of comparative cost data or competitive laboratory findings.

In positioning terminology, such a strategy is known as the "against position." By taking a market segment's common assumptions about a product category and turning them to the advantage of the communicated brand, it is possible to develop a strong and successful position. For instance:

> In the case of Beck's Beer, the repositioning is done at the expense of Lowenbrau. "You tasted the German beer that is most popular in America. Now taste the German beer that's the most popular in Germany."
> The strategy works because the prospect had assumed something about Lowenbrau that wasn't true.[7]

Once again, however, these techniques must be used carefully. The evidence suggests that if they are not carefully used, the communication campaign can boomerang by giving support to competitive brands and claims (see Chapter 10). Further evidence indicates that unless the audience is relatively sophisticated and highly involved with the product, it is unlikely to comprehend two-sided messages fully. And if the audience is sophisticated enough and involved, its attitudes may be quite difficult to change with any kind of message.

Strategy 6: Modifying the Composition Rule Used

Strategy 6 is so basic that it has been saved for the last so that its effect on the other strategies can be understood.

Strategy 3 discussed the underlying assumption about how communication relates to brand and product perceptions and the way these relate to brand preference. It was assumed that the purchase probability of any particular brand is the sum of the salient characteristics ratings multiplied by the brand ratings across all characteristics considered by a segment. This, in fact, is a *composition rule*. It refers to the pattern in which ideal characteristic ratings and brand perceptions relate, in combination, to the overall evaluation of the brand or product.

The most usual assumption in marketing-communication research is that, as suggested above, consumers consider all ideal product characteristics and brand perceptions and mentally multiply them out to come up with the chosen brand. This composition rule is called *linear compensatory*.

There are at least three other composition rules that consumers might use. The others are quite reasonable, especially in situations in which there is an overload of information and pressure to make a decision. One positioning strategy that might be effective, then, would be to get the consumer to change his or her composition rule in a way that would be favorable to the communicated brand.

First, consider the three other general types of composition rules.

For the *conjunctive* rule, the consumer would establish cutoffs on each evaluative dimension and require that a product surpass all of these to receive a high evaluation. In the toothpaste example, the mother would have some general idea of the minimum acceptable levels of decay prevention, child appeal, low abrasion, and cosmetic effect. The brand that surpassed all of these cutoffs would be purchased.

The *disjunctive* rule occurs when the consumer requires that the brand possess at least one distinctly superior characteristic in order to receive a high evaluation. Mediocre performance on other dimensions will not detract from the presence of an outstanding attribute. The singles toothpaste segment, for instance, may consider the cosmetic effect characteristic to be so important that outstanding performance on it would ensure purchase of the brand.

The *lexicographic* rule portrays the consumer making product comparisons one dimension at a time rather than using different dimensions concurrently. The consumer begins by comparing alternatives on the single most important dimension, and perceived differences here will determine his or her product evaluation. If a discrimination cannot be made on the most important dimension, then consideration is made among the brands on the second most important dimension, and so forth. If mothers were using this rule and were convinced that Crest and Aim were equivalent in terms of decay prevention, they then might move to the child appeal characteristic and choose Aim because it is distinctly better there.

It is initially important to know the consumer's composition rule in order to use any one of the first five strategies. As Peter Wright points out:

> Assume that Mrs. X has the following configuration of beliefs about our brand of toothpaste: (1) *slightly below average* in whitening power, (2) *average* in breath freshening capacity, (3) *average* in economy and (4) *slightly above average* in decay preventiveness. To simplify the example, assume that she thinks that each of these four dimensions is of equal importance in evaluating

toothpaste. If Mrs. X were using a compensatory rule and our promotional tactics succeeded in inducing a positive change in *any one* of her beliefs, then that change would have some positive effect on her overall judgment of our brand. Assume instead that she is using a conjunctive rule which requires that she believe a brand is at least average on each and every dimension to receive a favorable evaluation. In this case, promotional success in changing her beliefs about our brand's breath freshening capacity, economy, or decay preventiveness would be useless as long as she retains her current below-cutoff belief about whitening power. Or she may instead be using a disjunctive rule which requires a brand to possess at least one attribute that is *extremely above* average. Persuading her that our brand was average in whitening power was the key if she used the conjunctive rule, but such a change would be totally ineffective if she used this disjunctive judgment strategy. In this case, changing her "average" beliefs about our brand's breath freshening capacity and economy to "slightly above average" would likewise have absolutely no impact on her overall evaluation.[8]

Thus the real composition rule being used by the consumers is crucial to the decision as to which positioning strategy to use. And an additional strategy, Strategy 6, might be to attempt to induce consumers to use a composition rule favorable to your brand.

Much of the well-known positioning advertising consists of such attempts to alter the composition rule. The famous advertisement that introduced the Plymouth automobile was of this sort. The headline said "Look at all three," suggesting perhaps the use of a conjunctive rule.

In the present toothpaste market, Crest may actually lose out to other brands if compensatory or conjunctive rules are used. One effect of the constant Crest emphasis on decay prevention may be to force a disjunctive or lexicographic rule in evaluating toothpaste. If such a rule were used, Crest's outstanding performance on decay prevention would overwhelm its possible shortcomings on child appeal, low abrasion, and cosmetic effect.

THE PROCESS
OF POSITIONING ANALYSIS

The development of a position, like all creative acts, is aided immeasurably by complete information. In this case, good before-marketing-communication research on attitudinal structure provides almost all the information necessary to do positioning analysis.

This is not to say, however, that positioning analysis cannot be done without the detailed and extensive research that might go behind the perceptual matrices discussed here. It is also possible for creative strategists to do fact-gathering research on their own and come up with good estimates of the market's view in terms of perceptual matrices. Chapter 5 discussed a highly successful simple simulation model which accurately predicted shares in the cake-mix market. This model was developed on the basis of a perceptual matrix that was conceived by a group of campaign managers who felt they knew about consumer perceptions but usually did not have any detailed research.

It is possible, then, to make useful estimates of target segment perceptual matrices. The framework provided by attitude research is important enough in its effects on our thinking, even without the research. Development of these matrices, with or without research, is the first step in developing a position.

Of course, an infinite number of possible matrices could be developed in a situation. But fact-gathering analysis of product, consumer, trade, competition, and past experi-

ence should narrow the field to a workable few.

Then detailed consideration of each of the six positioning strategies should provide the breakthrough to a successful positioning strategy as exemplified in the message idea theme statement.

SUMMARY

In this chapter we have dealt more specifically with the heart of the message idea—its positioning. *Positioning* is a mental set developed to help consumers deal with the confusion in the environment. It is no longer enough to state a strong appeal or to work on an image for a brand. Both products and the competitive situation are too complex to allow some simple "We're better than them" statement. Consumers too are more sophisticated in their consideration of product and brand choices. By developing a position for the consumer to organize the brand's position in the marketplace, the marketer is making it possible for the consumer to deal with an entire configuration of possible appeals.

For instance, the Avis "We're number two, we try harder" message idea could be related to all kinds of appeals which originally may have to be covered in separate campaigns. A company with that sort of positioning would have to give fast service and would have a number of locations, clean cars, pleasant personnel, the best prices, and so forth. A positioning means more than an appeal or an image statement, even in a cluttered communication environment.

The positioning is the core of the message idea statement. It combines the appeal with the consideration of the target market segment, the trade, and the competition. By considering consumer information processing in terms of a linking of perceptions and preferences, it is possible to see the potential for six broad positioning strategies. Campaign managers can seek to (1) affect product-class linkages to goals and events, (2) add a salient characteristic, (3) alter the perception of existing product characteristics, (4) change perceptions of the brand, (5) change perceptions of competing brands, or (6) modify the composition rule used.

ISSUES AND PROJECTS FOR DISCUSSION

1. What is "positioning" and why has it taken over from such concepts as "appeal" and "image" in advertising and communication?

2. For a marketing-communication situation of your choice (or one assigned to you), answer the following questions:

    a. What is the brand-product?

    b. What is the target segment? The communication goal situation?

    c. What needs and events are critical to this brand-product and consumer?

    d. Which product attributes are salient or considered in purchasing this product?

    e. How important do you believe each of those attributes is to the consumer? (10= extremely important; 1 = extremely unimportant though considered)

    f. What are the three (or two) top brands considered by this consumer?

    g. How is each of these market offerings perceived by the target segment consumer in terms of the salient attributes? (10 = has attribute completely; 1 = lacks attribute completely)

    h. How would the target segment consumer go about ranking the brands in preference?

3. Construct a perceptions-preference matrix for this situation and note how the typical target segment would decide among the alternatives.

4. Using the matrix from Question 3, give an example of a positioning statement for each of the six strategies discussed in this chapter. Which do you feel is the best strategy in this situation? Why?

Notes

1. David Ogilvy, *Confessions of an Advertising Man* (New York: Atheneum, 1963).

2. David Ogilvy, "How to Create Advertising That *Sells,*" advertisement in *New York Times,* April 7, 1971.

3. James Adams, *Conceptual Blockbusting* (San Francisco: Freeman, 1973).

4. Charles Fredricks, "Aim Toothpaste vs. Crest and Colgate," *How Do You Tackle the Leaders?* (New York: American Association of Advertising Agencies, 1975), pp. 1–14.

5. A. H. Maslow, *Motivation and Personality* (New York: Harper & Row, Pub., 1954); and John C. Maloney, personal communication, 1966.

6. Jack Trout and Al Ries, "The Positioning Era Cometh," *Advertising Age,* April 24, 1972, pp. 35ff; "Positioning Cuts through Chaos in the Marketplace," *Advertising Age,* May 1, 1972, pp. 51ff; "How to Position Your Product," *Advertising Age,* May 8, 1972, pp. 114ff; "The Positioning Era: A View Ten Years Later," *Advertising Age,* July 16, 1979, pp. 39ff.

7. Trout and Ries, "The Positioning Era Cometh," p. 30; and "The Positioning Era" (New York: Ries Cappiello Colwell, 1972), p. 22

8. Peter L. Wright, "The Use of Consumer Judgments in Promotion Planning," *Journal Of Marketing,* 37 (1973), pp. 27–33.

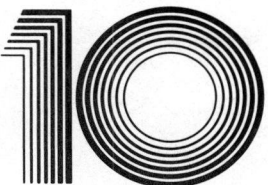

Developing Tone

• Assume you are the advertising manager for a large insurance company. Your agency account supervisor and creative director have brought the following four ads as examples of the type of message ideas they want you to consider. You know the target segment is young family men and women in growing families. The communication goals are to develop strong positive awareness with advertising and then convert this awareness into initial action in terms of contact with a salesperson. Comprehension, attitude change, and eventual purchase of a pol-

icy occur as a result of the entire mix. Your company is to be positioned as the capable, conscientious, larger company that can help.

Which direction would you take? Why?
Would you take some other direction? Why?

(Courtesy of United Pacific/Reliance Insurance Companies)

(Courtesy of New York Life Insurance Co.)

Although you may be able to make the decision between the four insurance ads and message ideas now, you will be able to do it with greater ease after reading this chapter. Here we are concerned with the main difference between these ads, *tone*.

It is even possible that after reading this chapter you may be able to create a new message idea with a tone that is truly distinctive and creates the strong awareness effect called for in communication goals.

If the message idea theme statement and copy platform include information only on the position, the message idea developer has missed a chance to clearly direct the creative effort toward a distinctive campaign theme. The Maytag theme mentioned earlier would have been meaningless if it was simply "Maytag will be positioned as the most dependable washing machine on the market." Such a theme would lack the distinctive aspects of testimonials from "real" people that were believable-unbelievable. Theme statements with just the position lack direction about tone.

This chapter deals with three key questions about the tone of the campaign message idea:

1. Should the tone of the message idea tend toward emotional or toward rational?
2. Should the campaign message idea deal with competitive brands and claims and, if so, how?
3. How strong or extreme should the campaign arguments be and how does this decision relate to believability?

The answers to these three questions can provide guidance to message idea developers who have to decide what tone or quality to put in the message idea.

EMOTIONAL VERSUS RATIONAL TONE

Perhaps the essence of tone, in a communication sense, is the degree of emotion in the message. Unfortunately, however, it is impossible to clearly define the word *emotional* or *rational,* nor is it possible to discriminate clearly between them. What may be rational to one person may be emotional to another.

Psychologists differentiate emotional from rational behavior on the basis of physiological reactions. Emotions have to do with feelings that are not normally under our physical control. More specifically, emotions such as anger, fear, excitement, joy, rage, and giddiness are all "felt" through reactions in our autonomic nervous system. This nervous system, which can be controlled only by extensive training, is the one that produces all the physiological aspects of emotion, including heavy breathing, increased pulse, dry mouth, sweaty palms, cold feet, and so forth. So for the present purposes, emotional can be differentiated from rational on the basis of whether a message idea or appeal is likely to be related to a reaction in the autonomic nervous system that would produce some feeling.

Rational message ideas would involve just reason, thought, and control on the part of the audience as opposed to the feelings, visceral excitation, and general lack of control related to emotional tone in a message idea.

Note that the emotional-rational distinction is not a clear dichotomy. Message ideas can range along a continuum from purely emotional to purely rational. Research conducted by Schacter has shown that people's emotions are dependent not only on the excitation of the autonomic nervous system but also to their perception of the situation they are in.[1] Thus rational thought is necessary to identify emotions, and the emotional-rational distinction is really a continuum.

We have all seen advertising that involves a heavy component of emotional appeal. Included would be advertising for perfumes, cosmetics, clothing, social causes, and travel. Rational appeals are more common in industrial, appliance, and commodity advertising.

For some product categories, both emotional and rational appeals are used. In the dentifrice market, Crest used rational appeals while Ultra-Bright tended toward emotional appeals. Automobile manufacturers, such as Ford, might try to generate the emotions of excitement and expectant pride for one line of cars while emphasizing the rational appeals of economy and durability for another line. Volkswagen used primarily emotional appeals for its Scirocco car and rational ones for its Rabbit. Most travel destination advertising emphasizes the emotional, but David Ogilvy has often filled his travel advertising with such facts as lodging and cost per day.

Appeals of price, durability, reliability, quality parts, and so forth, are usually considered rational. Appeals of fun, status, sex, and sensory enjoyment are usually considered emotional. But as our society moves up Maslow's hierarchy of needs, all goals might be seen as rational. Therefore a message idea that told consumers how they could achieve enjoyment, status, sex, and self-fulfillment might be considered rational if done in a very factual way. Only when these types of appeals are likely to affect the autonomic nervous system and result in feelings in addition to or instead of reason should the message tone be considered emotional.

Situational Factors

The question is, What factors determine whether a message will be successful in the emotional or rational tone? Some hint of an answer can be found by considering a simple model of human behavior.[2]

This model presumes that in order for behavior or the probability for behavior to occur, there have to be at least four components: a stimulus, a drive, a habit, and some promise of a reward. In some consumer communication behavior, some of these components are weak or almost nonexistent. But the drive and reward components are almost always somewhat present in connection with the kinds of appeals used in marketing communication. There must be some excitation or feeling in order for behavior to occur. One conclusion from this might be that in any communication transaction in which there is an attempt at attitude and behavior change, some emotion must be present to some extent.

In some situations, consumers are "driven" toward the product on the basis of its inherent characteristics, and there is no need for emotion to be present in the message itself. In other situations, consumers are making fairly habitual choices and are not inherently excited about the product or brand. In such situations, it would seem reasonable to include emotional content in the message.

Perhaps the best way to identify these two types—that is, those in which the emotion or drive is inherent in the consumer and situation and those in which the message idea should bring the emotion or drive to the situation—is to consider the product life-cycle concept from Chapter 4. For really new products with substantial consumer benefits in the introductory stage of the life cycle, there is already much "emotion" in the situation. It would seem that rational arguments about clear product benefits would be most effective at this stage. Of course, there are those deviant situations in which the product is so new that its use requires a dramatic change of typical consumer behavior. In such situations, it might be necessary to use some emotional content in the message itself.

But the need for emotion in the message itself probably is clearest in the late growth and maturity stages of the product life cycle. At those points, consumers have made some choice as to the brand of the product they habitually buy. The product category becomes somewhat boring because the nature of the product is very well understood and alternative brands typically represent quite close choices. Therefore emotion in the message seems called for in order to make the message distinctive, create attention, and motivate action.

Now what about the insurance ads at the beginning of this chapter? There may be some subsegments of the target segment for which insurance is laden with emotion. After all, for this young-family person, insurance may be in a fairly early part of the life cycle. But this emotion may not be manifest for many people in the target segment, and the goal for advertising may be strong positive awareness. The choice is yours.

Strength of Emotion

Given that emotional appeals are more appropriate in some situations than in others, how strong should the emotion be and to what extent should it be positive or negative?

Message idea developers can answer the first question by considering the simultaneous facilitating and inhibiting aspects emotion might have. Emotion can be facilitating if it heightens drive. Then there is the possibility of greater attention and interest in the product and message than if no drive were aroused. This aspect of emotion should be especially attractive in the context of the need in marketing communication for distinctive

approaches. A sufficiently strong emotion might lead to acceptance of the message recommendation by first inducing interest in the communication and then prompting action or at least attitude change related to the message idea.

But emotion also brings the important characteristic of inhibition into the picture. Too strong an emotional content may focus attention on the emotion rather than on the message itself. This may result in avoidance of the eventual communication, selective distortion of the message, or a view of the recommendations of the messages as being inadequate in relation to so important an emotion.

Figure 10-1 shows how the facilitating and inhibiting effects might work together to produce a curve of effect for different degrees of emotion in a message. In the particular situation depicted, both facilitating and inhibiting effects increase as emotion increases. What this means, in terms of the resulting effect curve, is that the optimal level of emotion is somewhere in the middle ranges.

One could imagine, however, a situation

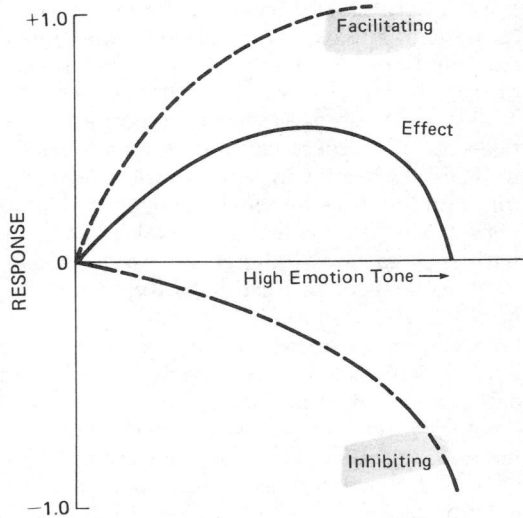

Figure 10-1. *Facilitating and inhibiting effects that might work to produce a nonmonotonic curve of effect for different degrees of emotion in a message*

in which there were no inhibiting effects connected with the use of emotion in a message. This may occur in the situation in which people have generally lost interest in the product category and have no base emotional investment in it. In that kind of situation, the effect curve becomes equivalent to the facilitating effects one in Figure 10-1. In other words, the greater the emotion, the greater the effect.

Examples of such strong facilitating effects of emotion in messages would include the toothpaste market for brands like Colgate, in which mothers have to be convinced that switching from Crest should be considered. This is perhaps one of the reasons that Colgate used such emotion-charged terms as the "cavity prone years."

The same thing can be said for the cereal market, where buyers may long ago have assumed that cereal is not a critical component in a proper diet. Thus emotional appeals such as Kellogg K's "Charge up, sleek down, feel like a healthy animal" and Total's "What's a mother to do?" can generate interest in a product category and appeal that otherwise might not exist.

In other situations, just the reverse is true, and the effects curve is equivalent to the inhibiting effects curve in Figure 10-1. In other words, a totally rational appeal is the only one that will work, and there are no facilitating effects of increasing emotion in the message. Therefore the highest level of effect is found at zero emotion. Effect would decrease as emotion is increased in the message in such situations.

Perhaps the best example of a situation appropriate for the rational appeal occurs when there is a dramatic new product with substantial benefits. Announcement of the Polaroid SX-70 was a model of the rational approach. Sir Lawrence Olivier simply talked about and showed the operation of the new camera.

Sometimes the rational approach that is appropriate in the introduction of the product is carried on too long into the growth stage, when emotional appeals might stave off competition. An example is offered by the introduction and growth period for freeze-dried coffee. General Foods' Maxim, which was the introductory brand of the product category, initially had campaign advertising that simply showed how freeze-dried coffee was made, and the company promised benefits as a result of this revolutionary new product. The advertising seemed in a sense to be quite technical and proud of the technical achievement without much emotion relating to the consumer. It may have generated sales for the Maxim brand early in the introduction, but when Maxim was met with quite emotional appeals by the rival Taster's Choice brand, it lost the leading share of market position.[3]

Thus in order to determine the strength of emotion that should be used in a message, the message idea developer should first determine how much emotion is already inherent in the situation. Then he or she should use that knowledge to make guesses about the nature of the facilitating and inhibiting effects that might be caused by increasing emotion in the message content. Inhibiting effects seem likely if there is already a great deal of emotion connected with the product category and brand choice. Facilitating effects seem likely if there is not a great deal of inherent interest in the product category or brand. In such cases there is not the emotion or drive or feeling necessary to get attitude change and action relevant to the communication message. Therefore a message with emotion can produce increasingly greater acceptance of the message recommendation.

Since inhibiting effects are likely to exist where there is already a great deal of emotion, a rational appeal that builds on this existing emotion can be quite effective. And a rational message in a situation in which all competitors are "shouting" with emotion might be quite distinctive and separate out the message from others in the field.

Again, what about the insurance problem? Is the segment likely to feel emotional about insurance? Is emotion likely to put your brand on the facilitating or inhibiting curve or something in between?

Negative versus Positive

Analysis of the possible facilitating and inhibiting effects of emotion can provide a guide to how emotional the message should be, but what guide is there for whether the emotion should be positive or negative? In fact, the curves drawn in Figure 10-1 fit best the research evidence on *negative* emotional appeals, specifically the effect of *fear* in the message.

The research shows, in general, that positive emotional appeals are unlikely to have a great deal of inhibiting effect. Therefore, if positive emotional appeals are appropriate, the facilitating effects curve is likely to be the equivalent of the actual effects from a positive emotional message. For fear or negative appeals, however, there have been found to be both facilitating and inhibiting effects, so that there is a resultant middle effect curve as shown in Figure 10-1. This means that fear messages, when they are appropriate, are most effective at some middle range.[4]

In marketing communication, the term *fear* is perhaps too strong to describe the negative emotional appeals that might be used. Typically, marketing communication deals with social fears or negative consequences which are psychological rather than physiological. In other words, the message might deal with needs at a higher level in the Maslow hierarchy of needs. There is not the danger of scaring people on questions of basic survival. Instead the negative emotional appeals that might be used tend to point out a problem that consumers might otherwise not recognize.

Segmentation analysis of the effects of fear appeals indicates that they work best with segments who have not seen themselves as part of the market for the recommended product or brand. Thus it might be surmised that strong Cancer Society appeals might be more effective for younger than older smokers, since younger smokers are less likely to see themselves vulnerable to the cancer threat.

In a similar way, insurance companies might find that fear appeals work best with groups who typically do not see themselves as needing insurance, even though they have already been exposed to insurance ads dealing with security, benefits, and so forth. Mouthwash advertisers might find that fear appeals work best with those who have not really considered the bad-breath problem. Dietetic foods might be sold with fear appeals to those on the verge of gaining weight who have not yet considered weight gain a problem. Safety features in cars might best be sold with fear to those infrequent drivers who have not considered the dangers of short trips in the city.

Figure 10-2 shows the possible resulting effect curves for two segments of the insurance market. The curve to the left is for a segment of young heads of families for which the initial concern about insurance would be quite high, so that the optimal level of emotion or fear in the message must be quite low because higher fear would only add to the already great concern inherent in the market segment. The curve to the right, showing a much higher optimal level of fear, is for middle-aged singles who may not have a great deal of

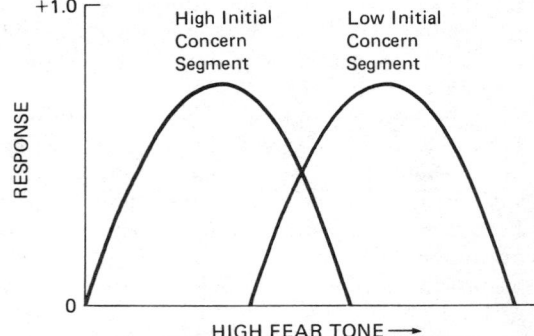

Figure 10-2. *Fear effect curves for two segments of the insurance market*

concern about the issue of insurance. For this group, a higher level of fear may be effective in getting concern about the product category and individual acceptance of recommendations.

The same sort of graph, showing curves of acceptance for different segments, might be drawn for positive emotional appeals. In the case of positive appeals, however, the curves would probably be monotonic; that is, they would never turn down in the extreme way that the curves in Figure 10-2 do. Instead the curve for the "old" segment would go up very quickly and would level off at a low level of emotion. The curve for the "new" segment would go up slowly and would reach an optimal or leveling-off point at a higher level of emotion.

Summary

There are several clear guides for message idea developers considering the question of emotional versus rational tone. First, although the distinction between the two types of appeals is hard to establish, the emotional type of message tone involves some feeling related to the autonomic nervous system. As such, emotional tone can provide the drive or excitation necessary to motivate attitude change and action.

The question of whether emotion should be part of the message idea seems to be related to whether there is some emotion or drive in the situation itself. If the message idea developer finds on the basis of analysis that there is inherent motivation to buy or use the product in the situation already, then the inclusion of emotion in the message may create confusion. A rational appeal would be best in such a condition. But if there is not inherent emotion in the situation, then it would be appropriate as part of the message idea and the eventual message.

The same sort of analysis answers the questions as to the degree of emotion and whether it should be positive or negative.

Considered in life-cycle terms, it seems that for products that are new and provide clear benefits, messages should be rational in the introductory and early-growth phases, moving to emotional in the late-growth and maturity phases. The tone of the messages should be positive into the maturity stage of the life cycle, shifting to negative emotional to grab those segments of the market who have not seriously considered the problem the market offering can solve. Once the problem is established for any particular segment, it might be wise to move to a negative rational appeal, since too heavy a fear level for concerned segments creates too many inhibiting affects.

Thus the standard cycle of emotion and direction of tone through the life cycle (or at least through the experience of any particular market segment with a product or market offering) should be

positive rational
to positive emotional
to negative emotional
to negative rational

Of course there are those segments that are initially brought into the product category only on the basis of a negative emotional appeal. This type of appeal seems best suited to the maturity stage of the life cycle in which the many competing brands have already skimmed off the prime market segments on the basis of positive appeals, both rational and emotional. The negative emotional appeal is unusual and can stand out among the noise of the communication environment. It is especially suited to a leader in the product category, since the negative appeal tends to be a primary demand one. That is, the negative emotional appeal tends to deal with problems that can be solved by the category as a whole.

Once consumers are attracted to the product category on the basis of a negative emotional appeal, it should be followed up or even accompanied by rational and also positive appeals for the product in question.

Again, which of the insurance ads represent the correct tone in terms of emotion?

These questions of the fine tuning of message tone begin to become questions of format, however. As we have already indicated, the nature of the format can actually change the actual tone developed by the message. Considering negative emotional or fear appeals, for instance, it will be seen in Chapter 12 that the success of a fear-laden message is heavily dependent on a series of format considerations, such as on the clarity and ease of recommended actions, the nature of the source and presenter, whether the fear is directed at the audience or loved ones, and the nature of the illustrations and wording. Similar considerations will be covered in Chapter 12 in regard to positive emotional tones such as humor, positive rational tone such as the straight sell, and negative rational problem-solving approaches. Remember that the message idea statements can set the tone, but the tone is implemented and often altered by the particular format developed by the creatives working in each marketing-communication situation.

COMPETITIVE TONE

The consideration of competition in marketing-communication campaign message ideas has been inadequate. For many years, just like the negative emotional tone or fear appeal, the use of directly competitive messages was almost totally neglected. Marketing communicators apparently reasoned that mentioning the competition simply gave them extra exposure at your expense.

But more recently, with an increasingly noisy and competitive communication environment, competitive tone is something that must be considered directly. It may be true that there are variations of competitive tone that increase message effectiveness without giving an extra boost to competitors.

Also, it should be realized that the capitalistic market system is based on the give and take of competition. In the communication area, this system should provide competitive sources of information that allow the consumer to make comparisons and fully informed choices. Competitive tone in messages is one clear way to provide this comparison.

Of the situations discussed at the beginning of the preceding chapter, the Goodrich, Mayor Lindsay, and Honeywell ones were the most directly competitive in message tone. Goodrich, it will be recalled, dealt directly with the name confusion with the market leader, Goodyear. Lindsay directly attacked the competitive notion that he had made mistakes during his initial term in office. Honeywell positioned the company directly against IBM in order to show their differences in providing computer services.

Even these three examples, however, are different in the way that they are competitive. Only Honeywell directly mentions the competition. Goodrich, in fact, uses a competitive promotional tool, the Goodyear blimp, to get across the name difference without even mentioning its main competition. Lindsay did not deal directly with any competitive candidate, but rather with competitive *ideas* that were being advanced against him. And couldn't it be said that all the examples in this chapter and all effective messages must be somewhat competitive in tone? What is competitive tone? And how can it be especially emphasized in a message idea?

There are actually three ways of being competitive in a message: positioning, attack, and refutation.

"Positioning" as Competitive Tone

The positioning approach is based upon the assumption that any communication message will have to be seen in the context of competitive messages. Therefore, picking and using one of the six positioning strategies discussed in the preceding chapter is in fact competitive. But it is possible to use at least five of those strategies without directly mentioning competition and without an actual competitive tone to the message. Thus, positioning is competitive but not necessarily with competitive tone.

"Attack" Competitive Tone

The "attack" form of competition is the one that has usually been rejected for marketing communication in the past. The attack strategy is suggested by positioning Strategy Five, which is an attempt to decrease the extent to which consumers see competition as possessing certain product attributes. But Strategy Five should not be interpreted to mean only a direct attack. There is some evidence that mentioning the competition, even in attack, can actually give them extra exposure without any special advantage to the communicating brand.[5] Thus simple attack is the form of competitive tone that should be avoided.

It should be recognized, of course, that the attack form of competition often becomes a legal rather than a communication issue. Various government bodies, primarily the Federal Trade Commission, have urged marketers to include comparisons in their messages. In cigarette advertising, this urging has led to the "battle" of tar and nicotine, in which ads indicated the specific amount of these ingredients. Carlton was successful with this attack approach by showing that ten packs of Carlton had less tar than *one* pack of the other brands. In the cereal market, Total cereal has directly attacked natural cereals in its advertising by exposing the small quantities of vitamins and minerals available in those cereals. In the analgesics market, the non-aspirin pain reliever Datril directly advertised its price against the Tylenol brand. This attack was quite ineffective, since Tylenol's price was immediately reduced.

If government bodies want to increase the amount of information available to consumers in marketing-communication campaigns, they should probably use a route other than the kind that would encourage the attack type of communication.

"Refutational" Competitive Tone

The third type of competitive content in messages is the refutational approach. This seems to be the most relevant to the questions about competitive tone that might be asked by message idea developers.

The refutational approach to competitive tone is really an approach for inducing resistance to persuasion. When the message idea developer sees, realistically, that consumers already have ideas that are counter to buying the product or brand, or when it is highly likely that competitors' communication will either directly or indirectly attack the product or brand, it is necessary to have a message that will deal with this difficult communication environment. Such a message would not only promote the positive aspects of the message idea developer's brand but also attempt to answer, or at least mute, the attacks on the brand that are implicit in the media and in consumers' minds. Thus this type of message, here called the refutational approach, attempts to induce resistance to the counterpersuasion in the communication environment.

Although there is considerable research and clear direction for message idea developers on the problem of inducing resistance to persuasion, very little of it has been directly applied to advertising. Usually there is thorough discussion of the first or positioning type of competitive approach accompanied by rejection of the attack mode.

For instance, almost none of the advertising textbook literature deals with what might be said in an ad in order to reduce the effectiveness of inevitable competitive claims, that is, inducing resistance to persuasion. To be sure, there are suggestions relating to positioning and the need to consider competitive claims, to be distinctive from competitive claims, and so forth. But these suggestions have to do with how the ad itself can be more persuasive rather than how the ad can induce resistance to the persuasion of competitive ads.

In the overcautious approach with regard to the attack mode, one often hears the suggestion to avoid mentioning the competition or their claims in advertising copy. When this happens, the advantages of competitive tone in some situations are lost. For instance, an American Motors ad had the headline "Now—American Motors fills the gap between the 'too-little-car' imports and the 'too-much-money' compacts." A writer in *Advertising Age* commented that the ad was "too defensive" and that "... we would have shown the car in a picture big enough to make it *look* large and then have written a headline that asked, 'Where else can you get a tough American-built car of this size for (this price)?' "[6]

The *Advertising Age* writer's suggestion ignores the realities of the competitive environment in which such an ad would be placed. Potential car buyers already have a number of negative impressions about American Motors products. In addition, there are so many cars, both American and foreign, available on the market that buyers need a guide in order to allow them to position an American Motors offering. All kinds of cars claim they are tough and American built and low priced. The American Motors headline took into account the competitive environment and showed potential car buyers where the car is positioned and how it might solve their problem.

Of course it is not always correct to use competitive tone of the refutational or inducing resistance to persuasion type. A message that attempts to deal with possible attacks at the same time that it promotes the positive attributes of the product is a complex one. If it is possible to simply lay out positive benefits and position the brand clearly and strongly in the consumer's mind, then this should be done without the confusion that sometimes occurs when competitive messages are used.

In order to determine whether competitive tone should be used, the message idea developer must carefully analyze the situation to determine if there are any consumer blocks or present or potential counterattacks against his or her brand in the communication environment. If there is no such potential or if the counterattacks are weak, unimportant, or made by a weak competitor, then the possible confusion of competitive tone should be avoided. In most cases, however, there is significant competition in the environment, and the message should answer it.

Let us look at how competitive messages might have an effect in one controversial situation. Figure 10-3 shows what happens to belief in the proposition "Capital punishment should be abolished" for groups of people (in this case high-school seniors) receiving various conditions of message exposure. The higher the attitude level on the vertical scale, the greater the agreement in that proposition. One group received no messages about capital punishment, and agreement is just above the midpoint of the scale at about 9. A sepa-

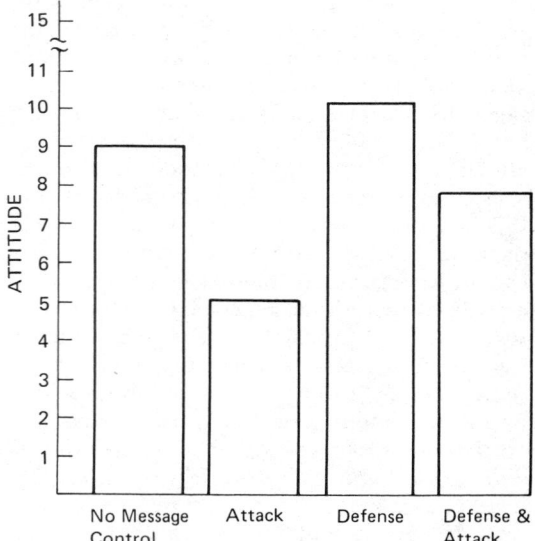

Figure 10-3. *Effects of various types of messages on the belief "Capital punishment should be abolished"*

rate group read an attack on the belief, and agreement is less, about 5 on the 15-point scale. A third group read a defense of the belief, and this seemed to increase agreement slightly, to about 10 on the scale. And finally, one group was exposed to a competitive situation of sorts, in that they read both a defense of abolishing capital punishment and an attack on that idea. This fourth group's agreement level was between the level of those who received only an attack and the level of those who received only a defense.[7]

It is obvious then that, even in this laboratory-type research, competitive messages have effects and countereffects. One of the questions that now becomes relevant is whether there are any differences in these levels depending on the nature of competitive tone in the defense message. For advertising, the broad question is the one mentioned above—whether the straight positive approach or the approach considering competitive claims would be most effective.

These are the two broad types of approaches the message idea developer has available. The supportive approach is equivalent to a straight "sell" without competitive tone. The refutational approach would mention briefly, and then refute, arguments attacking a brand or product. Listerine mouthwash has, for instance, used the supportive approach in the past with its claim that the brand "kills germs on contact"; while later the brand did use a refutational approach with the message that Listerine does not taste good but that this taste indicates how well it works. The straight-out attack taken by Procter and Gamble's Scope against the "mediciny" brand (Listerine) illustrates how effective the refutational approach might be, since Scope advertising probably reminded consumers of the medicine-tasting and therefore effective Listerine.

There is, in fact, a great deal of research evidence on the relative effectiveness of supportive and refutational appeals. Not only does this research indicate how well the two types of message work but it also indicates

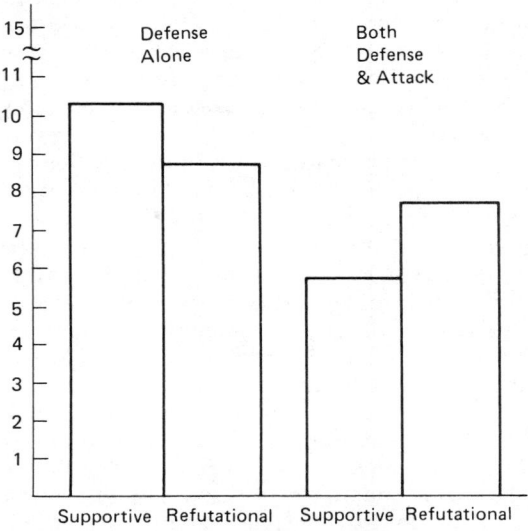

Figure 10-4. *Comparison of effects of "supportive" versus "refutational" defense messages*

under what conditions each is best utilized.

The left hand side of Figure 10-4 shows how supportive and refutational approaches work in isolation, after each of two groups has received either a supportive or a refutational message. The result here supports the advertising folklore that was mentioned above. A straight positive sell in isolation will outdistance one that attempts to deal with competitive claims. In this case the supportive messages do slightly better than the refutational in increasing belief related to a group of ten issues. This kind of result has been replicated over and over again in communication research and copy-testing studies.[8]

But advertising and marketing communication almost never stops with one exposure of one message. What happens to belief in our proposition after the competition has exposed the countering message? We know from Figure 10-3 on capital punishment that when a competitive attack is presented alone, it can be quite devastating. But is there any difference in the ability of the supportive and the refutational defenses to guard against persuasion?

The right hand side of Figure 10-4 shows that when the competitive attack follows exposure of the defenses, the refutational defense now becomes superior to the supportive in holding belief. This is just the reverse of the effect after presentation of the defenses alone. This reversal occurs so repeatedly in communication research that it has been called the "paper tiger effect." This effect suggests that the competitive tone of the refutational approach might often be superior to the supportive in advertising, despite the results in one-shot copy tests and despite the general belief that the competition should be ignored in advertising and marketing communication in general.

The results in Figure 10-4 and the bulk of similar communication research findings indicate that many message idea developers should be making a decision that has often been ignored in the past. They must decide to what degree their ads will deal with competitive claims. Their ads can ignore these claims and present only their brands' benefits. Or, at the other extreme, their ads can be composed entirely of answers to competitive claims.

There is some evidence that advertisers are making this decision and are often making it in favor of the refutational approach. The Avis and Hertz advertising could be offered as an example of the refutational and the supportive approach. Hertz in the past, of course, used a straight supportive approach, mainly selling the idea of renting a car for a wide variety of purposes and the convenience of doing this with Hertz. Avis, on the other hand, refuted the implicit claim that "number one equals the best" by suggesting that "number two tries harder." After a time, Hertz felt it was necessary to refute Avis's claims. But Hertz and Avis have not been the only ones using this refutational approach.

For instance, life insurance companies must very often face the counterargument that people would be better off putting less money in life insurance and more in stocks and bonds. Mutual of New York refuted that argument

with a picture of a stockbroker who said in the headline, "I'm in stocks and bonds. I'll take them over life insurance. But a MONY man gave me a new look at life insurance. As an investment cornerstone it would protect my family . . . and build cash, too!"

In the headache remedy area, there are constant claims that various products are stronger or better than aspirin. Bayer, which is nothing but aspirin, answered these claims on television and also in print with, for instance, ads showing a tower of products shaped like those of Bayer competitors and a headline that said "Tower of babble." Another ad simply said, in a large headline, "Does buffering it, squaring it, squeezing it, fizzing it, flavoring it, flattening it, gumming it, or adding to it improve aspirin?" And then this potential attack was refuted with the statement that nothing improves the power of aspirin.

At one point Encyclopedia Americana answered the implicit suspicion of encyclopedia salesmen with an ad that showed a typical family man who might be such a salesman. The headline of the ad stated the attack: "What kind of man sells encyclopedias for a living?"

The text of a Polaroid Color Pack Camera advertisement was a perfect refutational statement that must have come out of a message theme that asks copywriters to deal with the "luxury" image of the camera. The copy said:

> Sure you can live without it. The new Polaroid Color Pack Camera won't mow your lawn or drive you to the station. What it will do is deliver a beautiful color picture a minute after you take it. And bring a new kind of kick into your life.

When Kodak developed a cartridge-loading movie camera, it directly attacked that part of the potential market that had developed a whole series of arguments against home movie making. Kodak's headline and pictures stated four clear objections which were then refuted in the body copy.

"Movie cameras are too big and bulky."
"Sure, I'd like one, but the prices are a little steep."
". . . and loading them is a nuisance."
"I'm not sure movies are worth the trouble."
Kodak has changed all that.

In the same way, Goodrich refuted the argument that all good tires and good innovations in tires were developed by the leader Goodyear. Mayor Lindsay refuted the argument that he had made many mistakes in his administration and therefore should not be retained as mayor. Honeywell refuted the idea that all types of computers and computer services could be obtained from the leader IBM.

One of the most successful refutational advertising campaigns was the one for the Volkswagen Beetle. At a time when virtually all automobile manufacturers were attempting to show how beautiful, luxurious, and large their automobiles were, Volkswagen decided to directly refute the idea that its automobiles were too small, uncomfortable, and ugly.

The examples of Volkswagen refutational ads are so numerous that it is difficult to pick a few. One showed a picture of the basketball star Wilt Chamberlain standing next to the comparatively small Volkswagen. The headline said, "They said it couldn't be done. It couldn't." And the copy said in part, "So if you are 7 feet, 1 inch tall like Wilt our car is not for you. But maybe you are a mere 6 foot, 7 inches." And then the copy went on to refute the idea that a small car did not have advantages.

At another time, when several foreign manufacturers were introducing small-size station wagons with ads making them look big, the VW Squareback was introduced with an ad making its small size the focal point and turning it into an advantage. The headline simply said, "Anybody for half a station wagon?"

Situations for Competitive Tone

All of these examples and others that might be mentioned seem perfect for those situations. But there are obviously many situations for which competitive tone and the refutational approach would not be appropriate. How can the message idea developer decide? Perhaps the best first step is to understand how the refutational approach works.

Again, referring to the simple model of communication effect mentioned earlier, communications should develop drive, cue, reward, and information (habit).

If we apply this framework to the operation of refutational approaches, we can see that this type of message has the potential of satisfying all four of the criteria for effective messages.

First, in the drive and stimulus-cue area, refutations are more stimulating than supportive messages. They underline conflict and get people concerned about an area. Social psychological studies indicate that this motivating factor alone can be quite effective, since refutational defenses can work even if they deal with claims other than those that appear in subsequent attacks.

What this means for marketing communication and advertising is that competitive tone might be used even in those situations where competition is not particularly great, that is, when people are really not too concerned about the area. For instance, in rent-a-cars, although Avis and National competed ferociously, consumers may have been fairly placid and content with the situation. They may have devoted more attention to other expenditure decisions. But the Avis advertising set up a conflict which probably interested people in the rent-a-car area more than they would have been in the past. This conflict and concern should have benefited Hertz as well as Avis, especially if Hertz could have exercised the restraint necessary to avoid answering the Avis competitive messages.

The second reason that refutational defenses seem to be effective is related again to the stimulus and to the reward criteria for effectiveness: They refute counterclaims and thus make the competitive attacks seem less credible when they appear. The refutation is probably quite rewarding to the audience. In social-psychological terms, the statement of counterclaims can arouse dissonance or imbalance. The refutation can restore balance and thus make people feel better or reward them regarding the area.

A final reason for the effectiveness of refutational messages relates to the habit or informational component of effective communication. Refutational messages do contain some supportive information. Even though there is less than in supportive messages, this content probably contributes somewhat to the effectiveness of the message.

Thus, beyond the obvious situation in which a communicator must deal with a heavily competitive environment, the message idea developer should consider the use of competitive tone and the refutational approach in those situations where there is a need to develop the stimulus, drive, reward, and information components of effective communication.

Research both within and outside of marketing has indicated that competitive, refutational messages work best with a specific type of market segment. First, there seems to be some intelligence or knowledge requirement necessary before consumers can effectively process the refutational type of message. For instance, in two studies those respondents who had completed high school were more favorably affected by refutational-type messages than were those who had not completed high school.[9]

This finding can probably be generalized to imply that some understanding about the issues related to a product category is necessary if the refutational appeal is to work. It seems logical that unless an individual knows about the possible counterarguments to a brand or product, the refutational argument would make very little sense. Generalized even

further, this might mean that it would be necessary to have a segment of users or potential users of the product category in question. At a minimum, there would need to be some concern with the goals and events related to the product category. In short, the refutational and competitive types of messages are not very good messages for the introductory and growth stages of a product category.

Another segment consideration has to do not only with whether people are concerned but also with whether they are antagonistic to your brand in the first place. It seems that the refutational advantage over the supportive type of message is much greater with market segments that are users of competitive brands. For these people, a straight supportive noncompetitive message simply reinforces their past concepts of the brand as it fits their goals and event considerations. But a refutational approach seems to be effective in answering the negative thoughts they may have in their minds about a particular brand. Thus, for such a segment, competitive tone can be quite effective.

Table 10-1 shows headlines from both refutational and supportive messages that were used in a research project comparing the effectiveness of these message types in generating purchase intention.[10] The results of the study support the idea that competitive refutational messages work best for those segments who are somewht antagonistic to the brand. As Figure 10-5 shows, the repetitive effects of the refutational message were increasingly stronger against those segments who were regular users of the major competitor or regular users of some brand other than the test brand or its major competitor. In other segments, shown on the left side of the figure, the supportive messages seem to work much better.

Summary

Where are we then in the question of whether message idea developers should sug-

Table 10-1. Excerpts from Supportive, Refutational, and Competitive Ads

Repeated Ad	Supportive Appeal	Refutational Appeal	Competitive Ad
Bayer aspirin	"Bayer works wonders. Relax with Bayer . . . Bayer is 100% aspirin."	"Buffer it, square it, squeeze it, fizz it, . . . Nothing has ever improved aspirin. Bayer is 100% aspirin."	Bufferin. "Take aspirin. I did but I still have a headache. Next time take Bufferin."
Lava soap	"For real dirty hands, reach for Lava—the soap that can really clean . . ."	"Lava—world's worst bath soap! Lava users have revolted. They argue that Lava is not only a good soap for hands but for anything else too . . ."	Phase III. "Both a deodorant and a cream soap . . ."
Parker pen	"Just one could be all you ever need. At $1.98 it's the best pen value in the world. Up to 80,000 words . . ."	"Why pay $1.98 for a ball-point pen? You can get them for 49¢, 69¢, or for free. The kind that skip, stutter, etc., and run out of ink. You pay $1.98 for a Parker, but you never have to buy another."	Scripto. "Only 49¢."
Renault automobiles	"Sales are climbing. Renault's new features and fine construction are paying off . . ."	"Sure, they save money but I wouldn't want to take a long trip in one. Foreign cars are easy on the wallet but hard on everything else. Renault is changing all that."	Volvo. "The car that won't self-destruct in two years."
Slender diet drink	"The same appetite that made you fat can make you thin. Slender is a bonafide meal."	"A 225 calorie meal is easy. A good tasting 225 calorie meal is hard . . ."	Sego. "For the joy of a slender figure . . . Sego has more tasty flavors"

SOURCE: Alan G. Sawyer, "The Effects of Repetition of Refutational and Supportive Advertising Appeals," *Journal of Marketing Research,* 10 (February 1973). Used with permission.

gest in the theme and copy platform that the message should have a competitive tone? First, we have seen that all messages are competitive to some extent in that positioning always relates to how the brand is perceived in relation to the competition. Second, it seems that direct attacks that mention the competition, and are designed only to reduce consumer perceptions of their attributes, are almost never effective. Third, however, there does seem to be a variety of situations in which the refutational approach to competitive tone can stimulate interest in a product category and its brands and lead to consumers' seeing the communicated brand in a much stronger light.

The situations in which this type of competitive tone should be used seem to be those in which there are some competitive counterarguments or the potential for them. The target segments for these messages must have some minimal understanding about the product category, and the messages work best with those groups who are somewhat antagonistic to the brand or product in question. What about your insurance problem?

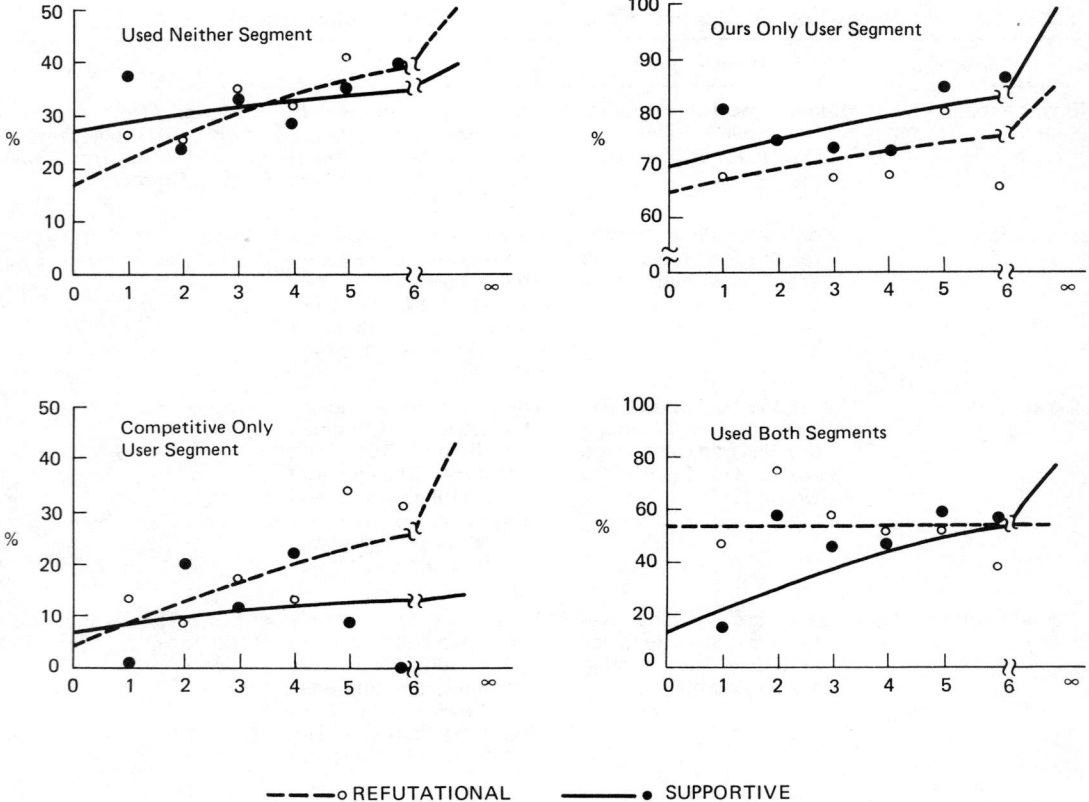

Figure 10-5. *Empirical and fitted functions for refutation and supportive appeals in four segments (Supportive empirical results are solid dots, fitted curve in solid line; Refutational—circles, dashed line). Number of exposures on baseline. Refutational ads seem to produce more repetition result in the antagonistic situations on the left.*

Reprinted by permission from Michael L. Ray and Alan G. Sawyer, "Behavioral Measurement for Marketing Models: Estimating the Effects of Advertising Repetition for Media Planning" *Management Science,* Vol. 18, No. 4, Part II, December 1971, Copyright 1971. The Institute of Management Sciences.

STRENGTH AND BELIEVABILITY

All marketing communication is an attempt to move people from one mental state to another. It would seem that the stronger the argument, that is, the more distant the new position recommended is from the audience's original one, the more effective the message would be. But this may not always be true. Too extreme a message may be rejected as ridiculous and unbelievable. It may be necessary to move people in small steps to the recommended belief and action. The question in terms of message tone is, How extreme a message should the message idea developer recommend in the message idea theme and copy platform statements?

Just as the questions about emotional-rational and competitive tone related to particular positioning strategies, the strength-tone question does also. In this case it relates to Strategy Three (altering the perception of existing product characteristics) and Strategy Four (changing perceptions of the brand). For both of these strategies, it is critical to know how strong the message should be in order to move consumers' perceptions of the ideal level of product characteristics (Strategy Three) or of the extent to which any given market offering has those characteristics (Strategy Four).

The dominant trend in contemporary marketing communications, especially advertising, seems to be to use the strongest tone possible. Automobile manufacturers, for instance, seldom just say that their cars have a quiet ride. Instead, Rolls-Royce used the famous advertising line, "At 60 miles per hour the only sound that can be heard in a Rolls-Royce is the ticking of the electric clock." In the United States the relatively low-priced Ford made the claim that its car was quieter than any other, even a Rolls-Royce.

In the energy crises of the 1970s and 1980s, many automobile manufacturers have taken a variety of positions in discussing their products' gas mileage. Some talked quite specifically about the gas mileage established for their automobiles by the Environmental Protection Agency. Others made very strong statements of this mileage, with vivid demonstrations of how far their cars would go on a tank of gas. Porsche advertising showed the car traveling from Los Angeles to San Francisco and beyond on one tank of gas.

Apparently, however, some American manufacturers felt that too strong a claim for their cars would wreck credibility. At the same time, they wanted to convince potential buyers that their mileage was better than those buyers had perceived. The strategy that was taken was a moderate one, showing that some of the American models had mileage that was comparable to that of foreign makes that were known for their outstanding mileage.

It would be recalled from the discussions of Strategies Three and Four that ideal points really consist of an optimal range within which consumers can accept brands on particular characteristics. Also, it seems that there are reciprocal relationships between characteristics like price and quality. People seem to believe that some low prices, although desirable in themselves, may be associated with low quality. This kind of reciprocal relationship poses special problems for marketers who want strong tone in their messages. There is always the possibility that a strong appeal on one characteristic may have a peripheral negative effect on another characteristic.

Such is the problem faced by marketers of low-tar cigarettes. It seems clear that consumers see low tar and nicotine as being associated with lack of taste in a cigarette. Much cigarette advertising attempts to make extremely strong taste claims at the same time that it is making extremely strong low-tar and nicotine ones.

In fact, if one surveyed contemporary advertising, he or she would find a plethora of strong claims. Detergent advertisers seem, without exception, to claim that their product will make clothes "whiter than white, brighter than bright." Pain-reliever advertisers always seem to claim that they have the strongest and fastest brand on the market. Deodorant advertisers seem to claim that their product is absolutely dry and will keep consumers completely dry, and some claim to do it for days on end after even a single application.

Still there does seem to be some advantage in an approach that attempts to move consumers a bit more slowly toward the advocated point. Also, it seems that marketing-communication messages would begin to lose credibility if all communicators took the extreme position. Just by virtue of contrast, appeals such as Bic's, "It's a pretty good lighter," would seem to stand out just because they are not overclaiming. Again, what guidance is there for determining the strength of message that should be recommended in the idea statement?

Two Theories

Some guidance on strength of message is provided by two theories: linear operator and assimilation-contrast. These two theories seem somewhat incompatible, but they are related in a way that allows message idea developers to more efficiently determine how strong messages should be.

The *linear operator* theory is that the degree of opinion or attitude change achieved by a message will be some constant proportion of the distance from the audience's initial position to the position advocated by the message. Let us assume, for instance, that you are responsible for introducing a new toothpaste with extra cavity prevention characteristics beyond the fact that it contains fluoride. Your target segment probably believes that a toothpaste like Crest provides about all the cavity prevention that is necessary. The linear operator theory would say that there is some proportion, perhaps 25 percent in this case, of your claim that people will believe and utilize. This means that if you were to claim that your toothpaste was half again as good as Crest, the audience might be persuaded to believe that it was about one-eighth better. Similarly, if you were to claim that your toothpaste was twice as good as Crest, the audience would believe it was about 50 percent better, and so forth, if the linear operator model held in this situation.

The other theory, *assimilation-contrast,* would argue that people have acceptable ranges of belief around their most preferred position. If a claim is within that acceptable range, people not only will move their most preferred position toward that claim but will also see it as being initially closer to their most preferred position (assimilation). On the other hand, if the claim is outside the acceptable range, assimilation-contrast theory argues that there will be a boomerang effect and the audience will move their own most preferred position in the opposite direction from the claim and see it as being even further from their own than it actually is (contrast).

In the toothpaste example, it can be seen that the claim that the new toothpaste is half again as effective as Crest may be within the acceptable range and will produce an effect similar to that posited above in the linear operator explanation. But a claim that the new toothpaste is twice as effective as Crest may be too extreme, especially considering that Crest has been seen as the standard in preventing tooth decay. Thus, such a claim, falling outside the acceptable range, might produce a contrast or boomerang effect, with the new brand being rejected and Crest more heavily favored for its decay preventive characteristics.

It seems clear that contemporary advertisers are making an assumption something similar to the linear operator one, because they seem to keep using stronger and stronger appeals as the noise in the communication environment increases. The assumption seems to be that the stronger the appeal, the greater the effect will be on target segments. The assimilation-contrast theory, however, would argue that it is possible to have too strong an appeal, with the resultant boomerang or contrast effect. Which is correct?

It may be that both theories are correct depending on the situation and the range of acceptable positions for any particular market segment. As Figure 10-6 shows, the assimilation-contrast theory posits that there are several zones of acceptance, noncommittal, and rejection. In the toothpaste situation, Crest represents the most preferred position or brand on the decay prevention continuum. As can be seen, there is a "latitude of acceptance" of decay preventive levels that the target market segment is willing to accept in a toothpaste. This range is narrow, probably because the main target segment, let us say mothers, would not be willing to buy a toothpaste for their family that did not have some minimal level of decay prevention capability. The upper level of the latitude of acceptance is probably caused by the consumer perceptions that a toothpaste product that has too much decay prevention capability must be deficient in some other desired characteristic.

The two "zones of noncommitment" are levels of toothpaste decay prevention that consumers cannot clearly discriminate as being

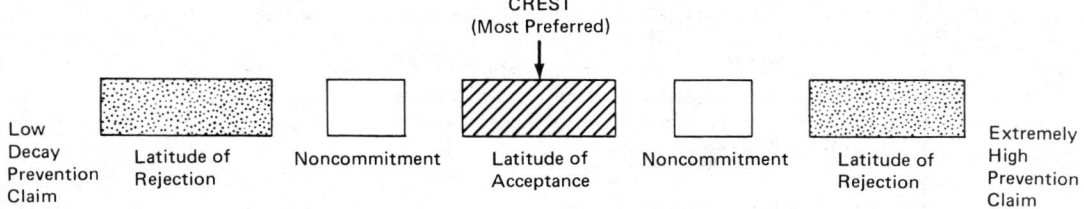

CREST
(Most Preferred)

Low
Decay
Prevention
Claim

Latitude of
Rejection

Noncommitment

Latitude of
Acceptance

Noncommitment

Latitude of
Rejection

Extremely
High
Prevention
Claim

Figure 10-6. *Toothpaste decay prevention strength of claim situation*

desirable or undesirable. The "latitudes of rejection," however, are clearly beyond anything that would seem reasonable to consumers. Note that there are latitudes of rejection for too much of a characteristic, in this case decay prevention, as well as those in the region where there is too little of that characteristic. Also note that there is not any clear symmetry here. That is, the rejection area at the top of the decay prevention scale is somewhat smaller than that at the bottom.

Now the *reconciliation of the two theories* that allows some planning ease for message idea developers is that the linear operator model may fit any appeals within the latitude of acceptance and the zone of noncommitment. Extreme positions within those ranges should make some proportional shift in the attitude or opinion or intention of the target segments. But where the linear operator idea seems to fall down is in the latitude-of-rejection areas. Therefore the message idea developer must have some information or intuition as to the range of acceptable appeals to his or her market segment. It seems that the strongest appeal possible should be used as long as it does not slip into the latitude of rejection.

Hierarchy Situation Analysis

It should be recognized that both the linear operator and the assimilation-contrast models assume a Learning hierarchy type of situation. That is, it is assumed that the message will be attended to and will lead either to acceptance or to rejection and that this will lead to some kind of action. When the situation is considered beyond the learning one, however, it can be seen that claims strong enough to be in the latitude of rejection might work. In fact, for the other types of hierarchy situations, there might be no clear latitude of rejection and much broader zones of noncommitment.

In the Low-Involvement hierarchy type of situation, for instance, the communication job seems to be, in a broad sense, to make some shift in gross positive awareness. Since by definition the situation is a low-involvement one, the zones of noncommitment must be quite broad. Thus it might be possible to use a very strong claim to cut through the noise of the communication environment and make enough of an impression to shift cognitive structure. This may be what is going on in the detergent market where a number of years ago a *Chicago Tribune*-commissioned study indicated that most women simply stop paying attention to the specific claims in detergent advertising. But as the discussion in Chapter 7 pointed out, some general impression from these claims could get through in a Low-Involvement situation and lead to a higher probability of action related to the market offering that is the subject of the messages.

It is also true that in the Dissonance-Attribution hierarchy situation, the latitude of acceptance might be much broader than it would be in the Learning hierarchy situation. In the Dissonance-Attribution situation, the function of advertising claims very often is to support an action decision that has already been made. Recent automobile purchasers are said to be (even though actual research is quite unclear on this point) heavy readers of advertising for the make of car they have purchased. The reason for this seems to be that they want support for the very important decision they have just made. In such a Dissonance-Attribution situation, a strong positive claim is what people want to hear. This is another way of saying that the latitude of acceptance would be rather broad and would accommodate strong message tone.

It seems, then, that although message idea developers must be very careful about the strength of claims made for Learning hierarchy and involved situations, very strong claims may realistically be made for those segments that are either uninvolved and non-committed (Low-Involvement hierarchy) or somewhat favorably disposed and seeking support for a recent decision (Dissonance-Attribution hierarchy). Strong claims can be made for a wide variety of situations unless there is a cacophony of extreme positive claims in the product category communication environment. In such situations a softer sell might be quite effective just from the standpoint of making the communicator's advertising distinctive.

It is still true that for the Learning hierarchy situation in which people are involved and may be antagonistic to our brand or product, great care should be exercised in utilizing strong message tone. As mentioned above, latitudes of acceptance, zones of non-commitment, and latitudes of rejection are likely to be clearly defined. There is always the risk that a strong appeal will fall in the latitude of rejection and promote lack of credibility or strong disbelief. This might lead to the kind of boomerang effect discussed above, a rejection of the message and an eventual loss in market share.

Believability and Curious Nonbelief

It is such problems that have led advertisers to be very concerned about message believability. A strong message may be desirable but may not be believable. Thus advertising theme and copy tests have usually included a question on believability. If consumers responding to these tests indicated even a residual amount of incredulity, message ideas and advertising copy were quickly rejected.

In contrast, however, the advertising psychologist John Maloney has examined the area of believability and this practice of being overconcerned with claims that are seen as being too strong.[11]

First Maloney defined what was meant by *believability*. A claim was seen as being believable, Maloney asserted, if it fits in with what we already know. In a way this meant that totally believable advertising was nothing more than reminder advertising. And reminder advertising can be dull.

Then Maloney went on to point out that instead of only two areas of believability—total belief and total nonbelief—there were really three levels of believability, roughly corresponding to the latitudes of acceptance and rejection and the zone of noncommitment. The third level of believability that he added to belief and disbelief was what he called "curious nonbelief." A message that was totally believed would probably fit in the latitude of acceptance. A disbelieved message would probably fit in the latitude of rejection. A curious nonbelief message would probably slip somewhere into the zone of noncommitment.

It is the "curious nonbelief" reaction that is most critical for determining the strength of message in a Learning hierarchy or involved audience communication situation. By restricting their messages to those that are simply totally believable and therefore in the latitude of acceptance, advertisers may be missing a chance to move from dull believable advertising to a strength of message that creates curiosity and eventual action.

In the automobile market, for instance, an ad that said that Ford was one of the best values might be believable but would not create much excitement. On the other hand an ad that said that the Ford LTD was as well made in every detail as a $50,000 Rolls-Royce might simply be dismissed completely as being too incredible. Ford's claim that its car is as quiet as a Rolls-Royce, however, may have created the curious nonbelief reaction of, "Can it be true?" Such a reaction is enormously valuable in generating interest (curiosity) and possibly moving people to the showroom and a trial ride to see for themselves.

The, "It can't be true, but is it?" type of reaction can be seen as the real or unintended objective of a variety of communication campaigns. For instance:

☐ Contadina once advertised that it put "8 great tomatoes in that tiny little can."
☐ Genesee beer's "fantastic fan" campaign featured testimonials from people who moved from the Genesee marketing area and desperately missed the beer.
☐ Mitchum deodorant featured ads with a man stating that he could skip a day and not use his deodorant because Mitchum was so powerful and would last several days.
☐ Bold detergent was advertised as creating brighter than bright colored wash.
☐ The Ford Granada was shown as looking like a very expensive Cadillac Seville but costing the same as a Volkswagen Rabbit.
☐ Heinz catsup advertising showed a family waiting for the catsup to come out of the bottle for what seemed to be an interminable amount of time.
☐ The Volkswagen Rabbit was advertised as one of the "world's 10 best cars" for under $3,500 (obviously a long time ago!).
☐ Ban Basic was claimed to be a nonaerosol that was more effective than an aerosol, and although it came in a very small bottle, actually lasted longer and cost less over the long run than did the typical aerosol deodorant.
☐ Second Nature, an egg substitute, was said to have all the flavor and quality of eggs without the cholesterol content.
☐ Sears power lawnmowers were said to start easily and every time, or nearly every time, as demonstrated on television.
☐ Testimonials for Maytag washing machines

contained fantastic claims as to the reliability and long-lasting qualities of the make.

The theme of these unusual and strong claims is to separate each brand from its competition and create more than believability without landing in the disbelief, latitude-of-rejection area. If, as you are exposed to them, you get the feeling of curiosity and the I'll-have-to-try-that-or-see-about-that response, then the message has been effective. It may be, of course, that the message is not strong enough and is merely believable. Or, on the other hand, it may be too strong and lead to rejection.

But there is some evidence that in situations corresponding to the Learning hierarchy, a message that generates curious disbelief is most effective. For instance, Maloney content-analyzed the responses of a group of women to some food advertising. Those women who had the curious disbelief type of response were more interested as a group in trying and serving the food products than those women who had the total belief or total disbelief responses.

Summary

Although the question of strength of message tone is one that could be related to all positioning strategies, it is most relevant to Strategies Three and Four, which involve changing the acceptable range of beliefs about product or brand characteristics. A message idea developer attempting to decide on strength of tone should consider two theories: linear operator and assimilation-contrast. The linear operator theory says that the stronger the message, the greater the persuasive impact of the message. The assimilation-contrast theory says that strong tone can be effective up to a point, after which it passes into the latitude of rejection and may actually have a boomerang effect because it may seem so incredible to the target market segment.

The message idea developer should consider the hierarchy situation in determining the strength of tone appropriate for his or her brand. In the Learning hierarchy situation, it seems that the assimilation-contrast model holds with the linear operator effect working in the latitude of acceptance and zone of non-commitment areas.

For the Low-Involvement situation, it may be that neither of the two theories fits because people simply do not care about the product category enough to make detailed choices as to whether a claim is too strong or not. In such situations, there seems to be almost no reasonable limit as to how strong a message tone should be. The only real consideration is whether a more moderate tone may be distinctive because it is different from the run of the mill in the product category.

This same sort of conclusion might be made for the Dissonance-Attribution hierarchy situation. Because mass-media messages can provide the support necessary for decisions consumers have made, the stronger the message tone, within some limits, the better.

When considering believability, it was seen that for all hierarchy situations, the practice of rejecting message ideas that produce some disbelief is probably a dysfunctional one. Maloney's analysis indicated that there is a third level of belief, which he calls "curious nonbelief." If it is possible to make messages strong enough to create this sort of response, then it seems likely that the tone of the message will be strong enough to create interest and intention to do something about the product. This sort of response should be the goal of all aspects of marketing communication.

SUMMARY

Without a statement on tone, no copy platform is complete. This was illustrated by three broad questions that were examined in this chapter: (1) Whether and to what extent should a message be emotional as opposed to rational? (2) Whether and how should competition specifically be considered in messages? and (3) How strong should the message be in terms of the relationship between the advocated position and the initial position of the target segment?

In answering these three questions about tone, it was necessary to first define each type of tone and then indicate the type of situational characteristics that determine whether and how each type of tone should be used.

The emotional-rational question involves a continuum rather than a dichotomy. Toward the emotional end of the continuum is the message tone that involves feeling. In general, emotion should be included in the message in those situations in which there is not a natural amount of emotion in the environment itself. Both facilitating and inhibiting aspects of emotion should be considered. The needs for positive and negative emotion vary throughout the life cycle. Negative emotional or fear appeals seem best suited to those segments of the market that have not considered the problems the market offering is designed to solve.

There are several types of competitive tone, but the one most emphasized and recommended here involves inducing resistance to persuasion. The best form of this competitive tone is a two-sided or refutational message. It is recommended in those situations in which the target segment is knowledgeable about the product category and in which there are antagonistic messages and ideas in the competitive environment that should be dealt with in the message. Like fear appeals, refutational messages also have the characteristic of being distinctive from the run-of-the-mill positive, noncompetitive message typical in marketing communication.

In general, message tone can be stronger than message idea developers typically realize. The goal should be to develop a message that is strong enough to stimulate interest but not so strong as to create incredulity.

Together, the positioning and tone cre-

ate the setting for message format development. It should be remembered, however,
that this is only the setting and that there are
many considerations in the format area that
will determine whether particular positionings, emotional tone, competitive tone,
and/or strength of appeal will indeed be successful. These format considerations, clearly
the capstone of the marketing-communication creative strategy process, are the focus of
the following chapters.

ISSUES AND PROJECTS FOR DISCUSSION

1. What is message idea "tone" and how does
it differ from "position," "appeal," "competitive
considerations," and "target segment"?

2. What is the tone of each of the four insurance ads at the beginning of this chapter? You
may use more than the three types of tone discussed in this chapter to answer.

3. Two types of automobile ads in this chapter were described as having two different levels
of strength. What aspects of tone do they share?

4. How can the communication planner determine how emotional or rational his or her
message idea statement tone should be?

5. Under what conditions would you recommend avoidance of fear appeals? Using mild fear
appeals? Moderate fear appeals? Strong fear appeals?

6. When and how much competitive tone
should be used? What are the three types of competitive tone? How do they differ?

7. What are refutational messages and when
should they be used?

8. How strong or extreme should campaign
arguments be? What two theories relate to this
question? What situational factors can affect
strength of argument? What research information on prospect attitudes should the manager
have before deciding on this issue?

9. Under what conditions is a curious nonbelief tone preferable to a total belief one?

Notes

1. Stanley Schacter, "The Interaction of
Cognitive and Physiological Determinants of
Emotional State," in *Cognitive Social Psychology,* ed.
Leonard Berkowitz (New York: Academic Press,
1978).

2. Michael L. Ray, "Psychological Theories
and Interpretations of Learning," in *Consumer Behavior: Theoretical Sources,* ed. Scott Ward and
Thomas Robertson (Englewood Cliffs, N.J.:
Prentice-Hall, 1973), pp. 45–117.

3. Walter Margulies, "How Nestlé Beat
General Foods in Freeze-Dried Coffee Battle,"
Advertising Age, June 21, 1971, pp. 51–52.

4. Michael L. Ray and William L. Wilkie,
"Fear: The Potential of an Appeal Neglected by
Marketing," *Journal of Marketing,* 34 (January
1970), 54–62; Brian Sternthal and C. Samuel
Craig, "Fear Appeals: Revisited and Revised"
Journal of Consumer Research, (December 1974),
22–34; Howard Penn Krishner III, Susan A.

Darley, and John M. Darley, "Fear-Provoking
Recommendations, Intentions to Take Preventative Actions, and Actual Preventative Actions,"
Journal of Personality and Social Psychology, 26 (May
1973), 301–8.

5. Alan G. Sawyer, "The Effects of Repetition of Refutational and Supportive Advertising
Appeals," *Journal of Marketing Research,* 10 (February 1973), 23–35.

6. "The Creative Man's Corner," *Advertising
Age,* June 26, 1967, p. 140.

7. William J. McGuire, "Inducing Resistance to Persuasion: Some Contemporary Approaches," in *Cognitive Social Psychology,* ed. Leonard Berkowitz, (New York: Academic Press,
1978); and Sawyer, "Effects of Repetition."

8. Ray, "Psychological Theories"; and Michael L. Ray, "The Present and Potential Linkages between the Micro-Theoretical Notions of
Behavioral Science and the Problems of Adver-

tising," in *The Behavioral and Management Science in Marketing,* ed. H. Davis and A. J. Silk (New York: John Wiley, 1978), pp. 91–141.

9. Ray, "Present and Potential Linkages."

10. Michael L. Ray and Alan G. Sawyer, "Behavioral Measurement for Marketing Models: Estimating the Effects of Advertising Repetition for Media Planning," *Management Science,* 18 (December 1971), Part B, 73–89.

11. John C. Maloney, "Is Advertising Believability Really Important?" *Journal of Marketing,* 27 (October 1963), 1–8.

MESSAGE FORMAT

. . . Development Procedures and Experience

. . . Relevant Research Guidelines

. . . Alternative Mix Implementations

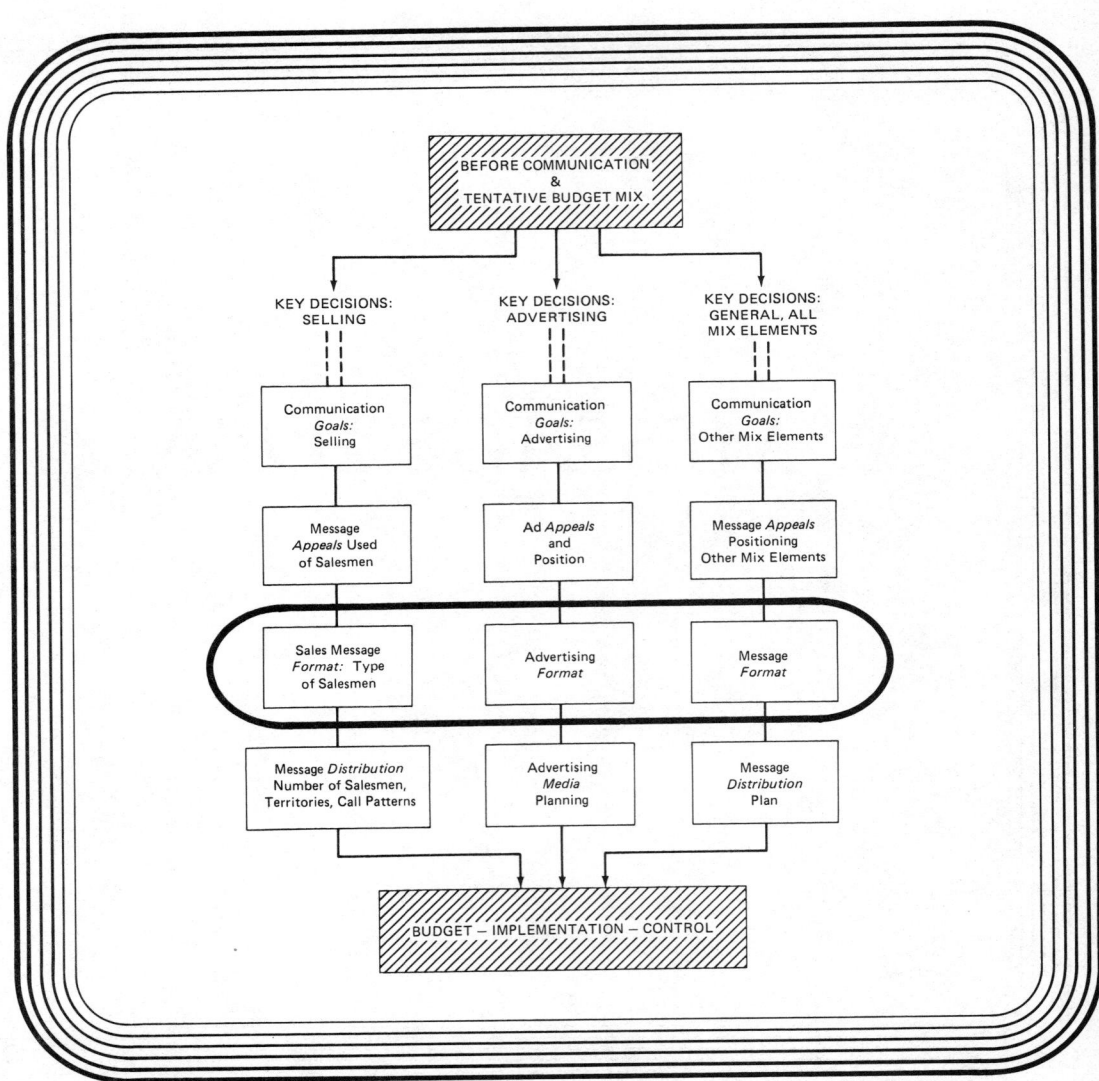

11

Message Format I: Procedures and Agency Philosophies

■ *The facts are not enough . . . don't forget that. Shakespeare used some pretty hackneyed plots, yet his message came through with great execution.* —William Bernbach

■ *Most agencies fit into two categories—they can arrive at the correct strategy, but they can't execute it in an exciting way; or they are creatively exciting, but are not aiming in the right direction. At Wells, Rich, Greene we try to be right in the first place, and wonderful in the second.* —Mary Wells Lawrence

■ *Every advertisement and every commercial should contribute to the complex symbol which is the brand image.* —Ogilvy & Mather advertisement

■ *I think it was 1955 when I first heard the concept of brand image expounded. There were 4,700 products in the average supermarket then. Today there are 7,000. Are there really enough distinctive brand images to go around?* —John O'Toole

■ *Advertising today refuses to take itself so seriously. The headlines are challenging, bold and sometimes outright sassy. Copywriters talk like professional debaters making opening arguments. Decorum be damned.* —Stephen Baker

■ *For the most part, creativity in advertising today means anything different from the run of the mill. In print this is generally a matter of graphic presentation. In television it means off-beat.* —Fairfax M. Cone

■ *. . . the copywriter and the art director . . . come up with blazingly brilliant puns and stunningly far out layouts . . . that don't relate in any way to the marketing situation or the products they are intended to sell or to the people who might be expected to buy them.* —Jo Foxworth

■ *It's beautifully written, but it is too smooth. It will slip into one side of the reader's consciousness and out the other without making a mark. Rough it up a little. Make a grammatical mistake or mess up the rhythm of a phrase so they will stop and have a chance to be aware of what they are reading.* —Leo Burnett

■ *Simple words are powerful words. Even the best educated people don't resent simple words. But they're the only words many people understand. Write to your broker or mechanic or elevator operator. Remember, too, that every word is important. . . . Once I changed the word "repair" to "fix" and the ad pulled 20% more.* —John Caples

■ *. . . my mind wandered back to those early days when George and I used to meet each other after work and I'd spend the afternoon anticipating the rush of joy when I'd first glimpse him coming down the block . . . As I sat there recalling those delicious days, the campaign for Nice 'n Easy shampoo-in hair color unfolded like a dream. And, as if in a dream, the man and woman in the commercial would float toward each other in slow motion across the fields or through the crowds with arms outstretched in anticipation.* —Shirley Polykoff

■ *The Dry Ban deodorant (FTC) case involved five commercials . . . where Dry Ban, sprayed on a surface, showed up clear, while a 'leading' competitive product showed white and gritty . . . Under an order . . . B-M would have been prohibited from using 'rigged' demonstrations . . . But the decision was reversed, and Commissioner Thompson said, 'If the American consumer has no more serious problem than the possibility of "dryness" of his underarm deodorant, he is in much better shape than I had been led to suppose at the time I joined this agency.'* —Stanley E. Cohen [1]

The development of message format, following and directed by the message idea statements, is the essence of creativity: imagination that fits and solves the problem. In this case the problem is to develop an advertisement, a commercial, a billboard, a package change, a publicity release, a promotion, or a sales presentation that gets the selling idea across with sufficient impact to a large enough group of people so that their actions fulfill total campaign objectives.

Most people trying to do this message format job fail miserably and often. Part of the reason for this failure is that the odds are against them. In other words, there are so many products and marketing offerings available that even a good message can pull only a fairly small proportion of them out of obscurity and into success.

But a good part of this failure is due to a lack of true creativity, which establishes a balance between the two components of creative strategy: the message idea and the message format. Bernbach, Wells Lawrence, and O'Toole point out that with too much emphasis on the proposition and not enough on the way it is stated, marketing communication messages might get lost in the clutter of today's communication environment. It is also true, however, as Cone and Foxworth state, that it is possible to go too far in message idea creativity, so that the idea is lost in the cleverness of the message. The balance between these two needs—to say something important and to say it in a way that will get heard—is a realistic goal achieved by creativity as exemplified by Ogilvy, Baker, Burnett,

Caples, and Polykoff. Even the watchful eye of the FTC sometimes does not stop a truly effective demonstration of product benefits like Dry Ban's if it is correct.

Part V of this book examines how this critical balance between idea and format can be achieved. As is mentioned in Chapter 2, message format development has a show business quality to it. It is something that the campaign manager is often counseled to leave entirely to those "creatives" who work on message format development for each element of the communication mix. The emphasis here, however, is on the way the manager can develop systems within which outstanding creativity can occur. We will examine what is known about what works and does not work in message format, both on the basis of experience of outstanding creative people and on the basis of behavioral science research. The discussion will concentrate on advertising, but what is said here holds true for all elements of the communication mix. Chapters 13 and 14 consider alternative format implementations for all components of the communication mix. Creativity is not all intuition. The procedure for format development in this chapter considers pretesting research that might be done to weed out inappropriate format alternatives.

CREATIVITY, THE APPROVAL PROCESS, AND ORGANIZATION

If you ask an advertising copywriter why a particular campaign failed, the copywriter will very often tell you it was because there was interference on the part of the brand or campaign manager. If you ask the same advertising copywriter why another campaign succeeded, the copywriter will tell you that it was because he or she was allowed the creative freedom to develop the best possible message. The issue in message format development is creativity. And the main question is how the managerial approval process can be organized so that the best work of the "creatives" can be applied to the problem situation.

Creativity is fostered in an atmosphere that defines the problem without putting too great a restriction on the creative imagination. Creative output is fostered by some pressure, but not so much pressure that the output is dull and unimaginative.

In trying to achieve the perfect relationship between the campaign manager and the creatives, the advertising industry has developed two rather extreme positions. One is the creative's position. And the other is the client's or campaign manager's position.

The Creative Power Extreme

The creative's position is typified by the system employed by William Bernbach of the Doyle Dane Bernbach advertising agency. Bernbach feels that a client is an expert in the marketing situation and the agency is an expert in advertising. Therefore the creative position on creative organization would have the client provide the advertising agency with all the information and general direction for the campaign, and the agency would then come up with a campaign to fit these restrictions. Some of those stating this creative position on the approval process even say that if clients do not like the message format idea presented to them, they should find a new agency. In any case, this approach is anti client approval and suggestions, anti multiple decision makers from the client organization getting involved, anti multiple alternatives

being presented to the client for choosing, and anti research that would be used to choose among such multiple alternatives.

Perhaps the most extreme example of putting power in the hands of the creatives is found in Jerry Della Femina's book, *From Those Wonderful Folks Who Brought You Pearl Harbor.* At one point Della Femina tells about a very tight situation in which he and his art director came into their office very early one Monday morning because they knew that one of their clients, representing an investment house, would be in soon to see the layouts for a new advertising campaign they had promised him. The two agency people bantered back and forth trying to come up with an idea for the campaign. Soon their discussion degenerated into a series of complaints about how hard they had to work and what an inconvenience it was to have to start so early on a Monday morning. Suddenly they realized that company pension fund managers, who represented their main target segment, probably felt that way too. This idea, with some refinement, was developed as a central one for their proposed campaign. They basically decided to sell the investment house to the pension fund managers on the basis of understanding about the difficult task the pension fund managers had in deciding how to spend money wisely. The art director quickly roughed out a series of advertisements that would express this message idea. These were presented to the client as his only alternative, and supposedly the campaign was quite successful.[2]

The Manager Power Extreme

The exact opposite of the creative's approach to message format development is that it would be run by the client. In the extreme, it would be typified by an analytical model developed by Irwin Gross. Gross's model was intended to determine the number of alternatives that should be considered in developing an advertising campaign and the amount of money that should be spent on pretesting them. Investigations using the model indicated that advertisers and their agencies should be developing many more alternatives and spending much more money on the process of message format development and testing.[3] The implication is that creative talent should be used to develop a number of alternatives, which can then be tested by a research organization designated by the client. Aside from creating the alternatives, the advertising format developers or copywriters would have no power to indicate which alternative should be selected.

Some advertising agencies purportedly take this managerial view and supply their clients with a large number of alternatives from which to choose. These agencies are sometimes known as "tie shops" because just like a tie shop they provide many selections without bias.

An Alternative: A Format Development Procedure

Of course neither the creative power alternative represented by Della Femina nor the client power alternative presented by the Gross model is ideal. The creative power alternative could produce the kind of off-target imaginative and wild advertising approaches criticized by Jo Foxworth in the quotation at the beginning of this chapter. The client power alternative would emphasize the message idea without careful attention to the importance of the format itself. It may very well be that creatives would become very discouraged in such a situation and that pretesting would incorrectly "pick" a campaign that was less than optimal.

The campaign manager should exercise some control without stifling the creative process of message format development. Creative workers should be given a clear idea as to the message idea and purpose of the campaign. They should have at their disposal and use all the information generated from fact-gathering research as well as past experience and communication research relative to the problem in question. More than one alternative should be developed for each campaign, but the agency-creative people should have a chance to indicate their favorite. Out of a large number of alternatives, the client and agency people should work together to pare down to a few that might be tested. Testing should be a part of the process, since actual results from consumers can add information to the deliberation as to which format to use.

Thus a four-step procedure is suggested as a process to ensure that all facts are used well and that creative talent is used to its best potential in solving the problem. *Step one* of the recommended process would be a clear definition of the problem. This is represented by message idea development and is done with the cooperation of both campaign managers and creative staff both within and outside the campaign organization.

Step two of the creative process in message format development should be a careful review of what is known about the types of format that might be used. The problem statement can indicate the general type of appeal that will be considered. Message ideas represent a distillation of the situation analysis in terms of product, consumer, trade, competition, and past experience. Given this distillation, the question is: What do we know about the kinds of formats that work best for this kind of message idea? There are two broad sources of this information. There is the experience of those people who have worked on other campaigns in this product category, and there are the substantive findings that have come from research on communication, both academic and commercial.

Step three of the approval and development process is the generation of specific alternatives in some rough to finished version. Like all the creative processes that have been discussed in this book, the message format development procedure discussed here can be seen as a continual narrowing down of the alternatives available. But no amount of past experience and research information is going to tell the copywriter or art director exactly what will be effective in any particular situation. Therefore it is necessary to develop specific alternative implementations that fit the situation at hand.

In *step four,* or the pretesting stage of the creative approval and development approach, the campaign team has a set of specific alternatives that are based on and fit a particular problem-message idea. The alternatives are usually in a form that would allow them to be pretested or at least examined in some helpful way by members of the campaign team.

The term "pretesting stage" may be misleading, since sometimes pretests are not done or they are done after a great deal of concentrated discussion and evaluation. Thus the pretesting stage might be called the "decision stage," since it is necessary to make some very hard decisions among the number of alternatives available.

Figure 11-1 depicts the four stages—problem formulation, review of available knowledge, development of specific alternatives, and pretesting-decision—of the creative approval and development procedure that is being suggested here. Notice that between the boxes depicting each of the stages there are feedback arrows. That is, there seems to be a flow of information and decisions both down the sequence and also up between each of the stages.

Note also that at the bottom of Figure 11-1 there is an additional box labeled "message distribution stages." These stages, which will be discussed in greater depth in Part VI, consist of computer simulation, field experimentation, and campaign monitoring, respectively. These three stages are implemented in a minority of situations but can be valuable in adding strength to the first four stages and moving decisions toward implementation.

Where does the procedure depicted in Figure 11-1 leave us in terms of the problems of approval and the critical interaction be-

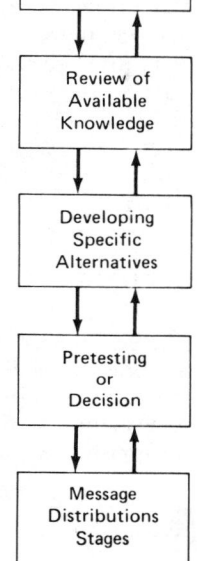

Figure 11-1. A procedure for developing message format

tween managers and creatives, client and copywriter, and so forth? At first glance, it might appear that this procedure is heavily biased toward the manager-client side. Certainly the type of last-minute turbulent interaction represented by the Della Femina example mentioned earlier does not seem to fit the procedure depicted in Figure 11-1. On the other hand, the procedure suggests just that, a procedure, rather than specific organizational and power relationships connected with each step. It would be possible for all of these stages to be carried out by one person—e.g., for mail-order advertising done by some mail-order houses. At the other extreme, every one of the stages would be done by different people or groups of people.

Neither of these alternatives—total control of the whole process by some single creative individual or a complete fragmenting of the process under control of management—is acceptable or optimal. Instead, it is necessary to have representatives of all four stages of the procedure involved from the beginning, under the control of the campaign brand manager.

In a real sense, then, the procedure recommended in Figure 11-1 is not necessarily an organizational one but is really a series of mental stages that individuals and organizations must go through in order to develop successful message format as part of a creative strategy. With this in mind, this procedure is used to organize the rest of Part V.

PROBLEM FORMULATION

The problem set for those people involved in developing message formats is well defined by the message idea statement, both theme and copy platform. As was indicated in Chapter 8, these statements should have five components:

☐ Market target
☐ Appeal or appeals
☐ Reference to competition
☐ Tone
☐ Rationale

These, along with the fact that the environment is a very noisy one and budgets are always tight, provide quite clear direction as to the nature of the job that has to be done.

But at the beginning of message format development there should be a careful delineation of exactly what the message idea implies in terms of possible difficulties that creatives might have in developing the format. These considerations will clearly direct the comprehensive review of past experience and research findings.

With regard to *target market,* the message format problem is different depending upon the socioeconomic, personality, psychographic, and brand-related attitudes of the key segments. If the segments are relatively knowledgeable about the product category, it may not be necessary to use attention-getting devices. Or it may be possible to use a particular type of humor or illustration that fits

that particular segment. For instance, in Chapter 5 there were illustrations of two advertisements that the Regis McKenna advertising agency prepared for a single client, Spectra-Physics, Inc. One of the ads for the Ion Laser Division of the company was aimed at a very sophisticated academic research lab target market. The illustration was quite futuristic and the copy quite sophisticated. The other Spectra-Physics ad shown in Chapter 5 was directed at the market segment that was much less sophisticated about lasers. Therefore the cartoon format used by Regis McKenna for this ad both captured attention and fit the needs of the segment. Considerations leading to this kind of outstanding format can come directly from clear discussions related to the target market aspect of the message idea statement.

When considering the *appeal* or *positioning* of the campaign, those people doing the message format should first examine the difficulty of communicating the position. The position simply indicating that the brand has more of a particular characteristic than other brands should be fairly simple to depict. But positions attempting to affect the goals and events considered, the composition rule consumers should use in making a choice or relating the brand in some way to competition, all require extra effort in terms of format. For instance, when Eastern Airlines was attempting to "sell" the whole idea of air travel, the format considerations were quite difficult. When the airline moved to a push strategy emphasizing schedules and the fact that it was the second-largest passenger airline in the free world, the format problems were much simpler.

The *competition* part of the format development problem is considered in a general sense in regard to the noisy and cluttered communication environment. More specifically, message format developers will have to examine carefully the format used by all major competitors. Printed advertisements should be pinned on a bulletin board for easy comparison. All broadcast advertising should be screened and played. Field staff should collect materials from competitive promotions. And publicity-public relations and selling efforts should be monitored as closely as possible.

Basically, the copywriter is attempting to understand the competitive message situation so as to try to move away from the sameness that seems to occur in each category. When all advertising looks alike in a product category, there is a tendency for consumers to credit it to the leading brand. The same sort of thing can be seen in insurance advertising where all advertisers probably wanted to get across the dual ideas of security and convenient handling of all insurance needs typified by Allstate's "You're in good hands with Allstate." Copywriters for agencies with competitive accounts were asked to develop a phrase or slogan similar in impact and intent to Allstate's.

In washing machine advertising, the long-running Maytag campaign attracted almost exact imitators.

For advanced 35-mm cameras, it seemed that celebrities like Bruce Jenner, Cheryl Tiegs, and John Newcombe were the rule. For microwave ovens, a simple picture of them was common.

When, as is often the case, there is a sameness in a product category's marketing-communication formats, creatives must investigate the possibility of either wildly different format approaches or approaches based on communication research knowledge.

The *tone* part of the message idea also has implications for the nature of the creatives' problem in developing message format. For instance, if the strength of argument to be used is so extreme that it might be in the latitude of rejection for the target segment, the creatives will have to look for ways that the argument can be presented so as to possibly soften the blow of such an extreme argument. If the competitive, refutational tone is to be used, then the creatives know that they have to find out how this rather convoluted type of approach can be presented efficiently and

with interest to the target segment. And, once again, emotional or fear appeals also have their own set of format questions—e.g., the nature of the presenter, whom the fear should be directed to, how the fear will be demonstrated, the use of colors and visuals, etc. These are some of the ways the tone part of the message idea should be considered by creatives developing the format of the message.

The last aspect of the message idea statement is that of *rationale*. It is an indication of how all the components of a message idea will work together to achieve both communication and total campaign objectives. These objectives often have little hope of achievement on the basis of the message idea alone. The format is usually quite critical in such situations. In the insurance example mentioned above, it is likely that for most companies, the bulk of the weight in achieving total campaign objectives of increased premiums would be placed on the selling efforts of the insurance agents themselves. People typically do not seek out and compare insurance companies, especially for life insurance. Therefore the function of advertising probably is to create some gross positive awareness that can be converted into comprehension and intention with publicity and promotional tools and finally into sales through the efforts of the insurance agent. The awareness goal for advertising would suggest a search on the part of creatives for techniques that might be used to promote greater awareness within well-defined budget limits. The comprehension and intention goals for promotion would stimulate a search for those promotions that would not only open the door for the agent but also convey something distinctive about the insurance company. The same kind of analysis would relate to publicity changes and sampling techniques for promotions that were intended to change attitudes related to a product that was reformulated or improved in some way. In these situations the problem is defined by rationale and objectives in such a way that creatives will look for particular kinds of alternatives when they comprehensively review their own experience and research information.

EXPERIENCE AND CREATIVE PHILOSOPHIES

How do creatives learn what works and does not work in particular message situations? They observe and examine what has succeeded and failed in similar situations in the past.

What do advertising agencies have to sell their clients and potential clients? Their main commodity is their creative philosophy, the sum total of their experience as to what works and does not work in advertising and marketing communication in particular situations.

The four creative philosophies reviewed in the following paragraphs seem, on the surface, to be quite different. Actually they espouse a series of common principles about message construction that work differently in the different situations for which each creative philosophy is appropriate. The agency heads and agencies reviewed here developed their philosophies because they were forced to face different situations and did so successfully. Some dealt with highly competitive drug marketing, others with selling luxury automobiles, and still others with situations in between. The fact that they were each able to deal with those situations successfully led to their dealing with more similar situations and receiving more reinforcement in terms of success. Thus each of the four men reviewed here—Rosser Reeves, Leo Burnett, David Ogilvy, and William Bernbach—were quite convinced and convincing that they each had *the* answer for constructing messages. If their statements are looked at as a guide to what seems to work in particular situations, they can provide an excellent overview of what experience has told us about effective message formats.

Rosser Reeves—The Hard Sell

No, sir, I'm not saying that charming, witty and warm copy won't sell.
I'm just saying
I've seen thousands of charming, witty campaigns that didn't sell.[4]

Rosser Reeves would rather be effective than charming. He would rather sell than please. He would rather be repetitive than ignored. He had a long and very successful career selling drugs, cigarettes, household products, and other items that cost very little and which people apparently have to be forced to think about. By being successful in selling these low-involvement products, such as Viceroy and Kool cigarettes, M&M candies, Anacin, and Colgate dental cream, Reeves has developed a set of what he calls "immutable principles of advertising," which he put forth in his book *Reality in Advertising*.

Some of Reeves's ideas were discussed in Chapter 8. His approach is essentially a hard-sell one. More than any of the creative strategists discussed in this chapter, he believes in the importance of finding the single differentiating characteristic of the product and then hammering away at this characteristic incessantly. He calls the distinguishing characteristic the USP, the unique selling proposition.

One gets the idea from reading Reeves that the USP is almost an entirely product-bound concept. In other words, it does not seem to matter much whether the USP is initially an important benefit to the consumer. That helps, of course, but the important thing is that the USP be "unique" and that it can be transmitted via a television demonstration. The Bates agency, of which Reeves was president before his first retirement, had an unusually high percentage of its billings placed in television. And as Chapter 7 pointed out, television is the best place to run campaigns for low-involvement communications.

Perhaps because Reeves very often worked with propietary drug products, he has a tendency to attempt to bring scientific evidence to bear in his commercials. This was certainly true in the Bates commercials for Anacin and later for Bufferin. Often, too, he discusses a special ingredient that his product has exclusively. Therefore the ads for Colgate talked about MFP fluoride. Commercials for Certs always mentioned "the magic drop of Retsyn." The initial ads for Viceroy filter cigarettes said that "only Viceroy gives you 20,000 filter traps in every filter tip."

Once Reeves and Bates discovered a USP and a good way of demonstrating it, they continued with it for a long time. Repetition was recommended both within the ad and of the ad itself. For instance, in one Fleischmann's margarine ad the USP of "corn oil margarine" was mentioned at least seven times!

Reeves felt that one of the greatest mistakes a client could make would be to change the advertising too early. He claimed to have an accurate research system that would spot when an ad was failing to create penetration (of the USP) and convert to usage pull (that proportion of those aware of the USP who bought the product). Once these figures fell below acceptable levels, Reeves would apparently feel that it was time to change the campaign. Certainly this was the case when Crest's ADA approval began to erode Colgate's leading share with the latter's old "Cleans your breath while it cleans your teeth" USP appeal. Bates quickly shifted to a fluoride appeal, saving a large chunk of the market and the client.

A key principle from Reeves's philosophy is that the message format should create interest in the product and make the product important, not the ad. He will use any technique that can forward that particular goal. This, of course, constitutes a dilemma in the modern communication environment with its tremendous amount of clutter and noise. If

we eschew the "borrowed interest" techniques abhorred by Reeves, then is it possible to make enough people aware of our advertising and communication messages in order to sell them on the product?

Reeves feels it is and sees great inefficiency in what he calls "distraction" techniques. These would be gimmicks such as putting a beautiful model into an ad to attract attention. Later in this chapter we will discuss distraction from another perspective; but Reeves's careful professionalism, which argues that everything about an advertisement or communication message should be aimed at getting across a clear point about the product, should be kept in mind.

The Reeves-Bates form of advertising has been attacked by others in the profession. For instance, in one judging in the mid-1960s, some of the Bates advertising was ranked with the worst category. Reeves, however, was fond of pointing out that the advertising that was judged worst was actually doing an excellent job in terms of producing sales. This brings up another question that must be considered by brand managers and creatives: "Is it possible for ads that are unpleasant, like some of the repetitive and intrusive work done by the Bates agency, to be successful in achieving communication and overall campaign goals?" The Reeves-Bates philosophy seems to suggest that the answer is yes as long as the product USP gets across.

Leo Burnett—Empathy for Middle America

We try to be . . . more straightforward without being flatfooted. We try to be warm without being mawkish.

I believe today that visibility, sheer visibility, is more important than it has been, speaking of printed advertising—and that applies to television, of course, too. Sheer visibility is important with today's rising advertising costs; if you don't get noticed, you don't have anything. You just have to be noticed, but the art is getting noticed naturally without screaming or without tricks.[5]

Burnett, like Reeves, anchored his creative philosophy in the main idea behind the message. But Burnett was not as mechanistic as Reeves. Instead of the USP, Burnett talked about the "inherent drama" in products. It seems that inherent drama is really a combination of the message idea and the format. In explaining inherent drama, Burnett suggested a particular way to look at products in format terms:

> Of course we, over and over again, stress this so-called inherent drama of things because there is usually something there, almost always something there, if you can find the thing about that product that keeps it in the market place. There must be something about it that made the manufacturer make it in the first place. Something about it that makes people continue to buy it . . . capturing that, and then taking that thing—whatever it is—and making the thing itself arresting rather than through relying on tricks to do it.[6]

The best examples of Burnett's application of the inherent drama idea come in the food product categories. Some of his classic campaigns were his original ads for Green Giant peas (including the headline "Harvested in the moonlight," which Burnett pointed out had so much more inherent drama than the typical line "Packed fresh"), the idea of showing a big multiple-layered Pillsbury cake on a pedestal with a slice cut out of it, or the idea of photographing raw, red meat on a red background for the American Meat Institute.

But Burnett had more than just food accounts. And we have already seen how Reeves handled Fleischmann's margarine. Burnett's work was previously mentioned in this book in terms of the Maytag washing machine "real people" testimonials and the Allstate insurance "You are in good hands with Allstate" ad, which showed a young family at play (see Chapter 10). The agency has also done the United Airlines "Friendly skies of your land" campaign and household products for Procter and Gamble. In fact, even in the Reeves-Bates area of cigarettes, Burnett takes a slightly different tack with the Marlboro Country campaign and Virginia Slims "You've come a long way, baby" effort.

What differentiates the Burnett advertising most clearly from the Bates advertising is the attempt to empathize with common folk. Much of the Burnett food advertising does have this corny sort of Middle America touch to it. The common touch was also seen in Burnett's country music singing for "Me and my RC" advertising, Kentucky Fried Chicken commercials, and scenes of families waiting for the ketchup to plop in Heinz commercials.

As the Burnett inherent drama and common-touch philosophy moved from print to television, it was very often implemented in terms of continuing characters and jingles in the advertising. This agency was the creator of Morris the Cat (for 9-Lives cat food), the Jolly Green Giant and the little sprout, the Marlboro man, Charlie the Tuna, the Pillsbury Dough Boy, the lonely Maytag repair man, and Tony the Tiger. In the next chapter we will discuss the research evidence bearing on the issues of source credibility and the use of various presenters. It is clear that the Burnett agency used many of these characters, both animated and live, to great effect. It is possible that these characters, instead of distracting from the product (as Reeves would allege they do), actually pull people into advertising in a natural way.

Most recently a president of the Leo Burnett agency, when asked to comment on the agency's philosophy of advertising, said that he called it the "non-school school of advertising."[7] The tendencies mentioned above that were instituted by Leo Burnett are still present in all Burnett advertising. But it is clear that, like any campaign manager attempting to find the appropriate format for a particular situation, Burnett is bending its approach to fit the problem.

David Ogilvy—The Image and Science

> Never do anything which violates the image.
>
> Advertising should be *charming*. People don't buy from salesmen who are bad mannered.
>
> Make your advertising editorially alert—and *contemporary*. The consumer is apt to be younger than you are.
>
> Ogilvy and Mather has created over $1,720,000,000 of advertising, and spent $5,700,000 tracking the result. Here, with all the dogmatism of brevity, are 32 of the things we have learned.[8]

David Ogilvy came to America from England and got into advertising. He brought with him all the sophistication and status overtones of that country. This eventually led to his concept of the brand image, that everything that is said and shown and indicated in the format of any communication message is part of the long-term investment in the image of the brand. This was in fact a combination of the message idea and the message format, the content and form of the advertisement. Part of the idea was that people may buy a product for the very reason that it has a particular image.

But Ogilvy has more than the status-laden concept of the brand image that is probably based in his British roots. When he first came to the United States, he worked as a researcher for the Gallup & Robinson Company. This started him on a quest for "principles" of good advertising. One of his early influences was Rosser Reeves himself, who transmitted to Ogilvy some of the rules he was learning in working with disciples of the great copywriter Claude Hopkins, who wrote the book *Scientific Advertising*. So while Ogilvy very often talks about a more sophisticated advertising than either Reeves or Burnett, he also has a tendency to express his philosophy in an almost scientific way in terms of lists of approaches that should be used.

While Reeves developed his philosophy out of early successes in the hard-sell low-involvement drug category and Burnett hit stride with more-involving food advertising, Ogilvy honed his style on high-priced, high-status products. One of his most famous advertisements was one for Rolls-Royce which had the headline, "At 60 miles an hour the loudest noise in this new Rolls-Royce comes from the electric clock." Not only did the ad show Ogilvy's concept of image quite clearly, but it also demonstrated a series of technical points which he believes can make the format of an ad successful.

The brand image aspects of the Rolls-Royce ad were quite clear. This is the most prestigious of all luxury cars, and it was shown in a setting and with people that enhance its prestige. In addition, all the wording in the ad was quite straightforward and at the same time low key. As would benefit as serious a product as the Rolls-Royce, there are long headlines and long body copy, because such a serious purchase should not be passed off in a few quick lines. All of this, as Ogilvy has said many times, contributes to the overall image of a brand, in this case a prestige one.

But the Rolls-Royce ad also indicated a number of technical points which are common to most of Ogilvy's print advertising. For instance, in terms of headlines, Ogilvy has pointed out that five times as many people read the headline as read the body copy. Therefore he suggests that the benefit must be in the headline, that the headlines must have news in them, that long headlines sell more merchandise than short ones. In addition, it is usually true that Ogilvy ads get extra push from the headline by including subheads that repeat and amplify the message of the original headline. Another of Ogilvy's principles, taken from readership research, is that captions under pictures are usually read by twice as many people as the body copy.

Ogilvy's philosophy is based much more on success in print advertising than is either Reeves's or Burnett's. Most of the prestige brands that were sold early in the history of his agency had to be sold through print because of limited budgets and very specific target markets. His successes in print very often involved a continuing character. This was seen in Ogilvy ads for Schweppes and Hathaway.

When Ogilvy's agency moved beyond the prestige products for which the Learning hierarchy is most applicable, to the more low-involvement products that are advertised on television such as Shell gasoline and Dove soap, there was an application of the basic Ogilvy idea, but there was also a movement toward a more hard-sell approach appropriate to television and that type of product.

William Bernbach—Honesty with a Twist

So the most important thing as far as I am concerned is to be fresh, to be original—to be able to compete with all the shocking news events in the world today, with all the violence. Because you can have all the right things in an ad, and if nobody is made to stop and listen to you, you have wasted it. When people first saw our advertising they said it's fine, but will it work?[9]

The Doyle Dane Bernbach advertising agency started what is generally thought of as a revolution in the message format in advertising and generally in marketing communication. Whereas the other creative philosophies reviewed here were based on highly competitive low-involvement products, somewhat involving food products or prestige, Learning hierarchy-type products, the Bernbach initial success and style are based on work with retailers, durable goods, and services that were definitely second rank in the market and had some problems connected with them as far as the consumer was concerned. The essence of the Bernbach–DDB style is to take such a problem and second rank in the market and turn it into an advantage with total honesty and a twist that makes a disadvantage into an advantage.

This essentially refutational approach is implemented with very clean and direct ads and commercials, a distinctive format, and, often, a touch of humor.

Probably the first campaign to have the Bernbach touch was for Ohrbach's, a women's apparel chain. This retailer's problem was that it had an image as a low-priced, often cheap dress shop with corresponding decor and selection. Bernbach directly attacked this objection by pointing out that Ohrbach's had outstanding fashions at reasonable prices.

The same sort of approach was carried over to Volkswagen, which was the advertising campaign reputed to have started the revolution in message format development. As Jerry Della Femina said, "In the beginning there was Volkswagen." The technique used for that campaign was very much like the one used for Ohrbach's. Volkswagen had several problems that all consumers knew about. It was too small. Its engine was in the back. It was a foreign car. It was seen as ugly. It had insufficient service facilities. Yet Bernbach and DDB were actually able to take these objections and turn them into positive benefits for the product with a series of clear, direct, humorous, and honest advertisements.

Bernbach is known as the one creative great who emphasizes form over content. But in discussing the evolution of the VW campaign, Bernbach pointed out that his agency group worked very hard visiting the factory in Germany and talking to engineers, production people, executives, workers on the assembly line. They saw everything about the production of the car, from molten metal to countless inspections. They eventually felt that the proposition was that VW was an honest car. But then all the work on format transformed that proposition into the continuing series of trail-blazing VW "Bug" advertisements and on to more recent ads for the VW Rabbit and other models.

The same kind of movement from problem or deficiency to clever implementation capitalizing on that deficiency was done for Avis ("We're number two, we try harder"), Levy's rye bread ("You don't have to be Jewish to love Levy's," with a picture showing people of various ethnic backgrounds enjoying Levy's), and the Jack-in-the-Box fast-food chain ("Watch out, McDonald's" and actually exploding the Jack-in-the-Box itself).

In television the Bernbach approach has been characterized by dramatic visuals and humor. It might be said that Bernbach's advertising is most diametrically opposed to the kind of television work that Reeves-Bates espouse, while at the same time often getting a key selling point across.

The Bernbach approach has had many imitators. Evidently it captured a spirit that was effective and rewarding.

Comparison of the Four Philosophies

What can be learned for message format development from the experience and creative-style philosophy statements reviewed above? For one thing, there is definitely no one best creative style. That would be a logical impossibility, given the communication environment. For if everyone were using the same creative style, a great deal of sameness would occur, and it would be necessary to move to a variety of other message formats.

Instead it seems that the appropriate message format depends on the particular situation. One guide to selecting a format seems to relate to the type of hierarchy. Reeves worked in a low-involvement, highly competitive, low-differentiation, mature stage of the life-cycle area. People were not ordinarily involved with the products he advertised. His reaction was to use television heavily, with very clear benefits and hard-sell demonstrations.

Burnett, on the other hand, seemed to favor a Learning hierarchy, since his early successes formed his philosophy and style. At least he was dealing with more pleasant products than was Reeves initially. Therefore the format Burnett favored was a more folksy, warm style, which tried to get across the inherent drama (note the naturally involving aspects) of the product in the language of the consumer.

Ogilvy initially dealt with true Learning hierarchy situations, prestige products of high cost which required both an image approach and a very careful copy follow-up to help people rationalize their decision. When he got into relatively lower priced products, such as drink mixers (Schweppes) and shirts (Hathaway), the establishment of the continuing character was important to remind people of the image of the brand for repeat purchases. When Ogilvy moved to television and more-low-involvement products, he tended to rely even further on his "scientific" lists of rules for good advertising. At that point his approach comes very close to that of Reeves-Bates.

When we consider Bernbach, it is impossible to analyze the appropriate situation for his style simply on the basis of a hierarchy analysis. Bernbach's style seems best suited to a noisy communication environment in today's media. In the early DDB successes, there was a clear emphasis on clients who had a problem and were definitely not leaders in their category. Budgets were usually small. Perhaps that is why the Bernbach style evolved into one that emphasized execution in order to make the advertising message stand out from all the noise.

Limits of the Creative Philosophies

Perhaps the most distinct impression that one gets from looking at statements on creative style is that, like the message idea, the appropriate message format is heavily dependent on the situation. There clearly are principles of creative execution. But they must be applied with care depending on the situation.

When one hears or reads the statements made by the creative leaders of the advertising industry, there is often the feeling of having only part of the story. Even the advertising greats have almost as many failures as they have outstanding successes. In fact, it may be that their relatively low failure rate of something under 50 percent is the reason why they are acclaimed. Is it possible that a more definitive answer might be found on the basis of communication research?

Reeves, for instance, argues against distraction techniques. Is there any evidence that indicates when distraction or borrowed interest or mood can be a facilitating factor in message format?

Both Bernbach and Burnett used humor, in slightly different ways, to seemingly great effect. Reeves, however, implies that humor is the kiss of death. Who is right? Under what conditions and in what way might humor work? How can a variety of other borrowed interest techniques such as sex and striking illustrations work?

Reeves's detractors claim that the problem with his advertising is that it is unpleasant. Yet it works. Under what conditions is this true? And what about repetition? The importance of testimonials? The refutational approach as practiced by Bernbach? The use of testimonials and demonstrations? Order effects and long-versus-short copy? The use of advertising techniques for other elements of the communication mix? Photographs versus artwork? Color versus black and white?

A comprehensive review of past experience can indicate which of these questions is critical for any given situation. And then a look at research evidence can prepare the way for the development of specific alternatives in message format. An overview of relevant research guidelines is the topic of the next chapter.

ISSUES AND PROJECTS FOR DISCUSSION

1. How do message format decisions differ from message idea ones?

2. If you had to choose between the two extremes, creative power or client power, which one would you choose? Why?

3. In what ways would the procedure for developing message format outlines in this chapter be better than the alternative you chose in Question 2? In what ways does it have disadvantages?

4. The following are some accounts at each of the agencies whose philosophies were discussed in this chapter. To what extent do you believe the advertising done by each agency reflects its philosophy? To what extent do you think the philosophy has been affected by the needs of the communication situation as opposed to the agency philosophy?

Bates: Breck, Brown & Williamson tobacco, Carter Products, Colgate toothpaste, Coors beer, Electrolux, Wonder Bread, M&Ms, Kal Kan pet foods, Maybelline eye prod-

ucts, Prudential insurance, Wyler drinks, U.S. Navy recruiting.

Burnett: Allstate insurance, Oldsmobile automobiles, Green Giant canned and frozen vegetables, Heinz ketchup and baby food, Kellogg cereals, Taster's Choice coffee, Marlboro cigarettes, Pillsbury, Cheer laundrey detergent, Gleem toothpaste, 7-Up, Star-Kist tuna, 9-Lives cat food, United Airlines, Kleenex.

Doyle Dane Bernbach: American Airlines, American Tourister luggage, Avis, Tickle deodorant, Clairol Nice 'n Easy, Mr. Goodbar, IBM office products, Mobil oil, Columbian coffee, Ore-Ida frozen potatoes, Polaroid cameras, Gain laundry detergent, Schaeffer pens, Stroh beer, VW and Porsche automobiles.

Ogilvy & Mather: American Express, Avon, British Tourist Authority, Swanson frozen dinners, Clairol Condition*, Maxwell House and Maxim coffees, Shake 'n Bake, Gaines Meal, Sugar Crisp cereal, Ex-Lax, Hershey chocolate, KLM Royal Dutch Airlines, Kotex, Dove soap, Aim toothpaste, Contact, Real cigarettes, Schaefer beer.

5. For the following clients, select one of the four agencies to handle the account and explain your choice. Assume that there would be no account conflicts and that all other things would be equal except the agency creative philosophy-experience. Also assume that the situation, budget, goals, and general message idea would be as you know them to be for the brand at about the time you are doing this assignment.

Litton microwave ovens	AT&T Long Distance telephoning
U.S. Post Office	Vantage cigarettes
Aqua-fresh toothpaste	Finish dishwashing detergent
BMW automobiles	Amtrak
India Tourist Board	Gant shirts

6. To what extent were your choices in Question 5 affected by product life cycle, segmentation, budget mix, or hierarchy situation?

7. Which agency philosophy is best for each of the three hierarchy situations? Explain.

8. Why would you want to consider more than just the philosophies and guidelines from experience in developing and evaluating message format? Read the following two quotations before giving your answer.

ON HUMOR:

Avoid it. What's funny to one person isn't to millions of others. Copy should sell, not just entertain. Remember there's not one funny line in the two most influential books ever written: the Bible and the Sears catalog. (John Caples, "Caples on Copy," *Wall Street Journal* ad, *Advertising Age,* October 9, 1978, p. 17.)

"Always in the past I've persecuted copywriters who wrote funny commercials," he told the audience, "I used to have the awful ordeal of going to conventions and seeing the Y&R reel, all as funny as hell. Made the audience laugh, made the clients want to go to Y&R. And I wouldn't let our people do it. I said you may not be whores.

"But I always envied Y&R," he continued. "Thank God, now we can be funny, too. Our new research reveals that humor can be very effective if the humor is concentrated on the product." (David Ogilvy, "David Says O&M Ads Can Be Laughing Matter," *Advertising Age,* November 12, 1979, p. 110.)

Notes

1. References for the quotations at the beginning of this chapter:
Carolyn Pfaff, "Bernbach Comments Ruffle Researchers," *Advertising Age,* April 13, 1981, p. 98.
Mary Wells Lawrence in Don Grant, "Secret of Wells, Rich Miracle? It's 'Nagging,'" *Advertising Age,* July 1, 1968, pp. 3ff.
Ogilvy and Mather, "How to Create Advertising That Sells," booklet, p. 2.
John O'Toole, "Let's Put More Advertiser into Advertising," (New York: American Association of Advertising Agencies, 1970), p. 2.
Stephen Baker, "Demise of Pomposity in Ads," *Advertising Age,* September 12, 1966, p. 124.
Fairfax M. Cone, "Blue Streak," memo #36 (Chicago: Foote, Cone & Belding, September 19, 1961), p. 1.
Jo Foxworth, "Jo Foxworth Decries Idiot Savants in Advertising," *Advertising Age,* August 15, 1966, p. 58.
Leo Burnett in Draper Daniels, "Leo Burnett: The Unlikely Giant," *Advertising Age,* June 21, 1971, p. 74.
John Caples, "Caples on Copy," *Wall Street Journal* ad, *Advertising Age,* October 9, 1978, p. 17.
Shirley Polykoff, "Remembrances of Things Past," *Advertising Age,* November 3, 1975, pp. 51–52.
Stanley E. Cohen, "Washington Beat," *Advertising Age,* May 26, 1975, p. 57.
2. Jerry Della Femina with Charles Sopkin,

From Those Wonderful Folks Who Brought You Pearl Harbor: Front Line Dispatches from the Advertising War (New York: Simon & Schuster, 1970), pp. 168–73.

3. Irwin Gross, "The Creative Aspects of Advertising," *Sloan Management Review,* Fall 1972, pp. 83–109.

4. Denis Higgens, *The Art of Writing Advertising* (Chicago: Crain Books, 1965), p. 94.

5. Ibid., p. 44.

6. Ibid.

7. L. Edwards, "Burnett Is Agency of Year; Zeroes in on Single Concept," *Advertising Age,* February 23, 1976, front cover ff.

8. Ogilvy and Mather, "How to Create Advertising That Sells."

9. Don Grant, "DDB Bosses Distribute Advice as Agency Marks Its 20th Birthday," *Advertising Age,* June 9, 1969, pp. 52 and 54.

Message Format II: Relevant Research Guidelines

As the marketing services manager of a multiproduct company, you are reviewing the overall work of several advertising agencies to determine whether and to where an account shift should be made. You must evaluate, and the people at each of the agencies must support with solid research evidence, the following approaches.

△ For its wine clients, one agency used a humorous interaction between two comedy stars; another used a famous actor-director who carefully intoned: "We will sell no wine before its time"; and a third used a situation in a liquor store and an "irritating" jingle.

△ For public service accounts, one agency showed emaciated children in foreign countries in an appeal for money; another used baseball star Reggie Jackson to elicit contributions to combat "Lou Gehrig's" ALS disease; and a third answered objections to contributing by stating the positive benefits donors received psychologically.

△ For detergent clients, one agency used a demonstration in which a dirty garment was ripped in half; another used a situation in a launderette; and a third used a series of implied recommendations from washing machine manufacturers.

△ For fast-food chains, one agency developed a campaign that attacked the major competitor by name; another featured a character for children; and a third hammered home the variety available at stores with a jingle.

△ For electronics manufacturing clients, one agency borrowed a consumer advertising slogan to emphasize the breadth of the line; another showed nearly complete competitive specifications which were mildly favorable to their line; and a third featured well-known applications of their components.

△ For airfreight forwarders, one agency emhasized the organization's size and dramatic pictures of its planes taking off; another showed humorous scenes of, for instance, a man who used the wrong forwarder hiding under his desk while his boss shouted his name angrily, and a third used a ten-second commercial that simply said (in a curfewlike tone), "It's eleven o'clock. Do you know where your package is?"—followed by the name of the company.

△ For financial institutions, one agency compared its bank client with savings and loan companies in a TV ad by having a cab driver tell his passenger on his way to such a company that the slightly greater interest wasn't worth the inconvenience of taking a cab (the driver passed many branch offices of the bank); another illustrated that its savings and loan client was number one by using commercials featuring such individuals as Fred Astaire and Helen Hayes, who were number one in their field; and a third took a historical perspective by emphasizing the tradition of a bank.

Which of the three approaches is best for each of the preceding situations? Is humor, a famous actor, or repetitive hard sell best for selling wine? Is fear, an endorsement, or objection answering to be preferred for eliciting contributions?

At this point in the development of format—after analysis of the problem situation and review of creative style suggestions—managers and creatives have only general and conflicting answers to such questions. Now it is necessary to consider the vast literature or communication research for further guidance. Managers have to be able to differentiate between various approaches to a particular problem, but they often are not knowledgeable in terms of what directions are provided by research.

The amount of research literature on communication format effects is tremendous. One review by McGuire listed over thirty communication research categories, each represented by numerous studies.[1] And much of this does not really apply to particular marketing-communication problems like the ones listed on the first page of this chapter.

Rather than try to review this literature category by category, this chapter deals simply with five key questions that are part of nearly every one of the managerial evaluations on the first page and that have been highlighted by the material of the preceding two chapters. Only a small proportion of the research is ever relevant in any given situation. In addition, the comprehensive review of creative styles further winnows down the list of relevant areas to a workable few. Further, there are strict limits to the conclusions that might be drawn from the research available. In other words, only a few areas have produced relatively solid findings that might be applied to the development of message format. In this chapter, the following five areas are discussed:

☐ *The effects of being warm, charming and witty.* This is the question brought up by the differences between Reeves and Bernbach. Is it possible for an ad to have these characteristics and sell? Or, on the other hand, can an irritating ad work? This section examines the effect of pleasantness and unpleasantness, of mood, of distraction, and of "borrowed interest" techniques such as humor and sex.

☐ *Testimonials and presenters.* Both Ogilvy and Caples advocate the use of testimonials to increase the effect of advertising. The Burnett agency uses testimonials freely to add warmth and reality to its advertising, such as in the Maytag campaign. But, as the McGuire list of available communication research indicates, the source of the message has many characteristics, including expertise, trustworthiness, similarity, familiarity, liking, and various kinds of power. Ogilvy's concept of the brand image and O'Toole's makers mark concept both imply that every advertisement and communication message contributes to that complex symbol which is the marketing company as a source. Research provides many guidelines for how to handle the source in communication.

☐ *The honest-twist approach.* The most recent "school" of creativity in advertising stems from the Bernbach touch on Ohrbach's, VW,

Avis, and extends to the work of Della Femina and Mary Wells Lawrence. This message format approach was characterized above as being honest about problems of a follower in the marketplace and turning them into advantages with clear, direct, and often startling message format. Research on how to implement the refutational approach, the use of order effects, and explicit versus subtle conclusions and recommendations is examined to determine when and how this message format alternative should be used.

☐ *Repetition and the hard sell.* Some creatives advocate pounding a message across with repetition, big illustrations, and overstatements. There is research evidence that relates to the use of this sort of approach. Some of it was reviewed in Chapters 7 and 8. But repetition and size or strength of statements are examined more thoroughly in this chapter in terms of research evidence.

☐ *Implementing fear.* Not one of the creative philosophies clearly advocated the use of a negative emotional appeal of fear. But it is possible to apply a variety of research findings on message format to the effective implementation of a fear appeals message strategy.

Both the brand manager and the creative dealing with any particular marketing communication problem should be looking for situationally related predictions on the basis of research. That is, since the creative philosophies indicated that each of these five general types of approaches is an important consideration, research should tell us under what conditions and how each of them will work. Thus in some situations a warm, charming, and witty format may be effective, and in others a more direct but unpleasant format may be effective. Research evidence should be examined in order to determine such interaction predictions. Then creatives can move the development one step further by coming up with alternative implementations of each approach. Chapters 13 and 14 explore how research suggestions can be carried out by creatives working on the various elements of the communication mix.

THE EFFECTS OF BEING WARM, CHARMING, AND WITTY

In order to sell, it is often necessary to be unpleasant and pushy. But in advertising and other parts of the communication mix, there is the opportunity to achieve various goals with a soft-sell, pleasant approach. Nowhere, perhaps, is this illustrated better than in radio advertising, which runs the gamut from hard-sell automobile dealers and stereo shop sales pitches to humorous and engaging approaches such as the following example from Blue Nun wines. This series was developed by the Della Femina, Travisano and Partners agency and featured the comedy team of Stiller and Meara.

STILLER: Excuse me, the cruise director assigned me this table for dinner.

MEARA: Say, weren't you the fellow at the costume ball last night dressed as the giant tuna? With the scales, the gills, and the fins?

S: Yea—that was me.

M: I recognized you right away.

S: Were you there?

M: I was dressed as a mermaid so I had to spend most of the night sitting down. Did you ever try dancing with both legs wrapped in aluminum foil?

S: No, I can't say I have. Did you order dinner yet?

M: I'm having the fillet of sole.

S: Humm. The filet mignon looks good. Would you like to share a bottle of wine?

M: Terrific.

S: I noticed a little Blue Nun at the Captain's table.

M: Poor thing. Maybe she's seasick.

S: No, Blue Nun is a wine. A delicious white wine.

M: Oh, we can't have a white wine if you're having meat and I'm having fish.

S: Sure we can. Blue Nun is a white wine that is correct with any dish. Your fillet of sole. My filet mignon.

M: Oh, it's so nice to meet a man who knows the finer things. You must be a gourmet?

S: No, as a matter of fact, I'm an accountant. Small firm in the city. Do a lot of tax work ... (fadeout).

VO (Voice Over):   Blue Nun. The delicious white wine that's correct with any dish. Another Sichel wine imported by Schieflin & Co., New York.[2]

This campaign featuring Stiller and Meara reportedly was very successful and contributed to the single wine's taking a large proportion of that market. On the other hand, the comedy team of Bob and Ray did a widely acclaimed series of advertisements for Piel's beer in New York a number of years ago. The commercials were so entertaining that newspapers listed when they were going to be shown so that consumers could see them. The beer, however, consistently lost market share. Why this difference? And how is it that the unpleasant, pounding, hard-sell approach with little visual, verbal, or print charm often seems to work so well?

Do Irritating Commercials Work?

There appear to be two kinds of findings and ideas about how pleasant as opposed to unpleasant messages work. One type of finding is that the more pleasant the message, the more effective it will be in terms of generating attitude change, intention, and general acceptance of recommendations. Another type of finding would indicate that the message must be stimulating in order to be effective. It can be either very pleasant or very unpleasant, but as long as it is not in the mediocre middle it will have an effect.

For instance, in a very old study involving the army, Schwerin (who later developed a heavily used television commercial testing technique) discovered that the two extremes of the pleasant-unpleasant continuum were most effective in inducing draftees to change their shoes.

One explanation for the differential effects of pleasant versus unpleasant messages may have to do with the desired response. Unpleasant messages seem to be able to cut through the noise in the communication environment and have some effect on awareness and possibly comprehension. In a Low-Involvement hierarchy situation, the unpleasant message can thus increase the probability that the product will be chosen just on the basis of an increase in awareness. For instance, in a test of anti-drug-abuse communications, two commercials called "Big Brother" and "Walkout" produced very different effects in terms of liking, and the disliked commercial seemed to be the more convincing overall.[3] These effects existed both in a laboratory experiment and in a field experiment during actual campaign exposure. The disliked "Walkout" commercial seemed to cut through the noise in the communication environment and made some cognitive impression on the target "parents" audience.

The effectiveness of the unpleasant advertisement in this case is possibly due to a Low-Involvement hierarchy situation similar to that in which Reeves and the Bates agency seem to work. An unpleasant ad may succeed because it can be effective in standing out and affecting gross awareness.

One phenomenon that has been discovered repeatedly in communication research may explain how this gross awareness can be converted to behavior at a later date. This phenomenon is known as the *sleeper effect*.[4] It was first discovered in studies of source credibility. In immediate measurement after the presentation of messages by a low-credibility and a high-credibility source, the high-credibility source was always more effective in producing acceptance of communication rec-

BIG BROTHER

Audio

You're 17—old enough to know about things like speed, grass, acid and smack. We don't intend to give you any advice. You wouldn't listen. But the trouble is neither will your kid brother. He doesn't know one-half of the things you know about drugs, like how they affect your body.

He's really a set up for the guy selling the stuff. We can't warn your kid brother but maybe you can.

Visual

Rear shot of a teenage boy—blond, walking under trees (dressed neatly in jeans).

—Camera points to little brother walking beside him (dressed like former)

—Closeup of both faces

—They walk away from camera across the street (the area resembles suburban springtime)

WALKOUT*

Audio

(Son) "Hey Dad what's happening?"

(Dad) "I'll show you what's happening, get in that room. Now your mother found that in your room, would you please explain it?"

(Son) "It's nothing."

(Mom) "What's it called Johnny?"

(Son) "Dope, grass, whatever you want to call it."

(Mom) "Then you must be known as Junkie?"

(Son) "No Dad, I'm sorry but it's just what I like to do. Look, you drink. I see you stumbling from the kitchen."

(Mom) "My son, my marvelous son is a junkie. We're just looking for respect in this town. Why are you tearing us down?"

(Son) "I'm not tearing you down. I'm the only one that I'll hurt."

(Dad) "What's the next step?"

(Son) "You people are fools, you don't know what you're talking about."

(Announcer) "Before you talk with your child you ought to read this free booklet about drug abuse. It's written by people who know what they're talking about. Write Drug Abuse Information, Box 1080, Washington, D.C. Do it before it's too late."

(Door slams as boy walks out)

Visual

—closeup of disturbed mother

—enraged father, talking with son in living room—three different still shots of all three disturbed faces

*Edited from 60-second to 30-second version

Figure 12-1. Two Anti-drug Abuse Commercials

ommendations. But when there was a delay of some time, the two communications seemed to be equal in their effect on acceptance of message recommendations: a sleeper effect for the low credibility message.

Although there have recently been other interpretations, it seems that the low-credible source was forgotten and only the message was retained over time. Extending this finding to unpleasant messages: It may be that a message that is unpleasant because it is shocking, direct, pushy, and so forth, may actually cut through the noise of the communication environment to develop awareness about the product and brand more efficiently than would a bland but pleasant message. This awareness may later be converted to purchasing behavior when unpleasant aspects are forgotten in a Low-Involvement situation.

Of course, the comparison here is between a strong unpleasant message and a bland pleasant one. It may be that it is more difficult to develop a strong pleasant message, but the fact remains that when messages of equal strength can be compared, pleasant messages seem to outdistance the unpleasant ones.

Some explanation for those situations in which the unpleasant type of message seems to work might be due to the effect of *effort*. For instance, in several studies where people are forced to comply with positions they really do not believe in or to do things they really do not like to do (e.g., eating grasshoppers), they seem to change their attitude more when they are forced by unpleasant rather than pleasant sources of messages. The rationale here fits the Dissonance-Attribution situation. That is, if a person made the effort to read or comply with an unpleasant message or source, then the only thing that person could attribute his or her behavior to would be that one's attitudes really were in accord with the action taken. Thus, in such a situation, if the audience can be induced to make some effort even though the message or source is unpleasant, it may actually be more effective than under pleasant conditions.[5]

The study of *mood* offers somewhat contradictory results to those suggested by effort. There are ample results indicating that when people are put in a pleasant mood during a communication, they are more likely to accept its recommendations. Perhaps this is an instance of a Learning hierarchy situation, whereas the sleeper effect phenomenon related to Low Involvement and the effort one to Dissonance-Attribution. Some researchers studying the effect of mood found that there was a greater effect of the communications when people were eating peanuts and drinking Pepsi than when this was not true during the communication exposure. Obviously the media environment may have a much greater effect in setting mood than the content of the communication itself. It may be that the relaxed and entertaining atmosphere of television, for instance, may produce such a positive mood that irritating and unpleasant commercials of the Reeves-Bates variety may be effective. The creative strategist must balance all aspects of the communication situation in order to produce effect.

What about Distraction?

Distraction is another aspect of pleasant commercials that may increase their effectiveness. In one of the early studies in this area, some audience members were asked to concentrate on the presenter while others were asked to concentrate on the message that was attacking the audience position. Those people who concentrated on the speaker were more likely to move toward the speaker's position than those who concentrated on the message.[6] This suggests that if message format developers can institute some aspect of the message that distracts from the actual arguments, it may be more effective.

Why would distraction work in this way? Some explanation was provided in connection with another study in which one group of college fraternity members saw an antifraternity movie showing the speaker making statements and another group of fraternity members heard the speech but saw a distracting cartoon presentation (from the film *Day of the Painter*). The second distraction condition produced more agreement with the antifraternity position. This situation provides an exemplar of the kind of condition in which distraction may work to improve the effectiveness of the message.

Distraction is posited to work by preventing involved and antagonistic audience members from making counterarguments against the position advocated by the message. In other words, the hypothesis is that the distracting *Day of the Painter* film helped to lower the fraternity members' perceptual defenses. Before they knew it, while they were watching the pleasant visuals, they heard and processed a great deal of information that led to a change in their attitudes. Without the distraction, they may have mentally argued against or shut off their minds to the commercial.

Of course the conditions under which such distraction would work are fairly clearcut. Essentially this has to be a learning situation in which people are involved and concerned about the issues at hand. In addition, they should initially be antagonistic to the message. Otherwise they would not be mentally developing counterarguments and there would not be any need to distract them from the fact that the message wants them to take a new position. Further, the message cannot have so much distraction that learning is impaired. In some later studies of the distraction effect, the distracting message was less effective. This seemed to be due to the distraction's being too strong, thereby eliminating any effect of the message at all.

Considered on the basis of this research it is easy to see why Reeves, who eschews the "warm, charming, and witty," and Bernbach and Burnett, who embrace it, are all correct in their particular situations for advertising. Reeves deals with a Low-Involvement situation in which it is important to get the message across or all is lost. Therefore any dis-

traction added in an attempt to make the message pleasant or attract attention by irrelevant means may endanger this goal. Bernbach and the others very often tend to deal with learning situations in which the consumer audience is initially antagonistic to the position advocated. For instance, the Blue Nun commercial can be seen as using the distraction of humor to get across the unusual idea of a white wine that can be served with everything.

Using Humor

This brings us to the use of *humor*. To what extent and under what conditions can being witty improve the effectiveness of a commercial? The available evidence seems to indicate that when humor can be used as a principal distractor to get across key points to otherwise antagonistic audiences, it can be effective. When the situation is such that it is difficult to get any information across at all, humor may be too great a distraction and may completely impair learning.

One study of forty TV commercial content and execution factors provides a valuable overview of the characteristics associated with high-performance and low-performance commercials. These guidelines are shown in Table 12-1.

Of course one of the key questions is, What is humor in the first place? Something that is funny to one audience may be silly or irrelevant to another. For instance, one study by Lynch and Hartman used factor analysis to classify humor into eight types.[7] These classifications—general knowledge, sophistication, sensitivity, simplicity, visualization, cuteness, staging, and abstraction—are not too important in themselves because the researchers did the study with a very small sample using only print advertisements. What is important, however, is that different types of humor would be appropriate for different audiences. If an audience were to appreciate humor that fit on the "sophistication" dimen-

Table 12-1. Guidelines for Creating Effective Humorous Commercials

Characteristics Associated with	
High Performance	Low Performance
Early brand product category identification	Late brand product category identification
Begin with the **key idea**	"Set the stage" or employ an indirect lead-in
Subtle/light humor—Designed to amuse rather than overwhelm	Bizarre/overdone humor
Relevant humor, well integrated with brand/key idea	**Irrelevant**—Humor for its own sake
Contain a relevant characterization	Contain either an irrelevant characterization or none at all
Satirize or parody familiar/universal subjects—viewer is in on the humor from the beginning	Conceal or delay the "punch line" or source of humor—viewer can't share in the fun
Belittle or kid the **brand** or the **subject matter**	Belittle the consumer

SOURCE: Harold L. Ross, Jr., "How to Create Effective Humorous Commercials, Yielding Above Average Brand Preference Changes," *Marketing News,* March 26, 1976, p. 4. Used with permission.

sion, it would have to be sophisticated in the sense of knowing what was going on in contemporary society, especially as it relates to the product situation involved in the advertising. Advertising humor that fits in the "general knowledge," on the other hand, does not require this kind of sophistication and presents humor rather obviously.

Once the message format developer and brand manager consider the types of humor that might be used, then this must be related to the nature of the campaign situation and the appeals that must be communicated. In considering the situation, it is especially important to learn whether humorous messages are being used by competitors. If this is true to any great extent, then it is not likely that humorous messages will perform their usual function of attracting attention. If everybody is trying to be funny, then your humorous message may get lost in the cacophony of laughter. If, on the other hand, the communication within a product category is rather somber, a humorous message can definitely stand out. A good example is offered by the New England Life ad in Chapter 7. There were no jokes in the insurance advertising category when that campaign appeared, and the use of humor may have created attention and the gross positive awareness necessary in that sort of total marketing communication campaign.

Another aspect of the communication situation that should be considered with regard to humor is the frequency with which the messages are designed to reach the typical member of the campaign target segment or segments. If the campaign objectives call for a strategy that goes after a particularly difficult segment with many repetitive messages, then a humorous format will be particularly difficult to use successfully. When advertising and communication are particularly intrusive, as they are on radio and television, it is likely that a fatigue factor will build up rather quickly and the advertising will become irritating. In any medium, a campaign for a product that requires constant repetition runs the risk of turning what might initially be an effective humorous message into something that not only becomes irritating but also drags a tremendous amount of attention away from the product. It is said that this is essentially what happened to the Burt and Harry campaign for Piel's beer on television. But this irritating and overly distracting effect occurs for many small low-level attempts at humor in slogans and radio commercials. For instance, commercials for Levitz's Furniture Stores ended with the play on words in the jingle, "You'll love it, you'll love it, you'll love it at Levitz's!" Advertising for Wrigley's Doublemint gum has for years included the slight humorous touch of doubling everything in the commercials. Many of the ads showed twins. One radio commercial had a chorus singing every word twice. The repetitive nature of the campaign can lead to these small jokes becoming very irritating.

One solution when the brand manager and creative staff are faced with such a campaign situation is to use variety in carrying out the campaign. Whereas Rosser Reeves could brag about one Anacin commercial being run to the tune of over $86 million, a humorous campaign must be implemented with many different commercials, ads, promotions, and so forth. Commercials for Benson and Hedges cigarettes each showed a different "disadvantage" of the longer brand in a humorous way. At one point there was a whole stable of commercials for Alka-Selzer ("I can't believe I ate the whole thing," "Try it you'll like it," etc.). A humorous campaign for Excedrin featured different kinds of situations that created headaches. This allowed a large pool of commercials that could be run without causing fatigue and irritation. The Stiller and Meara campaign for Blue Nun wine was another example of a witty campaign that consisted of a larger pool of commercials than would be required for a more direct approach. The VW campaign, too, is an example of the use of continuing changes in advertising within a consistent humorous framework. VW also used humor in the less-intrusive print medium, which is less likely to cause irritation with repetition. Also, durable goods like automobiles do not require as much of the entire communication effort to be directed through advertising on television.

Also relevant to the communication situation that affects the use of humor is the nature of the message idea itself. If the appeal is complex or there are a number of appeals loosely related to a central positioning, humor may not be too effective. The reason is that, as we already know, there is a limit to the amount of information consumers can process at any given time and with regard to any particular issue. If the message idea is complex already, humor may add another element that not only distracts from the message but makes the entire information load too ponderous. The examples of campaigns that have successfully used humor usually also have very clear positioning or simple, important appeals. For Blue Nun wine, the appeal is simply that this is the one wine that goes with any meal and eliminates the bother of attempting to select the right wine. For Benson and Hedges, the appeal is that this is an extra long cigarette with all of its advantages. One of the difficulties of fitting humor with the message is that the message itself is often too complex. There do seem to be more failures than successes with humor.

The effectiveness of humor can be looked at in terms of communication objectives. If the goal is to attract attention and generate general awareness, humorous messages, in a setting in which there is little competitive humor, can be quite effective. On the other hand, if communications are designed to achieve comprehension, humor might get in the way unless the point to be comprehended is very simple and clear. When we move to attitude change as a goal, there are pros and cons that make it difficult to say anything general about the effect of humor as opposed to more direct messages. On the positive side in terms of attitude change, humor may distract the audience, thereby reducing counterargumentation and increasing attitude change; humor may enhance source credibility because a source willing to laugh about the product may be seen as more honest; humor may fit a particular audience more precisely than would a direct communication; and humor may produce a positive mood which would possibly rub off on the message. On the negative side in terms of attitude change, humor initially may be irritating and actually not funny; humor may be too distracting and thus impair learning; and humor may just not wear well over the course of the campaign.[8]

These facilitating and inhibiting effects of humor might possibly be analyzed in the way similar ones were for fear appeals. It may be, in other words, that as the degree of humor is increased, both facilitating and inhibiting effects have greater strength. Thus the most effective amount of humor would be somewhere in the middle ranges. Too little humor would not serve to create attention, inhibit counterargumentation, improve the mood, and enhance source credibility. Too much humor, however, might produce irritation, might overly distract so that the message would not be learned, and might not fit the audience. As a result, something between too little and too much might be most effective if humor were to be used, especially over the long run in a campaign.

Evidently the few successful humor message formats are those that are mild and pleasant jokes that go along with the selling appeal. They wear well and can be used in all aspects of the marketing-communication mix. They fit their audiences particularly well. They make fun of the product, not the people who are in the market for the product. Campaigns like those for Benson and Hedges, Dr Pepper, VW, and others use the humor in a variety of ways in advertising, promotion, and publicity and throughout the communication mix to add effect to messages.

Other Borrowed Interest Techniques

The same kind of analysis that was made in the area of humor might be made for other techniques of "borrowed interest" or of the "warm, charming, and witty" genre. These would include such techniques as the use of *sex, exaggerated graphics and illustrations, slogans,* and *music and jingles.* The research on all the techniques that might fit into the "warm, charming and witty" category indi-

cates no final, general answer on whether these types of message format techniques are "better" than the more straightforward techniques suggested by Reeves and others. Instead, brand management and creative people must analyze the hierarchy situation, the audience, the effects of mood, the effects of distraction, the attention potential of these techniques, the relationship to communication goals, the communication environment, the fit of the technique with the message idea, and the long-term potential of the format over repetition and the entire scope of the communication mix.

TESTIMONIALS AND PRESENTERS

Every message has a source. There is the company behind the communication, the implied source of the media in which the message appears, the presenter if there is one, and the person giving a testimonial in that type of format. Both people in the communication industry and researchers have focused on source as perhaps the key variable affecting the success of the message format.

At one end of the source effects continuum is the company as a source. Legislation has been introduced that would literally force corporations to identify themselves in connection with brands whose names seemingly have high credibility.

The same sort of positive versus boomerang effect possibility exists with regard to people presenting or making testimonials for a product in advertising and other marketing communication. In the 1970s there was an increase in the use of both star presenters and presenters who were very "ordinary" as compared with professional announcers. Apparently this trend occurred because advertisers felt that such stars as Bill Cosby, Ricardo Montalban, Joe Namath, and Mark Spitz had certain aspects of attractiveness and power that would be conferred upon the products they endorsed. At the other extreme, "ordinary" people would generate a certain amount of identification and credibility because they would be similar to people in target segments.

Even the medium in which advertising appears can confer a certain source effect on the message. This was evident in a trade ad for *Business Week* which showed a picture of a typical *Business Week* subscriber playing tennis at his own tennis club with ex sports champions. The ad said:

> Can you imagine a man like this who doesn't read Business Week? . . . or a marketing plan that doesn't include him?
>
> Norton Mailman's menage includes son Bruce (17) who gardens and is writing a book about it, motorbiker Matthew (15), the compleat angler, Chris (8) and wife Ginny, partner in her own product promotion agency. All play serious tennis on their country home court and at the Montego Bay Racquet Club, where Mailman is Chairman of ". . . the spot for tennis buffs." (1974 Fielding's Guide.)
>
> Mr. Mailman is also chairman of Macrodyne Industries, Inc., manufacturers of aircraft component parts; 1974 sales volume $40–50 million. Amex Symbol MCT.
>
> Chairman Mailman is also chairman of the World Health Administrative Services, Inc., a medical facility in the NYC's World Trade Center, to provide health maintenance and emergency services for the lower Manhattan business community.
>
> Chairman Mailman began reading Business Week long before he was chairman of anything.

All of these kinds of source are laden with suggestions of meaning, possibly interest, and direction for action on the part of target segment consumers. They all have the chance of either great success or a terrible backfire. The question here is, What has communication research told us about the use of source in all of these forms?

First, it is possible to look at source in the same way that the "charming, witty, and warm" or "borrowed interest" techniques were looked at above. That is, a source can be used to attract attention to communications and little more. Even in this role, source has not much more than a fifty-fifty chance. For instance, in four Gallup and Robinson studies, it was found that a celebrity gave a television commercial an average 12 percent premium above normal recall levels, but 47 percent of celebrity commercials did not come up to the norm.

And, just like humor and other types of borrowed interest techniques, the celebrity source took up time and space that could otherwise have been devoted to appeals. When the use of source is evaluated in terms of comprehension, the general finding is that an arresting source adds one more component to the message that detracts from the positioning and appeals. For instance, Gallup and Robinson found that an average thirty-second commercial communicated 2.4 copy points per respondent, whereas a celebrity spot communicated just 1.4.

Further, when the extreme celebrity type of source is evaluated in terms of attitude, it also offers some room for doubt. The Gallup and Robinson research found that regular spots generated more "favorable buying attitude" than did television commercials with celebrities, on the average.

Most textbook discussion of the use of source tends to give the impression that source credibility is monolithic in its effect; that is, it is supposed to be a benefit in almost every situation. However, as these findings from Gallup and Robinson indicate, it is possible to overuse source in the message format or use it incorrectly. Message format developers should realize that testimonials in advertisements have been overused in the past. And there is evidence that consumers are jaded by endorsements.[9]

If it is true that people down to teens and subteens in age are highly cynical about advertising sources (and research does indicate that such seeds of cynicism start as early as around ten years of age), then the usual discussion of research evidence on source must be taken with a large grain of salt. Testimonials and presenters have to be used carefully, if at all, and the research evidence provides only general guidance for message developers.

Most of the research involves the effect of source on the acceptance and retention of recommendations, not the ability of source to generate attention and interest. Original findings were that messages were more effective with a "high-credibility" source as opposed to a "low-credibility" one. When measurements were taken at some time after the original message exposure, the "sleeper effect" phenomenon mentioned earlier occurred. That is, the high-credibility source message seemed to decrease somewhat in effect while the low-credibility source message seemed to increase to the point that, after some time, there was no difference in the effect of messages with different source credibility. Although the reason for the sleeper effect phenomenon has recently been disputed, its implication for the message format developer seems clear: Unless it is possible to firmly establish a connection between the source and the message over the course of the campaign, the source will probably not have any special effect beyond generating attention, if that.

Three Source Characteristics

Thus, as with other distinctive format aspects, the effectiveness of the source is highly dependent upon the particular marketing communication situation in which it is used.

Originally, communication researchers identified three critical characteristics a source might have.[10] One of these characteristics, *credibility,* involved the simple aspect of whether the source knew what he or she was talking about and was motivated to communicate it because it was the truth rather than because of being paid to do so. A perfect ex-

ample is the commercial for the E. F. Hutton investment house that was delivered by J. Paul Getty, who was reputed to be the world's richest man. Getty was highly credible because he above all people would know something about making investments, and he would not by any stretch of the imagination be someone who could be paid off in order to make the testimonial. Ordinary people caught with a hidden camera often have this same kind of credibility because they do not actually know they are making a testimonial, although they may be particularly well suited to be making one.

The second aspect of source is *attractiveness.* This is usually the basis for the use of celebrities in marketing communication presentations. Here it is not necessary that the source be an expert on the particular subject he or she is discussing. What is more important is that the personality can create a positive mood in relation to the message.

The third aspect of source is *power.* This is seldom directly applicable in advertising situations, but it is applicable with regard to personal selling, publicity, and some promotion parts of the communication mix. It is sometimes true that salespeople can use executives at higher levels of their organization to support their claims with promises of future concessions to the prospect company.

Two Source "Games"

The three components of source described above have been found to work differently depending on the hierarchy situation in which the message format developer finds himself or herself. In a Low-Involvement hierarchy situation, the attractiveness component is probably the most important one, since a strong presenter can create attention for the message and possibly a generally positive mood that would carry over to a gross positive awareness for the brand. In a Learning hierarchy situation, on the other hand, the effective source seems to depend upon the goals of the audience. As Bauer pointed out, if the audience is playing the "problem-solving game," then the credibility component of source effect is extremely important. People selecting an investment house or deciding upon what food to serve their families are going to look with some care upon the presenter and that person's expertise and motivation for endorsing and explaining the product. But if the audience is playing the "psychosocial game," the attractiveness and commonality of the communicator become more important. Here the audience members are concerned about what status will be conferred upon them by using a particular product or, alternatively, whether the product is used and understood by people like them.[11]

A good example of the Learning hierarchy situation in which both "problem solving" and "psychosocial" effects of source occur was provided by a study by Levitt which looked at the interaction of source, message, and audience on the effectiveness of sales presentations in the industrial area.[12] Levitt's respondents were actual industrial purchasing agents, chemists, and Harvard MBA candidates. Each of these groups saw either a good or a poor sales presentation on a new paint-suspending agent by a salesman from either a high-credible (Monsanto Chemical Company) or medium-credible (Denver Chemical Company) source. Just as would be expected for the Learning hierarchy situation, these variations in source did have an effect. The higher the credibility of the company, the better were its chances of getting a favorable first hearing for the product. But if the customer was asked to make a greater, and therefore more risky, commitment to the product, the effect of source was mitigated. Obviously, in such a situation, the audience would be playing the problem-solving game. Even beyond that, purchasing agents who were more likely to be used to playing the problem-solving game were less affected by company reputation than were chemists. In all, in this industrial learning situation, the three components of source, message, and au-

dience interacted in the ways that would be expected. It may be that message format developers working in this area with personal selling may be able to assume fairly straightforward effects of source.

The "Reverse" Source Effect

It is in the third hierarchy situation, Dissonance-Attribution, that the standard ideas about source most readily begin to fall apart and at the same time become more interesting. Recall that this sort of communication situation is the one in which the audience is involved and knows that there are possible differences between alternatives that it cannot actually discern. The members of the audience have usually been forced to take some favorable action with regard to one alternative, most often prompted by some personal interaction component of the communication mix. The products are usually in the mature stage of the product life cycle.

In such a situation, the audience members are usually considering source as one reason that they may have taken an action with regard to a particular alternative. Since they are involved, that action and their reason for taking it is very important. If they can rationalize their action on the basis of being unreasonably affected by the particular source of the message, then it is possible that the message can be completely discounted and rendered ineffective. That is, if the message format using source induces a typical audience member to say, "I felt favorable toward this product only because there was such an overwhelmingly favorable source, not because it was really a better product," then the message would be ineffective. This is precisely the reverse of what is usually hypothesized to occur as a result of source. In other words, a medium- or low-credibility source might actually be more effective than a high-credibility one.[13]

This sort of effect has so consistently been found in the communication research literature that it should not be ignored by message format developers. If it is necessary to attempt to persuade people to do something they do not want to do or to convince them of a point that they are slightly antagonistic to, it might actually be better to use a presenter who is somewhat deficient or neutral in credibility. If this is done, any attitude change or intention change that occurs would be credited by the audience members as being their own decision, not one that was forced upon them by an overly positive source.

This kind of attribution theory analysis fits the findings of "overheard" messages. Many advertisers, by using hidden cameras and testimonials from ordinary people who do not know they are giving the testimonials, attempt to give the illusion of the audience's overhearing a message presented by people who could not actually have any externally generated motivation (e.g., being paid off) to give the endorsement. Research on this point indicates that overheard messages have an advantage over straightforward presentation only in those situations where the audience is highly involved and somewhat antagonistic to the position being advocated. Thus, in many public service advertising situations, and in situations in which there are strange new-product offerings, the overheard message presentation may have important source benefits.[14]

Summary

In sum, it might be said that the creative philosophies' emphasis on testimonials and continuing presenters must be considered with some care. Highly credible sources have had uneven success, and this success seems to depend intimately on the nature of the communication situation. In some cases a "bad" source can be good. And the effect of the source can only be assessed on the basis of the total Gestalt of the company, the medium, the presenter, the endorser, and the very language used in the message. The source, like the brand image, is something that is a result of the interaction of all aspects of the marketing-communication mix.

THE HONEST-TWIST APPROACH

Perhaps the most common description of the new approach to creativity in advertising relates to the fact that it is honest and usually has a clever twist connected with it that is different from the usual run-of-the-mill approach. The advertising of Bernbach, Della Femina, and Wells provide examples.

The real question having to do with the new creative approaches typified by these leading creative figures is, When and how can these approaches be used effectively? The big problem with the "creative explosion" of the late sixties and early seventies was one of indiscriminate copying without developing message format appropriate to the situation. Creatives and brand managers need to know what communication research tells us about how these various approaches work.

First let us look at what the "honest-twist" approach is in terms of available communication research findings. One primary distinguishing characteristic, especially for the Bernbach–DDB advertising, is that this approach tends to be *refutational*. Campaigns such as those for Volkswagen and Avis seem to work by bringing up a competitive counterargument and then refuting it with supportive arguments for the advertised brand or company.

But it should be recognized that the "honest-twist" approach, especially as practiced by creatives copying the Bernbach style, is really more than just refutational. It tends more toward *comparative attack*-type messages that actually mention the competition by name and even disparage them. This is typified by the Total cereal advertising, which specifically compared Total's nutritional content with natural cereals; AMC's direct comparisons of its Buyer Protection Plan with the warranties of other automobile makers; and Datril's direct attack on the pricing of Tylenol. The Opel ad in Figure 12-2 is another comparative version of the honest-twist approach.

Chapter 10 examined the situations in which it is appropriate to use a competitive approach including both refutational and at-tack methods. In general, the suggestion there was that a refutational approach is probably more often effective than the attack one. It seemed most appropriate for those situations in which there was some clear competition or consumer reservations related to the advertised product. Also it seemed best suited to those audiences who were well educated, particularly with regard to the issues in any prod-

(Courtesy of Buick Motor Division, General Motors Corp.)

Figure 12-2. *Opel comparative attack version of the honest-twist approach. VW later used this ad in Rabbit advertising. By being ''honest'' Opel put itself in the consideration class.*

uct category. Now the question is, Given these conditions, how best can this sort of creative style be carried out?

It should be recalled that the refutational approach seems to work, because it can arouse interest in a product category, alter the consumers' perceptions of competitive messages, provide a reward in the form of refutation of discordant belief, and instill important supportive information along with the refutation. Thus, in the first place, it is important that the format of a refutational message capitalize on these advantages of the approach. Advertisements should clearly juxtapose opposing positions in order to develop controversy and create interest in the product category. The argument should be made as simple as possible in order to give the consumer something with which to characterize competitive messages and eliminate discordant beliefs. And a great amount of supportive information is necessary to bolster beliefs related to the brand rather than simply dealing with the competition. Research has shown that consumers have difficulty understanding refutational messages because they are so complex. There is some evidence that the typical consumer would prefer to read a simple supportive message rather than a convoluted refutational one. And it has been shown time and again that specifically mentioning the competition in communications actually does give competitors extra advertising. Further, the refutational approach would have to be used very carefully in the broadcast media, if it is to be used there at all. Consumers seem to be bothered by being forced to view a complex refutational message, and this tendency would be exacerbated in television or radio, since its time limits restrict the number of arguments that can be presented.

It has been said that the complex and sometimes irritating aspects of the refutational approach are better implemented in print than in television. Broadcast advertising is so intrusive that a message that is hard to understand may actually irritate rather than inform. Also, it is possible that a television message might have the effect of the audience actually carrying away only the negative message.

One successful implementation of the refutational approach on television shows how carefully this must be done. The Philadelphia Electric Company decided to deal directly with seething consumer complaints with the service, costs, and environmental impact of the company's business. Its agency developed a series of eleven commercials that featured actual customers making complaints and then being answered by a spokesperson for the company. The complaints were quite strong, such as the following:

☐ Philadelphia Electric Company has been named the number one polluter.
☐ I live out in Bucks County, and there are these huge power lines . . . Now, you know we have beautiful rolling hills out there and these huge monsters are sticking out . . . Why can't they run the lines under the ground?
☐ My [electric] bill runs $12 a month in a 2-room apartment which is ridiculous.
☐ When the thermal pollution gets into the streams it kills the fishes.
☐ No matter where you put nuclear power no one wants it.
☐ Anyone who has the money can pollute the air the way the system is set up now.

The format characteristics that apparently made this campaign successful included the commercials' length and the careful balancing between complaints and full answers. The commercials were two minutes in length, approximately four times as long as the standard television message. Use of length is supported by research, since it is difficult to implement a refutational message in a very short time span. Each Philadelphia Electric Company commercial featured only twenty seconds of what the utility critics had to say, followed by one hundred seconds from the company's spokesperson. Thus the supportive content was very high, once the stimulating counterarguments were used to pull people into the message.[15]

It seems more effective to deal with counterarguments that are general and not related to any particular competitor. A study by Ogilvy and Mather showed quite clearly that specifically mentioning competition only gives them additional exposure. Research by Sawyer on refutational versus supportive advertising showed that only when refutational ads specifically mentioned competition was there any benefit to competition. For this and other reasons, the specific way in which the refutational message is executed is important.[16]

As was noted above, the honest-twist approach tends to use shock and tries to involve the reader in drawing his or her own conclusions relative to the market offering. Communication research that deals with order effects and direct versus indirect approaches provides some guidance for creatives who want to use this general style. First, in regard to the use of shock, there is some evidence from the order effects research that it is possible initially to develop interest in an issue and then satisfy that interest with information and recommendations. Certainly it is clear that the order of interest-generating-materials-first is superior to just presenting information and recommendations before developing motivation to read and learn them.[17]

Thus the typical order of the honest-twist approach seems to be supported by research. But what evidence is there that the use of the shocking material alone can get people involved to the point that they draw their own conclusions favorable to the brand being advertised? The answer seems to be that if it is possible to get the audience members involved enough to draw their own conclusions from a message, then that message will be more effective than one in which all arguments are completely explicated. The difficulty, of course, is that it is almost impossible to get a significant proportion of the audience members to draw the right conclusions on their own. Because of this, messages that carefully draw explicit conclusions for consumers are usually found to be more effective than vague messages that simply state a problem or create motivation without actually providing clear recommendations.

Much public service advertising makes the error of incomplete or inexplicit recommendations. We are stimulated and made concerned about a variety of social issues, but we are not told what we as individuals are supposed to do as a result.

The successful honest-twist approach advertising does not make the mistake of letting the technique get in the way of the message. The refutational approach might be used, the advertiser admits that there are some negatives connected with the product, but this is followed by extensive copy that fully refutes counterarguments, supports the product, and provides clear recommendations for action. It also is true that the honest-twist approach is best used within an overall marketing communication strategy. Since it is ideal to involve the audience in the communication, it might be possible to generate this involvement on the basis of one part of the communication mix and provide a close toward specific recommendations with use of another component of the marketing-communication mix. For instance, the public service messages that generate concern might be followed up by promotional booklets and personal-selling campaigns that convert this concern into action.

REPETITION

The Reeves creative style in particular advocated the use of repetition both within each communication message and across the campaign. One of the most common mistakes pointed out by a number of creative philosophies is that of changing the campaign too frequently or diluting it with too many different message versions.

In general, research seems to indicate that repetition is worth the extra expense, especially in today's crowded media environment. It is difficult to get any message across when there is a great deal of noise. Repetition *can* help to cut through the noise and implant the message. It is also true, however, that there is a point at which repetition begins to become irritating. And there is the question of how many repetitions are optimal in any given situation. That is, there is probably some point beyond which further repetitions would not provide any added benefit in terms of communication response.

Research has shown that there is a general S-shaped function that underlies repetition effects. That is, it seems that there is only a small amount of effect at low levels of repetition, a quick up in effect in middle ranges of repetition, and, finally, a leveling off or even a decrease in effect once the repetition level is too high. Although this S-shaped curve seems to underlie most repetition results, it is seldom observed in its entirety in any particular marketing-communication situation. For very difficult situations, the early flat part of the curve is observed. When persuasion is easy, the strongly increasing effects part of the curve is shown. And in those situations in which the consumer has been heavily exposed to messages about a product category, the flattening-out part of the curve is observed.[18]

The effect and use of repetition is governed by the situation. If the purpose of the campaign is to produce rather easily influenced responses such as awareness or general recall, then repetition can be used to great advantage and will produce strong effects. Similarly in low-involvement situations in which the audience is not very familiar initially with the brand, repetition can be used to overwhelm the lack of involvement and familiarity.

If it is necessary to use a complex or vague message, then repetition might be used to carry that message across in the long run. There is some evidence that over the course of a campaign, a less-direct approach might actually be more effective with repetition. For instance, in one study the repetition effects of a campaign were compared for one-color versus black-and-white versions. The color version was more effective in generating immediate attention and worked better than the black-and-white version at low levels of repetition. But if the measure of effect was actual comprehension of the message, the black-and-white version seemed to be superior, especially at high levels of repetition. Apparently consumers were attracted to the color ad for a superficial reason and carried away little of the message. The black-and-white ad did not attract as many people with each exposure, but those it attracted carried away something of the message. Further repetitions reinforced this strong content transmission.

Both advertising folklore and research indicate that the ideal number of repetitions of key copy points and brand names within a message seems to be three. Krugman provides some theoretical basis for this finding. He posits that the first exposure to any message or message component produces an attention response and little more. The second exposure usually results in consumers' actually processing and comprehending the idea. Then the third and subsequent exposures, says Krugman, only serve to remind consumers of the message point.[19] Within a given message, then, it does not seem necessary to go beyond three mentions of any point. Across a campaign, it might be possible to repetitively expose target consumers far beyond the three-exposure level with effect, simply because additional exposures provide reinforcement that is valuable for its influence on action.

It is sometimes possible to go too far with repetition. When the audience is already very involved with the product category, is familiar with all arguments and alternatives related to it, and is somewhat antagonistic to the advertised position, repetition may be counterproductive. This was illustrated in some research that was done on political advertising. For political races that the voter was not particularly involved in or aware of, repetition seemed to have strong and continuing effects on awareness and voting intention. For other political races, such as the presidential one, voters seemed to be so aware and committed to a position that heavy repetitive advertising could produce actual *decreases* in voting intention. It has also been a consistent finding that advertising for well-known brands or market-share leaders does not have to be repeated with the intensity of that for newcomers in a product category. The reminder should be there, but it should not be so intensive that it begins to irritate those people who are already favorably disposed toward the brand.

Once again, the four-component idea— drive, habit, stimulus, reward—can be used as a guide for a message format implementation. [20] Repetition can be seen as effective in increasing the habit (information) and stimulus components of effect. When there is already a great deal of drive and reward in a situation, however, repetition must be used carefully, since consumers would probably be motivated to generate information and learn about the nature of the product stimulus on their own. In such situations, low levels of exposure to target segments should be maintained. Where higher levels are required, it may be best to utilize more complex messages and variation to mitigate the possible irritation that could be generated. Repetition is a much more reasonable format technique in low-involvement and dissonance-attribution situations than it is in learning ones. In the latter situations, it must be utilized with care.

THE IMPLEMENTATION OF FEAR

One format aspect that is inadequately discussed in creative philosophies is the implementation of fear appeals. Chapter 10 pointed out that medium levels of fear appeals (not too weak so as to be innocuous and not too strong so as to be overwhelming) appear to be most effective. In addition, fear seems called for in situations where key segments of consumers have overlooked a prob-

lem that might be solved by a particular product. In such situations, stronger levels of a fear may be optimal in attracting otherwise unconcerned consumers. But it may also be true that the effectiveness of a fear message, even in an ideal situation for one, could be totally altered by the nature of the message format.

Fortunately there has been a great deal of research on the components of a fear message that can improve its effectiveness. Creatives and brand managers can best understand how to implement fear messages by considering once again the fact that emotional messages can have both facilitating and inhibiting effects. The facilitating aspects of fear messages relate to their potential for increasing drive or interest and concern with a particular product. Fear messages can be inhibiting when they go too far in increasing this drive without providing reassuring recommendations. All aspects of format that have been found to be effective in implementing fear contribute to a proper balancing of facilitating and inhibiting factors.

For instance, it is especially important to state clearly recommended action to alleviate the fear that has been generated. One of the difficulties with some advertising using fear is that it generates concern without providing clear and actionable recommendations. Some fear research indicates that the effect of a fear message is almost directly related to the physical distance between the exposure location and the place where recommendations can be acted upon. Fear messages require especially strong recommendations that are clear and easily implemented. If it is not possible to provide this sort of format, some other type of appeal should probably be used.

Other research has indicated the optimal order of the fear and recommendation content within a message. It seems to be best to start the message with the fear content to generate concern and then follow quickly with a large component of recommendations that alleviate the fear and lean toward action.

As mentioned in the preceding chapter, consumers who have previously been unconcerned about particular problems can be affected by a higher level of fear than would be those who initially had some concern. This general principle seems to extend to the question of whom the format should direct the fear to and how illustrations should depict the fear. Research indicates that if the fear is directed toward someone close to the prospect rather than to the prospect himself or herself, it is more effective. For instance, one Mutual of New York ad showed a wife and two children, obviously after the husband had died. The headline was "My husband's life insurance covered everything. Except inflation." By concentrating on the effect on the family rather than the husband, the ad had a better chance of success.

Another format aspect that can increase the facilitating side of fear appeals is source credibility. Most studies indicate that the effect of source credibility and of fear is heightened when the two are used together. Fear appeals are more effective when they are delivered by, or are seen as coming from, a highly credible source. Consumers are less likely to discount the fear when it comes from a credible source.[21]

The fear appeals area is one example of several in which suggestions from communication research may actually feed back to affect creative styles. The implications of the research not only for message tone but also for specific format are quite telling, especially considering the bias that contemporary advertising has toward emotional and shocking approaches.

GENERALIZATIONS ABOUT RESEARCH ON FORMAT

Communication research seems to indicate that the situational perspective is important in determining the format for communication messages. Our review of creative styles

indicated that each one seemed to come out of and be appropriate to a particular type of marketing-communication situation. The communication research review provides further support for this perspective.

The situations seem to divide quite well along the lines suggested by the hierarchy analysis of Chapter 7. In a Low-Involvement hierarchy situation, it seems that the approach used by Reeves is best. That is, it is necessary to be direct and clear at the cost of possibly being unpleasant. Testimonials and presenters are only important in making the message clear, and, in the low-involvement situation, they should not become a major part of the message and distract from the product. The honest-twist approach is too complex for such a situation. Rather, repetition of very simple points can be used to drive the message home. Fear appeals stated strongly without clear recommendations are also likely to be too distracting in a low-involvement situation.

It is in the Learning and Dissonance-Attribution hierarchy situations that the other side of the coin in terms of message format seems most applicable. When people are in a Learning mode or attempting to gather in information that would support their previous decisions, it is possible to be "warm, charming, and witty" with great effect. In such situations the mood of the commercial can have positive benefits, distraction can be used to aid the transmission of possibly antagonistic beliefs, humor can smooth the transmission of ideas without becoming an overwhelming factor in itself. This is the kind of situation in which source credibility is used as a guide by consumers in order to evaluate the message. The honest-twist approach can be very effective because it uses a series of arguments that people are looking for when they are in a Learning or Dissonance-Attribution mode. In such settings, too much emphasis on repetition can be counterproductive after a certain point. People are too involved anyway, and they get irritated.

Of course not everything about message

format can be reduced to generalizations that come from hierarchy analysis. Every format decision must be looked at with regard to the facilitating as opposed to inhibiting effects that might be brought to the campaign. This chapter has emphasized that it is difficult to implement successfully such format characteristics as mood, distraction, humor, sex, shock, honest-twist, endorsements, repetition, and fear. It is difficult because they all contain a component of positive and negative effects, which must be balanced carefully if the message is to be successful.

Although there are some excellent general suggestions about message format that come from the communication research literature, these suggestions will only be valid depending on the way they are implemented in particular situations. The issues of alternative implementations and the way they might be pretested are ones of concern in the next two chapters.

ISSUES AND PROJECTS FOR DISCUSSION

1. Do irritating commercials work?

2. What is the sleeper effect, and how does it affect the pleasantness-unpleasantness of advertising and testimonial (source credibility) effects?

3. How does "distraction" affect message effect?

4. In what conditions can humor be (a) effective and (b) ineffective in marketing communication?

5. Can you do the same analysis as the humor one (question 4) for other techniques, such as the use of sex in advertising, exaggerated graphics and illustrations, slogans, and music and jingles? Give an example.

6. What type of source credibility is represented by this book's admonition to speak to real people in their own terms? In what sort of situation can low source credibility be more effective than high source credibility? Differentiate between Bauer's problem-solving versus psychosocial "games." Give examples of advertising situations for each. What are the implications?

7. When is the honest-twist approach right and when is it wrong in advertising?

8. Use the four-component model—drive, habit, stimulus, reward—to indicate when repetition and the hard sell are appropriate and when they are not.

9. How can format influence the effectiveness of fear appeals?

10. Now, assume again that you are the marketing services manager discussed at the very beginning of the chapter. For any two of the situations you are considering, rank the message format approaches in terms of potential effectiveness and indicate why you ranked them in this way.

Notes

1. William J. McGuire, "An Information-Processing Model of Advertising Effectiveness," in *The Behavioral and Managerial Sciences in Marketing,* ed. H. Davis and A. J. Silk (New York: John Wiley, 1978), pp. 156–80; and "The Nature of Attitudes and Attitude Change," in *Handbook of Social Psychology* (2nd. ed.), ed. G. Lindzey and E. Aronson (Reading, Mass.: Addison-Wesley, 1968), III, 136–314.

2. William D. Tyler, "Radio Turns to Interruption These New, Different Ways," *Advertising Age,* August 5, 1974, p. 24.

3. Michael L. Ray, Scott Ward, and Jerome B. Reed, "Pretesting of Anti-Drug Abuse Education and Information Campaigns," in *Communication Research and Drug Education,* ed. Ronald E. Ostman (Beverly Hills, Calif.: Sage Publications, Inc., 1976), pp. 193–219.

4. Thomas D. Cook, Charles L. Gruder, Karen M. Hennigan, and Brian R. Flay, "History of the Sleeper Effect: Some Logical Pitfalls in Accepting the Null Hypothesis," *Psychological Bulletin,* 86 (July 1979), 662–79.

5. Philip Zimbardo, M. Weisenberg, I. Fire-

stone, and B. Levy, "Communicator Effectiveness in Producing Public Conformity and Private Attitude Change," *Journal of Personality,* 33 (1965), 233–55.

6. Leon Festinger and Nathan Maccoby, "On Resistance to Persuasive Communication," *Journal of Abnormal & Social Psychology,* 68 (April 1964), 359–66; Stewart Bither, "Effects of Distraction and Commitment on the Persuasiveness of Television Advertising," *Journal of Marketing Research,* 9 (February 1972), 1–5; and Ray, Ward, and Reed, "Pretesting of Anti-Drug Abuse."

7. Mervin D. Lynch and Richard C. Hartman, "Dimensions of Humor in Advertising," *Journal of Advertising Research,* 8 (December 1968), 39–45.

8. Brian Sternthal and C. Samuel Craig, "Humor in Advertising," *Journal of Marketing,* 37 (October 1975), 12–18.

9. Eric Sevareid, "Sevareid on Endorsement Rules," *Advertising Age,* June 2, 1975, p. 15.

10. Carl Hovland and Walter Weiss, "The Influence of Source Credibility on Communication Effectiveness," *Public Opinion Quarterly,* 15 (1951), 635–50; and Carl Hovland, Irving Janis, and Harold Kelly, *Communication and Persuasion* (New Haven, Conn.: Yale University Press, 1953).

11. Raymond A. Bauer, "A Revised Model of Source Effects" (Paper presented at the annual meeting of the American Psychological Association, Chicago, September 1965).

12. Theodore Levitt, "Communications and Industrial Selling," *Journal of Marketing,* 31 (April 1967), 15–21.

13. Brian Sternthal, Lynn W. Phillips, and Ruby Dholakia, "The Persuasive Effect of Source Credibility: A Situational Analysis," *Public Opinion Quarterly,* 42 (Fall 1978), 285–314.

14. Timothy C. Brock and Lee Alan Becker, "Ineffectiveness of 'Overheard' Counter-propaganda," *Journal of Personality and Social Psychology* 2 (1965), 654–60.

15. "A Utility Puts Its Critics on Television," *Business Week,* September 9, 1972, p. 64.

16. J. J. Boddewyn and Katherine Mason, *Comparison Advertising* (New York: Hastings House, 1978); Alan G. Sawyer, "The Effects of Repetition of Refutational and Supportive Advertising Appeals," *Journal of Marketing Research* (February 1973), pp. 23–33; and William L. Wilkie and Paul W. Farris, "Comparison Advertising: Problems and Potential," *Journal of Marketing* (October 1975), pp. 7–15.

17. McGuire, "Nature of Attitudes."

18. Michael L. Ray (in collaboration with Alan G. Sawyer, Michael L. Rothschild, Roger M. Heeler, Edward C. Strong, and Jerome B. Reed), "Marketing Communication and the Hierarchy of Effects," in *New Models for Communication Research,* ed. P. Clarke (Beverly Hills, Calif.: Sage Publications, Inc., 1973), pp. 147–76; and Alan G. Sawyer, "The Effects of Repetition: Conclusions and Suggestions about Experimental Laboratory Research," in *Buyer/Consumer Information Processing,* ed. G. D. Hughes and M. L. Ray (Chapel Hill: University of North Carolina Press, 1974), pp. 190–220.

19. Herbert E. Krugman, "Why Three Exposures May Be Enough," *Journal of Advertising Research,* 12 (December 1972), 11–14.

20. Michael L. Ray, "Psychological Theories and Interpretations of Learning," in *Consumer Behavior: Theoretical Sources,* ed. Scott Ward and Thomas Robertson (Englewood Cliffs, N.J.: Prentice-Hall, 1973).

21. Michael L. Ray and William L. Wilkie, "Fear: The Potential of an Appeal Neglected by Marketing," *Journal of Marketing,* 34 (January 1970), 54–62; Brian Sternthal and C. Samuel Craig, "Fear Appeals: Revisited and Revised," *Journal of Consumer Research,* 1 (December 1974), 22–34; Howard Penn Krishner III, Susan A. Darley, and John M. Darley, "Fear-Provoking Recommendations, Intentions to Take Preventative Actions, and Actual Preventative Actions," *Journal of Personality and Social Psychology,* 26 (May 1973), 301–8; and Ray, "Psychological Theories," pp. 94 and 95.

Advertising Format Implementation and Pretesting

△ Assume that the television commercial depicted here is the single format implementation to be used to carry out a "health plus a fun-taste" appeal for Life cereal. Justify the continued use of this one commercial as the total Life advertising campaign. And suggest how the format could be implemented in other advertising media, as well as packaging, personal selling, sales promotion, and publicity-PR.

BBDO
Batten, Barton, Durstine & Osborn, Inc.

Client: **QUAKER OATS CO.**

Time: **30 SECONDS**

Product: **LIFE CEREAL**

Title: **"THREE BROTHERS" REV.** Comml. No.: **OAAL3664**

1ST BOY: What's this stuff?
2ND BOY: Some cereal. Supposed to be good for you.

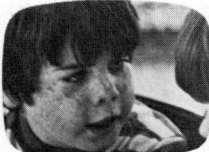

1ST BOY: D'you try it?
2ND BOY: I'm not gonna' try it, you try it.

1ST BOY: I'm not gonna' try it.

2ND BOY: Let's get Mikey!
1ST BOY: Yeah!

2ND BOY: He won't eat it. He hates everything.

2ND BOY: He likes it!

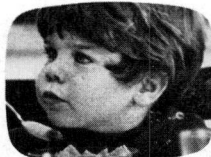

Hey Mikey!
ANNCR: (VO) When you bring Life home, don't tell the kids it's one of those

nutritional cereals you've been trying to get them to eat. You're the only one who has to know.

(Courtesy of The Quaker Oats Company)

The excitement of the process of message development is in the precise implementation of actual ads, selling propositions, sales promotions, and publicity activities. Throughout the first two stages of the procedure of format development, the seeds are planted for the later blossoming of alternatives. In step one, problem formulation, and step two, review of available evidence, there is a narrowing of possibilities. Now there is further narrowing to a small set of choices which are made with or without pretesting.

Let us examine what actually happened to Life cereal. This product had a nutritional story to tell that it had not been able to turn into a solid market share in the huge cereal market. Many television format approaches had been tried—humorous with the comedy team of Bob and Ray, animated protein characters, clinical tests. The brand did not seem to hold its own against such competitors as Kellogg's Special K and Total. Then the one commercial shown at the beginning of this chapter was developed and run in the early 1970s. It seemed to offer the right combination of nutrition and taste in a format that appealed to children and their parents. As soon as it started running, the brand's share started growing at a 20 percent rate. The agency tried other formats, but none seemed to work as well as that one. At the time this book was being written the commercial was still running, although it was accompanied by some other ones for the brand. "Mikey," the main character, was depicted on the brand's packages. The commercial was still getting high recall and identification scores. The implementation appeared to be correct.[1]

This point in the development of message format for any campaign is unique for each situation. It is impossible to represent the infinite variety of possible alternatives that might be considered within the constraints that are dictated by the problem, the message idea, past creative experience, and research findings. Instead this chapter attempts to review the range of possible alternatives and considerations in each of the forms of advertising, including television, newspapers, magazines, radio, outdoor, and other media. A section on pretesting shows how final format decisions might be made and closes out the chapter. Chapter 14 reviews implementation for other communication elements.

TELEVISION

The campaign manager is now being faced with a dilemma in television. The medium reaches more people than do any of the other media, with greater potential, excitement, and intrusiveness. On the other hand, the problem of "clutter" is more potent in television than in the other media. The average viewer was said to have seen thirty-eight thousand commercials a year during the mid-1970s. Usually by the end of May, two of the three major networks would have already stopped accepting orders for prime commercial time.

The standard alternative forms of the television commercial—stand-up presenter, demonstration, and animation—are still with us. But they have been developed with tremendous sophistication into a series of clear alternatives for campaign developers.

The stand-up *presenter* has been expanded into the possibility of testimonials, the continuing presenter, or the star. "Real person" testimonials give a feeling of authenticity, even in a short commercial. The continuing presenter—such as Mr. Whipple for Charmin bathroom tissue, Pete the butcher for Shake 'n Bake, or Mrs. Olson for Folger's coffee—presents the possibility of quick consumer identification with the brand name and claim in the short-commercial, cluttered environment of television.

Demonstrations have expanded beyond anything that was available to the standard pitchman. Now TV commercial viewers can see cars hurdling through the air and over test tracks to display products' durability.

Animation is the traditional television alternative that has shown the most growth in terms of providing alternatives for campaign developers. It is true that strict animation in the cartoon sense now comprises a small portion of all television advertising. But if one includes all the graphic and production techniques that have been developed for television advertising, the variety of alternatives becomes impressive.

In contrast, one of the most durable and often used alternatives in television is the *"slice of life."* This basic format involves a believer or persuader person who meets with a nonbeliever or uninformed person with regard to the brand being advertised. In the course of the commercial, the believer shows the nonbeliever the error of his or her ways. During this "slice of life" discussion or demonstration, the advertised brand is heavily promoted. In many cases the "slice of life" can be combined with a continuing presenter, as it is with all the continuing presenters mentioned earlier.

Laypersons often ignore the *audio* characteristics of television advertising. Music and jingles have always been clear alternatives underlying the types of television commercial techniques mentioned above. In addition, natural sound can be used to create a mood that is relevant to the message.

An examination of alternatives in television can provide new questions that might be resolved by reviewing the research literature. Television advertising brings up such questions as whether the message should start with a dramatic beginning (research says open strong), how specific the recommendation should be (research indicates the more specific, the better), the timing of motivating materials and selling recommendations (research says to motivate first and then recommend), color versus black and white (color can provide ID and beauty but black and white may stand out for some topics), videotape versus film (videotape provides realism and immediacy while film provides higher quality and more production latitude).

Campaign managers can make decisions on such alternatives on the basis of the broad framework of analysis that has been suggested in the message format chapters. In many cases it will be necessary to test specific alternatives to determine their effectiveness.

NEWSPAPERS

Although newspapers are the second-largest advertising medium for national advertising, they are by far the largest in terms of total expenditures.[2] Thus their strength is for local, mainly retailer, advertising. And in that strength lie many of the medium's weaknesses and its general neglect in terms of format development.

Because newspapers offer the quality of immediacy and newsworthiness, the preparation of ads for them is often left to the last minute. Because of their low cost, relatively high reader involvement, and control of viewing as well as the large page size, creatives often revert to long copy ads with little creative flair. Or ad formats from magazines are loosely adapted to the newspaper medium.

Of course newspapers do have a rather short life and in general do not offer the same quality of reproduction that is possible in magazines. Also there is a great deal of clutter in newspapers. So in total there is not the sort of effort on format development for the medium that it deserves on the basis of expenditures alone.

But look at any major city daily for a week, particularly the Sunday edition, and you will begin to see the many varieties of format that are possible in the modern newspaper. There are many forms of color available, including ROP (which means "run of paper" or color anywhere in the newspaper, available in newspapers representing more than 90 percent of total U.S. daily newspaper circulation), comics, special preprinted inserts, and magazine rotogravure. Many different shapes and sizes of ads can be used. They range from magazinelike preprinted inserts to the smallest classified ad. Big double-paged spreads can make announcements with great impact. Smaller-spaced ads can be repeated throughout a particular issue to make sure the reader gets the message. Sometimes white space can be combined with the page size of newspapers to fit advertising with the day's news.

Perhaps the range of possibilities can be seen in some of the winners of the AdConcepts contest, which was sponsored by the Newspaper Advertising Bureau and the International Newspaper Advertising Executives. For instance:

☐ A public service ad urging people to take part in a heart attack rescue program showed a circle of horrified office workers looking down on the reader. The headline said, "Pretend you're having a heart attack."
☐ The New Science Museum of Minneapolis had a tribal mask that could be cut out of its newspaper ad. The headline said, "Wear a smile to the New Science Museum of Minne-

sota." The ad copy had all sorts of details about the participative nature of the museum and included a map of directions as to how to get there.
☐ An employment ad with blurred type said, "We're looking for a sharp operator to work in our photo lab. Must have 2–4 years' experience and not be afraid of the dark. For a clearer picture, call . . ."
☐ A speculative layout for the United Way was in one-color purple and was made to look like a blanket. The headline said, "If you still wonder why there's a United Way, try using this newspaper as a blanket some night on a park bench."
☐ A speculative layout for a home center had a full-page calendar with a special on each day of the month. It said, "Save every day in June. Tear out and save this calendar for a full month of savings and valuable coupons!"
☐ A speculative ad for Scotch brand tape was laid out like Christmas wrapping paper. The copy was, "If you run out of wrapping paper you can use this, but what are you going to do if you run out of 'Scotch' brand magic transparent tape?"
☐ A speculative ad for a barbers' chain had a life-size picture of the bottom of a bearded face. The headline said, "Put this ad under your nose and see what it's like to have a beard."
☐ A speculative ad for a financial service had extensive copy at the top and the outline of a breakfast-table setting at the bottom. Obviously taking advantage of the fact that many newspapers are read at the breakfast table, the headline inside the outline of the plate said, "I'm glad we could have this breakfast. Set your plate here for a way to turn your taxes into personal wealth. Reading time: two eggs and an english muffin."

Obviously there are opportunities to create "salesmanship in print" and to reach people through creative format implementation in newspapers.

MAGAZINES

Like newspapers, magazines give people more time with and control of advertising exposure than do the broadcast media. People can be more involved and selective with advertising in the print media. Magazines differ from newspapers, however, in not having the local character and immediacy while having the advantages of better graphics and longer life.

As a result, magazine advertising has a greater opportunity to create a mood and work on the earlier stages of the decision process than does newspaper advertising.

Only a few of the decision points in magazine-advertising format implementation can be touched on here. They include

☐ The nature of the layout and the organization of illustration (if any) and the copy.
☐ The size of the ad and whether it is a "bleed" ad running all the way to the edge of the page.
☐ How much copy should be used. This depends on the situation. Although people can and do read more in magazines, there is a tendency toward verbal overemphasis in magazine advertising, just as there is a tendency toward visual overemphasis in television advertising.
☐ The nature of the illustrations. Should they be in color or just black-and-white photographs or art or some combination?
☐ Should the question-answer or one-two punch sort of format be used? For instance an ad for the Tobacco Institute said:

DOES THE GOVERNMENT SUPPORT THE TOBACCO FARMER?
NO, THE TOBACCO FARMER SUPPORTS THE GOVERNMENT.

This kind of approach can involve the reader and quickly get to the point, but there are times and market situations in which it is overused.
☐ Should there be an illustration at all? Should there be people in it? If so, should they look like ordinary people or professional models?
☐ Should the advertising fit the format of the magazine in some way or should it contrast with it? A gross example: use of scantily clad models in a *Playboy* ad as opposed to being in an industrial publication. These kinds of decisions trade off the possibilities of more thorough reading if the ads are compatible as opposed to the greater attention usually afforded to ads that contrast markedly with the magazine editorial.

One research method that has been used to provide information on such magazine format alternatives is the readership survey. After an ad has appeared in a magazine the readers are interviewed, either in person or by mail. As they look through the publication, they are asked about their readership of ads. Three scores are provided by the Starch readership service:

☐ *Noted:* percent who remember having previously seen the ad in the issue
☐ *Associated:* percent who saw any part of the ad which clearly indicates the brand of advertiser
☐ *Read Most:* percent who read 50% or more of the written material

Such a service is not a pretesting one, but it can provide guidelines as to how certain mechanical features of ads *may* affect readership. For instance, the three ads in Figure 13-1 were tested by the Starch service and are quite similar with the exception of the illustration and headline. They produced quite different Starch scores.

The middle ad in Figure 13-1 was the winner on the basis of all three scores. An official of the Starch company explained this by pointing out that pictures of food in women's service magazines (the ads appeared in *Family Circle* in May, June, and October respectively) work quite well, while models should be someone the female readers can either emulate or admire. Apparently the cropped picture of the mother in ad (a) is not something women like to see, particularly in this denigrated form. And the overweight women in the third ad do not seem to be the type that women want to identify with.[3] Such ad format speculation can only be done on the basis of a large number of readership scores. Even then the scores are subject to various interpretations. The Starch scores for the three ads are as follows:

THE SHORT STOP SNACK.

When the game's called on account of hunger, it's time for Mom to break out the Dole bananas. Every young ballplayer we know loves their fresh, natural sweetness and creamy texture. Bananas add vitamins and minerals to a child's diet too... without adding a lot of calories. A medium-size Dole banana contains only about 101 calories. Have a bunch ready when the team heads home. And get a big bunch of smiles in return.

The Dòle Banana. As a snack, it's a natural.

(a)

IT DOESN'T ADD UP.

It looks luscious. Tastes even better. Yet when you count up the calories, this new salad recipe from Dole has fewer than you might expect.

Start with a medium-size Dole banana, fresh and creamy. Add watermelon balls from a slice 10" by 1." A half-cup of sliced ripe peaches. One tempting Kiwi fruit. (If not available, substitute ½ cup green grapes.) Arrange on fresh lettuce. Only 306 calories so far.

Next whip up our new Pink Cloud dressing in your blender: ½ cup low fat plain yogurt, ½ cup low fat strawberry yogurt, 1½ teaspoons fresh lemon juice, and a dash of salt. Blend till smooth. Only 20 calories in two tablespoons of dressing. Or 326 in the entire salad. Go ahead, indulge yourself.

For a new banana recipe booklet, send your name, address, zip code to: Patricia Collier, Dept. BI, Castle & Cooke Foods, P.O. Box 7758, San Francisco, CA 94119.

The Dòle Banana. As a snack, it's a natural.

(Courtesy of Castle & Cooke, Inc. Dole)

(b)

WAIST NOT, WANT NOT.

Some things are not as they appear. Take a Dole banana. Sweet and plump and creamy enough to satisfy the hungries. Maybe you think it's loaded with calories. Uh-uh. A medium-size Dole banana contains only about 101 calories, no cholesterol and about as much fat as you'll find in lettuce. So when that 10 A.M. craving comes and you want to keep the scale tipped in your favor, grab a Dole banana. It's one snack that won't go to your waist.

The Dòle Banana. As a snack, it's a natural.

(c)

Figure 13-1. *Which ad attracted more readers?*

	Noted %	Asso. %	Read Most %
Ad (b) appetite appeal	60	56	16
Ad (c) diet food	52	48	5
Ad (a) snack for children	43	38	4

A more sophisticated approach was taken by Hanssens and Weitz.[4] Unlike the studies mentioned above, theirs concentrated on industrial advertising. Although they studied advertisements from only a single trade publication over a six-month period, they used an action measure, inquiries keyed to the ad, in addition to readership. And they were able to separate results for three different types of industrial product purchase: important, routine, and unique. The study results, summarized below, give another set of guidelines for magazine format, particularly in the industrial area. Note that the effect of format is not as great on the action measure of inquiring as it is on readership.

> These results indicate that the use of photographs, illustrations, and females are strongly related to the recall and readership of ads for routinely purchased products. Ad size and the use of multiple products and pointers have the strongest impact on inquiry generation for these products.
>
> Ad size, and the use of women and pointers have the largest impact on the readership and recall on unique products. Mentioning the name of a unique product in the headline has a negative impact on effectiveness. Inquiry generation is strongly related to the use of four color and free offers.
>
> All effectiveness measures of ads for important products are related to cost characteristics like ad size and color. Multiple products in important product ads decreases readership and recall.[5]

RADIO

Expenditures in radio advertising are less than a fourth of those in newspapers. There is some tendency for advertisers to neglect the particular creative needs and opportunities of the medium. But there is plenty of evidence that with careful attention to the details of format in radio, it is possible to achieve substantial sales success.

Radio advertising can create images that cannot be obtained with any other medium, simply because it is possible to rely on the listener's imagination. Radio is also inexpensive, so there is the possibility of using longer-length messages than in television. And it is possible to repeat messages more often, so there is the chance to construct messages that can both benefit from repetition and withstand it without becoming irritating.

In creating radio advertising format, it should not be forgotten that radio is essentially a local medium with stations targeted at specific segments. And messages can be timed for specific audiences, as Maxwell House coffee did with its radio advertising at breakfast time, Campbell soup with its advertising at noon lunchtime, and Datsun during drive time with its slogan, "Put your money in the bank, not in the tank." The specific area, segment, and time capabilities of radio put extra importance on the format decision.

Laid against the advantages of radio are the disadvantages—including the lack of visual aspects for package identification and the severe clutter that is found, particularly on AM radio.

The alternatives in radio must be seen in light of its advantages and disadvantages. There has been an emphasis on borrowed-interest techniques—primarily humor and arresting music. In order to provide package identification and cut through the clutter, for instance, a series of commercials for Kava coffee used humor and had the line, "The coffee with the really ugly label."

Both humor and music must be used carefully. Over and over the story is told of the person humming an advertising theme song while buying the competitive product. Or the jokes of the commercial are told, but the advertiser is forgotten.

But radio is loaded with fast-talking salespeople selling cars, stereo equipment, and the like. Are they easier to tune out, to hate? Should the soft-sell approach represented by humor and music be preferred to the hard-sell fast talker?

Well, all the evidence is not in and the hierarchy situation is the key to determining the proper approach. A series of studies in psychology and advertising indicate that time-compressed or speeded-up radio and television commercials are more effective than normal-speed ones. Time-compressed commercials, which make speakers seem more enthusiastic and committed, produced about 40 percent more brand name and commercial recall, more attention, and more favorable reaction to the commercials.[6]

Since a service is now available for compressing commercials, this alternative must be added to all the others for the radio creative and communication decision maker.[7]

OUTDOOR[8]

The outdoor industry consists of some 270,000 billboards in nine thousand U.S. communities. All of these are off-premise, that is, the outdoor advertising discussed here does not include business signs. And part of the standardization of the industry includes a selection of well-traveled urban arterials for the location of the two main types of board: the poster panel and the painted bulletin. The poster panel is about 12′ by 25′ and accommodates printed sales messages provided by the advertiser. These are usually sold on a monthly basis. The painted bulletin is typically about 14′ by 48′ and is painted individually from designs supplied by the advertiser. It is normally sold on a long-term basis, such as a year at a time.

Exposure opportunity information for outdoor is collected by the Traffic Audit Bureau, which develops data on about one hundred thousand billboards a year.

Outdoor has special advantages as a *sustaining* and *complementary* part of an advertising program.

In its sustaining role, the medium can provide new exposures to the essential message idea before, during, or after insertions in other media have been made. Because outdoor provides a *dramatic presentation* in size and color that is unmatched by any other mass medium, the essential message of the campaign can be strengthened and extended by these additional exposures. Outdoor is complementary in that it provides a reach and frequency, brand and package identification, and access to certain market segments superior to those of other media.

Since travelers have little time to read billboards, the main format decisions are somewhat constrained. Recommendations range from four to eight words. The outdoor industry's own publications are a little more broad in terms of the appropriate number of words. One booklet says that ". . . outdoor design can be summed up in a pair of two-word sentences: Be brief. Be clear."

OTHER ADVERTISING ALTERNATIVES

Direct marketing is often thought of in terms of direct-mail or mail-order advertising. In reality it is done in nearly all media, and the format alternatives that were discussed for other media apply when a direct response is sought. There are clearly some differences in terms of how letters should be written, and so forth. These are touched upon in the following sections on selling, promotion, and publicity.

A number of other media are either similar in their implications to those covered earlier or to the communication elements discussed in the next chapter. These include transit advertising, specialty advertising, matchbook advertising, and so forth.

PRETESTING: DIMENSIONS AND DECISIONS[9]

Advertising research exists at three stages of campaign development. First there is the type of situation analysis research that was discussed in the "before marketing communication" chapters and also in the chapter on developing the message theme. This first stage of advertising research leads to the message format, the problem statement for creatives developing the message format. The review of experience and past communication research as well as creativity results in a series of alternatives for pretesting, the second stage of advertising research. The third stage is posttesting or evaluation, which is covered in Chapter 18.

In this section we concentrate on the dimensions and decisions necessary for developing and using pretesting methods for selection and scheduling of various parts of the campaign, primarily advertising.

Three Broad Pretesting Objectives-Types

If the objective is simply to "rough test" some communication concepts, the procedures involved in what we have termed "developmental" or "format pretesting" are relevant. This kind of pretesting is done early in format development sometimes at the request of creatives, to test headlines, songs, visuals, models.

If the information needs are more complex, then the objectives are more extensive, needing "selection" or "scheduling" pretesting, that is, pretesting to examine such questions as the following: Should a particular format or piece of material be run? Which of two or several formats should be run, in which media, and how repetitively? What are the effects of competing messages?

Once the format is implemented in a finished form and can be run in media, it is possible to do "limited posttesting," the third broad type of pretesting.

Three sets of dimensions are relevant in evaluating selection or scheduling pretesting procedures:

☐ Design, measurement, and sampling dimensions
☐ Creative (or stimulus) research dimensions
☐ Cost and payout dimensions

For each set of dimensions, campaign planners must make decisions based on the naturalness or the artificiality of the pretest research setting. A *completely natural test* would involve posttesting, or running a complete media communication campaign and observing market responses. A *completely artificial pretest* would be a developmental pretest, the kind conducted early in development. Obviously, if there were unlimited funds and time, the most natural type of test would be desirable. It would be totally valid and would provide much valuable information for long-range development. On the other hand, less-natural forms of pretesting are less expensive and have great short-term value because they allow for changes in campaigns before running them full scale with possible damage.

The three types of pretesting discussed can be arrayed on a dimension from natural to artificial:

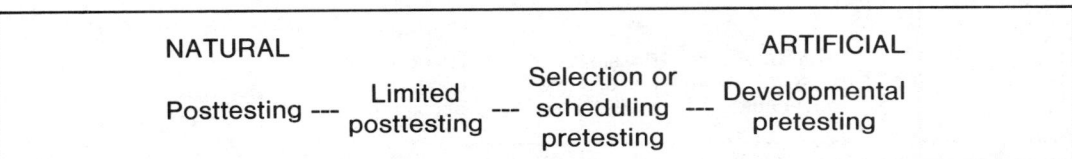

NATURAL			ARTIFICIAL
Posttesting ---	Limited posttesting	--- Selection or scheduling pretesting ---	Developmental pretesting

The selection/scheduling type of pretesting is near the middle of the natural-to-artificial dimension. This type of pretesting has the advantages of a relatively high degree of validity and precision which only a completely natural test can achieve, as well as the efficiency of the more artificial types of pretesting.

Design, Measurement, and Sampling Dimensions

The specific dimensions involved in design, measurement, and sampling considerations are arrayed on the natural to artificial scale in Figure 13-2.

Campaign planners must make decisions concerning research design: Should the research be conducted in the home, or in an artificial research facility? Measurement and sampling decisions must also be made: Should the measure be unobtrusive (i.e., totally natural)? Should repetition effects be taken into account? Should the sample be representative and random, or can an "accidental" sample be tolerated? Perhaps most important, Should the design and measurement plan be based on total experiment control (i.e., of temporal order in presentation of test stimuli)? or should the research be "one-shot," with no comparison or control possibility?

Creative (or Stimulus) Research Dimensions

A second set of dimensions involves decisions about what, specifically, subjects or respondents will respond to in the pretest. The pretest dimensions involved in subjects' responses to various types of test ads are arrayed on a natural to artificial scale in Figure 13-3.

Key decisions are whether individuals will view complete, finished ads or simply

```
NATURAL TESTING -------------- ARTIFICIAL PRETESTING
Design:
In home  --- Familiar quarters  --- Mobile unit  --- "Downtown"
or school
After-only measurement -------- Disguised measurement before
exposure  --------- Undisguised measurement before exposure

Measurement:
Natural unobtrusive  --- Coupon  --- Choice in test  --- Obtrusive
measure (behavior)               environment          measure

Repetition effect measured  ------------- One-shot measures
Lag effect measured ----------------- Immediate measure

Respondent alone  -- Self-administered with --- Interviewer makes
responds            interviewer supervision   responses

Sampling:
Individual or  --- Individual  --- Family group  --- Unusual group
family

Representative ---- Just random ---- Matched ---- Accidental
random sample                                     sample

Complete        Control of       Possibility of    No control or
experimental --- time of ------ correlational  --- comparison
control         observation      study             possibilty
```

Figure 13-2. Design, measurement, sampling dimensions

```
┌─────────────────────────────────────────────────────────┐
│  NATURAL TESTING – – – – – – – – – – – – ARTIFICIAL PRETESTING │
│  Stimuli:                                                 │
│  Campaigns  – – Representative ads  – – Ads  – – Idea with  – – Idea │
│                                                   explanation │
│  Finished – – – – – Rough – – Photo – – Art  – – – Storyboard – – Rough │
│  commercials    film      on film   skills               cuts │
│  Natural surround- – Program – Program – Other – – – – Surrounding │
│  ing material                      messages  material    │
│  (Magazine) – – – (Skeleton issue) – – – (Portfolio) – – – (Ads alone) │
│  Ordinary     On TV,      On TV,     Closed   Film into   Handy │
│  presenta-  – regular – – – special – – – circuit – – TV-like – – presen- │
│  tion         programs    programs             screen    tation │
└─────────────────────────────────────────────────────────┘
```

Figure 13-3. Creative (or stimulus) research dimensions

rough cuts or storyboards. Another important decision concerns whether people view test ads in isolation or in the context of other messages. If respondents simply view a test ad on a tear sheet, this is obviously more artificial than viewing the ad in the context of a dummy magazine. In the case of television messages, it is obviously more "natural" to view test ads via a television receiver rather than via a movie screen; and it is also more natural to include test messages in the context of programming and other messages than to show them in isolation.

Costs and Payout Dimensions

Finally, the campaign planner must make decisions based on costs, and on how quickly the results must "pay out." The pretest costs, time, and payout dimensions involved in planning media campaigns are shown on the natural-to-artificial scale in Figure 13-4.

Note that the most natural test would involve actually running the campaign for a sufficient time which would be very costly but provide long term information for developing future campaigns. The almost completely artificial developmental pretest costs little, takes little time, and does provide short-term information for the development of the present campaign.

Making Pretesting Decisions

There is no "ideal" pretest procedure, since the "technology" of pretesting is not very advanced, and since particular needs of campaign planners make it impossible for any single set of dimensions or any single procedure to be "ideal."

Moreover, time and money are often major determinants of what pretesting techniques will be employed, that is, which dimensions are crucial or less crucial. If there is limited time available for pretesting, it is impossible to measure lag effects of exposure to information campaigns. Limited funds preclude large, representative samples, and often force pretesting with "rough" or unfinished materials, rather than testing with finished messages.

At present the most popular type of pretest for television commercials is the limited posttesting type called day-after-recall. Examples are provided by Burke and Gallup-Robinson. Rough-cut or almost finished commercials are actually run on television in certain markets. Then telephone interviewing is done twenty-four hours after the exposure to measure mainly recall. A good commercial will garner 20 percent "proven" recall, although the standards and norms differ by product category. One commercial for Levi's, a futuristic corporate commercial that cost

```
┌─────────────────────────────────────────────────────┐
│  NATURAL - - - - - - - - - - - - - - - - - - - - - - - - - - - - ARTIFICIAL     │
│  High cost - - - - - - - - - - - - - - - - - - - - - - - - - - - Low cost       │
│  More time  - - - - - - - - - - - - - - - - - - - - - - - - Less time           │
│  Little short-term payout - - - - - - - - - - - More short-term payout          │
│  Much long-term payout - - - - - - - - - - - - Little long-term payout          │
└─────────────────────────────────────────────────────┘
```

Figure 13-4. Costs and payout dimensions

$250,000 to make, broke day-after-recall records with a 59 percent score.[10]

Despite its popularity, the day-after-recall method is heavily questioned in terms of reliability and validity. Used in concert with it is usually some form of theater or small-group testing in which respondents are carefully controlled as to exposure, which is usually in the context of a program and sometimes includes repetition. Examples are provided by Audience Studies Inc. (ASI), McCollum-Spielman, and ARS. Such "laboratory" television pretests allow deeper measurements, including attitude and intention (sometimes coupon-use action) as well as recall. The decision to use two of these pretest types (day-after-recall and laboratory) is usually based on the assumption that the natural exposure environment of the day-after-recall test is necessary to measure effectiveness adequately, while the laboratory test gives enough measures so that diagnosis can be done.

Similar considerations lead to pretesting forms for other types of advertising as well as for format alternatives in personal selling, sales promotion, and publicity–PR. Trends are toward a balancing of diagnostic and predictive uses of pretests. Measures are becoming more sophisticated, gauging cognitive reactions instead of just rote learning. And there is increasing realism in pretesting, including interactions between parts of the communication campaign by using such technological advances as split and two-way cable television and electronic checkout scanners.

There are actually more reasons now for including pretesting as part of the decision process for message format in the communication mix, although many format decisions are made without it.

When should pretests be done? Basically when the decision between alternatives is not clear. As was indicated in Chapter 11, research conducted by Gross indicates that more pretesting should be done in most situations.[11] Pretesting can improve ad effectiveness, ease decision maker's minds, settle organizational disputes, and help sell the format to the client. But if it is done for only cosmetic reasons, it should be avoided.[12]

SUMMARY: THE MESSAGE FORMAT DECISION PROCESS

In Part V (Chapters 11 through 13) the process of developing specific message format has been examined in terms of a procedure of four steps or stages. This procedure reflects an attempt to balance the power between the client campaign decision maker and the creative developing format.

This chapter focused on the third stage, developing specific alternatives, and the fourth stage, the pretesting or decision one.

A review of alternative formats in each of the advertising media indicated the variety possible and the many ways each component of the mix can contribute to the total goals of the campaign.

Various forms of pretesting can be used for nearly any communication format and situation. The job in selecting a pretest is one of balancing along the natural versus artificial continuum within certain cost constraints and short- and long-term goals. There is no ideal pretest, but some of the more popular ones for television format testing were discussed. Finally, the decisions about format can be made without pretesting in some cases, although pretesting is recommended as a check on both the client and the creative sides of format development.

ISSUES AND PROJECTS FOR DISCUSSION

1. Identify television commercials that fit the five types discussed in this chapter. Which of these do you feel is the most effective?

2. Rank the following media in terms of the advantage they afford for using color as opposed to black and white: television, newspapers, magazines, and outdoor. Explain your ranking.

3. It is relatively common practice to use the sound tracks from television commercials as radio commercials. Is this a good practice? Why or why not? How does the specific situation affect this?

4. What characteristics can affect the effectiveness of magazine advertising? How do product situations affect these relationships?

5. What are the opportunities and constraints in transferring a campaign from other media into outdoor?

6. When should pretesting be used?

7. What are the three types of advertising research, among which pretesting is only one? It is said that the more that is done effectively on earlier research, the less will be needed on later types. Why is this true?

8. In what sense might a record day-after-recall score be meaningless in terms of a commercial's effectiveness?

Notes

1. Milton Brown and others, "The Quaker Oats Company—Life Cereal," in *Problems in Marketing* (New York: McGraw-Hill, 1968), pp. 161–95; Larry Edwards, "How 'Mikey' Put Life into Life; Single TV Spot Now a Campaign," *Advertising Age,* March 8, 1976, p. 33; Dave Vadehra and Katey Cohen, "Outstanding TV Spots? How Northeast Views 'Em," *Advertising Age,* April 16, 1979, p. 50; and Peter H. Webb and Michael L. Ray, "Effects of TV Clutter," *Journal of Advertising Research,* 19 (June 1979), 7–12.

2. Examples in this section come mainly from "Creative Newspaper Ad Concepts 79," a newspaper insert published by the Times Publishing Company, St. Petersburg, Fla., 1979, and from Ann Sobczyaski, "Ad Creativity Goes Only So Far," *Advertising Age,* November 19, 1979, pp. S-30, S-32, and S-34.

3. Johanna Rock, "Starch Readership Scores: Which Ad Attracted More Readers?" *Advertising Age,* February 12, 1979, p. 61.

4. Dominique M. Hanssens and Barton A. Weitz, "The Effectiveness of Industrial Print Advertisements across Product Categories," Working Paper No. 73 (Center for Marketing Studies, University of California at Los Angeles, June 1979).

5. Ibid., pp. 28–29.

6. James MacLachlan, "What People Really Think of Fast Talkers," *Psychology Today,* 13 (November 1979), 112ff.

7. Jane Levere, "Compression Is Way to Beat the Television Time Squeeze," *Advertising Age,* July 23, 1979, p. S-30-1.

8. Institute of Outdoor Advertising, *The First Medium* (New York, 1975); Institute of Outdoor Advertising, *Outdoor Advertising Design* (New York, 1967); and Michael L. Ray, "The FTC Proposal and Outdoor Advertising" (Statement to the FTC hearings on a proposed nutritional advertising trade regulation ruling, 1976).

9. Michael L. Ray, "The Advertising Pretest as Part of a Multimeasure, Multimethod, Multisituation Validation and Application Research

System," in *Advances in Consumer Research,* ed. Mary Jane Schlinger (Ann Arbor, Mich.: Association for Consumer Research, 1975), II, 577–87; and Michael L. Ray, Scott Ward, and Jerome B. Reed, "Pretesting of Anti-Drug Abuse Education and Information Campaigns," in *Communication Research and Drug Education,* ed. Ronald E. Ostman (Beverly Hills, Calif.: Sage Publications, Inc., 1976), pp. 193–219.

10. Harry W. McMahan, "New $250,000 Levi's Commercial Scores All Time Burke High with Whopping 59," *Advertising Age,* October 31, 1977, p. 58.

11. Irwin Gross, "The Creative Aspects of Advertising," *Sloan Management Review,* Fall 1972, pp. 83–109.

12. Ray, "Advertising Pretest."

Format Implementation for Selling, Promotion, and Publicity–PR

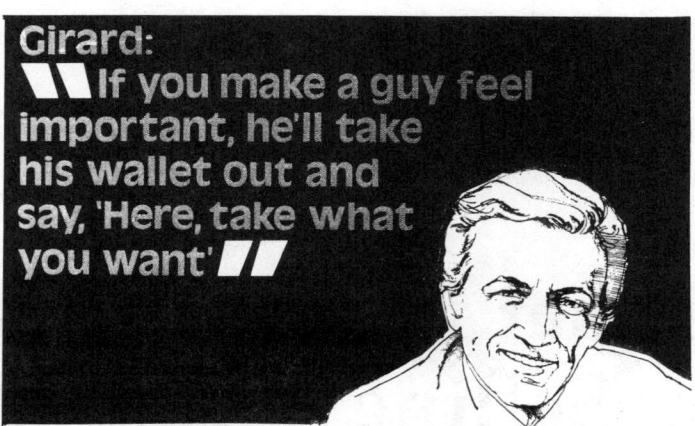

SELLING

(Courtesy of TWA Ambassador Magazine)

PUBLICITY–PR

(Courtesy of Geltzer & Company, Inc.)

SALES PROMOTION

Stri-Dex picked a popular teen fashion item, sport shorts, as premium offer to counter competitive inroads in the rapidly changing acne-remedy market.

Advertising and communication management is possible only because the same decisions must be made for all communication elements. Even though the preceding six chapters have concentrated on advertising, it should not be forgotten that the basic decisions about message idea and format apply also to personal selling, sales promotion, and publicity–PR. It is critical to the success of the campaign that there be full and coordinated development of the message inherent in every communication-mix element.

The message idea and questions of platform, positioning, and tone more obviously apply across all elements of the mix than do the format questions discussed in the preceding three chapters. Now, at the point of implementation, it is important that the communication campaign strategist consider message format issues as they apply specifically to components of the mix other than advertising.

The heart of creativity is in incongruous combinations that produce results beyond expectations. And the communication mix embodies these kinds of incongruities. Consider the disparities of the communication mix that can be put together with such power. While advertising is completely controlled, the message "units" for personal selling are living beings who present the actual format and are quite difficult to control. Every form of sales promotion provides a somewhat different opportunity to affect both short-term sales and long-term consumer franchise. Publicity and public relations combine characteristics of all of the other three mix elements. While they tend not to have the control of advertising, some parts of publicity–PR do not have the variability of personal selling and do present more long-term image potential than sales promotion.

Some of the drama inherent in the format decisions for these other mix elements can be sensed by the stories connected with each of the examples at the beginning of this chapter.

Joe Girard was listed in the *Guinness Book of World Records* as being the greatest salesman. In one year he sold 1,425 automobiles. In 1975 he collected $191,000 in commissions. In some sense, he is unusual as an example of format in personal selling. But it doesn't hurt to begin with one of the best. What did he do to be the number-one car and truck salesman in the world throughout the 1970s? First, he makes his prospects feel important. He sends out over thirteen thousand cards every month, just to let people know he is thinking of them. He offers cigarettes and drinks to parents and candy to children. He pays as much as $14,000 a year to customers who refer buying customers to him (at $25 apiece). He listens carefully to customers and claims to know when they are ready to buy. He knows his products so thoroughly that he does not have to look up features, and so forth. He makes a practice of never looking better in terms of dress or office than the customer does.[1] Yet there are many other alternatives to his approach to personal selling.

Stri-Dex medicated pads was one of the more mature brands in the acne-remedy field. The brand was growing faster than the category but was facing increasing competition. And it was dealing with the difficult teen-age segment. The purpose of the running shorts promotion illustrated earlier was to "increase sell-in volume, generate excitement and interest among our salesforce and the trade and get more shelffacings and displays." The sports shorts had the brand's advertising line "Come over to my pad," and the offer appeared to meet all of the promotion's objectives. The Stri-Dex promotion illustrated all the details of promotion implementation. This included minibooklets attached by elastic string to large-size packages and package inserts for small-size jars, shelf talkers with order form ads attached, and special trade allowances to encourage retailers to stock up. The promotion achieved a 40 percent greater volume in sales than the preceding year's spring promotion. And there was a record number of premium orders, even though twice as many proofs of purchase were required than for other Stri-Dex offers.[2]

Active was a nonadvertised detergent, which became the news slant for its exemplary publicity–PR campaign. Both consumers and consumerist groups were the targets. Feature stories appeared on women's, food, living, and business pages of daily and weekly newspapers throughout New England, the first market in the national rollout. Active hired a regional spokesperson, a home economist, who appeared on radio and television talk shows. She also spoke to women's, service, religious, and consumer organizations. At supermarkets she passed out coupons and spoke with consumers. And, without advertising, Active achieved 80 percent distribution in supermarkets in the first three months. The PR agency, Ries & Geltzer, claimed that more than 1.5 million New England consumers had been reached through the media.[3] Normally we think of public sector and industrial marketing as the main areas of PR application. But both Active and the new dairy product mentioned in Chapter 6 are examples of the powerful implementation of publicity in consumer marketing.

PERSONAL SELLING

The Problem

Personal selling provides the most direct route to the consumer with the quickest, most significant feedback. Salespeople should be able to determine whether they are getting through to the prospect and what can be done to help him or her as a consumer or industrial buyer.

That main advantage, the "personal" aspect of personal selling, is also its main disadvantage. Because personal selling is so personal, it is harder to control than other forms of marketing communication. This is particularly true in terms of message format which, in the case of personal selling, consists of a two-person communication situation that is always capable of changing depending on the people involved and all the many factors in the environment. Even if a salesperson is ordered to memorize a sales presentation, it is unlikely that those exact words will be used continually. The sales pitch will change to fit the prospect and the situation.

All the great salesmen and saleswomen do something beyond what their job description would dictate. Surely there was no manual that told Joe Girard to send out greeting cards, to have drinks and cigarettes and candy available for his prospects, and to do all the many little things he did to sell a record number of Chevrolets every year.

Every successful salesperson has the basics. Salespeople know and believe in their product. They feel the same way about their prospects. They believe in selling. They know the basic selling techniques, such as how to size up a consumer, how to meet objections, and how to close a sale.

There is something extra in an outstanding salesperson, however. Such salespeople are persistent. They will keep at it until they have found out how they can serve the potential buyer. They know that their job is to determine what it is that the consumer actually wants and needs. An example would be the following explanation of the secret of success of an outstanding real estate saleswoman:

> "Do you want to know June's secret?" Rich beams with pride. "She kills her clients with service! I mean it: she'll kill them with service, even after they purchased the home. For example, she'll see to it that their water is turned on. If it requires a deposit because it's been turned off by the previous owner, she'll make a deposit. She'll arrange to have the telephone installed. June will have a gift for the family which may be in the home before they move in. The first day in the home she'll cater a meal.
>
> "It's a privilege for a buyer to be fortunate enough to do business with her. A successful salesperson will provide so much service that the homeseeker will be ashamed to do business with anyone else."[4]

The problem is that not all salespeople can be motivated in this way. Perhaps more typical is the kind of lack of personal interest illustrated in the car-buying example in Figure 14-1. Instead of listening to the prospect and determining what he wanted, the people at the first car dealership made fools of themselves with deals that probably work for some prospects. Just think of the years of VW Beetle advertising that went into Barbara's deciding on a white convertible. Consider the promotions that heralded the end of that particular model. And see how message format at the personal-selling level ruined the sale for one dealer and made it easy for another dealer.

Examples of this kind of breakdown occur almost every day in retail stores. You see people come into a department store, interested in, say, home electronic equipment, and no one is there who is interested enough in the merchandise to help these potential customers. Thus the promise of a product is lost at the final stage.

The question this section seeks to answer, then, is not so much What are the alternatives for message format in personal selling? but rather, How can the campaign manager ensure that the message format will be close to the optimal one in all the many situations in which his or her product, service, idea, or candidate will be sold?

This question is discussed in successive approximations. First the campaign manager must decide on the general *type of selling* required. Then it is possible to determine the *type of salesperson* required. Selecting, training, and motivating the right salespeople are a large part of the battle in controlling selling format. Beyond that, however, it is important to consider *specific selling format alternatives* that salespeople might be encouraged to use.

Types of Selling

The decision on type of personal selling to use stems mainly from the earliest marketing decisions on distribution and whether a push or a pull strategy will be used for the product (see Chapters 1 and 6).

The longer the distribution channels, the greater the likelihood that less-intensive personal selling will be used. That is, the greater the number of wholesalers, retailers, and other types of middlemen, the greater the likelihood that the campaign will depend on advertising, sales promotion, and so forth, to "pull" the product through distribution. In these types of situations, it is more common for missionary-type salespeople to be used in working with the trade (e.g., when the sales forces of companies like General Foods, Lever, or P&G do the basic selling to the trade and prepare the way for advertising) and for clerks to be doing any selling that is necessary to consumers.

Short distribution channels are, by definition, those situations in which intensive selling is done. The shortest distribution channels are those in which the company has its own sales force to do all the selling. This is the most extreme push strategy.

Thus there are many types of selling, but they can be classified into intensive-sales

Sell Me a Car, Please!

A few weeks ago, we decided to buy Barbara a VW convertible. The 1972 Olds she was driving was a gas guzzler and fairly unreliable transportation. Anyway, we had talked about getting the car and Barbara's choice (with some prompting from our teenager-about-to-be-a-driver) was the white Beetle convertible. After checking with the credit union about a loan, making a guestimate of what I'd get for the Olds, and some quotes from brokers, I decided on a fair price. The only thing left to do was (1) find a dealer with a white convertible in stock, and (2) get him to agree to the price.

After several phone calls, the search narrowed down to two dealers. Both claimed they had a white convertible. At lunch I drove over to a local dealer. "I'd like to buy a VW convertible. I can tell you what I want on it and what I'm willing to pay. If you say yes, I'll give you the down payment now and deliver the balance tomorrow." With that, we went into the office for the negotiations. Remember, I had already told the salesman the conditions under which I'd buy. Evidently, he wasn't listening, didn't take me seriously, or thought my price was not acceptable—whatever. Out came the estimate sheet, the interest rate book, etc. "Frank, I can put you in that car for less than you're talking about. Let me have the keys to the Olds so my used car manager can give me an estimate." "Well, OK, Tom, but I really think I can do a lot better

selling the Olds myself. The price I want doesn't include any trade." After ten minutes of small talk, the used car manager re-appears and hands the estimate sheet to the salesman. "You know, Frank, the car has almost 80,000 miles on it and there's not much of a market for it. Besides the seats are dirty." (What the hell does he expect with a constant bombardment of muddy shoes, chocolate bars and wet swim suits.) Anyway, here's this salesman telling me what a piece of junk the Olds is and all I want to do is buy a car. But I'm beginning to enjoy the drama so I shut up. Besides, I can almost predict his next move. Right? Right. He goes to the payment book and says, "Frank, for $184.65 a month I can put you in the car." "That's great, Tom, but what's the price?" "Well, Frank, that's $5682." Suddenly, this guy is into the numbers game. And he's holding the calculator. "But, Tom, I told you that I'd pay $5982 without a trade. You're really giving me $300 for that bombed out Olds—$5982, yes or no?" For a moment, he's cornered. He excuses himself and goes to the office at the end of the hall. The door is closed. A few minutes later he comes back and says, "Frank, I've talked with the sales manager and we've worked it out. I can put you into that car for $168.50 a month" . . . and that's the way it went for the next 15 minutes—back and forth to the corner office.

Even though I'd already spent 30 enjoyable minutes with this guy I had to go. "Tom, I've really got to go." With that, he excuses himself again and disappears into the corner office. Only this time the sales mana-

ger comes out. I'm flattered. The full court press. This time we adjourn to another cubicle and the sales manager looks pensively at the estimate sheet —and starts playing "never give a sucker an even break" on the adding machine. Tape is spewing out the top and the tension is building . . . just like the $64,000 Question. Finally he says, "Think we can get those payments down to about $48 a week, and I'll upgrade the radio."

Shopping for a car can be fun. And, as I was driving back to the office, I kinda chuckled—it had been an enjoyable forty-five minute lunch. But I still hadn't bought the car and that was the purpose of the mission.

That night on the way home from work I stopped at Stevens Creek Volkswagen. "Hello, I'm Jack Mandel, may I help you?" "Yes, Jack, my name is Frank and I'd like to buy that white convertible." "Let's go in and sit down, Frank." "Tell me, Frank, what did you have in mind?" And Jack shut up and listened as I described the exact car I wanted, the options and the price. Jack wrote up an estimate sheet and my price and said, "As I understand it, Frank, if we can deliver this for $5982, you'll give me $1000 right now and the balance tomorrow. Is that correct?" "Yep." With that, he excused himself. In about three minutes he returned and said, "Fine— you can make the deposit out to Stevens Creek Volkswagen." I did. The whole transaction took about eight minutes. And Barbara picked up her new car the next day.

(Courtesy of Regis McKenna Inc.)

Figure 14-1. *Personal-selling breakdown and success*
Frank Burge, "Sell Me a Car, Please!" *Strategy 1* (Palo Alto, Calif.: Regis McKenna, May 1978), pp. 1–2.

closing, missionary, and clerk. Many companies use all three in the course of doing business, although some are really out of their direct control.

This is the point of decision making related to personal-selling format that provides greatest control to the campaign manager. In other words, the selection as to the type of selling to use determines, in a general sense, the limits of what the field sales force can do.

It does not ensure that they will do their jobs well or in line with total campaign format requirements, however. For this it is necessary to move to careful selection and training.

Types of Salespeople

Are great salespeople born or are they made? It is almost impossible to answer that question. But it is possible to identify characteristics that are appropriate for particular selling jobs.

There is some evidence, although it is not unequivocal, that different personality types are required for certain types of selling jobs and that salespeople tend to be more like the people they sell than the people they don't sell.

For instance, Howells studied four types of salesmen. His conclusions were that

☐ Technical representatives need closing and expository skills
☐ Van-based salesmen need just closing skills
☐ Retail salesmen need closing and "propagatory" (using emotional appeals and selling nonproduct benefits) skills
☐ Commodity salesmen require just propagatory skills

When Howells related these skills to personality variables, he concluded that sales positions requiring

☐ Closing seem related to high ego involvement or drive.
☐ Expository activities are best suited to those having an internal orientation.
☐ Propagatory activities seem to fit people with an external orientation.[5]

When these kinds of skill and personality characteristics findings are coupled with those on the similarity between salespeople and their sold prospects, it is possible to see how campaign and sales managers can achieve some assurance of format in personal selling just by hiring and training procedures. For instance, one study by Evans indicated (although later reanalyses questioned) that an insurance salesman's attitudes, personality, and demographics were more similar to the prospects he sold than to the prospects he did not sell.[6] And after an analysis of about twenty-two thousand insurance policies, Gadel found that agents' sales tended to be concentrated among persons who were in the same age group as themselves.[7]

A number of authors have pointed out that the findings of the studies reported here are sometimes equivocal.[8] This does not, however, mitigate the importance or the effectiveness of campaign and sales managers' attempts to find the right person for the selling job and the campaign format.

Selling Format Alternatives

The way a sales presentation is made and the way a salesperson interacts with the customer can undoubtedly affect the outcome in terms of sales and other campaign goals. A number of observers, most prominently Barton Weitz, have pointed out that each personal-selling interaction represents in some way the whole of campaign development.[9] A salesperson must analyze the customer, develop strategies, and carry out those strategies, often in the course of one communication interaction of the two-person type discussed in Chapter 1.

Campaign and sales managers can help salespeople in this difficult task by training and motivating them in directions that will make the job easier.

A number of studies have been done on the effects of the message in selling, and the findings seem to indicate that the specific situation is more important than anything else.

For instance, Swinyard and Ray found that verbally labeling a prospect for a Red Cross solicitation was a more effective technique than a straight sales pitch or one in which a small commitment was elicited. Their measure was intent to volunteer, and effects were even more prominent when interactions with later direct-mail advertising were considered.[10]

In a laboratory experiment "selling" a low-cost household item, Farley and Swinth found no significant difference between using product-related or personal messages.[11] Reizenstein showed that in one situation in selling drinking glasses, "soft sell" was more effective than "hard sell."[12] Two studies concerned with salesperson-prospect similarity found opposite results. Brock found that similarity was more important than expertise in selling paint.[13] Woodside and Davenport, on the other hand, found just the reverse—that expertise was more important than similarity in selling a technically complex product.[14] Once again, the "situation" is critical.

Such experiments provide some guidelines, but they do not deal with the extremely flexible situation the salesperson finds himself or herself in. Weitz has been particularly creative in applying the sort of perceptions-preference matrix discussed in Chapter 9 to the personal-selling situation. From the salesperson's viewpoint, the job is to determine the matrix of each prospect and then adjust strategies accordingly. Weitz gives this sales process the acronym ISTEA, which stands for the five main selling steps.

- [ ] *I*mpression formation
- [ ] *S*trategy formulation
- [ ] *T*ransmission
- [ ] *E*valuation
- [ ] *A*djustments

Weitz's research indicates that selling success is determined largely by the ability to accurately form impressions of consumers and formulate appropriate strategies.[15] The direction for sales management is to train salespeople not only in appropriate techniques but also in listening and formulating strategies in each individual selling situation.

Many of the campaign directions in this book have or should have led to directions for selling format. The Northwestern Mutual "Quiet Company" campaign quite naturally leads to a particular selling approach. The Spectra-Physics "Laser Man" yellow-colored cartoon approach to the construction industry led to its salesmen wearing yellow jackets to fit in with the strategy.

In addition, there are many selling gambits such as reducing the price of monthly payments, getting small successive commitments in the process of making the sale, an-

swering objections, and presenting the final close as a choice between two alternatives (for payment, for two colors, etc.) instead of a choice as to whether to buy or not.

Basically, however, the selling format decisions as to type of selling, salesperson, and format alternatives are rooted in tailoring the selling interaction to the needs, interests, perceptions, and preferences of individuals who happen to be consumers.

SALES PROMOTION

Sales promotion consists of nearly everything in the communication campaign that does not fall into the classifications of advertising, personal selling, and publicity–public relations. Included are sampling, couponing, consumer demonstrations, some consumer educational materials, price-off packs, premiums, specialty advertising, contests and sweepstakes, consumer refunds, trade allowances and incentives, trade shows, and point-of-purchase (POP) materials.

These types of sales promotion have been classified in previous chapters into those that are consumer franchise building (CFB) and those that are not. Basically the differences between these two types are in their ability to build the brand image in a long-term sense, to get across product attributes to consumers in a favorable way. It is important to realize, however, that this general CFB versus non–CFB classification does not hold up when specific alternatives are considered. For instance, in Chapter 1 premiums were categorized in the non–CFB class. Some alternatives examined later in this section, however, have promises of contributing to the brand's consumer franchise.

We have seen that the purpose of promotions tends more toward short-term sales and distribution stimulation. Sales promotion, in general, is more of a reaping than a sowing communication set of tools, to use some of the terminology of Chapter 6. Used judiciously, this set of tools can be used to perform critical short-term goals. But when it is overused, sales promotion cannot achieve long-term objectives and contributes to the weakening of a brand's position.

Specific alternative formats are critical not only for the above basic reasons but also because format must be distinctive enough to cut through the clutter in sales promotion—which if anything is worse than that in advertising! It has been estimated that well over 325 store coupons are distributed by manufacturers for every man, woman, and child in the United States each year. This would average more than 100 per month per family. Estimates indicate that the number is due to increase. And it does not even include all the other forms of sales promotion bombarding the consumer.[16]

Obviously there is a limit to the types of promotions that will stand out in the clutter. Only certain kinds of contests, premiums, coupon offers, and the like will cut through the clutter and at the same time contribute to promotion and overall campaign objectives.

This section identifies such sales promotion activities.

Sampling

Sampling puts the product, by some means, into the target consumer's hands so he or she can try it. This is done in a number of ways—direct mail, house-to-house placement, attached to a package of another brand, handed out in stores, or in print media.

When the product is outstanding and has features that cannot be transmitted through advertising (flavor, taste, unusual use characteristics, etc.), and when an adequate sample can be offered economically, there is probably no better single method of promotion—particularly for a new product. It is said that the best way to kill a bad product is a great advertising campaign. Everybody tries the product and determines that it does not live up to the promise of the advertising.

Contrariwise, the best way to introduce a truly fine new product is to conduct an outstanding sampling campaign. It is said that in the introduction of some Procter and Gamble products, over 90 percent of U.S. households were sampled by house-to-house delivery. This is the most expensive, but also the most efficient, method of sampling.

The sampling campaign should include educational materials with each sample and be coordinated with advertising. Swinyard and Ray suggest, on the basis of their study of advertising-selling interactions, that sampling should precede advertising and include some commitment.[17]

While sampling is the staple of new-product introductions, it can sometimes fit in with a particular campaign of an already established brand. A sampling ad for Gaines-burgers semi-moist dog food, stressed the economy of the brand versus canned dog food. The sampling plan appealed to the very market that currently used canned dog food, since six labels from any canned dog food could be used to get the free box of the semi-moist product. The commitment generated by such a plan would be considerable.

Sampling is not restricted to just grocery, drug, and cosmetics products. Makers of innovative home entertainment equipment must somehow get consumers into the store to actually hear, see, and try the product. Sometimes a free home trial is arranged. Museums and zoos will have free days. Orchestras give free concerts. Door-to-door vacuum cleaner salesmen give demonstrations that are like sampling. Of course, in automobile selling the standard was the trial ride, although more recently manufacturers have had agreements with rental companies—both for the extra advertising weight and (more importantly) to give consumers an adequate chance to have a thorough trial of their products. Note once again the important commitment that is generated by this sort of trial sampling.

Sampling is obviously considered to be a CFB activity, particularly if the product is good and if the message and commitment of the offers described here can be generated. Although it is sometimes said that samples, in addition to being expensive, are not as efficient as coupons in converting tryers to users, this probably is true only of sampling plans with little commitment on the part of the consumer.

Coupons Direct to the Consumer

In one sense, coupons are popular because they can achieve many of the goals of sampling but are much cheaper and require more commitment than the average sampling campaign.

Coupons too can be distributed in a variety of ways, and the method of distribution affects the format of the offer. Coupons can be sent by direct mail, delivered house to house, placed in a package of the same or of a different product, or inserted in print media.

Coupons are also a CFB type of activity, especially when they include a selling message. They produce short-term actions that can lead to long-term loyalty. They can get people to try the product, convert people to be regular users, increase the supply held by regular users (called "loading"), trade regular users up to larger sizes, and increase wholesaler-retailer stocking of the product at critical buying periods (called the "buy-in"). Obviously a well-timed coupon will prevent competitive inroads by causing present consumers to stock up.

The effect of coupons greatly depends on their form. For instance, a coupon in a package of the same product will attract primarily present users, while one in a related but more popular product will attract new tryers.

Certain basic decisions must be made about coupon format. For instance, where should the coupon be put? Normally it should be easily accessible in the lower right- or left-hand corner of the ad with dashed lines around it. Odd shapes or coupons that are hard to remove get less use. How large should

the coupon discount be? This depends on the face value of the market offering and the method of distribution.

How can coupon format make the offer stand out in the clutter of increasing couponing? There are several possibilities. Big offers get noticed, even though they have the economic problems mentioned earlier. It is important to tie the coupon to the basic message of the media campaign. For instance, P&G had a multiple coupon ad that featured, next to each coupon, a quick statement of each selling proposition, such as

☐ "You can't beat Crest for fighting cavities."
☐ "The Prells. For fresh, full-looking hair."
☐ "Secret. Strong enough for a man, but made for a woman."

Finally, the coupon promotion can be made in a dramatic way. When Foamy shaving cream introduced a new coconut fragrance, it was done with a print ad featuring Scratch 'n Sniff, which allowed readers to test the new fragrance right in the print ad. This was combined with POP displays on the promotion.

The disadvantages of coupons have to do with the clutter and their limited appeal. There are only certain segments that seem to use coupons. If coupons are not done properly, they can actually weaken a brand's image. To avoid this, they must be combined with a strong total campaign and format.

Consumer Demonstrations

Consumer demonstrations can be done in-store, for clubs, with corporate sponsorship, at consumer shows (e.g., outdoor, automobile, home, energy), or in classes or schools. Often there is the possibility of distributing samples. Since demonstrations offer the possibility of very strong product selling and image building, they are clearly consumer franchise-building activities. Sometimes they are included in personal selling or publicity–PR, but they are clearly part of sales promotion when their purpose is to demonstrate the product to a number of people without closing sales and with clear identification as to sponsor. Demonstrations have the problem of lack of targeting and relatively high cost but can be efficient when used as part of a coordinated program.

Consumer Educational Material

Consumer educational material would include cookbooks and recipe materials such as those sent out by companies like General Mills, teaching materials such as the comprehensive program developed by Procter and Gamble, recipe and service materials that are sometimes distributed through special company-controlled magazines, and materials distributed to people who can recommend the brand (such as doctors, pharmacists, auto mechanics, and home economists and their classes).

Obviously this sort of material can sometimes be almost directly connected to personal selling, as when the missionary salespeople called "detail men" distribute samples and literature to doctors and pharmacists. In other cases this sort of material relates to publicity and public relations. The P&G program mentioned above will be discussed more thoroughly in the publicity–PR section because its main intent is quite broad instead of concentrating on any particular product or brand sell.

There is the possibility of cutting through all kinds of clutter with consumer educational material, because in certain formats it allows the development of a separate "medium." If a program is developed for teaching oral hygiene in grade schools, for instance, the students will be dealing only with the sponsor's products and brands. There is no clutter, and there is a great deal of involvement. The same is true of educational materials in all sorts of industrial and public-sector situations.

Fan clubs and their magazines fit into this category. For instance, Mattel Toys developed Hot Wheels and Barbie clubs and associated regular magazines. This sort of promotion creates a separate market that can be sold through its medium on new toys as they are being introduced.

Educational materials can certainly stimulate trial and deepen loyalty and usage among present users. There is no doubt that this is consumer franchise-building activity. And because there is the possibility of creating a separate medium, there is little concern about attracting attention. In most situations a Learning hierarchy prevails. Format can be thorough with long copy, use of adequate sources, comparative tone, and so forth. There is a real chance to be of service to people.

Price-off and Bonus Packs

The price-off and the bonus packs category is the first category discussed here that is generally considered to be nonconsumer franchise building. The rest of the sales promotion categories are thought of in this way, even though format can sometimes add a CFB aspect.

There is no way to save price-off and bonus packs from the non–CFB designation, however. Special packaging materials are made up which give the offer. Or an extra product is attached in the bonus promotion.

Of course this sort of promotion can result in a sharp sales increase. This can help the sales force to load the trade, get in shelf talkers and special displays. Sometimes a price-off or bonus pack promotion can be a strategic competitive move, as when heavy price-off and bonuses are used to confuse a competitor's test market. On the consumer side, there is the possibility of loading consumers and passing on savings that might not get to them through trade allowances (although retailers sometimes rip apart bonus packs and sell the components separately at full price).

About all that can be said in terms of format is that the deal should be made clear and integrated with POP materials and trade selling effort. Also the price cut must be 15–20 percent for grocery brands; the smaller the brand's share (and, therefore, the loyalty to it) the bigger the price cut must be. These kinds of deals are truly non–CFB. They do not produce loyal users, since the people most likely to use them are those low in loyalty and in tendencies to loyalty.[18] Not only are these techniques unable to reverse share declines but the more they are used to the lack of CFB activities, the greater the decline is likely to be.

Premiums and Specialty Advertising

Although the premiums and specialty advertising category is clearly in the non–CFB range in general, there are possibilities for using premiums to get something across about the brand. It is when the premium has little to do with the product or the advertising theme that it becomes nothing more than a giveaway or reduced price. The key aspect in format is to choose a premium that fits the market offering and its message strategy, such as soup mugs for Campbell soup, western-theme wallets for Wells Fargo Bank, or special radiator caps with the name of the Prestone brand. Then the premium must be presented in such a way that both those consumers who participate in the promotion and those who just know about it will get a strong message about the brand.

There are two types of premiums. Some are *free* if the consumer buys and sends in enough proof-of-purchase labels, and so forth. The Stri-Dex running shorts promotion featured at the beginning of the chapter required four proofs of purchase of the medicated cream. The second type of premium is the *self-liquidating* kind in which consumers pay a reduced price for the premium. This results in no cost (self-liquidating) to the manufacturer

for the premium program. In most cases consumers are given the option of choosing either of the approaches to get the premium.

Although it is possible for premiums to do things on the consumer level, such as increase brand awareness and encourage sampling, the campaign manager should know that, on average, very low proportions of media audiences get involved enough to send for premiums. Seldom more than one percent of media circulation and an infinitesimal proportion of their audiences actually send for them.

Usually premiums are presented in the media and sent out by mail. But in some situations they are presented in-store or on the package.

Specialty advertising, such as that on pencils, cigarette lighters, calendars, and rulers, is obviously similar to premium promoting, since the consumer is offered a product with the market offering's name and message. The main difference is that the specialties are given to people with no proof of purchase required. An example would include a Hughes Air West specialty advertising program which went along with the "Top banana in the West" campaign illustrated in Chapter 8. The slogan and the airplane symbol were printed on celluloid buttons and bumper strips. These and balloons in the shape of the banana airplane were mailed to travel agents and employees, along with a free offer of an iron-on patch for T-shirts. At all Hughes reservation counters, customers received a metal lithographed tab with the Flying Banana insignia on it.[19]

Specialty advertising does not generate commitment or extra sales directly, and it certainly is not self-liquidating. But it can have a long life and provide many repeat, reminder exposures in the campaign. And it can fulfill specific campaign needs. For instance, one restaurant served only one special dish each evening. So many people called during the day to find out what the dish was going to be that evening that the restaurant decided to distribute a free calendar listing all the special dishes for the year. The bothersome telephone calls decreased and business increased markedly.[20]

Contests and Sweepstakes

Contests and sweepstakes promotions also fit into the non–CFB category in general but can, with the appropriate format, have a modicum of consumer franchise-building effect.

The normal purpose of sweepstakes is to develop awareness and reading of ads as well as building trade support for displays, and so forth. Since it is hard to set up a sweepstakes so that purchase of the product can legally be required, the normal short-term benefit of non–CFB promotions usually does not exist with sweepstakes. Only a limited segment of the population can be convinced to enter sweepstakes, even though they may have a more general effect on advertising readership. Clutter takes some of that benefit away, however. One examination of seventeen women's magazines showed that they had a total of more than twenty-one hundred different premium and sweepstakes offers during a year. This was more than ten such ads per issue. This does not include premium and sweepstakes offers that come through other types of magazines or media.[21]

Some contests that seem to relate well to the product and the theme include the Benson and Hedges "100's" contest in which a hundred of a variety of prizes could be won, Arm and Hammer baking soda's "1001 Uses" contest in which entrants named their favorite use and contended for one of 1,001 prizes, and Timex quartz watch sweepstakes in which entrants could rub clear the faces of watches in the ad which revealed parts of the advertising appeal good for prizes.

Some contests require actions such as answering questions about brand advertising, going into stores to special displays to find matching UPC (Universal Product Code—which is on supermarket packages) numbers,

and holding entries behind a clear green Palmolive bottle to get answers. These kinds of approaches promise some sales value from contests even though they are becoming increasingly difficult to use successfully.

Refunds and Trade Coupons

Consumer refunds involve a number of different ways, comparable to coupons, in which consumers can get money back on their purchases. Among the most well known refund schemes are the rebates that have been offered by automobile manufacturers. These refunds or rebates can stimulate business, but often not enough to cover their cost. Some sellers do not realize how much they lose through rebates. If they make $750 per car and the rebate is $250, sales will have to increase by 50 percent in order to cover the cost of the rebates. With a $500 rebate, sales will have to triple.

Since trade coupons are those in retailer ads for specific brands, they have all of the disadvantages of consumer coupons and almost no opportunity for the advantages, even though they can boost sales temporarily. They are usually found in cluttered newspaper ads, and there is almost no chance for a selling message. Again, this is a non–CFB sort of promotion.

Trade Promotions

Trade promotions would include per case or per unit allowances given to encourage stocking up of the brand, stocking of the brand at all (in the case of new products seeking distribution), off-shelf displays, and cooperation in connection with programs in other parts of the mix, such as contests or coupon programs. It is also possible to offer contests or other incentives to trade salespeople to get them to pay particular attention to a particular brand.

Even though these are non–CFB activities, they are essential for certain situations, such as when there is a need for trade support in introducing a new brand or in carrying out a particular promotional program. Some market offerings are highly seasonal in terms of sales pattern also, and this requires a trade promotion in order to ensure stocking and distribution at the critical seasonal period when competition is heavy.

Trade promotions offer little room for format alternatives, of course. Trade shows do have some leeway (see the next section on publicity–PR). The basic alternative in trade allowances is in terms of combinations with other types of promotion and communication. And even if the trade promotion is successful in getting POP displays in stores, they will face an increasingly cluttered situation. Louis Haugh estimates that it is not unusual for the typical supermarket to have more than one hundred displays from cut case to manufacturer spectacular at any one time.[27]

PUBLICITY AND PUBLIC RELATIONS

There are probably more forms of publicity and public relations than of any other type of marketing communication. We are more concerned with publicity here than with public relations, since the former deals more often with communication about particular market offerings—products, brands, services, candidates, and ideas.

The purpose of this class of tools is to use the media to spread the word about the product without actually running advertising that is clearly sponsored. Publicity and public relations should be used early in the campaign before selling, sales promotion, and advertising. Publicity and public relations are particularly effective when there is real news about the product. They can be used quite effectively even when budgets for the total communication campaign are quite small.

In most forms, publicity and PR have extra credibility as far as the consumer is concerned, because of the lack of obvious sponsorship. In other forms, the sponsorship is obvious, but the event or educational material is so involving as to make the sponsor's message compelling. With all forms, there is the problem of lack of control of the exact message or at least a need to be less than direct in actually selling a product.

Getting into the News

The major goal of most publicity work is to get into the news with stories about or related to the market offering. At least five general formats can be used to accomplish this: the press release, the exclusive feature, the feature release, the press conference, and the press kit.[23]

The *press release* is the staple of publicity. It should be used when there is real news about a product that can be stated in the form of a news story. It should be done so that it fits the needs of the print and the broadcast editors who can use the material. It is possible that some of the material will have to be changed for different markets and different media. For instance, in the industrial field it might be necessary to write different lead paragraphs of the release for each of the different types of trade publications that might be interested.

The *exclusive feature* is a story in broadcast news or an in-depth article that is in the print media. Usually this is done by extensive work and selling effort between the publicity people and, say, the editor of a trade publication. The exclusive feature does not have to be about something dramatically new and usually is not completely about the product or brand that is the focus of the communication campaign. Instead the feature can be about a concept, an industry trend, a fad, an event, how to do something, and so forth. The product or brand is simply featured as part of the article.

The *feature release* is a cross between the

preceding two formats. Like the press release, it is distributed widely without intensive consultation with editors. Like the exclusive feature, the editor has a complete story, which may not be about a new product but about a new use or trend. The article can be edited for print media and used as the basis for the start of a story or program in the broadcast media.

Press conferences have developed a clutter of their own. News people sometimes complain that they could spend a large proportion of their working hours attending this type of conference. With this type of clutter it is easy to see why press conferences should be used only sparingly in marketing communication. Something truly dramatic must be announced.

Press kits are used in connection with press conferences and along with some of the other forms of publicity–PR such as conferences, trade shows, and events. A press kit would include releases, in-depth stories, photographs, tapes and films, and case histories, and even product samples, complimentary passes, and the like.

The format for all five of these methods for getting the market offering in the news should definitely be a news format that fits the media. It is not wise to use superlatives or any of the strange language of advertising. The essence of creativity here is in solving the editorial or program people's problem of reaching the same people you are trying to reach with significant communication.

Getting into Entertainment

When a particular product is featured in a movie or a television program, it is usually as a result of some financial or other agreement between the producers and the marketers. Stars are shown flying on a particular airline, drinking a particular beer, driving a particular automobile, staying at a particular hotel, or eating a particular breakfast cereal. Sometimes the product or service

becomes the star or one of the stars of the program or movie (*The Love Bug, Plaza Suite, Solid Gold Cadillac, Corvette Summer*). In one case the Los Angeles Heart Association suggested scripts for "Sanford and Son" and other television programs in order to make some critical points about heart disease prevention to certain high-risk groups who would be most likely to get the message through one of their favorite television programs.

Like the exclusive feature, these entertainment program placements can be used in other parts of the communication campaign—by personal salespeople, in POP material, in advertising, as the basis for promotions, and even in press releases. But the campaign planner should be certain that the product will be used well and not be denigrated. And some entertainment features are better than others. For instance, research showed that one of the Heart Association programs was markedly better than others in getting across key information and in changing attitudes.

Events and Sponsorship

Examples of events and sponsorship would be the Virginia Slims (cigarettes) sports tournaments, the Macy's Thanksgiving Day parade, the Quaker 100 Natural Cereal running races, support for public television programs, and support for various local events. This is the first publicity activity discussed in which the sponsorship is made clear. Obviously with such events it is not possible to achieve anything of the credibility or endorsement value of the news or entertainment placements that seem to be unsponsored.

The value of events or sponsorship is in the awareness and favorable feeling that can be generated about the market offering doing the sponsoring.

Once again the campaign planner must be certain that positive awareness and image are generated about the market offering by the event or the sponsorship. An event that fits the message theme and can be integrated with other parts of the communication mix is best. The Kool cigarettes sponsorship of the Kool jazz festivals was a good example, while its sponsorship of the Newport Jazz Festival in 1980 was questionable, since "Newport" was the name of a directly competitive cigarette.

Appearing in Person; Speakers, Conferences, and Shows

Companies can provide speakers and can participate in various kinds of conferences and trade shows. Of course the sponsorship of any remarks or exhibits or show events is obvious. But there is a good chance to spread the word of the market offering to people who are already very interested, as evidenced by their attendance.

Educational Efforts

Once again, while educational types of publicity–PR efforts are usually clearly identified as to sponsor, they reach people who are already interested and have a real need for the information. The basic idea is that if people learn about a whole way of doing things with your product, they are more likely to use that product in the future.

There are a number of successful examples. Procter and Gamble, for instance, has an educational services division which prepares kits for students in such areas as laundering, home care, food preparation, and personal care.[24] Automobile dealers make their vehicles available for driver training programs. Active, the nonadvertised detergent brand featured at the beginning of this chapter, hired a home economist who made a number of speaking engagements. Computer markets will sponsor training programs. Several advertisers have sponsored national student competitions for the best advertising campaign for the product. It is hard to imagine much better commitment toward a product than that developed by going through all the research and decision making necessary to create an advertising and communication campaign.

Such educational efforts should concentrate on the education and not on selling. If the market offering is adequate, it will sell itself. The main job of the communication team in this instance is to develop materials that will actually contribute to education in an area they serve.

Controlled Media

Stemming partially from the educational efforts of many firms is a series of materials that are, in a sense, controlled media. These include various information books and booklets, pamphlets, manuals, inserts and enclosures in billing statements, newsletters, films, and tapes. Even annual reports can be used to transmit a product message to people who are naturally interested. Special telephone information lines can be called by people who want to hear jokes, sports scores, bedtime stories, health messages, weather reports, and so forth—along with mention of the sponsor.

Ortho Lawn and Garden products sponsored a seasonal and regional gardening book available in garden supply outlets. This led to a series of special gardening books developed for Ortho by Richard M. Ray. Hewlett-Packard, a large electronics firm, publishes its own technical journal; Apple Computer publishes a magazine for home computer hobbyists; and Big Boy restaurants publishes a comic book for children to read while they and their parents are waiting for their food.

These kinds of efforts have the possibility of reaching users and potential users in a very personal way. The main format concern is to keep the consumers' trust and present valuable information in an exciting and interesting way while at the same time including some product and brand-related information.

SUMMARY

Format implementation is quite different across the elements of the communication mix, even though the same basic decisions are made. It is the varying nature of personal selling, sales promotion, and publicity–PR that creates both problems and opportunities in implementation. The opportunities come when the different and incongruous aspects of communication elements are combined in powerful ways.

The main advantage of personal selling—the fact that it is personal and direct—is also its disadvantage in format terms. The problem is that it is simply not possible to control the format of sales pitches done by people in the same way that the format can be predetermined for advertising.

But managers do have three points of control of personal-selling format:

1. *Type of selling,* ranging from intensive sales closing to missionary to clerk, can be utilized.
2. *Type of salespersons* can be hired who are likely to present certain types of selling formats that are appropriate to the task at hand.
3. *Specific selling format alternatives* can be achieved, not so much by getting salespeople to memorize them, but actually more by training and motivation.

Sales promotion presents a greater opportunity for control of format than does personal selling. The main opportunity (and problem) with sales promotion is to select the correct tool for campaign purposes. Since the use of all sales promotion techniques is increasing, there is considerable clutter, and each sales promotion technique must be used with a great deal of flair and distinctiveness in order to cut through the noise and confusion.

The types of sales promotion format discussed could be placed roughly into two categories, depending on whether their effect is likely to be more long term (CFB) or short term (non–CFB). The following long-term types were discussed:

☐ Sampling
☐ Coupons direct to consumers
☐ Consumer demonstrations
☐ Consumer educational materials

The following short-term types were discussed:

☐ Price-off and bonus packs
☐ Premiums and specialty advertising
☐ Contests and sweepstakes
☐ Refunds and trade coupons
☐ Trade promotions

Note, however, that the specific format of each type of sales promotion is critical as to whether it will be successful or not. Premiums, for instance, although usually in the non–CFB range, can have long-term value if they fit the market offering and its message strategy.

There are probably more forms of publicity and public relations than of any other type of communication. Managers can choose or work with two general types (1) those that are not obviously sponsored and thus have the potential for extra credibility and long-term effect and (2) those that are obviously sponsored.

The format implications of the following types of publicity–PR were discussed: getting into the news (press releases, exclusive features, feature releases, press conferences, and press kits), getting into entertainment, events and sponsorship, appearing in person (speakers, conferences and shows), educational efforts, and controlled media.

ISSUES AND PROJECTS FOR DISCUSSION

1. How can campaign managers get some control over personal selling format? What alternatives in personal selling format are available to managers?

2. Think of a time when you tried to convince someone of something or tried to sell somebody something. Does Weitz's ISTEA description of the selling process fit your experience at all? In what ways does it fit and what ways doesn't it fit? Were you a good salesperson? Explain, using Weitz's model.

3. Which would be the best single sales promotion tool to

    a. Build a consumer franchise

    b. Attract new users

    c. Get distribution quickly

    d. Convert tryers into users

    e. Develop ad readership

4. Explain how format can make some sales promotion tools, normally thought to be non–CFB ones, into CFB activities.

5. Some publicity–PR activities work primarily because of their apparent nonsponsorship and others because of their involving nature. Which are which?

6. How can events differ in terms of their ability to build consumer franchise for the brand?

Notes

1. Robert L. Shook and Robert W. Shook, "The Sell Game," *TWA Ambassador Magazine,* January 1979, pp. 24–25; and Hubert K. Simon, *Classic Winners in the Marketplace* (Yonkers, N.Y.: Hubert K. Simon, 1976), pp. 8–9.

2. Edward Brutman, "Stri-Dex Pads Away with Record Response: Selling Teens Poses Special Challenges," *Advertising Age,* October 1, 1979, pp. S-2 and S-4.

3. Al Ries and Howard Geltzer, *Positioning in PR* (New York: Ries & Geltzer PR, no date), pp. 13–14.

4. Shook and Shook, "Sell Game," p. 28.

5. G. W. Howell, "The Successful Salesman: A Personality Analysis," *British Journal of Marketing,* 2 (Spring 1968), 13–23.

6. Franklin B. Evans, "Selling as a Dyadic Relationship," *American Behavioral Scientist,* 6 (May 1963), 76–79.

7. M. S. Gadel, "Concentration by Salesman on Congenial Prospects," *Journal of Marketing,* 28 (April 1964), 64–66.

8. Harry L. Davis and Alvin J. Silk, "Interaction and Influence Processes in Personal Selling," *Sloan Management Review,* 13 (Winter 1972), pp. 59–76; Orville C. Walker, "Current Directions in Sales Management Research" (Paper presented to the American Marketing Association Doctoral Consortium, Madison, Wis., August 2, 1979); Barton A. Weitz, "A Critical Review of Personal Selling Research: The Need for Contingency Approaches," in *Critical Issues in Sales Management Research,* ed. G. Albaum and G. A. Churchill, Jr. (Eugene: Division of Research, College of Business Administration, University of Oregon, 1979), pp. 76–126.

9. Walker, "Current Directions"; and Weitz, "Critical Review."

10. William R. Swinyard and Michael L. Ray, "Advertising-Selling Interactions," *Journal of Marketing Research,* 14 (November 1977), 509–17.

11. John U. Farley and R. L. Swinth, "Effects of Choice and Sales Messages on Customer-Salesman Interaction," *Journal of Applied Psychology,* 51 (April 1967), 107–10.

12. Richard C. Reizenstein, "A Dissonance Approach to Measuring the Effectiveness of Two Personal Selling Techniques through Decision Reversal" (Proceedings of the Fall Conference of American Marketing Association, 1971), pp. 176–80.

13. Timothy Brock, "Communicator-Recipient Similarity and Decision Change," *Journal of Personality and Social Psychology,* 49 (June 1965), 650–4.

14. Arch G. Woodside and J. William Davenport, "The Effect of Salesman Similarity and Ex-

pertise on Consumer Purchasing Behavior," *Journal of Marketing Research,* 11 (May 1974), 195–202.

15. Weitz, "Critical Review"; and Barton A. Weitz and Peter Wright, "The Salesperson as Marketing Strategist: The Relationship between Field Sales Performance and Insight about One's Customers," Report No. 78–120 (Cambridge, Mass.: Marketing Science Institute, December 1978).

16. Louis J. Haugh, "Promotion Hot Line: Cutting through the Nagging Clutter," *Advertising Age,* May 7, 1979, pp. S-14–15.

17. Swinyard and Ray, "Advertising-Selling Interactions."

18. Robert Blattberg, Thomas Buesing, Peter Peacock, and Subrata Sen, "A Loyalty Group Segmentation Model for Brand Purchasing Simulation," *Journal of Marketing Research,* 15 (August 1978), 369–77.

19. "24-karat Specialty Advertising" (Rolling Meadows, Ill.: Specialty Advertising Information Bureau, 1977), p. 21.

20. "The Case for Specialty Advertising" (Rolling Meadows, Ill.: Specialty Advertising Association International, 1977).

21. Louis J. Haugh, "A Crisis in Creativity: Promos Lose to Clutter," *Advertising Age,* September 17, 1979, p. 64.

22. Haugh, "Crisis in Creativity."

23. Will W. White III, "Techniques of Preparing and Placing Publicity," in *A Handbook for the Advertising Agency Account Executive* (Reading, Mass. Addison-Wesley, 1969), pp. 424–27.

24. "P&G Uses Pampers Story to Teach the Consumer about Marketing," *Advertising Age,* April 4, 1977, pp. 41, 42, and 44.

MESSAGE
DISTRIBUTION
AND MEDIA

. . . Advertising Media Planning

. . . Scheduling, Buying and Modeling Media

. . . Message Distribution Plans across The Mix

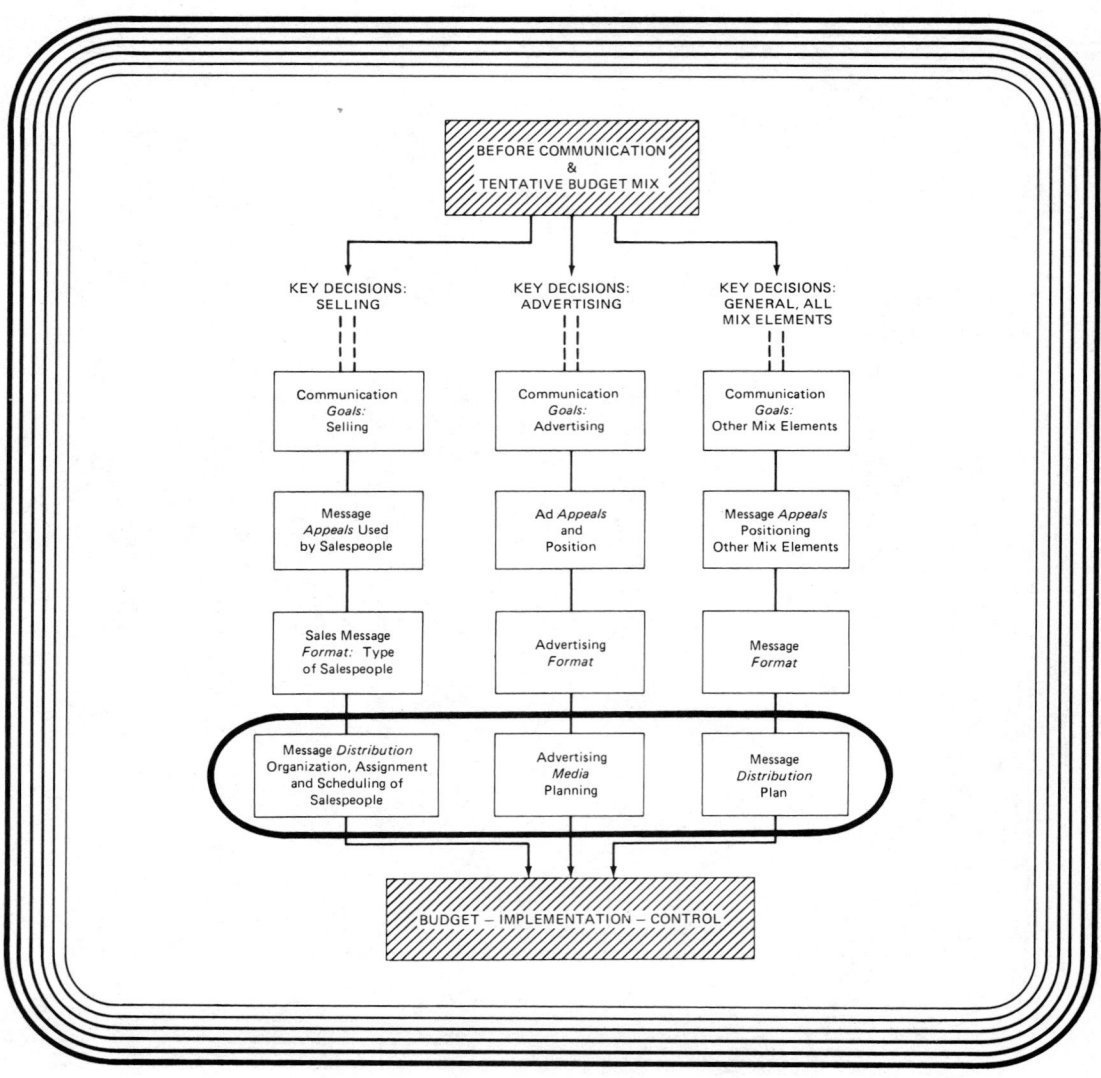

Advertising
Media Planning I

◁ *Problem:* The Shell Oil Company was continually having difficulty getting impact from its $13 million advertising budget. Shell sales seemed stagnant, and the company's advertising budget constituted only 0.1 percent of all advertising and 6.0 percent of all gasoline advertising.

▷ *Solution:* Shell put virtually all of its media advertising dollars into newspapers with the effect that it completely dominated that medium and moved into a new era of awareness and comprehension of the Shell advertising points. This dramatic move was converted into more conventional media budgets in subsequent years.[1]

◁ *Problem:* Z-Frank, a large Chicago Chevrolet dealer, was puzzled as to how it should spend its advertising money in radio. There was a plethora of radio stations available and practically no data to guide its choice.

▷ *Solution:* The company merely checked the radio-dialing buttons on cars that came into the dealership for service. Using the assumption that those stations that were preselected by the company's own customers would be excellent for its advertising, Z-Frank was able to substantially increase the efficiency of its media expenditures.[2]

◁ *Problem:* For a variety of reasons, Northwestern Mutual Life Insurance Company, Hunt's tomato sauce in the early days of its development, Hathaway shirts, Sunkist lemons, and Bell and Howell all faced the problem of getting attention against larger and more heavily advertising competitors.

▷ *Solution:* All of these advertisers made dramatic media purchases by scheduling their advertising in media that particularly fit their creative campaigns and allowed them to dominate. Northwestern Mutual Life put the bulk of its budget into the 1972 Olympics. Hunt Foods dominated matchbook advertising with recipes as its sole effort in the very early days of its existence. Hathaway Shirts, a very small New England shirtmaker in the beginning, put all of its budget into the *New Yorker* magazine. Sunkist Lemons moved similarily by putting all of its budget into the *Ladies' Home Journal.* Bell and Howell departed from the usual photographic magazine advertising distribution plan to sponsor "CBS Reports." All of these campaigns resulted in a successful change in the fortunes of the brands involved.[3]

The campaigns listed above owe their success not just to creative copy but primarily to creative planning in the message distribution or media area. The one characteristic that is common to all the examples above is the existence of scarce resources. The message distribution plan problem is always one of resource allocation under some constraint. Because of this, it is often looked at as a quantitative and economic problem as opposed to one that responds to creative moves and thorough understanding of the consumer in a qualitative sense.

The purpose of Part VI is to dispel this aura of mechanistic quantitative bias from the message distribution area. In this and the next chapter we will deal with advertising media planning and buying. It is an area that has to take into account the McLuhanesque idea that "the Medium is the Message." Consumers and buyers are exposed to the message and the medium as a unit. They do not differentiate between the two. Therefore it is necessary for media planners to understand everything that has gone on before in the development of the marketing-communication program. Then they can develop an excellent fit between the requirements of the creative messages and the medium and consumers for which those messages are intended. Of course, this task requires quantitative analysis, but it should be remembered that the media and message distribution decision is one that pulls the entire campaign together for a revision in the final budget allocation. As such, it is a task that requires full under-standing of the communication strategy and the consumers for which it is intended.

Perhaps one of the best introductions to this chapter was written by the *Advertising Age* columnist Herbert D. Maneloveg in a column entitled "The Two Media Departments."

■ Today, as media allocation becomes more precise, as the complexities of media selection become more of a science (a corny but true statement) major agencies find themselves having to look at media in at least two ways. One revolves around the planning function; the other concerns media purchasing. One diagnoses what to do. The other performs the surgery for buying.

As each broadens in scope, we have, in essence, two separate departments, each working separately, but still in close association with the other. Both call on the strong people within the department and we often end up working together in many of the daily searching media problems. Nevertheless, the pressures often lead us to make unilateral decisions and allow another group to carry them out. . . . But before the "buyer" can purchase a spot on KDKA or a one-half page in *Holiday,* he must be told by the "planner" that this is the proper medium for him to consider. . . .

■ For, the key element in the media department today is the planning group. These are the people who actually plot out the course of action from a well thought out set of marketing and copy objectives. They determine which mix of media do the best job in meeting those objectives. After consultation with the creative group, plus account and marketing personnel, the media planner sits down (either with a computer or a stubby, worn down pencil) and indicates that for these series of objectives and that desired reach and frequency level, and within this budget level, *this type of medium* best suits the purpose of the advertising campaign. Every resource in the media analysis section, the research and statistical department work towards guiding the planner in his final decision. And it is at this point that the general media pattern is established.

Because of a specific desire for long copy, perhaps magazines do a better job. Because of a need to concentrate against a certain consumer group (teen agers, for example) disc jockey radio might be the perfect effort. If a new product introduction aims specifically at young housewives for a new convenience grocery item, perhaps daily newspapers to introduce and daytime television abetted by supplements is the way to go. The planning group attempts to weigh all the various marketing and creative directions, and sets up the pattern for analysis of all feasible media. . . .

■ The principal aim of the media department is to get advertising messages to the right people, within the right environment, at the right time, with adequate frequency. It is, by no means, an easy job. There are many more media opportunities to consider today. And because of rising costs the job of targeting against the best group with that adequate frequency is a difficult one.[4]

Following Maneloveg's lead, this chapter will be devoted primarily to media planning; the next chapter, to buying. First in this chapter we discuss the general characteristics of media planning. Next we focus on the plan itself. Then we cover the intermedia and vehicle decisions. Once the media and vehicles are selected, it is necessary to determine how they will be scheduled, and scheduling is the first topic for discussion in Chapter 16. Then the issues of media buying and the requirements of media plans are discussed within a

media model framework. Chapter 17 deals with message distribution decisions for non-advertising parts of the marketing communication mix. Here we deal with just advertising.

THE NATURE OF MEDIA PLANNING

Media planning is very similar to creative planning with the exception that the media planner has one extra piece of information: the creative plan. Also, media planners usually have more information on the nature of alternatives. And planners tend to be working with combinations of entities that exist as opposed to developing new combinations.

Definitions and Decisions

In order to discuss the nature of media planning, it is necessary to make some very specific definitions, since there are many terms in the media area and they often get confused. An *advertising vehicle* is the specific entity into which you put your advertising. This might be a page in *Reader's Digest* or in *Industry Week,* a spot time on WGN, a "number 100" showing of billboards in Chicago, or a spot on the "ABC Wide World of Sports" broadcast. An *advertising medium* is a collection of vehicles. Examples would include magazines, newspapers, outdoor, television, and radio.

Given these definitions, three decisions must be made by the media planner:

1. Which media or medium will be used for the campaign?
2. Within each of those media, what general type of vehicle should be considered? For instance, if magazines are being considered, are we talking about the business press or consumer

magazines or farm publications? And if we are talking about consumer publications, should we be considering mass-circulation "books," newsweeklies, romance magazines, shelter books, women's service publications, or what? If television is part of the schedule, should the buyer be considering network versus local spots and then what kind of vehicles within those two categories? The same kind of decision as to general class of vehicle has to be made for all the media involved in a schedule.

3. How should the campaign be scheduled? That is, what time of the year should the messages be delivered? With what intensity and pattern? Should there be a fairly even campaign or is it necessary to saturate at particular times of the year?

The media plan, therefore, has to include a clear statement on all three of the issues—media, general type of vehicle, and scheduling. This plan provides direction to media buyers who must implement it. In addition, the plan will indicate the general cost of the campaign and the payout that is likely as a result of it. As such, the media plan leads directly to revision of the budget allocation. It is the end process of the objective and task or media-buildup approach to budgeting advertising and marketing communication in general.

Using the Situation Analysis

In developing a media plan, it is necessary to consider all the development that has gone on in marketing communication up to that point. Especially important is the situation analysis. Some managers feel that it is better to develop the media plan directly from the situation analysis rather than developing the creative strategy first. Although that sequence is not recommended in this book, we do not deny that media opportunities often lead to specific creative strategies rather than the other way around. In addition, the media planner should consider the

situation analysis in great detail in order to both develop and justify the plan.

In particular, it is important to consider the consumer market, the product and creative characteristics, and the promotional environment. With regard to the consumer market, the media planner should know the target segments to determine how they can be reached, with what necessary prestige, how often, when, and at what cost. With regard to the product and creative considerations, the media planner should know whether there is a need for demonstration, for color, for audiences' thorough consideration in detail, or whatever. With regard to the promotional environment, the media planner should know where competitors are advertising, how much money they are spending, and whether there seems to be some subsistence level of expenditure in the various media.

Consumer considerations are uppermost in importance, particularly for those planners who do not take the creative plan into detailed account. In some sense the media plan is simply an attempt to get to the right people, at the right time, with the right frequency. Since there are measurement services that provide information on readership and viewership of hundreds of media vehicles by consumer demographic, psychographic, and product usage categories, it is possible to target on segments with considerable accuracy.

Several of the creative media breakthroughs mentioned at the beginning of this chapter constituted outstanding work in consumer analysis use. Z-Frank used its own customers' radio-listening patterns to plan its radio schedule. Sunkist's choice of the *Ladies' Home Journal* was based on a psychographic analysis of various women's magazines. And the *New Yorker's* audience matched the market segment for Hathaway shirts.

Product and creative considerations sometimes dictate the medium and vehicle decisions with little room for argument. Media planners are given the word that an outstanding television campaign has been devel-

oped for a product "requiring" demonstration and that the plan "must" go in that direction. But a good media planner will resist overdirection of this type.

Chapter 13 indicated that such media as newspapers, radio, and outdoor are underemphasized by creative people. Virtually all the creative people in advertising today grew up with television. Most of them in consumer advertising work learned their trade in relation to television. And it is the most dramatic of the media for them. Added to this situation is the natural bias that large agencies have toward the extra income from television—no matter how much they guard against this bias.

To make a last check against all these sorts of bias toward a particular medium (sometimes it isn't television), vehicle, or plan, the campaign manager and media planner should consider the situation one more time from the perspective of the hierarchy situation analysis discussed in Chapter 7.

Those situations that are not the pure sort of low-involvement one force a consideration of media other than television. But even the pure low-involvement situation can use media other than television, such as outdoor and radio or magazines for certain target segments.

If involvement is high, the possibility for detailed reading of ads in the print media is possible. If there are true differences between products and these differences can be shown by dramatic illustrations, outdoor is a possibility as well as many forms of print. If sound is a key aspect of the product, as was true of Lanier dictating equipment and Baldwin pianos, then the media planner can take advantage of the low cost of radio. If the target segment is likely to get its information from print media, as in most industrial and large consumer durable situations, then print is a possibility. Newspapers can often provide a medium that delivers information seekers close to the point of decision. Products early in the life cycle can go several ways depend-

ing on their characteristics and the budget, but no one medium should be assumed automatically.

The *promotional environment* was crucial to all the outstanding creative media decisions highlighted at the beginning of this chapter. Creativity is coming up with new combinations, and it is by knowing the old combinations that media planners can come up with new creative ones that solve media and advertising problems. It is necessary to know not only how much money competitors are spending but, more importantly, what their plans are in terms of media, vehicles, and schedules.

Getting such information as competitive expenditure patterns is not easy in itself, although it has been helped considerably by use of the computer. It is because of the size of the task and the relative lack of assumptions that *competitive expenditure analysis* was one of the earliest advertising agency tasks to be done with the computer.

What the planner needs specifically is a breakdown of competitive expenditures by media, by season, and by market. At first it might appear that this would be readily available. But remember that in this competition it is not possible to just ask individual advertisers what they spend. Sometimes it is possible to get such information through the trade press, media representatives, and so forth. Normally, however, it is necessary to buy reports issued by a number of organizations which offer only estimates of expenditures for particular brands.

Some idea of the difficulty of getting good estimates is indicated by the nature of the reporting services themselves. *Broadcast Advertisers Reports,* for instance, provides estimates of expenditures in network television advertising. In order to do this, it continually tapes the audio portion of the New York transmission lines of three networks. At the time this book was being written, BAR was having some difficulty in working with CBS. But despite these sorts of problems, BAR provides expenditure data by parent company and brand, broken down by broad dayparts. The expenditures are estimates using the average costs by advertisers for each program each month. Thus estimates may be a little off from what each advertiser actually paid. When BAR develops its quarterly BAR-CUME report on network expenditures by local market, there are similar estimating problems. It monitors only a week each quarter and multiplies by 4.3 to get monthly data. It may be, of course, that a brand's activity during that one week is not representative of what was done during the month.

Similar estimating and data-gathering problems exist for other competitive expenditure sources such as BAR for Spot TV, *Radio Expenditure Reports, Publishers Information Bureau* (magazines), LNA (outdoor), and *Media Records* (newspapers).[5]

Planners should keep the limitations of the expenditure data in mind. It is worth the extra analysis to check and double-check the data in some situations. Some organizations have data banks and computer analysis packages that allow them to do this checking and provide quick expenditure reports. But for many it is a difficult manual task, sometimes depending too heavily on the LNA (Leading National Advertisers) summary report, which of course does not include newspaper and spot radio data. In the industrial field there was no regular expenditure service for business publications at the time this book was being written. In the public-sector field it is often difficult to determine exactly what one's competition is, much less develop a reliable expenditure analysis.

Despite all of these problems, competitive expenditures analysis offers good general direction for planners. Two broad approaches might be taken on the basis of competitive expenditures:

1. *Follow* competition on the basis that they are spending in the best pattern to reach the most important target market and that it will be possible to beat them at their own game.

2. *Diverge* from competitive spending to have impact in media they are not using.

For most advertisers, the first "follow" strategy is a senseless one. In the first place, campaign planners should know enough about the advertising situation and the market so that they do not have to use competitive expenditures as an indicator of where the market is. Second, there is substantial anecdotal and research evidence that one must be the market leader, have a compelling creative strategy, or simply have much more money to spend in order to succeed with a following strategy. In one regional beverage category, for instance, 94 percent of expenditures were in television, two-thirds of this in network.[6] One can imagine the difficulty of trying to outspend in this medium. If the brand is not the leader or does not have a tremendous creative strategy, there is no hope. And there is evidence that effectiveness can decrease with increasing expenditures in a medium.[7] This can occur, presumably, because each additional expenditure or insertion has the potential of exposing the brand to comparison and confusion with competing brands that are advertising more effectively and intensively in the medium.

Thus unless special conditions exist, it is probably best to diverge in some measure from the competitive expenditure pattern. Usually, however, there is a great deal of copying in media just as in the creative area. Take, for example, the competitive expenditure figures for soft drinks shown in Table 15-1. All competitors put over 60 percent of their expenditures in television. Coca-Cola dominated in this medium, in spot radio, in magazines, and in total. There was a real possibility that unless the creative work was outstanding (as may have been the case for Pepsi and 7-Up) or the TV buys unusual (as was the case for Dr Pepper, which sponsored specials appealing to the key subteen and teen market segments), all other competitors in the market might have been "buried" by Coca-Cola. Of course the dollar expenditures do

Table 15-1. Regular Soft Drink Competitive Advertising Year 1972 (In Thousands of Dollars)

Brand	Period	Total	% of Year	Network TV	Spot TV	Network Radio	Spot Radio	Magazines	Supps	Outdoor
Coca-Cola	1st Qtr.	$ 5,243.6	20.2	$1,696.7	$ 1,643.4	—	$1,591.2	$ 13.3	$ —	$ 299.0
	2nd Qtr.	7,186.1	27.8	2,261.3	2,407.9	—	2,121.9	78.6	—	316.4
	3rd Qtr.	7,238.6	28.0	2,093.9	2,014.3	—	2,363.0	399.0	—	368.4
	4th Qtr.	6,220.8	24.0	1,979.6	2,102.2	—	1,757.7	39.7	—	341.6
	Year	25,889.1	100.0	8,031.5	8,167.8	—	7,833.8	530.6	—	1,325.4
% of Total Media				31.0	31.5		30.3	2.1		5.1
Pepsi-Cola	1st Qtr.	3,873.9	18.5	491.6	2,191.0	—	982.4	11.8	—	197.1
	2nd Qtr.	6,165.7	29.5	502.8	3,493.3	—	1,915.2	23.6	—	230.8
	3rd Qtr.	6,892.0	32.9	1,264.2	3,690.7	—	1,733.2	51.2	—	152.7
	4th Qtr.	3,993.0	19.1	793.1	2,145.6	—	893.6	11.8	—	148.9
	Year	20,924.6	100.0	3,051.7	11,520.6	—	5,524.4	98.4	—	729.5
% of Total Media				14.5	55.2		26.4	.5		3.4
7-Up	1st Qtr.	3,341.9	23.6	1,185.5	1,723.2	—	186.3	2.0	—	244.9
	2nd Qtr.	3,889.5	27.5	619.5	2,068.4	—	514.8	—	—	686.8
	3rd Qtr.	4,468.1	31.6	827.0	2,567.5	—	485.3	—	—	588.2
	4th Qtr.	2,453.4	17.3	133.4	1,887.0	—	122.0	—	—	311.0
	Year	14,152.9	100.0	2,765.4	8,246.1	—	1,308.4	2.0	—	1,830.9
% of Total Media				19.6	58.3		9.2	—		12.9
Dr Pepper	1st Qtr.	614.8	10.8	—	392.6	—	140.4	18.6	—	63.2
	2nd Qtr.	2,215.6	39.2	661.8	867.8	—	626.1	30.4	—	29.5
	3rd Qtr.	1,769.0	31.3	345.4	736.9	—	606.6	49.1	—	31.0
	4th Qtr.	1,061.5	18.7	316.6	535.3	—	184.5	—	—	25.1
	Year	5,660.9	100.0	1,323.8	2,532.6	—	1,557.6	98.1	—	148.8
% of Total Media				23.3	44.4		27.3	2.0		3.0
Royal Crown	1st Qtr.	644.0	13.6	119.8	339.7	—	72.8	—	—	111.7
	2nd Qtr.	1,523.5	32.2	344.7	705.7	—	141.2	—	133.7	198.2
	3rd Qtr.	1,273.4	26.9	120.3	655.6	—	169.2	124.8	—	203.5
	4th Qtr.	1,297.8	27.3	436.0	473.9	49.0	128.4	—	—	210.5
	Year	4,738.7	100.0	1,020.8	2,174.9	49.0	511.6	124.8	133.7	723.9
% of Total Media				21.6	45.8	1.0	10.8	2.6	3.0	15.2

SOURCE: From Steven A. Greyser and Roger A. Strang, "Dr Pepper (B)," 9-576-140, Harvard Business School. Copyright © 1976 by the President and Fellows of Harvard College. Reproduced by permission.

not actually indicate the number of people reached in the target market segment. Frequency and impact are not indicated either. For instance, 7-Up, which at that point was using the Uncola campaign, probably was well advised to somewhat follow the cola brand expenditures, since it was the contrast that the "Uncola" brand was seeking. In a similar public-sector example, the effectiveness of anticigarette advertising was said to be heightened by the cigarette advertising itself on television. When the cigarette advertising was forced off broadcast media, the anticigarette forces lost not only the extra free exposure based on an equal-time ruling but also the bite of their anticigarette message without the contrast of the cigarette advertising right in the same medium.[8]

Both the anticigarette and the 7-Up situations were ones in which following the expenditures of the leaders or the product class made some sense from a creative standpoint. In most media-planning situations, however, the consumer, product, and creative considerations should be used wisely by media planners to diverge from what is being done by the competition.

Six Criteria for Judging Plans

The media planner uses specific aspects of the situation analysis and the marketing-communication plan to justify his or her plan on a number of criteria. Media plans can be considered to be good or bad depending on whether they meet the criteria of reach, frequency, continuity, flexibility, dominance, and mood.

Reach is defined as the number of audience members who have been exposed to the advertising at least once. One of the growing controversies in media planning is the definition of "exposed." That definition can range all the way from gross circulation and audience to exposure with some communication impact. The more the campaign and media plan are developed and evaluated on the basis

of impact, the better they tend to be. Media plans tend to be evaluated on the basis of a measure called *cost per thousand*. This is the dollar expenditure required to reach one thousand individuals. The reader should be careful to ask the questions, Cost per thousand who? Cost per thousand what? That is, most recent developments in media planning have been in the area of more precise definitions of reach within particular segments and on the basis of impact measures rather than gross circulation. Some media that have a tremendous audience may be very inefficient in "reaching target segments," or they may reach them with minimal impact. These are important considerations in developing and justifying a plan on the basis of reach.

Frequency is the average number of times an individual in the audience has been exposed to the campaign messages. The same types of considerations mentioned for reach apply to the question of frequency. That is, we should be concerned with frequency within particular segments and with particular impact. In justifying a media plan on the basis of frequency, the media planner has to be assuming some response function that relates the number of exposures to some effect measure. In some cases, it may be detrimental to reach people too often. In other cases, it may be impossible to reach people too often. In other words, it may take a great deal of frequency to get people past some inertial level. Frequency is therefore quite directly related to the issue of scheduling over time. In some cases, it may be necessary to use a jolt and fade campaign in order to build up enough frequency within particular time periods. Frequency is therefore not adequately described by just a single number that indicates the average number of times the average person in the segment has been exposed. The good media planner and media plan go beyond this gross statistic.

Continuity is defined as the extent to which the media plan keeps the product or service in the communication marketplace over the span of the campaign itself. The campaign should be allowed to build upon itself, and if it does not have continuity, this building cannot go on. The media planner should justify his or her plan on the basis that the schedule provides this kind of continuity.

Flexibility indicates the contingencies built into the campaign for changes that might be made as a result of competitive moves or consumer reaction to the early stages of the campaign or other environmental factors. An advertising campaign exists in a constantly changing environment. The media plan that is set up without allowing for contingencies or without recognizing that the environment may change is a bad plan. Some media provide more flexibility than others. For instance, the closing dates on newspapers, radio, and local television at certain times can be quite short. That is, it might be possible to move in and out of those media fairly quickly. Including contingency funds and media of this type allow a plan to have flexibility.

Dominance is the extent to which a plan would lead to your advertising's standing out against competition and the other advertising in each medium. Much has been said in this book of the clutter or noise that exists in the media. In this environment it is important that the media plan be justified on the basis of how well it will lead to the advertising's being distinctive. The assumption here is that only by perceptually standing out can the message get through to the consumer. One of the most consistent findings in the research on the current clutter situation is that there have been great increases in the extent to which people misidentify commercials and other advertising. That is, people will remember seeing an ad for a deodorant but will attribute it to the wrong company.

If everyone in an industry follows a typical pattern, then those advertisers spending the most money with the best creative campaigns are going to benefit from everybody else's advertising. Therefore the criterion of dominance is a particularly important one. For those advertisers with scarce resources, there is a need for great creativity and breaking with tradition in order to achieve dominance in the media plan.

Mood is the "medium is the message" characteristic of media plans. That is, mood is the extra effect the media bring to each exposure of the message. Much discussion of media plans has to do with the "qualitative value" of the media. Mood refers to this aspect of media exposure. It asks the question, If the same advertisement were exposed to equivalent groups of consumers but in different publications, what would be the differential effect of this exposure? It is assumed that differences in the media surroundings can produce differences in mood and therefore differences in effect. This type of qualitative value should be clearly differentiated from respondents' opinions of the media vehicles or the qualitative nature of the audiences of the vehicles. Media plans are justified in terms of mood when the planner discusses the particular fit of the creative message and product within the context of the vehicle itself. It is assumed, for instance, that women would react differently to a vaginal deodorant advertisement if it appeared in *Playboy* as opposed to *Ms.* as opposed to *Ladies' Home Journal* as opposed to *Time* as opposed to a TV program like "Soap," or "Three's Company." The critical difference is a difference in mood.

Earlier in this book we talked about creativity as the process of discovering new combinations for more efficiently solving problems. The reason the media-planning decision is a creative process is that it presents such an interesting problem. In order to develop the best media, general type of vehicle, and schedule, it is necessary to meet all of the criteria above in a situation with scarce resources. This is complicated by the fact that these criteria are in some respects reciprocal. For example, to the extent that one can achieve reach with a particular advertising budget, to that extent they will decrease frequency. Continuity is often achieved at the expense of frequency and flexibility. The media that one can dominate sometimes do not have the appropriate mood. It is the handling of all of these trade-offs that takes a great deal of creativity and represents the outstanding media plan.

THE PLAN ITSELF

Given that the media plan recommends media, general vehicles, and scheduling within the context of the situation analysis and with recognition of a series of important criteria, exactly what is required in terms of a plan statement?

Essentially a media plan statement or presentation puts forth in a convincing manner the nature of and rationale for expenditures allocation. Some people seem to think that a media plan is nothing more than a listing of the expenditures by media or a chart that shows insertions in the various media on a week-by-week basis. Others assume that it is books and books of data: competitive expenditures, reach of the various media by target segments, cost-per-thousand figures, frequency buildup charts, and so forth.

A good media plan is neither a single chart nor books of numbers nobody really sees. Instead it is an organized selling document for the people at the client organization who make the approval decisions. And it is a blueprint to be used by everyone in the agency, particularly the media buying group, to implement the plan in all its various forms.

A good media plan has six sections which are essential for all those working on the campaign:

1. Campaign needs
2. Media objectives and criteria
3. General recommendations—media, vehicles, and schedules
4. Rationale and alternatives
5. Specific spending and insertion plan
6. Contingency plans

Good plans can be organized in a variety of ways, but the six sections must be covered somewhere in the plan presentation. Usually the written plan statement also has an appendix with backup data. Perhaps such an appendix is inevitable, given the amount of data necessary in developing and supporting a plan. It is recommended, however, that critical data, charts, and tables, which will help people to understand and approve the plan, should be included within the plan document itself, not buried in an appendix. Only data that decision makers will actually use should be included in an appendix, if one seems necessary.

Campaign Needs

It might be said that this first section of the plan should include everything that has gone before in developing the campaign. This is both true and false. It is true in the sense that everything else should be represented in spirit. It is false in the sense that detailed marketing objectives, situation analysis, segmentation statements, budget details, communication goals, creative strategy, and message format discussions are *not* called for at this point. What is needed is a media plan statement of campaign needs that provides a context within which the plan can be considered. It is necessary to get to the "nut" of the problem for the media decision.

A typical mistake is to concentrate just on the target segment stated in a very sterile way. For instance, one media plan started with:

In order to define the current and potential purchase of———Beer, three demographic analyses have been prepared within the category of Regular Beers: . . .

The demographic profile for "Total Male Beer users" is determined to be:

☐ Men between the ages of 18 through 49
☐ County Sizes A and B
☐ Attended college/graduated college
☐ Employed full time
☐ Household income $15,000

The plan had no information or summary of marketing objective, lifelike information on target segment, creative strategy, or the like.

Sometimes there is a concentration on just marketing objectives, which again is not an adequate start for a media plan statement. Just stating a share objective is not enough.

One summarized statement of campaign needs that illustrates the kind of review needed in presenting a media plan is the following excerpt from a plan developed by Bob Reuschle of Henderson Advertising Agency for a reintroduction of Lux liquid detergent. Note that almost every sentence presents information that should lead to certain considerations in the next "media objectives" section. Note also that the market position and objectives of the product, the consumer, the competition, and the creative considerations are all touched upon. Of course there would be a bit more information on the nature of the consumer. But in the main, Reuschle presents the basis for action in media.

> *Discussion of marketing objectives*—The market situation clearly sets forth the challenge and requirements for the introduction of reformulated Lux Liquid. As a light duty liquid (LDL) detergent used primarily to wash dishes, Lux Liquid must restage its product and positioning more strongly in this highly competitive, but mature and declining category, where usage is shrinking rapidly due to growth of automatic dishwashing soaps.
>
> The restage of Lux Liquid with new package design, higher sudsing, and more pleasant aroma and an intrusive new creative approach to "convince" women that Lux is a superlatively mild dishwashing liquid, admittedly, *will not be the most startling and earthshaking news to the homemaker.*
>
> The Lux Liquid media budget (increased 25% to $4.5 million) remains fourth behind the brand leaders. With a relatively small share of category spending (15% of total), and at a rate only 75% of average spending for each of the three leading brands, *Lux Liquid may need more than one year to reach its 13 share goal.* If Lux Liquid is to achieve this

share, it must do so largely at the expense of the three leading brands (which account for 56% of total LDL volume and 62% of the non-Lux LDL volume).

> *Impressions must be concentrated* against selected user segments to achieve a realistic, but fair share of the noise level against key users. If a 45% increase in market share is to be achieved, the initial period of restage must receive very strong support, rather than generate a slow buildup of impressions over the year.[9]

Media Objectives and Criteria

Once the scene has been adequately set with the first section of the plan, it is important to lay out the objectives that must be met by the media program. Again, in the spirit of the media plan as a selling and organizing document, this section should allow everyone associated with the campaign to know how the planner sees the media requirements that come from the situation analysis.

The best statement of media objectives and criteria would be one that thoroughly touched upon all six of the criteria—reach, frequency, continuity, flexibility, dominance, and mood. Most media objectives statements deal with just reach and frequency, with only vague statements, if any, about the other criteria.

The following statement of media objectives and critera was prepared for a fictional new cigarette brand called Sputnik. The planner was G. Maxwell Ule, who was with the Kenyon and Eckhart advertising agency at the time. Ule uses the word "coverage" in a way that is synonymous with "reach." When he speaks of "gross rating points" or "rating points," he is referring to the total number of impressions, whether or not those impressions were against the same people or not. The term *gross rating points* simply means a multiplication of the reach number by the frequency number. In Ule's case it was felt that, in order to achieve a certain awareness and trial rate, the media program should reach 80 percent of U.S. households with an average of forty conscious advertising impressions. This translated to a goal of 3,200 (80 × 40) gross rating points. One should be careful in using the gross rating points idea, since it ignores *duplication* in which the same people are reached two or more times by different media or over the course of the campaign.

Nevertheless, the Ule statement of media objectives and criteria is an exemplary one. Note how he covered almost all of the six criteria in a coordinated way. This kind of statement, perhaps not in this exact form, is needed in all planning situations.

> To achieve our marketing sales objectives, we should attempt to reach 80 per cent of U.S. households with an average of 40 conscious advertising impressions per household reached during the introductory year. If we multiply our coverage objective (80 per cent) by our frequency objective, our communication objective for the first year should be equal nationally to delivering the equivalent of 3,200 rating points of conscious advertising impressions.
>
> a. The coverage goal will remain level throughout the year, since we must perform a three-fold process—com-municate to many people (80 per cent), build a brand awareness (un-aided) by the end of the year among this group, to produce enough trial buyers, who after typical customer loss will still produce regular customers equal to 8 per cent of all smokers.
>
> b. Frequency of impression will be intensified during the first 13 weeks of the introduction with an average of 16 conscious advertising impressions as the goal during this quarter. An average of 8 conscious advertising impressions per quarter against each household reached is our goal during the remaining 39 weeks.
>
> Each impression has the estimated net effect of creating an unaided brand awareness of 2 per cent among the households reached. Forty impressions will create 80 per cent awareness among the 80 per cent of U.S. households we reach. [See Figure 15-1.]

What requirements should media fill to meet marketing objectives and product demands?

MEDIA STRATEGY – SPUTNIK CIGARETTES
THEORETICAL GROWTH IN LEVEL OF PRODUCT AWARENESS

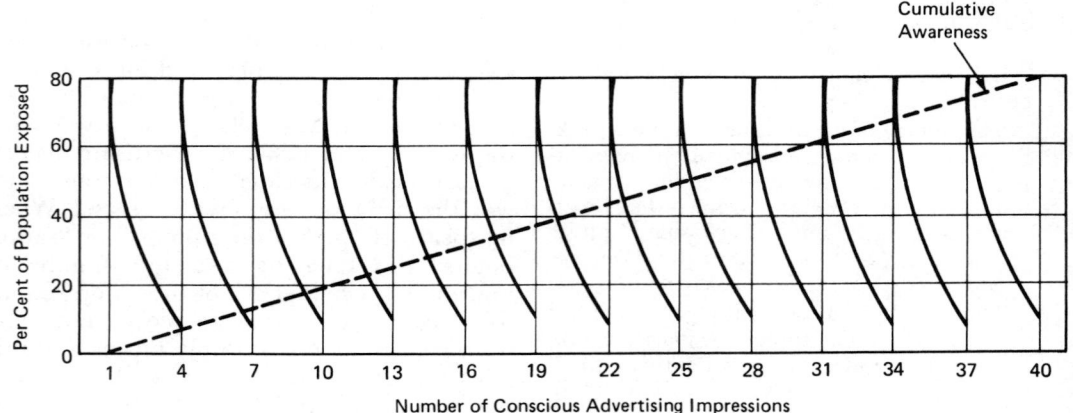

Figure 15-1. *Ule's "Chart 1"*

G. Maxwell Ule, "A Media Plan for 'Sputnik' Cigarettes" (New York: American Association of Advertising Agencies, November 20, 1957). Used with permission.

1. To provide broad coverage—to meet 80 per cent coverage goal.
2. To build balanced frequency of impression against the coverage area—to achieve desired level of awareness, as opposed to highly varied or uneven coverage.
3. To provide visualization—for product identification and maximum reinforcement of the product story or image desired.
4. To provide color—to reinforce package identification.
5. To emphasize metropolitan area coverage—to pinpoint best prospects for product.
6. To achieve an efficient cost-per-thousand conscious advertising impression.

Media should also be able to emphasize coverage and frequency against men who are by far our most numerous and best prospects. In most instances, however, those mass media which reach men and women in combination are as efficient as the selective media. These mass media can also be used selectively—for example, a network television Western will provide an extra bonus male audience but also deliver a sizable female audience.[10]

The General Program

It is possible at this point in the plan statement to indicate the nature of the media mix and schedule in a general way. The purpose is to give all concerned a set of recommendations for dealing with the problem in the context of the criteria.

The statement of the general program should be neither too detailed nor too general. It is too detailed when it includes pages of schedules, data or gross rating points, cost-per-thousand figures per insertion, and so forth—with no clear statement of how the recommendation relates to campaign needs and media objectives and criteria.

This statement can be too general when it just lists the media to be used. Lack of some statement of the general type of vehicle, an overview of scheduling, and a linkage with campaign needs and media criteria can destroy the ability of the plan to sell itself and organize the campaign effort.

The best compromise is a forceful statement that briefly states the recommendation in terms of the media, vehicles, and schedule. It usually helps to have a summary chart that shows the plan in a schematic form over the plan period. General budget allocation should be shown also.

The general plan recommendation is the heart of the media plan. Many people who are working on the campaign and therefore have an idea as to campaign needs and media criteria will turn directly to the recommendation before reading anything else. In some sense, then, a summary of the entire plan should be there for them to see. Because of this, the following example taken from a media plan for a "powdered tomato concentrate" introductory campaign is particularly apt. Note how the key chart lays out the entire recommendation almost in a glance.

Exhibit 1 shows how we have divided the $4 million appropriation by media.

The schedule for this appropriation is broken down in our planning into two periods:

☐ The national announcement period to be run in January and February 1960
☐ The sustaining period to run from March through the end of the year.

We would start our daytime network television at the outset of the announcement period. This would consist of a schedule of three daytime quarter hours per week in 125 markets. This would cost approximately $2,278,000.

Supplementary spot television will be added in 18 major markets with a frequency of 6 to 12 announcements per week to bolster the network television in areas of greatest sales potential. These larger multistation markets are also those where slightly lower than average network ratings can be expected.

Sunday supplements (or daily newspapers where supplements are not available) will be used during the initial two-month period with a schedule of one full page and three half pages in two colors.

A national weekly would also be used on the same schedule during this opening period and the sustaining campaigns in monthly women's magazines would start simultaneously, with one full page and one one-half page scheduled to carry announcement copy.

As you can see, during the national announcement, a very strong print advertising program has been provided in an effort to create excitement about the product in the maximum number of homes, to establish familiarity with the package, and to help induce sampling. This campaign will reach into areas where the regional adver-

tising may not have penetrated and will rekindle the interest on the part of both consumers and the trade in regions where the introduction of the product was completed months earlier. It will provide a second shot-in-the-arm, so to speak.

During the sustaining period, the objectives of the campaign will be limited to keeping the advantages of the product constantly in the minds of the housewives through media which will reach them efficiently and thus permit maximum frequency.

The network daytime television programs and the spot TV announcement schedules will be constant throughout and provide the basic advertising program. Supplements and the national general magazine would be dropped but the campaign in women's service publications will be continued with a one-half page insertion per month.

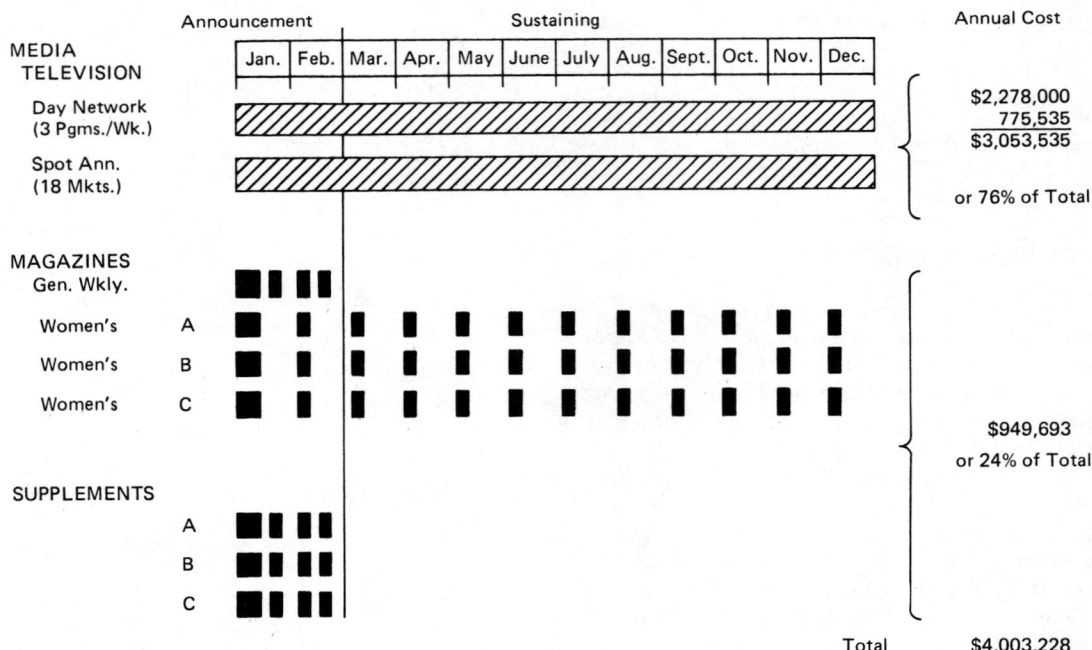

Exhibit 1. *Schedule of media plan—first year of national distribution*

Boyd and others, "Dorian Food Products," in *Cases in Advertising Management* (New York: McGraw Hill, 1964). Used with permission.

An effort will be made to distribute impressions in relation to market potential during this period. Television spots will provide the flexibility required for this purpose.

Following is our rationale on the choice of media for the national campaign.[11]

Rationale and Alternatives

The section involving the rationale and alternatives of the media plan is read carefully by those campaign managers who are doing their job of approval well. It is the section in which media planners present their reasoning for making the recommendations.

Once again, this section is sometimes overdone. It should not include all the work steps leading to the recommendation. If, for instance, media models are used to arrive at parts of the recommendation, it is sufficient to present the results of the model runs in terms of reasons supported by numbers. Overdoing it occurs when printouts of many of the model runs are exhibited in this section.

The arguments of this section should be two sided. No media plan is without faults. Pros and cons should be stated, and the reasons for recommending the particular alternative, even with its faults, should be supported with strong reasoning.

As part of this two-sided approach, there should be a clear statement of alternatives. If so, everyone involved in the campaign can make more informed judgments about the recommendations. For instance, in a media plan for an advertising campaign for the stage musical "The Wiz," there were two alternatives:

> One approach involved a four-week TV and radio campaign totalling about $70,-000, of which $47,000 would be spent in the first two weeks. The second approach called for a very intensive TV campaign costing $55,000 over about 2½ weeks.[12]

An adequate plan for "The Wiz" would first recommend one of the approaches and then present a rationale for it in contrast to the alternative rejected. Sometimes aspects of the rejected alternative can be held in reserve for contingencies.

Space limitations prevent the presentation of a complete "rational and alternatives" section. It should be organized by media recommended with rationale of vehicles and scheduling for each. Scheduling and the budget breakout usually require an additional section.

Some idea of what is required is indicated by the following excerpt from the powdered tomato concentrate media plan from which the general program recommendations were presented above. This excerpt is the rationale for the spot television part of the plan.

> The network programs meet the basic objectives of supplying a broad national base of advertising. However, as previously pointed out, extra weight in opportunity areas will be necessary in order to meet our objectives.
>
> Therefore, it is recommended that we buy an average of six television announcements per week in all of the 18 major markets except those on the West Coast. In this area, where TV ratings are generally lower than average, approximately 12 spots will be added. The markets selected are those where potential sales opportunity is greatest.
>
> Spot television has been selected for this localized advertising program for the following reasons:
>
> 1. A spot program, even at this relatively moderate frequency, will add considerably to the reach of the network schedule, bringing the coverage of homes in a four-week period from 40.7 to 53.8 per cent.
> 2. The flexibility of spot makes it possible to place this extra emphasis where it is most needed in the 18 key markets and on the West Coast.
> 3. It will permit us to obtain sufficient frequency when combined with the daytime programs to become a domi-

nant factor in the medium in these important areas.

4. Television offers the best method of implementing the creative strategy which at this stage will concentrate on various uses of the product and on ease of preparation, and consequently, spot television becomes a very effective local medium (see Exhibit 3).

It is also advisable to summarize the rationale and alternatives in the form of a chart that would list each medium, the types of vehicles, and the schedules for each alternative, accompanied by brief statements of rationale related to fulfillment of media objectives and criteria.

Specific Spending and Outcomes

This section involving the specific spending and outcomes of the media plan is for the hearty campaign worker who is interested in a truly detailed statement of expenditure recommendations and estimates of reach, frequency, and so forth. It is a section that allows media planners to present all the data that are behind the recommendations and rationale. This should not degenerate into an appendix or a repository for table after table of facts that were collected and developed on the way to the recommended plan. The media planner should never forget that the plan is both a selling and a guiding document. No section of it should get in the way of these purposes.

There is no doubt that substantial amounts of data can be developed. The author was visiting a very large marketer and asked if it would be possible to determine what it would cost to run a national campaign in local newspapers in the top two hundred markets. It was late morning when the request was made. The estimate and the schedule were ready after lunch. The computer data banks and analysis packages were such that reports of this kind can be spewed out quite quickly. If the media planner is not careful, the specific spending and outcomes section can become loaded with such data, seriously damaging the document's effectiveness.

Contingencies

The contingencies section of the plan is not always necessary. It represents both an attempt to meet the flexibility criterion and an attempt to show the need for budget alterations if certain conditions occur.

Any good plan is based on a set of assumptions as to what will happen in the future, particularly in response to the communication campaign. There should be flexibility in the plan as a way to be ready for any eventuality, such as unexpectedly higher or lower sales, an unusual competitive response, or a new media opportunity. Sometimes the alternatives from the preceding section can be contingency plans.

An example is offered in Ule's plan for the new cigarette brand. His use of a communication buildup approach indicated that a budget larger than that allocated by the client was required. In the final section of his

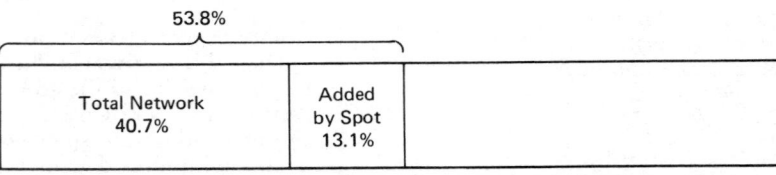

53.8%

| Total Network 40.7% | Added by Spot 13.1% | |

53.8 Per Cent of All Homes are Reached in a 4-Week Period

Exhibit 3. *Per cent of U.S. Homes Covered by TV*

Boyd and others, "Dorian Food Products," in *Cases in Advertising Management* (New York: McGraw-Hill, 1964). Used with permission.

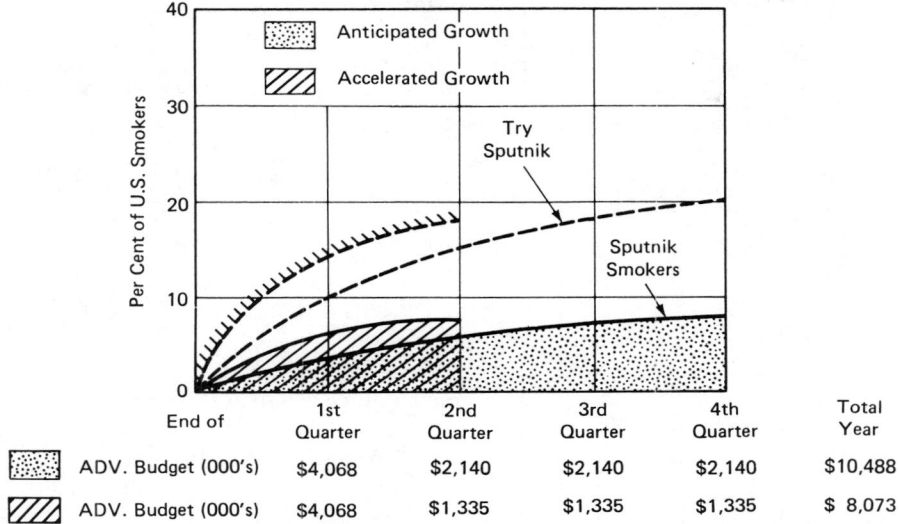

MEDIA STRATEGY – SPUTNIK CIGARETTES
ADVERTISING BUDGETS REQUIRED UNDER TWO ALTERNATIVE RATES OF SALES GROWTH

	1st Quarter	2nd Quarter	3rd Quarter	4th Quarter	Total Year
End of					
ADV. Budget (000's)	$4,068	$2,140	$2,140	$2,140	$10,488
ADV. Budget (000's)	$4,068	$1,335	$1,335	$1,335	$ 8,073

Figure 15-2. *One type of contingency plan*
Ule, "A Media Plan for 'Sputnik' Cigarettes." Used with permission.

plan statement, he shows how the budget might be reduced if results were actually better than expected. Figure 15-2 is a summary statement of Ule's contingency plan.

THE INTERMEDIA AND VEHICLE DECISIONS

The media plan includes all three critical choices—media, general vehicle type, and schedule—as well as some direction for buying. In this section we consider the more current information and approaches to making the first two decisions.

There are two broad ways that advertising media can be evaluated in order to make the decisions as to which media and which general types of vehicles will be included in the media plan. These two ways are the *qualitative* and the *quantitative*. The quantitative considerations all have to do with how effectively various media will deliver audiences for a particular advertising message. But before

the planner considers these quantitative aspects, he or she should pay careful attention to the more general qualitative aspects of media which are here related to the consumer and the creative strategy.

General Qualitative Considerations

Figure 15-3 has sample data from the *Media Cost Guide*. It indicates the media and, in some cases, vehicle alternatives available to the media planner in the consumer area. Another listing is available from the *Standard Rate and Data Service* books, which provide rates and data on consumer magazines, business magazines, farm publications, spot ratio, and spot television. These SRDS books are available in business and communication school libraries and advertising agencies.

The main impression one gets from looking at these listings of media and vehicles is that they differ not only with regard to their rates and audiences but also with regard to

III. COVERAGE AND COST DATA SELECTED DAILY PAPERS
(Top 50 Markets)

ADI Markets	Editions*	Circ. (000)	Metro H.H. Cov.	Line Rate
1. NEW YORK				
Daily News	M	1,555	23%	$12.60
Times	M	915	10	7.00
Post	E	654	10	6.15
2. LOS ANGELES				
Times	M	1,024	23	6.16
Herald Examiner	E	284	7	4.30
3. CHICAGO				
Tribune	A	790	26	6.56
Sun Times	M	657	24	5.80
4. PHILADELPHIA				
Inquirer/News	M/E	656	31	7.67
Bulletin	E	459	23	6.80
5. SAN FRANCISCO				
Chronicle/Examiner	M/E	666	29	5.49
Oakland Tribune	A	165	9	1.65
6. BOSTON				
Globe	A	492	24	4.18
Herald American	M	264	13	3.26
7. DETROIT				
News	E	631	38	5.26
Free Press	M	602	30	4.47
8. WASHINGTON D.C.				
Post	M	601	49	5.55
Star	E	346	30	3.65
9. CLEVELAND				
Plain Dealer	M	393	34	2.45
Press	E	301	31	2.35
10. DALLAS-FT. WORTH				
News	M	287	23	2.18
Times Herald	A	250	23	2.06
Star Telegram	M/E	241	23	1.70

I. DEFINITIONS
(Same as in the Magazine Section.)

II. CIRCULATION & RATES

	No. of Carrier Papers	Avg. Wkly. Circ. (000)	U.S. H.H. Cov.	One Time P4C Cost Mag. Size[3] (000)	One Time P4C Cost Digest Size[4] (000)	Eff. Date
FAMILY WEEKLY	355	12,350	16%	$ 59.9	$ 43.9	1/81
PARADE	129	21,644	28	106.3	75.4	10/80
SUNDAY	50	21,732	30	123.2	94.3	7/80
PARADE'S SMP[1]	165	38,790	51	218.0	161.6	10/80
NAT'L ROTO PLAN[2]	518	51,090	67	273.0	201.8	10/80

1. Includes Parade National, Sunday Waiver, L.A. Times, L.A. Herald, S.F. Examiner, Boston Herald and L.I. Newsday
2. PARADE'S SMP plus Family Weekly
3. 7″ x 10″ Magazine size = 3/5 in Sunday Magazines
4. 5″ x 7″ Digest size = 2/5 in Sunday Magazines

Source: The Various Publications.

III. SPOT RADIO

1. COST PER METRO RATING POINTS
(Top 100 Markets—Fall 1979)

ADI Markets	Cost Per Metro Rating Point* Men	Women	Teens
Top 10	$ 830	$ 735	$ 485
Top 20	1,140	930	725
Top 30	1,190	1,100	880
Top 40	1,580	1,275	1,005
Top 50	1,755	1,410	1,140
Top 60	1,835	1,470	1,200
Top 70	2,000	1,580	1,275
Top 80	2,060	1,690	1,345
Top 90	2,210	1,770	1,390
Top 100	2,255	1,835	1,470

*30 Second spots cost 20% less than 60's.

Note: Men and teen costs per point were based on schedules rotating through drive time (AM & PM) and evenings (7PM-MID) on weekdays and all time periods on weekends. Women costs per point were based on daytime (10AM-3PM) and PM drive schedules on weekdays and weekends.

Source: Editor's Estimates.

2. ONE & FOUR WEEK REACH FORMULA
(For well dispersed Spot Schedules)

One Wk. GRPS	AM&PM Drive 1 Wk.	AM&PM Drive 4 Wk.	PM Drive + Eve. 1 Wk.	PM Drive + Eve. 4 Wk.	Mon-Sun 6AM-12MID 1 Wk.	Mon-Sun 6AM-12MID 4 Wk.
50	26%	47%	25%	46%	28%	49%
100	37	63	36	62	41	65
150	45	69	43	68	50	71
200	50	72	48	71	55	74
250	53	75	51	72	58	76
300	56	76	54	74	61	78
350	57	78	56	75	64	80
400	58	79	57	76	65	80
450	59	80	58	77	66	81
500	60	81	58	78	67	82

Source: Editor's estimates.

Figure 15-3. *Selected sample data on media and vehicles available to the media planner.*

Source: *The Media Cost Guide*, *1st Quarter '81* (New York: The Media Book, 1981). All rights reserved. Used with permission.

II. CIRCULATION & RATES
(Selected Publications)

	Annual Issue Freq.	ABC Circ. 6/30/80 (000)	Rate Base (000)	Eff. Date	One Ti. Rate P4C	PB&W
AD FORUM	12	5[1]	NA	6/80	$2,500	$2,500
ADVOCATE	25	70	71	1/80	NA	1,080
AFTER DARK	12	54	62	1/80	2,100	1,400
AIR CALIF. MAG.	12	40[1]	50	1/80	2,325	1,750
AIR FORCE TIMES	52	107	NA	4/80	4,765	2,480
AIR NEW ENG. MAG.	6	25[1]	NA	1/80	1,030	770
AIR PROGRESS	12	150	NA	1/80	4,405	2,755
ALASKA	12	179	NA	1/80	2,880	1,973
ALL IN STYLE	10	1,200[1]	NA	1/80	19,200	14,405
AMERICANA	6	252	250	3/80	5,040	3,360
AMERICAN BABY	12	1,000[1]	1,000	7/80	21,710	15,700
AMERICAN BANKER	250	17[2]	NA	1/80	3,282	2,782
AMERICAN FILM	10	102	NA	4/80	2,350	1,595
AMERICAN LEGION	12	2,592	2,500	1/81	15,036	10,369
AMER. PHOTOGRAPHER	12	203	200	10/80	5,550	3,700
AMERICAN WAY	12	NA	250	1/81	8,590	6,960
AOPA PILOT	12	250	NA	1/80	6,365	3,960
APARTMENT LIFE	12	819	800	1/81	14,930	10,405
ARCHITECTURAL DIG.	12	483	500	1/81	14,260	9,505
ARMY TIMES	52	136	NA	4/80	4,515	2,230

III. SPOT TV
1. AVERAGE RATINGS BY DAY PART
(Top 100 Markets)

	4th Qtr. 1980	1st Qtr. 1981	2nd Qtr. 1981	3rd Qtr. 1981
a) PRIME TIME (Mon-Sun 8-11 PM)				
TV Homes	18.5%	19.0%	14.5%	12.0%
Men (18+)	12.0	13.0	9.0	8.0
Women (18+)	13.5	14.5	10.5	9.5
Teens (12-17)	11.0	12.0	9.5	8.0
Children (2-11)	10.0	11.0	9.5	6.5
b) DAYTIME (M-F 10AM-4:30PM)				
TV Homes	5.5%	6.0%	5.0%	5.5%
Women (18+)	4.5	5.0	4.0	4.5

IV. ESTIMATED OUTDOOR POSTER COSTS FOR TOP 300* METRO AREAS

Metro Market	Population (000)	#50 Showing Cost Per Month	#100 Showing Cost Per Month
Rank 1- 10	51,536	$ 382,199	$ 696,868
Rank 1- 20	70,520	555,222	1,034,176
Rank 1- 30	85,592	679,162	1,275,965
Rank 1- 40	95,227	762,167	1,436,909
Rank 1- 50	103,783	840,827	1,585,905
Rank 1- 60	108,862	895,871	1,686,471
Rank 1- 70	114,858	953,736	1,792,328
Rank 1- 80	119,557	993,981	1,869,769
Rank 1- 90	123,150	1,026,417	1,930,403
Rank 1-100	127,260	1,061,370	1,993,028
Rank 1-150	141,548	1,215,829	2,260,159
Rank 1-200	150,635	1,327,526	2,449,188
Rank 1-300	161,099	1,469,194	2,679,994

Source: Institute of Outdoor Advertising/Out-Of-Home Media Services, January 1980.
*Hawaii and Alaska excluded.

Figure 15-3. (continued)

II. NETWORK TV
A. AVERAGE RATING AND COST ESTIMATES
(Regularly Scheduled Programs)

	4th Qtr. 1980	1st Qtr. 1981	2nd Qtr. 1981	3rd Qtr. 1981
1. PRIME TIME (Mon-Sun 8-11 PM)				
a) Average Ratings				
TV Homes	19.0%	20.0%	15.5%	13.0%
Men (18+)	12.5	13.0	10.0	9.0
Women (18+)	14.0	15.0	11.0	10.0
Teens (12-17)	11.5	12.5	10.0	9.0
Children (2-11)	10.5	11.5	10.0	7.0
b) Cost per "30" ($000)	79.0	72.5	75.0	60.0
c) Cost per TV Home Rtg. Pt.	$4,158	$3,625	$4,839	$4,615
2. DAYTIME (M-F 10AM-4:30PM)				
a) Average Ratings				
TV Homes	6.5%	7.5%	6.0%	6.5%
Women (18+)	5.5	6.5	4.5	5.0
b) Cost per "30" ($000)	11.5	10.5	11.0	10.0
c) Cost Per TV Home Rtg. Pt.	$1,769	$1,387	$1,467	$1,538

their mood or qualitative characteristics. Some media are appropriate for doing certain things in terms of creative strategy and others are not. Some media seem to be more appropriate for introducing particular types of new products and others are not. Some fit particular hierarchy situations (Chapter 7) better. All of these aspects relate to qualitative considerations the media planner must make before getting into detailed coverage and frequency data.

As has already been mentioned, one way of looking at the "quality" of media is to consider the quality of the audience itself. Some media, for instance, such as television, tend to reach a lower-income, lower-socioeconomic class than other media such as magazines, particularly special-interest ones. Therefore, if the advertiser has a very well defined and small market segment, it might be extremely wasteful to go into the mass-circulation type of media such as television.

A second aspect of media quality has to do with the physical characteristics of the media. These relate to a number of creative possibilities for advertising. For instance, television allows demonstration. Magazines allow full quality reproduction as well as an in-depth message—i.e., long copy. Newspapers are published daily and may convey immediacy. Outdoor billboards are limited to short reminder messages that have the potential of building up a great deal of frequency. General vehicles within these media types also differ as to their physical characteristics and potential for advertising effect. For instance, broadcast soap operas usually have a continuing audience, which allows advertisers to establish frequency among a small proportion of the market.

A third aspect of media quality relates more directly to what was talked about above as mood. Here we are concerned with the interaction between the consumer and the physical characteristics of the medium itself. The question is, How likely is it that this particular medium or general type of vehicle will give an extra added effect to our messages?

The more basic issue is the way in which consumers interact with each of the media and general vehicle types. In this regard, there seems to be a continuum of media from those that are used with great purpose and activity on the part of the consumer to those that thrust themselves upon the consumer and are used primarily for entertainment. Probably the best representative of those media that are "used" by their audiences is business magazines. At the other end of the continuum, where the media or vehicle is more or less doing all the work for the consumer, is television, particularly the entertainment TV vehicle.

Obviously the continuum from business publications to television entertainment vehicles is primarily a hypothetical one that differs from situation to situation and from vehicle to vehicle. The decision as to media and vehicles on a qualitative basis should be made with cooperation between the media planner, the creative staff, and the line management concerned with the marketing-communication campaign. These people should be assisted by research evidence whenever available. Within vehicle classes, for instance, there are subtle differences in the extent to which consumers will be attuned to sophisticated information processing with regard to advertising.

In the business publication class, for instance, some publications are read for other than pure business, functional, or utilitarian purposes. And in the medical area, for instance, publications range from the *Journal of the American Medical Association* to *Medical Economics,* which emphasizes the business aspects of medical practice and has been the medical publication with the greatest readership, to some medical publications that discuss travel and entertainment for doctors. As we move across these three publication types, it is likely that doctors' involvement with pharmaceutical advertising will become less and less pronounced. On the other hand, management and creative staff may believe that pharmaceutical advertising in these less professionally oriented publications would be more effective, primarily because of the contrast or surprise value, which may lead to a low-involvement information-processing effect. Also, since the entertainment publications contain less competitive pharmaceutical advertising, any advertiser's pharmaceutical ads are more likely to stand out and be more effective.

The same kind of qualitative analysis can be done for different types of magazines, radio programming, and television programming. While we assume that television is a low-involvement medium, there may be some programming that will generate an audience response of higher-involvement information processing. Thus a special that is a "National Health Test" may be a particularly apt vehicle for a health insurance company.

Although the media provide some research evidence on the qualitative considerations, there is a need for media planners and other people involved in the campaign decision to use judgment in this area. They should examine the publications and view the television programs and other vehicles with some care. In many cases, the high level of judgment needed in making such decisions is disturbing to media planners and to management. However, it should be recognized that some assumption about the qualitative effects of the media is always being made in the process of recommending particular media and general types of vehicles for media schedules. And the exciting creative breakthroughs that are made in media planning tend to be those that recognize the distinct qualitative contribution that can be made by the media when used in combinations.

Quantitative Audience Considerations

It has been said that the comparisons that need to be made between media and also between general vehicle classes are like the comparisons that might be made between apples and oranges. That is, primarily because of qualitative considerations, it is hard to make a comparison between an exposure to a thirty-second television commercial and an exposure to a full-page, four-color bleed page (pictures and visuals that run all the way to the edge of the page without border) in *Time Magazine*. For many years advertising people struggled with this apples-and-oranges problem. Then the Audience Concepts Committee of the Advertising Research Foundation published a booklet entitled *Toward Better Media Comparisons*. The chart depicting the guide this committee developed for evaluating media is shown in Figure 15-4. The following is a report on the current state of data available for evaluating media at each stage of the ARF model.

As can be seen from the chart in Figure 15-4, the ARF committee posited something like a Learning hierarchy of levels of response to media. It suggested six stages in the effect of media on the advertising message: vehicle distribution, vehicle exposure, advertising exposure, advertising perception, advertising communication, and sales response. It should be noted, however, that the hierarchies discussed in Chapter 7 are most likely to be occurring at the fifth, or advertising communication, level in the chart. It is logically unlikely that there would be the sort of reversals among the stages of the ARF model that were suggested for the stages of the marketing-communication hierarchies.

The chart itself depicts the progress of the media effect from vehicle distribution to sales response. As you move from left to right on the chart, there is an increasing progression toward purchase or sales response. The heavy horizontal line divides audience members who are prospects from those audience members who are nonprospects. The multiple columns that are represented for the vehicle exposure, advertising exposure, and advertising perception stages are meant to indicate the proportions of the audience receiving that level of effect with various frequencies.

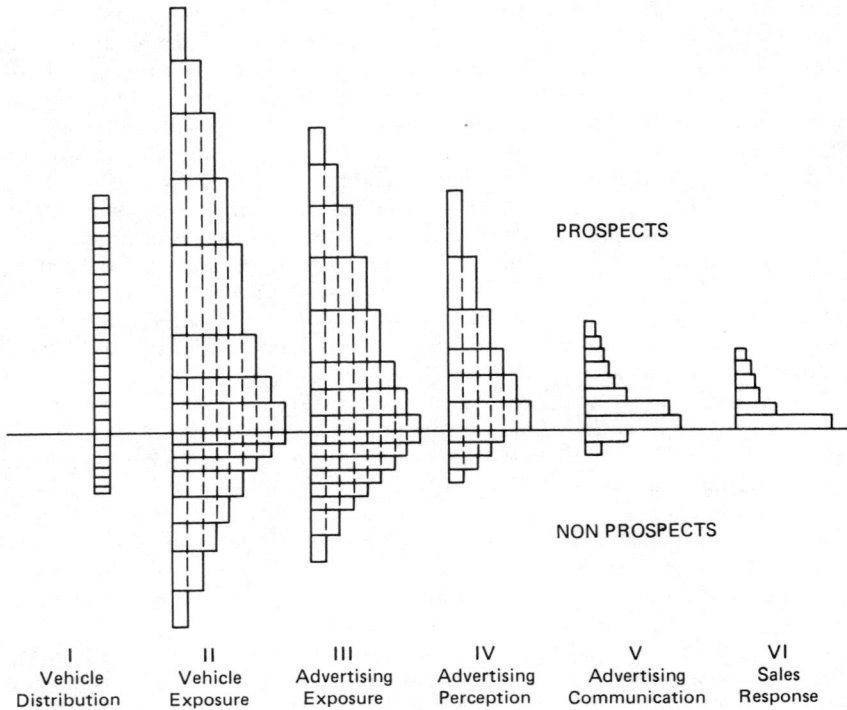

PROSPECTS

NON PROSPECTS

I	II	III	IV	V	VI
Vehicle Distribution	Vehicle Exposure	Advertising Exposure	Advertising Perception	Advertising Communication	Sales Response

Figure 15-4. *The ARF guide for evaluating media*

Audience Concepts Committee, *Toward Better Media Comparisons* (New York: Advertising Research Foundation, 1961), p. 15. Used with permission.

It should be noted that advertising has two parts: that transmitted (the message) and the means of transmission (the media). The purpose of the guide indicated in the chart is to try to separate these two parts and concentrate on the media component. As will be seen, these stages are differentially effective in separating the message and the media in terms of the message's effect. In addition, as we move from the vehicle distribution stage to the sales-response stage, there is increasing difficulty of both making this separation and attributing the response to the media themselves or, indeed, to the advertising component of the mix as a total entity.

Vehicle distribution, the first stage of the ARF guide, is defined as the number of physical units of the vehicle that are disseminated.

In television this is measured by the proportion of sets tuned, the familiar Nielsen or ARB ratings. For magazines or newspapers the measure is circulation, which is carefully checked or audited by the Audit Bureau of Circulations (ABC) or, for business publications, the Business Publications Audit (BPA). These circulation or vehicle distribution figures are given some qualitative value in that they are broken into free or controlled circulation as opposed to paid circulation, newsstand versus subscription, and renewal rate of subscription. But in the main they are still dealing with just physical units disseminated. The equivalent sort of measure for outdoor would be the number of billboards containing any advertiser's message. However, this is not what is used. A 100-GRP (gross rating point) package is enough billboards to deliver the equivalent of the population of a market in exposures in one day.

While it is true that vehicle distribution measures most clearly separate media from message effects, they have two critical problems. They do not indicate anything about the effect of advertising, and they do not consider people in any way. Thus, although circulation, ratings, or vehicle distribution figures provide a rough cut, we have to move on to other stages in order to get information on advertising effect and to consider the interaction of the media with people. The later stages all consider the interaction with people.

Vehicle exposure, the second stage, could be defined as open eyes confronted by the vehicle. It is the number of people who are exposed in some way to the vehicle. It should be noted that the columns in the model are much larger for the vehicle exposure stage than they are for the vehicle distribution one. The reason is that more than one person will probably be exposed to every physical unit of the vehicle distributed. For example, more than one person in any family is likely to read a particular copy of a magazine, be sitting in front of the television set, and so forth. This relationship would not be true, however, of the controlled or free circulation publications that are sent to people in industrial markets without their having taken out a subscription. In that case, many of the issues of these publications might simply be thrown away, which would mean that the vehicle exposure columns would be smaller than the vehicle distribution ones.

Another relationship that is important at the vehicle exposure stage is that there should be a greater proportion of the columns above the line in the prospect area as opposed to below the line in the nonprospect one. The reason is that those people who are in the audience for a vehicle are more likely to be prospects than nonprospects.

The best synonym for the vehicle exposure type of measure is *audience*. The audience studies that are done at this level are the most consistent source of intermedia and intervehicle comparison data available to the media planner. At the time this book was being written, there were two main services providing audience information, Simmons Marketing Research Bureau (SMRB) and Mediamark Research Incorporated (MRI). Essentially these services collect vehicle exposure data for television, radio, newspapers, and magazines. Their sample sizes are large enough so that these data are provided for various demographic, psychographic, and usage segments. As an example, the MRI report consists of about fifty volumes of survey results and an introductory volume, all based on an extensive interview survey with a sample of approximately twenty thousand adults in the United States. Well over forty product-class categories are covered in addition to over eighteen demographic characteristics, twenty psychographic categories, and a wide variety of media vehicles. There are local market reports for the top twenty markets also.

These kinds of data have allowed an extremely sophisticated set of comparisons to be made between media vehicles and across media types. That is, it is only with such data that the type of sophisticated media models that is discussed later in this chapter could be feasible.

Despite the value of such data, there are problems. Primarily there are the problems of determining the reliability and validity of the data. Most recently there have been controversies over the data presented in the SMRB and MRI reports.[13] There was a movement on the part of some publishers and broadcasters to develop a single audience service that would be supported by industry and rigidly controlled. The basic underpinning of these difficulties and this controversy is that the measure of vehicle exposure involved in these audience studies is really quite different from the operational definition given above. That definition was "open eyes" (and, if applicable, "attuned ears") confronted by the vehicle.

Very few studies meet this operational definition. The only studies done on a continuing basis are those for the outdoor media. Within that medium, there are studies that measure traffic going past certain outdoor billboards. There have also been studies that use a camera photographing traffic going past various types of billboards. The operational measurement here is literally "whites of eyes seen in the photographs." Similar vehicle exposure measures have been made on a sporadic basis for television by the means of cameras placed in homes to photograph the audience in front of the set at intermittent time periods. In other studies, participant observers have been hired to report the viewing behavior of other members of their families. For instance, college students were hired to watch the viewing behavior of other members of their families. In still other studies, mothers were hired to watch the viewing behavior of their children.

In contrast with these photographic and participant observer studies, the continuous audience studies made by SMRB and MRI have several obvious defects. They are not based on a strict operational definition but rather on respondents' recall or recognition of their viewing and reading behavior. The surveys are typically done during the last five months of one year and the first month of the year for which the report is issued. This means that respondents are asked in one sitting to indicate their vehicle exposure behavior over a long period of time. Such measurement is exposed to many noise and bias factors which would affect reliability and validity. It is likely that respondents put different weights on the amount of exposure that is necessary before they would consider themselves to be in the audience for a particular vehicle. This assessment can be effected by the length of time since they were last exposed and the nature of the interviewing process. Sampling problems also add to the difficulties.

Despite these problems, the audience studies are the only continuing, well-researched service that provide data allowing comparisons across media and vehicle types.

Advertising exposure, the third level of the ARF guide, is the first stage that considers the ability of the media to deliver an audience to specific advertising. Again, the operational definition would involve "open eyes and ears," this time confronted by the ad rather than the vehicle. The outdoor and television photographic studies mentioned above are a good operational definition of advertising exposure when they are applied to the ad itself. Another reasonable measure of ad page exposure for magazines was developed by Alfred Politz. He had tiny glue spots placed in the crevices between the pages of the magazines that were hand-circulated to consumers. A count of the broken glue spots indicated the pages that respondents had turned to. Another close representation of the advertising exposure level was developed by Cornelius Dubois when he experimented with fingerprint measures of magazine page exposure.

As in the vehicle exposure area, there are more viable but less representative measures of advertising exposure that are available on a more or less continuing basis. Perhaps the best example of these types of services is that provided by the Starch Readership Service. Starch researchers interview a sample of consumers by flipping through publications. For each advertisement, respondents are asked whether or not they looked at it, whether they related it to any particular sponsor (the advertiser's name is blocked out), and how much of it they read. The first or "noted" score is probably the closest representative of a continuing measure of advertising exposure.

Of course, Starch does not provide intermedia comparison data. For this, some individual advertisers do day-after-recall (DAR) studies for particular ads in various media. The most general and easy response criteria in these studies might be compared to what is meant by advertising exposure.

While advertising exposure is a better

measure of the media contribution to advertising effect than the previous two levels of the ARF model, it does present some difficulties. Starch is the main continuing service available for consumer publications (several are done for business publications), and it has various research difficulties. The primary one is that Starch "noting" is dependent on respondent self-report. Some research indicates that this self-report is based on the respondent's assessment of the subjective probability that he or she was exposed to a particular ad. Thus if a respondent is a user of a product category or if the product or brand has done a lot of advertising, it is likely that respondents will overclaim their exposure to those particular ads based on their "guess" that they were so exposed. In addition to the research questions with the advertising exposure measure, there are certain conceptual ones. For instance, there are likely to be differences in the value of exposure from medium to medium. In order to get at the value of exposure, we would have to move on to the subsequent stages of the ARF model.

Advertising perception, the fourth stage, is the first measure to consider the degree of response generated by the combination of the advertising message and the medium or vehicle. Here we are asking whether the individual saw or heard the message. The Starch service is one good example for the magazine medium. Another one for magazines is the service provided by Gallup and Robinson, in which the measure was recall without the respondent's getting to look at the ads. The latter seems to be a purer measure of advertising perception than is the Starch service. The Gallup and Robinson type of service is less subject to the kinds of biases mentioned above, although one problem with it is that the recall levels are so low. One aspect that should be noted here is that as we move along the stages of the model, there are fewer and fewer continuing services available. The biggest lack is in the area of services that will allow comparison across media. It is only at

the vehicle exposure stage that continuing services are available and can be used with regularity in media planning.

The main research problem with advertising perception measures is that we are not just simply getting "seen" or "heard"; we are getting memory and we have to depend on it. In addition, in comparing between media, we should recognize that advertising perception measures are quite far removed from sales. And it is at the ad perception stage that the factor of creativity itself becomes more important in the measure (as opposed to media capabilities). This becomes a major difficulty in making comparisons across media types and vehicle types. In intermedia comparisons different media are likely to have advertising with different degrees of creative quality and ability to achieve advertising perception. For instance, radio broadcasters often complain that the creative work devoted to their medium is substandard. Therefore an advertising perception comparison of radio and other media would be biased against that medium.

Two approaches might be used to get around the problem of differential creative input to various medium vehicles. One approach would be to take a large sampling of advertising from each vehicle and assume that you would get a sampling of the best and the worst usage of the medium. Thus, within-vehicle creative input is held constant. This still has the problem of intermedia comparisons that was mentioned with regard to radio. The other approach that might be used to get around this problem would be to make comparisons on a brand-by-brand basis. This would make the assumption that the same basic elements have been put in ads or commercials in all media. Thus the only creative differences would be those differences that are caused by the limits of the media themselves, which are important considerations in making the media or vehicle decision. However, if one is interested in comparing media on the basis of response, it seems fruitless to stop with just the advertising perception level. Since all the problems of differential creativity across media exist anyway, it seems reasonable to move on to the last two stages of the ARF model in order to make such comparisons of media effect.

Advertising communication is the level of the ARF guide that provides the kind of in-depth response that would be required to evaluate various media in terms of their effects. The advertising communication stage is best represented by the levels of the market-ing-communication hierarchies of effect that were discussed in Chapter 7. Thus, advertising communication measures would include measures of brand awareness, recall or recognition comprehension measures, cognitive response measures such as those relating to meaning or believability or comments, attitude or evaluation change measures, and indications of intention.

Note that in the chart depicting the ARF guide there are now a series of horizontal bars rather than the vertical columns indicated in the previous stages. These bars could be used to represent the levels of the hierarchy moving up from the awareness level to comprehension to cognitive response to conviction to intention to action.

Once again there is a great deal of difficulty in measuring the effect of media separate from the fact of creative strategy and implementation. Since there are no continuing studies or services in this area, most research is done on an individual advertiser and campaign basis. The most reasonable paradigm for such research would be an experimental study in which ads with the same creative strategy and basic elements would be placed in various media and vehicles. Then the response would be measured on the basis of some level of advertising communication. This would actually be a quantitative representation of the sort of qualitative analysis suggested earlier. The differences in response across the media would be due to the qualitative differences that were discussed earlier.

Other than the fact that there are few continuing services and that such research is quite expensive, there is the additional problem that the closer the evaluation across media gets to sales, the more the effects of variables other than advertising and media are being measured.

Sales response, the last stage of the ARF guide, is the most relevant to the advertiser. It is the easiest measure to make in terms of the gross response. Although there are problems, the basic thing measured is the number of units that move off the shelves. In other words, it is possible to make the measurement without depending on verbal responses and their obvious biases. But the main problem is that, of all the media measures, sales response is the least dependent on advertising and media. This is why sales-response measures are the ones that are most naturally considered at the tentative budget-mix level rather than in terms of some specific elements of the mix or some part of the elements such as media.

In summary, the ARF model in the preceding discussion has indicated that only at the vehicle exposure level are there continuing data on a large enough scale so that they can be used in media planning. As we move from left to right in the model, we get closer to the type of response of value. But it becomes increasingly difficult to relate this response to the contribution of the media alone. This is the basic problem in making the inter-media and general vehicle class decisions in media planning.

Conclusion: The Media and Vehicle Decision Process

Given the situation in terms of the variety of the media and nature of the data available to evaluate it, it seems reasonable that a simple four-step procedure will aid the media planner in making the decisions as to media and general types of vehicles:

1. The large number of alternative media and vehicles should be narrowed down on the

basis of a qualitative analysis stemming from consumer and creative considerations. As indicated earlier, the situation analysis, the nature of the rest of the campaign, and the creative strategy itself will typically dictate a certain type of medium or media as being necessary for the campaign. This analysis, in addition to an analysis of how the particular creative effort would interact with the media and vehicles, should indicate a workable set of vehicles to deal with. Some idea of the kinds of characteristics that might be considered for this analysis can be found in Table 15-2, which compares four media on thirty-five factors.

2. The alternative vehicle types should be compared on the basis of audience composition at the vehicle exposure level. It is important to get media that are efficient in terms of reaching target segments. The data from audience studies are available and good enough for making rough cuts suggested at this stage.

3. The planner should make some assessment of advertising exposure for each medium and general class of vehicle. If there is reason to believe that particular vehicle types would not produce a great proportion of advertising exposure among the vehicle exposure audience, then these vehicles should be dropped from consideration or certainly put in a lower-consideration class. The assessment of advertising exposure can be made on the basis of individual company and media studies (combined with judgment about the ability of the medium or vehicle to lead to advertising exposure). Table 15-2 provides some general indications. Greater specificity is needed of course.

4. Finally, some assessment should be made of the proportion of individuals who will reach some level of advertising communication as defined by the objectives of the campaign. For instance, in the media plan offered by Ule, awareness of the brand was the main communication objective. In each situation, the media planner makes some assessment of the conversion proportion from audi-

ence to advertising exposure to advertising communication.

These four steps are similar to the steps that a planner goes through in providing information to run an advertising media model. Whether or not a computer is used, they are critical steps in the efficient evaluation of media and vehicles for media plans.

SUMMARY

Advertising media selection is one type of message distribution planning within marketing communication. Often thought of as a dull clerical task, it actually offers great potential for creative problem solving. It is also an area in which the campaign planner can provide service to the consumers by getting messages to them when these messages are most appropriate. For the purpose of media selection is to get advertising messages to the right people, and at the right times and places, with adequate frequency and impact.

There are two broad areas of media decisions: planning and buying. The media plan provides decisions in three areas: medium or media to be used, general type of vehicles within each medium, and scheduling or weight of the campaign over time. Media buying is the task that takes the guidelines of the plan and implements it in terms of specific placements of ads in the media. It is at the buying stage that media models are most frequently employed.

This chapter covered media planning and the decisions about media and vehicles. The next chapter deals with scheduling decisions and media buying.

The media and all message distribution plans are vital links between what has gone before in campaign development and the implementation that is to follow. As such, the plan is based largely on the situation analysis and other plans. Consumer considerations are critical not only in identifying the target segment but also in indicating creative ways that

Table 15-2. Gross Media Comparisons

	TV	Radio	Magazines	Newspapers
Total population reach (Adults + Children)	Very Strong	Good	Fair	Good
Selective upscale adult reach	Fair	Good	Very Strong	Good
Upscale adult selectivity (Per Ad Exposure)	Poor	Fair	Very Strong	Good
Young adult selectivity (Per Ad Exposure)	Fair	Very Strong	Very Strong	Fair
Cost per 1000 ratios	Fair-Good	Very Strong	Strong	Good
National media availabilities + uniform coverage	Very Strong	Poor	Good	Poor
Local market selectivity	Good	Good	Poor	Very Strong
Ability to control frequency	Fair	Good	Good	Very Strong
Ability to pile frequency upon reach base	Very Strong	Very Strong	Good	Fair
Ability to exploit time of day factors (In Scheduling)	Fair	Very Strong	Poor	Poor
Ability to exploit day of week factors (In Scheduling)	Fair	Very Strong	Poor	Very Strong
Seasonal audience stability	Poor	Very Strong	Good	Good
Predictability of audience levels	Fair-Poor	Good	Good	Very Good
Depth of demographics in audience surveys	Poor	Poor	Very Strong	Fair-Good
Reliability and consistency of audience surveys	Fair-Good	Good	Fair-Good	Good
Ability to monitor schedules	Good	Poor	Very Strong	Very Strong
Ability to negotiate rates	Good	Fair	Poor	Poor
Fast closing + air dates	Fair	Good	Poor	Very Strong
Opportunity to exploit editorial "compatibility"	Poor	Fair	Very Strong	Good
Selective ad positioning	Poor	Fair	Good	Very Strong
Advertising exposure	Good	Good	Good	Good
Advertising intrusiveness	Very Strong	Good	Fair	Poor
Audience concern over ad "clutter"	Very High	High	Almost None	Almost None
Emotional stimulation	Very Strong	Fair	Fair	Poor
Sensory stimulation	Fair-Good	Fair	Very Strong	Fair
Brand name registration	Very Strong	Good	Fair	Fair
Product or efficacy demonstrations	Very Strong	Poor	Fair	Fair
Ability to exploit attention getting devices	Very Strong	Poor	Very Strong	Good
Ability to use humor	Very Strong	Good	Poor	Poor
Ability to use slice of life approach	Very Strong	Good	Poor	Poor
Ability to convey detail + information	Fair	Fair	Very Strong	Very Strong
Ability to stimulate imagination	Fair-Good	Very Strong	Fair	Poor
Package identification	Good	Poor	Very Strong	Good
Prestige and respectability of the medium	Fair	Fair	Very Strong	Strong
Ability to talk person-to-person with audience	Fair-Good	Very Strong	Poor	Poor

SOURCE: *The Media Book, 1978* (New York: Min-Mid Publishing, 1978), pp. 433 and 436. All rights reserved. Used with permission.

target segments can be reached in the context of the way they interact with media. Product and creative considerations dictate a bias toward media that provide the physical characteristics and context needed for the advertising. Competitive expenditure and exposure analysis leaves the planner with two broad alternatives: (1) follow the competition and attempt to beat them where they are advertising or (2) advertise where the competition are not putting weight, in order to be the dominant factor in these media.

Basically a media plan seeks to maximize effect on the basis of six criteria on which managers can judge the quality of any plan. These criteria are reach, frequency, continuity, flexibility, dominance, and mood. The creativity in media planning comes in balancing these criteria and the needs of the campaign. Only an advertiser with unlimited funds can maximize all the criteria. Since the criteria are somewhat reciprocal—reach is usually obtained only at the expense of frequency, for instance—clever media plans will break through these problems with new combinations.

The media plan itself is both a selling document to the client and a guideline for everyone working on the campaign. It should be presented very carefully with sections on campaign needs, media objectives and criteria, the general program recommendation, rationale and alternatives, specific schedules and output, and contingencies.

The intermedia and vehicle decisions are made on both qualitative and quantitative considerations. Media can be judged qualitatively in terms of audience character, physical characteristics, and mood, which is basically the nature of the consumer interaction with various media and types of vehicles.

Quantitative media and vehicle evaluation depends importantly on the types of data used. An ARF guide indicates that there are at least six types available; the best provided on a continuing basis appear to be of the vehicle exposure or audience type. Since adequate continuing data comparing media are not available on measures closer to sales, a four-step mixture of judgment and data is recommended for choosing media and vehicle types.

ISSUES AND PROJECTS FOR DISCUSSION

1. Define *vehicle, medium, schedule, cost per thousand, reach, frequency, continuity, flexibility, dominance, mood, gross rating points, duplication, audience, BAR, ARF, MRI, SRDS, qualitative value, Simmons, coverage, vehicle distribution.*

2. What do you think is the difference between a creative media plan and one that is not creative? Can you specify a noncreative alternative to one of the creative media ideas outlined at the beginning of this chapter? What is the essential difference between the creative and the noncreative alternatives?

3. What do you think is the major advantage of each of the following types of media vehicles: business magazines, news magazines, local television news programs, rock radio stations, outdoor billboards, outdoor spectaculars, morning big-city newspapers, Sunday supplements, public transportation car cards, matchbook covers.

4. Is there a best single medium or vehicle? Why or why not?

5. Assume the spending situation for soft drinks shown in Table 15-1 is approximately the same now in terms of competitive expenditure relationships. What general pattern of expenditures would you recommend for either Dr Pepper or 7-Up given their present message strategy? Support your recommendation.

6. Explain how it can be said that the six criteria for media plans are in some sense reciprocal, i.e., that achieving greater levels of some will mean lesser levels of others.

7. Describe the four steps you would go through to make the decision in Question 5.

8. What is probably the single most-read and important part of the media plan statement? How should it be presented to make it most effective?

9. Which levels of the ARF guide deal with people? With advertising effect? With audience response? With response that relates to the hierarchy of effects?

10. What are the advantages and disadvantages of each of the media solutions presented at the beginning of this chapter? Can you suggest better solutions for any of them?

11. Figure 15-3 provides some rates and data on a number of media and vehicles. Assume you are developing a plan for a revolutionary new and relatively inexpensive home water purifier. The message strategy is to convince "upscale" homeowners that water purification is important and now is simple and economical with this new unit. There is very little competitive expenditure. Pare the list in the table down to those types you would recommend as being suitable for the campaign. If you want to add any media or types of vehicles not represented in the table, go ahead. Support your recommendations.

Notes

1. "Shell Oil Company (A)," in *Cases in Advertising Management,* ed. Harper W. Boyd, Jr., Vernon Fryburger, and Ralph Westfall (New York: McGraw-Hill, 1964), pp. 259–65.

2. Eugene J. Webb, Donald T. Campbell, Richard Schwartz, and Lee Sechrest, *Unobtrusive Measures* (Chicago: Rand-McNally, 1966).

3. Stephen A. Greyser, *Cases in Advertising and Communication Management* (Englewood Cliffs, N.J.: Prentice-Hall, 1981).

4. Herbert D. Maneloveg, "The Two Media Departments," *Advertising Age,* March 18, 1963, p. 83.

5. Jack Hanrahan, "Measuring Services: Media Activity and Spending," *4A Media Letter,* 5 (April 1979), 2–5.

6. Richard Zackon, personal communication (January 1980).

7. John C. Maloney, "Attitude Measurement and Formation" (Unpublished paper, 1966).

8. Michael L. Ray and William L. Wilkie, "Fear: The Potential of an Appeal Neglected by Marketing," *Journal of Marketing,* 34 (January 1970), 54–62.

9. Bob Reuschle, "Solutions to Lux Media Problem," in *Media Planning Workbook,* ed. Jack Z. Sissors, Harry D. Lehew, and William B. Goodrich (Chicago: Crain Books, 1976), p. 147.

10. G. Maxwell Ule, "A Media Plan for 'Sputnik' Cigarettes" (New York: American Association of Advertising Agencies, November 20, 1957).

11. Boyd and others, "Dorian Food Products," in *Cases in Advertising Management* (New York: McGraw-Hill, 1964), pp. 242–44.

12. "Twentieth Century Fox—The Wiz," *Cases in Advertising and Communication Management,* ed. Stephen A. Greyser (Englewood Cliffs, N.J.: Prentice-Hall, 1981), pp. 497–515.

13. Bernice Kanner, "ARF Magazine Research Study Unable to Pick Best Method," *Advertising Age,* January 14, 1980, pp. 18–72.

Advertising Media Planning II: Scheduling, Buying, and Modeling

■ *It stands to reason that viewers who see a message only once may be less af-fected than viewers who see it four or five times. It also stands to reason that for many products there is a point of diminishing returns. . . . However, plan-ners with experience on a brand cannot count on these theories. Different brands within the same category can react differently to advertising stimuli. One brand can require heavy support—eight or more target audience exposures during pe-riodic four-week flights. Another may respond best with a low, continuing level of one or two exposures over an average four-week period. A third may show no pattern at all. This can be caused by variables in creative approach, promo-tional activities and distribution.*[1]

■ *The advertiser wants 100 rating points on spot TV in Market X. Buyer A is realistic. Buyer B is optimistic.* Both have the same assignment *(figures are hypothetical).*

Buyer A (Realistic	Buyer B (Optimistic)	Report to Client
Buys 12 non-preempt-ible spots at $100 each. Cost of buy is $1,200.	Buys 12 preemptible spots cost at least 25% less than fixed spots. 12 spots at $75 each gives total cost of $900.	Buyer B has saved the client $300, or 25%, and delivered the same number of spots as Buyer A.

In reality . . . *Without careful auditing, no one ever knows whether some of Buyer B's spots were preempted. The client assumed all spots ran as scheduled. In fact, some may never have run, and make-goods may have been of lower quality than originals, so dollar savings became invalid. Why else would the seller give Buyer B a discount? If Buyer A were willing to take the same preemtible risks, he could have paid the same lower price.*[2]

■ Yes we are heavily influenced by the computer. And I must confess I often find myself in the same position described by B. B. King, the great American blues singer.

In one of his mournful ballads he recounts his suspicion that his lady is sharing her favors with another man. The lyrics detail one piece of evidence after another and finally add up to Mr. King's colorful description of his plight: "I think I'm gettin' more help than I really need." Computers can give a man that kind of feeling too.[3]

■ The media planner's dilemma (which is essentially the high cost of digging deeper into what could be a dry well) . . . Media buyers in the past tended to recommend for maximum reach on the basis that "you can't sell 'em if you don't reach 'em." . . . for the panic mongers of the computer age who are still babbling that computers are idiots. . . . What they fail to realize is that the process of "counting faster" includes sorting faster and reporting faster. And just as a change in temperature can change molecular structure, the advent of speed in information management changes the structure and nature of information.[4]

As the quotations above indicate, there are many planning decisions left after the ones about media and types of vehicles are made. Scheduling indicates more precisely how the weight of the campaign will be applied to the selected media and vehicles across the year. Major changes can occur as a result of media-buying decisions. Media models sharpen the process of scheduling and buying so that planners know when they are making assumptions and when they need more data. And as the last quotation implies, with data arriving faster and in an improved form, there is greater opportunity for everyone working on scheduling and buying to be more creative.

Perhaps the areas of advertising planning with the greatest change in concepts, methods, and techniques during the past twenty-five years are the ones discussed in this chapter.

By the early 1980s a variety of models and data analysis computer packages could be and were being utilized by planners and buyers to deal with scheduling and buying problems. Now, however, there was disillusionment with audience data. Scheduling and buying were being made on the basis of "effective reach," a combination of reach and frequency that related to advertising communication and sales-response types of objectives for the campaign.

The result of all of this development is not just more numbers on computer printouts that take up space on our desks. Instead the scheduling and buying area has evolved to the point that the central concepts are not numbers per se. Rather media planners and this chapter concentrate on determining and estimating *response and decay functions*. These functions or curves indicate the *response* of the target audience at each level of advertising exposure and the *decay* that occurs over time in nonadvertising periods.

In essence, the scheduling task is one of determining what response is likely to be in the situation and how it is affected by various patterns of media schedules that might be bought. Current media models, when they are used, ask for assumptions about what response and decay are likely to be. And media planners and buyers make these assumptions every time they develop, approve, or buy a schedule. In many cases their assumptions are not even recognized or specified clearly.

The most important point of this chapter, then, is to help you to spot the most likely response and decay function in each situation. This is the main purpose of the next section, "The Scheduling Decision." This is followed by a section on media buying which illustrates that the best buy is often one that creates a separate medium, all alone for your advertising. Finally, media modeling is briefly examined as providing a comprehensive outline of the entire media-planning and buying process.

THE SCHEDULING DECISION

After the media and general types of vehicles have been selected, the media planner must determine how the total budget for advertising should be assigned to those alternatives. As a result of examining the general ways that money may be assigned, it is possible that the media planner will request an increase in budget in order to accomplish the overall communication goals of the advertising part of the campaign. This is what was requested by Ule in the part of the sample plan presented in the preceding chapter.

Scheduling in the media-planning sense is concerned with how the advertising budget will be spent over time in the campaign-planning period in the media and vehicles chosen. Not at issue here are the planner's choices in terms of time of day or days in the week. These are actually part of the media and vehicle decision, since particular vehicles are aimed at these time slots.

What is of greatest concern in the scheduling decision is the pattern of exposure to advertising that will be effected against target segments by various expenditure patterns. Thus the critical question is one relating to response functions to advertising and the decay or forgetting functions that occur when there are nonadvertising periods.

Some Typical Strategies

Assuming that virtually all but the largest advertisers have some limit on their budgets, there will almost always be time periods in which any given advertiser will be spending very little and other time periods in which this advertiser will be spending more than the average. This results in a pattern of expenditure that could be characterized as a *wave strategy*. The depth of the troughs and the height of the peaks of the waves differentiate an entire range of strategies that run from a constant level of expenditures to a situation requiring bursts or a "jolt-and-fade" pattern.

Figure 16-1 shows a number of these wave strategy patterns. While they sometimes relate to seasonality, there are evidently other factors causing the schedules depicted in the figure.

For the dog-food brand in Figure 16-1a, the schedule waving seems to be related to the television season. The peaks in the schedule in October, January-February, and April are due to the addition of network television expenditures to the schedule. The plan seemed to call for making the brand's presence felt in television at critical times (perhaps to convince the trade that the brand was well supported) and then pull away to maintenance levels in other media and vehicles. Note that with this jolt-and-fade scheduling there is only one month, May, that comes close to the average monthly expenditure.

Figure 16-1b quite clearly shows the effect of competition on scheduling in an industry that normally has a seasonal pattern. The three beers had very close total advertising expenditures but were quite different in expenditures during the first three quarters of the year. One interpretation might be that both Budweiser and Schlitz increased their expenditures in the fourth quarter to meet the

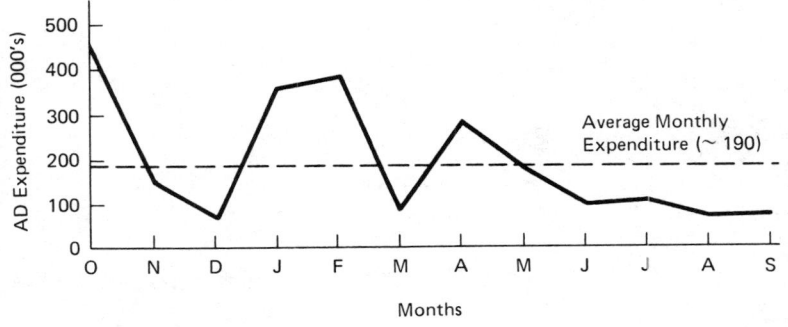

Figure 16-1a. *Recommended expenditure plan for a dog food*

Adapted from table in Jack Z. Sissors and E. R. Petray, *Advertising Media Planning* (Chicago: Crain Books, 1976), p. 296.

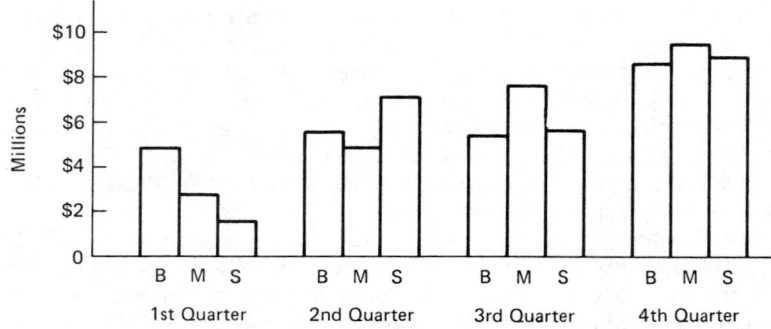

Figure 16-1b. *Quarterly advertising expenditures in six media for Budweiser (B), Miller High Life (M), and Schlitz (S) beers*

Constructed from data on 1978 expenditures provided by Richard Zackon of Air-Time Inc.

steady increases of Miller High Life during the year.

Figure 16-1c shows four types of scheduling strategies that are not uncommon. Note that the schedules are depicted in terms of the "Weight of Campaign" instead of just dollar expenditures. Showing the campaign in terms of such measures as gross rating points—even though they are not indicative of actual response—provides a bit more information than just expenditures. Note also that such exposure weight figures would relate to target segments only.

Looking at the upper left of Figure 16-1c, it can be seen that the solid-line schedule has some similarity to the dog-food one examined earlier. These are representative of an "introduction" sort of schedule in which the campaign is introduced with heavy

weight and then left to a maintenance schedule. The hope is that a concentration of money and weight will push up the reach and frequency to such a point that impact (by whatever measure) will be substantial and can be maintained with reminders during the year. The same sort of thing was done with the Northwestern Mutual Life Insurance campaign when nearly all of the company's budget was put into the sponsorship of Olympics broadcasts. Other aspects of the mix were used to provide reminders and maintenance of the tremendous impact generated by concentrating nearly all the media weight into the weeks of the Olympics.

An even more dramatic and perhaps risky scheduling strategy is represented by the three dashed rectangles at the bottom of Figure 16-1c. Such an advertiser goes in and out

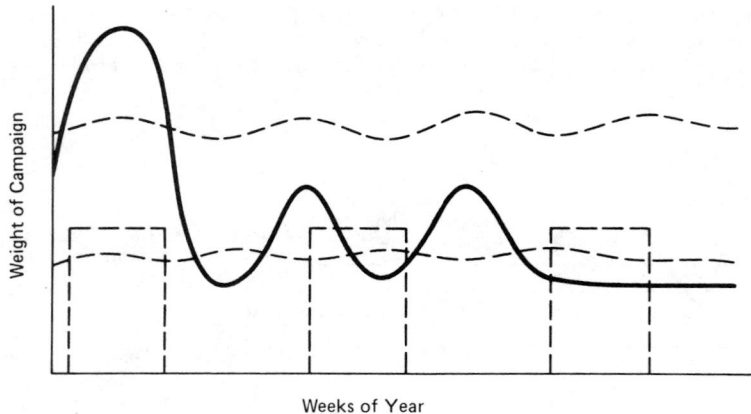

Figure 16-1c. *Four hypothetical wave strategies*

of the media, jolting and fading completely, as it were. The assumption is that only by concentrating efforts in certain periods will it be possible to develop sufficient frequency to have impact against key segments. Further it is assumed that during the nonadvertising periods, the impact will not decay to dangerously low levels. These are vital assumptions about response and decay functions that are *not* shown in the figure but will be discussed in the next section.

The two relatively flat schedules in Figure 16-1c seem less risky but may actually be more risky than the burst-type schedules. The higher one has to be representative of an advertiser with a great deal of money to spend. One example of such an advertiser may have been Budweiser before an experiment indicated that neither dropping advertising completely nor quadrupling it during the period of the experiment made any statistically significant difference in sales.[5] It seemed that Budweiser had been advertised at such a level and with such success over the years that the extremely high expenditures were not really necessary. In fact, the response to advertising might be so quick in such situations that constant high advertising weights might cause advertising to "wear out" (cease to have impact) or, less likely, to actually have a negative impact.

The lower relatively flat curve might actually represent the change made by Budweiser after it learned that it might have been spending too much money. Even the 1978 expenditure figures for Budweiser shown in Figure 16-1b indicate that Budweiser's expenditure pattern was actually at a reasonably flat low level for the first three quarters.

When an advertiser is in a position similar to Budweiser's—that is, being an extremely well known brand with an established image—the low-level, constant, noburst campaign with an emphasis on reach and continuity rather than frequency and dominance is probably the most reasonable.

If, on the other hand, an advertiser's brand needs frequency and dominance, the lower flat schedule could be a disaster. Note that there are few periods of the year when such a schedule is *not* dominated by more than one "competitor" in terms of the other schedules in the chart. And even these periods are very short indeed.

The solution for the low-budget advertising needing frequency might be in "media dominance" or "media concentration" scheduling strategies. In the *media dominance* approach, the expenditures are concentrated all in one medium or vehicle for part of the year and then moved successively to others. Thus while the overall curve at the bottom of Figure 16-c does not look too impressive, there may be substantial frequency and dominance within each medium. Even continuity may be adequate if there is substantial overlap between the audiences of the media successively dominated.

The *media concentration* strategy is similar to several of the creative approaches mentioned at the beginning of the preceding chapter. Instead of switching from one medium to another as with the dominance strategy, the advertiser concentrates everything, all year, in one medium. The extreme case of this was the one offered by Sunkist lemons. All the advertising for the brand was put into one *vehicle*, the *Ladies' Home Journal*, for a year. Thirty spread ads were placed, from one to four in each monthly issue.[6]

Two Key Response and Decay Functions

Whether to use various types of wave strategy or dominance or concentration strategies is dependent on the budget and on the reach, frequency, continuity, dominance, flexibility, and mood criteria of media plans. But what determines which of these criteria are most important? When is it better to emphasize reach and continuity over frequency and dominance, for instance?

The answer is that all the criteria are related to the response that might be expected to advertising exposure and the decay that occurs in response when advertising is absent.

And although there are probably countless numbers of response and forgetting functions in relation to advertising, two main patterns can be clearly considered by the planner for any given situation. Research has indicated when each of these two general types of response and decay are likely to occur. So the planner can examine situational characteristics, estimate response and decay, and plan accordingly.

The two key response and decay situations might be called the "Easy" and the "Difficult" ones.

In the *Easy response and decay function situation,* it is literally easy to have an effect on target segments with advertising and easy to maintain that effect. In response function terms, this means that each additional exposure after zero exposures produces some significant increase in the response as defined by the communication objectives for advertising. In addition, forgetting occurs slowly or almost not at all in the Easy situation. Decay functions are not steep. Sample curves are shown in Figure 16-2.

The Budweiser situation discussed above is an example of the Easy response and decay situation. The brand is extremely well known, a clear market leader with an established image and a need for reminder only. Thus a relatively low level of advertising and an emphasis on reach and continuity are possible. Since the response function to Budweiser advertising is likely to be linear or exponential, each additional exposure will have the reminder effect desired.

The only real problems in the Easy situation have to do with getting real reach in terms of effective exposures and with guarding against overexposure. It is true, for instance, that response is quite quick in Easy situations but that a point of diminishing returns may come quickly too. This not only constitutes a waste of money for the advertiser but may also lead to negative feeling toward the brand.

In the *Difficult response and decay function situation,* it takes a number of responses before there is any response at all. Even if substantial response is achieved with repetition, forgetting can be very quick. Sample curves are shown in the lower part of Figure 16-2. It should be remembered that these curves show the response of typical target segment consumers to clear exposures to the advertising.

The Difficult situation is the one faced by the majority of brand advertisers. Take the situation faced by Dr Pepper soft drink discussed in the preceding chapter. Only a heavily concentrated expenditure in television specials aimed at the target young people's audiences could push the brand awareness beyond the early flat part of the curve shown in the lower part of Figure 16-2. And even if the concentrated scheduling and the distinctive commercials push the brand up to the top of the curve, there is the chance for substantial decay during the nonadvertising period. Fortunately, as Herbert Krugman has pointed out, in package-goods markets like soft drinks the only response required is one like recognition—which has been shown not to decay quite as quickly as pure recall.[7] For marketers like Northwestern Mutual Life, on the other hand, responses like recall may be necessary and the decay may be quite quick.

A careful look at Figure 16-2 will show why the two situations are called "Easy" and "Difficult." In the top Easy situation, the response curve starts at a higher level and moves right up to a peak. There is a bit of decay early in the nonexposure period as some of the target segment people forget, but there is actually a plateau for awhile until the curve begins to decay at a very slow rate. Note that even without advertising it will take a long time to get down to the original starting place. And any modicum of advertising will create exposures that will push the response up again.

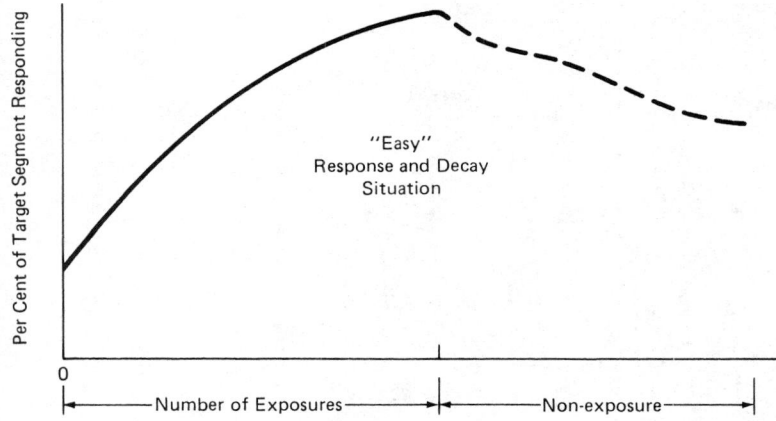

"Easy"
Response and Decay
Situation

Per Cent of Target Segment Responding

0

|—Number of Exposures—| |—Non-exposure—|

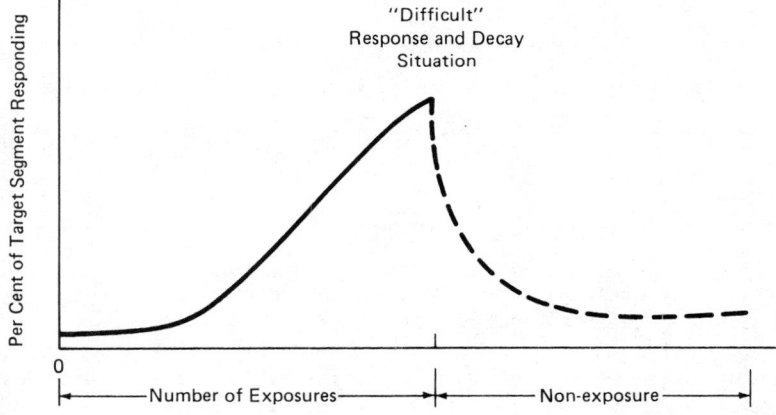

"Difficult"
Response and Decay
Situation

Per Cent of Target Segment Responding

0

|—Number of Exposures—| |—Non-exposure—|

Figure 16-2. *Two extremes in response and decay*

In the Difficult situation in the lower part of the figure, the target segment individuals must be exposed a number of times before there is any increase in the already low response level. And even if a concentrated schedule against a small target segment can produce a large number of exposures, forgetting is extremely rapid during nonadvertising periods. The forgetting curve dips quite rapidly almost down to the low starting level.

The dilemma of the media planner in the Difficult scheduling situation is quite clear. Those situational characteristics that make the S-shaped response curve requiring burst advertising are also those situational characteristics that make very fast forgetting likely to occur. This is a dilemma because the burst strategy is most likely to lead to very high peaks and very low troughs in terms of actual effect. For those advertisers who need to use a burst strategy because of scarce budget, there is the added problem that in the nonadvertising periods, forgetting is likely to be quite steep.

An experiment that illustrates the differences in effect caused by different schedules

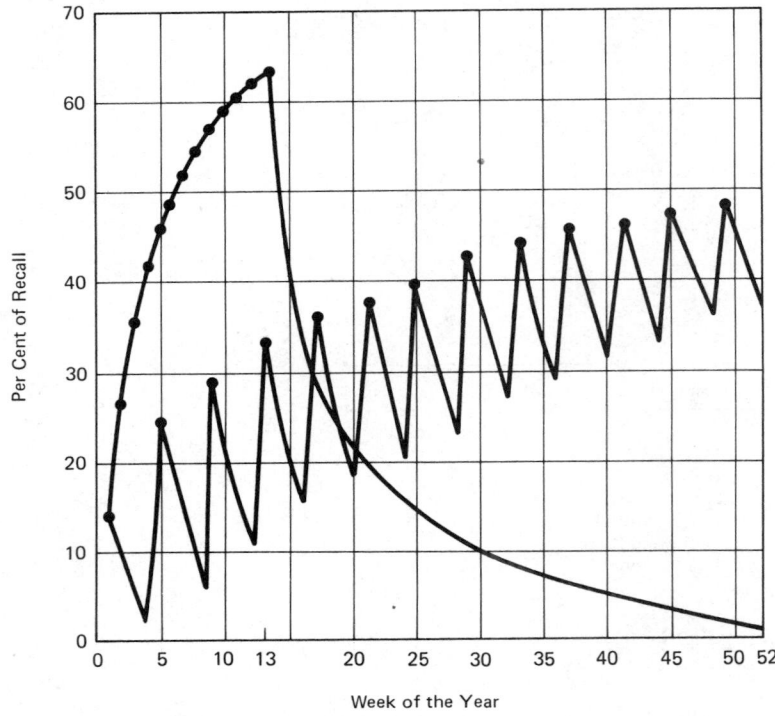

Per Cent of Recall

Week of the Year

Figure 16-3. Zielske's fitted results for two schedules (exposures are shown by dots)

and the dilemma of the "burst" scheduler was done by Hubert Zielske.[8] The experiment asks the basic question, If you have enough money for thirteen insertions in your selected medium, is the best schedule

☐ Once a week for thirteen weeks? or
☐ Once every four weeks throughout the year?

Zielske picked two experimental groups of housewives randomly and sent ads for a shortening to them in envelopes. The measure was advertising recall gauged by a short telephone interview. No housewife was interviewed more than once, and once a respondent was interviewed, she was dropped from the mailing list.

Zielske's overall results are shown in Figure 16-3. These are smoothed results but show general exponential response and forgetting curves for the advertising recall mea-

sure. Similar results have been found by Edward Strong in a replication of the Zielske research.[9] Strong did find much less decay, however, especially when the measure was something more rigorous than recall.

The implications of Zielske's results are fairly obvious. For product introductions, the short burst might be effective if it can be followed by adequate reminder and support advertising. But for the maximum average weekly number of people who remember the advertising, the spread-out campaign seemed better.

What is the solution to the dilemma posed to the media planner faced with a burst-type advertising situation? First, it is difficult to suggest an adequate solution until the planner is sure that the original situation is a burst one. The only way that this kind of assurance can be given is by some sort of continuing measuring program that indicates some kind of response. The sort of program suggested by the research system outlined in earlier chapters would also provide this information inexpensively. And some identifying situational characteristics are reviewed in the next section.

Once the planner is certain that a Difficult situation exists, several directions might be taken. First, it is critical that the creative strategy and implementation be developed to the point where each exposure will be maximally effective in terms of achieving communication goals. If this can be achieved, the flat early portion of the S-shaped curve will not exist. Effective creative work can also increase the memorability of the campaign.

Second, the burst dilemma can be alleviated by manipulation within the total communication mix. Thus it might be necessary to use a burst strategy with advertising but pick up the effect of the advertising with other components of the mix so that the troughs in advertising effect are totally nonexistent for the total effect of the campaign.

Third, it is possible to schedule the advertising across media in such a way that the pattern of exposure across a particular group can achieve a high constant level even though this may be a small group. This can be done with a media plan that goes against the traditional method of scheduling for any particular product class. Several of the examples given at the beginning of Chapter 15 are clear indications of this sort of strategy. Such advertisers as Northwestern Mutual Life Insurance, Hathaway shirts, Shell, Hunt's tomato sauce, Bell & Howell, and Sunkist lemons concentrated their expenditures in one medium or vehicle in order to become the dominant advertiser against that audience. This strategy can be varied so that instead of advertising in only one medium or vehicle across the entire campaign, the advertiser might switch from dominance in one medium to another in another period and so on. This latter dominance strategy develops high reach and frequency in specific vehicles during any given time period but sacrifices continuity throughout the year. The sacrifice in continu-

ity really depends on the extent of overlap between audiences. If there is a fair degree of overlap, then there is a reasonably good trade-off between the frequency and reach developed across the year.

Thus it is in the scheduling area that many of the interrelationships among components of the campaign are resolved. It is also here that a high degree of creativity can be applied through resolving the dilemmas of the media-planning situation.

Situation Analysis for Scheduling

The entire scheduling problem hinges on the nature of consumer response to exposures to advertising. That response could be the Easy or the Difficult or some type of response in between. Fortunately there has been some research and theory that indicates how various situations affect response. The wise planner can use these to determine strategy.

First there is the information-processing notion of Herbert Krugman that three exposures to television advertising are enough. Recall the discussion in earlier chapters of the difficulty we all have in processing information from television commercials. We are not terribly involved in the commercials in the first place. We can keep only a limited number of ideas in mind at any given time. And unless we rehearse an idea in our minds so that it can be put into long-term memory within thirty seconds of receipt, it is lost to us. Considering the clutter on television, the fact that we see shorter and shorter commercials in longer and longer strings, it is not surprising that little of great depth or accuracy is remembered.

Krugman builds on these facts and the research of others to assume that there is a three-step or three-exposure process of consumer information gathering from television commercials.

According to Krugman, the first exposure to a new commercial produces nothing more than a recognition that there is something new; and on the second exposure, the viewer does all the information processing he or she will ever do with the commercial. Since, as was pointed out in Chapter 7, television is a low-involvement medium, it is likely that something like "gross positive awareness" will be all that is generated by this second information-processing exposure. The third exposure and all subsequent ones, says Krugman, are merely reminders of the message generated by the second one.[10]

It is clear that this idea of Krugman's provides just the start for a consideration of response to and forgetting of advertising. His notion considers just television. Other media obviously produce other response patterns. And his measure seems to be recognition or recall at most. He does not clearly indicate how deeper comprehension (perhaps from media other than television), attitude toward the market offering, intention, or action is affected. Finally his idea gives us just a two-point curve with no effect until two exposures and then, presumably, a constant level of response following that. A substantial body of research indicates that there is wearout or viewer fatigue after a large number of exposures. There is also adequate evidence to indicate that people in different situations learn from and respond to advertising in ways that differ from those indicated by Krugman's three-exposure hypothesis.

You should be warned that campaign-planning and media-planning people have tended to grab on the Krugman hypothesis and apply it to media buying without considering the specifics of particular situations. In one sense, use of the Krugman three-exposure idea is better than just considering every exposure equal to every other one. On the other hand, the three-exposure idea is often being applied to the wrong situations, using the wrong data.

As was mentioned earlier, there has been a move toward "effective reach" instead of just gross rating points. One way effective reach is defined is by considering vehicle ex-

posure or audience figures (rather than *ad* exposure, as would be needed to use the Krugman idea) and counting just exposures after the third and up to some arbitrary wearout number (say, ten exposures) as being "effective."

What is wrong with this approach to scheduling situation analysis? Well, in the first place it is not situation analysis. It is taking a general idea and applying it to some specific situation. Beyond that it is not even doing a very good job of applying the general idea. Instead of using *advertising* exposure it uses *vehicle* exposure, and even this is only roughly estimated. Furthermore there is an upper effect limit, which Krugman never explicitly considered, although it should be determined in some way for each situation. Finally, the Krugman idea was posited for television and should not be applied uncritically to other media, particularly print.

In order to become more precise in determining the nature of response and forgetting in any particular situation, we must go beyond the general Krugman ideas. One program of research at Stanford University used both laboratory and field experimentation and indicated that there are at least seven factors that planners should consider in estimating the response and forgetting functions—or at least in determining whether the situation is likely to be an Easy or a Difficult one for scheduling.[15] These factors are

☐ Measure of effect or response
☐ Target segment brand and product usage
☐ Product type
☐ Brand
☐ Communication environment and competition
☐ Advertising appeal and tone
☐ Advertising format

In the following paragraphs the results and implications of this one extensive research program are summarized for the media planner. Note that many of the results indicate that a variable is important but is rather confusing in terms of specific scheduling implications. It is not possible to just add up the characteristics in any given planning situation and conclude that it is Easy or Difficult or something in between. Yet the following findings and implications do give adequate directions with which specific situations can be analyzed—instead of just mindlessly assuming that the more the GRPs, the better, or that only three to ten exposures count in every situation.

Measure of Effect or Response. This is the most important situational factor affecting response and forgetting and, ultimately, scheduling strategy. In general, if the response is on the lower levels of the response hierarchy (such as awareness, recognition, simple recall), it is easy to affect and easy to maintain—thus the Easy scheduling situation is most likely. And if the measure is more difficult to affect and maintain (such as detailed comprehension, attitude, or intention), the Difficult scheduling situation is most likely.

This dichotomy has certainly been found repeatedly in the Stanford research for the response to advertising and was suggested later by Krugman for the recognition measure.[12] Forgetting is not always as simple when measures are considered, however. Krugman points out that recognition seems amazingly impervious to forgetting; and if the product is a package-goods one that is bought on sight, it may be possible to assume very little forgetting and the complete Easy situation. Both Zielske and Strong, however, found very rapid forgetting curves for simple ad recall measures.[13] And Strong found that a difficult measure like attitude did not seem to decay at all during nonadvertising periods for well-known brands. Perhaps once any measure is attained by the weight of campaigns over the years—as is true of well-known brands—forgetting is not as rapid. This is probably a case of both measures and brand position (see discussion below) operating together to produce an Easy situation.

Target Segment Brand and Product Usage. The more the target segment is already in favor of the brand or market offering being advertised, the more likely the scheduling situation is Easy.

In one study in the Stanford program, for instance, there were four segments: (1) those buying the advertised brand most often, (2) those buying both the advertised brand and its major competitor more or less equally, (3) those buying neither brand, and (4) those buying the competing brand most often. For the first two segments, the Easy situation seemed to hold for straight supportive advertising appeals. For the last two segments, the Difficult situation seemed to hold.[14]

As Chapter 5 indicated, in almost all advertising and communication situations there are three segments on the basis of brand usage: "ours," "switchers," and "theirs." The "ours" segment, similar to the first one mentioned in the preceding paragraph, is already favorably disposed toward our brand and represents an Easy scheduling situation. The "theirs" segment considers the major competition to be its favorite brand and thus is already unfavorably disposed toward our brand—a perfect Difficult scheduling situation. In fact, the segment favoring the major competitor is often avoided by media planners because it is considered too difficult. The emphasis is then put on the "switcher" segment, which could be like the middle two segments in the Stanford study (buying both or buying neither). These segments could represent something between the Easy and the Difficult scheduling situations, but it is best to assume that they will be on the difficult side. Basically it is likely that switchers will respond more slowly than our own brand purchasers and will forget more quickly also. Thus some sort of wave strategy will be necessary in order to achieve the frequency and dominance appropriate to Difficult response and forgetting.

The Stanford study also found that a particular advertising appeal and tone—namely, a two-sided refutational appeal—was able to overcome somewhat the vagaries of the Difficult situation. This meant in one study using a media model that a greater total response in terms of purchase intent was possible in a Difficult situation by using an appropriate appeal and tone (see discussion below).

Product Type. It appears that certain product, service, or issue types require information sources other than advertising to a greater or lesser degree. To the extent that other information sources are used by consumers, the advertising media scheduling situation becomes Difficult. If advertising is the main source of information, then Easy scheduling tends to prevail.

One study in the Stanford program involved repetition of print ads for nine convenience-goods brands (heavy importance for advertising as an information source, Easy situation) and for nine shopping-goods brands (washing machines, television sets, and ladies' foundation garments, which should involve somewhat less customer dependence on advertising and thus a Difficult situation). Repetition of the convenience-goods ads produced a sharp linear curve for ad recall and a more gently sloping curve for purchase intention. The shopping-goods ads produced an ad recall repetition function that flattened after four exposures and a purchase intention function that was almost flat over six exposures.

The more important the purchase, the greater the likelihood that other sources of information will be used and that the situation will tend toward a Difficult scheduling one—i.e., it will be difficult for the advertising alone to have an effect and be remembered.

It is even possible that the three general types of communication situations discussed in the first chapter—consumer, industrial, and public sector—could be ranked with consumer marketing being most often Easy and the public sector being most often Difficult. One should take care in making such a ranking, however, since the example of the Stanford study mentioned above showed both the Easy and the Difficult scheduling situations within the consumer context. It seems that variables beyond the product type must be considered.

Brand Position. The stronger the brand position in terms of share of market and share of consumer mind, the greater the probability that the situation will be Easy. It is the also-ran brands and the not-so-well-known brands that face the Difficult scheduling situation. And it is doubly difficult because these brands are less likely to have substantial funds to spend on advertising.

This brand position relation to scheduling situation was found in both laboratory and field studies in the Stanford program. In laboratory research, ads for well-known brands produced higher and sharper curves than did ads for not-well-known brands. This occurred across several measures in two studies. In Strong's field experiment, it was the not-well-known brands that were likely to experience decay in effect during nonadvertising periods. The well-known brands not only experienced less decay but sometimes actually had increases during the nonadvertising periods.

Budweiser, Campbell soups, Morton salt, Chevrolet, RCA, and General Electric are all brand names well known enough to actually benefit even from competitive advertising of less-well-known brands when the latter are too similar. These kinds of brands almost define the Easy scheduling situation.

Putting together the segment, product type, and brand position factors makes it easy to see why public-sector campaigns often face a Difficult scheduling situation. Take a public health campaign. Usually it is trying to convince someone to stop doing something he or she is presently doing ("theirs" segment) about which most information has come from past and present personal sources and which is not well known or has a small share of market or mind. All of these lead to a Difficult scheduling situation.

Communication Environment and Competition. This factor is, in a sense, the reverse of the brand position one. That is, if the brand has a strong position and is well known, competition is not important, the communication environment is favorable, and the Easy scheduling situation probably holds. This may be true, but the communication environment and competition have an effect that is a bit more complex.

Basically the communication environment presents the problem of "noise." To the extent that the environment is cluttered with other advertising and with program or editorial material that is not supportive or is conflicting, there is the chance of slipping into the Difficult situation. This is true whether the brand has a strong position or not.

The studies in the Stanford program indicated that competitive effects could be quite complex and sometimes surprising. In one case, for instance, the repetition of one brand's advertising did more for the competitive brand recall than for the brand's own recall. In other cases the net effect was positive for the test brand's advertising. Sometimes the effect of the environment and competition depends on the measures of effect. Awareness and recall can be positively affected by competitive messages, particularly if the brand is in a strong position with distinctive advertising. But measures like deeper comprehension, attitude, and intention can be seriously affected by a competitive environment.

Remember that the communication environment is formed by more than just the competition. The environment can be set by the total context of the medium and also by other elements of the communication mix. In many advertising situations, the publicity–PR, personal selling, and/or sales promotion elements have occurred before or have at least been concurrent with the advertising. These other elements can contribute to the situation's being Easy or Difficult for advertising media scheduling. In one study in the Stanford program, for instance, Swinyard found that when a certain type of personal selling (which could also be implemented in the form of sales promotion) preceded advertising, something akin to an Easy situation was created for the advertising. Other forms of personal selling, which did not actually pave the way for the advertising, set up what might be considered a Difficult situation.[15] Suffice to say here that Media planners should be sensitive to aspects of the communication mix that might make the job for advertising either easy or difficult.

Advertising Appeal or Tone. Certain appeals and tones can fit the situation so well that they develop an Easy situation. And in other situations an appeal or tone is required by the situation even though it may create a Difficult scheduling setting.

Perhaps the best example of these potential effects of appeal and tone is in the use of refutational and supportive appeals. We have seen that the refutational appeal is a two-sided one that brings up and then refutes an argument competitive to the purchase of a brand. The supportive appeal is one that simply states the positive arguments in favor of the brand. In the Stanford research, it was found that the refutational sort of message produced an Easy response when the audience tended to be somewhat antagonistic or difficult to persuade. The supportive appeal tended to produce an Easy response in those situations that were already favorable to the brand.[16]

In the message chapters, the best example of application of the refutational approach is the "honest-twist" approach of Doyle Dane Bernbach for such campaigns as VW and Avis. Note that when these campaigns were developed, all other aspects of the situation—need for strong response, somewhat antagonistic segment, product information gathered mostly from sources other than advertising, brand in weak position, competition strong—tended to suggest a Difficult scheduling situation. While the preponderance of these factors and the limited budgets still required a media dominance strategy that is usually called for by a Difficult situation, the appeals (and to a great extent the format) of the advertising eased the situation somewhat for the media planner. Eventually the situations became Easy. Such can be the power of appeal and tone in scheduling.

Advertising Format. Since format is the last of the factors considered here, it is not surprising that its effect is interrelated with all the other factors already mentioned, particularly measures. An arresting format has been studied in the Stanford program in terms of being judged as a "grabber," responded to by consumers in an involving way, producing a great deal of cognitive response in terms of counterarguments, having an unusual illustration, or simply using color as opposed to black and white.

On the surface it would seem that the use of any of these format devices would make the advertising distinctive and produce something like the Easy scheduling situation. This seems to be true, but only for lower-level measures such as awareness and recognition. And even for those, strong format seems to work best in producing an Easy response function while forgetting during nonadvertising periods can be rapid.

For higher-level measures such as deeper comprehension, attitude change, and intention, unusual format can have a negative or null effect. In short, it seems that the media planner should concentrate on factors other than format in estimating potential response and decay for scheduling. For those cases in which it is desirable to have an important short-term effect on awareness response, certain types of format, particularly the involving one, can work. But the most important effects on the scheduling decision will be made by other aspects of the total plan and situation.

Summary. It would be simple to say that if (1) the response desired is awareness or recognition, (2) the target segment is favorably disposed toward our market offering, (3) the product type is one for which advertising is the main information source, (4) the brand is in a strong position, (5) the communication environment is supportive and has few competitors, (6) the appeal and tone are strong and appropriate, and (7) the format is arresting—the scheduling situation is Easy. These are the general indications across the seven factors. But these general guidelines should be used along with specific knowledge to estimate response and forgetting and plan schedules in each instance. All that can be said at this point is that it is usually true that one or several of these factors are not favorable, so that substantial skill and creativity must be used in scheduling.

The Scheduling Decision Process

The problem of scheduling was stated quite succinctly in the first quotation at the beginning of this chapter. That is, "One brand can require heavy support—eight or more target audience exposures during periodic four-week flights. Another may respond best with a low, continuing level of one or two exposures over an average four-week period. A third may show no pattern at all."[17]

This section has provided guidelines for determining which of these situations exists for scheduling at any given time. Scheduling certainly follows all the other decisions in the campaign, including the media and type of vehicle ones made for the media plan. Thus it is possible to analyze the situation thoroughly to determine what needs to be done.

The choice really involves the plan criteria of reach and continuity versus frequency and dominance. Relatively flat, low-level schedules over the year will give reach and continuity, especially when they are spread across media. Extreme wave approaches such as a burst or jolt-and-fade schedule will give frequency and dominance. So will media concentration or media dominance approaches.

Once the media planner knows the alternatives, it is time to determine what the consumer response to the campaign is likely to be. If something like the Easy situation is likely, reach and continuity are important. Overspending and overexposure are the potential problems.

Seldom is the situation purely an Easy one, however. Even the dominant market leader must take care to hold position and deal with new segments and new threats. And when a Difficult situation exists, there is a dilemma between the concentrated (burst, jolt-and-fade) schedules necessary to get adequate response and the resulting low or nonadvertising periods during which forgetting is rapid.

Sometimes this dilemma can be resolved by changes in other parts of the total campaign. Media more directly targeted at the key segment can be used so that frequency can be achieved at a lower cost. Message idea or format can be changed appropriately to lead to faster and more lasting response. Other communication elements can be used to pick up the slack during nonadvertising periods. In the Northwestern Mutual Life situation, for instance, the low-advertising period following the Olympics splurge was filled with promotional materials and the personal-selling efforts of insurance agents.

In most cases, however, the residual problems of scheduling are left largely to the media-buying team. It is up to them to use the available funds in such a way that there is enough frequency and dominance *and* continuity with reach enough to satisfy planners' nagging worries. The way buyers perform these minor miracles is the subject of the next section.

MEDIA BUYING

The preceding chapter began with Maneloveg's observation that the media decision process included two clear parts: media planning and media buying. Media planning is the decision as to media, general types of vehicles, and scheduling. This is done within the framework of a series of criteria. Once the media plan is developed, however, there is a great deal of work to do in implementing it in terms of media buying.

The main characteristic of the media-buying situation is enormous complexity. We have already noted that MRI issues audience reports in about fifty volumes every year. These reports cover over forty product categories, eighteen demographic classes, and twenty psychographic categories. The media buyer has to lay against these audience characteristics literally hundreds of vehicle options.

As an example, consider a media buyer who is given a plan with a budget of $1 million with which to purchase twenty spot announcements on prime-time television. If the general vehicle requirements of the plan indicate that the buyer should consider one hundred prime-time television programs, there would be 770 *sextillion* ways that this buyer could spend his or her television money. Clearly, this is a situation that could be improved by the application of computer assistance in the form of media models. Also, even with the models, creativity is the key.

Often it is at the buying stage that real breakthroughs in media take place. Buyers are the people who interact with the media representatives and thus are exposed to specific alternatives that may not be readily apparent to the planner. Sometimes in the course of executing the plan an opportunity or a problem comes up which can change the whole character of the media strategy. These may be the key to the solution which someone facing a Difficult scheduling situation needs. One can imagine how the following breakthroughs may have come from a media buyer trying to deal with what he or she must actually face in implementing a plan:

☐ "Why not see if we can bind a transcription right into the magazine?"
☐ "Why not run a series of half-page ads in the same issue on consecutive right-hand pages?"

☐ "Let's use an acetate overlay in the book preceding our ad and framing the main picture element . . . if the cost isn't too steep."

☐ "Maybe we could buy 3-second spots every hour and sponsor the time signals."

☐ "Let's make it an outdoor teaser campaign . . . paint the first word one week, the second the next, etc."[18]

The following media innovations, which came from the Ogilvy & Mather advertising agency, could also have been generated by media buyers dealing creatively with the problems and opportunities of implementing the plan:

☐ Open Pit barbecue sauce gained impact in radio advertising to Blacks by sponsoring a *disc jockey contest* for the best live delivery commercial.

☐ Maxwell House coffee explored new audiences by placing advertising in *paperback books.*

☐ Drāno advertised in the *Yellow Pages* of the telephone book, suggesting that people try Drāno before calling the plumber.

☐ NoDoz concentrated its *radio spots after 9 P.M.* to reach the tired driver.

☐ Merrill Lynch established a newspaper advertising position *opposite the stock market tables* to reach investors.[19]

Creating a Separate Medium

If you examine the media innovations above, you will note that they have a common characteristic. That is, they put the advertising message almost in a medium by itself. By knowing intimately the actual or potential interaction between the product and the consumer, campaign planners have found a place in the media that is like a personal store where the person in need almost naturally comes to get advice.

Consider the following description of reaction to one of a series of bread commercials which told a continuing story of a trucker and his waitress girlfriend. In addition to launching the career of the singer, C. W. McCall, these commercials were so popular that the company took newspaper ads to announce when they would be shown. And the effect on the bread company's sales was dramatic.

The din in the truck drivers' tavern near Interstate 80 in central Iowa suddenly ceased. Every eye focused on the TV set perched above the bar. Even the wafting smoke seemed to halt and the billowing froth in the beer mugs appeared to stand still. Sixty seconds later, the place erupted again. Laughter spewed across the room and the TV was swamped by the normal cacophony of the room. A hundred people—amazing as it sounds—had just been spellbound by a bread commercial.[20]

Of course this kind of moment in advertising communication is created by many separate elements and many separate people working on the campaign. But media buyers, because of their intimate contact with media problems and opportunities, can contribute importantly to creating such moments of communication.

What the Media-Buying Unit Does

Media buyers translate the plan into actuality by using the detailed cost and effectiveness data and meeting with media representatives to make actual purchases. Buyers are given certain objectives by the plan. They must achieve these objectives within the media, type of vehicle, and schedule assigned. And they must stay within the budget or at least have some strong reason for exceeding it.

Media buyers must often go beyond available numbers or at least use numbers from a variety of sources to make actual buying recommendations. For instance, in buying television time, it is necessary to go beyond cost-per-thousand figures based on ratings. Cost per thousand should be based on estimated target segment audience figures pared down by estimates as to what proportion of the audience will actually be exposed to the commercial and what response is likely to be at particular times. The buyers, media researchers, and media models all work together with data to determine which of the specific alternatives should be used. Sometimes the media themselves present the results of special studies or potential discounted buys which figure into the equation. It is said, in any case, that the buyer is the one person in the agency who could get a free lunch almost every working day just by meeting with a media salesperson at lunchtime.

Media-Buying Organizations

Sometimes the buying function is done outside of the advertising agency by a media-buying organization. Such organizations are at the forefront of attempts to develop new and more efficient forms of broadcast advertising alternatives. For instance, such a service might offer what is called *barter TV syndication,* in which a number of advertisers agree to support television programs which are then offered free to individual television stations. The stations get to control, say, 70 percent of the commercial time inventory on each show and make more money than they might with network programs. The advertisers get a more efficient, less-expensive television buy.[21]

In essence, the media-buying organization has evolved into one that does many or all of the functions of an advertising agency buying unit but also has some special capabilities to offer such packages as the one mentioned above, particularly in the broadcast area.

Buying Specific Media

Each medium or type of vehicle offers a particular set of data, rate structures, problems, and opportunities for buying.

Network television, for instance, is characterized as a seller's market. There is a limited amount of time to be bought in the first place. And there are many buyers. This means that

prices are high, and there is much negotition in order to arrive at actual prices.

When this book was being written, for instance, the rates for a thirty-second advertising time slot on network programming ranged from $55,000 to $150,000.[22] There were estimates that the average would reach $150,000 by 1985.[23] And for special programs such as the Super Bowl, the price rose to $275,000 per thirty-second time slot. In many instances these rates were whittled down by negotiation and the purchases of packages of participations on a number of programs.[24] But network television has been such a seller's market that the Super Bowl is often 80 percent sold over six months before it is broadcast. And certain time slots and programs tend to be controlled by particular advertisers. The best example is the dominance of package-goods companies such as Procter and Gamble over daytime serials.

The response of media buyers to all of the above has been to move to spot TV (in local markets on local stations), other media, and the kind of special program represented by the barter syndication one.

There is still an opportunity to get a bargain in network TV, of course. The pricing is based on expected ratings, and sometimes the ratings and audience size are much larger than expected, thus lowering cost per thousand substantially. Also, contrary to usual expectations, network television can sometimes be outstanding in reaching particular audiences, even on a psychographic basis.[25]

Spot TV is so difficult to buy, primarily because of the multitude of stations and markets, that one media director suggested that the agency commission be 20 percent for spot TV instead of the usual 15 percent.[26] Buyers are faced with mountains of data, battles for time with local advertisers, intricate variations in the amount of clutter or competing messages across markets, and alternatives such as buying into barter syndication. It is not surprising that the computer and media-buying organizations become important. It is also not surprising that barter syndication has pushed up to over 50 percent of some stations' operating costs or that special local program types and cable television advertising are alternatives increasingly being considered.

Cable and satellite TV are sometimes bought on a "network" basis in terms of satellite programming and sometimes on a local basis much like spot TV. The audiences are, relatively speaking, quite small. There were only about 17 million "wired" homes at the time this book was written. But this figure is expected to grow at a rapid rate.

Cable offers the possibility of direct targeting that is not typically available for television advertising. Costs are lower; however, data on actual viewing (vehicle exposure) are not usually available or solid.

Magazines have been one of the main beneficiaries of the lack of adequate low-cost availabilities on television. As buyers have moved more into magazines, they have discovered the dual problem and opportunity that there seems to be a magazine to reach almost every market segment. In fact, one firm has proposed personalized magazines based on a data file on each subscriber. Thus even the advertising could specifically meet consumer needs with, for instance, no cigarette advertising in the publication collated together for nonsmokers.[27]

The personalized magazine idea is an extreme of the kind of specificity that is available to the media buyer. Not only are there literally hundreds of publications each designed to reach a particular consumer, farm, or industrial market, but many of them have special regional and/or demographic editions. Buyers can also determine the size of an ad and its position within selected publications. An organization called Magazine Networks even allows local advertisers to buy ad space in inserts put into national magazines of various types.

Right-hand pages are said to have some advantage over left-hand pages in terms of generating response. Pages at or near editorial material also have an advantage, as do the inside and back covers. Special inserts can get more of the right kind of attention than ordinary single pages. Larger space in general seems to be better than smaller, although for all of these magazine variations, there are questions as to whether the advantage is worth the extra cost. Perhaps a guideline for specific situations would be an assessment of whether the extra expenditure is likely to develop something like a separate medium that will attract a target segment.

While availabilities are not a problem with magazines in the same way that they are with television (given enough lead time, magazines can simply add pages), solid data are difficult to get. At the time this book was being written, there was considerable controversy over the methods used to determine magazine audiences. Beyond audience data, media buyers must use some estimate of the value of exposure in particular magazines. This is a critical statistic, not only in media model work but also in all buying decisions, and good data comparing vehicles are hard to get.

Newspapers, being a print medium like magazines, have many of the same buying problems and opportunities and alternatives in terms of size of ad, position, and the like. At the same time, newspapers are a local medium and thus bear some relationship to spot TV buying. One twist still being practiced is higher rates for national as opposed to local advertisers in newspapers.

When considering a localized medium like newspapers, it is important to know what the environment is in each market. Not only must the buyer know the rates and audience figures. The buyer should also know whether in each market consumers tend to turn to particular newspapers to prepare for, say, grocery shopping. It may be that, in markets with substantial use of local media for shopping purposes, *cooperative advertising* involving shared expenditures between local and national advertisers would be effective.

Certain markets will have the bulk of local and national advertising in particular media or vehicles, the various newspapers, radio and television stations, and outdoor. The buyer must assess this carefully to determine where target segments might be reached and at the same time not be in an overly cluttered environment.

Sunday supplements are like the "network" version of newspapers in a magazine format. They are inserted in weekend newspapers around the country and have huge audiences and reasonably low costs per thousand. Although they share the short life of newspapers, they have some of the magazine characteristics of fine color reproduction and the like. In addition, their page size is larger than that of most magazines.

Radio is another medium that has blossomed in advertising billings due in part to the difficult buying situation in television. Radio is largely a local medium, although it is possible to buy it through a number of network formats and "nonwired" network packages set up by radio sales representatives.

Radio presents one of the most complex buying situations. Since it is a local medium, the buyer must consider markets and the situation within each market. Then there are stations appealing to specific audiences in both AM and FM. And each station offers a different pricing scheme for different special programs and for certain hours of the day—e.g., the 6–10 A.M. and 3–7 P.M. drive times, midday, evening.

Adding to this complexity is the difficulty involved in obtaining good data on radio audiences. However, many of the examples of creative media breakthroughs have utilized radio's relatively low cost and the ability to time messages so that they reach people when the product is salient—breakfast and break times for coffee, lunchtime for soup, late at night for NoDoz, and so forth.

Outdoor advertising can now be bought on a rating point basis. A 100 rating point buy would mean that the equivalent of 100 percent of the adult population would be covered in a day, although this would include duplication. Thus the average daily reach

would be perhaps 25 to 30 percent and over a month would be perhaps 85 percent and higher.

Taking into account the limited message that can be transmitted with outdoor, it can still be a very efficient medium for the buyer to consider. Prices are low, and there are adequate availabilities. Data are sufficient for making buying decisions by market.

MEDIA MODEL ASSISTANCE

This section examines computerized media models in terms of the structure they impose on the buying decision process. Despite the complexities and the difficulty of this process, media models are used only infrequently to deal with parts of it. The technology of media models has advanced to the point where much of the media-buying job can be done on the computer. This has not occurred, however, because objective data for use in the models have not kept pace with the development of the models themselves. The primary lack of data has been in the media information areas of advertising exposure effect, advertising communication effect (qualitative value), frequency curves (response functions), and forgetting curves.

In this section, therefore, instead of a detailed instruction on the use of media models, the general structure will be used to provide direction for the media-buying job.

The Adaptive Planning Trend

Several recent developments have occurred in the media models area, but the one that is most relevant for present purposes might be called the "management-based, adaptive planning, interactive" type.

They are "management-based" in that they are developed with the management view of media problems in mind. The model is only as complex as the data and experience of the media planner. If, for instance, the planner believes that advertising response does not vary by media option or if the planner feels there are inadequate data on that point, then he or she is not forced to include this as part of the model. The model is set up so that the advertising person can feel comfortable in using it, not so the mathematician can be proud of its elegance.

These are "adaptive planning" models in the sense that they are developed by adapting the form and content of the model on the basis of campaign and research experience. It is assumed that as more research is done, the media planner's information will become more complex and that he or she will ask the modeler to build more of this complexity into the model. In this way the model can be based on market experience and, as we shall soon see, on behavioral research inputs.

These models are interactive in two ways. The manager interacts directly with the model by use of an on-line computer terminal, time-sharing system. This is important because the manager then gets a chance to "feel" the way the model operates. These models are also interactive in the sense that they are often constructed so that the media model can interact with models in other parts of the marketing system. This is important because it can help put the advertising contribution to marketing goals in proper perspective.

The significance of these "management-based, adaptive planning, interactive" media models is that they require behavioral science inputs in order to develop to full capacity. This is the point made by Gensch who noted that advertising people need better inputs on such factors as the qualitative values of media, the effects of alternate creative approaches, the function of response to repetitive exposures of advertising, forgetting curves that occur under various advertising conditions, interactions between ad placements in a variety of media, and competitive advertising effects. Media models, Gensch noted, are highlighting the need for this behavioral information. In addition, media models provide a setting within which to actually use behavioral information and the outcome of behavioral research.[28]

Conclusion: The Media Model Framework for Planning and Buying

At this stage in the development of media decision making, we have a very complex situation that is being attacked by new data and the fresh tool of the media model. Until the data are developed to the point that managers feel confident about their inputs on advertising exposure, advertising communication, response functions, and forgetting curves, these media models will not be used on an everyday basis. Our argument here, however, is that the process of initializing and using these models provides an excellent framework for all the considerations that need to be made in order to plan and buy media. In fact, they are a decent outline of the message distribution decision area for any element of the communication mix. We conclude this chapter, therefore, with a brief statement of the steps a media manager must take in order to initialize and use the typical model.

Table 16-1 outlines the thirteen steps that a media manager must take in using the FOCUS model, which is representative of a heuristic-search-simulation media model.[29]

In order to highlight the framework of this book and media chapters, the list has been divided into four parts. The first part, "Situation, Goals, Creative," includes the inputs that come from the overall marketing-communication plan as well as the advertising creative strategy. Here we are concerned with the specific marketing targets and the alternative weights we apply to each of those segments. In addition, it is necessary to indicate to the model that there is a point of maximum frequency beyond which we assume that there would be negative returns. With the FOCUS model, one selects from a num-

Table 16-1. Steps for Using the FOCUS Model and for Making Media Decisions in General.

Situation, Goals, Creative:
1. Marketing targets
2. Segment weights
3. Maximum effective frequency
4. Reach-frequency response curve

Media Plan and Data:
5. Media-vehicle set
6. Media audience
7. Ad exposure
8. Ad communication
9. Constraints-budget

Model Runs:
10. Initial buy
11. Model runs
12. Buy decision

Application of Scheduling Plan
13. Scheduling

SOURCE: Michael L. Ray and Richard Clark, ''FOCUS'' (Unpublished paper, Graduate School of Business, Stanford University, 1971).

ber of reach-frequency response curves in order to indicate a repetition function that is expected on the basis of the situation and the particular creative strategy that is being used.

The second stage in initializing and using the FOCUS model involves a direct input of the "Media Plan and Data." On the basis of the media plan, the model user inputs the media-vehicle set that is to be considered, the media audience data for that appropriate set, an estimate of advertising exposure probabilities for each vehicle in the chosen set, an estimate of the advertising communication probabilities given the communication goal for the advertising campaign, and the con-

straint of budget thought necessary to achieve those goals. It is in these steps—5 through 9—that the media-planning and buying decision processes clearly interact.

Following the input of the media plan and data, the actual stage of "Model Runs" is reached. This consists of the media buyer's inputting an initial buy based upon his or her noncomputer expertise in media buying. Then the model runs by going through the heuristic-search-simulation process. It develops increasingly more improved buys. Finally, in step 12, the model user makes the decision to stop at some particular plan.

In the fourth and last stage, the buy plan that has been developed from the model is then developed into a schedule overtime as was indicated by the scheduling component of the original media plan. Scheduling is not a component of most media models, although the scheduling component of the original plan can be taken into account in terms of the advertising exposure and advertising communication weights the user applies.

The thirteen steps, then, are a responsible approximation of the requirements and techniques of the media strategy area and are analogous to the message distribution plan decisions that must be made for all elements of the communication mix. Recall also that use of a model consists of the fifth stage of the research system which started with the four steps (problem formulation, behavioral analysis, alternative generation, and pretesting) of message format development. As such, media strategy and the models that represent it are a link to the implementation of the total campaign.

ISSUES AND PROJECTS FOR DISCUSSION

1. In what sense has the use of media models actually changed the character of media planning and buying?

2. A promotional piece to the trade claimed that an advertising campaign generated "over 10 billion exposures to the American public." What

does this mean, if anything? What would be a more accurate, if perhaps not as impressive, number?

3. What is the difference between media scheduling and media buying?

4. How does the exposure definition or measure—i.e., vehicle exposure, ad exposure, ad perception or ad communication—affect whether you have GRPs or ERPs?

5. What alternatives do media planners have in terms of scheduling strategies? What sorts of situations would lead to the use of each of these strategies?

6. An industrial advertiser uses mainly trade magazines and claims to be using the Krugman three-exposure idea because he strives to get between three and ten exposures against his key segments. Is this an appropriate use of the Krugman idea? Why or why not? If not, what alternative could you suggest to him?

7. "If we can be funny in radio, we'll get response." Is this true? How does message format affect scheduling?

8. Under what conditions would you expect an Easy scheduling situation as opposed to the Difficult one?

9. Under what conditions would the clear market leader *not* expect an Easy scheduling situation?

10. Under what conditions would the planner try for reach and continuity, as opposed to frequency and dominance?

11. Which medium seems the easiest to buy and which the most difficult? Why?

12. Which medium or type of vehicle is best for frequency-dominance and which for reach-continuity? Why?

Notes

1. Walter Staab, "On the Media Front: Superman Has Effective Reach; Can Advertisers Duplicate It?" *Advertising Age,* April 2, 1979, p. 67.

2. "Media Buying Units: Grey Advertising Offers an Analysis," *Advertising Age,* May 25, 1970, p. 132.

3. Richard C. Anderson, "Do Computers Leave Room for Judgment?" *Advertising Age,* January 14, 1980, p. 47.

4. Paul M. Roth, *How to Plan Media* (New York). Pages are unnumbered, but quotations are from the second and last pages of Chapter 9, "Reach and Frequency—Whither They Goest?"

5. Russell L. Ackoff and James R. Emshoff, "Advertising Research at Anheuser-Busch, Inc. (1963–68)," *Sloan Management Review,* 16 (Winter 1975), 1–16.

6. "Sunkist Growers Inc.," in *Cases in Advertising and Communication Management,* ed. Stephen A. Greyser (Englewood Cliffs, N.J.: Prentice-Hall, 1981), especially Exhibit 20.

7. Herbert Krugman, "Memory without Recall, Exposure without Perception," *Journal of Advertising Research,* 17 (August 1977), 7–12.

8. Hubert Zielske, "The Remembering and Forgetting of Advertising," *Journal of Marketing,* 23 (January 1959), 239–43.

9. Edward C. Strong, "The Use of Field Experimental Observations in Estimating Advertising Recall," *Journal of Marketing Research,* 11 (November 1974), 369–78.

10. Herbert Krugman, "Why Three Exposures May Be Enough," *Journal of Advertising Research,* 12 (December 1972), 11–14.

11. Peter H. Webb and Michael L. Ray, "Effects of TV Clutter," *Journal of Advertising Research,* 19 (June 1979), 7–12; Michael L. Ray and Alan G. Sawyer, "Behavioral Measurement for Marketing Models: Estimating the Effects of Advertising Repetition for Media Planning," *Management Science,* 18 (December 1971), Part B, 78–89; and Michael L. Ray and others, "Marketing Communication and the Hierarchy of Effects," in *New Models for Mass Communication Research,* ed. Peter Clarke (Beverly Hills, Calif.: Sage Publications, Inc., 1973), pp. 147–76.

12. Krugman, "Memory without Recall."

13. Zielske, "Remembering and Forgetting"; and Strong, "Use of Field Experimental Observations."

14. Alan G. Sawyer, "The Effects of Repetition of Refutational and Supportive Advertising Appeals," *Journal of Marketing Research,* 10 (1973), 23–35.

15. William R. Swinyard and Michael L.

Ray, "Advertising-Selling Interactions," *Journal of Marketing Research,* 14 (November 1977), 509–17; and William R. Swinyard and Michael L. Ray, "Effects of Praise and Small Requests on Receptivity to Direct-Mail Appeals," *Journal of Social Psychology,* 108 (August 1979), 177–84.

16. Sawyer, "Effects of Repetition"; and Ray and Sawyer, "Behavioral Measurement."

17. Staab, "On the Media Front."

18. Holton C. Rush, "Ten Points the Account Executive Needs to Know about Media Strategy and Media Selection," in *A Handbook for the Advertising Agency Accoount Executive* (Reading, Mass.: Addison-Wesley, 1969), pp. 296–97.

19. Kenneth Roman and Jane Maas, *How to Advertise* (New York: St. Martin's Press, 1976), pp. 126–27.

20. Eric Levin, "The Hottest Romance in the Midwest . . . Is in a Bread Commercial," *TV Guide,* April 26, 1975, p. 10.

21. James P. Forkan, "Air Time Signs 5 for Bartered Shows," *Advertising Age,* February 11, 1980, p. 89.

22. Colby Coates, "CBS series top price list," *Advertising Age,* September 1, 1980, pp. 1 & 56.

23. Forkan, "Air Time Signs 5."

24. James P. Forkan, "Superspot: It's "275,-000 for a 30 on Super Bowl telecast," *Advertising Age,* January 12, 1981, pp. 1 & 66.

25. Ronald E. Frank and Marshall G. Greenberg, "Zooming in on TV Audiences," *Psychology Today,* 13 (October 1979), 92ff.

26. Herb Maneloveg, "Same Purchasing Rules Should Apply to All Media," *Advertising Age,* August 8, 1969, p. 60.

27. Jacques Neher, "Personalized Magazines Near?" *Advertising Age,* August 8, 1969, p. 60.

28. Dennis H. Gensch, "Media Factors: A Review Article," *Journal of Marketing Research,* 5 (November 1968), 414–24.

29. Michael L. Ray and Richard Clark, "FOCUS" (Unpublished paper, Graduate School of Business, Stanford University, 1971).

Communication Mix
Message Distribution

• As marketing division head for an insurance company, you are faced with one of the problems of success. You have just used nearly all of your advertising budget on a special television series. The results were astounding in terms of increased awareness. Now the question is, How can your sales force be organized to take advantage of the awareness and also to help fill in for the absence of advertising?

• You are planning the campaign for the introduction of an innovative video recording system. Your company is relatively successful in the television receiver market, even though it is not a leader. What will be your personal-selling message distribution plan? Specifically, would you deploy your resources where you are strong or where you are weak in television sales?

• As a brand manager for a leading bar soap, you have noticed the increasing spiral of expenditures in sales promotion. Competitive expenditures are in turn forcing you to participate also. You have also noticed, however, that there are different responses in different markets depending on whether consumer coupons are presented in newspaper ads or in-store. You are not sure how to deal with these confusing results.

• You have introduced your detergent brand with limited funds by using a publicity campaign based on the notion that the brand was not advertised. Now the question is, How should this campaign be extended to new regions and maintained in the present regions?

• As campaign manager for a senatorial candidate, you are perusing a computer-generated report on the candidate's strengths and weaknesses by precincts and in various areas of the state. Your job is to plan the deployment of the candidate for speeches, volunteer emphasis, rallies, and campaign material.

Everything a marketing organization does is a message about the marketing offering. Everything has the potential of communicating something about the product, service, candidate, or idea. And the distribution of these messages is critical to whether their potential is realized. This is just as true of personal selling, sales promotion, and publicity–PR as it is of advertising.

In fact, the insurance example at the beginning of this chapter is involved with personal selling in a nonadvertising period. A major advertising effort has ended and the question is how the "messages" of personal selling should be distributed. In this sort of situation, decisions very similar to the media, type of vehicle, and scheduling ones of media planning must be made. In addition, there is the opportunity to pick up the slack left by the absence of advertising.

The same sort of decisions and opportunities exist for sales promotion and publicity–PR. The soap brand problem outlined at the beginning of this chapter has to do with something like the media or type of vehicle decision in media planning. The detergent brand publicity example has those aspects as well as the need to make a decision about scheduling. Both the new video recorder and the senatorial candidate examples embody a typical distribution question for nonadvertising messages—that is, the geographic question of whether limited resources should be put where the brand is now relatively strong or relatively weak.

No campaign can be built on just one element of the communication mix. The distribution of messages across the mix is vitally important to the success of the total campaign. Neglect in any one area can mean failure to achieve goals. It simply is not possible to solve message distribution problems like those in advertising media without considering all the components of the mix.

This chapter describes how message distribution decisions can be made for personal selling, sales promotion, and publicity–PR. At first glance it may seem that there is little in common between, say, the distribution aspect of sales management and those of advertising media planning. But the similarities are greater than the difference. In both cases, resources must be allocated on the basis of goals across a series of clear alternatives. The communication elements can all be distributed in increasingly more specific ways, similar to the media-vehicle-scheduling-buying sequence of decisions for advertising media. Once again the response function and the nature of response are critical. Models are used and there are no total generalities. It is necessary to examine the situation carefully to determine the distribution plan.

At the same time that the general structure of message distribution decisions is similar across the elements of the mix, there are major differences caused by the nature of the messages. Thus each of the following sections treats one of the elements of the mix in terms of each of the decisions that must be made and the tools that are available for making those decisions.

SALES MANAGEMENT

Just as for advertising media, three decisions must be made for personal selling. Unlike media planning, however, sales management at the message distribution level is done after the basic decision analogous to media and type of vehicle has been made. That is, once the decision is made as to what role personal selling will play in the campaign, the type of selling (analogous to media) and the type of salesperson (analogous to vehicle) are determined.

It is also true that some general decision has been made about the size of the sales force effort to be devoted to the campaign. At the tentative budget-mix stage, a preliminary allocation has been made to personal selling for this product, brand, service, or market offering.

Given all of this, along with the fact that message distribution for personal selling must work within a distribution and sales organization that is relatively set or inflexible in order to serve all of the company's market offerings, the brand or campaign manager has three decision areas:

1. *Organization*—The question here is, How should the sales force be organized for the selling effort? The final basis is always some form of geographic territories, but there are also possibilities in terms of dealing with certain industries or types of customers, handling large accounts, systems selling with other products in the line, etc. And once the decision is made as to the horizontal organization, there are other decisions in terms of the vertical or line organization that should be maintained for the particular campaign.
2. *Assignment*—Where should salespeople be located? How should products be allocated to the available sales force given the overall organization? How much time should be devoted to a particular account or type of account?
3. *Scheduling*—Now, given the above, how should the selling effort with its various components be scheduled throughout the campaign?

Of course, these decisions for the campaign manager are also somewhat analogous to the media (organization), type of vehicle (assignment), and scheduling ones discussed for advertising media in the preceding two chapters. And, just as for those decisions, the personal-selling message distribution questions are quite dependent not only upon prior budget, goal, and message decisions but also on the company's traditional form of message distribution for this element of the communication mix.

The Context of Personal-Selling Message Distribution

Any company or public-sector organization will already have some sort of sales force in place at the time personal-selling distribution decisions are made for any particular campaign. Each division will have a sales force of a given size and type, and there will be a particular type of selling job expected of this sales force.

The message distribution plan for personal selling must take this situation into account. It is not possible to change the organization of the sales force for each campaign. Attention devoted to one product is attention that is taken from another product. It is difficult to convert a sales force that expects to close sales into one that simply does a missionary job or one that performs follow-up servicing functions after the sale is made.

The purpose of this section, then, is to discuss the context within which the selling distribution decisions of organization, assignment, and scheduling are made.

Types of Selling. We have seen that personal selling can vary from detailed, complex total selling of critically important products and services to missionary selling that does not even involve closing sales to simple order taking as is done in retail stores or by clerks in industrial companies. Many campaigns demand a combination of all three types—sales closing, missionary, and order taking. And the planner must consider that the sales-closing type of selling is likely to be more expensive than missionary selling, which is likely to be more expensive than order taking. Presumably all of this has been taken into account in making the message decisions for personal selling, but the present nature of the sales force will affect what can be done.

Creative Alternatives. In recent years it has been found that certain forms of selling can change the sales management decision situation. In many cases these creative alternatives are simply ways to better serve the customer distinctively.

A good example is *account management,* or systems selling. Used primarily in industrial marketing, it involves the salesperson's becoming a liaison between the customer organization and the seller. The salesperson can actually be a representative of the customer in terms of credit, billing, shipping, and so forth. The account management sort of seller in consumer marketing can advise retail stores in terms of what types of lines to carry to satisfy demand in particular areas. In such situations, the selling effort consists partially of knowing about the retailer's customers, in order to sell the retailer. In industrial situations, the account management forms of selling can mean knowing potential customers' whole production process so the product or service being sold can be fit to it. Or the account management team can actually provide training for their customers.

The main implication for message distribution from this type of selling is that geographic organization is passed over in favor of customer or market organization, with "salespeople" coming from several functional parts of the company.

Closely related to the account management approach are the ideas of *team selling* and *multilevel selling,* in which teams of people from the selling company are used to get to large accounts in particularly important industries. The teams can be composed of people from many functional areas and from several levels within the selling company—in order to deal with appropriate people in the customer organization.

Perhaps one of the best examples of these innovations is the consolidation that was made for large accounts at the American Telephone and Telegraph Company's Long Lines Division. Previously each regional operating company had responsibility for the large accounts in its operating territory. Then account management teams were set up to treat these accounts nationally. These teams could include several hundred people coming from not only sales but also engineering and operating divisions.[1]

Whether an enormous company like AT&T or a small public-sector volunteer organization is involved, the idea of serving customers with more than just selling-and-forgetting them is permeating much of personal-selling activity. This can increase the effectiveness of communication campaigns, but at the same time it presents problems for the planner.

Typical Consumer-Marketing Patterns. Large consumer firms in convenience-good fields have large sales forces to sell primarily to the trade: the retail chains, their individual stores, and the independents. This selling effort is usually done on two levels. First, buying groups at the national or regional level must approve the product. Then a different level of salesperson, sometimes a routeman, will sell to individual stores. Each brand manager must work hard to ensure that his or her product will be adequately supported in the personal-selling effort.

Consumer durable lines such as automobiles and television sets are often sold through a network of dealers. Again at least a two-stage selling process is necessary. First, it is necessary to sell dealers on carrying adequate stock, giving appropriate advertising support, and so forth. Very often dealer personnel are trained in selling and servicing the product also.

For both convenience goods, such as the products of Procter and Gamble or General Foods, or durable goods, such as the products of General Motors or RCA, there are often annual sales meetings for the company's own salespeople and for its customers. These annual meetings can serve to introduce the campaign. These meetings are extremely important from the standpoint of coordinating the selling effort with other parts of the campaign.

What does all this mean for the organization, assignment, and scheduling decisions for personal selling in the consumer field? For organization, it is clear that there are two major splits. A centrally located, more top management selling force deals with the buying offices, coordinates dealer activities, and develops the annual sales meetings or introductory national programs for new market offerings. In addition, there must be a dispersed local sales force that does the day-to-day selling, getting the individual dealer to stock the product, improving display, assisting in consumer selling, and handling servicing and complaints.

Assignment of sales effort at the national level depends on the importance and nature of the account or potential account. If the account is critically important in terms of sales, it will obviously get larger proportions of sales effort. But factors other than size will affect the assignment direction given by the campaign manager. For instance, if the product is an innovative one, prime prospects might be selected on the basis of whether they would be likely to try something innovative. Sometimes in such situations the retailer can give the product extra credibility just by carrying it. This might be true, for instance, of the new video recorder discussed at the beginning of the chapter. Starting distribution in electronics specialty outlets rather than high-volume discount houses or department

stores may be critical for achieving long-term success in the total market.

Scheduling is somewhat obvious at the national level for consumer products and services. There is a "selling in" season for seasonal products which usually precedes by a large margin the actual consumer buying season. For instance, trade shows for toys can take place in the spring, long before the actual heavy Christmas selling season. And, of course, for any new campaign, national-level selling to chains and major buyers must occur before other parts of the campaign. Nothing is worse than getting customers interested in your product at a time when it will not actually be in the store.

At the local or regional territory level, consumer field representatives must respond to the national campaign plans. Beyond that, however, they should be given guidance as to how to call on prospects over the course of the year. Since the decisions that local retailers make are usually minor compared with those made at the national level, there typically is not as great a need for extensive selling. Instead there is a need for the local salesperson to plan his or her visits to the retailer so that the product will always be available. Ideally the salesperson would arrive at the store at the point when the retailer is just about out of stock of the product. Just like the message distribution situation for advertising media, the personal-selling attempt is to get to the right people at the right time with the right message. While local store buyers are typically besieged by salespeople, the one with the product that is needed at the moment is always welcome. The campaign manager can provide tools for the local sales staff so that this type of coincidence of need and sales call occurs more often.

There is a story told about a Proctor and Gamble field representative who arrived at what was in fact the wrong time. The store manager was busy so the representative went back to the storeroom, hid the store's supply of Ivory Flakes behind some other boxes, and proceeded to show the store manager that he did not have any of the product and had better stock up. Of course this story is probably apocryphal as it relates to P&G, because of the normal quality of its campaign efforts. But it does illustrate what can happen to consumer selling if the message distribution part of sales management is not done properly. Other examples include high-pressure tactics employed by car salespersons, out-of-stock conditions in supermarkets, and inadequate service on insurance claims.

Typical Industrial-Marketing Patterns. It is harder to identify "typical" patterns of industrial sales message distribution, since the many types of industrial products require different types of selling effort. In addition, industrial buying decisions tend to be multiperson ones, with the need for selling to be done at several levels of the company. Sometimes, for instance, appropriation is made for a certain piece of equipment, such as an oscilloscope, and then the engineer in a specific department is free to make the purchase of any particular make, as long as it is within budget and general specifications. In such situations, where, when, and to whom should the selling effort be directed?

Probably the best way for the campaign manager to organize his or her thinking about industrial personal-selling patterns is to think in terms of the process of product adoption discussed originally in Chapter 5. Although there are many patterns of sales organization, assignment, and scheduling in the industrial market, they can be summarized by considering the degree to which a product is an innovation. On this basis, there are three general industrial-selling patterns for

1. Major innovations
2. New improved versions
3. Standard products

If the product is a *major innovation* that may promise many benefits but also may

threaten to change the way a customer company does business, there is a need for intensive selling and more. Obviously the personal-selling effort must be supported by the other parts of the communication mix. Then normally a team-selling effort is mounted, not so much by geographic area (although this is sometimes true) as by industry, by certain types of prospect companies within the industry, and by the several types of decision makers within the target type of company.

An example of a major innovation pattern in industrial selling was that offered by the Harlan Chemical Company (a fictitious name). The company was the single source supplier of a talclike substance that had certain advantages over talc in applications in the ceramic tile and paint industries. The clear advantage for the product was in the ceramic tile industry. The problem was that there was a very high initial cost for special dies associated with using the product. The selling job became one of trying to convince potential users that the high costs of the dies would be recouped quickly by costs savings through the use of the new ingredient. This was an especially difficult selling job when the prospects became concerned about having one source of supply.[2]

The best prospects in this instance seemed to be medium-sized growing companies that might be adding new dies anyway and could serve as opinion leaders for both larger and smaller companies. The Harlan sales staff had to deal with people at nearly all levels of the prospect companies, particularly management, production, and laboratory people. For some prospect companies, there were many calls made over a period of years.

Another type of industrial-selling pattern is that constituted by the *new improved version.* This type of product or service does not need as extensive selling as the major innovation, because it does not require a change in the way the customer does business. Many of the new versions of the products of the electronics industry would be examples. With a great reliance on publicity (in the form of trade press and journal articles) as well as advertising, the selling job can sometimes be reduced to order taking. There are, of course, instances in which it is necessary to have two levels of sales force, with one reaching the managerial decision makers and the other reaching the users and/or the purchasing agents. But when a company is turning out improved versions of already accepted products, it is possible to use a large sales force of people who sell at basically the purchasing agent/user level.

Examples of this sales message distribution strategy would include the electronics companies mentioned and pharmaceutical houses with their detail men who distribute samples and information to physicians and pharmacists. A specific company example was Sweda International Incorporated, a seller of electronic cash registers. The company was faltering in the market, and the new president tripled the U.S. field force to two hundred salespersons and three hundred customer-support people. What was even more indicative of the type of industrial-selling pattern represented by the new-improved-version type of situation (the company introduced twenty-five new products between 1976 and 1980) was that Sweda also relied on two hundred independent dealers, a practice frowned on in the industry. The organization consisted of a rather direct relation from the president to the sales force with concentration on specific industries.[3]

A third type of industrial message distribution for selling occurs when the purchase is more or less *standard*. The product is likely to be in the mature stage of the product life cycle, with a large number of competitors and a great deal of emphasis put on price and service. Some of these industrial products and services might be put into the commodity class, but it is probably more functional for the campaign manager to think of them in terms of the importance of the communication campaign in serving customers' needs. In other words, the particular way that marketers fit their standard market offering to the needs of their customers is what makes the difference. And this fitting process is done through all aspects of the marketing communication mix, particularly selling.

An example of this sort of industrial-selling situation is the steel service center industry where increasing personal-selling costs, greater buyer sophistication and size, competitive pressures, and the more important role of women as personal sellers have led to an almost equal role for inside and outside salespeople. Whereas inside salespeople have often been called clerks or order takers in the past, Enis notes that they are becoming equal in importance:

> There are two salespersons assigned to a given account—one outside representative who initiates contact with the account, performs an on-site inspection, and probes to determine needs.
>
> The outside rep works closely with an inside sales representative, who also becomes familiar with that account (and may also visit the customer's premises), but whose primary task is to be that customer's liaison with the rest of the operation—particularly inventory control, shipping, and billing.[4]

This same kind of attempt at selling teamwork for a "standard" industrial product is seen in the printing industry, in bank marketing, in the travel industry, and, frankly, in the majority of industrial selling. Organization tends to be along regional lines, with each salesperson or team assigned to a relatively large number of accounts. Scheduling against these accounts is more even across the year than is true of the other two types of industrial-selling situations.

Typical Public-Sector Marketing Patterns. So much emphasis is put on publicity and public relations in the nonprofit sector that the fact that personal selling exists is often denied. Indeed it is often true that much of this work is political by label, even though it is a selling activity. Nevertheless, all public-sector or nonprofit marketing campaigns embody some selling components. And all the types discussed previously for the consumer and industrial sectors are available and are used by public-sector campaign managers.

Some public-sector marketing activities are very close to *consumer product distribution.* For publication activities of museums and the Sierra Club, for instance, there is a need to distribute books to chains and then to individual bookstores. Although the budgets may be smaller than in the profit sector, the same kind of distribution and selling decisions must be made.[5]

Other public-sector activities rely very much on a *consumer "pull" strategy,* with publicity, advertising, and sales promotion doing nearly all the work and *order takers* doing the little remaining selling. This is true of the post office for many parts of its business (first-class mail, express mail, money orders, stamp collecting), for zoo and museum stores, for many types of arts programs (although some field selling goes on when representatives visit such groups as schools), and for public transit systems like Amtrak and municipal rapid transit districts (although again there is some selling of public transit commuting to business and school groups).

Still a third type of public-sector selling strategy involves *field workers,* who are very much like *consumer door-to-door salesperons* or *industrial missionary salesperons*—depending on whether a sale is closed or not.

The consumer door-to-door type of selling is most often used by charitable organizations when there are solicitation drives. For instance, the Stanford University annual alumni fund drive had the following message distribution organizational structure for personal selling:

> The Inner Quad, Quad and Phonathon programs were all organized on a regional basis, with the volunteer organization having a hierarchical structure. For instance, the Quad Program was headed by a National Chairman, under whom were ten National Vice-Chairmen, each responsible for an average of six Regional Chairmen.

The sixty regions were set up primarily by geographic location, but sometimes also by interest group. There were typically four or five Captains in a region, each supervising four or five workers, who in turn were assigned about five prospects each. The pyramidal nature of this organization reflected the large number of prospects (over 8,000) and the low prospect to volunteer ratio. Most of those in supervisory positions also solicited prospects themselves. The Phonathon Program, by contrast, had a much flatter organizational structure, despite its 30,000 prospects. This reflected the smaller number of regions (27), the much higher prospect to volunteer ratio, and the fact that the solicitation process was completed relatively quickly.[6]

The industrial or missionary-type salesperson is also used in the public sector, primarily in all types of political campaigning. The analogy is really quite close to industrial missionary selling. Just like the pharmaceutical detail man, for instance, the political campaign worker distributes literature and samples (ballots, buttons, bumper stickers). As in the senatorial candidate example at the beginning of this chapter, the message distribution question is often one of getting enough volunteers in certain geographic areas. Usually the precinct workers report to a precinct captain, who reports to a city or county director, who may report to a state or regional coordinator depending on the level of the political campaign or issue. All three sales management message distribution decisions (organization, assignment, and scheduling) must be made within this structure.

A fourth type of public-sector personal sales management structure is quite close to the *industrial, major innovation, extensive selling message distribution.* In all of these cases there is team selling, multilevel selling, and a need for the two-step sort of selling that occurs when a whole organization has to be persuaded that a particular program should be undertaken. Once this persuasion-selling job is done, then selling can go on at a lower or individual level.

Examples of this sort of public-sector selling exist for every program that has to be sold to some government group, then to special interest or industrial groups, and finally to individual companies or people.

☐ Community water conservation or energy conservation campaigns must be sold to government first, then departments, then institutions within the community, and then, sometimes, to individuals.

☐ The 911 or emergency services telephone number is introduced to a community often with sales presentations first to top management of organizations and then in meetings with specific departments or smaller groups.

☐ Agricultural information agents often present the idea of innovations to farm cooperative heads first and then present this idea to meetings of farmers to work out the details of adopting the innovation with individual farms.

☐ Federal government agencies such as the Urban Mass Transportation Administration (UMTA) will sell the idea of a mass-transit innovation to influential people in a community, then will help the process of implementation, and later will facilitate dissemination of information about the innovation to other cities.[7]

☐ University academic programs are sold by recruiters to high-school counselors, who then pass the word on to appropriate students. Sometimes the university recruiters, particularly those for graduate programs, will meet with individual students.

☐ The Peace Corps is sold at many different levels: to Congress for annual appropriation, to the host countries. But the heart of the total selling job is that involved with obtaining recruits. Often what must be done is that universities must be sold on the idea of allowing recruiters on campus. Then the recruiters must do the personal-selling job. The organization of this selling job, (shown in Figure 17-1), is not unlike that for such volunteer organizations as the armed services or for industrial sales forces that require extensive selling.

In all the nonprofit or public-sector selling organizations there is training, and there are periodic meetings like the sales meetings held annually for consumer or industrial companies. For instance, the Stanford alumni support solicitation organization held an annual Leadership Conference on campus each autumn to update volunteers on university activities, involve them in fund-raising planning and coordination, and provide a chance to revisit Stanford. Awards were presented to outstanding fund-raisers.

Centrality of the Selling Task. The typical organizational patterns for consumer, industrial, and public-sector organizations come from the task that must be done by the salesperson. This is dictated by all the decisions that have been made to this point in campaign planning for all elements of the communication mix, including personal selling. And these decisions are driven by what the sales prospect needs in terms of information and assistance.

Thus when the campaign manager is considering how the sales force effort should be distributed for his or her campaign, it is critical to keep in mind the task that must be accomplished in the end. In this way the key message distribution decisions can be made most effectively about sales force organization, assignment, and scheduling.

Organizational Issues

The organization of personal-selling efforts should be questioned repeatedly, particularly by the campaign manager whose concern is the effectiveness of the total communication campaign. The message distribution of the personal-selling communication element is likely to be severely affected by sales force organization. Yet that organization probably developed over the years on the basis of response to a series of short-run problems.

The campaign manager should concentrate on the personal-selling task to be done in light of the whole campaign. Then it is possible to develop an estimate of the number of salespeople that will be needed and the way

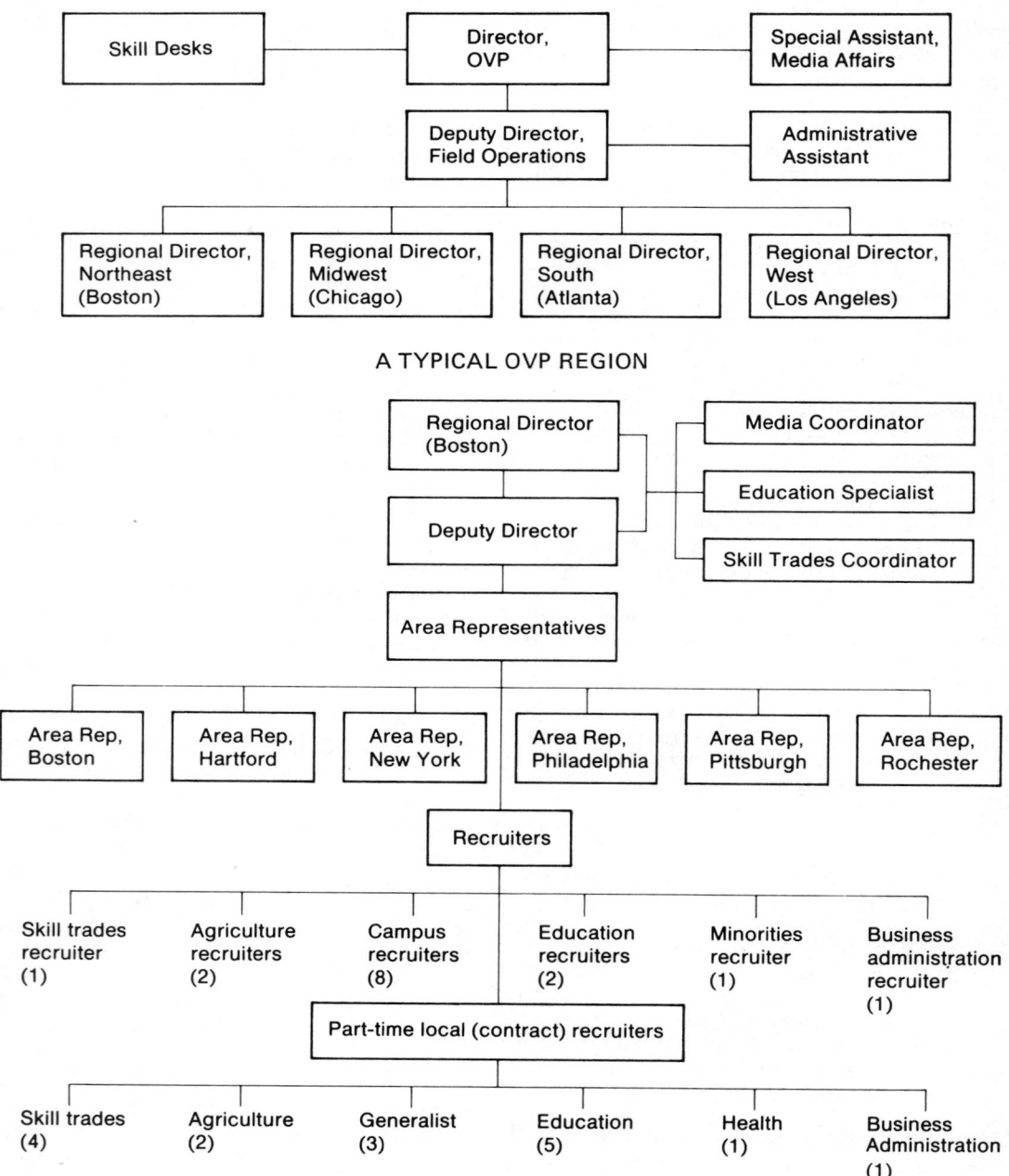

Figure 17-1. *Sales organization in the public sector, the Peace Corps' Office of Volunteer Placement (OVP)*

From Steven H. Star, "The Peace Corps," in *Cases in Profit and Nonprofit Marketing,* ed. Christopher H. Lovelock and Charles B. Weinberg (Palo Alto, Calif.: Scientific Press, 1977), p. 35.

they should be organized. At that point it is necessary to fit this estimate and organizational plan to the company's present sales force structure. If a comfortable fit cannot be made, then restructuring may be necessary. It usually is.

The campaign manager must recognize the context of personal-selling message distribution as was outlined in the preceding section. Not only are various types of selling possible, but there are also a number of creative alternatives to the standard approaches. And consideration of typical patterns in consumer, industrial, and public-sector marketing provides an opportunity to establish guidelines for possible innovation.

In sum, although the size of the sales force is tentatively given by the initial budget mix and the task for each salesperson is outlined by the message idea and format decisions, the campaign manager must still make organizational decisions and assessments as to

☐ The specific task in terms of the number of sales calls of what type it will take to reach certain criteria

☐ Whether salespeople should be assigned exclusively to the particular market offering or if sales time should be shared in some way with other market offerings of the company

☐ What extent there should be separate sales personnel for specific jobs such as missionary versus closing and large central office prospects versus small branch-type customers

☐ Horizontal organization in terms of general allocation of sales force by customer market and geographic territories

☐ Vertical organization in terms of the number of levels of management and the span of control (number of people controlled) at each level

Each of these five assessments and decisions (specific task, product concentration, functional concentration, horizontal organization, and vertical organization) are discussed briefly in the following paragraphs.

Specific Task. Assume that the campaign manager for the video recorder example at the beginning of this chapter has decided that the new product will be sold to the main buying offices of electronic and home entertainment retailers, that follow-up missionary sales efforts will be made to individual stores in the chains, and that eventually sales will also be made to independent retailers. At this point it would be necessary to make some estimate of the selling effort that would be necessary to make a sale or obtain a needed response at each level of selling. This can be determined on the basis of the results with other similar selling tasks in the context of the support the salespeople will receive from advertising, sales promotion, and publicity. For instance, if it was necessary to make a certain number of sales calls at chain headquarters before central buying committees accepted a previous introductory product, then the manager might use that number as an estimate for the present case—as modified by differences in advertising support, and so forth.

Such estimates are necessary to have any ideas as to what the sales organization should be for any given campaign. These estimates are usually made in terms of a range of possible outcomes and are not different in form from the response-function estimates for personal selling that were discussed in Chapter 6 on the tentative budget mix. The difference here is that the estimates can be made on the basis of a great deal more information on the nature of the campaign, particularly in the personal-selling area.

While it does not matter whether the manager puts his or her estimates in the form of specific curves or equations, these estimates are almost always the basis of models that are used to help make specific selling assignment decisions. Sometimes the estimates come from the salespeople themselves, such as when they have already had some experience in selling a product. And whether models are used or wherever the estimates come from, they must be the basis of subsequent decisions on sales organization.

Product Concentration. Is it possible for the present sales force to handle the campaign product along with the other products and tasks they have? Intuitively it would seem to be possible to answer this question by determining the tasks the sales force must perform for other products, along with the tasks already estimated for the campaign product. If in total there is too much to do, then the sales force should be expanded or salespeople should be concentrated by product.

This intuitive process is only an inadequate start to making the decision as to product concentration for salespeople, however. It is essential to consider the degree to which various products are complementary in terms of the selling task. A salesperson who has already sold television sets to department store central buying offices has established contacts; and for those prospects who are not now customers, the new video recorder may serve as an entree the salesperson did not have before. But those salespeople handling, say, refrigerators may not give adequate attention to the new video recorder line. For the missionary salespeople, however, it might be quite efficient to add another line, since they do not have to do the extensive selling after the line has been approved by chain headquarters.

These are some of the considerations that determine the degree of concentration of the sales force on any particular product. It all depends on a mixture of the selling jobs required for products of differing potential and profit. Every brand, product, or campaign manager would like to get a maximum effort from the sales force for each of his or her market offerings. But there must be a balancing so that each product is given a sales effort corresponding to its campaign needs.

Functional Concentration. The organization suggested earlier for the video recorder was a functional one. Some salespeople would handle the development of new accounts at the large chain outlets. Others would do missionary sales work at the individual outlets. And still others would sell to independents.

Certainly, dividing the work in this way

is in some sense natural. It makes the job of estimating the response to sales effort easier. As earlier sections indicated, it is not uncommon to find this sort of division in consumer-marketing selling to the trade—with one part of the sales force selling to chain buying committees and other parts dealing with individual stores and independents. In industrial selling for what was earlier called the "standard, mature" product, it has been noted that the selling job can sometimes be split between an outside contact representative and an inside salesperson who serves as a liaison with the rest of the seller organization.

Since Maytag washing machine advertising has been discussed relatively extensively in this book, it is interesting to note that the Maytag sales force has been organized with this sort of functional split. As the company's general sales manager said:

> Let me give you a specific example. Our Los Angeles market essentially consists of Los Angeles and Orange counties, with small portions of Riverside and San Bernardino counties. This area, for Maytag, is covered by eight salesmen. We have one lead salesman who covers eight major accounts. Each of these accounts has multiple outlets or branch stores. This man calls not only on the main buying office of each of these accounts, but also services each of the branch stores. The other seven men in the market are assigned geographical areas, exclusive of these eight principal accounts.
>
> This system has worked well for us in this particular case. In the first place, our lead man, the salesman who calls on the top eight accounts, has done an excellent job of developing the large accounts. He has developed these accounts to the point where they present a very favorable market image for products in the complete Los Angeles market. In the second place, the lead man in this particular market is highly respected by the other Maytag salesmen. This factor has led to a harmonious merchandising atmosphere and outstanding sales results. If I had to choose between the two factors, I think the lead man must be considered the

most important reason for success in this market.[8]

Of course, as the sales manager pointed out, the type of division of labor within a territory depends on the jobs to be done and the people involved. There are times when customers can become upset when they are passed from the initial contact person to someone else they see as being somewhat inferior in status. But if the market offering requires strong servicing and less selling after the original contact is made, some kinds of functional splits can be quite practical.

Horizontal Organization. When the horizontal organization of the salesforce is considered, attention usually turns to *geographic* territories. Actually, however, both the *product* and the *functional* divisions can be part of horizontal organization. In addition, it is necessary to consider organization by *customer type,* industry or market.

As was indicated in Chapter 5 on segmentation, one of the cleanest, easiest-to-apply organizations is by geography. As was also indicated there, however, geographic differences are sometimes not too important in terms of producing real differences in consumer and buyer decision making. Division by customer type, on the other hand, does promise to produce real differences in reasons and propensities for buying.

At some point there is need for geographic organization for any sales force, even if it is a small, one-person job shop. Even if the owner does his or her own selling, he or she will probably have to organize this effort by local areas. But even in such a very small business situation, there are great advantages to some additional structure's being imposed by market or customer type.

All of the advantage stems from being able to know intimately the needs of a particular type of customer. When salespeople have this kind of understanding of a market segment, they have greater ability to serve and thus to sell. And when there is a coincidence,

and division by product and market tend to coincide, salespeople usually have two strong advantages: (1) they know the product, and (2) they know the users and their needs. The coincidence of product and market segment can happen quite often if the campaign is well planned. As in the video recorder example mentioned earlier, the salesperson selling that product would probably call on a different buyer than the one from the same company who is selling refrigerators.

Total reliance on geographic territories does present some advantages in terms of original organization. Salespersons are simply put into territories to sell all of the products to all of the potential customers. There is not much wasted cost and travel time. There are not the problems of two different salespeople from the same company descending on the same prospects.

But with a total dependence on geographic organization, there is a certain loss of control on the part of the campaign manager and the sales manager. Unless there is almost constant contact, which is impossible to achieve, the salespeople themselves will determine what products and target customers should be given priority. Comfort, short travel time, and familiarity with old customers will be important factors in determining sales efforts. With the product and market organization imposed at some point, however, the campaign manager has the ability to fit personal-selling effort into the total campaign effort.

One example of a combination of geographic and market organization was discussed earlier in terms of Sweda cash register's effort to concentrate on the hotel-motel market with its large sales force and rather direct control from its president.[9]

With the exception of national accounts being handled in a national way as was illustrated by the AT&T Long Lines Division earlier,[10] geographic territories should be established for horizontal organization. But organization or at least emphasis on a product and/or market basis must be imposed in order that personal-selling message distribution can be integrated and work with the other elements of the communication mix.

Vertical Organization. The Sweda president was able to quickly impose a market direction on the sales force because there were not too many levels of command between him and the sales force itself. Vertical organization decisions must be made in order that this kind of control can be established for quick, decisive, and creative moves. The life insurance company mentioned at the beginning of this chapter was faced with a nonadvertising period. Vertical organization should allow the campaign needs to be quickly fulfilled during such periods.

As the discussion in Chapter 7 on the *compensation principle* indicated, the real art of campaign planning is to go so far in achieving one campaign goal with one element of the communication mix that it is almost dangerously necessary for another element to pick up the slack. This is the situation in which the insurance company finds itself. It has gone as far as it can go with advertising, and it now needs unusual support from the sales force. This is where a strong vertical sales organization can support overall campaign goals.

The vertical organization is built, at least conceptually, from the bottom up, from the field to marketing management in the home office. If the selling job is complex and there are functional splits as to specific selling jobs, it is necessary to have a narrow span of control (more second-level managers each controlling fewer first-level or field salespeople). On the other hand, some argue that a too-narrow span of control at this level can lead to overcontrol with a lack of salesperson initiative. Also too many levels of management between the field and the campaign manager can lead to an inability to move quickly and creatively.

Some authors argue that the ideal span of control at the second level is from six to eight.[11] The charts in Figure 17-1 indicate that the Peace Corps span at this level is from fifteen to thirty-one. Again, however, this may not be too large, since not much supervision of each field person may be necessary.

Making Specific Assignments

Once the overall organization is determined in terms of the five areas (specific task, product concentration, functional concentration, horizontal organization, and vertical organization) discussed in the preceding section, it is time to make more specific assignments of salespeople to territories and tasks. For instance, now that it has been determined that specific product lines will be sold to particular prospect types by teams of functional specialists within a series of territories, it is time to determine the nature of the territories, assign numbers of salespeople of various types to each territory, and provide guidance as to how the selling job should be distributed.

If the general organizational decisions of personal-selling message distribution could be said to be analogous to the medium or media decision of advertising media planning, the assignments are roughly equivalent to the second or type of vehicle decision in media planning. As such, the campaign manager does not really become fully involved in the assignment of people to territories, levels of sales management, or customer call patterns. These are the jobs of the sales manager, just as buying specific vehicles is the job of the advertising media buyer instead of the campaign manager. Again, however, as in the advertising situation, the campaign manager can provide guidance to the sales management team, so that their message distribution decisions contribute maximally to the campaign.

In a number of areas the brand or product manager can work with sales management to ensure that personal-selling message distribution will be appropriate for the market offering. One of the best reviews of research on these message distribution questions can be found in a series of reports by Ryans and Weinberg.[12] This forms the basis

ment decisions which is presented in the following paragraphs. This is followed by a brief description of models that can be used by management in assisting those who must eventually make specific assignments.

Importance of Potential. Ryans and Weinberg reviewed the results of their own study of four sales management situations, as well as the results of five other studies of a total of seven more situations. The review was quite conclusive: In nine of the eleven situations, the greater the potential in the salesperson's territory, the greater the sales he or she was able to obtain. Thus, within the limits of the other sales situation characteristics (particularly whether competition is strong or not), salespeople should be assigned more to territories or customer markets for which there is greater potential.

Emphasize Markets Where Presently Strong. This is the competition issue raised above and also by the video recorder and senatorial campaign examples at the beginning of this chapter. There is always the danger that the high potential may obscure the effect of other variables in planners' minds to produce a sort of "majority fallacy" in sales management.

The limited amount of research reviewed by Ryans and Weinberg on the question, "Should we put more of our selling resources where we are strong or where we are weak?" seems to indicate that the answer is, "Where you are strong." Ryans and Weinberg review only three situations in which a variable such as past market share was examined for its effect. In two of these studies, it had a significant positive effect on salespersons' performance in sales. This, combined with the results on total marketing support reported in the next section, as well as anecdotal evidence from other studies, provides adequate support for the recommendation that assignments should be made more heavily to strong territories or markets.

Of course it is possible that growth markets, where there is a chance of expanding sales, are the best sites for emphasis. This would certainly be supported by the general philosophy espoused by the growth-share matrix analysis discussed in Chapter 4.

This general suggestion to go with present strengths is often difficult for management to accept and implement. One oil company (Cities Service) had boasted about its thirty-seven-state marketing area. An analysis of strengths and weaknesses indicated that the company should actually pull out of seven of the states. It did so, despite the fact that its boast could not be as great and that some of the areas were the basis of the beginnings of its business.[13]

Coordinate with Other Communication Elements. In Ryans and Weinberg's own research, a very direct relation was found between the strength of campaign support and the individual salesperson's performance. One company in their research had a region that was restricted from marketing support activities such as direct mail, conferences, and user seminars. On average, a territory in the restricted region had 44 percent less sales than a territory in an unrestricted region.[14] Management knew support from other communication elements would have an effect, but it was surprised at the extent of the effect. Of course the results of this specific study cannot be directly applied to any other situation confronting a campaign planner. But the direction of the indication is clear: Personal-selling effort assignment should be coordinated with the message distribution of other campaign elements.

Pay Attention to Concentration in Large Accounts. Many marketers receive a disproportionate amount of their sales from large accounts. This is one of the reasons that separate national account selling teams are frequently used. In their review and research, Ryans and Weinberg found eight situations in which *concentration,* the degree to which potential is available in the larger accounts in the territory, was examined for its effect on personal-selling effectiveness. In half of these situations, there was a significant positive relationship. That is, the greater the concentration in larger accounts in the territory, the greater the sales of the individual salespersons in them. While a finding of only half of the situations showing significant findings may not seem impressive, the weight of evidence (including the direction of nonsignificant findings) seems to indicate that assignment should be made so that large accounts are covered well. At the same time, however, managers should be concerned with the majority fallacy, in that these large accounts are the very ones that competitors are bound to attack also.

Monitor Geographic Dispersion. In three of the five studies that Ryans and Weinberg reviewed, *geographic dispersion* (roughly, the size of the territory) was negatively related to sales performance. Of course this does not mean that sales managers should automatically listen to salespersons' complaints about driving time, traffic congestion, and the like. Innovative salespeople can sometimes handle much of the selling process by telephone and mail. Also it is possible that fewer visits of longer duration can do the job better. In general, the research results indicate that territories should be designed with geographic dispersion in mind—so that creative solutions to the dispersion problem can be instituted.

Workload Not Important. Normally it is assumed that a lower workload, or fewer accounts to sell and service, increases salesperson performance, since more time can be spent on each account. Ryans and Weinberg found, however, that in none of the five situations in which this variable was examined did it have the lower-workload-greater-sales effect. In two of the situations, just the opposite was found: more accounts, more sales. The conclusion is that, within normal ranges as respresented by the situations studied, workload is not a variable that must be seriously considered by personal-selling planners.

Span of Control. As mentioned earlier, recommended span of control has been six to eight. Since span of control in the three companies studied by Ryans and Weinberg themselves ranged from six to nine, six to eleven, and seven to eleven, predictions were that as span of control increased, sales performance would decrease. In three of four situations examined, this direction of result was observed. Two of these results were statistically significant.

It is not possible to say anything definitive about span of control, because needs for supervision differ so much in each situation. Also the results reported cover a rather restricted range (recall, for instance, that the span for the Peace Corps example earlier was from fifteen to thirty-one and the Stanford alumni example was as low as four or five). But, assuming that a company had information like that developed by Ryans and Weinberg, it would be possible to use the information to assess the need for adding additional regional managers to decrease the span and increase sales.[15]

Models for Assisting Assignment Decisions. The Ryans and Weinberg model was an econometric one which used data from experience to estimate the effect of each variable on sales response. Then these estimates can be used to ask "What if?" questions.

Other models take data and judgments from managers and salespeople to assist in such issues as

☐ Allocating salespersons' time across the multiple products they sell (e.g., the DETAILER model[16]).
☐ Allocating salespersons' time across the accounts in their territory (e.g., the CALLPLAN model[17]).
☐ Redrawing sales and service districts (e.g., the GEOLINE model[18]).
☐ Simultaneously locating the base offices of salespeople, assigning accounts to them, and allocating their time to each account (e.g., the TAPS model[19]).

These types of models have been used quite successfully to assist campaign and sales managers in making assignment or deployment decisions. For instance, the anticipated sales increases from the use of CALLPLAN have been reported to range between 5 and 25 percent.[20] In an actual experiment involving matched pairs of salespersons at United Airlines, the experimental group with access to CALLPLAN achieved 8.1 percent higher sales than a control group.[21]

The key factor in the majority of these decision calculus sales-planning models is the determination of the response that sales managers and their force expect from calls. Just like the models used in advertising media planning, these sales message distribution models mirror the steps management would take anyway in making plans. For instance, for the TAPS model mentioned above, the inputs and steps are:

1. Input the geographic structure of the problem in terms of the location of all accounts or customers being considered. This step represents the horizontal organization decisions of managers.
2. Input subjective judgments about the sales responsiveness of each account at various levels of calling effort. This step represents management's assessment of the task required of salespeople.
3. Input a starting solution or solutions in terms of a proposed location of sales representatives. This can represent management's best solution without model assistance. The step also shows how almost all personal selling message distribution decisions involve a restructuring of the organization and assignments.
4. These two steps involve the operation of the
& model program which uses the above data to
5. deploy sales representatives, develop territory alignment, and set account calling levels. The two steps are done over and over. After each iteration, an estimate of sales is produced. The iteration stops when sales estimates converge at a maximum level. These steps represent the normal process managers go through in trying to achieve the best organization and assignment scheme. Obviously the model serves as a data and judgment combinatorial device. It is up to management to evaluate the model output, see if it is realistic and determine if new runs of the model should be made with new judgments.[22]

In this way the decision calculus model becomes a tool that assists in the assignment decisions that must be made by the campaign and sales managers in any case, with or without a model.

Summary of Assignment Decisions. Once the general organization is set, it is necessary to determine how much sales force weight will be put against various divisions of the horizontal and vertical sales organization. Situation analysis considering potential, present strengths and weaknesses, the influence of other communication elements, concentration in large accounts, geographic dispersion, and span of control can assist in the making of the assignment decisions. Models of both the econometric and the decision calculus types provide further order in making these choices.

Scheduling

This third decision area for personal-selling message distribution is exactly equivalent to the third or scheduling decision discussed in the preceding chapter for advertising media planning. The brand, product, or campaign manager is not directly concerned with the scheduling of the work of individual salespeople. Instead, analogous to the media-scheduling decision, the question is one of how the total selling effort will be allocated for the market offering over the course of the planned communication campaign, usually a year in duration.

Predominance of the "Difficult" Response Scheduling Situation for Selling. Recall that media-planning scheduling was dependent on managerial judgments and data regarding whether the response and decay functions were likely to be "Easy" or "Difficult." With the Easy situation, it was easy to get response to campaign exposures, and easy to maintain that response during normal decay periods, when there was less or no exposure to the campaign. With the Difficult situation, it was difficult to both get and maintain response.

While many kinds of personal-selling situations require only easy responses similar to those in advertising, there is a tendency for the Difficult situation to predominate, particularly on the response side. This is true primarily because the response almost always required (except in the case of missionary selling) is a behavioral one of relatively great importance (or else personal selling of the sort discussed here would not be used). In order to get someone to buy something that will have relatively great consequences for him or her, it is necessary to work relatively hard—thus the predominance of the Difficult response situation in personal selling.

Of course it should be noted that a brand's market position can ease the burden. So can the target segment's brand loyalty, strong support from the rest of the communication campaign, company image, and the like. But despite all of this, it is better for the campaign manager to assume a difficult process in making sales, particularly initial ones.

Less Decay or Forgetting for Personal Selling. While the response situation for personal selling tends to be difficult in most situations, there is a countertendency for "forgetting" or "decay" to be less pronounced during nonexposure periods than is true of advertising.

Some of the reason for this relative lack of difficulty in maintaining the response created by personal selling is just a matter of definition. That is, once a person or an organization has bought a product, there is a certain lifetime to it. During that lifetime, it is extremely difficult for competitors to make inroads. Of course this varies for services, on which it is conceivable that prospects and customers could make switches daily. But buying a product or service does physically commit

the buyer to it, to a greater degree than does mere exposure.

Nearly as important is the psychological commitment one makes by buying a product or service. As indicated by the Dissonance-Attribution hierarchy situation, once somebody has made the commitment of purchase, there is a tendency to support that choice with favorable attitude change and favorably biased exposure to the mass media followed by further positive learning: the Do-Feel-Learn hierarchy.

Both the physical acts of buying and owning a product—coupled with the psychological commitment, attitude change, and learning that follows—are important to the relatively mild decay rates for personal selling.

Of course the campaign manager should not become complacent. There is a need for adequate commitment in making the purchase. And there are always competitors, changes in customers' needs, and other external factors that can hasten losses if satisfactory contact is not maintained with customers.

General Need for Wave Strategies in Personal Selling. Given the predominance of the Difficult response situation and the extremely high and increasing cost of personal sales calls, it is likely that relatively extreme wave strategies will be needed in personal-selling message distribution. That is, the pattern of selling will be characterized by heavy efforts against certain groups for each product during certain time period, followed by periods of nearly no personal-selling effort.

There is a *need* to do this because personal selling takes great effort. There is an *opportunity* to do this because the decay rate, after buyers or organizations have made a purchase, is not likely to be great when that commitment has been made.

Just as in advertising scheduling, the problem is one of limited resources. The campaign manager cannot expect the sales force to be working extra hard on his or her product at all times. So the manager must creatively schedule heavy efforts in places and times and with customer groups that will produce strong sales effects. Then the manager can follow with maintenance efforts, often on the basis of other parts of the communication mix.

Thus while it is true in general that it is difficult to change sales force size and effort during the year, it is possible to make shifts from product to product and customer type to customer type. Salespeople are always working during the year, but there are jolts and fades for target customer groups, in order that the Difficult response situation can be overcome. Some of the campaign situations in which this might occur are

☐ *Introduction campaigns.* When a product or a new version is introduced, there is a need for heavy personal selling to fit with the rest of the campaign effort, to get the product into distribution, and to make certain that early adopters and opinion leaders are in fact able to get the product or service.
☐ *Seasonality.*
☐ *Annual sell-in periods.* Usually a part of seasonality and certainly part of introductions is the "sell-in" period when the product is sold to retailers for consumer products or sold for general corporate approval for industrial products.
☐ *To compensate and interact with other mix elements.* This is discussed more thoroughly in the next chapter, but, just as in the insurance example at the beginning of this chapter, there is the possibility that another part of the mix has been pushed to its limits and personal selling must take up the challenge. For the insurance company, the total advertising budget had been used in an innovative media buy. Next it was up to the sales force of agents to capitalize on the effect of the expenditure and maintain campaign momentum.
☐ *Difficult but valuable customer groups or territories.* The Sweda electronic cash register concentration on the hotel-motel market was an example. Or, "What about the territory where the competition is knocking your ears off? How

about investing more in it if the business is really there? If you are selling industrial markets, take a page from consumer selling and saturate the territory until you succeed. Then pull the shock troops out, but leave a team behind to follow up."[23]

Summary: Creativity in Sales Management

Sales management, like its message distribution counterpart, advertising media, is often considered to be a dismal undertaking, devoid of opportunities for creativity. From the campaign manager's perspective, however, there are opportunities to use the limited resource of personal selling in creative ways that multiply its effect in the context of the campaign.

The three message distribution planning decisions for personal selling are analogous to the three for media planning, with organizational decisions being like the choice of media, assignment decisions being like the choice of type of vehicle, and scheduling decisions being directly comparable.

These three decisions must be made in the context of a sales force that is usually already in place, a traditional form of selling for the firm, and the personal-selling message decisions that have already been made as a part of campaign development. At the same time there are a series of creative alternatives such as account management, team, and multilevel selling. The campaign manager can choose or deviate from typical message distribution patterns in consumer, industrial, or public-sector marketing.

A sales force message distribution plan is built from the bottom up, from the actual contact between the salesperson and the prospect. Thus the first step in developing personal-selling organization is to specify the selling task. Then decisions can be made as to product concentration, functional division, horizontal organization, and vertical organization. The creative campaign manager will not forget the critical two-person selling interaction and will go beyond just territory organization questions.

Assignment decisions, putting sales force weight against various divisions of the horizontal and vertical organization, can be done creatively on the basis of situation analysis and the use of models. Then scheduling can be used to allocate the limited resource of personal selling effectively. Typically this is done with a jolt-and-fade scheduling pattern, necessary because of the difficulty of selling and possible because of the relative ease of maintaining customers. Creativity in assignment and scheduling come from making unusual concentrations in time and space, maintaining selling effort adequately during nonconcentration periods, and balancing sales efforts with other parts of the mix.

SALES PROMOTION

In some sense, the decision equivalent to the advertising medium decision is already made for sales promotion at the message format stage when one or more of the many types of sales promotion are selected. But there still are critical message distribution decisions. Planners must choose the method of delivery (equivalent to the media and vehicle decisions) and the way in which each form of promotion will be scheduled throughout the year.

Many of the decision criteria for sales promotion message distribution are similar to those used for advertising, particularly since some of the most popular delivery methods for promotions involve advertising. Thus such criteria as reach, frequency, and continuity are not unheard of in talking about how promotions should be delivered.

On the other hand, the goals of promotion are more frequently of the direct action type. Thus delivery methods are often considered in terms of whether nonusers, competitive users, or repeat usage is being generated

by the method. And the method of delivery can affect the degree to which a delivery method is consumer franchise building (CFB) or not. Usually, for instance, delivery through an advertisement with a message can increase the CFB or long-term loyalty effect of the promotion.

In the following sections we first consider delivery methods for sampling, coupons to the consumer, consumer demonstrations, consumer education material, price-off or bonus packs, premiums and specialty advertising, contests and sweepstakes, refunds and trade coupons, and trade promotions. Then there is a section on delivery of combinations of promotion types, such as samples combined with coupons. Finally there is a section on the scheduling decision for sales promotion.

Sampling

Sampling is used to introduce a product or to get nonusers to try a product already on the market. Thus this high CFB tool should be delivered by a method that encourages real trial that results in a positive experience. And this should be done with target segments at a reasonable cost-per-thousand actual use.

Samples can be delivered by direct mail, house to house, attached to packages of other products, handed out in-store, and offered in print or broadcast media. There are variations of each of these basic methods. Each offers particular advantages and disadvantages to the campaign planner.

Direct Mail and House-to-House Delivery. These methods ensure reach or coverage, even though there is the possibility of waste circulation and relatively high cost. If the product is one used widely by the population, then these methods will not result in great waste in reaching households that do not use the product. And direct-mail distribution can result in some more specific targeting when accurate lists for specific types of consumers or buyers are used. But for many products, particularly ones that are already on the market and have well-identified user groups, the specter of waste circulation would lead campaign planners to recommend other delivery systems.

Another issue with direct-mail and house-to-house approaches is that they require little psychological or physical effort on the part of buyers. This could mean that there will be a lack of commitment to actually using the sample. Planners should not asume that once a sample is delivered, it will be used. Even for categories as widely used as antiperspirants, there has been research showing that only 50 percent of the samples have been used. Findings of even lower sample usage are reported for food products that require in-home preparation.[24]

Package Enclosures or Attachments. Here there is the possibility of less waste circulation, particularly if the sample is attached to a related product. The fact that the buyer must spend money in order to get the sample can lead to greater psychological commitment and a greater probability that the product will actually be used. For products that are normally sold to relatively small proportions of the population and, in particular, take some effort to use, the attachment of a sample to a related product is an especially efficient method of delivery.

In addition, when samples are attached to related products there is an opportunity to develop frequency. That is, buyers may buy several of the sample packs at once or over time.

In-Store Delivery. This can be quite efficient (low cost and well targeted) and create some commitment to actually use the product. This is actually true when the delivery method does not force the sample on buyers. If the buyer has to step up to a fieldworker to get the sample, then there is some selectivity, commitment, and a greater probability that the sample will actually be used. If the sample

is forced on people, there is the possibility of waste and less consumer use.

In-store delivery is the way "sampling" is done for large durable items and services. This would be true of trial use of audio equipment and cars, free days at museums and zoos, and so forth. Note that most of these would have the sort of commitment that would lead to successful sampling. And there is strong assurance that the sampling actually took place.

Media Offers. In many ways, print or broadcast offers to send samples represent the least-expensive way to get to interested consumers who will be committed enough to actually use the sample. The reason is that the consumer or industrial buyer who sends or calls for a sample has actually made some effort to get it. Samples are sent only to those who have made this effort, so that there is little waste circulation. Those who have taken the trouble to send for a sample are more likely to use it and, psychologically, have the reason to favorably evaluate it. Also an advertisement for a sample can contain a CFB advertising message in addition to the sample offer.

Of course one of the main reasons that this sort of delivery has not been used as much as, say, house-to-house sampling is that the effort required tends to eliminate some important segments of the market. If the campaign has a need to get samples to nonusers (particularly in the case of new products) or competitive brand users, it is difficult to imagine media offers delivering these people. Typically media sample offers are best for getting to people who are already favorably disposed to the brand.

There have been some sampling innovations that deal with this problem of media distribution, however. For instance, in Chapter 14 there was a report of a Gaines-burgers print ad that would appeal directly to competitive users. The ad offered a sample box of the semimoist dog food to anyone who would send in labels from six cans of wet dog food, the competitive product.

Another media-sampling method that gets to nonusers is the free-standing insert coupled with a questionnaire that was developed by John Blair Marketing. The headline reads, "Send for your free samples. Sample some of America's favorites just for answering this questionnaire." The questions ask about product usage in a number of categories. Then samples can be sent to people on the basis of campaign objectives and the questionnaire answers. That is, sponsor samples are sent to all who check usage of a competitive brand. Consumers checking the sponsor's brand would get a coupon, a line extension sample, or no product at all in that category.[25] One use of this program in eight newspapers in the Northeast with a total distribution of 4,749,000 achieved a return rate of 8 percent.[26]

Note that this return is far from the 90 percent of American households that some companies claim to achieve for door-to-door sampling programs. But the free-standing insert can be more efficient in reaching competitive user targets, particularly for established brands.

It should be remembered that any sampling distribution system using advertising should be planned with the same care as that used for the planning of normal media advertising schedules.

Coupons to the Consumer

Coupons can be distributed in all the ways that samples are distributed, in addition to being distributed with samples themselves (the "bounce-back" coupon which is intended to be used by consumers after they have used the sample, in order to extend the trial). Many of the same considerations of sample distribution apply to coupon distribution. The exception is that coupons have even broader goals than samples. While samples are generally used to induce trial and mainly for products that are new to the market, coupons, in addition to inducing trial, can help convert competitive users to the promoted brand, get users to stock up more than they usually would, increase wholesaler-retailer stocking, and help decrease competitive inroads.

Thus getting coupons to people who at present are not users or competitive users becomes more important for coupons. Fortunately, their use requires some commitment, which can increase the value of the trial experience. Unfortunately, the need for consumer effort can sometimes decrease the extent to which competitive users redeem manufacturer coupons.

Direct Mail and House-to-House. Again there will be some waste circulation with these methods. But the cost of coupon redemptions comes only when they are redeemed. These mass methods of distribution offer some hope of reaching cost-conscious buyers of competing brands, particularly when the sponsor coupon is in packets with coupons for a number of other products.

In or on Packages. If the coupon is on a package of the same brand, then the goal of getting present customers to stock up can be achieved. If the coupon goes with a package of another product in the manufacturer's line, there is hope of drawing in new users.

In-Store or Mail. Usually the in-store method involves the problem of forcing coupons on people who are not really interested. The advantage is that consumers have the coupons with them as they enter the store. This allows impulse purchasing to be done with the coupons and eliminates the time lag between receiving a coupon in the mail and actually getting an opportunity to use it. Some research has indicated that when this time lag is reduced, coupon redemption rates rise about 300 percent.[27]

One of the most ambitious store-door sampling programs was tested in early 1980 by Donnelley Marketing, which also runs the

"Carol Wright" cooperative coupon distribution service with direct mailings of coupon packets to a group of 21 million frequent users of certain grocery store categories.

The Donnelley store-door program involved representatives handing out flip-through coupon books at store entrances. Shelf talkers signaled shoppers as to the products for which there were coupons in the books. Universal Product Code scanner data were used to compare results for couponed versus noncouponed brands in each category.[28]

Media Coupons. Once again, as with samples offered in the media, coupons offered this way require some effort on the part of the consumer. Thus the percentage redeemed is certainly not going to be as great as for some of the above distribution methods. But the effect of each redemption in regard to long-term franchise building is likely to be greater, simply because of the effort the consumer must make. Also there is the possibility of tying the coupon ad message to the message idea of the entire campaign. This cannot be done as easily with some of the other methods of distribution. Note that with media coupons, there is a need for precise advertising media planning in addition to the coupon distribution planning.

Consumer Demonstrations

The promotion technique involving consumer demonstrations is used most often for introductions, but it can have a secondary purpose in generating product exposure to competitive and noncompetitive users.

Message distribution here depends on where the demonstrations are made. The sites for demonstration will affect how efficiently the demonstration reaches various kinds of prospects and the impact the demonstration will have.

The alternatives include demonstrations in stores, for clubs, with corporate sponsorship, at consumer shows, or in school classes or other kinds of school-related activities. In general, the closer the demonstration is to the point of purchase, the greater the likelihood that prospects will be reached and that there will be impact in terms of trial purchase of the product. If the campaign manager is looking for a more long term image or CFB effect, however, demonstrations for organizations and school classes may be more effective, simply because they have a public service tone and possibly greater credibility.

An example of an in-store demonstration that got around the sample use problem for a difficult-to-prepare food item was conducted by General Foods for its Oven Fry batter mix coating for chicken. The company simply cooked chicken with the mix and handed it out to shoppers. Fryer sales increased 19 percent during the test and usage of Oven Fry increased 30 percent, with large-size packages accounting for more than half the dollar sales.[29]

Consumer Education Material

Consumer education material normally does not result in short-term sales increases such as with the other promotion devices mentioned above. Instead there is the hope that some trial will be stimulated when company products are featured and, more likely, that there will be an improvement in attitudes toward the brand as a result of the material.

This promotional tool can be delivered by missionary salespeople, as when information about products and their application is distributed to doctors, high-school coaches, teachers, nutritionists, architects, and contractors. Or, at the other extreme, an advertisement can be turned into educational material when it presents recipes or offers services related to the main market offering.

In between these two distribution extremes—by salespeople and by advertising—there are a variety of others that to a greater or lesser degree offer potential for putting customers in a separate medium and thereby fully achieve the attitude change goal. Such delivery methods would include cookbooks, fan clubs and their magazines, controlled magazines such as the Diner's Club *Signature,* and total teaching programs for the classroom.

These alternatives divide naturally into those that are more costly but have impact against a small segment and those, like the advertising delivery method, that may reach more people but do not have the impact of credibility and service offered by other forms.

Price-Off or Bonus Packs

With regard to price-off or bonus packs, very little can be done with these obvious non-CFB activities in terms of variations in delivery. Of the two, the price-off package is a more certain way of passing on savings to consumers. With bonus packs there is some possibility that retailers will rip the pack apart and sell the parts at full price.

Bonus packs do have the advantage of causing consumers to stock up with the product and get an extended trial. The packs can be used competitively to cloud the results of an opposing test market.

These promotional methods should be used where it is necessary to get trade loading, shelf talkers, and special displays. But, as mentioned in Chapter 14, they are more likely to attract buyers who are low in loyalty. Therefore they should be used sparingly.

Premiums and Specialty Advertising

Planners should do everything possible to use premiums and specialty advertising creatively so that they become consumer franchise building. Although these tools have some ability to generate trial, planners sometimes can fall into the trap of selling the premium or specialty item instead of the market offering.

For premiums, the message distribution choice is first between the free type and the self-liquidating type, for which consumers pay a reduced price with proof of purchase. Most premiums are distributed by mail after being offered in print or, possibly, broadcast advertising. Premiums can also be presented on packages, as is common for cereal premiums and in-store on shelf talkers and the like.

Advertising announcement of premiums is probably the most appropriate distribution approach, since the premium offer can generate extra advertising awareness. In addition, if the premium fits the message strategy for the campaign, this can be developed best in the context of advertising. Of course if advertising is used for the delivery, it is likely that the media strategy should parallel, in miniature or in part, the strategy for the main campaign.

Specialty advertising items are typically delivered by mail or by salespeople. The main issue in their distribution is to get them to the right people at the right time. Accurate prospect lists are the best aid in achieving this targeting.

Contests and Sweepstakes

Contests and sweepstakes occur almost solely in the context of advertising. They can generate awareness for the ads and sometimes fit with the message strategy in this delivery.

For services such as airlines and fast-food operations, there has been some trend toward presenting the contest in advertising but then holding it on the airplane or in the store with an "instant winner" promotion. This can help to build traffic during the period of the contest. But in the early 1980 battle of contests among the airlines, the originator, United, eventually switched to a more long term advertising strategy.

Refunds and Trade Coupons

Refunds are distributed in advertising and at the point of purchase. Trade coupons are the ones that are offered in, for instance, newspaper advertisements for supermarket chains. This type of trade coupon was one of the choices available to the bar soap brand manager discussed at the beginning of this chapter.

Nielsen research reveals the popularity and effectiveness of presenting refunds in advertising. Its studies show that 41 percent of refund offers are made in print advertising, 26 percent at the point of purchase, 16 percent in or on the package, and 17 percent use a combination of delivery approaches. Awareness of refunds was generated for 55 percent of people by print ads, 40 percent from the package, and 6 percent from shelf talkers.[30]

Trade Promotions

The key link in price concessions to the trade is the salesperson, although this and particularly other types of trade-oriented promotion are delivered by mail, at trade shows, or in advertising (e.g., contests).

Since the prime purpose of trade promotions is to produce quick action at that level in terms of sell-in period, developing in-store displays, and gaining retail support for other parts of the mix, the salesperson part of this message distribution is the key for the effect. The trade promotion is the extra offer that many salespeople can make to retail buyers. And when the brand has lost much of its consumer franchise, a deadly spiral of continued dealing can take place at the retail selling level, just so salespeople have something to sell.

Combined Promotions

Since the problem of clutter is probably more severe for promotions than for advertising, campaign planners try many combinations of promotion techniques. For instance, the free sample and the "bounce back" coupon have already been mentioned as one combination. Others might be a coupon and a refund, a coupon plus a self-liquidator, a coupon along with a sweepstakes, trade coupons (in newspaper ads) combined with manufacturer coupons, and trade promotions in support of promotions at the consumer level.

One observer has suggested that if there are twelve promotion techniques, there are more than 845 million possible combinations of them.[31] And this does not consider all the message distribution options for each of the techniques and their combinations.

The best guidance that can be offered is for concentration on the main campaign purpose of the promotion. For instance, the purpose of the sample and coupon combination is to give new users a favorable experience with the product through the sample and then extend that experience with the coupon use. Therefore the principles of sample distribution mentioned earlier are the first consideration. Then the coupon should be easily available to the satisfied sample user.

Scheduling for Sales Promotion

Much has been written about the lack of planning for sales promotions.[32] And perhaps nowhere is this apparent lack of planning seen more clearly than in the scheduling of the sales promotions themselves.

Unlike the message distribution scheduling of other parts of the communication mix, sales promotion tends not to be thought of as a year-round activity (except in the many cases where it has truly gotten out of hand). Instead it is planned for use in campaigns in two characteristic ways:

☐ For peaks in the campaign
☐ For firefighting

Use for peaks in the campaign would include sampling and coupons at the beginning of a campaign, particularly for an introduction. In addition, there are seasonal sell-in periods for retail products, at which time it is often important to offer trade promotion. And other products and services have seasons of the year when sales may need a boost. This is when promotions are used.

Firefighting is done with promotions when competition is making dangerously too much progress in certain areas. Promotion can be used to counter these advances. Much of the growth of sales promotion in recent decades has occurred as a result of this sort of competitive countermoving.

The reason for the nature of promotion scheduling is not that managers somehow fall to pieces when they try to deal with this communication tool. Instead, as was true of advertising and personal-selling message distribution, scheduling is based directly on the *type of response and decay* engendered by each communication element.

In the case of sales promotion, response and decay are quite different from what was discussed for either advertising or selling. While those curves could be said to be quite gradual, sales promotional ones are much sharper. Particularly for the non-CFB type of promotion such as refunds, price-off packs, or trade coupons, there are dramatic shifts in sales. First, during the promotion, sales can increase sharply. Then, after it is over, there can be a drop in sales *below* the normal sales level. This is usually caused by deal buyers using up the stock of product they bought during the promotion. Eventually, however, sales usually increase back to their original level.

Since promotions can have this dramatic effect, they turn into a method that is scheduled for peaks and saved for firefighting, rather than being a more regular device used during the campaign year.

Of course the nature of the response and decay depends on which sales promotion tool or combination is being used. Samples sometimes have a slower, more gradual effect than

do price deals. Demonstrations and educational materials can be used in different ways to support the campaign throughout the year.

One way to remember the sales promotion response and decay situation is to know that, at least in theory, it is perfectly complementary to the personal-selling one. While selling *response* is slow, promotion response is fast. While selling *decay* is gradual, promotion decay is not. This is why these two communication tools work so well together in scheduling throughout the year. Promotion tools can help the salesperson during, say, the sell-in period. Sales force effort can help to maintain sales after the promotion—no matter what the nature of the market offering.

PUBLICITY AND PUBLIC RELATIONS

For publicity and public relations, just as for personal selling and sales promotion, the message distribution decision that is somewhat akin to the "medium" or "media" selection is already partially made when one or several of the many forms of publicity–PR are picked as part of the message strategy. There are still quite critical message distribution decisions that have to be made, however. These remaining media, vehicle, and scheduling choices are the subject of this section.

The heart of making these message delivery decisions for publicity–PR is the target segment individuals and type of communication sought with them. Publicity–PR is restricted mainly to awareness, information, and attitude-image effects, with only indirect effects on action. But what can be done with publicity–PR can be done quite well, because it can have both extra excitement and credibility. The goal of achieving awareness, information, and attitude-image effects through the heightened excitement and credibility of this communication-mix element should always be kept in mind while planning message distribution for it.

In publicity–PR distribution decision making, it is both easy and dangerous to confuse inputs with outputs. Since there is almost no regular control research to measure the impact of these efforts, there is a tendency for managers to think about them in terms of inputs—e.g., number of magazines that featured a story about the new product, the movie that showed the star buying a hamburger at one of our stores, the number of press conferences held, the number of people who attended the event—rather than outputs in terms of effects on awareness, information changes, and attitude-image. Even if no research exists, attention to the individual effects of these messages will help the manager to guard against planning on the basis of something less than objectives. With message distribution decisions for publicity–PR, the role of introspection is a critical aid to a planner's thinking.

The criteria for planning here are much like those for advertising: effective reach at an efficient price with mood, flexibility, continuity, and impact to fit with the rest of the campaign. Very often it is not as feasible to achieve frequency with publicity as it is with other communication elements.

The key problem in message distribution planning for PR is a lack of control. Instead of being able to simply purchase a news story about the market offering, the planner must depend on the PR people to persuade key magazines or broadcast vehicles people to run such a story. This makes message distribution planning for publicity–PR difficult and, at the same time, exciting.

Getting into the News

Three ways for getting into the news can be planned much like advertising media, because message distribution is actually done by separate media. If there is a good story about

the market offering, it can be distributed to the media in terms of a *press release,* an *exclusive feature,* or a *feature release.* For any of these formats, it is necessary to plan in terms of which media and types of vehicles would be appropriate and would contribute to publicity and overall campaign goals. In some cases it is necessary to develop longstanding relationships with the editorial people who can use the information to develop stories. In other cases it is necessary only to send out press releases and materials to the publications and news departments that could produce the desired exposure.

In one example, the Burson-Marsteller public relations agency convinced a battery manufacturer client to send its experts to key trucking publication editors. The goal was to place stories that would break through the skepticism the trucking industry had about maintenance-free batteries which were supposedly developed for their needs. The media tour produced these "inputs" (note the critical difficulty of erroneously assuming these are the outputs for publicity–PR): mentions in fifty publications, including feature articles in twelve publications which reached the target market particularly well. Note the possible buildup of frequency in this case. The main output reported was the development of forty thousand sales leads even before the first ad was run for the new maintenance-free battery.[33]

Press conferences and related *press kits* tend to be distributed geographically as opposed to the media vehicle and target segment approach used for news placement with the three formats above. Conferences are held in particular locations and the local media people are invited to attend. Sometimes the conferences are held in connection with some event, such as a general consumer show, a trade show in the industrial area, or the beginning of a new service in the public-sector area. In these cases the press conferences would be held at a location in proximity to the event. It is hoped that media stories will result from the conferences and that these stories will have effects that match campaign goals.

Getting into Entertainment

If the "entertainment" is some continuous type such as a television series, then there is some opportunity to plan for attempted placement to reach specific target segments. For instance, as mentioned in Chapter 14, the Los Angeles Heart Association campaign succeeded in affecting the scripts of television programs meant to reach people who had a high risk of heart problems. And there is a regular procedure used for offering products for prizes on game shows.

In many other instances, however, it is difficult to plan such placements in advance. A good public relations agency can make known the fact that the product is available for placement in certain types of entertainment vehicles. But quite often the producers of such material will actually make unsolicited offers to marketers. Then the message distribution decision is whether such a placement would have any advantage at all in the context of the campaign.

Events and Sponsorship

Some events and sponsorship opportunities occur regularly or fit the seasons, and they can be planned in almost the same way that advertising media schedules are planned. In other cases they are developed to fit certain problems. The nature of the distribution in these types of cases normally fits the segment and geographic nature of the problem. For instance, a food processor having difficulty breaking into the institutional feeding market held a series of seminars in key markets. This event was rolled out over the company's sales territories. Success in early markets, as indicated by sales force reports of dozens of new

accounts that were directly related to the seminars, led to subsequent seminars in additional territories.[34]

In still other cases opportunities present themselves and campaign planners must be ready to evaluate and act. When Kool cigarettes, which had already sponsored its own annual jazz festival in a number of cities, was presented with the opportunity of sponsoring the Newport (coincidentally the name of an opposing brand) Jazz Festival, there had to be careful concern about this "medium" for the brand's public relations effort.

Appearing in Person: Speakers, Conferences, and Shows

In all kinds of marketing, there are opportunities to use speakers, conferences, and shows. The senatorial candidate campaign manager discussed at the beginning of this chapter, for instance, has a number of these types of tools that can be sent to the various areas and events in the state. Primarily the candidate, but also other people speaking for the candidate, can appear at noontime speakers' areas, picnics, luncheons, dinners, and meetings of various kinds. The same sorts of options are available for campaign managers in the consumer and industrial areas.

In many cases this part of the message distribution plan is not even planned. Sometimes it is seen as just an obligation. In other cases there is a tendency to follow a traditional pattern instead of planning for a specific campaign. Thus the senatorial candidate and his or her people make the same round of speaking engagements that "have always been done." Similarly, the company in any given industry feels obligated to participate in a certain number and type of conferences, public or trade shows, and speaking engagements.

In contrast to this normal lack of planning, there is the benefit that can be derived from proper use of personal appearances of all types. This is an opportunity to reach people with certain well-defined interests. And the impact can be great, both in terms of numbers and in terms of the effect for each individual reached.

Personal appearance opportunities should be considered anew for each campaign. The needs of the campaign in terms of overall objectives, target segments, communication goals, message strategy, and message format for various aspects of the mix—all of these affect whether any personal appearances are necessary and, if so, what their nature should be.

It is always possible, to some degree, to lay out the options for personal appearances during message distribution planning before the campaign begins. In this way personal appearances can be evaluated in much the same way that advertising media are: in terms of the audience likely, the impact possible, the timing, and so forth. At this time it is also wise to include obligations as part of the decision process, but only after the options have been analyzed without this factor interfering. This initial analysis can also be valuable *during* the campaign when, say, speaking engagements come up and can be evaluated in terms of the total campaign context.

Since key shows and conferences are scheduled far in advance, it is possible to schedule them into the campaign so that they meet objectives and work with other elements of the mix. Fortunately, most of these public events are already timed to fit in with the selling season or decision period in relevant markets. Thus they bring together a group of decision makers who have come to the event or the show expressly to be exposed to personal appearances, exhibits, and the like.

Each personal appearance demands other publicity–PR materials for support. These should be considered in initial planning. They offer the opportunity to greatly multiply the effect of each appearance in terms of its goals.

Educational Efforts

Message distribution planning involving educational efforts consists mainly of determining the types of educational settings that are most appropriate, the audience that should be reached, the geographic location, and the timing. Of course when the work is done with schools of various types, all of this is dependent on the schools' needs and timing—in addition to the needs of the campaign.

In one example, a communication company specializing in teletype and Mailgram had long recognized that decisions about these types of services were made by administrative secretaries. But union rules prevented the company from giving in-house demonstrations to these important decision makers. The company did learn, however, that secretarial schools had a need for sessions on office communication equipment. After two years its program had been presented to more than seventeen thousand business and secretarial students at sixty-one schools in twenty-seven states.[35] Unfortunately, no information was available on the actual effect of the campaign. But the planning in terms of selecting the right educational setting, audience, location, and timing was exemplary.

Controlled Media

Controlled media efforts, stemming often from educational activities, can present a separate medium all alone for the campaign message both in stories and in enclosed advertisements. Many examples are offered in Chapter 14. And unlike some other kinds of publicity–PR, they offer the opportunity to specifically control message distribution.

Usually this distribution is to people who have already expressed some interest—as in the case of annual reports, enclosures in billing statements, magazines sent to credit-card holders, and magazines sent to owners.

Other types of controlled media attract attention on the basis of something other than interest in the market offering itself. Examples would include special telephone information lines (which mention the sponsor) and information inserts in other publications. For instance, the Ford Motor Company sponsored a series of supplements for college newspapers. Called *Ford's Insider,* they included fairly deep treatment of such issues as career planning, which would be of great interest to a significant buying group. The supplement would include, say, eight pages of ads in a twenty-four-page format.

With both types of controlled media, the issues are once again the ones of objectives, target segment, reach, frequency, continuity, flexibility, mood, and impact.

SUMMARY

The encouraging aspect of message distribution planning is the commonality of the decisions that must be made across the components of the mix. All of the elements, including advertising, have strong direction from the message format decision, which in some sense limits the message distribution decisions equivalent to "media" and "type of vehicle" selection.

But even the message format decision must be reconsidered in light of the assessment of message delivery alternatives. In personal selling there are decisions about organization, assignment, and scheduling. Sales promotion delivery questions depend very much on the particular form of promotion, but again the issues are ones of satisfying campaign needs and criteria with choices

quite similar to the media-vehicle-scheduling ones. For sales promotion, it is remarkable how these choices can lead to various levels of commitment on the part of consumers and thus to various levels of achievement or nonachievement of objectives.

Publicity–PR also occurs in a number of different forms, each of which presents a slightly different message distribution setting. Other than the methods used for getting into the news, however, these publicity–PR approaches tend to be done almost without distribution planning, on the basis of what has always been done or in reaction to particular opportunities. Suggestions are offered here as to how each of these types of publicity–PR message can be distributed in a planned, efficient way.

All four elements of the communication mix perform overlapping and complementary tasks. This complementarity importantly affects scheduling. For instance, the response and decay of sales promotion effects are almost the opposite of the response and decay of personal selling. This means that personal-selling response is difficult to achieve, while sales promotion response is easier. For decay, the reverse is true. Thus sales promotion (and publicity) techniques are used to help the sales force achieve sales, and personal selling (and advertising) can be used to help to maintain the sales level in periods when there are no promotions.

This balancing of components of the communication mix is central to campaign success. Certainly message distribution scheduling can help to achieve the balance needed. But the integration of the total campaign, covered in the next chapter, is necessary for successful implementation.

ISSUES AND PROJECTS FOR DISCUSSION

1. Compare and contrast the message distribution planning problem for the four elements of the communication mix.

2. What is the value of using models to help make sales management decisions?

3. What is the difference between the horizontal and the vertical organization of the sales force?

4. Make an audit of the various sales promotions with which you come in contact during one week. What kinds are they? Evaluate them from the standpoint of their potential effect on you. To what extent is the nature of that effect due to the way the promotions were delivered to you?

5. Do the same kind of audit mentioned in Question 4, but this time for publicity–PR. Remember that you will have to assume that certain media and entertainment placements are there because of the effort of some marketing organization.

6. In your opinion, what message unit is distributed for each of the four elements of the communication mix? Does that unit differ at all depending on the method of distribution?

7. Explain how response and decay effects can lead to particular scheduling strategies for personal selling and sales promotion. What causes these response and decay effects?

8. How can methods of distribution affect the effectiveness of sampling, coupons, premiums, and publicity news features?

9. What situational factors would you monitor in order to make the "assignment" decisions of sales management?

10. What actions would you take in each of the vignette situations described at the beginning of this chapter? Use chapter material to support your decisions.

Notes

1. Benson P. Shapiro, "Account Management and Sales Organization: New Developments in Practice," in *Sales Management: New Developments from Behavioral and Decisions Model Research,* ed. Richard P. Bagozzi (Cambridge, Mass.: Marketing Science Institute, 1979), p. 269.

2. "Harlan Chemical Corporation," Harvard Graduate School of Business Administration Case #9-574-011, 1973.

3. "Sweda: Aggressive Marketing Produces a Spirited Turnaround," *Business Week,* March 31, 1980, pp. 101–2.

4. Ben M. Enis, "Role Gap Narrows between Inside and Outside Industrial Salespersons," *Marketing News,* April 4, 1980, pp. 3 and 7.

5. Arthur Segel and Charles B. Weinberg, "Sierra Club Publishing Division," in *Cases in Public and Nonprofit Marketing,* ed. Christopher H. Lovelock and Charles B. Weinberg (Palo Alto, Calif.: Scientific Press, 1977), pp. 7–18.

6. Christopher H. Lovelock, "Stanford University: The Annual Fund," in *Cases in Public and Nonprofit Marketing,* ed. Christopher H. Lovelock and Charles B. Weinberg (Palo Alto, Calif.: Scientific Press, 1977), p. 83.

7. Kathleen P. Magill, Thomas E. Shanks, and Everett M. Rogers, "The Innovation Process for Three Mass Transportation Innovations" (Institute for Communication Research, Stanford University, April 1980).

8. Gerald E. Ankeny, "Basic Factors in Sales Territory Design-II," in *Allocating Field Sales Resources: A Symposium* (New York: National Industrial Conference Board, 1970), pp. 17–18.

9. "Sweda."

10. Shapiro, "Account Management."

11. William J. Stanton and Richard H. Buskirk, *Management of the Sales Force* (Homewood, Ill.: Richard D. Irwin, 1974). p. 91.

12. Adrian B. Ryans and Charles B. Weinberg, "Managerial Implications of Territory Sales Response," *Proceedings of the 1979 American Marketing Association Educators' Conference,* August 1979, pp. 426–30; "Territory Sales Response," *Journal of Marketing Research,* 16 (November 1979), pp. 453–65; and "Determinants of Sales Force Performance," Marketing Science Institute Report No. 79-113, December 1979, 27 pages.

13. Stanley D. Breitweiser, "An Organizational Tune-up," in *Allocating Field Sales Resources: A Symposium* (New York: National Industrial Conference Board, 1970), pp. 2–7.

14. Ryans and Weinberg, "Managerial Implications," p. 430.

15. Ryans and Weinberg, "Determinants of Sales Force Performance," pp. 18 and 19.

16. David B. Montgomery, Alvin J. Silk, and Carlos E. Zaragoza, "A Multiple-Product Sales Force Allocation Model," *Management Science,* 18 (December 1971), P-3 to P-24.

17. Leonard M. Lodish, "CALLPLAN: An

Interactive Salesman's Call Planning System," *Management Science,* 18 (December 1971), P-25 to P-40.

18. Sidney W. Hess and Stuart A. Samuels, "Experiences with a Sales Districting Model: Criteria and Implementation," *Management Science,* 18 (December 1971), P-41 to P-54.

19. Thomas A. Glaze and Charles B. Weinberg, "A Sales Territory Alignment Program and Account Planning System (TAPS)," in *Sales Management: New Developments for Behavioral and Decision Model Research,* ed. Richard P. Bagozzi (Cambridge, Mass.: Marketing Science Institute, 1979), pp. 325–42.

20. Lodish, "CALLPLAN," p. P-39.

21. William K. Fudge and Leonard M. Lodish, "Evaluation of the Effectiveness of a Model Based Salesman's Planning System by Field Experimentation," *Interfaces,* 8 (November 1977), II, 97–106.

22. Glaze and Weinberg, "Sales Territory Alignment Program."

23. James Girdwood, "Restructuring Sales Territories," in *Allocating Field Sales Resources: A Symposium* (New York: National Industrial Conference Board, 1970), p. 30.

24. Lou Haugh, "Build Franchise through Sampling," *Advertising Age,* November 5, 1979, p. 64.

25. Ibid.

26. Louis J. Haugh, "Service Companies Filling Void in Promotion Research Frontier," *Advertising Age,* April 21, 1980, p. 56.

27. " 'Carol Wright' to Distribute Coupons at Supermarket Doors," *Marketing News,* February 22, 1980, p. 12.

28. Ibid.

29. Haugh, "Build Franchise through Sampling."

30. Louis J. Haugh, "Promotion: Cash Refunds Multiply," *Advertising Age,* May 5, 1980, p. 48.

31. William A. Robinson, "Economics to Change Promo's Look," *Advertising Age,* February 18, 1980, p. 54.

32. Roger A. Strang, The Relationship between Advertising and Promotion in Brand Strategy (Cambridge, Mass.: Marketing Science Institute, 1975).

33. John D. LaSage, "Objectives-oriented PR Programs Boost Sales in Industrial Markets," *Marketing News,* April 4, 1980, p. 19.

34. Ibid.

35. Ibid.

THE TOTAL MIX

. . . Budgeting, Implementation, and Control

. . . Society and the Future

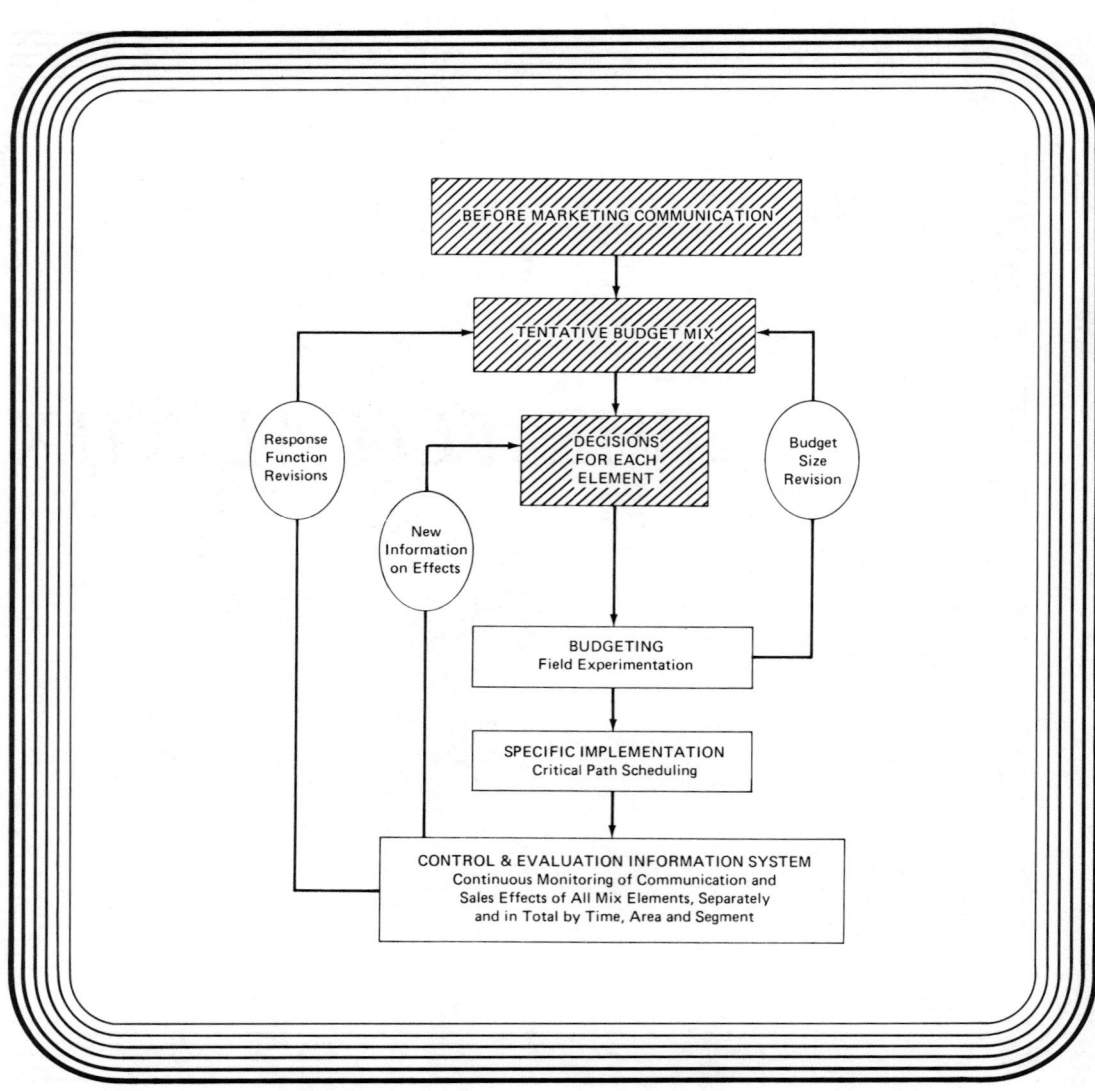

BEFORE MARKETING COMMUNICATION

TENTATIVE BUDGET MIX

Response Function Revisions

DECISIONS FOR EACH ELEMENT

Budget Size Revision

New Information on Effects

BUDGETING
Field Experimentation

SPECIFIC IMPLEMENTATION
Critical Path Scheduling

CONTROL & EVALUATION INFORMATION SYSTEM
Continuous Monitoring of Communication and
Sales Effects of All Mix Elements, Separately
and in Total by Time, Area and Segment

Budgeting, Implementation, and Control

• As product manager for a division of a large microcomputer corporation, you are puzzled by budget figures for next year's campaign for one of your products. Although you have worked reasonably closely with the departments and suppliers, you find that the personal selling, sales promotion, and publicity–PR budgets total exactly to their original allocations, while advertising is almost double what was initially proposed.

• Your biscuit mix has been on the market for generations and had been allocated a reasonably small communications budget. But people working at your advertising agency have come up with what you believe to be a breakthrough in terms of new uses for the product. How can you convince top management to substantially increase your budget for the campaign? Should any additional research be recommended to support your position?

• Each year the controller of your small coffee company attempts to evaluate your advertising effort in terms of sales effects in that year. What type of advertising research and control system can be set up to show him, and the other members of top management, how advertising and other aspects of the communication mix are working for the company?

• Responding to a breakthrough by company engineering staff which produced a photovoltaic cell with triple the efficiency of any on the market, your staff people have developed outstanding programs for each of the elements of the communication mix. Now these separate programs have to be scheduled into the introductory campaign. You must achieve maximum impact without warning competitors who either have made or are about to make the same sort of breakthrough.

• Your mayor's reelection campaign was fully planned and is in operation. Suddenly there is a strike by city workers. What should be done to adjust the message and the scheduling of the campaign in order to deal with this dramatic development?

• You have been public events director at a small private university for approximately nine months. Working with faculty and students in the marketing and communication departments, you have developed a campaign strategy for the performance series that is literally revolutionary. Even though the strategy is based on solid marketing communications principles, you know that the school administration is likely to be shocked by it. How can it be presented to them so that it will be approved? Should some middle or moderate position be taken instead of going all the way in recommending the strategy?

Someone once said, "Ideas are cheap." In many ways, that would be a terrible thing to say to a person who has labored over the creation of ideas that go into the making of an advertising and marketing-communication campaign. But in all of the six examples above, ideas—probably considered by their creators to be great ideas—were developed for campaign strategy, only to be faced with a series of circumstances that might kill them or substantially alter their effectiveness.

Yes, ideas are cheap. So many come to mind, some are even developed a little, but very few are truly implemented in an exciting and effective way. And how do we know whether they really worked?

This chapter presents the basic principles by which communication campaign ideas can be given value. Here the *final budgeting procedure* is discussed as another point in campaign development at which it is possible to add value to individual communication elements in combination. *Implementation* is seen as the only way that ideas for the campaign will have reality. The actual method by which the campaign is done is the real nature of the ideas, not just the concept in someone's mind. The people carrying out the campaign also have to have many ideas in order to bring it to fruition. And *control procedures,* such as advertising evaluation research, can provide an indication as to how well the campaign is doing, why it is performing that way, and what new kinds of ideas will be needed for the next campaign.

Some Examples

Consider the examples at the beginning of this chapter. An industrial product manager is faced with some budget requests that are exactly what was allocated to some communication elements originally in the tentative budget mix. But the advertising people are asking for almost double the tentative allocation. Both the exact budgets and the advertising budget should be questioned. The exact ones may be like that because there has been a lack of creativity. Since personal selling, sales promotion, and publicity–PR are traditionally important in this industrial company's budget, they may have been planned with no thought of change. Advertising, on the other hand, has not traditionally been important here. It may be that the people planning this communication element have come up with a way to make it work effectively for this *microcomputer company*. The double-allocation request should not be rejected automatically. The life of the idea may be saved. It is at the final budget adjustment phase that campaign ideas can actually come to life.

What can be a more startling idea to top management than to learn that a brand it thought was a "cash cow" heading into decline is going to need a communication budget close to that of an introductory brand? This is the situation faced by top management in the *biscuit mix* example. More appropriately, it is the problem situation faced by the campaign manager. The new ideas developed by the people at the advertising agency may have tremendous effect, but no one will ever know unless the campaign manager can convince top management to fund the effort. And the manager might be able to do this by first requesting a budget for some experimental research to test the campaign and spending levels in the field.

The position of the *public events director* outlined at the beginning of this chapter is not an uncommon one for campaign managers in the public sector. Resistance to using proper marketing tools is not uncommon. This public-sector situation only highlights the pervasive marketing-communication problem of having to get approval for strategies before they can be implemented.

Anyone faced with the opportunity of introducing a breakthrough in *photovoltaic cell* efficiency is literally dealing with great amounts of energy and the potential of a multibillion-dollar industry. Given fine strategies for each of the elements of the communication mix, however, how will they be scheduled? How will the announcement and marketing-communication campaigns roll out? It is in this scheduling task that many great campaign plans either falter or succeed.

Financial people are often characterized as the idea crushers in many companies. In the case of the *small coffee company*, a controller repeatedly questions advertising expenditures on the basis of sales effects. This is not unusual in a market in which price-off promotions can have strong short-term effects. A regular control procedure must be developed and agreed upon by everyone concerned so that it is possible to determine not only how well advertising and other communication elements are doing but also why they are performing in that way.

It is an unusual campaign in which nothing new comes up and everything works more or less as planned. Instead there are generally so many possibilities that campaign managers should have contingency budgets,

contingency plans, and a great deal of flexibility in order to respond to the environment. Very often a mediocre campaign can be turned into a great one by the response made to an unexpected event. This could turn out to be true in the case of the *incumbent mayor* faced with a city worker strike in the middle of her reelection campaign. Perhaps she should stay out of sight and out of the news. Maybe she should attempt to rally the voters to her support in the time of crisis. Whatever is done will be the essence of campaign implementation in this situation and others like it in other parts of marketing. Even as a communication campaign is running, it is continually being developed, for better or worse.

Feedback as Shaping and Development

Recall that in an earlier discussion of creativity, the last stage of a technique for producing ideas was called "shaping and development." By this was meant that after the insight of an idea came, it was necessary to work it into something that could be implemented. That shaping and development process has been discussed throughout this book as successively more specific decisions have been the focus.

Now the shaping and development reaches its ultimate form in terms of final budgeting, implementation, and control. And each of these shaping and development steps has its effect in terms of *feedback*. In other words, by doing these steps we learn something about response or likely response that feeds back in terms of altering earlier or subsequent decisions. Three feedback loops are shown in the figure at the beginning of this part of the book to represent the actions that might be taken as a result of the final decision stages.

The budgets reviewed by the campaign manager at this point, for instance, are the result of vastly more information than was available at the time the tentative budget mix was set. All the work of goal setting, message strategy development, and message distribution planning has taken place. In the course of this work, many people have contributed ideas based on a great deal of research and personal experience information and thinking. The feedback loop entitled "Budget Size Revision" graphically portrays management action as the tentative budget mix is altered, on the basis of all this information, into the final budget recommendation.

Specific implementation can lead to changes in strategy as experiences in the marketplace, changes in the environment, and new ideas that come from the work of actually producing campaign materials all begin to provide feedback on the original strategy concepts. This is shown in the figure in terms of the feedback loop to the decisions called "New Information on Effects," which connects to previous decisions on the communication elements.

Finally, the control and evaluation information system stage provides feedback both to the past strategy decisions and to the feedback loop entitled "Response Function Revisions," which cycles back to the tentative budget mix. In other words, if such control exists, it will be possible to determine quite early in the campaign whether the original response estimates were correct. And once the campaign is finished, there should be enough information to make more accurate estimates during the planning for the next campaign.

The Process
of Making Combinations

At this point in the job of advertising and communication management, the planner finds himself or herself making more and more specific and final combinations. This is not surprising. The advantage of looking at all the activities that constitute marketing communication together, instead of separately, is that they might be combined for synergy, a total effect that is greater than the parts acting separately.

Although this kind of synergy can happen when the communication elements are planned in combination, the process of making combinations is a difficult one. It becomes even more difficult with the time pressures present at the end of the campaign.

One major message of this chapter is that the campaign manager should not become discouraged and stop making combinations at the final budgeting, implementation, and control stages. If the powerful combinations of strategy are not implemented, it is as if they never existed in the first place. It is hoped that the suggestions in this chapter will ensure that strategy will be carried through to the field.

FINAL BUDGET SETTING

Budgeting is an activity that is always going on in some form with regard to communication campaigns. Larger budgets are successively divided into smaller pieces. In this book, however, budgeting has been discussed at three stages: total communication budget for the market offering, the tentative budget mix, and now the "final" budget setting.

Although each of the stages has its own importance, this final one is probably the most decisive because it represents all the previous planning and work in terms of actual monies to be spent. In addition, the assessment of the individual budgets and their combination can cause changes in both the tentative budget mix and the total budget for the product. Such changes were implied in the microcomputer and the biscuit mix examples at the beginning of this chapter. Even further, the final budget setting—in a way similar to the tentative budget-mix allocation, communication goal setting, and message strategy position—allows the manager to look across the components of the mix and balance them into powerful combinations.

The Objective and Task Method

By separating the budgeting task into three stages, the manager has used several commonly mentioned but seldom used budgeting methods. In setting the total communication budget, the product portfolio concept as well as cash flow and environmental analysis is used. In developing the tentative budget mix, the marginal economic budgeting method is applied in a general sense. This is done when managers estimate response for each element of the communication mix. It can be done even more formally if decision calculus models are utilized.

Now, at the final budget-setting stage, the manager will have in his or her hands a series of budget estimates or requests for each of the communication elements. And each of these should have been prepared by the use of some form of the objective and task method.

The Budget Statements: Selling Documents

The way in which the objective and task method should have been applied for each of the communication elements has already been described in great detail in this book. At this point the budget request statement for each communication element should be a selling document that builds from the individual goals (objectives) and demonstrates how those goals can be achieved by undertaking certain tasks.

The format of the budget plan request for each communication element should generally follow the procedure described in the following sections.

Executive Overview. Since the budget statement for each element of the communication mix is a selling document, it is vital to have this summary statement which presents the main points of the budget proposal. The overview should clearly state the budget requested and whether and in what way it may vary from the tentative allocation. This

variation should be supported by a brief statement of what will be achieved by the program (particularly in comparison with last year's results), the tasks that are necessary to achieve those results, and the cost implications of all of this.

Communication Goals. Those responsible for each of the elements (advertising, personal selling, sales promotion, and publicity–PR) should restate the communication goals as specifically as they can be stated for that element. There should be a statement of what the level of the criterion measure was before the campaign and what it is hoped to be at the close of the campaign—for which target groups and areas of the country. This goal statement should be supported briefly by background on the hierarchy situation analysis that led to the original assignment of these goals to be the communication element. If the proposal contains any changes or additions to this initial analysis, this should be clearly stated also.

Message Strategy. It is not necessary to go into great detail in this area in the budget statement, since everyone who will be using this statement is familiar with the general strategy. Only the salient facts that affect the budget should be outlined here. Usually, for the individual budget elements, this means a concentration on message format after some review of the message idea. If unusual opportunities in format—such as the opportunity to use a particularly appropriate celebrity presenter in advertising, to hire more high-priced technical salespeople, to use a particular premium, or to sponsor a special event in a number of key market areas—have come up and are critical to the specific budget recommendation, they should be explained in terms of both their budget impact and their likely efficacy.

Message Distribution Plan. This is the area where the budget is usually built. Once we know what goals are to be achieved, what message is to be communicated, and what format is to be used, it is possible to examine exactly how this message will be distributed to target consumers and buyers.

This plan—as exemplified by the media plan statements in Chapter 15—is usually stated in units (e.g., pages of ads, sales calls, samples distributed, controlled publication copies), each of which requires a certain expenditure. By relating goals and message and target segment to this distribution purchase, a budget is "built up" and justified.

For instance, if personal-selling goals consist of selling a certain volume in a certain industry by using a certain type of salesperson and message, the unit of sales calls can be related to this objective. That is, a certain number of sales calls, each costing a certain amount, will be necessary to achieve each sale with a certain amount of volume. Logically, the total amount to be sold can be divided by the amount achieved per sales call to determine the number of sales calls needed. This can be multiplied by the cost per sales call to give the total budget requested for personal selling for the brand.

In this general way, the budget for each element of the communication mix is developed.

Formal Budget Statement. At this point the components of the budget should be stated for each element of the mix. The campaign manager should know exactly where the money is to be spent, when it is going to be spent, and what was spent on each of the categories in previous years. Although the form of these budget statements differs for various companies, Figure 18-1 shows a budget proposal form used for the R. T. French Company. Note that all four elements of the mix are covered on this one form. In contrast, this section discusses a step before this consolidated budget, even though it provides a good example.

Explanatory Notes. There may be a need to explain some aspects of the formal budget

statement. This is another opportunity to make the budget clear and to sell the thinking behind it.

Summary. An expanded version of the executive overview, this section should complete the selling job on the budget proposal. In particular, the buildup or objective and task aspects of the budgeting process should be highlighted for justification. There should also be a mention of alternative budgets and of how this proposed budget is superior.

Assessing Budgets Separately

A brand, product, or campaign manager will receive budget statements like the above either from his or her own staff or from outside organizations representing each element of the mix. Or, depending on the situation, the manager may develop some or all of them personally. Now the manager must take the two steps that will complete the budgeting process before implementation of the campaign: (1) assess each budget separately and (2) develop a combined budget for the campaign. This section deals with the first activity.

There are three ways to check each of the budget proposals. The easiest and most effective way is to use logic and judgment based on the experience of working with the people who developed each budget. The second is to use decision analysis to supplement the logical analysis. And the third is to do field experimentation, which can be done in only a small minority of instances.

Logical and Judgment Analysis. Since the campaign manager should have been working closely with the people who did the detailed work for all four communication elements, he or she is no stranger to the thinking behind the proposals. The manager was directly involved in assigning the tentative budget and balancing goals across the mix. He or she worked with representatives of all the organi-

MARKETING BUDGET PROPOSAL FOR _____

SUMMARY	19 ACTUAL	19 ACTUAL	19 ORIGINAL VOTE	19 ESTIMATED	19 PROPOSED	19 APPROVED
Sales $						
Income Before Marketing $						
Income before Marketing to Sales %						
Marketing (A) $						
Marketing to Sales %						
Marketing includ Allocations (B) $						
Operating Income before Adj. (D) $						
Operating Income to Sales %						
Population M						
Sales Milex ($/1000 pop.) $						
Marketing Milex ($/1000 pop.) $						

MARKETING BUDGET CATEGORIES

1 Magazines						
2 Newspaper Rop						
3 Newspaper Supplements						
4 Radio						
5 Television						
6 Posters						
7 Special Media						
8 Agency Fees						
9 Trade Media						
11 Consumer Non-Price Incentive						
13 Consumer Price Incentives						
14 Sales Conferences						
15 Merchandising Materials						
17 Trade Allowances						
18 Trade Free Goods						
19 Sundries						
MARKETING (A)						

Allocations of Publicity						
Alloc. of Fgt. on Un-ident. Merch. Mat.						
Alloc. of Military Food Marketing						
MARKETING INCLUD. ALLOC. (B)						

Package Development (C)						
Market Research (C)						

(A) Marketing — Total of Budget Categories
(B) Marketing including Allocations — Marketing plus Allocations of Publicity, Freight on Un-Identified Merchandising Materials, and Military Food Marketing.
(C) Already deducted via Administration Expense in arriving at Income before Marketing.
(D) Operating Income Before Adjustments — "Income before Marketing" less "Marketing including Allocations", before Corporate Adjustments.

PER _____ DATE _____

Figure 18-1a. *Excerpt from a marketing budget proposal form for R. T. French Company*
From David S. Hopkins, *The Short-Term Marketing Plan* (New York: Conference Board, 1972), pp 51–52.

QUARTERLY MARKETING AND SALES BUDGET

19 ____ PRODUCT _____

	1 ST QUARTER	2 ND QUARTER	3 RD QUARTER	4 TH QUARTER	12 MONTHS TOTAL
Estimated Sales					

MARKETING BUDGET CATEGORIES

1. Magazines					
2. Newspaper Rop					
3. Newspaper Supplements					
4. Radio					
5. Television					
6. Posters					
7. Special Media					
8. Agency Fees					
9. Trade Media					
11. Consumer Non Price Incentive					
13. Consumer Price Incentives					
14. Sales Conferences					
15. Merchandising Materials					
17. Trade Allowance					
18. Trade Free Goods					
19. Sundries					
MARKETING (A)					

Allocation of Publicity					
Allocation of Freight on Un-Ident. Merch.					
Allocation of Military Food Mkt.					
TOTAL MKTG. INCLD. ALLOC. (B)					

Package Development (C)					
Marketing Research (C)					

(A) Marketing — Total of Budget Categories
(B) Marketing including Allocations — Marketing plus Allocations of Publicity, Freight on Un-Identified Merchandising Materials, and Military Food Marketing
(C) Already deducted via Administration Expense in arriving at Income before Marketing.

MERCHANDISING AND ADVERTISING HIGHLIGHTS, INCLUDING PROMOTION DATES.

1 ST QUARTER   3 RD QUARTER
2 ND QUARTER   4 TH QUARTER

Per _____ Date _____

Figure 18-1b. Quarterly budget format for R. T. French Company

zations in developing the message idea and the copy platform, particularly positioning and tone. Neither the message formats nor the distribution plans for the elements will be a surprise to this manager. One way of looking at the assessment of the individual budget proposals is as a check on the manager's own work.

Of course there is more to it than that. If the campaign manager has applied just the correct amount of supervision, not too much and not too little, to stimulate creativity, there will be aspects of the budget proposal that will either be new to this manager or somewhat unfamiliar in the details.

On these aspects of the campaign, the campaign manager should analyze the recommendations to see if their basic facts are correct, if they are mathematically correct (this can be done by having an assistant run a check), and if they are internally consistent in terms of assertions. Beyond this, the manager must assess whether the forecasts of the effects of the expenditures are reasonable. This part of the analysis is facilitated by the budget proposal when it compares the proposed budget with alternative actions. The brand or campaign manager can better assess the likelihood of goals being achieved by the recommended plan if there is something to compare it with.

The brand manager should be open to new ideas at this point in the process. This certainly should have been true of the microcomputer situation at the beginning of the chapter. The recommendation of nearly double the budget for advertising may seem strange in an industrial marketing situation where publicity and personal selling are so important. But an increase in effort for advertising may be just what the division needs to make gains in its market.

Decision Analysis. Decision analysis, decision theory, or decision trees is an approach that could be used by the campaign manager to quantify his or her judgments about budget proposals for single elements. Sometimes this quantification can produce insights that would not otherwise be apparent. Also, clear statement of areas of uncertainty is achieved, so that direction for further fact gathering is given.

This book is not the place to provide a thorough treatment of decision analysis. There are literally entire books that do that.[1] But the rudiments can give some idea of the kind of thinking that underlies the approach.

Basically the manager would provide four aspects of the situation: the alternatives being considered, the possible market response or outcome for each alternative, the monetary payout associated with each response for each alternative, and the probability that each response would occur for each alternative. There are many refinements and many types of decision analysis, but this sort of problem fits the communication situation quite well.

An example of the microcomputer budgeting situation is shown in Figure 18-2. At the top might be the way the manager would structure the problem. The alternatives being considered are the normal advertising expenditure versus a nearly double-sized budget. The possible responses on the part of the buyer target segment could be very favorable, favorable, or unfavorable. The payout for those three responses are all zero for the normal expenditure, since the payout here is an estimate of what additional response might be estimated over the one that would be achieved by the normal budget. The payout for the nearly double-sized budget varies greatly depending on consumer response. And the manager attached probabilities of .5, .3 and .2 (adding to 1.0 because these would represent the total of the responses possible to the campaign) to the three possible responses, respectively.

Note that at the bottom of each column there is a total expected payout for each alternative. This is calculated by multiplying the expected payout for each response for each alternative by its respective probability and then summing the results for each alter-

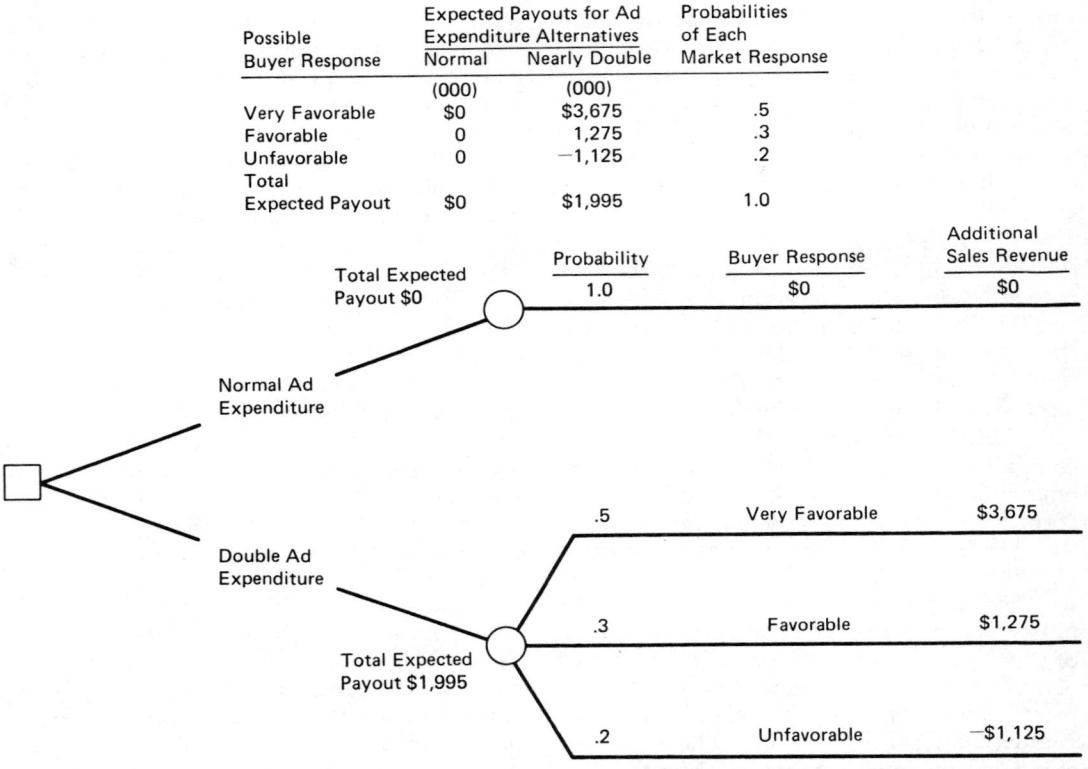

Possible Buyer Response	Expected Payouts for Ad Expenditure Alternatives		Probabilities of Each Market Response
	Normal	Nearly Double	
	(000)	(000)	
Very Favorable	$0	$3,675	.5
Favorable	0	1,275	.3
Unfavorable	0	−1,125	.2
Total Expected Payout	$0	$1,995	1.0

Figure 18-2. *Decision analysis resolution of microcomputer division advertising expenditure increase problem*

native. In the figure this does not have to be done for the normal advertising case, since there are no payouts expected above the normal level. For the nearly double budget case, however, the sum of the products of the payouts and the probabilities is $1,995,000. Assuming that this overall expected value is larger than the cost of nearly doubling the budget, decision analysis would recommend that the product manager go ahead with the extra expenditure.

The bottom of Figure 18-2 gives the same situation and solution in the form of a decision tree. Many people prefer to work with decision analysis in this way.

It should be obvious that this is a highly simplified example. When the alternatives and the possible outcomes increase, decision analysis becomes quite complex and difficult to solve. In addition, the use of quantification sometimes gives the impression that the analysis is based on something more than judgments. All the analysis in the figure is based on judgments as to the alternatives, the possible outcomes, the value of the outcomes, and the probabilities of the outcomes. Conceivably there are many more alternatives than the two considered. There are also many other possible outcomes. For instance, it would be possible to consider competitive response as another set of outcomes. Even further, the manager's ability to estimate payouts in sales is questionable, especially since the advertising may have some intermediate communication goal. And where do the probabilities come from?

The reader may have been somewhat uncomfortable with the solution presented in the example also. This may be because the decision rule, based on total expected payout, can sometimes seem unsatisfactory. There are some rules, such as the minimax rule (minimize the maximum loss), that would favor the normal advertising expenditure—because at least it would not produce sales below normal level in any outcome. Still other decision rules would concentrate on the most likely outcome.

Again, however, despite all of these problems and complications, decision analysis does force explicit consideration of judgments the manager may be making anyway. Sometimes the analysis can point out where additional information is needed. A set of methods for obtaining such information is discussed in the next section.

Field Experimentation. Various methods can be used to test proposed spending levels for individual communication elements. Basically these are all some form of experimentation in which different spending levels are tried in different markets that are equivalent or matched on other relevant characteristics.

Field experimentation is the sixth stage of the adaptive research system that spans the message, distribution, budgeting, and control states of advertising and communication management. It is a stage and procedure that should be done only seldom, in conditions where there is a great deal of uncertainty to resolve and when the rest of the campaign, particularly the message, is strong enough to merit the extra time and expenditure of a test.

Of course there are several levels of experimentation that might be done. They differ in time and expenditure and, conversely, in the amount of payout in terms of uncertainty reduction. Some of the alternatives would include, in decreasing order of cost:

1. *Random assignment of cities to experimental and control groups.* This is the most expensive approach and has less often been used because of this. Examples would include Du Pont's test of *advertising weight* (spending level) for Teflon-coated cookware and Budweiser's lengthy spending test for the beer. The Du Pont test indicated that Teflon could be reintroduced with adequate advertising.[2] Budweiser's test showed no difference despite expenditure variations from 0 to 300 percent of normal weight across the test markets.[3]

2. *Matched samples of cities in experimental and control groups.* The beauty of random assignment is that if the numbers of cities are large enough, all the nontest variables are statistically controlled. When matching is used instead of random assignment, there is an attempt to find cities that are equivalent on as many characteristics as are obvious. Matching can never achieve complete equivalence. So it always leaves a question as to whether different effects from different spending levels are caused by the different cities instead of the spending levels. Despite this problem, advertisers and others tend to use this method, probably because it is cheaper. Sometimes it is used with only two cities, one with the old spending level and another with the new level.

3. *Split cable facilities.* Markets are available in which it is possible to run one level of advertising (or other communication element) in one part of the market and another level in the other part. Services providing research in these markets indicate that spending tests are quite frequent.[4] In some markets it is possible to measure effects in terms of sales to individuals. Panels of people use a special credit card which is keyed to Universal Product Code scanning devices at the supermarket checkstand.[5] Of course one problem with such systems is that they can develop markets that are saturated by tests.

4. *Store-by-store experimentation.* This is more appropriate for testing sales promotion expenditures than advertising ones. But stores can be randomly assigned to spending treatments. When UPC checkout scanners are used, the tests can be done quite efficiently.[6]

Many other variations of field experimentation could of course be used to answer questions about individual element spending proposals. A review of the pretesting framework presented in Chapter 13 gives a broader indication of the alternatives available. Suffice to say here that each form of field experimentation has its own positive and negative aspects in addition to the general problems of cost, time, and possible warning to competitors. But field experimentation of some kind should be employed in those situations in which something unusual in spending has been proposed. The microcomputer and the biscuit examples at the beginnning of this chapter are good examples of such situations.

Combining Budget Proposals

The most powerful aspect of coordinating the various activities of marketing communication under one brand, product, or campaign manager is that the activities can be balanced for a greater total effect. The final budgeting stage offers a major opportunity for doing this. Once again, there are several methods by which this combining can be done. These methods can be used alone or in sequence.

Logical and Judgment Combination. At this point the campaign manager has more than an adequate knowledge of the nature of the job each component of the mix can do for the campaign. Each of the budget statements gives further information and reasoning on this. Just the previous work of assessing each of the budgets separating can give a tremendous amount of insight as to how the components of the mix will work together.

The first choice the manager has is to simply combine the budgets in just the amounts that have been requested separately, as revised by the assessment the manager has done. Unfortunately, this can sometimes lead to the sort of situation facing the biscuit mix brand manager discussed earlier—i.e., the individual budgets may add up to something more than the original budget allocated to

the campaign. Of course it might be argued that an increase in the total budget is necessary, but this argument should not be made until other possible combinations of expenditures have been explored.

In making this exploration, the manager should keep the *compensation* principle in mind. It may be possible that an unusually large effort for one component of the mix may be compensated for by using milder efforts with other components of the mix. For instance, it could be that the biscuit mix campaign could be handled with increases in advertising and some decreases in personal selling and sales promotion. Or it could be that, at the start of campaign planning, publicity had not been considered for this old brand. Perhaps with the new ideas developed by the advertising agency, it will be possible to use publicity and PR to develop awareness in a less costly way than would be necessary with advertising.

The campaign manager is in an unusual position to see such combination possibilities. In some cases it may be that particular components of the mix will be seen as having potential for effect that could not be seen by even the people working on those components. Sometimes, of course, as may be true of the biscuit mix example, there is a need to increase the budget for all or nearly all of the components of the mix because of an unusual opportunity.

Thus combination by logic and judgment is always the first step and sometimes the last in developing the final budget proposal. In many cases, however, other methods such as the following are used.

Decision Analysis. As was indicated in the preceding section, this method can become almost too complex to handle for a problem such as combining the budget for the final proposal. And if the alternatives are reduced to something like "increase total budget versus maintain total budget level," the problem can become too far removed from reality. Despite these problems, however, decision analysis might help the manager to order his or her thinking and might also highlight areas where further information is needed.

Field Experimentation. The methods discussed earlier could be used to test combinations of elements in a total campaign. In fact, this is what is done in *test marketing*. But it should be made clear that tests done in this way really are not experiments. They are really just trial runs for the campaign in several different ways in several different markets. Test marketing can be extremely expensive, take valuable time, yield confusing results, and warn competitors of the nature of the campaign. For instance, the test-marketing program for General Foods' Maxim freeze-dried coffee was said to be too long. While Maxim was being tested, Nestlé's competitive Taster's Choice brand was introduced and eventually took the lead in the market.[7]

Of course the use of some of the other methods mentioned earlier would allow limited testing of various spending combinations without the cost or time expenditures of test marketing. It should be noted, however, that these approaches would constitute only limited tests, in that the effect of various combinations of communication elements often takes time and a large-scale presentation.

Adaptive Planning and Decision Calculus Models. These models can be thought of as quantitative representations of the manager's logical and judgment approach (see Chapters 6 and 18). The value of the models is that they can bring order to this approach and use data as they become available.

An example of a model that could be used to assist the process of combining budgets is Little's BRANDAID.[8] It uses factual data, judgments, and assumptions about how the market works to provide indications of how various combinations of price, promotion, and advertising would work. There is no reason why personal selling and publicity could not be added to the model's activities.

The introductory stage in using such a model includes management orientation, forming a model-using team, selecting and formulating a problem (which might be the budget allocation and combination one), calibrating the model (seeing if it will reproduce past results accurately), and initial use. Then, as the model is used repeatedly and some confidence is developed with it, each year's budgeting can be done with the model's assistance. If members of top management have accepted the use of the model, it can be a valuable tool in convincing them to accept budget proposals.

IMPLEMENTATION

The implementation of an advertising and communication campaign is a tangible summary of all the planning work that has been discussed in the preceding parts of this book. But implementation is more than this summary. It can also be an extension or even an alteration of those plans as the realities of the marketplace cause certain plans to be rejected in favor of new opportunities.

The campaign manager cannot be involved in all the aspects of implementation. But four areas demand his or her attention, so that the planning can be carried efficiently to the field. These four areas are:

1. Timing and mixing issues
2. Contingencies and feedback planning
3. Presenting the plan and getting approval
4. Scheduling the work effort

Timing and Mixing Issues

The effectiveness of the campaign can be affected drastically by the timing of the components of the campaign. For instance, the stories of advertising creating demand at the stores before the product is actually there are enough to cause any brand manager to wince. Even further there is evidence that certain timing of campaign elements can substantially improve campaign efficiency.

The timing and mixing of campaign elements are totally determined by an assessment as to how the eventual consumer or buyer will be exposed and react to them. As in the painful example above, if the sales force has not sold the product into the stores, then there is no chance that advertising effect will be important to individual consumers.

Perhaps the best way to summarize the considerations of timing is in terms of the hierarchy situation analysis. No matter what the product or marketing situation, the mental steps through which the consumer or buyer must move are critical to the order in which he or she should be exposed to communication elements. Beyond the indications of the hierarchy there are issues of cost—e.g., whether it is cheaper to develop awareness through publicity or advertising first.

Learning Hierarchy Situations. In such situations people tend to move from awareness to comprehension to conviction to action. Usually there is actually something to learn about the marketing offering. Major purchases such as new durable consumer goods or industrial goods would be good examples. The most likely order would seem to be:

☐ First, publicity–PR to capitalize on the newness and get the message in highly credible print media from which awareness, comprehension, and even some conviction can occur.
☐ Second, advertising to expand awareness and comprehension and pave the way for salespeople.
☐ Third, personal selling, possibly preceded by some promotional incentive to visit a retailer in consumer marketing. This stage can lead to further conviction and, of course, action.

This is a fairly standard order of elements in new-product and innovation marketing. It would be appropriate, for instance, for the new photovoltaic cell situation depicted at the beginning of this chapter. The only variation comes in instances when it is necessary for selling to take place earlier, not to the ultimate buyer or user but rather to the trade of distributors, wholesalers, and retailers. In those instances the trade selling effort should take place before the advertising so that the product will be available when the advertising stimulates people to come in for the ultimate selling event.

Low-Involvement Hierarchy Situations. In these situations the products or services are mature, and the buyers have had ample opportunity to learn about the product category and its brands. The purchases are not very involving and not much effort is expended in learning about the products. Good examples would include consumer convenience goods. The most reasonable order would seem to be:

☐ First, selling in to the trade by the sales force in order to make sure the product has adequate distribution before advertising can have effect. Some trade promotion usually accompanies this effort.
☐ Second, advertising, usually on broadcast media in order to develop the large amount of gross positive awareness needed for this kind of product category.
☐ Third, during the advertising effort both sales promotion and publicity–PR events can take place to maintain distribution, develop trial, and, in general, maintain interest in a low-involvement situation.

Note that the selling must precede the advertising, and the advertising must precede the other two types of consumer activities. If advertising does not precede sales promotion and publicity events, they will not have the same degree of long-term effect for this kind of hierarchy situation.

In industrial marketing it is unusual to find anything like the Low-Involvement hierarchy situation. There is some similarity, however, in the scheduling of mix elements for what were called "standard" products in the preceding chapter. With such industrial products, there is selling (to a trade of distributors), maintenance advertising, and some use of promotional events.

Dissonance-Attribution Hierarchy Situations. In these situations there is involvement but a sameness between alternative market offerings. Consumers have had some experience with the product category but not enough to get over the nagging doubt that there are hidden differences between brands and that they, the purchasers, may have made the wrong choice. Some action or strong intention to act has occurred, and this is followed by attitude change and increases in knowledge. This is the Dissonance-Attribution hierarchy.

This hierarchy situation points out the advantage in many categories of getting consumers to take some action with regard to the market offering in order to commit them to it. Once this commitment is developed, there is the possibility of greater response to subsequent communication elements.

Recall, for instance, the research by Swinyard mentioned in Chapters 6 and 14. In that study, Red Cross volunteers, acting as missionary salespeople, elicited this sort of commitment from individuals with a "labeling" statement or by getting them to comply with a small request. Individuals who received this sort of sales call before advertising responded more dramatically to advertising than did those who did not receive such calls or received them after the advertising.[9]

What this research and the Dissonance-Attribution hierarchy situation suggest is that in many campaigns there is the possibility of creating this sort of commitment even before target segments are heavily exposed to advertising. The tools used to engender this commitment could be sampling or consumer coupons in many consumer categories. In industrial markets and some public-sector categories, the type of sales call utilized by Swinyard could create the commitment during or before the more mass-media distribution of the message occurs.

In sum, the order that seems to be most reasonable for the Dissonance-Attribution hierarchy situation is one starting with some commitment-producing action, followed by advertising (and, if possible, publicity–PR ac-

tivities), which can develop the attitude change and knowledge necessary for the final action of purchase.

Other Situations and Factors. Of course the three hierarchy situations are not the only ones in advertising and communication. And costs and other practicalities often cause variations from the timing suggestions made above. The brand manager should keep in mind that the timing of the elements of the campaign is done best when it serves consumers best—i.e., providing information and product and offers when they are needed for the purchase decision process. Also there is opportunity for creativity in timing the campaign. Sometimes timing the campaign in a nontraditional way can lead to strong effects. One example is the suggestion from the Swinyard research that selling effort should sometimes precede advertising in the campaign. This is the reverse of what had been assumed in industrial marketing. The new order can produce strong extra effects in certain situations.

Contingencies and Feedback Planning

According to Murphy's law, "If anything can go wrong, it will." In advertising and communication campaigns, it is probably better to not be this negative. Instead it should be realized that new opportunities for planning will occur during the campaign itself. Unexpected events may come up even during the campaign preparation—*before* the campaign is actually exposed to the public.

It is best to be ready for both problems and opportunities right from the beginning of implementation rather than assume that everything will go as planned and that nothing new will come up. The more that is done in implementing the plan, the more managers and their staff learn about how communication can actually be accomplished. If the plan and the brand manager are too rigid, this new information is not used. New possibilities are lost.

Nearly all the examples at the beginning of this chapter are situations in which the manager has to react to unexpected events. The biscuit mix brand manager must consider increasing the budget because the advertising agency has come up with some new uses for the mix. Another executive has to scrap all previous plans when engineers come up with a dramatically new photovoltaic cell. The mayor's campaign is interrupted by a city workers' strike.

How can one be prepared for the unknown future in communication planning? Obviously there should be a contingency fund. Recommendations for such funds range from 2.5 to 10.0 percent of the budget.[10] Some recommend just padding the budget everywhere, instead of having a specific fund. Probably the best resolution is to be realistic about budget figures (take the trend in costs into account) while having a small budget for contingencies. In addition, there should be an understanding that unexpected events may occur which will require even more than a contingency fund can provide.

But contingency planning is more than just budgeting. It has to be a general sensitivity to the likelihood of unexpected events occurring. Part of the planning process should use decision analysis to lay out the planners' expectations as to the probability of certain events occurring. What is the probability that there will be a strike and what will be its effect? What if the product name turns out to be legally owned by someone else? What if an opportunity to sponsor a program or an event comes up? How likely is it that the competition will react in certain ways? What is the probability that an improved advertising format will be developed? Some prior assessment of the known possible "unknowns" should be made.

Of course it is impossible for the brand manager to predict during planning or even to consider much of what will happen during campaign implementation. It is important to set up feedback mechanisms that will allow the manager to know when something unusual has happened. One type of feedback mechanism is the control and evaluation information system that is discussed later in this chapter. This system, however, will cover only the effects of the campaign in operation. In addition, during campaign operations there should be an open policy so that new information and occurrences can be brought to the attention of someone who can do something about them. People working on the campaign should not feel that they must abide by the original plan, no matter what.

If the manager first assumes that the unexpected will occur and gets ready for it in terms of contingency funds, futures analysis, and the institution of adequate feedback mechanisms, the problems of the future can be turned into opportunities.

Presenting the Plan and Getting Approval

Once all the groups responsible for the communication elements have submitted their plans, the final budget adjustment has been done, timing has been determined, and allowances for contingencies have been made, it is time for the brand manager to put together an overall plan. The audience for this plan is the top-management committee that will approve it and authorize the funds necessary for it to become a reality.

The plan is both a written document and a presentation to top management. Both of these should be efforts to sell the plan, based on a solid foundation of the activities that occurred before marketing planning per se. That is, the plan statement and presentation should refer to the situation analysis, the overall marketing objectives, and the total communication budget for the brand—as the bases on which the plan was built. These bases should be detailed quite specifically in the written plan statement. They can be mentioned more briefly in the presentation, since at that point the top-management audience need only be reminded.

The outline of the plan statement can vary somewhat to fit the situation. The outline of this book provides one alternative. For instance, the sections could be: executive overview; situation; marketing objectives; communication goals; message strategy; message format and distribution individually for advertising, personal selling, sales promotion, and publicity–PR; timing throughout the year; budget overview including contingencies and research-control expenditures; and a summary emphasizing the expected payouts from the campaign.

The oral presentation cannot possibly cover all of those points. Instead it should concentrate on the distinctive methods of the campaign and the way in which it will pay out for the organization. Since this is a selling presentation, it is important that it fit the audience well. The same sort of care that is done in communicating to consumers should be taken in communicating with top management.

Figures 18-3 and 18-4 present short-term marketing plan directions for R. J. Reynolds and a food company. Although they differ in the structure recommended for the plan statements, they have common elements which were summarized in the outline suggestion above. They both ask for specificity. The mark of an outstanding plan is that it clearly indicates what is to be accomplished, how it will be accomplished, and how management will know it has been accomplished.

Scheduling the Work Effort

The campaign manager cannot get involved in the scheduling of all the detailed activities that have to be completed in order to implement an advertising and communication campaign. Each organization responsible for a part of the campaign is responsible for detailed scheduling to complete that activity. For instance, advertising agencies have account service and traffic departments that keep the schedule going with regard to the production and placement of advertising.

The brand or campaign manager is responsible, however, for making certain that the timing of the campaign fits the timing of the plan. This means that the manager must encourage efficiency from each of the individual working units, obtain firm estimates from them as to completion times, and schedule the overall work effort.

Probably the best approach to all of this, both at the brand manager level and at the agency level, is *critical path scheduling,* sometimes called PERT (*p*rogram *e*valuation and *r*eview *t*echnique). This method, which was originally developed to avoid delays on government missile projects, simply asks the manager of any project to keep track of all events and activities connected with it. This means learning when each event occurs in the process and how long it will take (optimistic, most likely, pessimistic).

By mapping out the order of events, their time, and their interrelationships, a manager of any project, including a communication campaign implementation, can immediately see how long the total project will take if nothing is changed. The manager can also see how the scheduling might be improved by changing or eliminating activities or by increasing efficiency on certain of them. This can save time and money and improve campaign quality itself.

This can be done without the computer programs and quantitative analysis of critical path scheduling and PERT. They provide two benefits, however. First, they allow analysis of the tremendous number of activities that are necessary to implement the campaign. For instance, a critical path network for a new-product introduction is shown in Figure 18-5. Note the tremendous complexity even when activities are considered at this gross level and time estimates are omitted.

The second benefit of the computer program is that it determines the *critical path,* that sequence of activities on which all other activ-

I. STATEMENT OF BUSINESS

    A. Brief summary statement of brand's performance during current year
    B. Share trend of brand
    C. Volume trend of brand

II. FINANCIAL SUMMARY

    A. Brief summary of brand's current financial picture -
        current year vs. next year
    B. Brand's P&L for current year and next year
    C. Brand's P&L for latest five-year period

III. MARKETING PLAN

    A. Statement of brand's marketing objective
    B. Statement of brand's marketing strategy -
        how the marketing objective will be achieved
    C. Marketing rationale - supporting points for
        marketing strategy

IV. ADVERTISING PLAN

    A. Statement of brand's advertising copy objective
    B. Statement of brand's advertising copy strategy
    C. Advertising rationale - support for strategy

V. MEDIA PLAN

    A. Objective
    B. Strategy
    C. Rationale
    D. Request for funds and itemized budget

VI. SALES PROMOTION PLAN

    A. Objectives
    B. Strategy
    C. Rationale
    D. Request for funds and itemized budget

VII. BACK-UP MATERIAL

    (Supporting data for foregoing section)

Figure 18-3. *Outline of annual marketing plan for each company brand—R. J. Reynolds Tobacco Company.*

Source: Hopkins, *Short-Term Marketing Plan,* p. 26.

<u>Marketing Plan Implementation</u>

The approved marketing plan is the central point in setting the direction for the activities of other functions in relation to the product. Product Management is responsible for the communication of this direction.

Other operating functions then construct their plans to carry out their related activities as outlined in the marketing plan.

1. <u>R&D</u> works to formulate new products and to modify or improve existing products.

2. <u>Production</u> must provide the proper items in sufficient quantities at the right time at the lowest cost to meet marketing demands. This begins with procuring required ingredients and materials, primary commitments for seasonal crops and cans or other containers.

Marketing staff groups prepare specific ingredients of the marketing mix:

3. The <u>advertising agencies</u> must create selling messages that effectively communicate the selling appeal to meet the specific advertising objectives for the product.

4. The <u>packaging</u> department designs labels or packages to implement marketing objectives; e.g., a cents-off label, an on-pack premium.

5. The <u>merchandising</u> department designs display materials, consumer promotions, etc., as needed to meet specific marketing objectives.

6. <u>Marketing</u> research recommends and implements methods of providing essential information feed-back on which to assess current programs and recommend future action.

Once prepared in final form, all of these components are then delivered to the people they are aimed at -- either through our distribution channels or directly to consumers.

7. <u>Distribution</u> must insure that products are kept in stock, meaning that inventory levels must be coordinated with upcoming marketing programs designed to accelerate turnover. Also, offer a customer service plan on shipping, warehousing, etc., to meet the grocery store needs.

8. <u>Sales</u> must be prepared to communicate marketing programs effectively to the grocery trade and to follow through with sufficient retail store coverage to generate maximum exposure and availability of the product to consumers. Communication includes the total marketing mix -- product differentiation, advertising support designed to "pull through" the product, packaging innovations, allowances, etc.

9. <u>Advertising and Merchandising</u> messages are delivered through media that reach consumers considered the best prospects for the product frequently enough to convince and/or remind them to buy the Libby brand.

Corporate staff functions, concurrently, tie together the individual product marketing plans with regard to financial planning requirements. Upon completion of all operational plans <u>profit planning</u> translates the sum of the operational plans into a total company plan.

Figure 18-4. *Excerpt on implementation from marketing planning instructions—a food company.*
Source: Hopkins, *Short-Term Marketing Plan, p. 68.*

ities depend. Once the manager can determine the critical path, he or she can zero in on the activities that, if improved in efficiency, will lead to marked improvement in the overall project. The critical sequences in Figure 18-5 are signified by darker lines.

Whether the brand manager and the organizations working for him or her use the entire critical path technique or not, careful scheduling can lead to substantial benefits. In the development of one standard copytesting technique, for instance, attention to the critical path of activities led to the possibility of a 78 percent reduction in the time to complete the activity.[11] And this is only one of the many subactivities necessary for the successful implementation of an advertising and communication campaign.

CONTROL AND EVALUATION

Once planning is done and implementation is under way, everyone associated with the campaign wants answers to two broad questions: (1) How are we doing? and (2) Why are we doing it that way? These are the main questions of control and evaluation.

The first question must be answered because corrections can be made in the campaign while it is still running. Or the next campaign can be improved if the results of the present one are known.

The second question is essential because unless it can be answered, there is no way to make corrections in the present campaign or improvements in the next one. The brand manager simply would not know where or how to make improvements if he or she did not know what was causing the effects of the present campaign.

The Centrality of Goals

Every step in the process of planning and implementing an advertising campaign has implications for the issue of how it will be controlled and evaluated. At each step, the consideration is whether what is being planned or implemented will contribute to the goals of the communication element and the objectives of the campaign. And considering the contributions to goals and objectives automatically leads to the question of how these contributions will be measured.

In a sense, we have come full circle, because one of the quotations at the beginning of the first chapter was John Wanamaker's "I know half the money I spend on advertising is wasted; but I can never find out which half." Throughout this book approaches have been discussed that could have helped Mr. Wanamaker to "find out which half." Basically these approaches involve setting down very clear and specific goals in writing—so that everything that is done on the campaign can be done with the thought of those goals and how they can be measured. Now in this penultimate chapter we can discuss how these approaches can be brought together for control and evaluation of the campaign.

In order to set goals, it is essential to have benchmark measurements of where the brand is—in terms of awareness, knowledge, attitudes, intentions, or sales—at the time the goals are set for the future. If there is information on the brand's present level of, say, awareness among people in target segments, then at a minimum it will be possible to measure the level of awareness in these segments during and after the campaign also. Thus the stating of goals in terms of actual measurements is the first step to determining how well the campaign is doing.

Of course it is possible that awareness could have been caused by any or several of the elements of the communication mix. Or it could have been shifted by some external factors. In order to tease the effect of the campaign or any part of it from these other factors, it is necessary to do some experimentation or develop statistical models that can tentatively determine causes. If there are no measurements, however, none of these techniques will be possible. And the clear

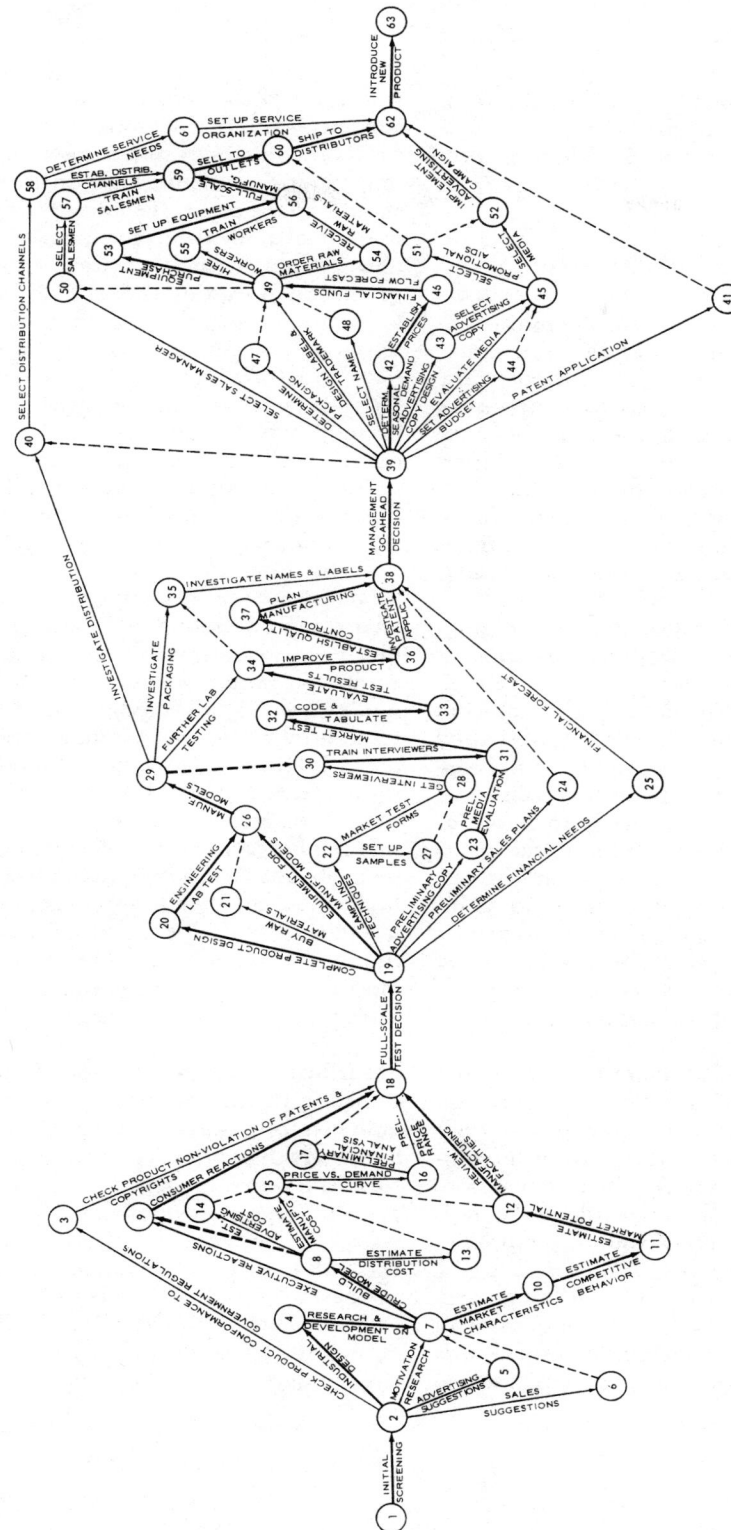

Figure 18-5. *Critical path network for a new-product introduction*

From Yung Wong, "Critical Path Analysis for New Product Planning," *Journal of Marketing*, 28 (October 1964), p. 55. Used with permission.

statement of goals, along with the consideration of goals in planning and implementation, is central to the control and evaluation process.

The Information System Concept

The only way to know how communication works in a market is to have experience. The greater the experience, the greater the knowledge that can be used to plan future campaigns. The control and evaluation done on a campaign are the only way that brand managers can have experience with how the campaign is working. And probably one of the best forms of control and evaluation is found in a continuing *marketing-communication information system.*

In its full-blown form, an information system includes the continuous collection of both primary and secondary data, statistical techniques that put the data in a useful form and assess their value, and decision-oriented models that use the data along with judgments to help in various planning tasks.

It is not necessary to have an information system in its full-blown form to realize its benefits, however. In the beginning it is necessary only to keep the concept in mind as information about campaign effects naturally comes in. Let us examine the components of the information system concept and the way they relate to control and evaluation.

Continuous Data Collection. This rather frightening aspect of the information system concept is actually a structuring of what organizations very often do anyway. For instance, no matter how small the organization, sales records are kept, salespeople and retailers give indications of how well the campaign is doing in their areas, trade publications give hints about competition and trends, regularly published services are available for data of all sorts related to the campaign, warranty cards are sent in, coupons are redeemed, and so

forth. What the information system concept suggests is that these kinds of data be checked for their contribution to campaign evaluation and control. If some have little value, they should be dropped. If there are gaps in information with regard to certain campaign goals and campaign elements, then some means of getting such information should be explored. Creative and inexpensive data sources can be developed for almost any situation.[12]

Measurement should be made regularly, at least as often as every quarter and preferably every month. It is *not* necessary to collect data *continuously,* although one corporation comes quite close to this by conducting a national probability sample survey by telephone every night of the week!

In order to develop regular data from target segments, some consumer and industrial companies use panels of people who regularly give information on media and other campaign exposure along with their purchasing, awareness, knowledge, attitudes, and intention related to the product category. Such panel information can be obtained relatively inexpensively when bought from a service that spreads the expense over a number of subscribing companies. Although there can be problems in linking panel responses to actual campaign effects, the collection of data in a regular way helps in the understanding of the data. Then statistical techniques and models can be used to convert the data into satisfactory forms for decision making.

Statistical Techniques. Data of the sort discussed in the preceding section become available in a form that cannot actually be used by managers. Statistical techniques must be used to, at the very least, develop average scores for areas of the country, segments, or times of the year.

Of course these techniques can become increasingly sophisticated as more data are collected. For instance, if any kind of sample data is collected, statistical techniques can be used to determine if differences between samples (e.g., of areas, segments, or times) are statistically significant (not due to just sampling variation). Other techniques will go beyond indicating just whether there was a significant difference. They will indicate how big the difference was and which factors in the marketplace were likely to have caused the difference.

Remember that the use of these techniques is dependent on having data that are collected regularly and relates to both the communication inputs and the goal-related outputs. As will be discussed later, it is important to have a solid base of good measurement for each of the elements of the communication mix. Collecting data continuously is one of the best assurances that the measures and procedures will be both managerially and scientifically adequate.[13]

Decision-Oriented Models. These types of models have already been discussed in Chapters 6, 16, and 17, as well as earlier in this one, in regard to the assistance they can give in setting the final budget. Decision calculus models are not absolutely necessary for control and evaluation, any more than they were absolutely necessary for any of the other uses. Just as for the other uses, however, these models can add a great deal of power to the information system.

They add power by helping to answer the second or "Why" question of control and evaluation. They show where judgment is important and where additional data should be gathered. They take early data from a campaign, project these data to later, and indicate what steps can be taken to improve that future prediction. Their predictions and strategy suggestions have often proved to be quite accurate.[14] This is probably because the models are based on the judgments of experienced managers. Also, solid theory and findings from the behavioral sciences are used to develop the models. Perhaps the most important of all is that once an information system with models is started, it keeps improving

with additions of information, analysis, and decisions using the models. And what is even better, there should be substantial improvements in the quality of campaigns.

Advertising Measures of Effect

The issues of the measurement of advertising effect were treated quite specifically in Chapter 7 on communication goals where the general point was that the measurement plan should be stated at the same time as the goals. In Chapter 13, the framework for considering pretesting indicated the kind of research procedures that could be used for posttesting, after the campaign began. The point there was that posttesting typically involved measures, samples, designs, and materials that were more "natural" and more costly than those used for pretesting. Finally, the types of measures available on a continuing basis were outlined in Chapter 15 on media planning. There they served as examples of the levels of the ARF guide for evaluating media.

For measures of specific advertisement effects, readership services such as Starch's or day-after-recall techniques such as Burke's are adequate. Measurement of more than the individual ads can be accomplished with one or more of the field experimental techniques discussed earlier in this chapter. If a continuous program of measurement is under way, the advertising effect can be determined on the basis of survey or panel responses, with care being taken to avoid questions that ask respondents to indicate the extent to which they are affected by advertising. The indication of advertising effect should be determined from surveys on the basis of a comparison of people who would have had different degrees of opportunity to be exposed to the advertising.

Measures of advertising effect tend to be states of mind or intentions rather than actual purchasing effect. Usually the goal of advertising tends to be in terms of these types of measures. It should be noted, however, that with certain field experimental techniques—with measures like those that are available from supermarket scanning devices and with continuous measuring programs—companies are determining the sales effects of advertising with some regularity. Some companies are evaluating their advertising agencies on the basis of their ability to make sales quotas.[15] There is no question, however, that in order to learn about *why* ads work, it will be necessary to use some sort of state of mind measure.[16]

Measures of Personal-Selling Effect

For most personal-selling situations, it is possible to measure effect on the basis of actual sales. As was discussed in Chapter 17, the only difficulty is in separating selling performance from the effect of external factors, such as the potential of the territory. There are many kinds of information that can be used to get at selling effectiveness.

Of course for all types of selling, but particularly the type that does not involve sales closing, it is possible and necessary to get information on sales effects on buyer knowledge and attitude. With this sort of measurement it is possible to make strategy changes that may improve personal-selling effectiveness.

Measures of Sales Promotion Effect

Measurement of sales promotion effect depends on whether the sales promotion device is consumer franchise building (CFB) in intent or not. If it is, measurement in addition to sales must be used. If the device is not franchise building in intent, then immediate sales are usually the logical measure.

Once again, however, measures other than sales are often applied for both types of devices. For instance, even with non–CFB instruments such as trade promotions, it is im-

portant to get some idea of their effect on trade attitudes toward the brand. And some CFB forms allow a follow-up with promotion users to determine if there was an effect. One example would be the free-standing sampling insert in newspapers that was mentioned in the preceding chapter. Consumers answered questions about their purchasing habits, and those who had not chosen the brand were sent a sample. It was then possible to send a later questionnaire to these people to determine if the sample had achieved its purpose of converting other-brand users.[17]

It is possible to do more experimental work with sales promotion than with almost any other element of the communication mix. The reason is that an offer, for instance, can be distributed to very specific groups of people within a community. Realistic random assignment of sales promotion to various people or stores allows an extremely low cost assessment of the effects of sales promotion programs.

Publicity–PR Effects Measures

The publicity–PR element of the communication mix is often incorrectly measured in terms of inputs (number of pages of editorial material, number of visitors to a booth at a show, etc.) rather than real effects. When there are effects measures they can sometimes be very specific, such as the number of orders signed at a trade show or the number of inquiries that were accompanied by a mention of seeing an article about the market offering.

In other instances the effects of public relations programs are measured with a quite inadequate experimental design. A measure is taken with a national survey both before and after the campaign. If there is a change in the attitude that the public relations program is intended to affect, then the program is said to be effective. This is, of course, illogical. If there is a change in the attitude, it could have been caused by a variety of causes instead of or in addition to the public relations program.

A better design would involve use of the program in some areas and not in others. And no matter what the design, measurement should be in terms of effects, usually in the awareness, knowledge, and attitude areas.

SUMMARY

This chapter on the final steps of planning and the beginning steps of implementation serves as a summary for much of the rest of the book—just as these steps tend to do in actual campaign planning and implementation. The steps of final budgeting, implementation, and control all require an assessment and combination of the plans and directions that have been taken earlier. And this assessment and combination lead to three kinds of feedback which may alter earlier tentative decisions.

The budgeting discussed in this chapter is the third type of budgeting in communication campaign development. The first is the determination of the total campaign allocation. The second is the tentative budget mix. Now the final budget setting is done. The brand or campaign manager must both assess the recommended budgets for the individual communication elements and develop a combined budget for the total plan. Both of these tasks can be done on the basis of logic and judgment alone, using the underlying objective and task method. Or the manager can use decision analysis, field experimentation, or decision calculus models.

Implementation issues for the campaign manager are those that involve timing and mixing campaign elements, contingencies and feedback planning, presenting the plan and getting approval, and scheduling the work effort. Timing can be assisted by using hierarchy situation analysis. Contingency planning is necessary to make unforeseen events into opportunities. The presentation of the plan in both written and oral form should be seen as a selling exercise that leads to approval. The outline of the written presentation can be quite close to the parts of this book. Scheduling the effort of implementation can be improved with the sort of thinking exemplified by the critical path scheduling technique.

Campaign control and evaluation should move quite naturally from the goal and measurement-oriented approach to planning. The information system concept should be used in the sense that there should be regular measurement throughout the campaign year. Statistical techniques and decision-oriented models can make this information relevant to managers. Each element of the communication mix embodies particular types of measurement problems and opportunities.

ISSUES AND PROJECTS FOR DISCUSSION

1. How would you deal with the small coffee company financial officer in the example at the beginning of this chapter?

2. In what sense does feedback relate to the creative problem-solving process? What kinds of feedback are present in the communication decision process? How do they actually take effect?

3. How does communication goal setting affect the final budgeting, the issue of timing of campaign elements, and control and evaluation?

4. Assume the microcomputer product manager made the following judgments for the "Normal" Ad Budget situation: Very Favorable—$2.5 million with a .7 probability, Favorable—$900,000 with a .2 probability, and Unfavorable—minus $500,000 with a .1 probability. How would the decision analysis change? What effect would use of a minimax or a most-likely decision rule have on the outcome? What other kinds of market response or outcomes should be considered in this situation?

5. What kind of research might be used by the biscuit mix brand manager to justify an increase in the total campaign budget? Should the whole combination be tested? Just individual elements? Could experimentation be used? What type(s)?

6. What would be the most likely ordering or timing of campaign elements for the following market offerings?

Bathroom tissue
A new type of coffee
A redesigned business computer
A mayoral candidate
A theater subscription series

Explain your proposed scheduling plans.

7. The president of a large food company once said, "The importance of advertising spending versus advertising message is like the comparison between a teaspoon and a steam shovel. We only test budgets when we have an outstanding new message." Comment on this. Do you agree with the spending-message comparison? Are there other situations in which testing of budgets should be done?

8. The preceding two chapters discussed the response and decay of various communication elements. How do these general indications affect the scheduling of campaign elements, i.e., advertising, personal selling, sales promotion, and publicity–PR?

9. How could the mayoral campaign manager have prepared for the unexpected strike discussed at the beginning of the chapter?

10. What are the benefits of critical path scheduling and how should this concept be used by the brand, product, or campaign manager?

11. How can the information system idea be used by even small marketing organizations?

12. What are the major considerations in choosing effects measures for advertising, personal selling, sales promotion, and publicity–PR?

Notes

1. See Joseph W. Newmann, *Management Applications of Decision Theory* (New York: Harper & Row, Pubs., 1971); Robert Schlaifer, *Analysis of Decisions under Uncertainty* (New York: McGraw-Hill, 1969); or Charles Holloway, *Decisions under Uncertainty. Models and Choices* (Englewood Cliffs, N.J.: Prentice-Hall, 1979). Also most marketing research textbooks provide an elementary treatment of decision analysis.

2. James C. Becknell, Jr., and Robert W. McIsaacs, "Test Marketing Cookware Coated with Teflon," *Journal of Advertising Research,* 3 (September 1963), 2–8.

3. Russell L. Ackoff and James R. Emshoff, "Advertising Research at Anheuser-Busch, Inc. (1963–1968)," *Sloan Management Review,* 16 (Winter 1975), 1–16.

4. John Adler, "How to Test and Measure the Sales Effectiveness of Television Advertising," *Advertising Age,* July 14, 1975, pp. 27–29.

5. "Market Research by Scanner," *Business Week,* May 5, 1980, pp. 113–16; and Edward Tauber, "Checkout Scanner Ultimately a Marketing Goldmine," *Marketing News,* May 18, 1979, pp. 1, 11, and 13.

6. Ibid.

7. Victor A. Bonomo, "The Do's and Don't's of Test Marketing a New Product," General Foods Corporation (undated); and Walter P. Margulies, "How Nestlé Beat General Foods in Freeze-Dried Coffee Battle," *Advertising Age,* June 21, 1971, pp. 51–52.

8. John D. C. Little, "BRANDAID: A Marketing-Mix Model," Parts 1 and 2, *Operations Research,* 23 (July-August 1975), 628–73.

9. William R. Swinyard and Michael L. Ray, "Advertising-Selling Interactions," *Journal of Marketing Research,* 14 (November 1977) 509–16.

10. Jeremy Bacon, *Managing the Budget Function* (New York: National Industrial Conference Board, 1970); and Richard H. Stansfield, *Advertising Manager's Handbook,* 2nd ed. (Chicago: Dartnell, 1977), p. 1446.

11. Michael L. Ray, Scott Ward, and Gerald Lesser, *Experimentation to Improve Pretesting of Drug Abuse Education and Information Campaigns,* Part II of a final report to the National Institutes of Mental Health on Contract NIMH-OC-72-156, August 1973, pp. 39–41.

12. Michael L. Ray and Peter N. Sherrill, "Unobtrusive Marketing Research Techniques," in *The Marketing Manager's Handbook,* ed. Steuart H. Britt (Chicago: Dartnell, 1973), pp. 316–30.

13. Ibid.; and Roger M. Heeler and Michael L. Ray, "Measure Validation in Marketing," *Journal of Marketing Research,* 9 (November 1972), 361–70.

14. John D. C. Little, "Decision Support Systems for Marketing Managers," *Journal of Marketing,* 43 (Summer 1979), 9–26.

15. "Measuring How Well Ads Sell," *Business Week,* September 13, 1976, pp. 104, 107–8.

16. "Attitude Share of Market Predicts Better Than Behavioral Measures," *Marketing News,* May 16, 1980, p. 7.

17. Lou Haugh, "Building Franchise through Sampling," *Advertising Age,* November 5, 1979, p. 64.

Society and
the Future

■ *Media portrayal of women has been a concern of the women's movement since the 1960s. Early criticism focused on commercials like "Fly me—I'm Barbara." Advertisers felt that women were overly sensitive to "unintended" connotations in individual advertisements.*

—Matilda Butler and William Paisley (1980)

■ *The experiments of the psychologists indicate definitely that women are more neurotic than men. This means that they are more inclined to be nervous, moody and emotionally unpredictable than are men. Men display more emotional maturity than their sisters . . . Because of the sex differences just described, the emotional appeal is especially to be preferred in promotional material, either oral or written, designed to motivate women.[2]*

—R. S. Alexander (1947)

■ *The National Assn. of Broadcasters turned thumbs down last week on clown Ronald McDonald's claim that "Nobody can do it like Ronald can." In response to a complaint filed last June by J. Walter Thompson Co., New York, with the knowledge and approval of its client Burger King Corp. . . .[3]*

■ *Every business has its tools of the trade, and, in addition to CBS standards, commercials are also subject to industry and related guidelines. NAB, FTC, FDA, FCC, BBB . . . put them all together, they don't spell "mother" . . . they spell confusion.[4]*

■ *I think that when the last recourse is advertising which will offend, the creative well has run dry.[5]*

■ All advertising is dependent upon economic growth, which further concentrates wealth and power while destroying the planet.[6]

■ How better to use the science to persuade humanity to save itself? With world wide laser communications, advertising can, in the next couple of decades, reach everyone in the world, and advertology will then be called upon to develop techniques that will make it possible for world cooperation to be placed on a firm foundation.[7]

—Isaac Asimov

■ For 30 years, the television industry's aims have been clear and single-minded: continued growth in importance and advertising revenues. Now, suddenly—with ad volume at $12 billion annually—the medium faces a confusing, misty tomorrow.[8]

■ By 1990, a 30-second spot on a "Mork & Mindy"-type favorite show, which today goes for $116,000, will sell for $342,000. And a comparable spot on a daytime serial such as "As the World Turns," now priced at $15,500, will cost $45,500.[9]

■ Along with the de-massification of production and marketing—in fact, one of the elements that will make it possible—is the de-massification of the media, a phenomenon Mr. Toffler points out is already visible. Media segmentation will continue to accelerate as fast as the computer makes it cost efficient. Special interest magazines will continue to flourish, while their counterparts in cable TV, videocassettes, videodiscs, electronic newspapers and even regular newspapers grow with the individual—instead of the mass—consumer in mind.[10]

People in advertising and communication campaign management, like people in many other occupations, have often questioned the value of what they do for a living. Does advertising make people buy what they shouldn't? Is it just irritating? Should something be done to stop the flow of over one hundred coupons per month per household? Can all of this be changed in the future, when presumably the entire nature of marketing communication will be changed?

As the quotations at the beginning of this chapter indicate, these kinds of questions are not just the idle questions of malcontents. They are real issues that any thinking brand, product, or campaign manager must confront every day in some form. This final chapter provides some initial insights into the societal issues and future considerations of advertising and communication management so that people who work in the field can have a positive understanding of what they do.

Getting to the Right People

This entire book has been based on an underlying mission that is central to the questions of society and the future. That mission is to produce communication campaigns in marketing that get to the right people with the right message at the right time. At the beginning of the Preface it was stated that if this kind of communication was accomplished, advertising could be one of the most pleasurable, effective, and moral forms of communication. In the pages since, this book has contained presentations of an interlocking sequence of methods that are and should be used by managers to achieve efficient communication.

It is the position of this final chapter that if such efficient communication is achieved, most of the problems of advertising and marketing communication and society disappear. The question remains, however, as to whether this ideal form of communication can actually be achieved in any great number of instances. And to what extent are changes in the future going to impede or assist this sort of communication?

Social Questions and the Future Intertwined

While questions of advertising and society should not be considered in terms of the future, the future should be considered in terms of what it will mean for social questions. In that sense, the two—social questions and the future—are intertwined.

Of course, it is irresponsible to claim that current social problems can be ignored because new technology in the future will solve them. As Eugene J. Webb once said, "The future is not."[11] We can plan for it, but that does not mean that we should ignore the problems of the present.

On the other hand, there is potential for increasing ability in the future for the kind of efficient communication that is the goal of this book. For instance, if the kind of demassification of the media discussed by Toffler actually occurs, the control of communication will increasingly be under the control of consumers. Then it would be possible that more efficient communication would have to occur, simply because consumers would not let themselves be exposed to irrelevant messages at the wrong time. Is this just a dream? The purpose of this chapter's discussion of the future is to provide some initial answers to that question.

The Players Involved in the Game

There are "players" involved in the "game" of society and the future with regard to advertising and communication management. It is significant that they correspond to the parts of the model of communication presented in Chapter 1.

The first and most important is the *consumer or receiver* of the messages of marketing-communication campaigns. If this player does not receive the right message at the right time, then there are likely to be societal problems. And the future may bring new definitions of what is "right" (note, for instance, the more than thirty-year difference in the advertising consideration of women expressed by the first two quotations at the beginning of this chapter), as well as new ways to get the right message to the right person at the right time.

The second player in the society and the future game is the *sender,* the advertising and marketing-communication organization. These are the people attempting to achieve efficient communication. That there are times when they do not try or do not use the right methods is evidenced by those instances in which efficient communication does not take place. These people, the managers in the communication organizations, are the ones asking the questions about whether the work they do has value. If those questions can be answered in the positive and expansive way exemplified in the seventh quotation at the beginning of this chapter (which is from Isaac Asimov, the

scientist and science fiction writer), then the work of advertising and communication management will be more fulfilling.

The third player in the society and the future game consists of the people and the technology in the *channels* of advertising and marketing communication. The technology of the media and of distribution at the retail, wholesale, and industrial levels affects the ability to achieve efficient communication. And there is evidence that both media and distribution technology are becoming more and more individualized. In fact, there is some possibility that these two types of channels will become indistinguishable in terms of marketing. More on this later.

The fourth player in the society and future game consists of the government and other regulatory agencies and pressure groups watching over marketing communication. These people, mentioned in the McDonald's and the commercial regulation quotations at the beginning of this chapter, could be said to constitute both *feedback* and *noise* in the communication process. They are "feedback" in that if there is trouble from any of them, this trouble can signify that communication has not been efficient. They are "noise" in the sense that they have the potential of getting in the way of effective communication. This can happen when they impose their own idea of "right"—in terms of right message, right people, and right time—on all the other players in the process of effective communication.

There is evidence of several kinds of trends occurring for the future for these government and pressure groups. One trend is toward deregulation and less activity from the government types. At the same time, there is another trend toward more pressure groups, with more people getting involved in responding to marketing communication in ways other than as strict communication receivers. For instance, one network commercial clearance director remarked:

Consider, for example, such groups as: The Right to Life, Planned Parenthood, The

Gay Activist Alliance, The Knights of Columbus, Justicia, The Italian-American Anti-Defamation League, The American Indian Movement, The Council of Catholic Bishops, The Chinese-American Media Committee, The Council of Rabbis, The Black Media Council, The Council on Children Media and Merchandising, The National Citizens' Committee for Better Broadcasting, The Asian-American Council, The Southern Baptist Convention, and The National Organization for Women. And there are others, ranging from Action for Children's Television to morality in the media.[12]

In sum, it is necessary to examine every link in this process of communication to determine if efficient communication has occurred. This determination, however, will do much to answer the key questions of society and marketing communication, to which we now turn.

THE SOCIAL QUESTIONS: A DIALOGUE

Assume that we have run into someone who has read a little about advertising and marketing communication and wants to know more. He must have been reading some fairly negative books and magazine articles because his questions are "attacking" in nature. We will discuss some of his questions with him. He has questions first about how advertising works in selling individuals. Then he moves to economic issues and finally to specific types of marketing communication.

Low Salience for Advertising and Marketing-Communication Issues

Before we begin to deal with this fellow, it should be noted that he is reasonably unusual in his concern about advertising and communication and their social effects. It appears, in fact, that advertising and other communication elements are not of high involvement to most people most of the time. People may be upset by individual ads, a pesty salesperson, coupons cluttering their favorite magazines, or the odd public relations "event." But, in the main, these marketing communication activities seem to do their work without making themselves too obvious.

For instance, in two studies done by the American Association of Advertising Agencies in 1964 and 1974, national probability samples of consumers were asked to select, from lists of ten, those social concerns that were the three or four most talked about and those that needed immediate attention and change. Advertising ranked *last* among the ten concerns in both 1964 and 1974 in terms of number of mentions as being among "three or four topics talked about most." It ranked sixth in 1964 and seventh in 1974 in terms of "needing immediate attention and change."[13]

Note that these rankings tended only to indicate the degree of salience and concern rather than presence or absence of negative feelings about advertising. In fact, when favorable-unfavorable feelings toward five social institutions were elicited in the 1974 study, they ranked as follows in terms of favorability: the press, *advertising,* labor unions, big business, and federal government. There was the same ranking for another question asking, "Can you depend on what they tell you?" And there seemed to be a particular group that was negative about all institutions, not just advertising. Thus it was a general feeling of a particular group of respondents across all the institutions rather than a concentration on advertising by all or a majority of respondents.[14]

A more recent study provides some support for the 1964 and 1974 research. In a telephone survey conducted in ten major U.S. markets in early 1979, researchers found that "ad complaints and dissatisfactions do exist but at lower levels than suggested by many peoople, and they're less significant than the levels of complaints we found for some brands of some kinds of products."[15] The study did not ask about specific advertising experiences. Instead respondents were asked if they had seen or heard advertising that: made them upset or angry (28 percent said they did), they felt to be dishonest (18 percent said yes), they found to be amusing (40 percent agreed), made them want to buy or try something (30 percent said they had). Again, while the two negative responses are reasonably high, they are global responses, and they are lower than the positive responses and apparently significantly lower than negative responses to specific products.[16]

All of this is not to say that the concerns of our questioning friend are not important. There are critically important social issues connected to advertising and communication campaigns. But it is extremely unusual to find any individual at any one time who is as concerned about advertising as our friend. There are more important issues in people's lives. The manager or student can see that this is true by just introspecting as to his or her own attention to advertising before becoming more seriously interested in studying about it. Of course, our friend would say that such introspection and the research studies are really off the point. "It's precisely because people don't care about advertising that it has such a deleterious effect on society and the economy! It's like being beaten to death with a sponge. Who notices the individual blows? Eventually though, there's an effect."

It sounds as though we had better start answering this fellow's questions. He really represents the kinds of attacks that make communication planners not only wonder whether what they do has value but also wonder whether they are doing a disservice to society. So let's get to his first question.

Isn't It True That Advertising and Communication Make People Buy Things That They Don't Need?

This question really gets to the heart of all the complaints and questions about advertising and society. You have really implied two issues by your question. The first issue has to do with what people *need*. The second issue is whether, given that an adequate definition of "need" has been established, advertising and communication can actually *make* people do anything in the marketplace. Let's take them one at a time, and then see if we can answer your overall question satisfactorily.

Defining Need. Almost any basic economics textbook will have some statement of the amount of money a person would have to spend to live at a subsistance level. It is relatively little. If this is your definition of what a person needs, then advertising actually might be accused of leading people to buy something they don't need. It doesn't take much money for people to eat soy beans, wear pelts, and live in a cave or under some trees. Very few people in the United States live under those conditions by choice, however. Perhaps a better perspective would be *Maslow's hierarchy of needs,* which was presented in Chapter 10. Recall that Maslow hypothesized that people move from basic subsistence needs to social ones to the grand one of self-actualization. Once needs at any one level are satisfied, people seem to move up to higher levels. You wouldn't want to keep people artificially down at some level of need they have already achieved, would you?

"Well, that's already happened to millions of people around the world in underdeveloped countries. There are thousands of people in the U.S. who are artificially being kept at subsistence levels. Advertising keeps people trapped at lower income levels!"

Wait a minute! You're going into a whole series of other questions which we will be glad to answer. First, though, let's get at what you mean by "need." In both Chapter 5, in discussions of segmentation and attitudinal analysis of segments, and Chapter 9, covering positioning strategies, there are descriptions of how needs can be determined so that products and services can be developed to meet them.

By determining needs and then the attributes people find important to satisfying the needs (or the problems they are having with current products), it is possible to develop market offerings. Then communication planners find out how their market offering is perceived in comparison with competition—among segments of the market who use our brand, the main competition, both, or neither.

This allows the planning of communication campaigns to take into account the specific "needs" of specific groups of people—not all needs or all people. In campaigns that are intended to reach those at the subsistence level or those who have some needs or problems that cannot be met by relatively expensive products, the message would be entirely suited to that group. The point is to get the right message to the right people at the right time—not some global group who wouldn't really want to get the message. Of course, sometimes there are mistakes and the messages can't be delivered precisely. But that's no reason to eliminate the general benefit of communication.

"I'm beginning to understand a bit. The need has to be determined for each individual by that individual. That is the purpose of the research you do to develop communication campaigns. You try to find homogenous groups or segments that have the same set of needs and desired attributes. Then you develop products or services to fit that, and you try to communicate that need and attribute set to specific segments."

That's right. That's what we mean by getting the right message to the ri——

"OK, OK! But isn't that making people buy?"

Making People Buy? This part of your question touches on a whole series of related issues, such as whether advertising manipulates, persuades, or just presents information. The answers to these questions really depend on how well the brand, product, and campaign manager and all the people working for him or her have done their job. If communication is efficient in the way I've defined efficient (I'll try not to repeat that phrase with all the "rights" again), then communication campaigns just present the . . . correct . . . information, and consumers and buyers decide. They are not persuaded or manipulated.

Of course at several points in this book, notably in Chapter 9 on positioning, it is suggested that, to the extent that nothing distinctive can be said about a brand, product development should take place in order to provide information that will be useful. A message that is all format and no substance will certainly not be consumer franchise building and may lead to single customer purchases or investigations without any purchase or repeat purchase. You know you have to remember that you are asking about "buying" here. There are many more influences beyond the communication campaign that can affect whether a person searches for, tries, buys, and/or eventually adopts any particular market offering. Advertising is only one part of the communication mix. Its goals are usually to affect some state of mind before action. And the consumer is exposed to all kinds of personal and impersonal information about each market offering, each of which might have greater impact on the action of buying.

This reminds me of the cartoon that showed a group of executives in a planning session. One of them said something like, "Let's use about 12 million dollars of word of mouth." Don't we wish we could do that! In fact, the thing that can be most damaging to a brand is an advertising campaign that is *too good*. Such a campaign would present the wrong information, build up people's expectations, lead them to find out about or try the product or service once but never again.

"OK, I'm beginning to understand more about how advertising and communication work. But wouldn't such an advertising campaign like you just mentioned be misleading? And isn't it possible for other parts of the communication mix to be misleading in the same way? For instance, sales people, just by presenting information, can create unrealistic expectations."

Do Advertising and Marketing Communication Mislead?

Yes, there is no question that some small proportion of advertising and communication in marketing is misleading depending on how that word is defined. In fact, it could be said that some proportion of the audience exposed to any message *misperceives* it. Note that I said *any message*, whether marketing communication in orientation or not. The job of perceiving correctly the mass of messages in the media today is more than the human information-processing mechanism can handle, particularly since many of the messages really are not relevant to people at particular times. One study sponsored by the AAAA Educational Foundation provides some support for this idea of misperception occurring for almost any kind of message, whether it is advertising or not. In the study, twenty-seven hundred viewers in twelve geographically dispersed shopping malls each watched two thirty-second communications. Each communication was followed by six true-false questions relating to the broadcast message. Only 3.5 percent of the respondents answered all twelve questions correctly. In other words, 96.5 percent of the respondents misunderstood some part of what they saw—even though all they had to do was watch one commercial at a time by itself and not in the busy context of television, even though they probably watched with greater intensity than they normally watch commercials on television, and even though the message could be either a commercial or some part of a regular program. In fact, the respondents were slightly less likely to misunderstand commercials than thirty-second communications

coming from news or entertainment programs.[17]

Of course, your question said "mislead," not "misperceive." You may actually mean that advertising and communication actually get people to do something under false pretenses. Although the AAAA study did not deal with this issue, it is unlikely that those thouands of people who misperceived something from the commercials or other messages would actually act on those misperceptions. Since advertising and other media are so crowded and cluttered, consumers seem to use advertising messages, particularly those on broadcast media, to get general information about the availability of products and services. Then other types of messages, either from the communication campaign or elsewhere, will determine if they will act on that general information. So even if there is misperception, consumers seem to have adapted to the information explosion in such a way that they are not likely to let their minor misperceptions mislead them. There are just too many sources of information and experience to allow a minor misperception from a television commercial to lead to incorrect consumer action.

"You talked about crowding, clutter, and information explosion. Isn't all of this pretty irritating? Wouldn't we be better off if we didn't have so many messages bombarding us every day? Aren't a lot of these messages, particularly the advertising ones, irritating, offensive, and in bad taste? If consumers take so little information from ads, why do they have to go through all of this unpleasantness?"

Is Advertising in Bad Taste, Irritating, Offensive?

There is no question but that advertising, personal selling, sales promotion, and publicity–PR add considerably to the number of messages we must either deal with or ignore every day. In one year alone, the CBS network clearance people handled 22,725 commercial submissions.[18] And this was only one network, one part of one medium for only one part of marketing communication.

These numbers should not fool us into thinking that large proportions of people are necessarily being irritated or offended, either by the sheer magnitude of the information or by its poor aesthetic quality.

What seems to be happening instead is that consumers are developing ways of avoiding messages in general. Thus when marketers, as a group of senders, and the media, as representatives of channels, overload the environment with messages, consumers will avoid them. This is true not only of such passive messages as print advertising and mailed sales promotion, where the page can be turned (only an average of four seconds is spent on average per advertising page in magazines) or the mailer thrown away unopened. It is also true of more intrusive messages like television commercials, which it seems would take a physical act to avoid.

A series of studies by Webb, for instance, showed how consumers can avoid even television commercials under rather forced conditions. In one of Webb's experiments, consumers were exposed to three different patterns of twelve thirty-second commercials while viewing half-hour television programs. When the break pattern was unusual for a program compared with the way it was usually shown on the air, consumers would notice it. The lowest scores for commercial recall, coded attention, and other measures of effect tended to be for those break patterns that were most typical for each program. This indicated that consumers seemed to have built up mental methods for recognizing the commercial pattern in a show and thus avoiding the messages.[19]

In another of Webb's studies there was clear evidence of how consumers had a limit as to the number of messages they would process. Although the number of commercials shown ranged from sixteen to thirty-eight across the five conditions in the study, there was virtually *no difference* in the average number of commercials recalled per individual across the conditions. The average was about four and one-fourth recalled, and a little over three were recalled with their correct brand name.[20]

This all seems to mean that consumers have discovered ways of avoiding the glut of messages that face them. This may also mean that very few marketing communication messages are actually irritating or offensive to people.

Remember that one study mentioned earlier found lower proportions of respondents who reported ever having seen or heard advertising that made them upset or angry or which they felt to be dishonest than who reported positive experiences with advertising. And in the AAAA study in 1974, it was the issues of consumer benefits, credibility, and entertainment values that contributed most to attitudes toward advertising. They contributed to nearly two-thirds of the variance in such attitudes, whereas a clutter or intrusiveness factor accounted for only about one-fourteenth. Of course, the reverse of the entertainment value factor included some pretty negative reactions. But the number of commercials itself did not seem to affect attitudes as much as it did the effect measures like recall in Webb's study.

The loser in all of this seems not to be the consumer, who is certainly somewhat inconvenienced by having to avoid messages, but the advertiser or marketer, who is spending more to get even fewer exposures to and effects from target audiences. It seems that campaign managers will have to find other means of getting messages to people when they need them, rather than just trying to send them out en masse. Some of the developments in technology in recent years offer promise of solving this problem, although it seems that consumers have even now solved it temporarily on their side.

"I'm not sure I'm totally satisfied with your statistics. A lot of my friends are irritated by advertising. Anyway, let me move on. You talked about getting messages to specific people. I'm wondering about that. To what extent does advertising serve people in special or minority groups? It seems to me that most of the communication from industry tends to be focused on the majority and not only doesn't serve the small groups, but actually treats them very badly."

How Do Advertising and Communication Treat Special-Interest Groups?

The answer to your question has both positive and negative components. On the positive side is the fact, brought out in the segmenting and also the message distribution chapters, that effective marketing communication is nondiscriminatory. Socioeconomic and demographic descriptors do not actually do very well in segmentation. For both this and message distribution, psychographic measures or measures closer to purchase behavior seem to discriminate between people better than anything that would make someone a member of a minority group.

So, on the surface, effective marketing communication is nondiscriminatory. But, on the negative side, groups that really need special treatment might be ignored. And often these special groups were and are treated poorly in commercials and print advertisements. For instance, one review of sixty-seven studies of female sex stereotyping in advertising concluded:

> . . . advertising portrays the typical woman in a limited and traditional role, that woman's place in advertising is seen to be the home, and that her labor force roles are underrepresented. Women are typically portrayed as housewives and mothers, as dependent upon men, and sometimes as unintelligent and subservient. Women are often "used" as sexual or decorative objects

in advertising but are seldom shown or heard in authoritative roles, such as announcers or voice-overs. On the other hand, men are depicted as the voices of authority, the older and wiser advice-givers and demonstrators. They are shown in a wider range of occupations and roles in their working and leisure lives or as beneficiaries of women's work in the home.[21]

It seems that although the quotation from Alexander at the beginning of this chapter was made over three decades ago, it was still being heeded by marketers in the 1970s. The authors did say that there was some steady improvement in the treatment of women as characters in ads, but little change in the use of them as announcers.

All that can be said at this point is that this kind of stereotyping seems to be a problem in advertising for successively different groups. Campaigns that go for the big target segments of heavy users in most product and service categories tend to make this unfortunate majority fallacy-type of error. Then there are complaints, and corrections are often made in the tone and role depiction. Unfortunately, the advertising that is most likely to make this sort of error is that which is most visible. Need I repeat again that this kind of stereotyping is less likely to happen if campaigns are well targeted and achieve efficient communication?

"No, it won't be necessary to say that. It is easy to see how the drive for high volume leads to a most common denominator that is bound to hurt someone. I am interested in something more than that though. In what way does advertising affect our very values and the way we perceive the world? I mean, even though people seem to do a pretty good job of avoiding detailed processing of advertising messages, there is a certain commonality about all the messages. Doesn't that lead to dysfunctional attitudes of materialism, outer as opposed to inner beauty, worship of youth, competition instead of cooperation, and a kind of sameness?"

How Do Advertising and Communication Affect General Values?

This is a very common question with no easy answer. Everyone on both sides of the argument seems to agree that advertising has some role in perpetuating our culture's general consumer and capitalistic ethic. The differences come in assessing the strength of that role. Advertising's advocates point out that it is an effect, not a cause, and that just in order to work well, all components of marketing communication campaigns must follow the society's values closely. The detractors, on the other hand, say that nonetheless, advertising fuels these values beyond the point that they would otherwise have effect.

Unfortunately, or fortunately I suppose you would say, I have no research data to offer on this point. Detractors offer ingenious content analyses in which they point out how individual advertisements show an enormous variety of hidden meanings.[22] Social psychological research on *incidental learning* has shown that children can "learn" aggression and fear by being shown films with these sorts of themes.[23] It is possible that this same kind of process could be occurring in the effect of advertising on certain types of values. So far, however, there is little convincing research evidence in the advertising area. And if the trends in stereotyping discussed above continue—that is, if early errors in stereotyping are corrected—there may be areas in which advertising is actually leading society in breaking down old and dysfunctional values and perceptions.

You will note that virtually all the suggestions of this book were for careful monitoring to fit the message and message delivery to the target segment. If campaign managers and those who worked for them followed this procedure, they would be likely to pick up changes in values. It seems that people who are so shocked by the detractors' statements about advertising leading values are also the ones who follow the procedures recommended here. They cannot understand how anyone can accuse advertising of anything other than following society.

"Your arguments seem most weak when you run out of research evidence. Let me pursue the value question a bit more and ask whether any of advertising deals directly with social problems."

Does Advertising Have Any Effect on Social Problems?

Well, throughout this book we have discussed public-sector marketing communication in parallel to consumer and industrial marketing. Part of public-sector marketing includes social marketing and advertising which certainly deal with issues. This kind of communication is found in two forms, public service advertising and controversy advertising.

Public service advertising in the United States gets a big boost from the Advertising Council, an organization that coordinates volunteer efforts of the entire advertising community. Advertiser and agency people donate their planning, research, and creative skills and efforts. The media donate free time and space, over a half-billion dollars a year in value.

In any given year the Advertising Council might be coordinating twenty-five national campaigns or more. Many of them have been credited with enormous success. For instance, the Smokey the Bear Forest Fire Prevention Campaign is said to have cut forest fires in half and saved over $17 billion of natural resources. Another campaign on high blood pressure is supposed to have resulted in increased testing for the disease, a doubling of patients on adequate therapy, and a three-year increase in life expectancy.[24]

There are some difficulties with the Advertising Council from your perspective, of course. The council stays away from any campaign that has political overtones. Thus it was involved in a lively controversy with the National Organization of Women a number of years ago when the Advertising Council refused to take on the National Organization's account. And the council has done an American Economic Systems campaign which was criticized by some as contributing to perpetuating the values of the economic system. This is a bad thing to only a minority of people in this country, however, and the campaign has received an award from the Freedoms Foundation.

All volunteer and donated campaigns often have their limitations too. For instance, there is limited control over media scheduling and often less than prime time and space. Normally, there are not adequate funds for research either.[25] Recognizing these difficulties, the U.S. government often pays for its own advertising to the point that government is one of the nation's largest advertisers.

Controversy advertising is a form of social issue advertising that, as its name indicates, does not shy away from social issues. The only criticism that might be made of it is that the advertising is very often sponsored by large industrial corporations, who have the money to mount such campaigns. There is a question of whether there is equal advocacy on both sides of the controversial issues. The television networks have often shied away from accepting this sort of broadcast, probably to avoid the question of providing equal time to non-paying advertisers.[26]

So most controversy advertising is in the print media. There have been some outstanding success stories. For instance, two Doyle Dane Bernbach creatives were indignant over the U.S. House of Representatives defeat of a "Rat Extermination" bill. They developed an ad showing an ugly picture of a rat with the headline, "Cut this out and put it in bed next to your child." The ad actually ran only three times, but the national furor it caused was enough to get the bill passed.[27]

More recently there has been attack by large advertisers and certain members of Congress against the Federal Communications Commission's Fairness Doctrine, which has been used successfully by broadcasters to prevent controversy advertising from appearing on the air. Marketing companies are particularly incensed by treatment on television newsmagazines, which they are not allowed to rebut on TV itself. Instead they have run print ads and developed public relations campaigns.[28]

In general, then, I guess you could say that there is a fair amount of diversity in social advertising in terms of dealing with social problems in a way that is quite different from the normal campaign.

"I'd appreciate moving away from this psychological and social stuff now. Let's talk about money. Does advertising actually have any economic value, or does it just increase prices?"

What Is Advertising's Economic Value?

There is no simple answer to this question. Of course, it would be easy to say that advertising keeps the economy moving. But there are a whole series of separate questions that should be dealt with individually.

First, it should be pointed out that there is really no conclusive set of data or findings on advertising's effect on the total economy. The reason for this is that the situation is too complex. Even though it is possible to determine advertising effect for a single company (see Chapter 6), there are just too many variables, including the other elements of the communication mix, operating in too many different ways to clearly pull out the effect of advertising alone on the economy or any one market.

One of the best recent reviews cautioned against making any conclusions, and then, for the reader's peace of mind, the authors did list what their beliefs were. They believe that

☐ Advertising increases prices in general but also allows what is probably a lower cost form of retailing and decreases consumers' search costs. So the social-economic value of advertising is ambiguous.

☐ Advertising can increase profits for some companies at the expense of others within a given industry. The relation between advertising expenditures and industry profits is probably a function of risk as well as a number of other factors.

☐ Advertising alone cannot create industry concentration because it does not have significant scale economies. Product innovation is more important.

☐ Advertising can accelerate the growth of new markets.[29]

In addition, several places in this book offer situational analyses of the factors that lead to increased advertising and sales promotion budgets. The discussion in Chapter 6 is the best example.

Finally, I would be remiss in answering your question on economic effects if I did not point out that advertising pays a large share of the enormous costs of the media. Thus the argument is often made that, without advertising, television either would be a prohibitive expense for all but the most well off families or would have a very different character.

The other side of this media support argument is that there is danger of advertisers controlling the content of the media. There is not much evidence for this in network broadcasting, although this is not to say that it might not have happened in some local instances. At this point, someone usually compares the advertising-supported system with the state-supported system. I will not attempt that comparison, however.

"If I were to summarize your answers, such as they are, I would say you leaned pretty heavily on your idea of efficient communication. Am I right?"

Summary: Efficient Communication and Society

Yes, you are right. In the Preface to this book the point was made that one of the goals

here was efficient communication which would be fulfilling to those doing it and to those receiving it. The heart of efficient communication is the targeting of messages so that people who are not supposed to get them are not bothered by them.

Of course, efficient communication is not easy to achieve. But those who operate with efficient communication as a goal will find that they are (1) not making people buy things they don't need, (2) not causing misperception or irritating people, (3) reaching individuals and portraying special-interest groups with dignity, (4) reflecting the best in the value of the culture, (5) performing a public service and dealing with controversial issues, and (6) contributing to the economy and a specific industry in a positive way.

"Thank you for spending this time with me. Maybe I'll consider reading your book more thoroughly. Who knows, I might want to get into this communication field in marketing. Anyway, I think I'll do more reading."

You're welcome and thank you. Your questions were provocative.

REGULATION: NOISE AND FEEDBACK

There are four players in the game of interaction between advertising and marketing communication and society: the consumer receivers, the marketer senders, the distribution and media channels, and the regulators who represent noise and feedback. To this point the discussion has concentrated on the first three of these. Now it turns to the last group, the regulators.

Regulation comes in many forms. The most prominent is the Federal Trade Commission (FTC), with its substantiation, disclosure, and other programs which lead to actions against advertisers whose work is charged to be false and misleading. Then there are a series of other government agencies at both the federal and the more local levels. Finally, there is the nongovernment form of voluntary regulation carried out by the media, industry groups, and the like.

If all advertising and communication were perfectly efficient, there would be no need for any of this regulation. But such perfection does not exist. So the regulation is actually a critical part of the process of achieving efficient communication in many situations.

Regulation as "Noise"

Regulatory activities constitute "noise" in a communication theory sense because these organizations represent another source of messages to the public about the nature of the communications coming from marketers. In some cases, this is in the form of news stories about, say, FTC actions. In other cases, settlements or consent decrees include a provision for *corrective advertising,* in which the advertiser agrees to run a certain amount of advertising or include statements in its advertising that "corrects" misperceptions from previous campaigns. Sometimes the order even asks for research results that would show that the previous misperception has been corrected. This kind of advertising, and mass-media stories about FTC activities, all constitute *noise.* They provide another and often competing message in the total communication environment.

Regulation as "Feedback"

Regulator activity constitutes "feedback" simply because it is another source of information as to how campaign messages are communicating. With company and advertising agency procedures the way they are, this feedback often occurs before advertising appears on a full scale. Advertising is routinely checked with attorneys and experts in the area of, say, network clearance. These people are familiar with the FCC and other regula-

tors' standards, which in turn are supposed to reflect the best interests of consumers. Thus this early check could be thought to reflect a kind of feedback of how efficient the campaign would be in reaching consumers.

In addition, on-air tests of advertising are seen by regulators and competitors, and sometimes legal actions are brought before the advertising is actually run on a full-scale basis. Often injunctions to stop the running of the offending ads are sought. This can lead to agreements to change the ads to make them more acceptable or to drop the advertising approach entirely. Again this is really a sort of feedback loop that can change the advertising and make it more efficient.

It should be noted that many campaign managers do not see the regulators as being a very accurate form of feedback. To have lawyers at the FTC and elsewhere judging advertising is not considered to be a true indicator of whether the advertising was efficient or not. Many people would prefer to let the market forces, communication research, or control and evaluation information systems serve as feedback. Their argument is that the regulators are operating on the basis of many motivations which are counter to efficient communication as described in this book.

The Federal Trade Commission

The Federal Trade Commission was formed by a 1914 act of Congress which basically gave it the right to deal with unfair competition. However, the FTC did not move into advertising matters in earnest until 1938 when the Wheeler-Lea Amendment changed Section 5 of the FTC act to read "Unfair methods of competition in commerce and unfair or deceptive acts or practices in commerce are hereby declared unlawful." Apparently, because of the "deceptive" part of that statement, the FTC from that time on did not have to justify its actions against advertisers in terms of effects on competition. This interpretation was supported in subsequent court cases, and the FTC effect on the advertising industry has been substantial ever since.[30]

Since the FTC is continually being challenged by industry, it is impossible to give a final definitive statement of the nature of its activities. For instance, until May 1980 the commission was vigorously pursuing a children's advertising rule that maintained that advertising to this special group was unfair, simply because children were alleged to have insufficient discriminatory abilities. Then a compromise congressional bill eliminated the power of the FTC to pursue a trade rule on the basis of "unfairness." This means that the development of the children's rule, which was intended to govern this area of communication activity, was suspended. It may have been started up again, however, even though the premise of it during the three-year life of the compromise congressional bill which started in 1980 must be "false" or "misleading" rather than "unfair."

The overall nature of FTC activities is indicated by the chart in Figure 19-1, which describes the process that follows commission identification of the advertisement for consideration. The FTC has a continuous national ad-monitoring program. Ads are monitored by product category, by medium, and by ad technique and are closely reviewed by attorneys on a biweekly basis. Each ad monitored could go through the following five steps, which are shown in Figure 19-1:

1. Erroneous beliefs? If there is a judgment that this is true or if there is research supporting such a judgment, there would be the possibility of obtaining an injunction to stop the ad from running.
2. Is the ad running now? If so, there is the possibility of obtaining the injunction.
3. Do the erroneous beliefs still exist? Even if the ad has stopped running, there is the possibility that the consumer segment still has the erroneous beliefs. This may then lead to corrective advertising recommendations. Corrective advertising has been ordered in about a dozen cases since first proposed in 1969.

4. Might this company use this deceptive practice again? If so, the FTC might attempt to obtain a cease and desist order. It is usually successful.
5. Is the problem common to the industry? If this seems to be the case, three types of action might be taken. Since these types of action represent some of the most significant work the commission has done, they are reviewed in the following paragraphs.

Advertising Substantiation. The national ad-monitoring program could be concentrated on offending industries. The staff would request substantiation of any offending claims. This has been done in, for instance, the case of product safety advertising for pesticides and plastics, foods and nutrition advertising, cosmetic advertising, and with regard to uniqueness claims.

Trade Regulation Rules. Although these were pursued quite vigorously by the FTC during the middle to late 1970s, they proved extremely difficult to implement. The idea was to have trade regulation rules (TRRs) that would specify the types of advertising and communication activity appropriate in each industry. Usually the proposed rule would require certain disclosures to be made. For instance, in the proposed food-advertising trade regulation rule, there was to be disclosure as to the nutritional content of foods in advertising. Thus, something equivalent to the RDA (recommended daily allowance) nutrition information on cereal packages would appear in television advertising if the rule were ever actually implemented.

In the commission's proposed over-the-counter (OTC) drug TRR, the idea was that Food and Drug Administration requirements for OTC drug packages, labels, and inserts wording and warnings be applied to advertising. As in the food TRR proposal, the round of hearings was long indeed. Industry and consumer group spokespeople had their say, many disagreeing with the FTC's contention

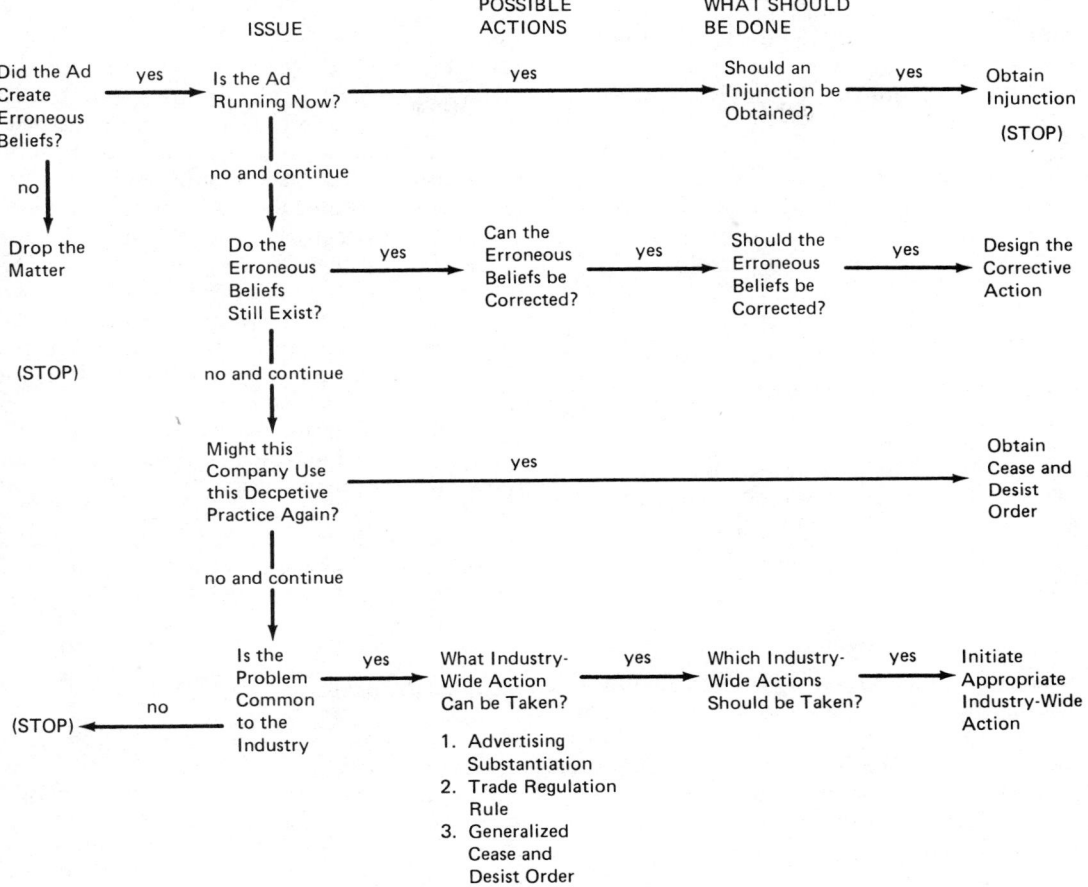

Figure 19-1. *Decision points in FTC deceptive advertising matters*

Benjamin J. Katz and others, eds., *Advertising and Government Regulation,* Advertising and Government Panel of the American Academy of Advertising, Marketing Science Institute Report No. 79–106, April 1979, pp. 1–6.

that a problem existed and with the proposed TRR as a solution.

Many of the principles in this book indicate why the FTC's TRR program ran into so much difficulty. It seemed to be based on a view of marketing communication that did not differentiate between the distinctive nature of the elements of the communication mix. What's more, the FTC staff seemed to accept a model of consumer information pro-cessing that assumed high consumer interest, involvement, and ability to perceive and pro-cess detailed nutritional information, and so forth, in television and other advertising. As indicated earlier in this chapter, consumers seem to process advertising in very general ways and avoid a good deal of the marketing communication that comes their way. It is this fact of consumer information processing that the FTC staff seemed to ignore as they attempted to win approval for a variety of TRR proposals. Perhaps this is why the process was so difficult.

The reaction to the TRR idea was so negative that the congressional bill of 1980 established a mechanism for review of FTC trade rules by both houses of Congress within thirty days of promulgation. Action by both the Senate and the House could veto a rule without the president's signature.

Generalized Cease and Desist Order. This power of the FTC, if continually upheld, would eliminate the need for the other two forms of remedy. The generalized order would mean that if one firm in an industry were found guilty of a particular practice, a cease and desist order would apply to all the firms in the industry. This has been called trial without a hearing, but the FTC will attempt to test it.

Summary: The FTC as Noise and Feedback. What has the FTC accomplished? At a minimum, the FTC has stimulated industry's investigation of its own practices. Usually the result of such investigation results in quite positive findings without a major industry change being required, but still the FTC has provided a feedback mechanism.

The commission has not been as effective as noise. Although some of the hearings held generate considerable publicity, the message is mixed. And when offending advertisers pay fines and run corrective advertising, the effects have not seemed to be dramatic. Again, however, the evaluative research has not been fully adequate.[31] One promising direction is when the FTC runs its own ads, as was true of campaigns on consumer direct-mail rights and on credit rights for women.[32]

Other Federal Agencies

Other federal agencies would include the Food and Drug Administration, which concentrates on product and packaging communication; the Justice Department, which brought a suit against the National Association of Broadcasters alleging that the Television Code limitation of advertising on television is a restraint of trade; and the Federal Communications Commission, which applies the Fairness Doctrine used by broadcasters to refuse much controversy advertising.

Many of the activities of the Justice Department impinge on communication activities other than advertising. For instance, in implementing the Robinson-Patman Act, the Justice Department affects message distribution for sales promotion.

Other government agencies have only minor advertising and communication interests. These would include the Consumer Product Safety Commission; the Alcohol, Tobacco and Firearms Unit of the Treasury Department; the Department of Agriculture; the Post Office; and the Securities and Exchange Commission.

State and Local Agencies

State and local governments have consumer protection agencies that perform many of the same kinds of activities regarding communication that the FTC does on the national level. Of course, the FTC does have regional offices, but these local activities have caused the commission a great deal of trouble. The state and local government agencies in a variety of capacities, such as in auto repair and state licensing of professionals, can affect the nature of communication. This was certainly true in the nationwide move to make it possible for lawyers to advertise.

Some of the best indications of the economic and other social effects of advertising are found in comparisons of states that allow certain kinds of advertising with ones that do not. For instance, such a comparison with regard to the cost of eyeglasses in states that allowed and did not allow advertising for them found that advertising lowered retail prices.[33]

Voluntary Regulation

The advertising industry has set up its own regulation procedure which deals with the content of advertising. The process is sponsored by the American Association of Advertising Agencies (AAAA), the American Advertising Federation (AAF), the Association of National Advertisers (ANA), and the Council of Better Business Bureaus (CBBB). These organizations make up the National Advertising Review Council (NARC), which sponsors the National Advertising Review Board (NARB). The CBBB alone sponsors the National Advertising Division (NAD).

Now that this melange of letters has been presented, how does this national voluntary regulation work? There are the following steps:

1. A complaint or question to the NAD.
2. The NAD evaluates and sometimes dismisses.
3. If not dismissed, the complaint is referred to the advertiser in question; substantiation is requested.
4. If the substantiation is not acceptable, the advertiser is asked to change or discontinue the message.
5. If the advertiser disagrees, the case is appealed to the NARB by the NAD or by the advertiser.
6. The NARB chairman will appoint a panel.
7. If the panel finds against him, the advertiser is asked to change or discontinue the message.
8. If the advertiser refuses, the case is referred to the appropriate government agency.

By this process over two hundred complaints have been processed per year. Many of them come from consumers. Many of them have dealt with *comparative advertising,* which the FTC specifically encouraged networks to accept in 1972. Complaints involving comparative ads jumped to over 25 percent of the cases reviewed by the voluntary process. In one year, 38 percent of the cases involved comparative advertising.[34] The FTC was encouraging comparative advertising, and evidently the only recourse for many complainants was the industry regulation body.

Media Clearance

Clearance of advertising for airing on the networks is one example of regulation that is carried out by all types of media. The National Association of Broadcasters (NAB), for instance, is mentioned twice at the beginning of this chapter, once as an acronym and another time in terms of turning back a McDonald's advertising appeal—at the request of Burger King. The quotation that lists a series of acronyms at the beginning of this chapter comes from a network clearance director. These directors judge commercials on the basis of taste, possible double entendre, offensiveness, and negative portrayals of certain types of people, as well as the standard questions of accuracy and substantiality. They are quite responsive to the complaints of consumers.

Often the media will maintain their own testing facilities which determine whether the products will do what advertising says they will. The *Good Housekeeping* seal of approval emanated from such a testing program.

It is not unusual for advertisers to ask the network clearance people to stop the running of a competitive message that is felt to be unfairly damaging. Again, comparative ads that are felt to be disparaging sometimes cause this sort of reaction on the part of complainants. Going directly to the media is sometimes faster than working with either the government or the voluntary procedures.

There was speculation that such a complaint process might be started in the early 1980's when Olympia Gold (a light beer) began running comparison advertising that not only named competitors but also compared calorie content and advertising appeals. The Bureau of Alcohol, Tobacco and Firearms seemed to be allowing the commercials to continue, even though they called Michelob Light "almost regular" and asked "Less what?" of the Miller Lite slogan, "Everything you ever wanted in a beer and less." The Olympia Gold commercial said, "Certainly not calories" and pointed out that Miller Lite had 37 percent more calories.[35] This kind of advertising is loaded with information for the consumer but is often the subject of complaints from competitors to the networks.

Individual Suits

When marketers feel they are being treated unfairly or consumers do not seem to be able to get help in any other way, they often bring a legal action of their own. Some of these can set precedents for the way marketing communication should and can be done.

Consumer Action Organizations

Some of the innovations in regulation of advertising and communication have come from the work of consumer action organizations. The idea of corrective advertising, for example, was first suggested by an organization called SOUP (Students Opposed to Unfair Practices). Action for Children's Television was a prime mover in getting the FTC to act in that area. Organizations in the nutritional area have affected the work on food advertising. Environmental, ethnic, women's, and senior citizens groups are others that have had effects on the nature of advertising and marketing communication.

Conclusion and a Modest Proposal

The "game" of regulation of advertising and marketing communication and their social effects is now being played in the form of an advocacy system. The quality of the noise and feedback provided by the regulators and the other players in response to regulation has been mixed indeed. There has probably been some increase in efficient communication as a result of all of this activity, but that is questionable. And there is some possibility that regulation in its present form hampers many brand, product, and campaign managers in their drive toward efficient communication.

One "modest proposal" to improve all of this would involve *supplemental advertising*. The idea would be to set up a supplemental advertising fund based on a small assessment per sales dollar from every competitor in each industry. Then a campaign team would be assigned to the fund for each industry. An advertising agency would be selected. The fund would provide a total advertising budget that was the equivalent of that of a major competitor in each market. The campaign would be designed to provide efficient communication of messages of general information on the product category. To some extent, this kind of work is already being done by various agricultural cooperatives in terms of their advertising funds. But the purpose of supplemental advertising would not be to increase the primary demand for the product. Instead the purpose would be to supplement the normal type of advertising with information consumers need on the product category. It would be hoped that the existence of supplemental advertising would eliminate many of the needs for legal actions in the field now. This type of advertising would lead to much more diversity in communication with consumers at the national and regional levels than exists at the present time.

But, who knows, the way that advertising and communication are done in the future may change so radically that such dramatic proposals as supplemental advertising will not be necessary.

THE FUTURE

If the goal of efficient communication is crucial to advertising and communication's relationship to society, then developments shaping up now for the future would seem to make that relationship look positive indeed. The reason for this is that all the trends in all the media are moving toward more specialization, more diversity, greater ability to get to target consumers without waste. On the other hand, it seems likely that all of this will cost advertisers a great deal more and change the way advertising and mass communication are done. The basic, underlying change will be that the power in the communication process will move from sender to receiver, from marketer to consumer.

Developments in the Media

Predictions of developments in the media have been difficult to make. Much of the technology has been available for quite some time, but for a variety of reasons the changes have not come as quickly as people originally expected. Here are some of the possibilities.

Cable TV. This method allows consumers to have many channels of television of many different types. There is also the possibility of two-way interactive television, which allows such communication and distribution combinations as home shopping. There were between 15 and 16 million cable homes at the beginning of the decade. But the figure was growing at a rate of eight thousand new subscribers every day, including weekends. Predictions were for 30 million cable homes by 1985, 60 million by 1990.

Satellite Communications. Satellite communications are another way that programming possibilities are increased, since these satellites can transmit large numbers of messages.

Home Computers. Home computers are one of the biggest growth industries in the country. The home computer has the potential to link all the other communication technology. People will literally be able to make their own newspaper or magazine which can be printed in the home.

Superstations. These can beam additional programming off the satellites to local stations into the home.

Home Receiving Stations. It is already possible to buy a home dish antenna that will pick up pay television signals. Less-expensive versions are being planned and tested. This offers the possibility that every home will be able to pick up the messages coming off the satellites.

Videodiscs and Videocassettes. These offer the potential of an entire industry (which has already started), which could sell television programs and movies in almost the same way that pop music records are sold today. Videocassette equipment also provides another way for consumers to avoid commercials. Devices now available on this equipment allow fast forward and reverse with the picture clearly in view. In this way, viewers can skip the commercials quite easily. Preliminary Nielsen rating results indicate that only 22 percent skip commercials with the fast forward button and 14 percent delete the messages entirely. Of course, the rest of the people who rerun the programs at home will have a repeated viewing of the messages.[36]

Holography. This is truly futuristic, but holography offers the possibility of three-dimensional images being transmitted to the home (or available through recording). Imagine the potential for home shopping when combined with the other techniques mentioned.

Specialization and Targeting

If even part of the above comes true, there will be a great deal more specialization in the media. At the time this book was being written, cable systems were capable of carrying thirty-six channels, and increases in capacity were not difficult. One prediction suggested that by 1990 there would be twenty national networks and many more regional and specialized ones.

Interactive cable systems are already in place. Magazines, newspapers, and radio stations, as well as television stations and networks, should become more and more specialized to reach specific groups of people with particular needs. All of this should lead to the possibility that marketing communicators will be able to target messages to people more precisely than ever before. Brand managers will be able to talk to people in their own terms at a time when these people want to talk.

Blurring of Communication Element Distinctions

Once it is possible to target more and more precisely, and consumers are requesting long interactive messages in order to assist them with their product purchases, there will not be a major distinction between the four elements of communication as discussed in this book. Long messages, somewhat akin to selling messages, will be coming into the home in the same medium formerly used to transmit television commercials.

Of course, not everything will be thrown away. There may still be television commercials as we know them today. But they may be bulked up together for particular categories on one channel or one time of day. Cable systems already have shopping channels that give comparative price information for food and drug items.

Power to the Consumer

If all the above happens, the consumer should have greater choice and therefore greater power in the interaction with the marketer. Instead of having to mentally turn off the television commercials, this futuristic consumer will simply choose not to be exposed to commercials at all or only to commercials of a certain type. This kind of future will be interesting, indeed, for the marketing communication campaign manager.

Why It May Not Happen

These predictions usually forget about the people who will have to use the technological innovations. Is it possible that people really will not want to have or take all the choice implied? Could it be that people do not really want to go into the great deal of detail in purchasing that is possible with the new technology? And what about the political and competitive realities? Isn't it possible that the same sort of thing that happened with radio and then with television in their early days will also occur for these new technologies? Why is it that there are really so few formats available on radio and television now? Could it be that consumers really are not that interested in the variety? Or that broadcasters do not really know how to provide it?

The principles for effective communication presented in this book will undoubtedly fit any scenario for the future, if the campaign manager of the future stays in touch with his or her audience.

ISSUES AND PROJECTS FOR DISCUSSION

1. Try to answer the questions on social issues in this chapter yourself. See if you can add anything to the answers given by the author. Use directions from the rest of the book.

2. What other questions about social issues do you feel need to be asked? Can you provide any answers to them?

3. This chapter concentrated largely on the social effects of advertising. What questions would you ask about the effect on society of personal selling, sales promotion, and publicity–PR?

4. How does marketing communication meet people's needs?

5. What is "efficient communication"? How does or would it affect advertising and communication's role in society?

6. At the end of the first chapter you were asked to find ads you liked and disliked. Now find two ads (or describe television or radio commercials) that you believe are misleading or deceptive. Try to be as thorough as an FTC attorney in building a case for the deceptive or misleading nature of the ads.

7. If you personally had a complaint about an ad, what could you do about it? If you were the brand manager of a competing brand, what could you do?

8. In what way could the job of advertising and communication campaign planning be easier in the future? In what way could it be more difficult?

9. Use the hierarchy situation analysis to discuss the FTC proposal to put detailed disclosure of nutritional information in TV ads.

10. Use the hierarchy situation analysis to assess the potential of consumers actually using the benefits of the new telecommunications technology.

Notes

1. Matilda Butler and William Paisley, *Women and the Mass Media* (New York: Human Sciences Press, 1980), p. 68.

2. R. S. Alexander, "Some Aspects of Sex Differences in Relation to Marketing," *Journal of Marketing,* October 1947, p. 166, as quoted in Alice E. Courtney and Thomas W. Whipple, "Sex Stereotyping in Advertising: An Annotated Bibliography," Marketing Science Institute Report No. 80-100, February 1980, p. v.

3. Christy Marshall and Richard L. Gordon, "McDonald's Told to Alter Claim: Nobody Can Do It in Kid Ads," *Advertising Age,* November 5, 1979, p. 1.

4. Jack E. Hinton, "Offending People in Advertising: Do Unto Others . . ." (Paper from the 1975 Eastern Annual Conference of the American Association of Advertising Agencies), p. 1.

5. Ibid., p. 7.

6. Jerry Mander, "Four Arguments for the Elimination of Advertising," in *Advertising and the Public: Sandage Symposium II,* ed. Kim B. Rotzoll (Urbana: Department of Advertising, University of Illinois, 1980), p. 23.

7. Isaac Asimov, "Advertising in the Year 2000," *Advertising Age,* May 9, 1977, p. 48.

8. "Television's Fragmented Future: A Scramble to Find the Right Approach and the Right Technology as Competition Widens," *Business Week,* December 17, 1980, p. 60.

9. Bernice Kanner, "Prime Time 30 at $342,000 Seen by '90," *Advertising Age,* March 10, 1980, p. 16.

10. Jacques Neher, "The World According to Toffler: Hang Ten on 'The Third Wave,'" *Advertising Age,* April 28, 1980, p. 53.

11. Quoted by Harold J. Leavitt in a presentation to the course "Creativity in Business," Graduate School of Business, Stanford University, May 1980.

12. Hinton, "Offending People in Advertising," p. 5.

13. Rena Bartos, "The Consumer View of Advertising—1974" (Paper from the 1974 Annual Meeting of the American Association of Advertising Agencies, 1975), pp. 1–11.

14. Ibid., pp. 13–19.

15. Gene Telser, "Pilot Survey Finds Consumers More Upset with Poor Products Than Dishonest Ads," *Marketing News,* January 11, 1980, p. 20.

16. Ibid.

17. "AAAA Measures Miscomprehension of Televised Communications," *AAAA Newsletter,* April-May 1980, p. 3.

18. J. J. Boddewyn and Katherine Marton, *Comparison Advertising* (New York: Hastings House, 1978), p. 11.

19. Peter Webb and Michael L. Ray, "Effects of 'Clutter,' on American TV," *Advertising Quarterly,* Winter 1976/77, pp. 18–19.

20. Peter H. Webb and Michael L. Ray, "Effects of TV Clutter," *Journal of Advertising Research,* 19 (June 1979), 7–12.

21. Courtney and Whipple, "Sex Stereotyping," p. vii.

22. See, for example, Wilson Bryan Key, *Subliminal Seduction* (Englewood Cliffs, N.J.: Prentice-Hall, 1973); and Judith Williamson, *Decoding Advertisements* (London: Marion Boyars, 1978).

23. Albert Bandura, *Social Learning Theory* (Englewood Cliffs, N.J.: Prentice-Hall, 1977).

24. Barton A. Cummings, "How the Advertising Council Supports Public Service Programs," in *Advertising and the Public,* ed. Kim Rotzoll (Urbana: Department of Advertising, University of Illinois, 1980), pp. 53–66.

25. Michael L. Ray, Scott Ward, and Jerome B. Reed, "Pretesting of Anti-Drug Abuse Education and Information Campaigns," in *Communication Research and Drug Eduction,* ed. Ronald Elroy Ostman (Beverly Hills, Calif.: Sage Publications, Inc., 1976), pp. 193–221.

26. Albert Stridsberg, *Controversy Advertising* (New York: Hastings House, 1977).

27. Ibid., pp. 108–9.

28. "The Business Campaign Against 'Trial by TV,'" *Business Week,* June 2, 1980, pp. 77–79.

29. Mark S. Albion and Paul W. Farris, "Appraising Research on Advertising's Economic Impacts," Marketing Science Institute Report No. 79-115, December 1979, pp. 172–74.

30. Benjamin J. Katz and others, eds., *Advertising and Government Regulation,* Advertising and Government Panel of the American Academy of Advertising, Marketing Science Institute Report No. 79-106, April 1979, pp. 1–6.

31. Kenneth L. Bernhardt, Thomas C. Kinnear, and Michael B. Mazis, "An Evaluation of Corrective Advertising Effects: A Field Study," Research Paper No. 538 (Graduate School of Business, Stanford University, February 1980).

32. "FTC Spots Note Direct Mail Rights," *Advertising Age,* March 17, 1980, p. 12.

33. Lee Benham, "The Effect of Advertising on the Price of Eyeglasses," *Journal of Law and Economics,* 15 (October 1972), 337–52.

34. Boddewyn and Marton, *Comparison Advertising,* pp. 50–51.

35. "Oly Gold Makes Tough Comparisons," *Advertising Age,* June 23, 1980, p. 90.

36. "The Videocassette Bonus," *Advertising Age,* May 5, 1980, p. 16.

Index

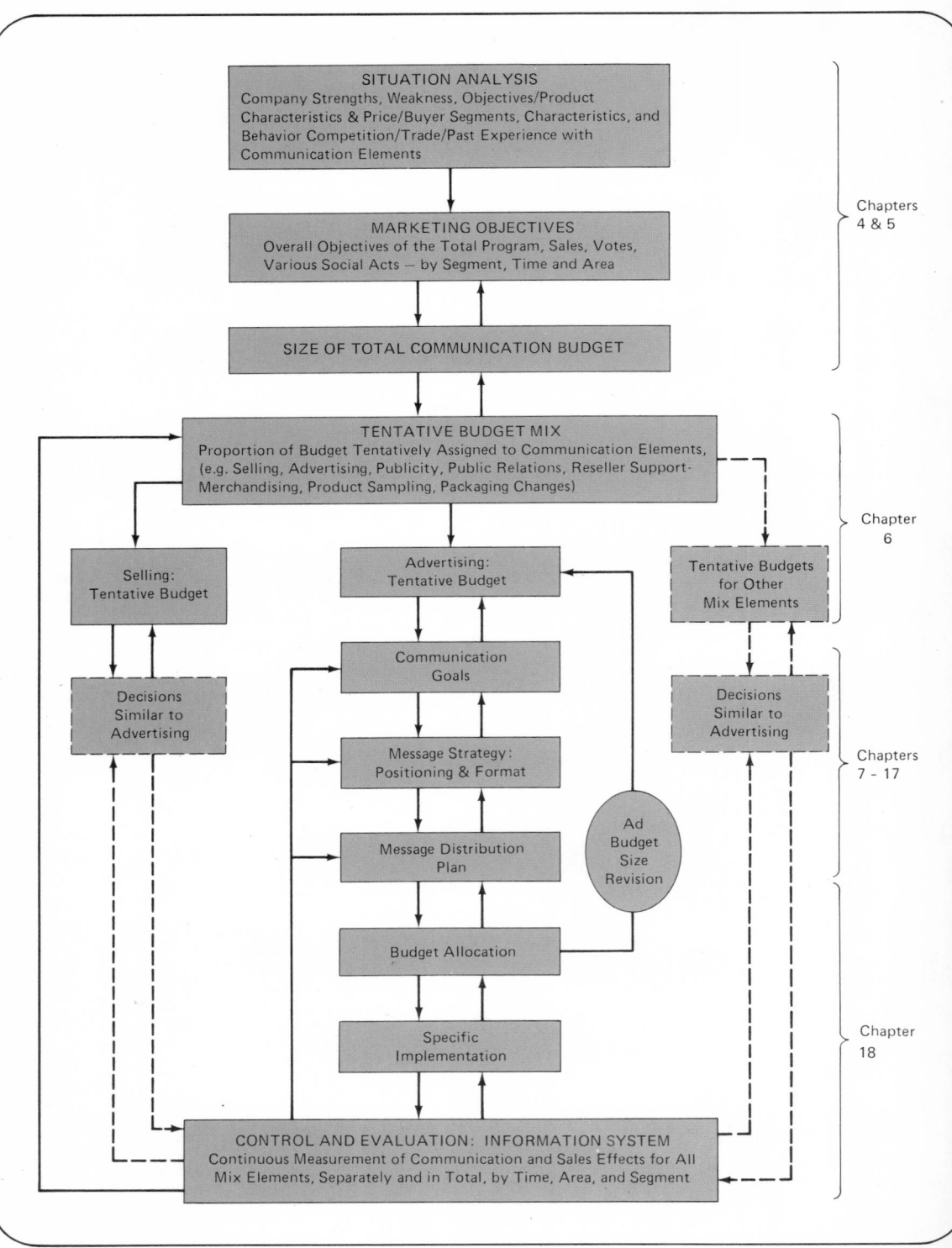

SITUATION ANALYSIS
Company Strengths, Weakness, Objectives/Product Characteristics & Price/Buyer Segments, Characteristics, and Behavior Competition/Trade/Past Experience with Communication Elements

MARKETING OBJECTIVES
Overall Objectives of the Total Program, Sales, Votes, Various Social Acts — by Segment, Time and Area

SIZE OF TOTAL COMMUNICATION BUDGET

Chapters 4 & 5

TENTATIVE BUDGET MIX
Proportion of Budget Tentatively Assigned to Communication Elements, (e.g. Selling, Advertising, Publicity, Public Relations, Reseller Support-Merchandising, Product Sampling, Packaging Changes)

Chapter 6

Selling: Tentative Budget

Advertising: Tentative Budget

Tentative Budgets for Other Mix Elements

Decisions Similar to Advertising

Communication Goals

Decisions Similar to Advertising

Message Strategy: Positioning & Format

Ad Budget Size Revision

Chapters 7 - 17

Message Distribution Plan

Budget Allocation

Specific Implementation

Chapter 18

CONTROL AND EVALUATION: INFORMATION SYSTEM
Continuous Measurement of Communication and Sales Effects for All Mix Elements, Separately and in Total, by Time, Area, and Segment